The Oxford
Reverse Dictionary

D0169841

Oxford Paperback Reference

The most authoritative and up-to-date reference books for both students and the general reader.

The Oxford
Reverse
Dictionary

Compiled by
DAVID EDMONDS

OXFORD
UNIVERSITY PRESS

OXFORD
UNIVERSITY PRESS

Great Clarendon Street, Oxford OX2 6DP

Oxford University Press is a department of the University of Oxford.
It furthers the University's objective of excellence in research, scholarship,
and education by publishing worldwide in

Oxford New York

Auckland Bangkok Buenos Aires Cape Town Chennai
Dar es Salaam Delhi Hong Kong Istanbul Karachi Kolkata
Kuala Lumpur Madrid Melbourne Mexico City Mumbai Nairobi
São Paulo Shanghai Taipei Tokyo Toronto

Oxford is a registered trade mark of Oxford University Press
in the UK and in certain other countries

Published in the United States
by Oxford University Press Inc., New York

© Oxford University Press 1999

Database right Oxford University Press (makers)

First published 1999
Reissued, with corrections, 2002

British Library Cataloguing in Publication Data

Data available

Library of Congress Cataloging in Publication Data

Data available

ISBN 0-19-280113-9

3

Typeset in Nimrod and Arial
by Interactive Sciences Limited, Gloucester
Printed in Great Britain by
Clays Ltd, St Ives plc

Introduction

We all have words 'on the tip of our tongue', and we all know how hard such words often are to coax back into consciousness, and how bad our speech or writing will look without them: "that bit of the wall that turns into the window" can never really replace *reveal* without the decorator thinking us a fool, and "the sort of magistrate who conducts inquiries into the causes of someone's death" is no substitute for *coroner*—indeed, no other term can be. This dictionary is designed to solve these problems quickly and efficiently, grouping the tongue-tip terms under their key concepts: so *coroner* will be found in the article **magistrate**, *reveal* at **wall**, and *kriegspiel* at both **war** and **game**.

The *Oxford Reverse Dictionary* will guide you to the standard terms for things most people have heard of: it is not an English-learner's dictionary, nor will it help you to literary or archaic words, or to slang; colloquialisms are offered only where standard speech offers no workable substitute. The cabinet minister's tonguetip has of course a different population from the schoolboy's, and the diversity of the 31,000 listed items takes this into account; but words from specialist vocabularies have been omitted, as have core vocabulary words such as *dog* and *family* which are usually immediately available to any native speaker.

Items sharing a key concept will be found as entries within the article devoted to that concept (so entries for *topiary, spudder,* and *trug* will all be found in the article **gardening**), and items sharing a single definition (such as *agent* and *representative*, or *symposium* and *colloquium*) are nested together in a single entry within the appropriate concept article. Such nested items are related in sense, but not necessarily interchangeable: they are listed alphabetically, and any item moved to the back of such a list may be considered an inferior match.

Articles are arranged in a single alphabetical sequence through the dictionary. Within each article entries are arranged alphabetically where that is possible, or in an appropriate sense-progression such as life–death, top–bottom, eldest/largest–youngest/smallest: there is also a general tendency to move out from core items to those that are more peripheral to the senses of the article headword. Each entry is glossed in the briefest possible way consistent with clarity—the user already *knows* what the tonguetip term means, and so only needs a pointer; not an exhaustive definition.

Where any exist, suffixes or prefixes bearing the basic meaning of the article headword are listed next after it (for example, -wise after **manner**), together (unless one is found elsewhere in the article) with an example of their use: they may serve as a spur to recollection of many further terms semantically related to the topic treated in the article but not specifically mentioned in it, or assist users in correctly coining their own *mot juste* where none is shown/exists. Similarly, adjectives related to the article headword in meaning but not in appearance (for example, *dental* at **tooth**), or whose formation may present other difficulties if imperfectly remembered, are listed at the beginning of the article. Item plurals are also given when irregular; but not where a regularly-formed plural of equal currency exists.

Dictionary-writing is a lengthy and lonely process, and I am grateful to many people for help and encouragement along the road. A special acknowledgement is due to Patrick Hanks for detailed advice during the earlier stages of the project, and to Kate Wandless for smoothing the bumpy road of author–publisher relations. Thanks are also due to Dr Adrian Young for information on medical terms, Tim Parry for clarification of some psychiatric concepts, and Alasdair Cross for legal definitions. The typescript benefited at a late stage from a thorough read conducted by Lucinda Coventry.

DJE

Abbreviations

a.m.	before noon
fem.	feminine
pl.	plural
e.g.	for example
esp.	especially
km	kilometre(s)
m	metre(s)
MP	Member of Parliament
NHS	National Health Service
p.m.	after noon
RAF	Royal Air Force
RC	Roman Catholic
UK	United Kingdom
US, USA	United States (of America)
VDU	visual display unit
19th-c.	nineteenth-century (and so on)

In memoriam
CAROLINE MARY FRASER
optimae amicae

Aa

abandonment ●abandonment of a legal claim: **waiver** ● abandonment of religious or political adherence: **apostasy** ● person abandoning such adherence: **apostate, turncoat**

abbot ● *adjective*: **abbatial** ● female abbot: **abbess** ● abbot's assistant: **prior** ● abbess's assistant: **prioress**

abbreviation ● abbreviation pronounced as a string of letters: **initialism** ● abbreviation pronounced as a word: **acronym** ● abbreviated title of a book or document: **short title** ● abbreviated version of a statement or document: **precis, resumé, summary**

abdomen ● *adjectives*: **coeliac, ventral** ● severe abdominal pain caused by wind or intestinal obstruction: **colic** ● stress-associated abdominal pain with diarrhoea or constipation: **irritable bowel syndrome** ● fibreoptic inspection of the abdomen: **laparoscopy** ● incision into the abdomen: **laparotomy** ● membrane lining the abdominal cavity: **peritoneum** ● inflammation of the peritoneum: **peritonitis**

Aberdeen ● *adjective*: **Aberdonian**

able ● *combining form*: **-able, -ible, -uble** ● adequate ability: **proficiency** ● person with exceptional abilities: **genius, prodigy** ● demonstrate one's abilities: **prove oneself**

Aboriginal ● Aboriginal club: **nulla-nulla, waddy** ● Aboriginal dance ceremony: **corroboree** ● Aboriginal medicine man: **koradji** ● Aboriginal throwing stick: **boomerang** ● Aboriginal wind instrument: **didgeridoo** ● land set aside for Aboriginal settlement: **reservation**

abortion ● advocating abortion: **pro-choice** ● deprecating abortion: **pro-life, right-to-life** ● start an abortion artificially: **induce** ● drug causing abortion: **abortifacient**

about ● *combining forms*: **circum-** (*e.g.* circumambient), **peri-** (*e.g.* perimeter) ● about to happen: **imminent, impending**

above ● *combining forms*: **epi-** (*e.g.* epidermis), **over-** (*e.g.* overhang), **super-** (*e.g.* superstructure), **supra-** (*e.g.* supramundane), **sur-** (*e.g.* surreal)

abrasive ● abrasive powder: **emery**

abroad ● person living abroad: **émigré, exile, expatriate** ● done or registered abroad: **offshore** ● sell abroad: **export**

absence ● absence without permission: **French leave** ● absence from school without permission: **truancy** ● permission to be absent: **leave, furlough** ● grant of brief absence from school: **exeat** ● person who is absent: **absentee** ● employee's statement that his absence was due to illness: **self-certification** ● in absence: **in absentia**

absurdity ● absurd misrepresentation: **travesty** ● seemingly absurd but in fact true statement: **oxymoron, paradox** ● proof of a statement's falsity by demonstrating the absurdity of its logical consequences: **reductio ad absurdum**

academic ● academic conference: **colloquium, symposium** ● academic thesis: **dissertation** ● academic essay: **dissertation, paper, memoir**

academic dress ●academic hat: **bonnet, mortarboard, square** ●academic cloak: **gown** ●coloured headcovering worn over the back of a gown: **hood** ●hood tail: **liripipe** ●dark clothing worn with academic dress: **subfusc**

accent ●East London accent: **Cockney** ●Irish accent: **brogue** ●Northumberland accent: **burr** ●South East England accent: **Estuary English** ●actors' sham rustic accent: **Mummerset**

accepted ●generally accepted or believed: **received**

accommodation ●available accommodation: **vacancy** ●accommodation unit that is part of a larger building: **flat, maisonette** ●stable blocks converted to accommodation units: **mews** ●denoting accommodation with its own kitchen and bathroom: **self-contained** ●denoting accommodation available as part of a work contract: **tied** ●institution offering basic accommodation: **hostel** ●wardened accommodation for the elderly or handicapped: **sheltered housing**

account ●account showing the assets, liabilities, and capital of a business at a particular point in time: **balance sheet** ●denoting a balance sheet showing no debts: **ungeared** ●temporary account for items awaiting final allocation: **suspense account** ●account to which credit purchases may be charged: **charge account** ●official examination of accounts: **audit** ●accounting record of money received: **credit** ●accounting record of money spent or owed: **debit** ●accounting system with each item entered both as a credit and as a debit: **double entry** ●difference between debits and credits in an account: **balance** ●accounting item rejected by the auditor, and repayable by those responsible: **surcharge** ●account-book

for the current day's transactions: **daybook, journal** ●account-book for minor transactions: **cash book** ●large book in which financial accounts are written up: **ledger** ●enter an item in a ledger: **post** ●make one account consistent with another: **reconcile** ●comparison of totals from a double entry account: **trial balance** ●money coming into an account: **receipts** ●person assembling and recording financial data: **bookkeeper** ●person recording or verifying financial data: **accountant** ●preparation of financial data to aid management decisions: **management accounting** ●analysis of operational costs: **cost accounting** ●British government's general account at the Bank of England: **Consolidated Fund** ●considered account for legal or publicity use: **statement**

accusation ●counter-accusation: **recrimination**

achieve ●achieve by skill or deviousness: **contrive** ●best achievement: **record** ●past achievements: **record, track record**

acid ●dye indicating acidity: **litmus**

acquaintance ●influential acquaintance: **connection** ●helpful acquaintance: **contact**

acrobat ●acrobat performing on a tightrope: **wire-walker** ●acrobat's tights: **maillot** ●acrobat's pair of long poles with foot supports: **stilts** ●swinging bar used by acrobats: **trapeze** ●acrobatic stunts on the wings of an airborne aircraft: **wing walking**

across ●*combining forms*: **dia-, trans-** (*e.g.* transatlantic) ●measurement taken across a circle: **diameter**

act ●daring act: **escapade, stunt** ●illegal act: **crime, offence** ●kind or helpful acts: **offices, good offices** ●act without preparation: **improvise** ●act on another's behalf: **represent** ●person acting on behalf of another:

agent, representative ●sudden urge to act: **impulse** ●repeatedly performing the same act(s): **serial**

acting ●*combining form*: **pro-** (*e.g.* pronoun) ●person acting for an absent doctor: **locum** ●person acting for a monarch who is absent or incapacitated: **regent** ●acting without forethought: **impetuous**

action ●*combining form*: **-ation** (*e.g.* hesitation), **-ence** (*e.g.* reference), **-tion, -ure** (*e.g.* closure) ●action done in automatic response to a stimulus: **reflex** ●action done purely for appearance: **gesture, window dressing** ●action consisting of spoken or written words: **illocution** ●established series of actions: **procedure, process, routine** ●freedom of action: **carte blanche, free hand** ●ability to take independent action: **initiative** ●incapable of effective action: **effete** ●still requiring action: **outstanding** ●out of action: **hors de combat**

activity ●*combining form*: **-ery** (*e.g.* archery), **-ism** (*e.g.* exorcism) ●recreational activity: **hobby, pastime, pursuit** ●menial or boring activity: **drudgery** ●pointless cycle of activities: **merry-go-round**

actor ●*adjective*: **histrionic** ●experienced actor: **trouper** ●actor who overacts: **ham** ●actor in a folk play: **mummer** ●actor who performs in silence: **mime** ●actor taking a principal role: **leading lady, leading man** ●actor taking minor roles: **bit player** ●actor appearing only in crowd scenes: **extra, figurant** ●actor who has prepared another actor's role, in order to replace him or her if necessary: **understudy** ●sardonic term for actor: **Thespian** ●group of actors playing together: **ensemble** ●actors participating in a performance: **cast** ●actor's part: **role** ●actor's try-out for a role: **audition** ●actor's make-up: **greasepaint** ●actor's flesh-coloured tights: **fleshings** ●actor's dressing-room assistant: **dresser** ●actor's pre-performance nerves: **stage fright** ●actor's arrival on stage: **entrance** ●actor's signal to speak: **cue** ●actor's long speech: **monologue** ●actor's speech when alone on stage: **soliloquy** ●actor's words not intended to be heard by others on stage: **aside** ●actor's words made up on the spur of the moment: **ad-lib** ●actor's mistake in speaking: **fluff** ●actor's loud whisper: **stage whisper** ●actors' sham rustic accent: **Mummerset** ●actor's movements, gestures, etc.: **business** ●plan of an actor's movements: **blocking** ●actor's departure from the stage: **exit** ●actors' backstage rest room: **green room** ●actor's return to the stage to acknowledge applause: **curtain call** ●noise made by actors simulating indistinct conversation: **rhubarb** ●denoting an actor who has learnt his or her role completely: **word-perfect** ●denoting an actor dressed as a member of the opposite sex: **en travesti** ●tendency to offer an actor roles of a type in which he or she has already been suucessful: **typecasting** ●play for one actor: **monodrama** ●scene for two actors: **duologue** ●(of an actor) forget one's lines during a performance: **dry** ●remind an actor what he or she must say: **prompt** ●acting technique encouraging emotional identification with the character portrayed: **the Method, method acting** ●troupe of actors presenting several plays at the same venue in the course of a season: **repertory company** ●euphemism denoting an unemployed actor: **resting**

acupressure ●Japanese acupressure therapy: **shiatsu** ●spot where pressure is applied: **acupoint**

add ●extra section added at the end of a book: **appendix** ●add something not part of the original design: **retro-fit**

addict ●*combining form*: -holic (*e.g.* alcoholic, workaholic) ●addict's phased abandonment of addictive drugs: **withdrawal** ●addict's instant abandonment of addictive drugs: **cold turkey** ●firm treatment of addicts: **tough love** ●clear an addict's body of drug residues: **detoxify**

addition ●*combining form*: epi- (*e.g.* epiphenomenon) ●addition to a book etc.: **addendum, appendix, supplement** ●addition to a building: **annex, annexe, extension** ●addition to a collection: **accession** ●addition to a document: **annex, schedule, rider** ●special addition to a price or payment: **premium, surcharge** ●addition to will: **codicil**

address ●address used as a collecting-point for mail: **accommodation address** ●address for a letter to be left at a post office until called for: **poste restante**

adhesive ●synthetic resin used in paints and adhesives: **polyurethane** ●join with adhesives: **bond**

adjective ●characterizing adjective: **epithet** ●denoting an adjective that precedes its noun: **attributive** ●denoting an adjective that is placed after the verb: **predicative, postpositive**

adjust ●adjust a mechanism: **regulate, set** ●make small adjustments: **finesse, fine-tune, titivate** ●thin strip of material used to make an exact fit: **shim**

admiration ●uncritical admiration: **adulation** ●object of admiration: **cynosure** ●deserving admiration: **commendable, estimable, laudable, praiseworthy**

admission ●admission ritual: **initiation** ●university admission ceremony: **matriculation** ●right of admission: **entrée, entry**

adolescence ●adolescent love: **calf love** ●period in which adolescents reach sexual maturity: **puberty** ●skin disease of adolescents, with black pustules: **acne**

adult ●age at which adulthood is reached: **majority, coming of age** ●suitable for children and adults: **family**

adultery ●man whose wife has committed adultery: **cuckold** ●married woman's male lover: **cicisbeo** ●condoned adulterous relationship: **ménage à trois** (*pl.* ménages à trois) ●person alleged in a divorce case to have committed adultery: **respondent** ●person alleged in a divorce case to have committed adultery with the respondent: **co-respondent**

advance ●advance payment: **ante** ●performance in advance of official opening: **preview** ●advance publication: **preprint**

advantage ●advantage granted to few: **privilege** ●take unfair advantage of: **exploit** ●use of various ploys to gain psychological advantage over one's rivals: **gamesmanship**

advertisement ●advertisement making exaggerated claims: **puff** ●advertisement discrediting rival products: **knocking copy** ●advertisements shown between television programmes: **spot advertising** ●preliminary advertisement not naming the product: **teaser** ●advertisement written by an aircraft smoke trail: **skywriting** ●catchphrase used in an advertisement: **slogan** ●simple tune used in an advertisement: **jingle** ●advertisement's quotation of a supposedly impartial and unsolicited commendation of the item advertised: **testimonial** ●large board to display advertisements: **hoarding** ●pair of advertisement boards linked by shoulder straps: **sandwich boards** ●small handbill: **flyer** ●promotional material on the outside of packaging etc.: **outsert** ● appearance of an advertisement in a newspaper etc.: **insertion** ● newspaper advertisement presented as editorial material: **advertorial** ● small newspaper advertisements grouped by topic: **classified advertisements** ● advertising campaign: **promotion** ● postal advertising campaign: **mailshot** ● unsolicited advertising sent by post: **junk mail** ● advertising using images or sounds not registered by the conscious brain: **subliminal advertising** ● advertisement's subliminal meaning: **metamessage** ● person who writes the text for advertisements: **copywriter** ● person who sticks up unauthorized advertisements: **fly-poster** ▸ *see also* **publicity**

adviser ● respected personal adviser: **guru, mentor** ● professional adviser: **consultant** ● group nominally advising the sovereign: **Privy Council** ● group of experts researching specific government problems: **think tank** ● influential but unofficial advisers to a person in authority: **kitchen cabinet** ● person serving as a mouthpiece for divine advice: **oracle, prophet**

aerial ● horizontal rod aerial: **dipole** ● aerial having a series of short rods: **Yagi antenna** ● bowl-shaped aerial receiving satellite signals: **satellite dish**

aerobatics ● vertical circle: **loop the loop** ● aircraft's fast revolving motion: **spin** ● acrobatic stunts on the wings of an airborne aircraft: **wing walking**

aesthetics ● aesthetic expert: **connoisseur** ● person with no aesthetic sense: **boor, philistine**

affection ● be uncritically fond of: **adulate, adore, dote upon** ● adolescent affection: **puppy love** ● feel unrequited affection for: **carry a torch for**

affirmation ● official affirmation: **confirmation, ratification** ● denoting a process of enquiry conducted by affirmation: **cataphatic**

afraid of ● *combining form*: **-phobe** (*e.g.* xenophobe) ▸ *see also* **fear**

African ● African club: **knobkerrie** ● African machete: **panga** ● long narrow African drum: **tom-tom** ● African hut village: **kraal** ● African itinerant storyteller: **griot** ● expedition to hunt or observe wild animals: **safari** ● African fly causing sleeping sickness: **tsetse**

after ● *combining forms*: **epi-** (*e.g.* epilogue), **meta-** (*e.g.* metacarp), **post-** ● after dinner: **postprandial** ● after sexual intercourse: **postcoital**

afternoon ● *adjective*: **postmeridian** ● afternoon performance: **matinée** ● afternoon sleep: **siesta**

again ● *combining forms*: **ana-** (*e.g.* anagram, *where the letters are 'written again' to form another word*), **re-** (*e.g.* redo) ● request for a performance to be given again, or such a performance: **encore**

against ● *combining forms*: **anti-** (*e.g.* antihistamine), **cata-** (*e.g.* catapult, *literally 'throw against'*), **contra-** (*e.g.* contraception), **counter-** (*e.g.* countermeasure), **ob-** (*e.g.* object, *literally 'throw against'*)

age ● age of early childhood: **infancy** ● age at which sexual activity becomes possible: **puberty** ● age between puberty and adulthood: **adolescence** ● age at which consent to sexual intercourse becomes legally valid: **age of consent** ● person under the age of legal responsibility: **minor** ● age of youthful immaturity: **nonage** ● too young to legally engage in a certain activity: **under age** ● age at which a person is considered capable of managing his own affairs: **age of discretion** ● age of legal adulthood:

majority ●achieve this: **come of age** ●age at which sexual activity declines: **climacteric** ●person of the same age: **contemporary** ●person below the age of full legal responsibility: **juvenile** ●person in his or her sixties: **sexagenarian** ●person in his or her seventies: **septuagenarian** ●person in his or her eighties: **octogenarian** ●person in his or her nineties: **nonagenarian** ●person a hundred or more years old: **centenarian** ●mental and physical decay associated with old age: **senility** ●loss of memory and control of bodily functions amongst the aged: **senile dementia** ●age of senile dependency: **dotage**

agent ●confidential agent: **henchman** ●agent arranging sea transport: **shipbroker** ●agent for the purchase and sale of shares, insurance policies, etc.: **broker** ●broker's fee: **brokerage** ●sporting or artistic agent searching for promising recruits: **talent scout, talent spotter**

aggression ●policy of yielding to the demands of a potential aggressor: **appeasement** ●diplomacy enforced by threats of aggression: **gunboat diplomacy, power politics, sabre-rattling**

agreement ●apprenticeship agreement: **indentures** ●formal agreement: **compact, pact** ●general agreement: **consensus** ●interim agreement: **modus vivendi** ●legally enforceable agreement: **contract** ●agreement between the pope and a secular state: **concordat** ●agreement between states: **treaty** ●imagined agreement between members of a society to forego certain personal freedoms for the general good: **social contract** ●agreement to suspend hostilities for a stated period: **armistice** ●agreement reached through concessions: **compromise** ●agreement reached by parties to a dispute

or lawsuit: **settlement** ●informal treaty: **convention** ●informal understanding reached between states: **entente** ●draft of an agreement: **protocol** ●bargaining to reach an agreement: **negotiation** ●bargains made to mutual advantage: **horsetrading** ●demand that must be satisfied before agreement is reached: **stipulation** ●condition attached to an agreement: **proviso** ●exceptions specified in an agreement: **saving clause** ●proviso added to an agreement: **rider** ●in full agreement: **unanimous** ●one side to an agreement: **party** ●denoting an agreement between two parties: **bilateral** ●denoting an agreement between three or more parties: **multilateral** ●person forwarding an agreement though not party to it: **intermediary, mediator** ●breach of an agreement's terms: **infringement** ●formal announcement of intention to end an agreement: **notice** ●reject an agreement already made: **renounce, repudiate, rescind**

agricultural machinery ●device turning over the soil: **plough** ●tined framework breaking the soil: **harrow** ●sowing machine: **drill** ●reaping and threshing machine: **combine, combine harvester**

agriculture ●combining forms: **agri-, agro-** ●agriculture perceived as a technocratic activity: **agribusiness, agro-industry** ●agricultural system of abandoning land as it becomes exhausted: **shifting cultivation** ●denoting a shifting system in which vegetation in new areas is cut down and burnt: **slash-and-burn** ●denoting agriculture producing small per-acre yields by cheap methods: **extensive** ●denoting agriculture producing high per-acre yields by expensive methods: **intensive** ●denoting agriculture whose yields are just sufficient to feed the farmer: **subsistence** ●denoting agriculture avoiding the use of artificial chemicals: **organic** ●denoting agriculture that preserves an ecological balance: **sustainable** ●denoting agriculture or land devoted to crop-growing: **arable** ●denoting agriculture or land devoted to stock-grazing: **pastoral** ●denoting agriculture involving both of these: **mixed** ●introduction of intensive agriculture to developing countries: **green revolution** ●denoting agricultural property or methods: **agrarian** ●intensive stock-rearing methods: **battery farming, factory farming** ●building for intensive poultry raising: **broilerhouse** ●dark and constricted pen in which a calf is raised for veal: **veal crate** ●crate-free environment for stock-raising: **loose housing** ●ingathering of crops: **harvest** ●celebration of this: **harvest festival, harvest home** ●feeding cattle on cut grass brought in: **zero-grazing** ●minimization of erosion by ploughing along contours: **contour ploughing** ●denoting agricultural land left unsown: **fallow** ●medieval allocation of agricultural land: **open-field system** ●agricultural machinery: **deadstock** ●agricultural animals: **livestock** ●seasonal movement of livestock to different pasture: **transhumance** ●livestock fattened for slaughter: **fatstock** ●animal's weight as saleable meat: **deadweight** ●book recording livestock pedigrees: **herd book** ●supply water for agricultural purposes: **irrigate** ●study of soil management and crop production: **agronomy** ▸*see also* **crop, farm, tool**

Aids ●sexual activity with precautions against Aids: **safe sex** ●cancer suffered by Aids victims: **Kaposi's sarcoma**

air ●*combining forms*: **aero-, atmo-** (*e.g.* atmospheric), **pneum(o)-** ●in the air: **aerial** ●containing air: **pneumatic** ●rising current of warm air:

thermal ●admit air to: **aerate, ventilate** ●allowing the passage of air: **porous** ●designed for minimum air-resistance: **streamlined** ●operated by air pressure: **pneumatic** ●in the open air: **alfresco** ●denoting air having less oxygen than normal: **rarefied** ●airless region: **vacuum** ●die through lack of air: **suffocate** ●kill through deprivation of air: **suffocate, asphyxiate** ●air-pollution filter for the nose and mouth: **mask** ●retarding effect of air on a moving object: **drag** ●study of air movement: **aerodynamics** ●study of air travel: **aeronautics**

aircraft ●*combining form*: **aero-** ●small light aircraft: **microlight** ●aircraft with one pair of wings: **monoplane** ●aircraft having two sets of wings: **biplane** ●denoting an aircraft that can move its wings from a right-angled to swept-back position: **swing-wing, variable geometry** ●aircraft taking off from and landing on water: **seaplane** ●aircraft taking off and landing on water or land: **amphibian** ●jet aircraft landing and taking off vertically: **jump jet** ●engineless fixed-wing aircraft: **glider** ●powered aircraft kept buoyant by gas: **airship, dirigible** ●wingless aircraft with powered horizontal rotor: **helicopter** ●wingless aircraft with unpowered horizontal rotor: **autogiro, autogyro** ●aircraft capable of space travel: **spaceplane** ●aircraft equipped to carry liquids in bulk: **tanker** ●aircraft observing enemy positions: **spotter plane** ●aircraft designed to evade radar detection: **stealth plane** ●aircraft's main body: **fuselage** ●aircraft with little or no fuselage: **flying wing** ●far from the fuselage: **outboard** ●near to the fuselage: **inboard** ●inside the fuselage: **inboard, onboard** ●outermost layer of an aircraft's structure: **skin** ●lights showing an aircraft's position:

navigation lights, running lights, sidelights ● aircraft carrying goods: freighter ● pilotless aircraft packed with explosives: flying bomb ● aircraft manufacture and technology: aerospace ● part of an aircraft's structure specially curved to give it lift: aerofoil ● streamlining structure on an aircraft: fairing ● flattened projection improving stability: fin ● wheels etc. supporting an aircraft while on the ground: landing gear, undercarriage ● cables etc. controlling flight surfaces and engines: rigging ● aircraft's single triangular wing: delta wing ● hinged rear edge of an aircraft's wing: aileron, flap ● aircraft wing flap projected to create drag: spoiler ● aircraft's door: hatch ● detachable unit on an aircraft: pod ● front and rear of an aircraft: fore and aft ● part of an aircraft for the flight crew: cockpit, flight deck ● transparent cover of an aircraft cockpit: canopy ● flight crew's powered seat for emergency escape: ejection seat, ejector seat ● cockpit instrument panel: console, dashboard ● instrument showing an aircraft's height: altimeter ● instrument showing the rate of climb or descent: variometer ● rod controlling direction of flight: control column, joystick ● persons responsible for flying an aircraft: flight crew ● person in command of an aircraft: captain, pilot ● captain's assistant: first officer, co-pilot ● person directing an aircraft's route: navigator ● device keeping an aircraft on a set course: automatic pilot ● electronic aviation equipment: avionics ● removable cover for an aircraft engine: cowling ● aircraft engine's outer casing: nacelle ● section divider in an aircraft: bulkhead ● aircraft's small window: porthole ● aircraft's kitchen: galley ● maintenance of atmospheric pressure inside a high-flying aircraft: pressurization ● aircraft's cargo area: hold ● person in charge of cargo: loadmaster ● aircraft crew responsible for passengers or cargo: cabin crew ● list of aircraft passengers or cargo: manifest ● person hiding on an aircraft in order to travel without paying: stowaway ● aircraft's paying passengers and cargo: payload, useful load ● behind or to the back of an aircraft: astern ● on the outside of an aircraft: outboard ● use of a powered aircraft to pull a glider into the air: aerotowing ● bulk air transport of troops or supplies: airlift ● flying or operation of aircraft: aviation ● aircraft's planned or actual course: flight path, vector ● route regularly used by aircraft: air lane, airway ● permitted air route: air corridor ● official record of an aircraft's journey: log ● aircraft's flight recorder: black box, flight data recorder ● flight path of an aircraft waiting to land: holding pattern ● aircraft circling a given point at different altitudes while waiting to land: stack ● aircraft's path between takeoff and level cruising: climb-out ● tilt an aircraft to make a turn: bank ● aircraft's steep climbing turn: chandelle ● level an aircraft: flatten out ● aircraft's maximum possible altitude: ceiling ● maintain an aircraft at a steady altitude: trim ● aircraft's deviation from course due to wind: drift ● aircraft's speed relative to the ground: ground speed ● aircraft's speed relative to the ambient air: airspeed ● trail of disturbed air left behind a moving aircraft: slipstream, wake, wash ● trail of condensed water left by an aircraft at high altitude: vapour trail ● instance of two aircraft passing each other closer than is permitted: airmiss ● denoting an aircraft in difficulties: in distress ● region of low or uneven pressure destabilizing an aircraft: air pocket, turbulence ●aircraft shake caused by turbulence: **buffet, buffeting** ●(of an aircraft) rock from front to back: **pitch** ●(of an aircraft) rock from front to back: **roll** ●(of an aircraft) twist from side to side: **yaw** ●violent swing of an aircraft on or near ground: **ground loop** ●aircraft's steep downward plunge: **nosedive** ●aircraft's fast revolving motion: **spin** ●aircraft's unpowered landing: **deadstick landing** ●aircraft's rough emergency landing: **crash-landing, hard landing** ●aircraft's emergency landing with a final vertical drop: **pancake landing** ●aircraft's gradual descent to the runway: **approach** ●aircraft's circling course after aborted approach: **goaround** ●aircraft's landing descent: **glide path** ●runway contact by the wheels of a landing aircraft: **touchdown** ●landed aircraft's deceleration along the runway: **roll-out** ●aircraft's slow ground movement to or from the runway: **taxiing** ●airport personnel servicing an aircraft between flights: **ground crew** ●prepare an aircraft for its return journey: **turn round** ●housing for an aircraft: **hangar** ●official unveiling of a new aircraft: **roll-out** ●hire an aircraft for a trip: **charter** ●hire of an aircraft without crew: **dry lease** ●hire of an aircraft with crew: **wet lease** ●enter or place on an aircraft: **embark, emplane, enplane** ●throw from an aircraft: **jettison** ●leave an aircraft: **disembark, deplane** ●denoting an aircraft safe to fly: **airworthy** ●establishment monitoring aircraft movements: **tracking station** ●service monitoring and directing aircraft movements: **air traffic control** ●permission for an air movement given by air traffic control: **clearance** ●details of a proposed flight submitted to air traffic control: **flight plan** ●computerized mock-up of an aircraft cockpit used in pilot training: **flight simu-**

lator ●prohibit an aircraft from flying: **ground** ●illegally seize control of an aircraft: **hijack, skyjack** ●air force unit of six aircraft: **flight** ●anti-aircraft fire: **flak** ●military aircraft's emergency takeoff: **scramble** ●military aircraft's wartime operation: **mission** ▸*see also* **aerobatics, airliner, navigation**

aircraft carrier ●airstrip on an aircraft carrier: **flight deck**

airfield ●military airfield: **airbase** ●hard-surfaced area on an airfield where aircraft may park or manoeuvre: **apron, flightline** ●strip for taking off and landing: **runway** ●illuminated runway: **flarepath** ●flexible cylinder showing wind direction and force: **drogue, sleeve, windsock** ●large building for housing aircraft: **hangar**

airliner ●airliner carrying many passengers: **jumbo, jumbo jet** ●short-haul airliner carrying many passengers: **airbus** ●part of an airliner for the passengers: **cabin** ●most expensive class of passenger accommodation: **first class** ●middle class passenger accommodation: **club class** ●cheapest passenger accommodation: **economy class, tourist class** ●persons attending to passengers' needs: **cabin crew, flight attendants, stewards** ●bag suitable for transport in the cabin: **carry-on, flight bag** ●air-traveller's luggage beyond his or her allowance: **excess baggage** ●list of airliner passengers: **manifest** ●person hiding on an airliner in order to travel without paying: **stowaway** ●company providing scheduled public air transport: **airline** ●product promotion giving vouchers redeemable for stated distances of free air travel: **Air Miles™**

airport ●airport building for departing and arriving passengers: **terminal** ●airport reception counter:

desk ●those parts of an airport terminal that lie between its street entrance and customs and passport control: **landside** ●those parts of an airport terminal that lie between the aircraft and customs and passport control: **airside** ●desk where departing passengers have their tickets inspected: **check-in** ●non-appearance of booked passenger: **no-show** ●refusal to honour a ticket, due to overbooking: **bumping** ●ticket-holder waiting for a seat to become available: **standby** ●airport information board or screen: **indicator** ●airport lounge for passengers changing planes: **transit lounge** ●airport exit to a particular flight: **gate** ●raised passageway to an aircraft: **pier** ●movable steps giving access to an aircraft: **ramp** ●airport's non-flying staff: **ground staff** ●airport employees servicing an aircraft: **ground crew** ●rotating machine from which luggage is collected: **carousel** ●arrival or departure of an aircraft: **movement** ●elevated office from which flight movements are controlled: **control tower** ●tiredness felt after a flight across time zones: **jet lag**

airship ●mechanically propelled airship: **dirigible** ●German military airship used in First World War: **Zeppelin** ●airship's gas container: **envelope** ●cabin suspended beneath an airship: **gondola**

alcohol ●courage gained by drinking alcohol: **Dutch courage** ●apparatus for distilling alcohol: **still** ●person authorized to sell alcoholic drinks: **victualler, licensed victualler** ●denoting a place authorized to sell alcoholic drinks: **licensed** ●denoting an alcoholic drink served without further dilution: **neat, straight** ●denoting a region where alcoholic drinks cannot be purchased: **dry** ●add alcohol surreptitiously to a drink: **spike** ●make alcohol unfit to drink: **de-**

nature ●alcohol denatured by methanol: **methylated spirit** ●abstinence from alcoholic drinks: **teetotalism, temperance**

alcoholism ●delusions caused by alcoholism: **delirium tremens** ●intermittent craving for alcohol: **dipsomania** ●child's mental and physical retardation caused by the mother's consumption of excessive alcohol during pregnancy: **fetal alcohol syndrome**

algae ●proliferation of algae in water: **algal bloom** ●study of algae: **algology**

algebra ●algebraic expression of the sum or difference of two terms: **binomial** ●expression of more than two algebraic terms: **polynomial** ●number multiplying an algebraic variable: **coefficient**

alien ●fictional mechanical alien organism: **dalek** ●imagined alien being: **little green man** ●person claiming to have had dealings with alien beings: **contactee** ●wartime imprisonment of resident aliens: **internment** ●resident alien in ancient Greece: **metic**

alkali ●dye indicating alkalinity: **litmus** ●non-alkaline substance: **base**

all ●*combining forms*: **omni-, pan-, panto-** (*e.g.* pantomime, *originally* (*referring to a mime artist*) *'imitator of all'*) ●for all persons or things: **universal** ●all at once: **en bloc, simultaneously** ●all-in: **freestyle** ●all-knowing: **omniscient** ●all-powerful: **omnipotent** ●all together: **en bloc, en masse** ●disease breaking out over all parts of a country or over all the world: **pandemic**

allergy ●allergy causing breathing difficulties: **asthma** ●allergy caused by pollen: **hay fever** ●substance causing an allergic reaction: **allergen** ●denoting a substance unlikely to cause an allergic reaction: **hypo-**

allergenic ● itchy red spots caused by food allergies: **hives, nettlerash, urticaria** ● compound released into cells to combat allergens: **histamine** ● medicine used to treat allergies: **antihistamine** ● cure allergy by gradual exposure to its cause: **desensitization** ● skin allergy test: **patch test**

alliance ● informal alliance: **entente** ● secret alliance between firms to prevent competition: **cartel** ● secret alliance of purchasers at an auction to force down prices: **ring** ● temporary alliance between political parties: **coalition, front** ● temporary alliance between businesses: **consortium**

allowance ● money paid to a carer for looking after an invalid: **attendance allowance** ● money paid to local councillors for time spent on council business: **attendance allowance**

alloy ● alloy used to join metal: **solder** ● mercury alloy used to fill teeth: **amalgam** ● alloy of gold and silver: **electrum** ● goldlike alloy of copper and zinc: **pinchbeck** ● silver-like alloy of nickel, zinc, and copper: **nickel silver, German silver** ● alloy of which monumental brasses are made: **latten**

almond ● almond paste: **marzipan** ● scald almonds to remove their skin: **blanch**

almost ● *combining form*: **quasi-** (*e.g.* quasi-autonomous) ● strip of land almost detached from the mainland: **peninsula**

alone ● person who lives alone: **hermit, recluse** ● person who enjoys being alone: **loner, solitary**

Alps ● beyond the Alps: **ultramontane** ● this side of the Alps: **cismontane** ● traditional Alpine wooden house: **chalet**

alphabet ● ancient Anglo-Saxon and Scandinavian alphabet: **futhark,** **runes** ● ancient British and Irish alphabet: **ogham** ● Indian alphabet: **Devanagari** ● alphabet of raised dots for blind people: **Braille** ● former alphabet of raised letters for blind people: **Moon** ● pronunciation sign written above or below a letter: **diacritic** ● write in a different alphabet: **transliterate**

altar ● chief altar: **high altar** ● portable altar: **superaltar** ● altar canopy: **baldacchino, ciborium** ● ornamental cloth covering the front of an altar: **frontal** ● ornamental cloth behind an altar: **dossal** ● shelf behind an altar: **retable** ● ornamental screen behind an altar: **reredos** ● painting placed behind an altar: **altarpiece** ● railing round an altar: **parclose** ● altar cabinet for the reserved sacrament: **tabernacle** ● drain near an altar: **piscina**

alternative medicine ● medical system associating parts of the hands and feet with different parts of the body: **zone therapy** ● massage system based on zone therapy: **reflexology** ● joint manipulation: **chiropractic** ● regime of massage, exercise, and diet control: **naturopathy** ● medicinal use of plants: **herbalism** ● healing by spiritual means: **faith healing** ● healing by crystals: **crystal healing**

amateur ● amateur dabbler in an art or skill: **dilettante** ● person falsely claiming amateur status: **shamateur**

ambassador ● papal ambassador: **nuncio** ● nuncio sent to a non-Catholic country: **pro-nuncio** ● ambassador's deputy: **chargé d'affaires** ● ambassador's assistant: **attaché** ● ambassador's residence: **embassy** ● ambassador's introductory letter: **credentials, letter of credence** ● dress of an ambassador who is presented to the head of state: **court dress** ▸ *see also* diplomacy

ambiguity ●statement made ambiguous by its grammar: **amphibology, amphiboly** ●statement designed to have a second (usually indecent) meaning: **double entendre, double entente**

American Indian ●American Indian thought to have magic powers: **medicine man, shaman** ●American Indian axe: **tomahawk** ●American Indian peace pipe: **calumet** ●American Indian shoe: **moccasin** ●American Indian spell: **medicine** ●American Indian tent: **lodge, teepee, wigwam**

ammunition ●ammunition for a single shot: **round** ●denoting ammunition containing explosive: **live** ●denoting ammunition containing explosive but no projectile: **blank** ●ammunition store: **magazine**

among ●*combining form*: inter- (e.g. international) ●among others: **inter alios** ●among other things: **inter alia**

amount ●tiny amount: **iota, jot, soupçon, trace, vestige** ●required or permitted amount: **quantum, quota, ration** ●insufficient amount: **short measure** ●amount left over: **surplus** ●express or measure an amount: **quantify** ●assessed by amount: **quantitative, quantitive**

anaesthetic ●anaesthetic affecting the whole body: **general anaesthetic** ●spinal anaesthetic given in childbirth: **epidural, extradural** ●denoting an anaesthetic affecting a specified part only: **local**

analysis ●detailed critical analysis: **critique** ●analysis of complex procedures to improve efficiency: **systems analysis**

ancestor ●earliest ancestor: **progenitor, primogenitor** ●enumeration of a person's ancestors: **genealogy, pedigree** ●related through a common male ancestor: **agnate** ●related through a common ancestor: **cognate** ●relationship by descent from a common ancestor: **consanguinity** ●resembling or deriving from ancestral characteristics: **atavistic**

anchor ●small anchor with several flukes: **grapnel** ●small anchor used to haul a ship: **kedge, kedge anchor** ●straight part of an anchor: **shank** ●triangular plate on an anchor's arm: **fluke** ●stone used as an anchor: **killick**

ancient ●*combining forms*: **archaeo-, palaeo-** ●excavation and study of the physical remains of ancient civilizations: **archaeology** ●study of fossil animals and plants: **palaeobiology** ●study of fossil plants: **palaeobotany**

angel ●angel of the first order: **seraph** ●angel of the second order: **cherub** ●angel of the third order: **throne** ●angel of the fourth order: **domination** ●angel of the fifth order: **virtue** ●angel of the sixth order: **power** ●angel of the seventh order: **principality** ●angel of the eighth order: **archangel** ●angel of the ninth order: **angel** ●feast of the archangel Michael: **Michaelmas** ●local group of Hell's Angels: **chapter**

anger ●anger at unfair treatment: **indignation, offence, outrage, resentment** ●expression of public anger: **outcry** ●public outrage or the event causing it: **scandal** ●public display of anger: **scene** ●childish outburst of anger: **tantrum** ●easily angered: **irascible, irritable, short-tempered, testy, tetchy, truculent** ●intended to cause anger: **provocative** ●remark made to provoke anger: **taunt** ●sulky bad temper: **petulance, pique** ●natural proneness to anger or equanimity: **temperament** ●petulant expression of the lips: **moue, pout** ●angry frown: **scowl** ●angry rebuke: **scolding** ●denoting a bad-tempered person: **curmudgeonly, dyspeptic** ●cause persistent resentment: **rankle** ●soothe anger: **appease, mollify, pacify, placate, propitiate**

angle ●*combining form*: **-gon** ●angle smaller than 90°: **acute angle** ●angle of 90°: **right angle** ●angle between 90–180°: **obtuse angle** ●denoting an angle not a right angle: **oblique** ●denoting an angle that combines with another to make 90°: **complementary** ●denoting an inward-pointing angle: **re-entrant** ●denoting an outward-pointing angle: **salient** ●figure with many angles: **polygon** ●having three angles: **triangular** ●having four angles: **quadrangular** ●having five angles: **pentangular** ●having eight angles: **octangular** ●tool for marking angles: **bevel** ●instrument to measure or draw angles: **protractor, set square** ●instrument measuring angles precisely: **goniometer**

Anglo-Saxon ●ancient Anglo-Saxon alphabet: **futhark, runes** ●Anglo-Saxon prince or noble: **atheling**

animal ●*combining forms*: **theri-, zoo-** ●animal without a backbone: **invertebrate** ●animal having a backbone: **vertebrate** ●animal having two feet: **biped** ●animal having four feet: **quadruped** ●warm-blooded animal suckling its young: **mammal** ●animal carrying its young in a pouch: **marsupial** ●scaly-skinned cold-blooded animal: **reptile** ●cold-blooded terrestrial animal having an aquatic larval stage: **amphibian** ●variety of animal developed by breeding: **strain** ●animal used to pull carts, ploughs, etc.: **draught animal** ●set of draught animals: **team** ●animal used to carry loads: **beast of burden** ●animal regarded as symbolizing a group or bringing good fortune: **mascot** ●animals bred or raised for profit: **livestock, stock** ●animal hunting others: **predator** ●hunted animal: **prey** ●animal used by hunters to attract others: **decoy** ●animal eating its own species: **cannibal** ●animal eating flesh: **carnivore** ●animal eating plants: **herbivore** ●animal feeding on refuse: **scavenger** ●animal in its second year: **yearling** ●animal that chews the cud: **ruminant** ●animal dependent upon external sources of heat: **ectotherm** ●animal creating its own bodily heat: **endotherm** ●animal maintaining a steady body temperature: **homeotherm** ●male animal kept for breeding: **sire** ●animal's female parent: **dam** ●young born to an animal at one time: **brood, litter** ●smallest member of a litter: **runt** ●give birth to young: **throw** ●malformed or mutant animal: **monster** ●offspring of animals of different species: **crossbreed, hybrid** ●large group of animals: **herd** ●group of herded animals: **drove, herd, flock** ●animals of a particular region or time: **fauna** ●underwater animal life: **epifauna** ●denoting an animal native to a particular region: **endemic** ●wild animal's home: **den, lair, lie** ●area regularly traversed by an animal: **home range** ●animal's seasonal change of habitat: **migration** ●panicked rush of a number of animals: **stampede** ●animal's bedding of straw etc.: **litter** ●animal's projecting nose and mouth: **snout** ●animal's flexible snout: **proboscis** ●animal's frightening jaws: **maw** ●hind part of an animal's body: **rump** ●animal's skin with the hair: **pelt** ●clean an animal's coat: **groom** ●skin disease of hairy and woolly animals: **mange** ●animal's seasonal loss of plumage or fur: **moult** ●animal's internal organs eaten as meat: **offal, pluck** ●animal's flexible grasping appendage: **tentacle**

●animal's track or scent: **spoor** ●denoting animals adapted to a very dry environment: **xerophilous** ●ability of certain animals to change colour: **metachrosis** ●denoting a tamed animal: **domestic, domesticated** ●denoting an animal returned to the wild: **feral** ●establish an animal in a foreign habitat: **naturalize** ●denoting an animal bred for research: **laboratory** ●denoting an untethered animal: **loose** ●animal's dose of medicine: **drench** ●climb onto an animal for riding: **mount** ●(of a male animal) climb onto a female animal for copulation: **mount** ●animal excrement: **droppings, dung** ●remains of prehistoric animals found in rock: **fossil** ●taking the form of an animal: **theriomorphic, zoomorphic** ●animal trainer: **handler** ●exploitation of animals justified by alleged human superiority: **speciesism** ●protected area for wildlife: **reserve, sanctuary** ●enclosure for keeping animals in semi-natural conditions: **vivarium** ●place for keeping stray animals: **pound** ●collection of wild animals for exhibition: **menagerie, zoo** ●doctor treating animals: **vet, veterinary surgeon** ●allegedly unjustifiable experiments performed on animals: **vivisection** ●book describing different kinds of animals: **bestiary** ●study of animals: **zoology** ●study of animal behaviour: **ethology** ●study of animals whose existence is doubted: **cryptozoology**

ankle ●ankle-covering: **gaiter, spat** ●ankle ornament: **anklet**

anniversary ●25th anniversary: **silver jubilee** ●50th anniversary: **golden jubilee** ●25th or 50th anniversary: **jubilee** ●denoting a 40th anniversary: **ruby** ●denoting a 60th anniversary: **diamond** ●100th anniversary: **centenary** ●150th anniversary: **sesquicentenary** ●200th anniversary: **bicentenary** ●300th anniversary: **tercentenary** ●400th anniversary: **quatercentenary** ●500th anniversary: **quincentenary** ●600th anniversary: **sexcentenary**

announcer ●announcer at a public event: **master of ceremonies** ●announcer at a variety show: **compère**

annoy ●easily annoyed: **irritable, peevish, tetchy** ●until it becomes annoying: **ad nauseam**

anointing ●ritual anointing for religious purposes: **unction** ●oil used for ritual anointing: **chrism**

answer ●sharp answer: **retort** ●witty answer: **rejoinder, riposte** ●witty answer thought of too late: **esprit de l'escalier** ●refusal to give straight answers: **stonewalling**

ant ●*combining form*: **myrmec(o)-** ●*adjective*: **formic** ●female ant: **queen** ●male ant: **drone** ●sterile ant performing most basic tasks: **worker** ●African and Asian animal that eats ants: **pangolin, scaly anteater** ●study of ants: **myrmecology**

antibiotic ●antibiotic produced from blue moulds: **penicillin** ●denoting an antibiotic effective against a large range of organisms: **broad-spectrum**

antidote ●serum containing antidotes: **antiserum, antivenin** ●supposed antidote to all poisons: **mithridate**

antique ●interesting antique: **objet de virtu** ●person who studies or collects antiques or antiquities: **antiquarian, antiquary**

antler ●flat section of antler: **palm** ●prong of antler: **tine**

anus ●*combining form*: **proct(o)-** ●*adjective*: **anal** ●muscle closing the anus: **sphincter** ●inflammation of the anus: **proctitis** ●swollen veins in the anus: **haemorrhoids, piles** ●instrument for inspecting the anus:

proctoscope ●surgical construction of an artificial anus: **colostomy** ●study of the anus: **proctology**

anxiety ●abnormally tense or anxious: **neurotic** ●showing no anxiety: **nonchalant**

apart ●*combining forms*: **dia-** (*e.g.* diagnosis, *literally 'telling apart'*), **se-** (*e.g.* separate)

apartheid ●former domination by whites in South Africa: **baaskap** ●term under apartheid for a South African black: **Bantu** ●offensive former South African term for any black person: **Kaffir** ●offensive former South African term for a person of mixed ethnic origins: **Coloured** ●homeland for South African blacks under apartheid: **Bantustan** ●urban settlement for South African blacks under apartheid: **location, township** ●township drinking place: **shebeen**

ape ●*adjective*: **simian** ●large powerful ape: **gorilla**

apex ●*adjective*: **apical**

Aphrodite ●*Latin name*: **Venus**

appeal ●passionate appeal: **cri de cœur** (*pl.* cris de cœur) ●litigant who appeals to a higher court: **appellant**

appearance ●*combining form*: **-morph** (*e.g.* polymorph), **-phany** ●appearance of a god to mortals: **epiphany, theophany** ●first appearance of an artist in public: **debut** ●sportsman or -woman playing in public for the first time: **debutant** ●surface appearance of a manufactured article: **finish** ●done merely for the sake of appearance: **token** ●denoting pleasant appearance and manner: **personable** ●misleading appearance: **guise, illusion**

appendix ●inflammation of the appendix: **appendicitis** ●surgical removal of an appendix: **appendectomy**

appetite ●*adjective*: **orectic** ●person with a gross appetite for food: **gourmand** ●person with an insatiable sexual appetite: **lecher**

appetizer ●first course of a meal: **hors d'oeuvre, starter** ●small open sandwich served as appetizer: **canapé** ●alcoholic drink taken before a meal as an appetizer: **aperitif**

applause ●loud and long applause: **ovation** ●persons hired to applaud: **claque**

apple ●apple that is green when ripe: **greening** ●alcoholic drink made from apple juice: **cider** ●apple brandy: **Calvados** ●apple of one's eye: **cynosure**

appointment ●appoint to a post: **nominate** ●where no appointments are needed: **drop-in** ●person not keeping an appointment: **no-show**

apprenticeship ●apprenticeship agreement: **indentures** ●having completed an apprenticeship: **time-served**

Arab ●Arab leader: **sheik** ●Arab scholar or man of high social standing: **effendi** ●nomadic desert Arab: **Bedouin** ●Arab living in Israel or Palestine: **Palestinian** ●Arab who does not want a negotiated peace with Israel: **rejectionist** ●Arab guerrillas: **fedayeen** ●Arab sailing boat: **dhow** ●Arab quarter in a town: **kasbah** ●Arab covered market: **bazaar, souk** ●Arab meat ball: **kofta** ●Arab dish of spiced durum semolina: **couscous** ●Arab dish of mashed chickpeas: **felafel, hummus** ●Arab cracked-wheat salad: **tabbouleh** ●Arab fruit-juice drink: **sherbet** ●Arab hooded cloak: **burnous, djellaba** ●Arab headdress: **keffiyeh** ●Arab headband: **agal** ●Arab man's long robe: **dishdasha** ●Arab eye make-up: **kohl** ●Arab gesture of greeting: **salaam** ●Arab name for God: **Allah** ●dried-up river channel in some Arab countries: **wadi**

● Arab term for marijuana: **kif**
● spirit in Arab folklore: **genie** (*pl.* genii), **jinn** (*pl.* same) ▸ *see also* **Muslim**

arbitrator ● *adjective*: **arbitral** ● arbitrator's formal decision: **arbitrament, determination** ● denoting an arbitrament that the parties must obey: **binding**

arch ● row of arches: **arcade** ● stone at the centre of an arch: **keystone** ● area behind the shoulder of an arch: **spandrel** ● underside of an arch: **soffit** ● support for an arch: **pier** ● structure supporting the lateral thrust of an arch: **abutment**

archaeology ● *combining form*: **archaeo-** (*e.g.* archaeometry) ● urgent archaeological investigation of a site about to be disturbed: **rescue archaeology** ● systematic inspection of a ploughed field: **field walking** ● analysis of layering of remains: **stratigraphy**

archdeacon ● *adjective*: **archidiaconal** ● title of an Anglican archdeacon: **venerable** ● archdeacon's formal inspection: **visitation**

archer ● astrological term: **sagittarius**

archery ● *adjective*: **toxophilite** ● archery range: **butts** ● mound for the target in a range: **butt** ● distant target: **rover**

architect ● *adjective*: **architectonic** ● architect working in consultation with local inhabitants: **community architect**

architecture ● architecture designed to sympathize with its environment: **landscape architecture** ● denoting architecture in the styles of ancient Greece and Rome: **classical** ● denoting architectural style manifested in functional buildings: **vernacular** ● upper part of a classical building: **entablature** ● rounded roofing vault: **dome** ● slender spire:

flèche ● ornamental porch with columns: **portico** ● covered walk round a quadrangle: **cloister** ● cloistered quadrangle: **cloister garth, garth** ● window projecting from a sloping roof: **dormer** ● denoting an opening wider at one end than at the other: **splayed** ● splayed window opening: **embrasure** ● ornamental stone openwork above a window: **tracery** ● semicircular alcove: **lunette** ● large polygonal recess: **oriel** ● projecting support for a wall: **buttress** ● arch-shaped buttress: **flying buttress** ● moulding round the edge of a ceiling: **cornice** ● moulding round a door or window: **architrave, dripstone, hood mould, label** ● wall filling the end of a pitched roof: **gable** ● decorative triangular gable above a door or wall: **pediment** ● pediment's recessed central area: **tympanum** ● decorative band at a wall top: **frieze** ● projecting wall above a fireplace: **chimney breast** ● projecting support: **corbel** ● ornamental woodwork at a gable end: **bargeboard** ● ornamental battlements: **castellation** ● ornament at the top or corner of a building: **finial** ● ornament covering a joint in ribwork: **boss** ● Norman pointed ornamentation: **dog-tooth** ● ornamental moulding of semicircular section: **beading** ● ornamental framing for an inscription: **cartouche** ● ornament covering converging vaulting: **boss** ● grotesquely carved water spout: **gargoyle** ● decoration in the Chinese style: **chinoiserie** ● outer covering for a wall: **cladding** ● lower part of an interior wall: **dado** ● smooth, square-cut masonry: **ashlar** ● steps and platform before a main entrance: **perron** ● elaborately decorated entrance: **portal** ● row of arches: **arcade** ● exterior gallery on an upper floor: **loggia** ● open courtyard in the centre of a building: **atrium** ● underside of an architectural feature: **soffit** ▸ *see also* **beam, brick, building, column, dome, ornament, vault, wall, window**

archive ●archived record: **muniment** ●person in charge of an archive collection: **archivist**

Arctic ●Arctic plain: **tundra** ●Arctic sledge dog: **husky**

area ●large area: **tract** ●long narrow area: **belt** ●remote area: **hinterland, interior** ●area with a particular use or character: **zone** ●key area: **nexus** ●area radically different from those surrounding it: **enclave** ●area cut off from those to which it is related: **exclave** ●surrounding area: **purlieu** ●area with controlled access: **exclusion zone** ●wet and boggy area: **quagmire** ●area devoted to buildings of a particular kind: **estate** ●area of influence or concern: **purview** ●area covered or available: **range**

Ares ●*Latin name*: **Mars**

argument ●*adjective*: **eristic** ●argument presented in court: **submission** ●argument carefully ignoring unfavourable facts: **special pleading** ●noisy but trivial argument: **squabble** ●likely to cause argument: **contentious** ●prone to argue: **disputatious** ●refutation of another's argument: **rebuttal** ●allowing no argument: **final** ●denoting a superficially plausible argument: **prima facie** ●denoting a fallacious argument got up to convince: **specious** ●user of dishonest arguments: **casuist, sophist**

arm ●*combining form*: **brachio-** ●*adjective*: **brachial** ●arm of an octopus: **tentacle** ●dinosaur with short armlike front legs: **brachiosaurus** ●ornament worn round the upper arm: **armlet**

armed forces ●*adjective*: **military**

armour ●armour made of small metal rings: **chain mail** ●helmet's plume: **crest** ●helmet's face-guard: **beaver, visor** ●throat armour: **gorget** ●armour for the chest and back: **cuirass** ●sleeveless mail coat: **habergeon** ●full-length mail coat: **hauberk** ●arm armour: **vambrace** ●armoured glove: **gauntlet** ●thigh armour: **cuisse** ●shin armour: **greave** ●cloth garment worn over armour: **surcoat**

arms ●*adjective*: **heraldic** ●system by which coats of arms are devised: **heraldry** ●expert in this: **heraldist** ●official controlling the College of Arms: **Earl Marshal** ●official overseeing state ceremonial and grants of arms: **herald, officer of arms, persuivant** ●chief herald: **King of Arms** ●herald's emblazoned coat: **tabard** ●shield bearing a coat of arms: **escutcheon** ●smaller shield drawn inside another: **inescutcheon** ●section of an escutcheon: **quarter** ●coat of arms with its bearers etc.: **achievement** ●diamond-shaped board showing this: **hatchment** ●heraldic design: **device, emblem** ●left-hand side of a coat of arms: **dexter** ●right-hand side of a coat of arms: **sinister** ●depict a coat of arms: **emblazon** ●display two coats of arms on one shield: **impale** ●denoting a coat of arms that represents the bearer's name: **canting**

army ●*adjective*: **military** ●citizen army: **militia, home guard** ●irregular resistance force: **militia** ●front part of an army: **van, vanguard** ●side of an army: **flank** ●ground between opposing armies: **no-man's-land** ●army training school: **military academy**

aromatic ●aromatic ointment made from a tree resin: **balsam** ●massage treatment using aromatic oils: **aromatherapy**

around ●*combining forms*: **amphi-** (*e.g.* amphitheatre), **circum-** (*e.g.* circumference), **peri-** (*e.g.* perinatal)

arrange ●arrange in sequence without overlaps: **stagger** ●arrangement of battle forces: **disposition** ●possible arrangement of a set of items: **permutation**

arrest ●arrest performed by an ordinary person: **citizen's arrest** ●immunity from arrest: **sanctuary** ●diplomat's immunity from arrest: **extraterritoriality**

arrival ●person dealing with arrivals at a hospital, office, or hotel: **receptionist** ●non-arrival: **no-show**

arrow ●arrow for crossbow: **bolt** ●arrow's central wooden section: **shaft** ●back-turned spike on an arrow head: **barb** ●feathered end of an arrow: **flight** ●feather an arrow: **fletch** ●case for arrows: **quiver**

art ●creative art: **fine art** ●vulgar or sentimental art: **kitsch** ●art intended to arouse sexual desire: **erotica** ●art produced by the untrained: **outsider art** ●art giving a minute reproduction of reality: **hyperrealism** ●realistic depiction of current social conditions: **social realism, verismo** ●denoting grimly realistic art: **kitchen-sink** ●artistic norms promulgated under Stalinism: **socialist realism** ●denoting art depicting physical appearances in a natural way: **figurative, realistic** ●denoting art not depicting physical appearances in a natural way: **abstract** ●denoting unconventional art: **avant-garde, underground** ●type of art: **genre** ●genres created before an audience: **performing arts** ●denoting those genres involving three-dimensional modelling: **plastic** ●genres based on line and tone: **graphic arts** ●recurrent feature in an artwork: **motif** ●conveyance of feeling in art: **expression** ●faculty of artistic origination: **creativity** ●artistic discernment: **taste** ●knowledge of the fine arts: **virtu** ●artwork turned out to make a living: **potboiler** ●artist's complete output: **oeuvre** ●outstanding artistic creation: **masterpiece, masterwork, pièce de résistance** (*pl.* pièces de résistance) ●artwork imitating other styles: **pastiche** ●amateur dabbler in an art: **dilettante** ●art exhibition: **salon** ●put works of art on show: **exhibit** ●artefact assembled at the exhibition: **installation** ●presentation of artefacts which includes performers: **performance art** ●found object considered as a work of art: **objet trouvé** (*pl.* objets trouvés) ●organized series of artistic events: **festival** ●spontaneous artistic event: **happening**

Artemis ●*Latin name*: **Diana**

arthritis ●arthritis in the joints: **osteoarthritis, rheumatoid arthritis** ●swimming exercises as a cure for arthritis: **hydrotherapy**

artificial ●artificial body parts: **prosthetics** ●artificially created: **factitious, synthetic**

artist ●major artist of the 13th–17th centuries: **old master** ●artist's workshop: **studio, atelier** ●artist's dummy: **lay figure, manikin** ●artist's personal style: **idiom** ●artist's youthful output: **juvenilia** ●artist's complete output: **corpus, oeuvre** ●artist's most important creation: **magnum opus** ●group of artists having a similar approach: **school** ●person posing for an artist: **model**

ash ●*adjectives*: **cinerary, cinerous** ●container for cremated ashes: **urn**

Asian ●light Asian cart drawn by one or more people: **rickshaw** ●Asian savoury pastry: **samosa** ●rainy season in southern Asia: **monsoon** ●yellow powder used to flavour and tint Asian dishes: **turmeric** ▶*see also* **Chinese, Indian, Japanese**

assembly ●assembly by the purchaser: **self-assembly** ●supplied ready for easy assembly: **prefabricated**

assessment ●analytical assessment: **critique** ●formal assessment of an employee's performance: **appraisal** ●person giving an assessment of an artistic work or performance: **critic** ●difficult or impossible to assess: **imponderable**

asset ●denoting assets not easily convertible into cash: **fixed, illiquid** ●denoting assets easily converted to cash: **disposable, liquid, near-money** ●denoting assets expected to be sold within a year: **current** ●sale of assets: **disposal** ●selling off assets of a purchased company for quick profit: **asset-stripping** ●simultaneous trading of assets in different markets to profit by price differences: **arbitrage** ●convert assets into cash: **realize** ●gradual increase in an asset's value: **appreciation** ●gradual decrease in an asset's value: **depreciation** ●progressive write-off of an asset's purchase value: **amortization** ●charge upon assets: **encumbrance** ●prevent the use of assets: **freeze** ●legal document disposing of one's assets after death: **will**

assimilation ●gradual assimilation: **osmosis** ●assimilation of cultural minorities: **integration**

assistant ●*combining form*: **sub-** (*e.g.* subeditor), **vice-** (*e.g.* vice-president) ●general assistant: **gopher, factotum, mate, office boy** ●author's or composer's assistant, taking down dictation or copying drafts: **amanuensis** ●criminal's assistant: **accomplice, abettor** ●hunter's or fisherman's assistant: **gillie** ●golfer's assistant: **caddie** ●civil servant assisting a senior government official: **private secretary** ●administrative assistant to a senior military officer: **adjutant** ●confidential assistant to a senior military officer: **aide-de-camp** ●priest's liturgical assistant: **acolyte**

assumption ●assumption made as a basis for further reasoning: **hypothesis** ●based upon assumptions: **supposititious**

asthma ●*adjective*: **asthmatic** ●person suffering from asthma: **asthmatic** ●drug taken by asthmatics to widen the bronchi: **bronchodilator** ●instrument measuring asthmatics' lung capacity: **peak flow meter**

astrology ●astrological forecast of future events: **horoscope** ●astrological chart: **zodiac** ●sector on an astrological chart: **house, sign**

astronaut ●trainee astronaut: **space cadet** ●astronaut's protective clothing: **spacesuit** ●astronaut's period of physical activity in space outside the spacecraft: **space walk, extravehicular activity** ●astronaut's supply line during extravehicular activity: **umbilical** ●imagined distortion of space–time enabling astronauts to breach the laws of physics: **space warp**

Athena ●*Latin name*: **Minerva**

athletics ●athletic contest with two events for all competitors: **biathlon** ●athletic contest with three events for all competitors: **triathlon** ●athletic contest with four events for all competitors: **tetrathlon** ●athletic contest with five events for all competitors: **pentathlon** ●athletic contest with seven events for all competitors: **heptathlon** ●athletic contest with ten events for all competitors: **decathlon** ●international athletic contest for the disabled: **Paralympics** ●athletic event not a race: **field event** ●athletic event involving racing: **track event** ●balanced series of athletic exercises: **circuit** ●disc thrown by an athlete: **discus** ●large heavy ball thrown by athlete: **shot** ●athlete

competing in short races: **sprinter**
● athlete competing in middle or long
distance races: **distance runner**
● athlete's warm oversuit: **tracksuit**
● weatherproof tracksuit: **shell suit**

Atlantic Ocean ● equatorial region of the Atlantic with uncertain winds: **doldrums** ● warm current running northwest from the Gulf of Mexico: **Gulf Stream, North Atlantic Drift**

atmosphere ● having a stale warm atmosphere: **frowsty, fuggy, fusty, stuffy** ● device to improve a room's atmosphere: **ionizer** ● map line joining points of equal atmospheric pressure: **isobar** ● regions of the earth's crust and atmosphere inhabited by living organisms: **biosphere** ● successive regions of the earth's atmosphere: **troposphere, stratosphere, mesosphere, thermosphere, ionosphere** ● interface between troposphere and stratosphere: **tropopause** ● interface between stratosphere and ionosphere: **stratopause** ● ozone-rich layer in the stratosphere: **ozone layer** ● thin area in this: **ozone hole** ● proportion of moisture present in the atmosphere: **humidity** ● elongated region of high atmospheric pressure: **ridge** ● elongated region of low atmospheric pressure: **trough** ● area of atmospheric pressure lower than those around it: **depression** ● unstable atmospheric pressure: **turbulence** ● instrument measuring atmospheric pressure: **barometer**

atom ● atom with a net positive or negative charge: **ion** ● atom's central core: **nucleus** (*pl.* nuclei) ● force holding atoms together: **bond** ● bonded group of atoms: **molecule** ● group of atoms behaving as a unit: **radical** ● constituent of an atom: **particle, subatomic particle, elementary particle** ● force holding quarks, neutrons, and protons together within the nucleus: **strong force** ● technology

for manipulating atoms and molecules: **nanotechnology** ● atomic clock: **caesium clock**

attach ● inessential extra item attached to something: **appendage** ● attachment between newborn infant and its mother: **umbilical cord**

attack ● *combining form*: (of a disease) **-lepsy** (*e.g.* epilepsy) ● brief attack: **foray, incursion, sally, sortie** ● fierce attack: **blitz, onslaught** ● sudden attack: **strike** ● sudden surprise attack: **coup de main** (*pl.* coups de main) ● sudden attack from a defensive position: **sally, sortie** ● attack on an enemy position: **assault** ● unprovoked attack: **aggression** ● attack designed to disable a perceived threat: **first strike, pre-emptive strike** ● response to attack: **counterattack, counteroffensive, second strike** ● attack by aircraft: **air raid** ● repeated attacks from low-flying aircraft: **strafing** ● denoting a military attack carried out with great precision: **surgical** ● crime of attacking a person: **assault** ● person or thing vulnerable to attack: **soft target**

attendant ● group of attendants upon an important person: **entourage, retinue, train** ● protective attendant: **bodyguard, minder**

attention ● focus the attention: **concentrate** ● centre of attention: **cynosure** ● forcing the attention: **intrusive, obtrusive** ● activity designed to distract attention: **diversion** ● avoidance of attention: **low profile** ● craftily avoiding attention: **furtive** ● time spent devoting one's attention to another: **quality time**

attitude ● set of attitudes: **mentality, mindset** ● set of attitudes opposed to those currently prevailing: **counterculture** ● confrontation of different attitudes: **culture shock** ● spread of middle-class materialism: **embourgeoisement** ● person with outdated attitudes: **fogey** ●still adhering to old attitudes: **unreconstructed, unregenerate**

attract ●bargain offered to attract customers: **come-on, loss-leader** ●attractive but worthless: **meretricious**

aubergine ●aubergine in Greek cuisine: **melitzanes** ●aubergine in Indian cuisine: **brinjal**

auction ●auction at which the price is progressively reduced: **Dutch auction** ●item sold at an auction: **lot** ●price which an item must reach before being sold: **reserve, reserve price, upset price** ●secret alliance of purchasers at an auction to force down prices: **ring**

audiotape ●audiotape machine recording telephone messages: **answering machine, answerphone** ●container for audiotape: **cassette**

Australian ●native Australian: **Aboriginal** ●Australian wild dog: **dingo** ●ostrich-like Australian bird: **emu** ●river backwater in Australia, filled only by floods: **billabong** ●large area of pasture: **run** ●Australian term for a British person: **Pommy** ●Australian term for an unskilled farmhand: **rouseabout, roustabout** ●Australian terms for the rural hinterland: **backblocks, outback**

Austrian ●title of former Austrian emperors: **Kaiser** ●Austrian mayor: **burgomaster** ●Austrian province: **Land** (*pl.* Länder) ●Austrian folk dance: **ländler** ●Austrian chocolate cake: **Sachertorte** (*pl.* Sachertorten)

author ●author employed to write for another: **ghostwriter** ●author of film and TV scripts: **screenwriter, scenarist** ●author's youthful output: **juvenilia** ●author's inability to think of new material: **writer's block** ●author's assistant, taking down dictation or copying drafts: **amanuensis**

●false name used by an author: **nom de plume, pseudonym** ●right of authors to royalties from libraries: **public lending right** ●person in charge of a dead author's works: **literary executor** ●assign authorship: **attribute**

authority ●with full authority: **ex cathedra** ●showing authority: **magisterial** ●shared authority: **partnership** ●intrusively authoritarian: **officious** ●misuse of authority: **misfeasance** ●area of authority: **remit, terms of reference** ●legal authority to act for another: **power of attorney** ●person authorized to act for another: **proxy**

authorization ●authorization to proceed: **commission, mandate, remit** ●be absent without authorization: **take French leave**

automatic ●introduction or use of automatic equipment: **automation** ●done in automatic response to a stimulus: **reflex**

autumn ●fine weather in late autumn: **Indian summer, St Luke's summer, St Martin's summer**

available ●available but not obligatory: **optional** ●available to all: **open** ●general availability: **open access, open door** ●acceptance of what happens to be available: **pot luck** ●not available: **inaccessible**

avocado ●Mexican dish of mashed avocado: **guacamole**

avoid ●have no dealings with: **boycott** ●avoid skilfully and repeatedly: **elude, evade** ●avoid a need or difficulty: **obviate**

award ●person receiving an award: **laureate** ●statement of reasons for bestowing an award: **citation**

away ●*combining forms:* **ab(s)-** (*e.g.* abduct), **ap(o)-** (*e.g.* apogee), **de-** (*e.g.* deduct), **out-** (*e.g.* outbound)

axe ●small axe: **hatchet** ●American Indian axe: **tomahawk** ●animal-slaughterer's axe: **poleaxe** ●climber's ice axe: **piolet** ●axe handle: **haft**

Aztec ●Aztec temple: **teocalli**

Bb

baby ●*adjective*: **infantile** ●baby less than four weeks old: **neonate** ●baby with insufficient blood oxygen: **blue baby** ●one of two babies born at a birth: **twin** ●one of three babies born at a birth: **triplet** ●one of four babies born at a birth: **quadruplet** ●one of five babies born at a birth: **quintuplet** ●set of clothes for a newborn baby: **layette** ●baby's bed: **cot, cradle** ●baby's small portable bed: **carrycot** ●baby's wickerwork cot: **Moses basket** ●baby's plastic teat: **comforter, dummy** ●baby's long-legged feeding chair: **high chair** ●baby's babbling: **lallation** ●wind suffered by a baby: **colic** ●feed a baby whenever it cries: **demand-feed** ●breast-feed a baby: **suckle** ●woman employed to suckle another's baby: **wet nurse** ●discourage a baby from breast-feeding: **wean** ●liquid baby food to replace breast milk: **formula** ●bounce a baby: **dandle** ●first faeces of a newborn infant: **meconium** ●unexplained death of a sleeping baby: **cot death, sudden infant death syndrome** ●abandoned baby of unknown parentage: **foundling** ●baby secretly substituted for another: **changeling** ●scaly skin on a baby's head: **cradle cap** ●space between the parts of an baby's skull: **fontanelle** ●apparatus providing special environment for a premature baby: **incubator** ●pouch for carrying a baby: **sling** ●institution offering daytime care of babies: **crèche** ●killing a baby: **infanticide**

Bacchus ●*Greek name*: **Dionysus** ●male follower of Bacchus: **bacchant** ●female follower of Bacchus: **bac-**chante, maenad ●staff carried by Bacchus' followers: **thyrsus**

back ●*combining forms*: **dors-** ●*adjectives*: **dorsal,** (*lower back*) **lumbar** ●back sloping forward at the top: **humpback, hunchback** ●back of a leaf of paper: **verso** ●lying on one's back: **supine** ●bag strapped to the back: **haversack, knapsack, rucksack**

back again ●*combining forms*: **ana-** (*e.g.* anamnesis), **re-** (*e.g.* return)

backbone ●*adjectives*: **spinal, myeloid** ●having a backbone: **vertebrate** ●having no backbone: **invertebrate** ●joint of meat containing a backbone: **chine**

backer ●person lending money to finance a film or play: **angel** ●person betting on a racehorse: **punter**

backwards ●*combining form*: **retr(o)-** (*e.g.* retrospect)

bacon ●side of bacon: **flitch** ●slice of bacon: **rasher** ●cube of bacon: **lardon** ●tough outer layer on bacon: **rind** ●denoting bacon having alternate strips of fat and lean: **streaky**

bacterium ●bacteria in contaminated food: **Escherichia coli, listeria** ●bacterium causing gonorrhoea: **gonococcus** ●bacterium causing pneumonia and dental decay: **streptococcus** ●bacteria cultivated for experimentation: **culture** ●test for bacteria: **Gram stain** ●substance arresting the multiplication of bacteria: **bacteriostat** ●substance killing bacteria: **antiseptic, bactericide, disinfectant** ●study of bacteria: **bacteriology**

bad ●*combining forms*: **caco-** (e.g. cacophony), **dys-** (e.g. dysfunction), **mal-** (e.g. maladministration), **mis-** (e.g. misadventure) ●exceptionally bad: **egregious** ●famously bad: **notorious** ●gradually getting worse: **insidious** ●a thing's bad aspects: **downside** ●bad breath: **halitosis**

badge ●flower-shaped badge of coloured ribbon: **rosette** ●school or sports team badge: **colours**

badger ●male badger: **boar** ●badger's burrow: **earth, sett**

badly ●*combining form*: **cata-** (e.g. catachresis), **mis-** (e.g. mismanage)

badminton ●badminton bat: **racket** ●feathered cork used as a ball: **shuttle, shuttlecock** ●strike the ball to commence play: **serve**

bad taste ●person having bad taste: **boor, groundling, vulgarian** ●vulgarly showy: **garish, gaudy, lurid**

bag ●plastic or paper bag with handles: **carrier bag** ●capacious bag: **holdall, tote bag** ●small bag for cosmetics: **vanity bag** ●small sealed bag: **sachet** ●travelling bag: **grip, suitcase** ●small travelling bag: **valise** ●two-sectioned travelling bag: **Gladstone bag, portmanteau** ●bag strapped to the back: **haversack, knapsack, rucksack** ●school bag on a long strap: **satchel** ●cylindrical canvas bag with a drawstring: **duffel bag** ●sailor's bag: **ditty bag** ●soldier's bag: **kitbag** ●air-travellers' shoulder bag: **carry-on, flight bag** ●bag for carrying a child on the back: **papoose** ●large bag at the side of a motor cycle, beast of burden, etc.: **pannier** ●bag used to remove a corpse from an accident, battlefield, etc.: **body bag** ●large bag for protection against exposure: **survival bag** ●small piece of plastic-covered wire used to secure the neck of a plastic

bag: **twist tie** ●baglike bodily membrane: **sac**

bagpipes ●Irish bagpipes: **uillean pipes** ●small bellows-powered bagpipes: **musette** ●pipe on bagpipes on which the tune is played: **chanter** ●pipe on bagpipes used to produce a continuous bass note: **drone** ●shrill sound of bagpipes: **skirl**

bail ●pay bail money for another: **stand bail, stand surety** ●abscond, having gained release by bail: **jump bail**

baking ●mixture of flour and yeast for baking: **dough** ●yeast substitute used in baking: **baking powder**

balance ●*adjective*: **equilibrious** ●*astrological term*: **libra** ●state of balance: **equilibrium** ●balance of forces or interests: **equipoise** ●person performing balancing feats: **acrobat, juggler, funambulist** ●self-balancing flywheel: **gyroscope** ●lose balance: **overbalance**

Balinese ●Balinese percussion orchestra: **gamelan**

Balkan ●Balkan guerrilla: **chetnik**

ball ●large black ball used in bowls: **wood** ●small white ball used in bowls: **jack** ●ball used in ice hockey: **puck** ●ball that is out of play: **dead ball** ●heavy exercise ball: **medicine ball** ●large metal ball thrown in athletics: **hammer, shot** ●spiked metal ball used as a war obstacle: **caltrop** ●ball of decorated blown glass: **witch ball** ●forward spin on a ball: **topspin**

ballet ●ballet company: **corps de ballet** ●chief female ballet dancer: **prima ballerina** ●leading ballet dancer: **coryphée** ●rank-and-file ballet dancers: **corps de ballet** ●female ballet dancer: **ballerina, danseuse** ●male ballet dancer: **danseur** ●rail supporting ballet dancer doing exercises: **barre** ●ballerina's short skirt:

tutu ●ballet shoes with strengthened toes: **pointe shoes** ●ballet step: **pas** ●arm movement: **port de bras** ●spin made on one foot: **pirouette** ●posture with one leg lifted at right angles: **arabesque** ●series of steps for a ballet: **choreography** ●person devising these: **choreographer** ●person teaching ballet dancers their steps: **répétiteur** ●solo dance: **pas seul** ●dance for two people: **pas de deux** ●dance performed on the tips of the toes: **pointe, en pointe** ●short dance to display technique: **divertissement** ●ballet enthusiast: **balletomane** ▶ *see also* **dancer**

balloon ●large balloon, moored in groups to frustrate air attack: **barrage balloon** ●balloon's gas container: **envelope** ●enclosed passenger compartment below a balloon: **gondola**

ban ●ban on trade: **embargo** ●ban on implementation of a decision: **veto** ●ban on dealings with a person, organization, etc.: **boycott**

band ●band conductor: **bandmaster** ●chief musician in a band: **bandleader** ●roofed outdoor band platform: **bandstand**

bandage ●bandage supporting an injured arm: **sling** ●loosely woven dressing: **gauze** ●bandage twisted tight to stop the flow of blood: **tourniquet** ●bandage stiffened with plaster of Paris: **cast, plaster cast** ●pad applied to stop bleeding: **compress** ●protective or healing material placed on a wound: **dressing** ●absorbent pad: **swab** ●absorbent plug: **tampon** ●soft moist mass applied to relieve inflammation: **poultice**

bank[1] ●artificial bank: **berm** ●steep bank: **bluff, scarp** ●large defensive bank: **earthwork** ●long bank built to prevent flooding: **dyke, embankment** ●artificial bank carrying a road or railway: **embankment**

bank[2] ●bank dealing in commercial loans and investment: **merchant bank** ●deposit-taking cooperative offering cheap loans to members: **credit union** ●bank account for frequent deposits and withdrawals: **current account** ●bank account for longer-term deposits: **deposit account** ●bank account for several persons: **joint account** ●bank account deficit: **overdraft** ●customer's book recording deposits and withdrawals on his account: **bank book, pass book** ●bank card giving access to cash dispensers: **cash card** ●management of a bank account by telephone or computer modem: **direct banking, home banking, telebanking** ●remove from a bank account: **debit** ●arrangement for a third party to draw on one's account: **direct debit** ●money paid into a bank account: **deposit** ●money taken out of a bank account: **withdrawal** ●bank deposit that cannot be withdrawn before a set date: **time deposit** ●instruction to a bank to make regular payments: **standing order** ●sudden withdrawal of deposits by many investors: **run** ●cheque drawn by a bank on its own funds: **bank draft, banker's draft** ●bank's printed order for payment of a specified sum: **money order** ●cheque guaranteed by a bank: **certified cheque** ●banks' establishment for the exchange of cheques: **clearing house** ●banks' trading in short-term loans: **money market** ●banking transaction effected via the telecommunications network: **electronic transfer of funds** ●wall-mounted deposit box used when the bank is closed: **night safe** ●secure store for valuables: **safe deposit, safety deposit** ●bank's secure storeroom: **vault**

banknote ●thin line inside banknote paper: **thread mark** ●banknote design visible only when held up to the light: **watermark**

bankrupt ●official appointed to manage the affairs of bankrupts: **receiver** ●release a bankrupt from further payments: **discharge**

baptism ●baptism by dipping: **immersion** ●baptism by pouring water over: **affusion** ●baptism by sprinkling: **aspersion** ●person making promises for a child being baptized: **godparent**

bar ●short bar attaching a collar to a shirt: **stud** ●bar at which drinks must be paid for: **cash bar** ●bar at which the drinks are free: **open bar**

bar code ●bar code reader: **light pen, wand** ●pass a light pen over a bar code: **wipe**

bargain ●bargain offered to attract customers: **come-on, loss-leader** ●shrewd bargaining to mutual advantage: **horse-trading** ●refuse to honour a bargain: **renege**

barge ●large light barge: **wherry** ●barge towed by another boat: **butty** ●person who works on a barge: **bargee**

bark ●remove a tree's bark: **decorticate** ●bark bruised as a source of tannin: **tan, tanbark** ●tanbark used as a ground-cover: **tan, spent tan** ●bitter extract of cinchona bark: **quinine**

barometer ●denoting a barometer using a vacuum box to measure atmospheric pressure: **aneroid** ●liquid metal used in a barometer: **mercury, quicksilver**

barrel ●large barrel: **hogshead, tun** ●small barrel: **keg** ●person who makes barrels: **cooper** ●plank from which barrels are made: **stave** ●metal band compressing a barrel's staves: **hoop** ●small hole in the side of a barrel: **vent** ●plug for a barrel vent: **spigot** ●allow air to enter a barrel: **vent** ●open a barrel: **broach** ●wooden peg to seal a barrel: **spile**

barrier ●crowd barrier: **crush barrier** ●roadside barrier preventing accidents: **crash barrier** ●improvised barrier blocking a street: **barricade** ●insurmountable barrier: **Chinese wall** ●imagined invisible barrier: **force field**

barrister ●barristers regarded collectively: **the bar** ●barrister's apprenticeship: **pupillage** ●barrister advising a court martial: **judge advocate** ●barrister serving as a part-time judge: **recorder** ●barrister's office: **chambers** ●barrister's advice on a point of law: **opinion** ●barrister's wig, gown, etc.: **court dress** ●case information and instructions given to a barrister: **brief** ●brief given to a barrister chosen by the accused while in court: **dock brief** ●brief to follow a case for a client not directly involved in it: **watching brief** ●initial fee paid to a barrister: **retainer** ●subsequent fee paid to a barrister in a long case: **refresher** ●honorific title bestowed on a senior barrister: **King's Counsel, Queen's Counsel** ●such barristers collectively: **the inner bar** ●other barristers collectively: **juniors, the outer bar** ●organization training and regulating barristers: **Inn of Court** ●forbid a barrister to practice: **disbar**

base ●base for a statue etc.: **pedestal** ●military base: **garrison** ●fortified base established on an enemy shore: **beachhead** ●fortified base established inside enemy territory: **bridgehead** ●proposition used as a base for further reasoning: **hypothesis**

basket ●food basket: **hamper** ●basket for soft fruits: **punnet** ●basket for garden vegetables: **trug** ●basket for dirty clothes: **linen basket** ●basket for sewing items: **workbasket** ●basket on a cycle or donkey: **pannier** ●wooden neck-frame for carrying baskets: **yoke** ●willow

cropped for basket-making: **osier**
●shoot from this: **withy**

basketball ●attempt at goal
awarded after a foul: **free throw** ●ad-
vance the ball by continuous boun-
cing: **dribble** ●aggressive marking of
opponents: **full-court press**

Basque ●Basque ball game: **jai alai,
pelota** ●court for this: **fronton**
●Basque separatist terrorist organization: **Eta**

bath ●*adjective*: **balneal** ●bath with
underwater jets: **jacuzzi™** ●bath
with hot aerated water: **spa, spa
bath, spa pool** ●steam bath: **Turkish
bath** ●hot-air bath: **sauna** ●bath
only large enough to sit in: **hip bath**
●mark left on a bath's sides by receding water: **tidemark** ●dried tropical fruit used as a bathing sponge:
loofah

batter ●thin fried cake of batter:
pancake ●sweet batter baked with a
fruit filling: **clafoutis**

battery ●rechargeable battery storing electricity as chemical energy: **accumulator** ●point at which current
enters or leaves a battery: **electrode**
●slow battery charger: **trickle charger** ●denoting an exhausted battery:
flat

battle ●small battle: **incident,
skirmish** ●close aerial battle: **dog-
fight** ●battle area: **field, front** ●posi-
tioning of troops for battle: **deploy-
ment, disposition** ●join battle:
engage ●bravery in battle: **gallantry**
●official report from the battlefront:
dispatch ●regroup after defeat:
rally ●the ultimate battle, or one
causing huge destruction: **Armaged-
don** ●battlefield hospital: **field hospital**

bay ●small sheltered bay: **cove**
●large bay: **gulf**

beach ●*adjective*: **littoral** ●barrier
preventing beach erosion: **groyne**

●defended beach position: **beachhead**

beads ●large string of beads used in
prayer: **rosary** ●small string of beads
used in prayer: **chaplet**

beam ●metal beam: **girder** ●verti-
cal underground beam supporting
foundations: **pile, spile** ●beam laid
horizontally in a wall: **wall plate**
●beam or plate distributing weight
along a wall: **template** ●beam supporting a floor: **joist** ●beam supporting joists or rafters: **summer** ●hori-
zontal beam connecting rafters: **tie
beam** ●short beam supporting a rafter or arch: **hammer beam** ●roof
beam supporting rafters: **purlin**
●beam at the apex of a roof: **ridge
piece** ●long beam supporting and
connecting a framework: **stringpiece**
●beam fixed at one end: **cantilever** ●beam above an opening: **lintel**
●beam across a fireplace: **manteltree**
●short horizontal wall-post to carry
scaffolding beams: **putlog** ●horizon-
tal beam dividing a window: **transom**
●vertical beam dividing a window:
mullion ●beam between a door and a
fanlight: **transom** ●beam across the
tops of columns: **architrave** ●over-
head beam supporting equipment:
gantry ●denoting a beam carrying
the structure above it: **load-bearing**
●use of beams: **trabeation** ●small
piece of stone or wood supporting a
beam's end: **tassel** ●heavy beam
used to knock down walls: **ram,
battering ram** ●floating beam restricting access to a harbour etc:
boom

bean ●*adjective*: **leguminous**
●small French kidney bean: **flageolet**
●bean giving bean sprouts: **mung**
●curd made from mashed soya beans:
tofu

bear ●*adjective*: **ursine** ●young
bear: **cub**

bearer ●*combining forms*: **-fer, -phore** (*e.g.* semaphore, *literally 'sign-bearer'*) ●person carrying the cross in Christian processions: **crucifer** ●person carrying a censer: **thurifer**

bearing ●*combining forms*: **-ferous** (*e.g.* odoriferous), **-gerous** (*e.g.* cornigerous)

beast ●*adjective*: **bestial, animal, feral** ●beast-like characteristics: **animality**

beauty ●*combining form*: **calli-** ●products claiming to improve the appearance of the skin: **cosmetics** ●exercises designed to improve strength and appearance: **callisthenics** ●not beautiful: **plain**

beaver ●young beaver: **kit, kitten** ●beaver's den: **lodge**

becoming ●*combining form*: **-escent** ●becoming liquid: **deliquescent** ●becoming rotten: **putrescent** ●becoming sexually mature: **pubescent**

bed ●bed without head- or footboard: **divan** ●bed with a canopy supported by posts: **four-poster** ●matching pair of single beds: **twin beds** ●narrow bed, often one of a tiered set: **bunk** ●canvas bed suspended by cords at its ends: **hammock** ●portable bed for the injured: **stretcher** ●enclosed bed carried on poles: **litter** ●fixed bed on a train, ship, etc.: **berth** ●NHS hospital bed for which a charge is made: **amenity bed, pay bed** ●bed made up as a practical joke with a single sheet folded back on itself: **apple-pie bed** ●bed's solid frame: **bedstead** ●canopy over a bed: **tester** ●panel at a bed's head: **headboard** ●thick upper bed-covering sewn in sections: **eiderdown, quilt** ●fabric case stuffed with feathers etc. as a mattress or pillow: **tick** ●ornamental cloth bedcover: **bedspread** ●bed-covering consisting of a quilt with a detachable cover:

continental quilt, duvet ●confined to bed: **bedridden** ●long-handled brass pan formerly used to warm a bed: **warming pan** ●Japanese quilted mattress used on the floor as a bed: **futon** ●animal's bedding of straw etc.: **litter**

bee ●*adjective*: **apian** ●female bee: **queen** ●male bee: **drone** ●sterile bee doing most of the tasks of the group: **worker** ●large group of bees: **swarm** ●hexagonal wax structure built by bees: **honeycomb** ●substance fed to potential queens: **royal jelly** ●structure for bees to live in: **beehive, hive** ●group of beehives: **apiary** ●person who studies or keeps bees: **apiarist**

beef ●cut of beef from the outside leg: **silverside** ●cut of beef from the breast: **brisket** ●cut of beef from the lower part of the spine: **loin** ●best part of this: **sirloin** ●high-quality beef taken from the hindquarters: **steak** ●lean cut from the rump: **topside** ●boned sirloin steak: **entrecôte** ●thick steak of fillet beef: **chateaubriand** ●small thick slice of fillet beef: **tournedos** ●seasoned dish of raw steak and egg: **steak tartare** ●beef stew with onions and beer: **carbonnade** ●French beef stew: **grillade** ●beef cooked in a sour cream sauce: **beef stroganoff** ●seasoned smoked beef: **pastrami** ●flat cake of minced beef: **burger**

beer ●beer brewed and stored traditionally: **cask beer, real ale** ●beer stored with carbon dioxide: **keg beer** ●beer served from a bulk container: **draught beer** ●nitrogen device in some beer cans: **widget** ●dark hoppy beer: **mild** ●dark beer made with roasted malt: **stout** ●dark beer made with charred malt: **porter** ●light effervescent beer: **lager** ●treated grain for brewing: **malt, grist** ●water used in brewing: **liquor** ●malt and liquor mixture: **mash** ●breakdown of sugars in brewing: **fermentation** ●mature further after fermentation: **condition** ●clarify a brew: **fine** ●final taste of beer: **finish** ●foam on beer: **head** ●beer mixed with a soft drink: **shandy** ●drink of lager and draught cider: **snakebite** ●tall beer mug with a handle: **tankard** ●large earthenware beer mug: **stein** ●person making beer: **brewer** ●beer cart or lorry: **dray**

beetle ●*adjective*: **coleopterous** ●beetle infesting kitchens etc.: **cockroach** ●ticking wood-boring beetle: **death-watch beetle** ●luminescent beetle: **glow-worm** ●sacred beetle of ancient Egypt: **scarab** ●student of beetles: **coleopterist**

before ●*combining forms*: **afore-** (*e.g.* aforementioned), **ante, fore-** (*e.g.* foreplay), **pre-, pro-** ●act or happen before (some other event): **anticipate** ●acting beforehand: **proactive** ●thing or person coming before another: **forerunner, precursor, predecessor** ●before the war: **antebellum, pre-war** ●feeling, when in a new situation, of having experienced it before: **déjà vu**

beg ●living by begging: **mendicant** ●begging the question: **petitio principii**

beginner ●keen or ambitious beginner: **aspirant** ●inexperienced beginner: **novice, tyro** ●suitable for beginners: **entry-level**

beginning ●*combining form*: **-escent** (*e.g.* pubescent) ●*adjectives*: **embryonic, incipient, inceptive, inchoate, initial, nascent** ●sudden beginning: **outbreak, outburst** ●from the beginning: **ab initio, ab ovo, de novo**

behaviour ●*combining form*: **-ery** (*e.g.* foolery) ●generally accepted behaviour, or its rules: **convention, etiquette, protocol** ●person's distinctive behaviour: **trait, quirk, mannerism, idiosyncrasy** ●unconventional behaviour: **eccentricity, deviance** ●child's playful misbehaviour: **mischief** ●morally correct behaviour: **conformity, decorum, propriety, rectitude, virtue** ●behaviour intended to fulfil social expectations: **role playing** ●behaviour aimed at others' benefit: **altruism** ●servile behaviour: **toadying, truckling** ●dishonest behaviour: **sleaze, skulduggery** ●immoral behaviour: **vice** ●employee's improper behaviour: **misconduct** ●engrained pattern of maladaptive behaviour: **personality disorder** ●stiffly well-behaved: **prim** ●strict and reserved in behaviour: **unbending** ●breaching propriety or convention: **transgressive** ●denoting behaviour expressing one's feelings of social superiority: **supercilious** ●imitation of behaviour: **mimesis** ●encouragement of desired behaviour by rewards: **reinforcement, positive reinforcement** ●encouragement of desired behaviour by cessation of punishment: **negative reinforcement** ●scientific study of human or animal behaviour: **behavioural science**

behind ●*combining form*: **retro-** (*e.g.* retrochoir) ●behind with payments: **in arrears**

being ●*combining form*: **onto-** ●study of the concept of 'being': **ontology**

belief ●system of beliefs: **doctrine, dogma** ●system of religious belief: **faith** ●firm belief: **conviction** ●mistaken belief: **fallacy, misapprehension** ●belief that all matter has an element of consciousness: **panpsychism** ●belief that plants and inanimate objects possess souls: **animism** ●doctrine of design and purpose in the material world: **teleology** ●traditional beliefs of a community: **folklore** ●credulous belief in the supernatural: **superstition** ● belief that one's nation is superior: **chauvinism, ethnocentricity, jingoism** ● person dying for his beliefs: **martyr** ● person changing his or her beliefs to suit prevailing fashion: **time server** ● correct a mistaken belief: **disabuse** ● publicly disown a belief: **recant** ● still adhering to old beliefs: **unreconstructed, unregenerate** ● person abandoning religious or political beliefs: **apostate** ● unable to believe: **incredulous**

bell ● bell rung to instruct people to return to their houses: **curfew** ● bell rung for the recitation of Roman Catholic prayers commemorating the Incarnation: **angelus** ● bell rung at death or a funeral: **knell** ● alarm bell: **tocsin** ● bell's tongue: **clapper** ● bell tower: **campanile** ● art of bell-ringing: **campanology** ● set of bells for campanology: **peal** ● large set of bells for musical performances: **carillon**

belonging to ● *combining form*: -ine (*e.g.* Alpine) ● sense of 'not belonging': **alienation**

below ● *combining forms*: hypo- (*e.g.* hypodermic , *literally 'beneath the skin'*), infra- (*e.g.* infrastructure), sub- ● below the threshold of consciousness: **subliminal**

belt ● ornamental belt: **sash** ● ornamental belt worn with men's evening dress: **cummerbund** ● ornamental belt won by champion boxer: **Lonsdale belt** ● belt worn by a beginner in martial arts: **white belt** ● belt worn by an expert in martial arts: **black belt** ● belt worn by certain police and army officers, with a strap over the shoulder: **Sam Browne** ● similar belt, carrying cartridges: **bandolier** ● shoulder belt supporting a sword etc. on the opposite hip: **baldric** ● belt-attachment to hold a sword: **frog** ● padded belt supporting a hernia: **truss**

bench ● long backless bench: **form** ● long wooden bench with high back: **settle** ● upholstered bench against a wall: **banquette**

bend ● U-shaped bend in a road: **hairpin bend** ● deflection of light or radio waves passing from one medium to another: **refraction** ● bending readily: **flexible, pliable** ● full of bends: **flexuous, sinuous**

beneath ● *combining forms*: hypo-, infra- (*e.g.* infrastructure), sub- ● beneath the earth's surface: **subterranean** ● beneath the skin: **hypodermic, subcutaneous** ● beneath one's dignity: **infra dig**

benefit ● reciprocal benefit: **quid pro quo** ● state benefit paid to disabled persons needing home care: **attendance allowance** ● state benefit offsetting a disabled person's loss of earnings: **disability benefit** ● state benefit paid to those temporarily off work through illness: **sickness benefit** ● state payment to the long-term sick: **incapacity benefit** ● state benefit assisting travel for the disabled: **mobility allowance** ● state payment to a family on low income: **family credit** ● situation where any increase in income triggers a counterbalancing withdrawal of state benefits: **poverty trap** ● seeming benefit designed to cause its recipient trouble: **poisoned chalice**

beside ● *combining form*: para- (*e.g.* parathyroid)

best ● best of all: **crème de la crème, par excellence** ● best available: **faute de mieux, pis aller**

bet ● bet recommended as a near certainty: **nap** ● bet placed by those with expert knowledge: **smart money** ● bet in which winnings and stake from a first event are placed on a second: **double** ● bet in which initial winnings are placed on a series of subsequent events: **accumulator** ● bet with cumulatively doubled stakes: **martingale** ● bet naming the first two in their correct order: **perfecta** ● bet naming the first two, but not giving their order: **quinella** ● bet naming the first three in their correct order: **tricast** ● bet that a horse will finish in the first three: **place, place-bet** ● denoting a bet placed on a horse before the runners are announced: **ante-post** ● denoting a bet made for a win or a place: **each-way** ● final odds at the start of a horse race: **starting price** ● money etc. put down on a bet: **stake** ● system where those backing the first three divide the total stake: **pari-mutuel** ● system where winnings are calculated from the total staked, not from odds offered: **totalizator, totalizer, tote** ● person who takes bets: **bookmaker** ● person holding bets laid: **stakeholder** ● make a bet: **place**

betrayal ● betrayal of one's country: **treason** ● person doing this: **renegade, traitor** ● person deserting one side to join the other: **trimmer, turncoat**

better ● *combining form*: **out-** (*e.g.* outsmart) ● better than what is on general offer: **preferential** ● progressively beneficial cycle of cause and effect: **virtuous circle**

between ● *combining form*: **inter-** ● between two other things: **intermediate** ● between living people: **inter vivos**

beyond ● *combining forms*: **extra-** (*e.g.* extraterritorial), **hyper-** (*e.g.* hypersonic), **meta-** (*e.g.* metaphysical), **para-** (*e.g.* paranormal), **super-** (*e.g.* supernormal), **supra-** (*e.g.* supranational), **sur-** (*e.g.* surreal), **trans-** (*e.g.* transnational), **ultra-** (*e.g.* ultramontane) ● beyond one's authority: **ultra vires** ● beyond what is necessary: **supererogatory, de trop** ● go beyond: **transcend**

bias ● unfair bias: **discrimination, favouritism, partiality, parti pris, prejudice** ● deliberate bias in favour of those usually discriminated against: **positive discrimination**

Bible ● first part of the Bible, containing the Jewish scriptures: **Old Testament** ● first five books of the Old Testament: **Pentateuch** ● first six books of the Old Testament: **Hexateuch** ● first seven books of the Old Testament: **Heptateuch** ● second part of the Bible, containing further Jewish scriptures not found in the Hebrew canon: **Apocrypha** ● third part of the Bible, containing the Christian scriptures: **New Testament** ● Jewish commentary upon the Old Testament: **Masorah, Midrash** ● Jewish mystical interpretation of the Old Testament: **Kabbalah** ● Greek version of the Old Testament: **Septuagint** ● textual criticism of the Bible: **lower criticism** ● biblical exegesis from a comparative historical and cultural standpoint: **higher criticism** ● interpretation of biblical symbolism: **typology** ● biblical passage read liturgically: **lesson** ● list of biblical readings: **lectionary** ● biblical etc. passage upon which a sermon is preached: **text**

biblical figures ● the first human: **Adam** ● his wife: **Eve** ● the first murderer: **Cain** ● his victim: **Abel** ● Noah's grandfather, said to have lived 969 years: **Methuselah** ● patriarch in charge of the ark: **Noah** ● father of the Jewish nation: **Abraham** ● his wife: **Sarah** ● his son, offered as a sacrifice: **Isaac** ● grandson of Abraham, later called Israel: **Jacob** ● Jacob's son, later a ruler in Egypt: **Joseph** ● Israelite leader in the Exodus: **Moses** ● Moses' assistant: **Aaron** ● Moses' successor, leader in the conquest of Canaan: **Joshua** ● national Israelite leader in emergencies: **judge** ● Israelite leader famous for his strength: **Samson** ●Philistine seductress of Samson: **Delilah** ●first king of Israel: **Saul** ●second king of Israel: **David** ●Philistine giant slain by David: **Goliath** ●son of David: **Absalom** ●third king of Israel: **Solomon** ●skilled hunter: **Nimrod** ●furious charioteer: **Jehu** ●proclaimer of the will of God: **prophet** ●prophet ascending to heaven in a chariot: **Elijah** ●Elijah's successor: **Elisha** ●Jew cast into the lions' den: **Daniel** ●prosperous Jew suddenly deprived of everything: **Job** ●biblical sea monster: **leviathan**

bicycle ●bicycle for general use: **roadster** ●bicycle with broad tyres and many gears: **mountain bike** ●bicycle whose rider lies on his back: **recumbent** ●bicycle for two riders, one seated behind the other: **tandem** ●bicycle with one wheel: **monocycle, unicycle** ●three-wheeled bicycle: **tricycle** ●early bicycle with one very large and one small wheel: **penny-farthing** ●early bicycle pushed along by the rider's feet: **velocipede** ●support for a bicycle wheel: **fork** ●small wheel steadying a child's bicycle: **stabilizer** ●racing cycle's sealed tyre: **tubular tyre** ●bicycle's mileage meter: **cyclometer** ●bicycle handlebars with handles below the bar: **drop handlebars** ●bicycle handgrip that may be twisted to change the gears: **twist-grip** ●particular cycle gear ratio: **speed** ●bicycle gears that move the chain to different cogs: **derailleur** ●U-shaped slot for quick wheel-changing: **dropout** ●cycle without pedalling: **freewheel** ●jump made on a bicycle while standing on the pedals: **bunny hop** ●cyclist's trick of riding with the front wheel off the gound: **wheelie** ●bag beside a cycle's rear wheel: **pannier**

bile ●*combining form*: **chol-** ●X-ray examination of the bile ducts: **choliangography**

bill ●hotel or restaurant bill: **account, tab** ●itemized bill: **invoice**

billiards ●billiard-player's stick: **cue** ●cue support: **rest** ●long stick to support the cue: **bridge, jigger** ●stroke made with an inclined cue: **massé** ●stroke in which the cue slips: **miscue** ●ball struck by the cue: **cue ball** ●ball at which the cue ball is aimed: **object ball** ●revolving motion imparted to the ball: **spin** ●backspin given to the cue ball: **screw** ●sidespin given to the cue ball: **side** ●stroke in which the cue ball strikes both the others: **cannon** ●pouch into which the ball is struck: **pocket** ●strike a ball into a pocket: **pot** ●stroke pocketing a ball: **hazard** ●direct pocketing of the cue ball: **coup** ●brush past another ball: **kiss** ●successful turn at play: **break** ●score-keeper: **marker**

bingo ●person announcing the numbers drawn: **caller** ●card with every number marked off: **full house**

binoculars ●outdoor binoculars: **field glasses** ●theatre binoculars: **opera glasses**

biology ●biological classification: **taxonomy** ●biological classes: **family, genus, species** ●biology of possible life on other planets: **astrobiology, exobiology** ●health or environmental risk posed by microbiological experimentation: **biohazard**

bird ●*combining form*: **avi-, ornith-** ●*adjectives*: **avian, ornithic** ●bird too young to leave the nest: **nestling** ●bird just able to fly: **fledgling** ●group of birds: **flight** ●bird hunted by man: **game bird** ●earliest known bird, a kind of flying dinosaur: **archaeopteryx** ●mythical bird, said to burn itself every 500 years and rise again from the ashes: **phoenix** ●large extinct flightless bird: **dodo**

• tall pink wading bird: **flamingo**
• birds imitating human speech:
budgerigar, mynah, parrot • denoting a bird able to feed itself soon after
hatching: **precocial** • denoting a bird
unable to do this: **altricial** • bird's
claw: **talon** • outer part of a bird's
wing: **pinion** • forked bone between
the neck and breast of a bird: **wishbone** • bird's muscular stomach: **gizzard** • membrane between the toes of
a swimming bird: **web** • group of
eggs laid by a bird at one time: **clutch**
• massed birdsong at daybreak: **dawn
chorus** • birds' seasonal change of
habitat: **migration** • glide or soar
without wing movement: **plane** • loss
of a bird's markings due to moulting:
eclipse • bird's cleaning its feathers
with its beak: **preening** • mass of
bones and feathers regurgitated by a
bird of prey: **pellet** • place where
birds rest at night: **roost** • enclosure
for keeping birds: **aviary** • aluminium identification strip round a bird's
leg: **ring** • tie up a bird's wings and
legs: **pinion, truss** • person who
rears or keeps birds: **aviculturist**
• study of birds: **ornithology**

birth • *combining form*: **-genesis**
• *adjective*: **natal** • close to the time
of birth: **near-term, perinatal** • obstetrics dealing with this period:
perinatology • expulsion of a fetus
before it can survive independently:
miscarriage • vaginal discharge at
the onset of labour: **show** • shortening of uterine muscles before and during birth: **contractions** • inducing
uterine contractions: **ecbolic** • newborn offspring: **neonate** • birth of
offspring already dead: **stillbirth**
• matter discharged after birth: **afterbirth, lochia** • denoting or occurring
in the time immediately before or
after birth: **perinatal** • first milk produced by a cow or goat after giving
birth: **beestings** • giving birth by
means of eggs: **oviparous** • giving

birth to live offspring: **viviparous**
• giving birth from eggs hatched
within the body: **ovoviviparous**
• producing one offspring at a birth:
uniparous • producing several offspring at a birth: **multiparous**
• group of animals produced at a
birth: **litter** • one of three offspring
born at a birth: **triplet** • one of four
offspring born at a birth: **quadruplet,
quad** • one of five offspring born at a
birth: **quintuplet, quin** • one of six
offspring born at a birth: **sextuplet**
• one of seven offspring born at a
birth: **septuplet** • one of eight offspring born at a birth: **octuplet** • placenta and foetal membranes discharged after giving birth: **afterbirth**
• difficulty in giving birth: **dystocia**
• virgin birth: **parthenogenesis** • rebirth in another body: **reincarnation**
• present from birth: **congenital, connate** • following birth: **post-partum**
• hormone stimulating milk production after giving birth: **prolactin**
• ratio of births to size of population:
birth rate, natality • equivalence of
birth and death rates: **zero population growth** ▸ *see also* childbirth

birth-giving • *combining form*:
-parous (*e.g.* viviparous)

biscuit • thin crisp biscuit: **wafer**
• thin crisp biscuit made of flour and
water: **water biscuit** • thin dry biscuit: **cracker** • thin narrow biscuit:
langue de chat • hard biscuit: **nut**
• rich crumbly biscuit: **shortbread,
shortcake** • currant biscuit: **garibaldi** • light almond biscuit: **macaroon** • biscuit of nuts in a chocolate
base: **florentine**

bishop • *adjectives*: **episcopal, pontifical** • bishops collectively: **episcopacy** • chief bishop: **patriarch, primate** • senior bishop: **archbishop,
metropolitan** • bishop in charge of a
diocese: **diocesan** • assistant bishop:
coadjutor, suffragan • sovereign's

letter nominating a bishop: **letter missive** ●bishop's ordination: **consecration** ●bishop's hat: **mitre** ●bishop's over-vestment: **dalmatic** ●bishop's long surplice: **rochet** ●bishop's staff: **crook, crozier, pastoral staff** ●bishop's ceremonial chair: **throne** ●bishop's folding chair: **faldstool** ●archbishop or metropolitan's area of authority: **province** ●bishop's area of authority: **diocese, see** ●bishop's period of office: **episcopate** ●bishop's letter to all his clergy: **pastoral letter** ●bishop's inspection of his diocese: **visitation** ●move a bishop to another see: **translate**

bite ●take small bites: **nibble** ●bite persistently: **gnaw**

black ●*combining forms*: **melan-** ●'black box' in an aircraft: **flight recorder** ●'black hole' in astronomy: **collapsar** ●boundary of a 'black hole': **event horizon** ●'black lung' caused by miners' inhalation of coal dust: **anthracosis, pneumoconiosis** ●black hairstyle with tight braids giving a geometrical scalp pattern : **cornrows** ●person having one white and one black parent: **mulatto** ●person having one white and one mulatto parent: **quadroon** ●person of mixed European and black descent: **Creole**

blackboard ●wooden frame supporting a blackboard: **easel**

blackcurrant ●French blackcurrant liqueur: **cassis**

blacksmith ●blacksmith's workshop: **forge, smithy** ●blacksmith's metal workblock: **anvil**

bladder ●*combining form*: **cyst(o)-** ●*adjectives*: **cystic, vesical** ●inflammation of the bladder: **cystitis** ●internal examination of the bladder: **cystoscopy** ●surgical cutting of the bladder: **cystotomy** ●surgical

operation to remove the bladder: **cystectomy** ●thin tube for draining the bladder: **catheter**

blade ●rotating blade: **vane** ●sharpen a metal blade: **whet**

blame ●person made to bear the blame for another's wrongdoing: **scapegoat, whipping boy** ●free from blame: **exculpate, exonerate, vindicate**

blind ●blind with angled slats: **jalousie** ●blind with pivoting slats: **venetian blind**

blindness ●partial blindness: **scotoma** ●blindness over half the field of vision: **hemianopia** ●inability to see in the dark: **night blindness, nyctalopia** ●dog trained to lead the blind: **guide dog** ▸*see also* **colour blindness, sight**

blood ●*combining forms*: **haem-, haemat-, -aemia** ●*adjectives*: **haemal, haematic, sanguineous** ●blood cell: **corpuscle** ●proportion of corpuscles in blood, or the determination of this: **blood count** ●red blood cell: **erythrocyte** ●white blood cell: **leucocyte** ●small lymphatic leucocyte: **lymphocyte** ●abnormal leucocyte in leukaemia: **lymphoblast** ●substance colouring erythrocytes: **haemoglobin** ●colourless fluid part of blood: **plasma** ●disc-shaped cell fragment in blood: **platelet, thrombocyte** ●amber liquid produced by coagulating blood: **serum** ●blood movement round the body: **circulation** ●denoting the heart and blood vessels: **cardiovascular** ●denoting the brain and its blood vessels: **cerebrovascular** ●coagulated blood: **clot, thrombus** ●inadequate supply of blood: **ischaemia** ●obstruction of the blood supply: **infarction** ●stoppage of blood to the brain: **stroke** ●stop blood flowing from a wound: **staunch, stem** ●substance stopping bleeding: **styptic** ●pad applied to stop bleeding: **compress** ●point where an artery may be pressed against a bone to stop bleeding: **pressure point** ●periodic uterine bleeding: **menstruation, period** ●blood substance aiding coagulation: **factor** ●deficiency of red cells in the blood: **anaemia** ●red cell antigen: **rhesus factor** ●denoting blood having the rhesus factor: **rhesus positive** ●denoting blood lacking the rhesus factor: **rhesus negative** ●blood disease causing proliferation of white cells: **leukaemia** ●blood protein counteracting antigens: **antibody** ●blood poisoning caused by bacteria: **septicaemia, toxaemia** ●blood poisoning caused by pus: **pyaemia** ●septicaemia caused by a retained tampon: **toxic shock syndrome** ●excessive glucose in the blood: **hyperglycaemia** ●insufficient glucose in the blood: **hypoglycaemia** ●sufficient glucose in the blood: **normoglycaemia** ●presence of parasites in the blood: **parasitaemia** ●excessive accumulation of blood: **congestion** ●swelling caused by collected blood: **haematocele** ●substantial discharge of blood: **haemorrhage** ●presence of blood in the urine: **haematuria** ●determination of the number of corpuscles in a specific volume of blood: **blood count** ●blood protein transporting oxygen: **haemoglobin** ●protein found in the blood of a diseased person: **paraprotein** ●study of the blood: **haematology** ●blood transfer: **transfusion** ●person providing blood for transfusion: **donor** ●store of blood for transfusion: **blood bank** ●set of types of human blood that are mutually compatible for transfusion: **blood group** ●baby with insufficient blood oxygen: **blue baby** ●the injection of oxygenated blood to enhance a sportsman's performance: **blood doping** ●artificial purification of the

blood: **dialysis, haemodialysis** ●feeding on blood: **haematophagous** ●blood-sucking parasite: **leech** ●blood relationship: **kinship**

blood clot ●*combining form*: **thrombo-** ●clotting of the blood: **thrombosis** ●swelling caused by thrombosis: **haematoma** ●reduced clotting capacity of the blood: **haemophilia** ●substance preventing blood clots: **anticoagulant** ●dissolution of a blood clot: **thrombolysis**

blood pressure ●high blood pressure: **hypertension** ●high blood pressure in pregnancy: **pre-eclampsia** ●low blood pressure: **hypotension** ●having normal blood pressure: **normotensive** ●temporary loss of consciousness through a fall in blood pressure: **syncope** ●pituitary hormone tending to increase blood pressure: **vasopressin** ●drug reducing blood pressure: **beta blocker** ●instrument measuring blood pressure: **sphygmomanometer** ●inflatable bag used with this: **cuff**

blood vessel ●*combining forms*: **angio-, arterio-, phleb-, vaso-, ven-** ●*adjective*: **vascular, venous** ●full of veins: **venose** ●in or into a vein: **intravenous** ●network of blood vessels: **circulatory system, vascular system** ●blood vessel running from the heart: **artery** ●blood vessel running to the heart: **vein** ●artificial blood vessel replacing one that is blocked: **bypass** ●main artery from the heart: **aorta** ●main artery of the neck: **carotid artery** ●artery supplying the heart: **coronary artery** ●artery supplying the lungs: **pulmonary artery** ●progressive hardening of the arteries: **arteriosclerosis, atherosclerosis** ●arterial obstruction by a blood clot or air bubble: **embolism** ●large vein returning blood to the heart: **vena cava** ●vein carrying blood to the liver: **portal vein** ●fine blood vessel: **capillary** ● breakage of capillaries below the skin: **rupture, contusion** ● inflammation of vein walls: **phlebitis** ● patchy inflammation of smaller veins: **angiitis, vasculitis** ● swollen vein in the legs: **varicose vein** ● varicose veins on the spermatic cord: **varicocele** ● treatment of varicose veins by injections to harden their walls: **sclerotherapy** ● swollen veins in the anus: **haemorrhoids, piles** ● narrowing of blood vessels: **vasoconstriction** ● widening of blood vessels: **vasodilation** ● drug narrowing blood vessels: **vasoconstrictor** ● drug widening blood vessels: **vasodilator** ● causing the constriction or dilatation of blood vessels: **vasomotor** ● throb of an artery as blood passes: **pulse** ● place where arterial bleeding may be stopped by pressure: **pressure point** ● medical puncturing of a vein: **venepuncture** ● surgical opening of a vein: **phlebotomy, venesection** ● X-ray examination of a vein: **angiography, venography**

blue ● *combining form*: **cyano-** ● *adjectives*: **azure, cyanic** ● brilliant light blue: **electric blue** ● dark blue: **royal blue** ● yet darker blue: **navy blue** ● brilliant deep blue: **ultramarine** ● blue-tinged skin due to poor circulation: **cyanosis**

blunder ● social blunder: **gaffe, faux pas** ● blunder in speaking: **slip of the tongue, lapsus linguae**

blush ● *adjective*: **erubescent** ● cosmetic reddening the cheeks: **blusher**

board ● board made of thin layers of wood with alternating grain: **plywood** ● board made of plaster set between paper: **plasterboard** ● board made of layers of glued paper: **pasteboard** ● strong pasteboard used in book covers: **millboard** ● board with a network of small holes: **pegboard**

● horizontal boards with overlapping edges: **weatherboarding**

boarding ● Continental boarding house: **pension** ● boarding establishment for cats: **cattery** ● boarding establishment for dogs: **kennels**

boat ● floating platform: **raft** ● boat hollowed out of a log: **dugout** ● flat-bottomed square-ended boat: **punt** ● flat-bottomed boat supporting a bridge: **pontoon** ● small sailing boat: **dinghy** ● light fast boat: **yacht** ● Malayan sailing boat: **proa** ● small oared boat used in the Far East: **sampan** ● light rowing boat for one person: **scull, skiff** ● traditional Nile boat: **felucca** ● small boat carried on a ship: **cutter, jolly boat** ● large boat carried on a ship: **longboat** ● small boat plying between a ship and the shore: **tender** ● boat conveying sailors on shore leave: **liberty boat** ● large motor boat: **launch** ● motor boat with living accommodation: **cabin cruiser, houseboat** ● fast motor boat designed to skim over the water: **hydroplane** ● fast motor boat with a vaned hull: **hydrofoil** ● rescue boat: **lifeboat** ● fast coastal patrol boat: **cutter** ● small naval patrol boat: **vedette** ● small powerful boat towing ships: **tug** ● inshore fishing boat: **smack** ● fishing boat using nets: **trawler** ● unpowered boat used to unload ships: **barge, lighter** ● flat-bottomed boat carrying freight on inland waterways: **barge** ● boat plying to and fro across a stretch of water: **ferry** ● pleasure boat on the Seine at Paris: **bateau mouche** ● anchored boat marking the course of a race: **stake boat** ● light racing boat: **shell** ● round wickerwork boat: **coracle** ● small pedal-operated pleasure boat: **pedalo** ● boat with one hull: **monohull** ● boat with parallel twin hulls: **catamaran** ● boat with three parallel hulls: **trimaran** ● boat's secondary hull: **outrigger** ● boat's stabilizing float: **outrigger** ● boat with a vaned hull: **hydrofoil** ● protective strip along a boat's side: **rubbing strake** ● denoting a deckless boat: **open** ● space at the bow or stern of an open boat: **sheets** ● flat surface forming a boat's stern: **transom** ● unmoor a boat: **cast off** ● (of an open boat) receive water over the gunwales: **ship water, ship a sea** ● scoop water out of a boat: **bail** ● group of boats: **flotilla** ● boat's side above water: **freeboard** ● top of this: **gunwale** ● boat's continuous line of planking: **strake** ● sailing boat's liftable keel: **centreboard, daggerboard** ● keel block to take the mast: **step** ● vertically hinged flap for steering: **rudder** ● horizontal bar fixed to the top of the rudder: **tiller** ● boat's rudder socket: **gudgeon** ● rudder pin: **pintle** ● boat's bow rope: **painter** ● boat's steersman: **cox, coxswain, helm, helmsman** ● boat's sudden change of course: **sheer** ● boat race on a course round obstacles: **slalom** ● secure a boat to an anchor or land: **moor** ● wedge supporting a beached boat: **chock** ● depth of water needed by a boat: **draught** ● passable by ships and boats: **navigable** ▸ *see also* ship, sailing

body ● *combining forms*: **somat-, -some** (*e.g.* chromosome) ● *adjectives*: **corporal, corporeal, personal, somatic** ● permanently damage a body part: **maim** ● body opening: **meatus, orifice** ● body's chemical processes: **metabolism** ● pliable body partition or lining: **membrane, septum** ● denoting this: **parietal** ● baglike bodily membrane: **sac** ● outer membrane enveloping the brain and spinal cord: **dura, dura mater** ● inner membrane enveloping the brain and spinal cord: **pia, pia mater** ● nerve tissues controlling the body: **central nervous system** ● bodily substance conveying a stimulus or

other information: **messenger** ● digestive passage through the body: **alimentary canal** ● cavity behind the nose and mouth: **pharynx** ● main part of the body without head or limbs: **torso, trunk** ● tube from mouth to stomach: **gullet, oesophagus** ● tube from the throat to the lungs: **trachea, windpipe** ● inflammation of the trachea: **tracheitis** ● part of the body between neck and abdomen: **thorax** ● area between the breasts: **cleavage** ● bodily organs used in breathing: **respiratory tract** ● muscular partition between thorax and abdomen: **diaphragm** ● part of the body between the thorax and groin: **abdomen** ● depression in the belly: **navel** ● organs of the main bodily cavities: **viscera** ● organ producing chemicals for bodily use: **gland** ● regulatory substance produced by glands: **hormone** ● supposed regulatory system for the metabolism: **biological clock, body clock** ● tube from stomach to anus: **intestine** ● side between the ribs and hip: **flank, loin** ● front between chest and waist: **midriff** ● membrane lining the abdomen: **peritoneum** ● inflammation of this: **peritonitis** ● duct conducting urine from the kidney to the bladder: **ureter** ● duct conveying urine out from the bladder: **urethra** ● inflammation of the urethra: **urethritis** ● lower abdominal area: **groin** ● area between the top of the legs: **crotch, crutch** ● final opening of the intestine: **anus** ● area between the anus and scrotum or vulva: **perineum** ● lower part of the abdomen: **pubes** ● tissue covering the pubic bone: **mons pubis, mons Veneris** ● strong elastic connective tissue: **cartilage** ● hormone oxidizing body sugar: **insulin** ● body sac containing liquid: **cyst** ● disease's chief bodily location: **focus** ● swollen, hot, and painful bodily state: **inflammation** ● exceptionally

sensitive bodily state: **irritability**
●colourless tissue fluid: **lymph** ●excess of fluid in the body: **dropsy, oedema** ●excessive discharge of fluids:
flux ●insufficient fluid in the body:
dehydration ●inability to control
bodily functions: **incontinence**
●blockage of a bodily passage: **obstruction** ●excessively low body temperature: **hypothermia** ●denoting
creatures maintaining a constant
body temperature: **warm-blooded**
●denoting creatures whose body temperature varies with that of their
surroundings: **cold-blooded** ●production and discharge of substances
by a bodily organ: **secretion** ●bodily
organ secreting chemicals: **gland**
●slipping down or forward of a bodily
organ: **prolapse** ●wasting away of an
organ or tissue: **dystrophy** ●unwanted air in body tissue: **emphysema** ●damaged body area: **lesion**
●small bodily swelling: **nodule**
●general bodily swelling: **dropsy, oedema** ●bursting of an organ or tissue: **rupture** ●listening to bodily
sounds with a stethoscope: **auscultation** ●study of the body by dissection: **anatomy** ●machine examining
the body by radiation, ultrasound,
etc.: **scanner** ●medical imaging of
bodily organs or tissue: **magnetic resonance imaging** ●X-raying a section
through the body: **tomography, computerized axial tomography** ●substance whose course through the body
may be monitored: **tracer** ●examine
the body by touch: **palpate** ●diagnostic tapping of the body: **percussion**
●clinical measurement of bodily functions as indication of continued life:
vital signs ●use of electric currents
to heat the body's inner organs: **diathermy** ●rubbing the body to relieve
pain etc.: **massage** ●person skilled
at this: **masseur** (*fem.* masseuse)
●physical treatment of bodily injuries
or deformity: **physiotherapy** ●enter-

tainer who twists his or her body into
abnormal positions: **contortionist**
●elegant bodily movements: **deportment** ●bodily position: **posture**
●bodily movements or posture taken
to indicate thoughts and feelings:
body language ●awareness of the
body's position: **kinaesthesia** ●excessive bodily sensitivity: **erethism**
●form and development of the body:
physique ●body type: **somatotype**
●person with a lean and delicate
body: **ectomorph** ●person with a
compact and muscular body: **mesomorph** ●person with a plump body:
endomorph ●non-reproductive bodily characteristics manifested at
puberty: **secondary sexual characteristics** ●tissue etc. inserted into
the body by surgery: **implant** ●artificial body part: **prosthesis** ●violent
and uncontrollable body movement:
convulsion ●body's incapacity for
self-movement: **paralysis** ●localized
death and decay of bodily tissue: **gangrene, necrosis** ●dead body: **corpse**
●rebirth in another body: **reincarnation** ●lacking a physical body: **discarnate, disincarnate**

boil[1] ●purify by boiling off: **distil**
●immerse briefly in boiling water:
scald

boil[2] ●formation of pus in a boil:
maturation ●cut a boil: **lance**

bolt ●large bolt with a rounded
head: **coach bolt** ●piece of metal
with an internal thread to receive a
bolt: **nut**

bomb ●bomb or its casing: **shell**
●hand-thrown bomb: **grenade**
●crude hand-thrown petrol bomb:
Molotov cocktail ●bomb containing
jellied petrol: **napalm bomb** ●bomb
hidden under earth or water and exploding on contact: **mine** ●bomb exploding at a fixed depth under water:
depth charge ●bomb travelling
under its own power or remote-controlled: **missile** ●denoting a

bomb equipped to find its target: **homing** ●bomb releasing projectiles on impact: **cluster bomb** ●bomb exploding into fragments: **fragmentation bomb** ●these fragments: **shrapnel** ●denoting a bomb causing fires: **incendiary** ●denoting a bomb destroying living beings rather than structures: **anti-personnel** ●artillery and bombs: **ordnance** ●bomb detonator: **fuse** ●prepare a bomb by activating its fuse: **arm, prime** ●peg deactivating a hand grenade: **pin** ●bomb an area intensively: **carpet-bomb** ●defusing or removal of unexploded bombs: **bomb disposal** ●defuse a bomb: **disarm** ●fierce fire caused by bombs: **firestorm** ▸ *see also* **nuclear weapon**

bone ●*combining forms*: **oss(i)**, **osteo-** ●*adjectives*: **osseous, osteal** ●bone-formation: **osteogenesis** ●set of bones supporting a body: **skeleton** ●head bones: **skull** ●principal bone of the upper arm: **humerus** ●principal bones of the lower arm: **radius, ulna** ●wrist bones: **carpus** ●hand bones: **metacarpus** ●bone connecting the breastbone and shoulderblade: **collarbone, clavicle** ●flat bone protecting the upper chest: **breastbone, sternum** ●curved bone protecting the lower chest: **rib** ●set of these: **ribcage** ●interlocking set of bones from the skull to the small of the back: **backbone, spine, spinal column, vertebral column** ●one of these bones: **vertebra** (*pl.* vertebrae) ●flat bone in the upper back: **shoulderblade, scapula** ●bones at the base of the spinal column: **sacrum, coccyx** ●bony structure to which the legs are attached: **pelvis** ●projection of this below the waist: **hip** ●triangular bone forming the back of the pelvis: **sacrum** ●penis bone in certain mammals: **baculum, os penis** ●principal bone of the upper leg: **thighbone, femur** ●bone

covering the knee joint: **kneecap, patella** ●bones of the lower leg: **fibula, shin, shinbone, tibia** ●ankle bones: **tarsus** ●foot bones: **metatarsus** ●turn into bone: **ossify** ●soft substance in bone cavities: **marrow** ●opening in a bone: **foramen** ●joint between bones: **commissure** ●close joint between bones: **symphysis** ●fusion of bones in a joint: **ankylosis** ●rigid seamlike junction between bones: **suture** ●cord connecting a muscle to a bone: **sinew, tendon** ●bone decay: **caries** ●bone softening: **osteomalacia** ●break or crack in a bone: **fracture** ●arrange the parts of a broken bone: **set** ●(of broken bones) re-fuse: **knit** ●rigid support for a broken bone: **splint** ●steel rod rejoining fractured bones: **pin** ●bone brittleness: **osteoporosis** ●bone inflammation: **osteitis** ●bone cancer: **osteosarcoma** ●degeneration of bone and cartilage in joints: **osteoarthritis** ●death of bone tissue: **osteonecrosis** ●medical treatment of bone and muscle deformities: **orthopaedics** ●therapeutic manipulation of bones and muscles: **osteopathy** ●bone-house: **charnel house, ossuary**

bone marrow ●*adjective*: **myeloid** ●inflammation of the bone marrow: **osteomyelitis** ●malignant tumour of the bone marrow: **myeloma**

book ●*combining form*: **biblio-** ●book made as a continuous roll: **scroll** ●ancient hand-written book: **codex** (*pl.* codices) ●early printed book: **incunabulum** (*pl.* incunabula) ●strong cloth book for young children: **rag book** ●account-book: **ledger** ●account-book for the current day's transactions: **daybook, journal** ●account-book for minor transactions: **cash book** ●ship's record book: **journal, log** ●book listing property-holdings in 1086: **Domesday**

Book ●denoting a book with removable pages: **loose-leaf** ●publicity booklet: **brochure, prospectus** ●instruction book: **handbook, manual** ●student's book giving instruction in a subject: **coursebook, textbook, workbook** ●elementary textbook: **primer** ●book giving systematic information: **companion, compendium, encyclopedia, handbook** ●book intended for consultation on specific topics, not discursive reading: **reference book** ●book for constant reference, giving immediate guidance: **companion, vade mecum** ●book's treatment of a topic: **coverage** ●book containing a collection of writings etc.: **anthology, collectanea, commonplace book, florilegium, miscellany, omnibus** ●book describing different kinds of animals: **bestiary** ●book compiled to honour a scholar: **Festschrift** ●book listing a region's animals: **fauna** ●book listing events etc. of the current or preceding year: **yearbook** ●book with samples of good handwriting: **copybook** ●book listing herbs: **herbal** ●large lavishly-illustrated book: **coffee-table book** ●book giving the rules of a language: **grammar** ●book recording livestock pedigrees: **herd book** ●Mass book: **missal** ●book listing names and addresses: **directory** ●book of psalms: **psalter** ●book of sermons: **homiliary** ●list of books: **bibliography** ●list of books regarded as correctly attributed to an author, or as classics: **canon** ●book's page-size and layout: **format** ●white space created by a book's inner margins: **gutter** ●part of a book preceding the main text: **front matter** ●pictures in a book: **illustrations, plates** ●drawn material in a book: **graphics** ●illustration facing the title page: **frontispiece** ●small decorative design at the end of a chapter etc.: **tailpiece** ●illustrate a book with material taken from others:

grangerize ●insert blank pages between the printed ones: **interleave** ●short introduction to a book: **foreword** ●list of chapters etc. in a book: **contents** ●list of errors found in a book: **corrigenda, errata** ●list of contributors to a book: **acknowledgements, credits** ●book's abbreviated title: **short title** ●book's section title: **half-title** ●page headline: **running head** ●short quotation at the start of a book or chapter: **epigraph** ●summary of a book's contents: **abstract, epitome, synopsis** ●separate section of a book, dealing with a point of detail: **excursus** ●book's final summing-up: **conclusion** ●closing section of a book: **epilogue** ●extra section added at the end of a book: **appendix** ●small dictionary at the back of a book: **glossary, vocabulary** ●extra page(s) replacing a defective section: **cancel** ●drawn illustration in a book: **figure** ●photograph reproduced in a book: **plate** ●blank page at the start or end of a book: **flyleaf** ●large fold-out page: **gatefold** ●count a book's pages: **paginate** ●piece of paper with a page printed on each side: **folio, leaf** ●count a book's leaves: **foliate** ●book composed of sheets folded once: **folio** ●book composed of sheets folded twice: **quarto** ●book composed of sheets folded three times: **octavo** ●right-hand page of an open book: **recto** ●left-hand page of an open book: **verso** ●decorative paper inside the covers: **endpaper** ●part of this attached to the cover: **paste-down** ●list of a book's printing errors: **errata** ●part of a book published separately: **fascicle, instalment, offprint, preprint** ●inserted slip bearing the owner's name: **bookplate, ex libris** ●note in a library book showing where it is shelved: **shelf mark** ●preparation and public sale of a book: **publishing** ●details of a book's printer and publisher: **imprint, colophon** ● denoting a book with worn pages: **dog-eared** ● denoting a book with discoloured pages: **foxed** ● book stand: **lectern** ● support for a row of books: **bookend** ● production of machine-readable books: **electronic publishing** ● book-collector: **bibliophile** ● passionate enthusiasm for collecting books: **bibliomania** ● itinerant bookseller: **colporteur** ● pornographic books: **curiosa, erotica** ▶ *see also* **publishing**

bookbinding ● glued unsewn binding: **perfect binding** ● binding having the spine in a different material from the rest: **quarter binding** ● fine goatskin for bindings: **morocco** ● sheepskin used as a substitute for morocco: **roan** ● calfskin impregnated with birchbark oil: **Russia leather** ● binding in limp leather which overhangs the pages: **yapp** ● strong pasteboard used in book covers: **millboard** ● part of a binding into which the pages are fixed: **spine** ● embossing of a book cover: **stamping, tooling** ● embossing of a book cover without a coloured inlay: **blind stamping, blind tooling** ● book's paper cover: **dust jacket, dust-wrapper, jacket, wrapper**

bookmaker ● bookmakers' signalling system: **tic-tac** ● bookmaker's assistant: **runner**

boot ● high waterproof boot: **wader** ● spiked plate for a climber's boot: **crampon** ● heavy nail strengthening a sole: **hobnail** ● small projection to a sole, giving improved grip: **stud**

border ● borderland between England and Wales or Scotland: **marches** ● sharing a border: **conterminous, contiguous** ● having the same borders: **coterminous** ● border post for passport and customs control: **checkpoint** ● earthwork marking a border: **dyke**

boredom ● listless boredom: **ennui** ● bored through lack of variety: **stale** ● tedious period: **longueur** ● lengthy and boring: **long-winded** ● become boring: **pall**

born ● born in wedlock: **legitimate** ● born out of wedlock: **bastard, illegitimate, natural**

borough ● *adjective*: **municipal** ● chairperson of a borough council: **mayor**

both ● *combining forms*: **ambi-, amphi-, bi-** (*e.g.* biconcave) ● able to use both hands equally well: **ambidexterous** ● able to live or operate on both land and water: **amphibious**

bottle ● small cylindrical bottle: **phial** ● pocket-sized bottle: **flask** ● unmarked bottle for serving wine or water: **carafe, decanter** ● large bottle protected by a frame: **carboy** ● large bottle for home winemaking etc.: **demijohn** ● double-sized wine bottle: **magnum** ● wine bottle 4 times the normal size: **jeroboam** ● wine bottle 6 times the normal size: **rehoboam** ● wine bottle 8 times the normal size: **methuselah** ● wine bottle 12 times the normal size: **salmanazar** ● wine bottle 16 times the normal size: **balthazar** ● wine bottle 20 times the normal size: **nebuchadnezzar** ● very small bottle of spirits: **miniature** ● metal bottle cap with a crimped edge: **crown cap, crown cork**

boundary ● limiting boundary: **parameter** ● boundary line: **perimeter** ● assert territorial boundaries: **beat the bounds, perambulate**

bow ● traditional Muslim bow of greeting: **salaam** ● former Chinese bow of greeting: **kowtow**

bow and arrows ● skill or sport of shooting with these: **archery** ● large bow drawn by hand: **longbow** ● bow's string notch: **nock** ● powerful bow on a wooden frame: **crossbow**

● missile shot by this: **bolt** ● arrow notch: **nock** ● shaped like a bow: **arcuate**

bowel ● difficulty in emptying the bowels: **constipation** ● flushing out of the lower bowel: **colonic irrigation, enema** ● stress-related bowel pain: **irritable bowel syndrome** ● remove the bowels: **disembowel, eviscerate** ▸ *see also* **intestine**

bowl ● crushing bowl: **mortar** ● church holy-water bowl: **stoup**

bowls ● large black ball used in bowls: **wood** ● small white ball used in bowls: **jack** ● session of play in one direction: **end** ● captain of a bowls team: **skip** ● kind of bowling green that rises towards the middle: **crown green** ● section of a green used for a match: **rink** ● uneven ground making a bowl change course: **rub** ● French bowls: **boules, pétanque**

box ● large metal box of a standard design: **container** ● large light wooden box: **tea chest** ● small ornamental box: **casket** ● box for a set of cutlery: **canteen** ● insulated foodbox: **cool box** ● light circular hatbox: **bandbox** ● open-ended box for papers: **pigeon-hole** ● box for sewing materials: **workbox**

boxing ● boxing match: **bout** ● programme of bouts: **bill** ● a bill's supporting bouts: **undercard** ● standard boxing rules: **Queenberry Rules** ● boxing shorts: **trunks** ● boxer's attendant: **cornerman, second** ● boxer's official weighing before a bout: **weigh-in** ● boxer's defensive posture: **guard** ● pretended blow: **feint** ● blow made with a bent elbow: **hook** ● upwards blow made with a bent elbow: **uppercut** ● blows with alternate fists: **one-two** ● grappling at close quarters: **clinch** ● time allowed for a standing boxer to collect himself: **standing count** ● denoting a boxer knocked to the floor: **down** ● denot-

ing a boxer knocked unconscious: **out** ● time allowed for a fallen boxer to get up: **count** ● knock down a boxer for a count of ten: **knock out** ● denoting a boxer so knocked down: **out for the count** ● victory awarded because the opponent is unfit to continue: **technical knockout** ● complete a bout: **go the distance** ● boxer's deformed ear: **cauliflower ear** ● ornate belt as championship prize: **Lonsdale belt** ● practice boxing, with light blows: **sparring** ● suspended stuffed bag for boxing practice: **punchbag** ● suspended stuffed ball for boxing practice: **punchball**

boy ● boy singing in a church choir: **chorister** ● winged boy portrayed in Renaissance paintings: **amoretto, cherub, putto**

brain ● *combining form*: **cerebro-, encephalo-** ● *adjective*: **cerebral, encephalic** ● half of the brain: **hemisphere** ● brain area concerned with a specific activity: **centre** ● front part of the brain, controlling memory and thought: **cerebrum, forebrain, prosencephalon** ● section of this: **lobe** ● denoting the foremost part of the frontal lobe: **prefrontal** ● brain area coordinating muscles: **cerebellum** ● outer layer covering the brain: **cortex** ● membrane covering the brain and spinal cord: **meninx** (*pl.* meninges) ● inflammation of the meninges: **meningitis** ● outer membrane enveloping the brain and spinal cord: **dura, dura mater** ● inner membrane enveloping the brain and spinal cord: **pia, pia mater** ● brain and spinal cord: **central nervous system** ● denoting the brain and spine: **cerebrospinal** ● inflammation of the brain and spinal cord: **encephalomyelitis** ● nerve transmitting signals from the eye to the brain: **optic nerve** ● nerve transmitting signals from the ear to the brain: **auditory nerve** ● denoting the brain and its blood vessels: **cere-**

brovascular ●stoppage of blood to the brain: **stroke** ●arterial bleeding into brain tissues: **cerebral haemorrhage** ●inflammation of the brain: **encephalitis** ●syphilitic inflammation of the brain: **paresis** ●brain disorder with sudden loss of consciousness or convulsions: **epilepsy** ●inability to express or understand speech due to brain damage: **aphasia** ●impaired muscular coordination due to brain damage: **cerebral palsy** ●person suffering from cerebral palsy: **spastic** ●persistent impairment of reasoning or memory due to brain disease or injury: **dementia** ●fluid accumulation in the brain: **hydrocephalus** ●disease which indirectly affects the brain: **encephalopathy** ●surgical cutting of the brain's white nerve fibres: **leucotomy, lobotomy, stereotaxis** ●brain surgery to treat mental illness: **psychosurgery** ●supposed memory trace in the brain: **engram** ●electrical activity of a relaxed brain: **alpha rhythm** ●electrical activity of an alert brain: **beta rhythm** ●record of the brain's electrical activity: **electroencephalogram** ●computer system modelled on the human brain: **neural net, neural network** ●computer model of the brain's ability to recognize and discriminate: **perceptron**

brake ●broad cylinder attached to a braked wheel: **brake drum** ●curved block pressing against the drum: **brake shoe** ●thin block pressing against a disc brake: **brake pad** ●hard material attached to the shoe or pad: **brake lining** ●denoting a hydraulically enhanced braking system: **power-assisted**

branch ●*adjective*: **ramose** ●local branch of certain trade unions: **chapel**

brass ●inscribed brass plate in a church etc.: **monumental brass** ●greenish surface colour of oxidized brass: **verdigris** ●person working with brass: **brazier** ▸*see also* **monumental brass**

brassière ●brassière giving firm support for active pursuits: **sports bra** ●part of a brassière supporting one breast: **cup**

bread ●dry bread: **hardtack** ●bread baked twice: **rusk** ●bread aerated by soda: **soda bread** ●very small loaf of bread: **roll** ●ring-shaped bread roll: **bagel** ●small thin bread roll: **bridge roll** ●light sweet bread roll: **brioche** ●flat bread roll for toasting: **muffin** ●flat hollow unleavened bread: **pitta** ●large loaf with diagonal slashes on a rounded top: **bloomer** ●loaf made of two round lumps of dough, the smaller on top: **cottage loaf** ●brown loaf with whole wheatgrains: **granary loaf** ●small piece of fried or toasted bread: **crouton** ●small piece of bread to dip into sauce etc.: **sippet** ●slice of bread: **round** ●slice of bread soaked in egg and fried: **French toast** ●long narrow French loaf: **baguette, French loaf, French stick** ●German rye bread: **pumpernickel** ●Italian aerated bread made with olive oil: **ciabatta** ●thin Italian breadsticks: **grissini** ●toasted Italian bread drenched in olive oil: **bruschetta** ●mixture of flour and liquid for breadmaking: **dough**

break ●sudden and complete break: **rupture** ●break off through structural strain: **shear** ●broken piece of pottery, glass, etc.: **shard**

breakfast ●light breakfast: **continental breakfast** ●substantial breakfast including hot food: **English breakfast** ●breakfast and lunch combined: **brunch**

breast ●*combining form*: **mast-** ●*adjectives*: **mammary, mamillary, pectoral** ●small pinkish projection from a breast: **nipple** ● hollow between the breasts: **cleavage** ● breastbone: **sternum** ● inflammation of the breast: **mastitis** ● enlargement of a man's breasts: **gynaecomastia** ● X-ray location of breast tumours: **mammography** ● surgical removal of a breast lump: **lumpectomy** ● surgical removal of a breast: **mastectomy** ● chemical polymer used in breast implants: **silicone** ● leaving the breasts uncovered: **topless** ● baglike mammary gland of cattle etc.: **udder**

breath ● *combining form*: spiro- ● *adjective*: **respiratory** ● process of breathing: **respiration** ● single intake of breath: **draught** ● breathing in: **inhalation, inspiration** ● breathing out: **exhalation, exspiration** ● excessively fast breathing: **hyperventilation** ● excessively slow breathing: **hypoventilation** ● breath needed for physical exertion: **wind** ● take short quick breaths: **pant** ● difficulty in breathing: **dyspnoea** ● difficulty in breathing due to constriction of the bronchi: **asthma** ● easily becoming breathless: **short-winded** ● breathlessness caused by enlargement of the air sacs of the lungs: **emphysema** ● denoting breathing that is noisy and laboured: **stertorous** ● breathe with a whistling sound: **wheeze** ● office workers' headaches and respiratory problems, thought to be caused by poor ventilation: **sick building syndrome** ● bad breath: **halitosis** ● temporary cessation in breathing: **apnoea** ● bodily organs used in breathing: **respiratory system, respiratory tract** ● instrument recording breathing movements: **spirograph** ● mechanical or manual restoration of a person's breathing: **artificial respiration** ● machine providing prolonged artificial respiration: **iron lung, respirator**

breed ● breed two species together: **cross-breed, hybridize** ● breed from

closely related stock: **inbreed** ● population improvement by controlled breeding: **eugenics**

bribe ● willing to take bribes: **corrupt, venal** ● refusing bribes: **incorruptible** ● payments made to an influential person to promote a product or interest: **payola** ● bribe someone to commit an unlawful act: **suborn**

brick ● bricks made from sun-dried clay: **adobe** ● brick made from cinders: **breeze block** ● heat-resistant brick: **firebrick** ● brick suitable for exposure to view in the finished building: **face brick** ● brick-making mixture: **loam, pug** ● furnace for bricks: **kiln** ● bake bricks in a kiln: **fire** ● stack of bricks for firing: **hack** ● denoting bricks not yet fired: **unburnt** ● brick laid at right angles to a wall: **header** ● brick laid parallel to a wall: **stretcher** ● built row of bricks: **course** ● horizontal decorative band of bricks: **string course** ● brickwork in a timber frame: **nogging** ● piece of brick used as a missile: **brickbat** ● cement or mortar filling the joints in brickwork: **pointing** ● builder's brick-carrier: **hod** ● appearance of crystallized salts on brickwork: **efflorescence**

bridge ● many-arched bridge carrying a road or railway: **viaduct** ● many-arched bridge carrying a river or canal: **aqueduct** ● bridge rising steeply to its centre: **humpback bridge** ● bridge supported by cables: **suspension bridge** ● bridge for pedestrians: **footbridge** ● raised passageway between buildings: **walkway** ● bridge that may be erected quickly from prefabricated parts: **Bailey bridge** ● bridge with a raisable section: **bascule, bascule bridge** ● raisable bridge at a castle entrance: **drawbridge** ● arch of a bridge between its supports: **span** ● supporting framework for a bridge: **truss** ● floating object used to support a bridge: **pontoon**

• pile set upstream of a bridge to protect it from floating objects: **starling**

bristle • *adjective*: **setaceous** • hedgehog's bristles: **spines**

broad • *combining form*: **platy-** (*e.g.* platypus)

broadcast • simultaneous broadcast of a programme on radio and television: **simulcast** • television broadcast: **screening** • broadcast news report: **news bulletin, newscast** • person reading such a report: **newscaster** • denoting broadcasting receiving no state funding: **independent** • denoting broadcasting funded by advertisements: **commercial** • room equipped for broadcasting: **studio** • broadcasting equipment: **transmitter** • frequencies used by a broadcasting station: **channel** • denoting an unauthorized broadcasting station: **pirate** • adjust a receiver to receive a particular station: **tune** • immediate rebroadcast of incoming signals: **relay** • deliberate generation of interference to render a broadcast unintelligible: **jamming** • broadcast sound covering a censored word: **bleep** • denoting broadcasting without the use of satellites: **terrestrial** • text of a broadcast: **script** • music associated with a particular programme or broadcaster: **signature tune** • list of recordings broadcast on a radio programme: **playlist** • selection and scheduling of broadcasts: **programming** • estimated audience of a particular broadcast: **rating** • time devoted to a particular type of broadcast: **airtime** • spoken linkage between broadcast items: **continuity** • broadcaster providing continuity between a number of contributors: **anchorman, linkman** • out-of-studio setting for a broadcast: **location** • description of a broadcast event: **commentary, voice-over** • denoting broadcasts transmitted at the time of occurrence: **live** • sample broadcast made to assess audience response: **pilot** • set of related broadcasts: **series, serial** • serial about ordinary people: **soap opera** • broadcast containing several episodes of a serial: **omnibus** • broadcast advertisement: **commercial** • broadcasting to a small or selected audience: **narrowcasting** • broadcast programme featuring phone-calls made to the presenter: **phone-in** • type of broadcasting featuring phone-ins and topical discussions: **talk radio, talk show** • broadcast programme in which celebrities are interviewed informally: **chat show** • time at which broadcasting attracts the greatest audiences: **prime time** • broadcast news reporter: **journalist, correspondent** • organization supplying news stories: **news agency** • unscheduled broadcast of important news: **newsflash** • end of a day's broadcasting: **close-down** • person employed to listen in to foreign broadcasts: **monitor**

bronze • *combining form*: **chalco-** (*e.g.* chalcolithic) • oxide film on bronze: **patina, verdigris**

brother • *combining forms*: **frater-, fratri-** • *adjective*: **fraternal** • brother sharing only one parent: **half-brother** • religious brotherhood: **fraternity** • killing one's brother: **fratricide**

brown • greyish brown: **dun** • light yellowish brown: **fawn** • reddish brown seen in old photographs: **sepia**

Buddhist • Buddhist religious teacher: **bonze** • Buddhist scriptures: **Tripitaka, sutra** • Buddhist mystical text: **tantra** • Buddhist concept of universal law: **dharma** • Buddhist policy of non-violence toward all living things: **ahimsa** • central Buddhist beliefs: **four noble truths** • Buddhist tradition emphasizing self-salvation: **Theravada** • Buddhist tradition emphasizing mutual salvation: **Mahayana** ●final goal of Buddhist spiritual progress: **nirvana** ●way of life leading to nirvana: **eightfold path, Middle Way** ●Buddhist's personal fate: **karma** ●degree of spiritual insight freeing from the cycle of rebirth: **enlightenment** ●Buddhist state of supreme happiness: **ananda** ●word repeated in Buddhist meditation: **mantra** ●disk symbolizing the universe: **mandala** ●Buddhist tower temple: **pagoda** ●domed Buddhist shrine: **stupa** ●Buddhist monastic order: **sangha** ●Japanese Buddhism, emphasizing meditation: **Zen** ●Japanese Buddhist festival of the dead: **Bon** ●Tibetan Buddhism: **Lamaism** ●Tibetan Buddhist shrine: **chorten** ●leader of Tibetan Buddhists: **Dalai Lama** ●Tibetan Buddhist monk: **lama** ▸*see also* **Tibet**

builder ●designer of buildings: **architect** ●construction labourer: **navvy** ●builder in stone: **mason, stonemason** ●builder in brick: **bricklayer** ●builder in wood: **carpenter** ●glass-fitter: **glazier** ●pipework-installer: **plumber** ●builder specializing in high work: **steeplejack, spiderman** ●person minding a building or site overnight: **nightwatchman** ●builder undertaking a whole project: **contractor** ●builder undertaking part of the project for the contractor: **subcontractor** ●builder's V-shaped brick trough: **hod**

building ●*adjectives*: **architectural, tectonic** ●buildings and their equipment regarded as an investment: **plant** ●building of historical importance: **monument** ●round domed building: **rotunda** ●very tall building: **high-rise, skyscraper** ●squalid or decrepit building: **slum** ●detached subsidiary building: **outbuilding, outhouse** ●group of buildings: **complex** ●buildings erected to fill space between others: **infill** ●sham building:

folly ●sham cave mouth: **grotto** ●denoting a building not joined to any other: **detached, freestanding** ●denoting a building joined on one side only: **semi-detached** ●denoting a building joined at the ground floor only: **link detached** ●denoting a building with few internal divisions: **open-plan** ●denoting a building having some rooms higher than others by less than a storey: **split-level** ●denoting a building having four pillars: **tetrastyle** ●denoting a poorly constructed building: **jerry-built** ●base of a building: **foundation, footings** ●side of a building: **elevation, facade, front, frontage** ●drawing or diagram of this: **elevation** ●building's principal facade: **frontispiece** ●projecting part of a building: **wing** ●external angle of a building: **quoin** ●project beyond a building's lower part: **oversail** ●denoting a timber-framed building: **half-timbered** ●part of a building made with stone: **stonework** ●part of a building made with brick: **brickwork** ●part of a building made with wood: **woodwork** ●large open area before or within a building: **concourse** ●open area before a building: **forecourt** ●open area at the centre of a building: **atrium, court, courtyard, well** ●area where visitors are dealt with: **reception** ●large oblong hall with interior colonnades: **basilica** ●vertical shaft for a staircase: **stairwell** ●roofed exterior platform at ground level: **veranda** ●this at a higher level: **balcony** ●floor of a building: **storey** ●person who designs buildings and supervises their construction: **architect** ●erection of buildings: **development** ●replacement of existing buildings: **redevelopment** ●denoting a building site with no previous development: **greenfield** ●denoting a previously developed building site: **brownfield** ●area where development is forbidden: **con-**

servation area, green belt ●adaptation of a building to new uses: **conversion** ●declare a building unfit for use: **condemn** ●unlawful occupation of a building: **squatting** ●walls, roof, and floor of a building: **fabric** ●standardized building unit: **module** ●plate strengthening a beam or joint: **fish** ●beam supporting a floor: **joist** ●built support for an arch or bridge: **pier** ●narrow area under a floor or roof, giving access to wiring or plumbing: **crawl space** ●channel within a building's walls for ventilation, cables, etc.: **duct, trunking** ●direction faced by a building's windows: **exposure** ●smooth surfaces of building stone: **dress** ●strip of material covering adjoining surfaces: **fillet, flashing, flaunching** ●waterproof filler: **mastic** ●vertical layer of cement: **perpend** ●levelled layer of floor cement: **screed** ●concrete layer under a building: **oversite, raft** ●reinforce a building by assuring or improving the strength of its foundations: **underpin** ●planking supporting setting concrete: **shuttering** ●framework suspended by ropes, for working on the exterior of a high building: **cradle** ●builders' framework of planks and poles: **scaffolding** ●raised walkway on this: **catwalk** ●building's intrinsic weight: **dead load** ●weight of people or goods in a building: **live load** ●allowance or charge made for a building's wear and tear: **dilapidations** ●area devoted to buildings of a particular kind: **estate** ●technical inspection of a building: **survey** ●property in buildings and land: **real property, realty** ●building with its land and appurtenances: **premises, property** ●denoting a building of certified architectural importance: **listed, scheduled** ●control of building development: **planning, town planning** ●building along the sides of a road: **ribbon development**

●large open container for building debris: **skip** ●structural subsidence: **settlement** ●completely destroy a building: **raze** ●structure of an unfinished or gutted building: **shell** ●fragments of a collapsed or demolished building: **rubble** ▸*see also* **architecture, beam, roof, wall, window**

building materials ●stiff clay: **pisé** ●crushed stone and gravel: **aggregate** ●lime and clay mixture: **cement** ●lime and cement mixture: **mortar** ●thin mortar: **grout** ●cement, sand, and gravel mixture: **concrete** ▸*see also* **brick, cement**

building society ●denoting a building society distributing its profits amongst its members: **mutual** ●restructure a building society as a public company: **demutualize**

bulge ●*adjectives*: **bulbous, tumescent**

bull ●*adjective*: **taurine** ●astrological term: **taurus** ●stab with the horns: **gore** ●Spanish bullfighter killing the bull: **matador** ●Spanish bullfighter on foot: **torero** ●Spanish mounted bullfighter: **toreador** ●matador's mounted assistant: **picador** ●bullfighter's decorated dart: **banderilla**

bullet ●plastic or rubber bullet used in riot control: **baton round** ●bullet expanding on impact: **dumdum** ●bullet emitting smoke etc. so that its course may be traced: **tracer** ●diameter of a bullet: **calibre** ●groove round the cylindrical part of a bullet: **canellure** ●bullet's rebound: **ricochet** ●explosive firing bullets: **propellant**

bun ●fruit bun eaten toasted and buttered: **teacake** ●iced yeast bun with currants: **Bath bun** ●flat bun sprinkled with sugar: **Chelsea bun** ●bun eaten on Good Friday: **hot cross bun**

bunch ●bunch of bananas: **hand** ●bunch of fruit: **truss**

bundle ●*adjectives*: **fascicular, fasciculate** ●wrapped or bound bundle: **bale** ●bundle of cloth or papers: **wad**

burden ●*adjective*: **onerous** ●unreasonable burden: **imposition**

burglar ●burglar's crowbar: **jemmy** ●burglar climbing the outside of a building: **cat burglar**

burial ●*adjectives*: **funerary, sepulchral** ●preparation of a corpse for burial: **last offices, laying out** ●burial with appropriate rites: **interment** ●chamber used for burials: **vault** ●ancient stone burial chamber: **cist** ●burial of the dead as a cultural phenomenon: **inhumation** ▸*see also* **tomb**

burn ●start burning: **kindle** ●blacken by burning: **char** ●burn superficially: **singe** ●burn unsteadily: **gutter** ●burn slowly and smokily: **smoulder** ●medical treatment by burning: **cauterization, cautery** ●grade of flesh-burn: **degree** ●denoting a burn affecting the skin surface only: **first-degree** ●denoting a burn causing blistering but no permanent scarring: **second-degree** ●denoting a burn affecting tissue below the skin: **third-degree**

burner ●laboratory burner: **Bunsen burner** ●portable burner giving a hot flame for removing paint: **blowlamp**

bus ●bus for 10–15 passengers: **minibus** ●two-storey bus: **double-decker** ●bus driver's compartment: **cab** ●extending framework connecting with overhead power lines: **pantograph** ●wheel on a pole extending to overhead power lines: **trolley, trolley wheel** ●person taking fares on a bus: **conductor** (*fem.* conductress)

bush ●dense group of bushes: **thicket** ●bushes etc. growing round a tree: **undergrowth**

business ●business owned by its employees: **cooperative** ●business not under state management: **private enterprise** ●business's established reputation: **goodwill** ●denoting a business demanding large capital investment: **capital-intensive** ●denoting a business needing a large labour force: **labour intensive** ●transfer a business to state management: **nationalize** ●free business from government controls: **deregulate** ●region offering government incentives to incoming businesses: **development area, enterprise zone** ●enter new areas of business: **diversify** ●item of business: **transaction** ●routine business matters: **administration** ●person setting up a business: **entrepreneur** ●number of persons employed in a business: **headcount** ●employees regarded as a business asset: **human resources** ●business's buildings and equipment: **plant** ●business agent: **factor** ●business agent for sportsmen, musicians, etc.: **manager** ●association advancing the interests of local businesses: **Chamber of Commerce** ●excess of business income over expenditure: **profit, surplus** ●total money entering or leaving a business: **cash flow** ●dishonest means of gaining business advantage: **graft, sleaze** ●disposal of subsidiary business interests: **divestment, divestiture** ●person engaging in dishonest business dealings: **racketeer** ●business collapse: **failure**

businessman ●powerful businessman: **magnate, tycoon** ●dishonest businessman: **racketeer, shark** ●person managing large sums of money: **financier** ●industrial manager or proprietor: **industrialist** ●young urban professional: **yuppie** ●young black urban professional: **buppie** ▸*see also* **manager**

butcher ●butcher's chopper: **cleaver** ●butcher's cutting table: **block**

butter ●purify butter by melting: **clarify** ●Indian clarified butter: **ghee** ●machine for making butter: **churn**

butterfly ●butterfly pupa: **chrysalis** ●butterfly expert: **lepidopterist**

button ●stitching anchoring a button: **shank** ▸*see also* **fastener**

buyer ●purchaser by telephone or computer link: **teleshopper** ●protection of buyers' interests: **consumerism** ●assessment of buyers' needs and preferences: **market research** ●let the buyer beware: **caveat emptor**

buzz ●buzzing device announcing a phonecall: **pager** ●buzzing in the ears: **tinnitus**

bypass ●bypass encircling a town: **orbital road, ring road**

Cc

cabbage ●cabbage's tight head: **heart** ●cooked cabbage and potato fried up together: **bubble and squeak**

cabinet ●cabinet minister responsible for finance: **Chancellor of the Exchequer** ●cabinet minister responsible for foreign affairs: **Foreign Secretary** ●cabinet minister responsible for home affairs: **Home Secretary** ●cabinet minister with no permanent responsibilities: **Minister without Portfolio** ●cabinet for hi-fi equipment: **console**

cable ●cable for securing a ship to a pier: **hawser** ●cable for steadying a mast: **guyrope**

cafe ●small cafe selling alcoholic drinks: **estaminet** ●cafe with computers for customers' use: **cybercafe**

cake ●fancy cake: **gateau** (*pl.* gateaus *or* gateaux) ●sweet cake or tart: **torte** (*pl.* torten) ●light cake made with little or no fat: **sponge** ●cylindrical sponge cake with a jam filling: **Swiss roll** ●layer cake with a filling: **sandwich** ●small breadlike cake: **scone** ●small rich cake: **madeleine** ●small crisp batter cake: **waffle** ●rich fruit cake eaten on Palm Sunday: **simnel cake** ●rich cake with equal amounts of each ingredient: **pound cake** ●cake made of bread dough, lard, and currants: **lardy cake** ●Austrian chocolate cake with a jam and cream filling: **Sachertorte** (*pl.* Sachertorten) ●dense oatcake: **flapjack** ●small hard currant cake: **rock cake** ●dark gingerbread: **parkin** ●thick sweet decorative paste: **fondant** ●silver ball for decorating cakes: **dragée** ●small coloured sugar balls: **hundreds and thousands** ●skill of decorating cakes with sugar paste: **sugarcraft** ●small seedless grape used in cakes: **currant** ●small seedless raisin used in cakes: **sultana** ●shop selling fancy cakes and pastries: **patisserie**

calcium ●*combining form*: calci- ●containing or producing calcium: **calciferous** ●harden by addition of calcium: **calcify**

calendar ●calendar now in general use: **Gregorian calendar** ●denoting a date from this calendar: **New Style** ●calendar formerly used in Europe: **Julian calendar** ●denoting a date from this calendar: **Old Style** ●annual publication containing a calendar and other statistical information: **almanac** ●calendar adjustable for any year: **perpetual calendar** ●denoting a day or month occasionally added to the calendar: **intercalary**

call ●call for someone via a bleeper: **page** ●sense of being called to follow a particular career: **vocation**

calm ●calm and dignified: **sedate** ●calmness in trying circumstances: **sangfroid**

Cambridge University ●*adjective*: **Cantabrigian** ●part of the term when undergraduates are expected to be resident: **full term** ●autumn term at Cambridge: **Michaelmas term** ●winter term at Cambridge: **Lent term** ●summer term at Cambridge: **Trinity term** ●Cambridge first-degree examination or course: **tripos** ●person gaining first-class honours in the Cambridge mathematical tripos: **wrangler** ●member of a university sports team: **blue** ●governing body of Cambridge University: **senate** ●member of a senate committee: **syndic** ●chief administrator of Cambridge University: **registrary** ●member of the Cambridge university police: **bulldog** ●Oxford and Cambridge universities considered together: **Oxbridge** ●Cambridge undergraduate receiving financial help from his college: **sizar** ●Cambridge college annual feast: **Commemoration** ●Cambridge college servant: **bedder, bedmaker, gyp** ●Cambridge college relaxation room: **combination room** ●confine within the college: **gate** ●suspend a student: **rusticate** ●expel a student: **send down**

camel ●camel with one hump: **dromedary** ●camel with two humps: **Bactrian camel** ●frenzied state of rutting male camels: **must**

camera ●type of camera producing a print after each exposure: **instant camera** ●type of camera in which the image is reflected onto a glass screen: **reflex camera** ●denoting a reflex camera whose viewfinder uses the aperture lens: **single-lens reflex** ●denoting a reflex camera whose viewfinder has a separate lens: **twin-lens reflex** ●difference in angle of view between lens and viewfinder: **parallax** ●hole on the front of a camera admitting light to the film: **aperture** ●device for varying aperture size: **diaphragm** ●denoting a camera with a large aperture: **fast** ●effective aperture size: **stop** ●focusing glass: **lens** ●device set in front of the lens to screen out certain types of light: **filter** ●device admitting light to the aperture: **shutter** ●opening of the shutter, admitting light to the film: **exposure** ●wire allowing the shutter to be activated from a distance: **cable release** ●duration of exposure: **speed** ●exposure for longer than usual shutter settings: **time exposure** ●lens

cover: **hood** ●camera socket for accessories: **shoe** ●camera attachment producing a brief very bright light: **flash** ●camera device delaying exposure: **self-timer** ●single-legged camera stand: **unipod** ●camera stand with three sloping legs: **tripod** ●crosswise camera movement: **pan** ●vertical camera movement: **tilt** ●move a camera towards or away from object: **track** ●bring an object into close or distant camera focus: **zoom** ●wheeled platform for a film or television camera: **dolly** ●liftable platform for a film or television camera: **crane**

camp ●temporary camp: **bivouac** ●camp for volunteers doing community projects: **work camp** ●former German prisoner-of-war camp for officers: **Oflag** ●former German prisoner-of-war camp for other ranks: **Stalag** ●former Soviet labour camp: **gulag** ●prison camp enforcing a regime of hard labour: **labour camp, work camp** ●camper's enamelled lidded cooking pot: **billycan**

campaigner ●person advocating something's abandonment or prohibition: **abolitionist** ●vigorous campaigner: **activist**

Canadian ●Canadian game of sliding stones across ice: **curling** ●member of the French-Canadian nationalist movement: **Québecqois**

canal ●canal boat: **barge, narrowboat** ●path beside a canal: **towpath** ●pivoting counterbalanced canal bridge: **bascule bridge** ●bridge carrying a canal: **aqueduct** ●short canal section whose water level may be raised or lowered: **lock** ●set of locks: **flight** ●boat used on Venetian canals: **gondola**

cancel ●*combining forms*: **dis** (*e.g.* disallow), **un-** (*e.g.* unsettle)

cancer ●*combining forms*: **carcin-, -oma** ●*adjective*: **carcinomatous**

•cancer suffered by Aids victims: **Kaposi's sarcoma** •surface cancer of the skin or internal organs: **carcinoma** •likely to develop into cancer: **precancerous** •substance causing cancer: **carcinogen** •herpesvirus causing certain cancers: **Epstein–Barr virus** •start of cancer: **carcinogenesis** •excessive growth as an indicator of cancer: **hyperplasia** •enlargement of an organ in an early stage of cancer: **dysplasia** •abnormal tissue growth caused by cancer: **neoplasm** •protein found in the blood of a diseased person: **paraprotein** •specimen taken from the cervix to detect cancer: **cervical smear** •denoting cancer that tends to spread: **invasive** •development of secondary cancers distant from the first: **metastasis** •cancer treatment by drugs: **chemotherapy** •cancer treatment by X-rays: **radiotherapy, radiation therapy** •denoting therapy applied after successful treatment of a cancer to suppress secondary tumours: **adjuvant** ▸ *see also* **tumour,** *and under the individual organs affected*

candidate •potentially successful candidate: **papabile** (*pl.* papabili) •candidate entered to divide the vote: **spoiler** •candidate initiating an election but expecting stronger candidates to come forward: **stalking horse** •offer oneself as a candidate: **stand** •list of a political party's election candidates: **slate** •list of candidates for final choice: **shortlist** •check on a candidate's background and general suitability: **screening, positive vetting, security check, vetting**

candle •waxed wick for lighting candles: **taper** •rendered fat used to make candles: **tallow** •dealer in candles: **chandler** •candle trimmer: **snuffers** •extinguish a candle: **snuff**

candlestick •candlestick attached to a wall: **sconce** •branched candlestick: **candelabrum** •suspended multi-light candlestick: **chandelier** •Jewish liturgical candlestick: **menorah** •candlestick's spiked top: **pricket**

cane •cane carried by military officers: **swagger stick**

cannabis •cannabis fibre: **hemp** •cannabis cigarette: **joint, reefer**

cannibal •*adjective*: **anthropophagous**

cap •round flattish brimless cap: **beret** •academic cap: **square, mortarboard** •woman's openwork cap: **Juliet cap** •French military peaked cap: **kepi** •Scottish beret: **bonnet, tam-o'-shanter**

capable of •*combining form*: **-acious** (*e.g.* efficacious) •capable of sexual intercourse: **potent**

captain •captain of a merchant ship: **master** •captain's assistant: **mate**

car •car made before 1905 (or before 1916): **veteran car** •car made between 1917 and 1930: **vintage car** •old and inefficient car: **banger, jalopy, rattletrap, tin lizzie** •ordinary car strengthened for racetrack collisions: **stock car** •car modified to give high performance: **hot rod** •car modified for drag races: **dragster** •small racing car with skeleton body: **go-kart** •low-built car designed for speed: **sports car** •car offering comfort and high performance: **gran turismo** •car offering basic comfort with high performance: **sports car** •large and comfortable car: **limousine** •long car offering extra accommodation: **stretch limousine** •police patrol car: **squad car** •small fuel-efficient car: **microcar** •open two-seater car: **roadster** •small open car for difficult terrain: **buggy** •opening panel in a car roof: **sunroof, sunshine roof** ●car's folding roof: **hood** ●car with a folding or detachable roof: **convertible** ●car wheel with narrow metal spokes: **wire wheel** ●two-door car with a sloping rear: **coupé** ●luggage space at the back of a car: **boot** ●car with a large luggage area: **estate car** ●car with upward-opening rear door: **hatchback** ●car provided by an employer: **company car** ●car provided to a client without charge: **courtesy car** ●open shelter for a car: **carport** ●car's small interior light: **courtesy light** ●car seat with a rounded back: **bucket seat** ●car seat with a flat back: **bench seat** ●person employed to drive a car for another: **chauffeur** (*fem.* chauffeuse) ●person employed to clean or park cars: **valet** ●registration plate with numbers etc. chosen by the purchaser: **vanity plate**

caravan ●large caravan: **mobile home** ●motor vehicle with living accommodation: **camper, camper van, caravanette**

carbohydrate ●*combining form*: **-ose** (*e.g.* lactose)

carbon ●circulation of carbon between living organisms and their environment: **carbon cycle**

card ●card held up for pupils to see: **flashcard** ●card indicating where a person should sit at table: **place card** ●card printed with one's name and address: **visiting card** ●card shown to a footballer who is being cautioned: **yellow card** ●card shown to a footballer who must leave the field: **red card** ●card sent on 14 February: **valentine** ●plastic card with built-in microprocessor: **smart card** ●plastic card with magnetically encoded information: **swipe card** ●bank card guaranteeing cheques: **cheque card** ●bank card giving access to cash dispensers: **cash card** ●bank card en-

abling purchases to be made on credit: **credit card** ●bank card issued to persons with a high credit rating: **gold card** ●bank card enabling electronic transfer of payments from purchaser's to vendor's accounts: **debit card** ●card usable only in branches of the shop etc. issuing it: **store card** ●store card enabling purchases to be made on credit: **charge card, option card** ●store card accruing bonus points for purchases made there: **loyalty card** ●cheque or credit card giving a donation to a specified charity for each transaction made: **affinity card** ●card unlocking a door: **key card** ●card giving unlimited use of a specified transport network for a specified period: **travel card** ●electronic swipe card reader: **card swipe** ●pull a card through this: **swipe, wipe**

cardinal ●cardinal representing the pope: **legate** ●denoting a legate with full powers: **a latere** ●cardinal's short hooded cloak: **mozzetta** ●council of cardinals: **consistory**

cards ●card that is a king, queen, or jack: **court card** ●card that beats all others not of its suit: **trump** ●card that may be assigned any identity by its holder: **wild card** ●set of playing cards: **pack** ●set of cards with a particular symbol: **suit** ●set of cards with a fifth suit of elaborately illustrated trumps: **tarot pack** ●rearrange a pack of cards: **shuffle** ●shuffle cards dishonestly: **stack** ●divide a pack of cards: **cut** ●distribute cards in rotation: **deal** ●box from which cards are dealt at a casino: **sabot, shoe** ●cards dealt to a player: **hand** ●player who is dealt to first: **elder, elder hand, forehand** ●dealer in a two-handed game: **younger hand** ●cards remaining undealt: **stock, talon** ●cards held by a player: **hand** ●hand played exposed: **dummy** ●announce trumps, or the possession of certain cards: **declare** ●player making a successful bid: **declarer** ●hand with no card above a nine: **yarborough** ●set of cards of the same suit and adjacent values: **sequence** ●suit of which a player holds many cards: **long suit** ●suit of which a player holds several high cards: **strong suit** ●suit of which a player holds only one or two cards: **short suit** ●card that is the only one of a suit in a hand: **singleton** ●lack of cards of a particular suit: **void** ●cards laid down in a round of play: **trick** ●card played when unable to follow suit: **discard** ●failure to follow suit when able to do so: **revoke** ●card ranked at its player's will: **joker, wild card** ●scoring card combination: **meld** ●sequence of cards of the same suit: **run** ●denoting cards identifiable from their backs: **marked** ●conceal a card in the hand: **palm** ●play a trump: **ruff** ●force the play of particular cards: **draw** ●play the first card to a trick: **lead** ●win a trick cheaply: **finesse** ●person who cheats at cards: **card sharp, card sharper** ●closing rounds of play: **endgame** ●organized meeting to play cards: **drive** ●card game in which there are no partnerships: **round game** ●card games won by gaining tricks bid: **contract bridge, solo whist** ●card games won by gaining the most tricks: **auction bridge, piquet, whist** ●bridge tournament with all competitors playing the same hands: **duplicate bridge** ●bridge victory taking all the tricks: **grand slam** ●bridge victory taking twelve tricks: **small slam** ●card games won by combinations held: **poker, rummy** ●card game won by spotting similar cards: **snap** ●card game won by acquiring family sets: **happy families** ●fortune-telling from cards: **cartomancy**

care ●failure to take care: **negligence** ●failure of an injured person to take proper precautions: **contributory negligence** ●careful and thorough: **painstaking, scrupulous**

career ●summary of a person's career and education: **curriculum vitae** ●descriptions of the careers and connections of important people: **prosopography** ●desire to follow a certain career: **vocation** ●cultivation of contacts that may further one's career: **networking** ●person with great career potential: **high-flyer, self-starter** ●person only interested in career success: **careerist** ●tacit barrier to career advancement: **glass ceiling**

careless ●careless and hasty: **slapdash** ●idly careless: **negligent** ●wilfully careless: **reckless**

caretaker ●resident caretaker: **concierge** ●security official in a public gallery: **invigilator** ●official keeping order in a public recreation ground: **park keeper** ●employee looking after sports pitches: **groundsman**

carpenter ●carpenter making stairs, doors, etc.: **joiner** ●carpenter making furniture: **cabinet maker**

carpet ●long narrow strip of carpet: **runner** ●small carpet: **mat, rug** ●soft raised surface of a carpet: **pile**

carriage ●light one-horse carriage: **gig** ●two-wheeled horsedrawn taxi: **hansom, hansom cab** ●enclosed carriage: **coach** ●Irish light carriage: **jaunting car** ●Russian three-horse carriage: **troika** ●Russian open carriage: **droshky** ●hooded wheelchair for invalids: **Bath chair**

carrying ●*combining forms*: **-fer** (*e.g.* conifer), **-ferous** (*e.g.* odoriferous), **-phore** (*e.g.* semaphore, *literally* '*sign-carrying*') ●carriage of a boat or its cargo between navigable waters: **portage**

cart ●small cart: **float** ●small cart pushed or pulled by hand: **handcart, trolley** ●light Asian cart drawn by one or more people: **rickshaw** ●cart used in the French Revolution to convey condemned persons to the guillotine: **tumbril** ●ancient two-wheeled cart: **chariot** ●cart's pole to which draught animals are attached: **shaft** ●fastening attaching a draught animal to the shaft: **trace** ●wooden crosspiece on the necks of draught animals: **yoke**

Carthage ●*adjective*: Punic

cartilage ●*combining form*: chondro- (*e.g.* chondrocyte) ●*adjective*: **cartilaginous**

cartridge ●cartridge containing powder but no bullet: **blank** ●belt with loops for cartridges: **bandolier**

carving ●*adjective*: glyptic ●grotesque carving: **gargoyle** ●carve upon something: **inscribe**

cash ●available cash: **liquidity** ●cash available for immediate use: **cash in hand** ●cash kept in hand to settle minor expenses: **petty cash** ●cash that must be accepted in payment: **legal tender** ●cash refund given to a purchaser: **cashback** ●bank card giving access to cash dispensers: **cash card** ●cash given to a customer at a supermarket checkout, and debited to his charge card: **cashback** ●possession having a cash value: **asset** ●assets easily convertible into cash: **liquid assets, near money** ●convert assets into cash: **realize**

caste ●member of the Hindu priestly caste: **Brahman** ●member of the Hindu worker caste: **Sudra** ●member of the lowest Hindu caste: **Dalit, untouchable** ●official name of the lowest Hindu caste: **scheduled caste** ●person of no caste: **outcaste, pariah** ●Hindu forehead mark indicating caste: **tilak**

casting ●hollow container shaping material being cast: **mould** ●casting method using a wax model which is melted away: **cire perdue, lost wax** ●clay mould around a wax model: **mantle** ●made in a single casting: **monobloc**

castle ●castle overlooking a city: **citadel** ●castle mound: **motte** ●castle's central tower: **keep, donjon** ●castle's underground cell: **dungeon** ●castle ditch: **moat** ●raisable bridge over a castle's moat: **drawbridge** ●castle's fortified gatehouse: **barbican** ●heavy grating lowered from above: **portcullis** ●castle's defensive wall: **rampart** ●castle's outer wall: **bailey** ●castle's outer wall between towers: **curtain wall** ●area enclosed by a castle wall: **bailey, ward** ●low wall sheltering troops on a castle wall: **parapet** ●parapet with regular openings for shooting through: **battlement, crenellation** ●walled part between these openings: **merlon** ●having battlements: **embattled** ●opening for dropping missiles on people below: **machicolation, murder hole** ●projecting fortification built where two walls meet at an angle: **bastion** ●room set in a castle wall: **casemate** ●castle's longdrop lavatory: **garderobe** ●inward slope of a castle wall: **batter** ●small outer door: **postern, sally port** ●bank sloping down from a castle: **glacis** ●flat open area in front of a castle: **esplanade** ●governor of a royal castle: **constable** ●troops stationed in a castle: **garrison** ●French castle: **chateau** (*pl.* chateaux)

cast off ●(of a snake) cast off an old skin: **slough** ●the skin so cast off: **slough** ●action of casting off a skin: **ecdysis**

castrate ●castrate a male animal: **geld** ●castrated man: **eunuch** ●castrated male singer in baroque opera or the papal chapel: **castrato** ●castrated bull: **ox** ●castrated cockerel: **capon** ●castrated stallion: **gelding** ●castrated ram: **wether**

cat ●*adjective*: **feline** ●male cat: **tom** ●adult unspayed female cat: **queen** ●young cat: **kitten** ●tailless breed of cat: **Manx** ●(of a cat) give birth: **kitten** ●imagined cat with a broad grin: **Cheshire cat** ●howl like a cat: **caterwaul** ●small door for a cat: **cat flap** ●inflammation of a cat's ear: **canker** ●cat with mottled fur: **tabby** ●dark brown fur on a Siamese cat: **sealpoint** ●plant cats like to smell: **catmint, catnip** ●boarding establishment for cats: **cattery**

cathedral ●covered walk in a cathedral complex: **cloister** ●cathedral precinct: **close** ●cathedral governing body: **chapter** ●meeting place for this: **chapter house** ●priest presiding over a cathedral chapter: **dean, provost** ●priest belonging to a cathedral chapter: **canon** ●denoting a cathedral chapter: **capitular** ●canon required to reside in the precincts: **residentiary canon** ●priest in charge of cathedral music: **precentor** ●deputy precentor: **succentor** ●priest assisting in cathedral services but not a chapter member: **minor canon**

cathode ●electron beam emitted by a cathode in a vacuum tube: **cathode ray** ●vacuum tube for this: **cathode ray tube**

cathode ray tube ●surface of this: **screen** ●movement of the electron beam across the screen: **sweep**

cattle ●*adjective*: **bovine** ●group of cattle: **herd** ●divided foot of cattle: **cloven hoof** ●one of a hornless breed of cattle: **poll** ●infectious cattle diseases: **murrain, rinderpest** ●cattle disease affecting the central nervous system: **bovine spongiform encephalitis, mad cow disease** ●cattle disease affecting the skin and lungs: **anthrax** ●cattle disease ulcerating hoofs and mouths: **foot and mouth disease** ●inflammation of the udder: **garget** ●cattle disease infecting the milk, and thereby transmitted to humans: **brucellosis** ●stick for prodding cattle: **goad** ●open trough for cattle fodder: **manger** ●beet grown to feed cattle: **mangold, mangel-wurzel** ●US cowherd: **cowboy** ●cattle-rearer: **grazier** ●round-up of cattle on a ranch: **rodeo** ▸*see also* **cow**

cause ●*combining forms*: **-genic, -genous, -facient, -fic, -ible, -otic** ●*adjective*: **aetiological** ●causing abortion: **abortifacient** ●causing cancer: **carcinogenic** ●causing drowsiness: **narcotic, soporific** ●caused by medical treatment: **iatrogenic** ●having an internal cause: **endogenous** ●having an external cause: **exogenous** ●without apparent cause: **spontaneous**

cave ●*combining form*: **speleo-** ●small artificial cave: **grotto** ●deep natural cave: **pothole** ●cave dweller: **troglodyte** ●cave dweller in Scandinavian mythology: **troll** ●pointed calcium carbonate excrescence hanging from a cave roof: **stalactite** ●tapering calcium carbonate column rising from a cave floor: **stalagmite** ●study or exploration of caves: **speleology**

ceiling ●denoting a ceiling hung from the floor above: **suspended** ●access panel in a ceiling: **trapdoor**

celebrity ●entertainment celebrity: **star** ●treat as a celebrity: **lionize**

cell ●*combining forms*: **cyto-, -cyte, -blast** (*e.g.* erythroblast), **-plast** (*e.g.* protoplast) ●cell identical to another: **clone** ●sexually mature germ cell: **gamete** ●cell formed by union of two gametes: **zygote** ●body cell able to absorb bacteria: **phagocyte** ●network of nerve cells: **ganglion** ●abnormal aggregation of cells: **nodule** ●grouping of cells, esp. in the brain: **cytoarchitectonics, cytoarchitecture** ●colourless material comprising the living part of a cell: **protoplasm** ●protoplasm excluding the nucleus:

cytoplasm •natural substance controlling body-cell activity: **hormone** •hostile reaction of body cells to implanted tissue etc.: **immune reaction** •compound released into injured cells: **histamine** •medicine able to target particular cells: **magic bullet** •growth of natural cells in an artificial environment: **culture, tissue culture** •poisonous to cells: **cytotoxic** •cell disintegration: **lysis** •study of living cells: **cytology**

Celtic •ancient Celtic priest: **Druid**

cement •cement used between bricks: **pointing** •cement used between tiles: **grout** •cement used to cover a floor: **screed** •cement used to cover a wall: **parget** •vertical layer of cement: **perpend** •cement hardening under water: **Portland cement** •liquid cement sealing a joint: **lute** •lime and cement mixture: **mortar**

cemetery •underground cemetery: **catacomb** •large cemetery: **necropolis**

censorship •moral censorship of texts: **bowdlerization** •deliberate generation of interference to render a broadcast unintelligible: **jamming** •broadcast sound covering a censored word: **bleep** •government notice to news editors forbidding publication of specified information: **D-notice** •legislation empowering censorship of information: **Official Secrets Act**

census •person gathering census data: **enumerator** •completed census form: **return**

centre •*combining form*: **centr-, mes-** (*e.g.* mesolithic), **-centric** •central point: **epicentre, nexus** •moving from the centre: **centrifugal** •moving to the centre: **centripetal** •having a common centre: **concentric** •having no centre: **acentric**

cereal •cereal stalks remaining in the ground after harvesting: **stubble**

•fungal disease of cereal crops: **ergot** •human disease caught by eating the infected grain: **ergotism** •breakfast mixture of cereals, dried fruit, and nuts: **muesli**

ceremony •admission ceremony: **initiation** •ceremony to make an award: **investiture** •ceremony to place a person in office: **induction** •ceremony to mark a turning-point in a person's life: **rite of passage** •memorial ceremony: **commemoration** •elaborate ceremony: **solemnity, pomp and circumstance** •perform a ceremony: **solemnize** •person directing ceremonial: **master of ceremonies**

Ceres •*Greek name*: **Demeter**

cinder •brick made from cinders: **breeze block**

chain •chain restricting an animal's movement: **tether** •chain controlling a dog by neck pressure: **choke chain** •U-shaped link at a chain's end: **shackle** •crosspiece through a chain link: **toggle**

chair •ceremonial chair: **throne** •dining chair with arms: **carver** •high-backed armchair with projecting sidepieces: **wing chair** •infant's long-legged chair: **high chair** •folding chair of wood and canvas: **deckchair** •enclosed chair carried on poles: **sedan chair** •piece of thin wood in a chair back: **splat** •rod between chair legs: **stretcher**

chalk •*adjective*: **calcareous**

chamber •*adjective*: **cameral** •denoting a single-chamber legislature: **unicameral** •denoting a two-chamber legislature: **bicameral** •denoting a three-chamber legislature: **tricameral**

chamber pot •piece of furniture containing a chamber pot: **commode** •contents of a chamber pot: **slops**

champagne ●champagne exclusive to one shipper: **monopole** ●denoting unsweetened champagne: **brut** ●champagne and orange juice: **Buck's Fizz**

chance ●*adjective*: **fortuitous** ●subject to chance: **probabilistic, random, stochastic** ●chance happening: **fluke** ●fortunate development of events by chance: **serendipity** ●person seizing offered chances: **opportunist** ●loss of other chances when one is taken: **opportunity cost**

chandelier ●cut-glass chandelier: **lustre**

change ●*combining forms*: meta- (*e.g.* metamorphosis), -tropic (*e.g.* psychotropic), tropo- (*e.g.* tropophyte) ●extreme change: **makeover, quantum leap, revolution, sea-change, transmutation, upheaval, U-turn, volte-face** ●involving extreme change: **radical** ●adaptive change: **acclimatization** ●minor change: **amendment, variation** ●subtle change: **nuance** ●unpredictable change: **vagary** ●capricious change of mind: **whim** ●change of appearance: **metamorphosis** ●change of the eucharistic elements: **transubstantiation** ●moment of decisive change: **turning point** ●improve by basic changes: **reform** ●constant change: **flux** ●capable of infinite changes: **protean** ●resistance to change: **inertia** ●open to change: **negotiable** ●easily changed: **flexible** ●favouring steady change: **progressive** ●changing unpredictably: **mercurial, volatile, wayward** ●change sides: **apostatize** ●adapt to suit individual requirements: **personalize** ●initiate new areas of activity: **diversify** ●process of change: **transition** ●general direction of change: **trend** ●thing that initiates or accelerates change: **catalyst** ●after essential changes: **mutatis mutandis** ●person advocating gradual change: **reformist**

●person opposed to all change: **reactionary** ●person who changes his principles to suit the times: **trimmer, time-server** ●'change of life': **menopause** ●denoting something that cannot be changed: **flat, sacrosanct** ●situation or action that cannot be changed: **fait accompli** ●inability to cope with change: **future shock** ●unwilling to change: **hidebound** ●things never change: **plus ça change, plus c'est la même chose** ●keep unaltered: **preserve** ●unchanging: **uniform**

channel ●channel for fast-moving water: **race** ●drainage channel: **ditch, dyke**

Channel Islands ●Channel Islands magistrate: **jurat** ●French name for the Channel Islands: **Iles Anglo-Normandes**

chapel ●chapel for the use of parishioners living far from the main church: **chapel of ease** ●small domestic chapel: **oratory**

charge ●extra charge: **surcharge** ●charge for as separate items: **unbundle**

charity ●*adjective*: **eleemosynary** ●day of street charity collections: **flag day** ●legally binding undertaking to make payments to a charity: **covenant**

Charlemagne ●*adjectives*: **Carolingian, Carlovingian**

Charles I and II ●*adjectives*: **Carolean, Caroline** ●supporter of Charles I: **Cavalier, Royalist** ●opponent of Charles I: **Parliamentarian, Roundhead**

cheat ●person who cheats at cards: **card sharp, card sharper** ●dishonesty in business or public life: **sleaze**

check ●check truth or validity: **verify, vet** ●check against a standard: **calibrate** ●check a job applicant's background: **vet** ●place where checks are carried out: **control**

cheek ●*adjectives*: **buccal, malar** ●drooping cheek: **jowl**

cheese ●*adjective*: **caseous** ●small whole cheese: **truckle** ●soft cheese made from skimmed milk: **cottage cheese** ●French soft white cheese: **Brie** ●French goat's cheese: **chèvre** ●soft cheese from Normandy: **Camembert** ●Danish soft white cheese with blue veins: **Danish blue** ●round Dutch cheese with a yellow rind: **Gouda** ●Greek goat's cheese: **feta** ●Italian soft blue-veined cheese: **Dolcelatte™** ●Italian hard blue-veined cheese: **Gorgonzola** ●Italian cream cheese: **mascarpone** ●firm white Italian cheese: **mozzarella** ●rich blue-veined Leicestershire cheese: **Stilton** ●sweet brown Norwegian cheese: **Gjetost** ●hard Swiss cheese: **Emmental** ●pale Swiss cheese with holes: **Gruyère** ●cheese's tough outer skin: **rind** ●protein present in cheese: **casein** ●curdling agent used in cheesemaking: **rennet** ●denoting unripe cheese: **green** ●sprinkled with grated cheese and browned: **au gratin** ●melted cheese on toast: **rarebit, Welsh rarebit** ●melted cheese on toast with a poached egg: **buck rarebit**

chemical ●*combining forms*: **chemi-** (*e.g.* chemisorption), **chemo-** (*e.g.* chemotherapy) ●chemical liquid destroying bacteria: **disinfectant** ●eat away by chemical action: **corrode**

chemical reaction ●self-sustaining series of chemical reactions: **chain reaction** ●substance used in a chemical reaction: **reagent** ●substance changed in a chemical reaction: **reactant** ●substance formed by a chemical reaction: **product** ●production of compounds by reaction from simpler materials: **synthesis** ●substance accelerating a chemical reaction: **catalyst** ●biochemical catalyst: **enzyme** ●substance slowing or preventing a chemical reaction: **inhibitor**

chemistry ●chemistry of compounds containing carbon: **organic chemistry** ●chemistry of compounds not containing carbon: **inorganic chemistry** ●chemistry of plants: **phytochemistry** ●chemistry of living organisms: **biochemistry** ●chemistry of radioactive substances: **radiochemistry** ●chemistry of the stars and space: **astrochemistry** ●medieval chemistry, seeking to turn base metals into gold: **alchemy** ●chemical analysis of a compound, expressed in symbols: **formula** (*pl.* formulae) ●substance used in chemical analysis: **reagent** ●substance having the same crystal structure as another: **isomorph** ●chemical decomposition by electric current: **electrolysis** ●chemical decomposition by water: **hydrolysis** ●not subject to chemical decomposition: **stable**

cheque ●cheque for a fixed amount usable abroad: **traveller's cheque** ●cheque drawn by a bank on its own funds: **bank draft, banker's draft** ●cheque guaranteed by a bank: **certified cheque** ●cheque counterfoil: **stub** ●person writing a cheque: **drawer** ●institution that must honour a cheque: **drawee** ●person benefiting from the cheque: **payee** ●writing on the back of a cheque: **endorsement** ●payee named in an endorsement: **endorsee** ●denoting an uncrossed cheque: **open** ●denoting a cheque that is invalid because drawn long before: **stale** ●credit a cheque to the payee's account: **clear** ●pay a presented cheque: **honour** ●refuse to pay a presented cheque: **dishonour** ●instruct one's bankers not to honour a cheque: **stop**

cherry ●sour cherry used in cooking: **morello**

cherub ●*adjective*: **cherubic** ●cherub in Renaissance paintings: **amoretto, putto**

chess ●chess played on separate boards: **kriegspiel** ●opening tactic: **gambit** ●chess pieces in order of importance: **king, queen, bishop, knight, rook** *or* **castle, pawn** ●bring a back-line piece forward: **develop** ●denoting a piece that can be taken: **en prise** ●attack upon the opponent's king: **check** ●repeated checking of the king: **perpetual check** ●closing moves: **endgame** ●winning position: **checkmate** ●concede defeat without checkmate: **resign** ●situation in which a player cannot move except into check: **stalemate** ●situation in which the need to make a move is itself a disadvantage: **zugswang** ●declaration when adjusting a piece: **j'adoube** ●side of the board on which both queens stand at the start of play: **queenside** ●half-move in computer chess: **ply** ●expert chess-player: **master** ●chess-player of the highest class: **grand master**

chest ●*adjectives*: **pectoral, thoracic** ●deformed human chest with projecting breastbone: **pigeon chest, pigeon breast (pectus carinatum)** ●chest murmur: **souffle**

chew ●chew the cud: **ruminate**

chicken ●brood of chickens: **clutch** ▸ *see also* **fowl**

chickpea ●chickpea paste: **hummus** ●chickpea rissole: **felafel**

chief ●*combining form*: **arch-** ●chief beam: **architrave** ●chief bishop: **archbishop** ●chief monk: **abbot, prior** ●chief nun: **abbess, prioress**

chilblain ●ulcerated chilblain: **kibe**

child ●*combining form*: **paed-** ●*adjective*: **filial** ●early childhood: **infancy** ●denoting a child born within wedlock: **legitimate** ●denoting a child born out of wedlock: **bastard, illegitimate** ●child that has been abandoned by its parents: **foundling** ●child whose parents are dead: **orphan** ●child substituted for another in infancy: **changeling** ●parental responsibility for a child: **custody** ●child cared for by a guardian: **ward** ●child under state guardianship: **ward of court** ●bring up another's child: **foster** ●children killed by Herod: **Holy Innocents** ●child's leading reins: **harness** ●child's playful misbehaviour: **mischief** ●exceptionally talented child: **child prodigy, wunderkind** ●children's part of a house: **nursery** ●day nursery for young children: **crèche** ●child who comes home to an empty house: **latchkey child** ●project offering pastimes for children during school holidays: **playscheme** ●person supervising children in public: **chaperone** ●supervise children while their parents are out: **babysit** ●study and treatment of the diseases of children: **paediatrics** ●dentistry of children: **paedodontics** ●giving priority to the interests of children: **child-centred** ●denoting something that children cannot open or use: **childproof** ●suitable for children and adults: **family** ●state agency organizing child maintenance payments: **Child Support Agency** ●person sexually attracted to children: **paedophile** ●representation of a naked winged child in Renaissance art: **amoretto, cherub, putto**

childbirth ●*adjective*: **obstetric, puerperal** ●process of childbirth: **delivery** ●childbirth at home: **home delivery** ●childbirth under water: **water birth** ●device for this: **birthing pool** ●childbirth via a cut in the mother's abdomen: **Caesarian, Caesarian section** ●childbirth with minimum medical and technological intervention: **natural childbirth** ●denoting a woman capable of childbirth: **fecund** ●woman who has never given birth: **nullipara** ●woman giving birth for the first time: **primipara** ●woman bearing a child for another: **surrogate mother** ●medical care and study of those giving birth: **obstetrics** ●doctor providing such care, or person making such study: **obstetrician** ●assist the birth of a child: **deliver** ●nurse attending at childbirth: **midwife** ●hospital for the care of childbirth: **maternity hospital** ●hospital area for the final stages of labour: **delivery suite** ●start labour artificially: **induce** ●hormone stimulating womb contractions and milk secretion: **oxytocin** ●hormone making the cervix dilate: **relaxin** ●period between the start of contractions and delivery: **labour** ●spinal anaesthetic given in childbirth: **epidural, extradural** ●drug easing labour pains: **pethidine** ●position of the fetus at the time of delivery: **presentation** ●presentation with feet or buttocks first: **breech delivery** ●surgical cutting of the vagina at childbirth: **episiotomy** ●large pincers assisting childbirth: **forceps** ●suction device assisting childbirth: **vacuum extractor, ventouse** ●greasy deposit covering a newborn infant: **vernix** ●prediction of a future child's genetic disorders: **genetic counselling** ●denoting the period before childbirth: **antenatal, antepartum** ●denoting the period after childbirth: **postnatal, post-partum** ●denoting the period from the child's conception until weaning: **maternity** ●first liquid from the breasts: **colostrum** ●substance encouraging breastmilk: **glalactagogue** ●excessive production of breastmilk: **galactorrhoea** ●breastfeed a baby: **nurse** ●woman's fever after childbirth: **milk fever** ●fever caused by uterine infection after childbirth: **puerperal fever** ●period after childbirth in which the reproductive organs return to normal:

puerperium ●government office where births are recorded: **register office** ▸*see also* **birth, pregnancy**

chimney ●free-standing part of a chimney: **stack** ●hooded chimney top: **cowl** ●duct inside a chimney: **flue** ●partition between flues: **withe**

Chinese ●*combining form*: Sino- ●Chinese official: **mandarin** ●Chinese native labourer: **coolie** ●Chinese secret criminal gang: **Tong, Triad** ●Chinese idol: **joss** ●Chinese temple: **joss house** ●Chinese Buddhist teacher: **bonze** ●absolute principle in Chinese philosophy: **Tao** ●active male principle in Chinese philosophy: **yang** ●passive female principle of Chinese philosophy: **yin** ●Chinese philosophical system advocating humility and piety: **Taoism** ●Chinese woman's close-fitting silk dress: **cheongsam** ●stick for eating Chinese food: **chopstick** ●Chinese frying pan: **wok** ●soup made from a coating on bird's nests: **bird's nest soup** ●Chinese egg dish: **foo yong** ●Chinese dish of grilled meat in a spicy sauce: **satay** ●Chinese-style dish of meat, mixed vegetables, and rice: **chop suey** ●Chinese-style dish of fried noodles with shredded meat and vegetables: **chow mein** ●Chinese pancake filled with vegetables: **spring roll** ●small Chinese savoury dumpling: **wonton** ●prawn-flavoured rice-flour crisp: **prawn cracker** ●Chinese snack of small dumplings: **dim sum** ●small white Chinese dessert fruit: **lychee** ●Chinese sauce with sugar and vinegar or lemon: **sweet and sour sauce** ●food additive used in Chinese cuisine: **monosodium glutamate** ●illness caused by excessive monosodium glutamate: **Chinese restaurant syndrome** ●Chinese sorghum spirit: **mao-tai** ●Chinese game played with small tiles: **mah-jong** ●Chinese gambling game: **fan-tan**

• Chinese geometrical puzzle: **tangram** • Chinese martial art: **kung fu** • Chinese plant with medicinal root: **ginseng** • Chinese therapy by needles: **acupuncture** • bodily energy path in Chinese medicine and acupuncture: **meridian** • life force in Chinese medicine and philosophy: **chi** • Chinese exercise systems: **t'ai chi ch'uan, qigong** • Chinese divination manual: **I Ching, Book of Changes** • former Chinese bow of greeting: **kowtow** • principal Chinese languages: **Mandarin, Putonghua** • transliteration systems from Chinese: **Wade–Giles, Pinyin** • architectural decoration in the Chinese style: **chinoiserie** • famous type of medieval Chinese porcelain: **Ming** • Chinese sailing vessel: **junk** • Chinese traditional racing boat: **dragon boat** • imitation of Chinese motifs in Western art: **chinoiserie** • study of Chinese culture and politics: **Sinology**

Chinese communism • party official in charge of political education: **commissar** • individual political indoctrination: **thought reform** • political wallposter: **dazibao** (*pl.* same) • jacket in Chinese communist style: **Mao jacket**

chip • denoting chips with wavy edges: **crinkle-cut**

chivalry • glove thrown down by a knight as a challenge: **gage** • patroness's ribbon etc. worn by a knight: **favour** • moral obligations of the nobility: **noblesse oblige**

chocolate • denoting chocolate made without milk: **plain** • greyish deposit on the surface of stored chocolate: **bloom** • maker or seller of chocolate: **chocolatier**

choice • choice where both options have disadvantages: **dilemma** • choice with no real alternatives: **Hobson's choice** • choice made to allocate scarce resources: **triage** • excess of available options: **embarras de choix** • wrong option in a multiple-choice question: **distractor**

choir • *adjective*: **choral** • section of a church choir standing on the north side: **cantoris** • section of a church choir standing on the south side: **decani** • choir divided to sing antiphonally: **double choir** • boy member of a choir: **chorister**

choose • choose as candidate for an election: **adopt** • choose at random: **draw, select by lot**

chorus • *adjectives*: **choral, choric**

Christ • *combining form*: **Christo-** • *adjective*: **dominical** • centred on Christ: **Christocentric** • representation of Christ's descent from Jesse: **Jesse tree** • Christ's birth, or a representation of it: **Nativity** • model of the stable, with figures: **crib** • commemoration of the birth of Christ: **Christmas** • period of fasting preceding this: **Advent** • commemoration of the visit of the Magi: **Epiphany** • commemoration of the presentation of the infant Christ: **Presentation, Purification, Candlemas** • commemoration of Christ's fast: **Lent** • commemoration of Christ's appearance in glory to three disciples: **Transfiguration** • commemoration of Christ's entry into Jerusalem: **Palm Sunday** • commemoration of Christ's institution of the Eucharist: **Corpus Christi** • Christ's suffering and death: **the Passion** • place of Christ's betrayal: **Gethsemane** • Christ's route to Calvary: **Via Dolorosa** • place of Christ's crucifixion: **Calvary** • marks of Christ's crucifixion bestowed on others through prayer: **stigmata** • representation of the dead Christ in his mother's arms: **pietà** • site of Christ's burial: **Holy Sepulchre** • Christ's freeing of the righteous dead: **Harrowing of Hell** • celebration of Christ's resurrection:

63 Christian | church

Easter ●commemoration of Christ's return to heaven: **Ascension** ●commemoration of the descent of the Holy Spirit: **Pentecost, Whit Sunday** ●expected return of Christ to earth at the Last Judgement: **Second Coming** ●representation of Christ as universal ruler: **pantocrator** ●doctrine of Christ's two natures: **dualism** ▸*see also* **Lent**

Christian ●member of Christ's immediate circle during His earthly ministry: **disciple** ●member of this continuing group, perceived as leaders and founders of the Church: **apostle** ●Christian love: **agape** ●medieval Christian expedition to regain the Holy Land: **crusade** ●Christian observing Sunday as the sabbath: **sabbatarian** ●Christian preaching intended to make converts: **evangelism** ●Christian thanksgiving for the harvest: **harvest festival** ●Christian tradition emphasizing scriptural authority and personal conversion: **evangelicalism** ●Christian Church following the Pope: **Roman Catholic Church** ●Christian Church following the Oecumenical Patriarch: **Orthodox Church** ●denoting those Western Christian Churches following the principles of the Reformation: **Protestant** ●denoting Christian unity: **ecumenical** ●officially exclude someone from the Christian sacraments: **excommunicate**

chromosome ●female chromosome: **X chromosome** ●male chromosome: **Y chromosome** ●number and appearance of an organism's chromosomes: **karyotype** ●chromosome defect causing intellectual impairment and physical abnormalities: **Down's syndrome** ●study of chromosomes: **cytogenetics**

church ●*adjective*: **ecclesiastical, ecclesial** ●principal church of a diocese: **cathedral** ●church exempt from diocesan control: **peculiar** ●denoting a church endowed for a chapter of canons: **collegiate** ●large church originally part of a monastery: **minster** ●small private chapel: **oratory** ●sanctify a church for use: **consecrate** ●assign a church to a saint's protection: **dedicate** ●church usher: **verger** ●senior layman responsible for church property etc.: **churchwarden** ●churchwarden's assistant: **sidesman** ●church caretaker and gravedigger: **sexton** ●official in charge of vestments and sacred vessels: **sacristan** ●church robing room: **vestry** ●official leading processions etc.: **verger** ●forms of church service: **liturgy** ●church assembly: **synod, convocation** ●church court: **consistory** ●church law: **canon law** ●expel from a church: **excommunicate** ●courtyard before a church: **parvis** ●church porch: **galilee** ●church antechamber: **narthex** ●holy-water basin near a church door: **stoup** ●main part of a church: **nave** ●wooden congregational bench: **pew** ●pew with high sides giving privacy: **box pew** ●kneeling cushion: **hassock, kneeler** ●space for access between pews: **aisle** ●raised enclosed platform for preaching: **pulpit** ●reading stand for a Bible: **lectern** ●broad aisle or passageway: **ambulatory** ●wooden seat for choir or clergy: **stall** ●ledge on this supporting a standing person: **misericord, miserere** ●section of a church choir standing on the north side: **cantoris** ●section of a church choir standing on the south side: **decani** ●booth for priest to hear confessions: **confessional** ●part of a church containing the high altar: **sanctuary** ●sanctuary cupboard: **aumbry** ●side table in a sanctuary: **credence** ●stone seats for the celebrants, built into the south sanctuary wall: **sedilia** ●view onto the altar, cut through a pillar: **hagioscope, squint**

•part of a church round the sanctuary: **chancel** •wood or stone partition at the chancel entrance: **rood screen, screen** •part of a church between nave and altar: **choir** •part of a church built out to form one of the arms in a cross-shaped plan: **transept** •part of a church where nave and transepts join: **crossing** •part of a church to the side of a nave or chancel: **aisle** •part of a church beneath the main floor: **crypt, undercroft** •set of windows overlooking aisle roofs: **clerestory** •gallery running over an arcade: **triforium** •section of a church east of the main altar: **retrochoir** •curved or polygonal extension to the east end of a church: **apse** •apse with an ambulatory: **chevet** •part of a church, or building adjacent to it, used for baptisms: **baptistery** •chapel dedicated to the Blessed Virgin: **Lady chapel** •water container for baptisms: **font** •chapel or altar endowed for Masses for the founder's soul: **chantry** •icon screen in an Orthodox church: **iconostasis** •room where vestments etc. are kept: **sacristy** •grotesque stone figure on the outside of a church: **gargoyle** •roofed gate into a churchyard: **lychgate** •building in a churchyard for exhumed bones: **charnel house** •a tenth of one's income given to the Church: **tithe** •authorization from a Church authority: **faculty** •denoting a Church having state control or support: **established** •sever formal links between Church and state: **disestablish** •Church administrative district: **parish** •study of the Church Fathers and their writings: **patristics, patrology** •study of church building and decoration: **ecclesiology** ▸ *see also* altar

Church of England •*adjective*: Anglican •group of Churches worldwide that are in communion with the Church of England: **Anglican Com-** munion •Anglican provincial synod: **convocation** •parish's contribution to diocesan funds: **quota** •priest supervising a group of parochial clergy: **rural dean** •parish priest formerly receiving tithes: **rector** •parish priest not formerly receiving tithes: **vicar** •priest's house: **rectory, vicarage** •job as parish priest: **benefice, living** •priest in charge of a benefice: **incumbent** •formal bestowal of a benefice: **induction** •period between incumbents: **interregnum**

cider •strong rough cider: **scrumpy** •drink of draught cider and lager: **snakebite** •pulpy fruit left after cider-making: **pomace**

cigar •long straight-sided cigar: **corona** •long thin cigar: **panatella** •cigar tapering at the ends: **perfecto** •open-ended cigar: **cheroot** •stub of a cigar: **butt** •airtight cigar box: **humidor**

cigarette •cigarette with a filter: **filter tip** •stub of a cigarette: **butt**

cinema •small cinema: **cinematheque** •cinema programme offering two full-length films: **double feature** •building housing several cinemas: **multiplex** •ratio of width to height of projected image: **aspect ratio**

circle •*combining form*: cycl- (*e.g.* cyclorama) •imagined circle joining the earth's poles: **meridian** •imagined circle round the earth equidistant from its poles: **equator** •prehistoric stone circle: **henge** •distance across a circle: **diameter** •distance round the outside of a circle: **circumference** •line from the centre to the circumference of a circle: **radius** •half-circle: **semicircle** •quarter-circle: **quadrant** •circular movement of water or smoke: **eddy** •circular movement of the axis of a spinning object: **precession**

circus ●large circus tent: **big top** ●place where circus animals are kept: **menagerie** ●enclosed area for a circus performance: **ring** ●person directing a circus performance: **ringmaster**

citadel ●ancient Greek citadel: **acropolis** ●Russian citadel: **kremlin** ●North African citadel: **kasbah**

citizen ●*combining form*: **-ese** (*e.g.* Viennese) ●*adjective*: **civil** ●gift of honorary citizenship: **freedom**

city ●*adjectives*: **civic, urban** ●chief city: **metropolis** ●city formed by the joining of several towns: **conurbation** ●huge composite city: **megalopolis, metroplex** ●central part of a city: **inner city** ●outlying part of a city: **suburb** ●suburb inhabited by daily commuters: **dormitory suburb** ●city area inhabited by a particular ethnic or social group: **ghetto** ●preserved open land round a city: **green belt**

clairvoyance ●having powers of clairvoyance: **fey** ▶*see also* **spiritualist**

clan ●clan's female head: **matriarch** ●clan's male head: **patriarch** ●distinctive plaid of a Scottish clan: **tartan**

class ●lowest social stratum: **underclass** ●working classes: **proletariat** ●middle-class person with conventional views: **bourgeois** ●the provincial middle classes: **Middle England** ●salaried classes: **salariat** ●member of the upper middle class: **haut bourgeois** ●privileged and influential section of society: **overclass** ●admirer of the upper classes and their ways: **snob** ●admirer of the lower classes and their ways: **inverted snob** ●dialect of a particular social class: **sociolect** ●class structure: **social scale, social ladder** ●improving one's social status: **upwardly mobile** ●person keen to improve his or her social status: **social climber** ●involving social groups of equal status: **horizontal** ●acceptable in the best circles: **pukka**

classification ●classification of plants and animals by shared features: **taxonomy** ●classification of plants and animals based on inherited characteristics: **cladistics** ●classification of plants and animals by genus and species: **Linnaean nomenclature, binomial nomenclature** ●classification by general type: **typology** ●classification according to rank: **hierarchy** ●classification according to shared ancestry: **cladistics**

clause ●clause that is in itself a complete sentence: **main clause** ●clause that is not in itself a complete sentence: **subordinate clause** ●clause in a contract stipulating exceptions: **saving clause** ●contractual clause freeing a party from obligations under stated conditions: **escape clause** ●contractual clause allowing for price increases: **escalator clause**

claw ●front claw of a lobster or crab: **pincer** ●having non-retactile claws: **cynopodous**

clay ●clay used for bricks and walls: **adobe** ●clay used for china: **kaolin** ●clay worked for making pottery or bricks: **pug** ●thin clay used to decorate pottery: **slip** ●clay used to make reddish pottery: **terracotta** ●mixture of clay and straw used for walls: **cob** ●clay used as a filter: **fuller's earth** ●liquid clay sealing a joint: **lute**

clean ●clean without using water: **dry-clean** ●clean by hard rubbing: **scour** ●clean by pressurized sand: **sandblast** ●cleanly practices: **hygiene** ●sterilize food by gamma radiation: **irradiate** ●disposable piece of paper etc. for cleaning: **wipe** ●mass of matted fine wire used for cleaning: **wire wool**

clear ●translucently clear: **pellucid** ●clarity of a picture or sound: **definition, focus**

clergy ●the clergy collectively: **the cloth** ●group of clergy responsible for several parishes: **team ministry** ●cleric assisting a priest: **deacon** ●cleric serving a prison, college, ship, etc.: **chaplain** ●military chaplain: **padre** ●clerical rank: **order** ●clerical ranks below deacon: **minor orders** ●Protestant clergyman: **minister, pastor** ●minister's lay assistant: **deacon** ●clergyman attached to a ship or military unit: **chaplain** ●make someone a priest or minister: **ordain** ●person peparing for ordination: **ordinand** ●clergyman's job, and the income derived from it: **benefice** ●piece of black material worn below a clerical collar: **stock** ●person who is not a cleric: **layman, layperson** ●such persons collectively: **laity** ●reduce a cleric to lay status: **defrock, laicize** ▶ *see also* Church of England, priest, Protestant, Roman Catholic Church

clerk ●*adjective*: **clerical** ●clerk preparing legal documents: **scrivener**

cliff ●steep cliff: **bluff, crag, precipice** ●collapse of part of a cliff face: **landslide, landslip**

climate ●dry climate with hot summers and cold winters: **continental climate** ●denoting a mild climate: **temperate** ●special climate of a small region: **microclimate**

climax ●*adjective*: **climactic** ●sexual climax: **orgasm** ●crucial moment in a play: **catastrophe**

climb ●climb down using a doubled rope: **abseil, rappel** ●climb by gripping with the hands and feet: **swarm up** ●place for a climber's hands or feet: **hold** ●climber's insecure foothold: **smear** ●pin driven into the rock: **piton** ●secure a climber's rope round a piton, rock, etc.: **belay** ●rock climbing using prepositioned aids: **aid climbing** ●rock climbing without prepositioned aids: **free climbing** ●climbing alone and without equipment: **solo climbing** ●spiked plate for a climber's boot: **crampon** ●climber's ice axe: **piolet** ●climber's attendant carrying supplies: **porter**

clinic ●clinic giving general practitioner and specialist services: **polyclinic** ●clinic for women: **well-woman clinic**

clitoris ●enlarged and rigid state of the clitoris: **erection** ●erectile tissue in the clitoris: **corpus cavernosum** (*pl.* corpora cavernosa) ●rounded part at the end of the clitoris: **glans** ●fold of skin surrounding this: **prepuce** ●removal of the clitoris: **clitoridectomy, female circumcision** ●excision of the clitoris and stitching together of the vulva: **infibulation**

clock ●precise clock: **chronometer** ●atomic clock: **caesium clock** ●large longcase clock: **grandfather clock** ●smaller longcase clock: **grandmother clock** ●small rectangular clock with a handle: **carriage clock** ●clock mechanism: **escapement, movement** ●clock's swinging weighted rod: **pendulum** ●art or study of clock-making: **horology** ●denoting a clock dial with moving hands: **analogue** ●denoting a clock dial with a changing numerical display: **digital** ●following the direction of a clock's hands: **clockwise** ●circulating in the opposite direction to a clock's hands: **anticlockwise, widdershins** ●set a clock to the same time as another: **synchronize**

cloister ●*adjective*: **claustral** ●land in the middle of a cloister: **garth**

cloth ●cloth impregnated with oil: **oilcloth, waxcloth** ●strong cloth used for sails and paintings: **canvas**

●cloth to cover a corpse: **shroud, winding sheet** ●cloth placed over a chair back to protect it from hair-oil: **antimacassar** ●roll of cloth: **bolt** ●cloth-maker: **clothier** ●person cleaning and thickening cloth: **fuller** ●clay used by a fuller: **fuller's earth** ●cloth-merchant: **mercer, draper, clothier**

clothes ●*adjective*: **sartorial** ●all the clothes owned by a person: **wardrobe** ●set of clothes worn together: **outfit, ensemble** ●items completing an ensemble: **accessories** ●denoting clothes suitable for both men and women: **unisex** ●denoting clothes in a timelessly elegant style: **classic** ●casual clothes: **leisure wear** ●style of women's clothes having a low neck and high waist: **empire line** ●denoting women's clothes shaped to fit the body: **fully fashioned** ●denoting clothes revealing glimpses of the body: **peekaboo** ●denoting clothes that are functional rather than decorative: **sensible** ●ceremonial clothes: **full dress, robes** ●clothing specific to a certain activity: **kit** ●clothes other than uniform or regulation dress: **mufti** ●maker of clothes: **tailor** ●design and manufacture of fashion clothes: **couture** ●designer of fashion clothes: **couturier** (*fem.* couturière) ●couturier's trademark: **label** ●couturier's shop: **salon** ●denoting clothes from a fashionable couturier: **designer** ●maker of theatrical or fancy-dress costumes: **costumier** ●full-sized model for displaying clothes: **dummy** ●colours on a garment: **colourway** ●part of a garment contrasting in colour with the main fabric: **facing** ●turned-back edge of a garment: **revers** ●part of a garment covering the shoulders: **yoke** ●glittering substance as clothes ornament: **paillette, sequin, spangle** ●flattened stitched fold in a garment: **tuck** ●tapered tuck shaping a garment:

dart ●double fold held by stitching: **pleat** ●sharp narrow pleat: **knife pleat** ●decorative frill or pleat: **ruche** ●strip of ornamental material on a skirt or dress: **flounce** ●length of cloth trailing behind a dress: **train** ●slit at the back of a jacket etc.: **vent** ●slit covering fastenings or for a pocket opening: **placket** ●pocket sewn onto the surface of a garment: **patch pocket** ●pocket set into a garment: **slash pocket** ●gradual widening of a garment: **flare** ●turned and sewn edge of a garment: **hem** ●thin stripe for business clothes: **pinstripe** ●garments that can be worn in various combinations: **separates** ●clothing etc. collected by a bride before her marriage: **trousseau, bottom drawer** ●clothes for a new baby: **layette** ●baby's short coat: **matinee coat** ●baby's one-piece garment: **playsuit, rompers** ●couturier's range of new clothes: **collection** ●liturgical clothes: **vestments** ●long strip of cloth worn over the shoulders or round the waist: **sash** ●fabric triangle worn over the shoulders: **shawl** ●long scarf or shawl: **stole** ●long scarf of fur or feathers: **boa** ●small shawl: **fichu** ●fabric head-covering: **kerchief** ●square of cloth worn round the neck: **neckerchief** ●small shiny decorative disk: **sequin** ●clothes indicating membership of a team etc.: **colours** ●guardsman's tall fur cap: **bearskin** ●dark clothes worn with university robes: **subfusc** ●one-piece garment leaving only the head, hands, and feet exposed: **boiler suit, coverall, jumpsuit, siren suit** ●one-piece undergarment covering arms, trunk, and legs: **combinations** ●loose overall: **smock, blouse** ●loose garment reaching the knees: **tunic** ●sleeveless tunic: **tabard** ●athlete's warm oversuit: **tracksuit, sweatsuit** ●weatherproof tracksuit: **shell suit** ●casual trousers: **slacks**

●denim trousers with a bib: **dungarees** ●shaped trousers for horse-riding: **jodhpurs** ●trousers ending gathered at the knee: **knickerbockers** ●baggy knickerbockers: **plus fours** ●ankle-covering: **gaiter, spat** ●length of cloth wound round the lower leg: **puttee** ●short jacket with elasticated waist and cuffs: **bomber jacket, windcheater** ●sleeveless jacket: **jerkin** ●silk jacket with an upright collar: **mandarin jacket** ●belted jacket with box pleats: **Norfolk jacket** ●lightweight belted jacket with patch pockets: **bush jacket, safari jacket** ●jacket in Chinese communist style: **Mao jacket** ●jacket with slits at the side or back: **hacking jacket** ●outdoor jacket waterproofed with wax: **waxed jacket** ●long waterproof jacket pulled over the head: **cagoule** ●thick double-breasted jacket: **reefer, reefer jacket** ●warm hooded jacket: **anorak, parka** ●jacket worn when sitting up in bed: **bedjacket** ●short sleeveless cloak: **cape** ●short cloak with a mask: **domino** ●woollen cape with a slit for the head: **poncho** ●thick blue sweater: **guernsey** ●sweater's high turned-over collar: **polo neck, roll-neck, turtleneck** ●sleeveless sweater: **pullover, slipover** ●motorist's short coat: **car coat** ●sailor's short overcoat: **pea coat, pea jacket, pilot jacket** ●long heavy overcoat: **greatcoat** ●loose overcoat belted at the back: **ulster** ●heavy woollen hooded coat with toggle fastenings: **duffel coat** ●waterproof coat: **mackintosh, raincoat** ●bullet-proof coat: **flak jacket** ●denoting a coat with a single row of buttons: **single-breasted** ●denoting a coat with two rows of buttons and an overlapping front: **double-breasted** ●front edge of a jacket that is folded back: **lapel** ●short-sleeved casual top: **T-shirt** ●loose shirt or dress: **kaftan** ●orna-

mental shirt frill: **jabot** ●starched neck frill: **ruff** ●long shirt worn in bed: **nightshirt** ●loose coat worn over nightwear: **dressing gown** ●elastic strip supporting a stocking: **garter** ●sleeveless vest: **singlet** ●strip of material covering the genitals: **G-string, thong** ●piece of cloth wound about the hips and crotch: **loincloth** ●woman's all-in-one undergarment: **teddy** ●woman's figure-shaping undergarment: **foundation, foundation garment, corset, girdle, roll-on** ●woman's light belt with stocking suspenders: **suspender belt** ●woman's undergarment supporting the breasts: **bra, brassiere** ●woman's vest: **bodice, liberty bodice** ●loose-fitting bodice: **camisole** ●woman's short vest exposing the stomach: **crop top** ●ballerina's short skirt: **tutu** ●woman's close-fitting garment covering the trunk and arms: **body, bodysuit, leotard** ●woman's close-fitting garment covering the trunk, arms, and legs: **catsuit, unitard** ●woman's close-fitting garment covering the trunk and legs: **body stocking** ●woman's two-piece swimsuit: **bikini** ●woman's swimsuit consisting of the lower half of this: **monokini** ●woman's light loose robe: **housecoat, peignoir** ●tight-fitting strapless top for women or girls: **boob tube, bustier** ●woman's close-fitting sleeveless top: **tank top** ●strap supporting a sleeveless top: **halter** ●part of a dress above the waist: **bodice** ●close-fitting bodice: **basque** ●woman's matching cardigan and jumper: **twinset** ●woman's short open jacket: **bolero** ●woman's shirt: **blouse** ●close-fitting dress: **sheath, sheath dress** ●dress hanging straight from the shoulders: **chemise** ●dress flaring out from shoulder to hem: **tent dress** ●long formal dress: **gown** ●denoting a dress having a low neckline: **décolleté** ●dress or skirt of a single piece of cloth wound round and tucked in: **sarong** ● dress or skirt of a single overlapping piece with one fastening: **wrap-around, wrap-over** ● dress or skirt ending well above the knee: **mini** ● dress or skirt of mid-calf length: **midi** ● coat or skirt of ankle length: **maxi** ● divided skirt: **culottes** ● full wide skirt with a tight waistband: **dirndl** ● padding formerly worn under the rear of a skirt: **bustle** ● loose underdress: **chemise** ● light underskirt or underdress: **petticoat** ● short petticoat: **slip** ● hoops formerly supporting a skirt: **farthingale** ● hooped petticoat: **crinoline** ● woman's light dressing gown: **negligee** ● loose dress worn by a woman in bed: **nightdress, nightgown** ● women's underwear and nightclothes: **lingerie** ● furry tube to warm the hands: **muff** ● workman's heavy jacket with leather-patched shoulders: **donkey jacket** ● man's heavy double-breasted overcoat: **ulster** ● man's long-tailed coat for formal day wear: **morning coat, tail coat** ● man's suit for formal daytime wear: **lounge suit** ● man's formal evening jacket: **dinner jacket** ● man's velvet jacket: **smoking jacket** ● man's long-tailed coat for formal evening wear: **dress coat, tailcoat** ● man's long-tailed coat for outdoor formal wear: **frock coat** ● man's false shirt front: **dicky** ● sash worn with male evening dress: **cummerbund** ● opening at the front of trousers: **flies** ● man's shorts for swimming or boxing: **trunks** ● man's long underpants: **long johns** ● decorative pouch for the male genitals: **codpiece** ● man over-eager to dress smartly: **dandy, fop** ● denoting a neatly dressed man: **dapper, spruce** ● elegantly dressed: **soigné** (fem. soignée) ● basket for dirty clothes: **linen basket** ● dummy to display clothes: **mannequin** ● person employed to wear clothes for display:

model ● women's clothes when worn by men: **drag** ● wear clothes of the opposite sex: **cross-dress** ● put on clothes: **don** ● wear informal or scruffy clothes: **dress down** ● wear smart clothes or fancy dress: **dress up** ● take off clothes: **doff** ▸ see also **glove, hat, uniform, robes, vestments** ▸ for items of foreign clothing see under the appropriate national adjective

cloud ● adjective: nebulous ● towering cloud-mass: **cumulonimbus** ● rounded cloud-mass: **cumulus** ● mass of fast-moving cloud: **wrack** ● low grey cloud: **nimbostratus, nimbus** ● low layer of clumped grey cloud-masses: **stratocumulus** ● cloud forming a continuous grey sheet: **stratus** ● height of cloud base: **ceiling** ● study of clouds: **nephology**

club[1] ● adjectives: clavate, claviform ● heavy club: **bludgeon** ● spiked metal club: **mace** ● Irish club: **shillelagh** ● Australian Aboriginal club: **nulla-nulla, waddy** ● South African club: **knobkerrie**

club[2] ● veto someone's proposed membership of a club etc.: **blackball**

clutch ● disengage a motor's clutch: **declutch**

coal ● soft brownish coal: **lignite** ● hard smokeless coal: **anthracite** ● coal heated in a vacuum: **coke** ● coal dust with small pieces of coal: **slack** ● semi-liquid mixture of water and coal particles: **slurry** ● black liquid distilled from bituminous coal: **coal tar** ● wood preservative distilled from coal tar: **creosote** ● area with many coal deposits: **coalfield** ● coal mine: **colliery** ● coal miner: **collier** ● coal miner's basket: **corf** ● coal mine safety official: **deputy** ● ship transporting coal: **collier** ● coal store: **bunker** ● fireside ornamental coal-box: **scuttle** ● stony residue from burnt coal: **clinker**

coast ●*adjective*: **littoral** ●coastal region with a subtropical climate: **riviera** ●coastal area regularly covered by tides: **salting** ●curve in a coastline: **bight** ●scenic coast road: **corniche** ●urban seaside road: **esplanade** ●coastal watchman: **coastguard**

coat ●coat with flour or sugar: **dredge** ●coat with plaster or cement: **render** ●coat a wall with planking: **clad** ▸*see also* **clothes**

cocaine ●potent hard form of cocaine: **crack** ●purified cocaine: **freebase**

cockney ●cockney's traditional dress: **pearlies** ●cockney wearing these: **pearly queen, pearly king**

cocktail ●advocaat and lemonade: **snowball** ●brandy with flavoured water and ice: **smash** ●brandy, lemon juice, and orange liqueur: **sidecar** ●gin and angostura bitters: **pink gin** ●gin and cherry brandy: **Singapore sling** ●gin and dry vermouth: **martini** ●gin, vermouth, and Campari: **negroni** ●gin, orange liqueur, and lemon juice: **White Lady** ●rum and water: **grog** ●rum and lime juice: **daiquiri** ●rum, pineapple juice, and coconut: **pina colada** ●spirits with beaten egg and milk: **egg-nog, egg flip** ●tequila and champagne: **slammer, tequila slammer** ●vodka and orange juice: **screwdriver** ●vodka and tomato juice: **Bloody Mary** ●whisky and ginger wine: **whisky mac** ●whisky with lemon or lime juice: **whisky sour** ●wine or spirits with fruit juices, spices, etc.: **punch**

coconut ●coconut fibre: **coir** ●dried coconut kernels: **copra**

code ●deciphering of codes: **cryptanalysis** ●word enabling this: **keyword** ●text written in code: **cryptogram** ●encode a text: **encipher, encrypt** ●encode electronically:

scramble ●denoting a text sent out of code: **en clair** ●signalling code composed of longs and shorts: **Morse code** ●study of codes: **cryptography, cryptology** ●code composed of parallel lines of varying thickness: **bar code, universal product code** ●light-emitting device reading bar codes: **light pen**

coffee ●strong black coffee made under steam pressure: **espresso** ●coffee topped with frothed milk: **cappuccino** ●stimulant in coffee: **caffeine** ●coffee sediment: **grounds** ●coffee pot with a plunger: **cafetière** ●coffee pot passing heated water though the grounds: **percolator**

coffin ●stone coffin : **sarcophagus, cist** ●inner coffin: **shell** ●framework on which a coffin may be set or carried: **bier, catafalque** ●coffin-carrier: **pallbearer**

cog ●cogwheel with teeth at 90°: **crown wheel** ●cogged or toothed bar or rail: **rack**

coil ●rotating coil in a dynamo or electric motor: **armature**

coin ●*adjective*: **numismatic, nummular** ●face of a coin: **obverse** ●back of a coin: **reverse** ●impression stamped on a coin: **incuse** ●ridges on a coin's edge: **milling** ●coin manufactory: **mint** ●collection of specimen coins at the Royal Mint: **pyx** ●deprive a coin of monetary status: **demonetize** ●study of coins: **numismatics**

cold ●*combining forms*: **cryo-** ●cold and damp: **dank** ●feeling of extreme cold: **nip** ●sleepy state brought on by extreme cold: **hypothermia** ●tissue damage caused by extreme cold: **frostbite** ●thermometer for low temperatures: **cryometer** ●substance producing low temperatures: **cryogen** ●deep-freezing of corpses in hope of subsequent medical advances that could reverse the cause of death: **cryo-**

genics, cryonics ●medical treatment using intense cold: **cryotherapy** ●surgery using intense cold to destroy tissue: **cryosurgery**

collapse ●inwards collapse: **implosion**

collar ●high stiff collar with turned down corners: **wing collar** ●high turned-over collar on a sweater: **polo neck** ●bar attaching a collar to a shirt: **stud**

collection ●collection of related items: **compendium** ●collection of miscellaneous items: **farrago, job lot** ●collection of writings: **anthology, collectanea, commonplace book, florilegium, miscellany, omnibus** ●collection of historical documents: **archive** ●collection of texts: **corpus** ●collection of essays on a particular topic: **symposium**

collective farm ●collective farm in Israel: **kibbutz** ●collective farm in Russia: **kolkhoz**

collector ●collector of bygones: **antiquary** ●collector of beer mats: **tegestologist** ●collector of books: **bibliophile** ●collector of butterflies and moths: **lepidopterist** ●collector of coins and medals: **numismatist** ●collector of matchboxes: **phillumenist** ●collector of stamps: **philatelist**

college ●*adjectives*: **collegial, collegiate** ●college for pupils in their final years of secondary education: **sixth-form college** ●further education college providing courses in practical or technical subjects: **technical college** ●military college training potential officers: **military academy** ●military college training officers for staff duties: **staff college** ●music college: **conservatoire** ●Orthodox Jewish college: **yeshiva** ●college site and buildings: **campus** ●college doorkeeper's room: **lodge** ●college courtyard: **quadrangle** ●college dining room: **hall, refectory** ●table in

this for senior teaching staff: **high table** ●college room where provisions are sold: **buttery** ●college relaxation room for fellows: **senior common room** ●this for postgraduates: **middle common room** ●this for undergraduates: **junior common room** ●college principal's apartments: **lodge, lodgings** ●college doorkeeper: **porter** ●college financial manager: **bursar** ●cleric serving a college: **chaplain** ●senior member of a college: **fellow, don** ●college fellow in charge of discipline: **dean** ●college teacher responsible for a particular subject: **tutor** ●college tuition session for an individual or small group: **tutorial** ●annual college feast: **gaudy, commemoration** ●money deposited with college authorities to pay for breakages: **caution money** ▸*see also* **Cambridge, Oxford, university**

colony ●*adjective*: **colonial** ▸*see also* **state**

colour ●*combining forms*: **chromato-, chromo-** ●*adjective*: **chromatic** ●one of a group of basic colours combining to form all the others: **primary colour** ●colour made by mixing two primary colours: **secondary colour** ●range of colours: **spectrum, palette** ●band of colours produced by refraction of a light source: **spectrum** ●denoting a colour that combines with another to make white or black: **complementary** ●colour intensity: **saturation** ●producing colour: **chromogenic** ●using only one colour: **monochromatic** ●in a single uniform colour: **self-coloured** ●having several colours: **particoloured, pied, polychromatic, polychrome** ●denoting colours that are burnt into a surface: **encaustic** ●small patch of colour: **fleck** ●subtle shade of a colour: **tint** ●faint trace of a colour: **tinge** ●quality of a colour: **tone** ●marked with patches of colour: **dappled, mottled, variegated** ● colouring matter: **pigment**

colour blindness ● complete colour blindness: **monochromatism** ● ability to discern only two of the three primary colours: **dichromatism** ● red-blindness: **daltonism, protanopia** ● green-blindness: **deuteranopia** ● blue-blindness: **tritanopia**

column ● rectangular column: **pilaster** ● short ornate column supporting a rail: **baluster** ● ornamental fencing made of these: **balustrade** ● denoting a column attached to the wall: **engaged** ● engaged column at the end of an arcade: **respond** ● row of columns: **colonnade** ● row of columns defining a space: **peristyle** ● head of a column: **capital** ● slight concave curve in a column: **entasis** ● beam across the tops of columns: **architrave** ● ornamental porch with columns: **portico** ● cylindrical stone forming part of a column: **tambour** ● arrange (statistics etc.) in columns: **tabulate**

comb ● projecting point on a comb: **tooth** ● comb wool or hemp before spinning: **card**

combat ● medieval mock-combat between mounted knights: **joust** ● place for such combat: **lists** ● combat game played with counters on maps: **kriegspiel**

combatant ● Spanish bullfighter on foot: **torero** ● Spanish mounted bullfighter: **toreador** ● Spanish bullfighter killing the bull: **matador** ● matador's mounted assistant: **picador** ● person who fought in a Roman arena to entertain: **gladiator** ● nation or person engaged in warfare: **belligerent** ▸ *see also* **soldier, troops**

combination ● combination into a single unit: **consolidation** ● combination into a coherent whole: **synthesis** ● combination of businesses: **conglomerate, consortium, corporation, syndicate** ● combination of

traders to fix prices: **cartel, price ring**

comet ● solid head of a comet: **nucleus** ● luminous tail following a comet: **coma**

comfort ● comfortable and cosy: **snug** ● degree of material comfort enjoyed: **standard of living**

command ● *adjectives*: **mandatory, preceptive** ● arbitrary command: **diktat, ukase** ● command that must be obeyed: **dictate** ● oriental ruler's command: **firman** ● sovereign's command advised by the Privy Council: **Order in Council** ● binding official instruction: **directive** ● carry out a command: **execute**

comment ● comment made in passing: **obiter dictum** ● perceptive comment: **aperçu** ● witty comment expressing a general truth: **aphorism, epigram**

commitment ● morally committed: **engagé** ● avoid committing oneself: **hedge**

committee ● committee establishing an organization's general principles of operation: **steering committee** ● committee appointed to advise on a particular problem: **working group, working party** ● parliamentary committee appointed for a special purpose: **select committee** ● invitation to join a committee given by its current members: **co-option** ● fill a committee with persons sympathetic to one's aims: **pack**

Commonwealth ● Commonwealth embassy: **high commission**

commune ● member of a commune: **communard**

communication ● communication by posture or gesture: **body language, kinesics** ● establish or facilitate communication: **liaise** ● organs of mass communication: **the media** ● communications company: **carrier** ● communication over a distance by telephone, radio, etc.: **telecommunication** ● work from home using telecommunications: **telecommute** ● discussion involving three or more persons at different sites using telecommunications: **teleconference** ● centre linking ground communications to satellites: **teleport** ● international communications system using teleprinters: **telex** ● international communications system using electronic scanning: **fax** ● telecommunications channel with a bandwidth sufficient for voices: **voice channel**

communism ● kind of communism retaining elements of Western liberalism: **Eurocommunism** ● central policy committee of a communist state: **politburo** ● standing legislative committee of a communist state: **presidium** ● opposition to the official Party line: **splittism** ● underground publishing in a communist state: **samizdat** ● countries not controlled by communism: **free world** ▶ *see also* **Chinese communism, Soviet**

compact disk ● compact disk player able to play several disks in succession: **multiplayer**

company ● *adjective*: **corporate** ● company operating in several countries: **multinational, transnational** ● company whose shares are not on public sale: **private company** ● company whose shares are traded on the stock exchange: **public company** ● capital raised by a company's sale of its shares: **stock** ● funds used in a company's day-to-day trading: **working capital** ● companies under common ownership: **group** ● company created to control others, whose shares it holds: **holding company** ● company controlled by a holding company: **subsidiary** ● combination of two companies into one: **merger** ● buy-out of one company by another: **takeover** ● denoting a takeover resisted by its victim: **hostile** ● person

or company making an acceptable counterbid to a hostile takeover: **white knight** ● company controlled by its shareholders: **joint-stock company** ● nominal company: **shell company** ● company section with a specific function: **division** ● denoting a highly efficient company: **lean** ● transfer a state-run company to private ownership: **denationalize, privatize** ● worker involvement in company government: **industrial democracy** ● transport or communications company: **carrier** ● company's preferred style of presentation: **house style** ● tax on company profits: **corporation tax** ● internal to a company: **house** ● company department responsible for recruitment, training, and welfare: **personnel** ● company department responsible for product innovation and improvement: **research and development** ● chart showing the interrelation of company posts: **organization chart** ● colours and symbols on a company's vehicles: **livery** ● spying to gain company secrets: **industrial espionage** ● denoting companies whose shares are quoted on the London Stock Exchange: **listed** ● (of a company) extend or vary its operations: **diversify** ● reorganize a company on a smaller scale: **downsize, rationalize** ● close a company down: **liquidate, wind up**

comparison ● standard against which other items may be assessed: **benchmark, control, datum line, yardstick** ● having no such common standard: **incommensurable** ● giving an annual comparison: **year-on-year**

compass ● gyroscope-aligned compass: **gyrocompass** ● denoting one of the four main compass points: **cardinal** ● deflection of a ship's compass needle by iron in the ship: **deviation** ● direction in which a compass needle will turn: **magnetic north** ●deflection of a compass needle from true to magnetic north: **declination**

competition ●competition's preliminary rounds: **heats** ●free pass to the next round: **bye** ●competition in which each round's losers are eliminated: **knock-out** ●denoting a competition open to all: **open** ●list of competitors in order of achievement: **league table** ●main bunch of competitors: **pack, van** ●compete closely: **vie** ●disadvantage imposed on a superior competitor: **handicap** ●denoting a player receiving no handicap: **scratch** ●group of clubs competing together over a season: **league** ●outside the competition: **hors concours**

compilation ●*combining form*: **-logue** (*e.g.* catalogue)

complaint ●*adjective*: **querulous** ●trivial complaint: **quibble** ●cause for complaint: **grievance** ●government official investigating complaints: **ombudsman**

complementary medicine ●treatment by minute doses of substances causing the disease: **homeopathy** ●manipulation and massage of bones and muscles: **osteopathy** ●manipulation of the spinal culumn: **chiropractic** ●massage treatment using fragrant oils: **aromatherapy** ●massage system based on zone therapy: **reflexology** ●inserting needles into the skin: **acupuncture**

complete ●*combining form*: **hol(o)-** (*e.g.* holocaust)

completely ●*combining form*: **cata-** (*e.g.* cataclysm), **de-** (*e.g.* denude), **holo-** (*e.g.* holograph), **over-** (*e.g.* overjoyed), **per-** (*e.g.* perfect)

complexion ●having a pale complexion: **ashen, pallid, wan** ●having a red complexion: **florid, ruddy** ●having a yellowish complexion: **sallow, jaundiced**

compliance ●strict compliance: **specific performance** ●minimal compliance: **tokenism**

composer ●composer's assistant, taking down dictation or copying drafts: **amanuensis** ●composer's personal musical style: **idiom**

compound ●compound with the same formula as another, but different atomic disposition: **isomer** ●denoting a compound containing carbon: **organic** ●denoting a compound not containing carbon: **inorganic** ●chemical analysis of a compound, expressed in symbols: **formula** (*pl.* formulae) ●breakdown of a compound into its constituent substances: **decomposition**

compressed air ●*adjective*: pneumatic

compromise ●compromise between two mutually incompatible objectives: **trade-off** ●middle way of compromise: **via media** ●admitting no compromise: **categorical, dogmatic**

compulsion ●done without compulsion: **voluntary**

computation ●computational device using beads on wires: **abacus** ●machine making mathematical calculations: **calculator** ●ruler with a sliding central section: **slide rule**

computer ●*combining form*: **cyber-** ●*adjective*: **computational, cyber** ●computer that can be held in the hand: **palmtop** ●hand-held microcomputer serving as a diary: **personal organizer** ●small portable computer: **notebook** ●portable computer: **laptop** ●computer for use by one person at a time: **personal computer** ●computer using a microprocessor: **microcomputer** ●computer sized for desk use: **desktop** ●production of camera-ready copy by this: **desktop publishing** ●general purpose computer more powerful than a personal computer: **workstation** ●medium-sized computer: **minicomputer** ●powerful computer supporting many peripherals: **mainframe** ●multimedia computer and entertainment system: **multiplayer** ●denoting activities performed by computers: **electronic** ●manufacturer's test of a computer component before releasing it for use: **bench test** ●time during which a computer is out of action: **downtime** ●time during which a computer is operational: **uptime** ●detect and repair computer faults: **debug** ●computer or program for creating and editing texts: **word processor** ●physical components of a computer: **hardware** ●part of a computer where operations are executed and controlled: **central processing unit, mainframe** ●integrated circuit replacing this: **microprocessor** ●other devices connected to these: **peripherals** ●computer part storing data and programs: **memory** ●computer programs, routines, and procedures: **software** ●set of hard and software units devoted to a particular application: **system** ●exclusively assigned to a particular function: **dedicated** ●denoting computing equipment compatible without modification to that of other manufacturers: **plug-compatible** ●start a computer: **boot** ●gain access to a computer system: **log in, log on** ●string giving user access to a system or part of it: **password** ●service or administrative computer tasks: **housekeeping** ●coded instructions controlling a computer: **command, program** ●reverse a previous command: **undo** ●allow the use of a program etc.: **support** ●self-operating program with reasoning capacity: **knowbot** ●repeated sequence of programmed instructions: **loop** ●single instruction expanding into a set: **macro** ●time taken by a system to implement commands: **re-**

sponse time ●denoting systems processing data as it is generated: **real-time** ●short time during which a computer deals with one user or program before switching to another: **time slice** ●device displaying data on a screen: **visual display unit** ●computer's displayed list of commands or facilities: **menu** ●movable indicator on computer screen: **cursor** ●strip of icons used to perform certain functions: **toolbar** ●hand-held device selecting items shown on-screen: **mouse, puck** ●ball moved to control the cursor: **rollerball** ●pad on which this is moved: **mat** ●display device receiving commands by touches on the screen: **touch screen** ●pull an icon across the screen: **drag** ●small command panel with touch-sensitive areas: **touch pad** ●mark a displayed item for particular treatment: **select** ●device allowing direct input of handwritten material: **stylus** ●photosensitive device inputting material via the screen: **light pen, stylus** ●onscreen warning of system malfunction or bad instruction: **error message** ●onscreen request for user input: **prompt** ●program replacing an unchanged screen display with a moving image: **screen saver** ●optional background pattern on a computer screen: **wallpaper** ●damage to computer screen from long use: **burn-in** ●linear sequence of characters etc.: **string** ●convert pictures or sound into computer-processable form: **digitize** ●computer scanning of existing images: **digital imaging** ●computer-aided recognition of printed characters: **optical character recognition** ●visual images produced using computer technology: **graphics, computer graphics, videographics** ●computer model of the brain's ability to recognize and discriminate: **perceptron** ●language defining operating tasks: **job control**

language ●character string identifying a program: **identifier** ●character with no assigned identity used in a search string: **wild card** ●character string identical with that searched for: **match** ●proceeding by trial and error: **heuristic** ●copy data to a storage location: **save** ●extra copy of data taken for security: **back-up** ●conducting an operation in simultaneous parts: **parallel processing** ●chief printed circuit board: **motherboard** ●transfer a program or data to memory: **load** ●denoting a program or device directly accessible to the user: **front-end** ●background computer process handling peripheral tasks: **daemon** ●system of interconnected computers: **network** ●directly controlled by a computer: **online** ●not directly controlled by a computer: **offline** ●study of electronic data processing for storage and retrieval: **information science, information technology, informatics** ●printout of computer data: **hardcopy** ●onscreen display of data: **soft copy** ●printout of what is shown on the screen: **screen dump** ●onscreen mockup of page layout before printing: **page preview** ●series of jobs waiting for the printer: **print queue** ●show an input character onscreen: **echo** ●temporary area opened onscreen to display a program's output: **window, viewport** ●component transferring electrical signals to the recording medium: **head** ●computer device able to switch between disks: **changer** ●smallest unit of electronic information: **bit** ●group of eight bits: **byte** ●series of characters stored in a computer: **string** ●back-up of changed files only: **incremental back-up** ●device giving high-speed back-up to tape: **tape streamer** ●flat plate for data storage: **disk** ●device accessing this: **disk drive** ●rigid non-

removable disk: **hard disk, hard drive** ●removable flexible disk: **floppy, floppy disk** ●floppy disk drive using a laser: **floptical** ●digital–analogue interface: **modem** ●modem converting digital to sound signals: **acoustic coupler** ●convert an image into digital form for computer use: **scan** ●computer's operating speed: **clock speed** ●computer's ability to interconnect systems: **connectivity** ●connected set of data items: **record** ●data stored under a particular name: **file** ●search directions for a file: **path** ●description of a file's whereabouts: **pathname** ●list of files: **directory** ●directory at the highest level of a hierarchy: **root directory** ●access to data requiring file readthrough: **sequential access** ●text stored in a file: **document** ●computer manipulation of texts: **text processing, word processing** ●word processing feature starting a new line to avoid word-division: **word wrap** ●insert material into a document: **paste** ●defined structure for data processing, storage, or display: **format** ●formatting software: **filter** ●restructuring and computer loading of data: **computerization** ●company restructuring to utilize computers: **business process re-engineering** ●analysis of complex procedures with a view to their computerization: **systems analysis** ●piece of computer code that can corrupt or destroy data: **virus** ●harmful self-replicating computer program: **worm** ●messages sent over a computer network: **electronic mail** ●denoting a computer terminal lacking independent processing capability: **dumb** ●denoting a terminal having this: **intelligent** ●denoting a computer serving several terminals: **multi-access** ●link a smaller computer to a larger one: **dock** ●device allowing use of audio components: **sound card** ●cafe with computers for customers' use: **cybercafe** ●rural establishment with computers for customers' use: **telecentre, telecottage** ●ordering goods by direct computer link: **teleshopping** ●increased availability of information due to computers: **information revolution** ●legal controls over use of electronic data: **data protection** ●person using codes to access a computer network: **cypherpunk** ●person gaining illicit access to secret computer data: **hacker** ●sexual pleasure obtained via computer technology: **cybersex** ●half-move in computer chess: **ply** ●ability to use computers: **computer literacy** ●fear of computers: **cyberphobia** ●instruction book for a computer user: **manual** ●technical assistance to a computer user: **support, technical support** ●notional environment for computer communication: **cyberspace** ●computer-generated model of future events: **simulation** ●computer-generated three-dimensional environment: **virtual reality** ●fiction set in a computer-dominated society: **cyberpunk** ●control for computerized video games: **console, joypad, joystick, light gun** ●denoting a computerized game playable over the Internet: **multi-user** ●computer application allowing the combination of animated and live-action elements in a film: **rotoscope** ●human thought mechanisms or processes when compared with those of a computer: **wetware** ●denoting logical systems reflecting the inexactness of human thought: **fuzzy** ▸ *see also* **computer disk, computer graphics, computer hardware, computer keyboard, computer memory, computer system, computer window, electronic data, file, program, virtual reality, word processor**

computer disk ●rigid non-removable disk: **hard disk, hard drive**

●removable flexible disk: **floppy, floppy disk** ●floppy disk drive using a laser: **floptical** ●denoting a disk of double storage capacity: **double density** ●concentric circle on a disk: **track** ●subdivision of a track on a magnetic disk: **sector** ●device accessing a disk: **disk drive** ●computer device able to switch between disks: **changer** ●disk storage device allowing data access from any of them: **jukebox** ●protect the contents of a disk from overwriting or erasure: **write-protect**

computer graphics ●small on-screen graphic: **glyph** ●graphic serving as a menu item: **icon** ●control system using windows, icons, etc.: **graphical user interface** ●screen graphic of a box posing questions to the user: **dialog box, dialogue box** ●computer drawing device: **graphics tablet** ●gradual change of an image by computerized techniques: **morphing** ●ready-made artwork in software packages: **clip art** ●denoting systems creating three-dimensional displays: **immersive**

computer hardware ●surface area taken up by a piece of hardware: **footprint** ●hardware standard determining what software it can run: **platform** ●denoting hardware that can be operated independently: **stand-alone** ●number of hardware units sold as a package: **bundle** ●hardcopy describing the uses and design of hardware: **documentation** ●device or program connecting two items of hardware: **interface** ●provide a user interface for software: **encapsulate** ●hardware manufacturers' after-sales advice service: **technical support** ●sudden hardware failure: **crash**

computer keyboard ●computer key giving quick access to a function: **hot key** ●computer key altering the function of another: **control key, shift**

key ●computer key used to arrest an operation: **escape key** ●computer key assigned a function by the current program: **function key** ●computer key used to execute a command: **enter key** ●computer key used to start a new line of text: **carriage return** ●computer key that alternately initiates and arrests a function: **toggle, toggle key, toggle switch**

computer memory ●computer's temporary memory area: **buffer, clipboard** ●computer's auxiliary memory: **cache** ●fast temporary memory: **scratch pad** ●fast memory for material in current use: **working memory** ●memory used for storage of interim results: **working storage** ●memory retaining data without electricity: **flash memory** ●denoting memory that can only be written once: **read-only** ●denoting memory that is cleared with loss of power: **volatile** ●denoting a memory able to retain data despite power cuts: **non-volatile** ●memory facility giving direct access to each location: **random access** ●memory facility allowing access only in a certain order: **sequential access** ●memory section: **partition** ●part of a computer memory where programs must be loaded: **conventional memory** ●security copy of memory contents: **dump** ●memory store not part of the main processor: **external memory** ●binary number identifying a memory location: **address** ●circuit board giving extra memory: **expansion board, expansion card** ●board containing extra memory chips: **memory board** ●key data into a computer's memory: **capture, enter, input** ●enter data into non-volatile memory: **save** ●destroy data in a computer's memory: **delete, erase** ●transfer a program or data to memory: **load, write** ●permanent software programmed into the read-only memory: **firmware**

●denoting software not kept permanently in the memory: **non-resident**

computer network ●network operating within a building etc.: **local area network** ●network of independent computers: **distributed system** ●network serving distant computers: **wide area network** ●international computer network: **Internet** ●electronic network for rapid transfer of digital information: **superhighway, information superhighway** ●computer providing network services: **host** ●network computer or program managing access to a central resource: **server** ●workstation networked to a server: **client** ●user point on a network: **terminal** ●connect several devices in series: **daisy-chain** ●device connecting two networks: **gateway** ●denoting a device accessible without the network: **local** ●denoting a device accessible only via the network: **remote** ●network protocol allowing a user on one computer to log in to another computer on the same network : **telnet** ●socket connecting devices to a network: **port**

computer software ●software available free of charge: **freeware, shareware** ●software made available over a network or television system: **telesoftware** ●software programmed using artificial intelligence techniques: **expert system** ●software allowing extensive cross-referencing: **hypertext** ●software supporting basic computer functions: **operating system** ●software for collective use: **groupware** ●software devised to meet a particular user's needs: **application** ●permanent read-only software: **firmware** ●formatting software: **filter** ●container for loading computer software: **cartridge** ●denoting software not kept permanently in the memory: **non-resident** ●denoting software able to exchange data without conversion: **interoperable**

• able to use specified software without modification: **compatible** • series of coded software instructions: **algorithm, program, routine** • electronic device enabling the use of protected software: **dongle** • provide a user interface for software: **encapsulate** • transfer software from one system to another: **port** • ready-made artwork in software packages: **clip art** • software manufacturers' after-sales advice service: **technical support** • sudden software failure: **crash**

computer system • computer system modelled on the human brain: **neural net, neural network** • theory and development of computer systems able to think like humans: **artificial intelligence** • denoting systems employing artificial intelligence: **expert, fifth-generation** • logic employed by such systems: **fuzzy logic** • control system using windows, icons, etc.: **graphical user interface** • part of a computer system preventing unauthorized access: **firewall** • denoting a system simultaneously usable by several people: **multi-user** • system multi-use: **time-sharing** • denoting systems able to exchange data without conversion: **interoperable** • denoting a system making input data immediately available as feedback: **real time** • denoting systems processing data as it is generated: **real-time** • denoting systems creating three-dimensional displays: **immersive** • arrange and adjust the elements of a computer system: **configure** • copy data from one computer system to another: **download** • transfer data to a larger computer system: **upload** • re-express data for use with a different system: **convert** • computer's ability to interconnect systems: **connectivity** • logical organization of a computer system: **architecture** • denoting an architecture allowing several instructions to be loaded and executed simul-

taneously: **superscalar** • gain access to a computer system: **log in, log on** • string giving user access to a system or part of it: **password** • means by which user and system interact: **user interface** • onscreen warning of system malfunction: **error message**

computer window • subsection of a window: **pane** • simultaneous use of several windows: **windowing** • reduce a window to an icon: **iconify** • arrange windows so that they do not overlap: **tile** • bar at the foot of a window giving information on the document edited or the program running: **status bar**

concern • lack of concern: **apathy, indifference** • showing no concern: **insouciant, nonchalant**

concert • concert for an unseated audience: **promenade concert** • concert given by one or a few players: **recital**

conclusion • conclusion derived by logic: **deduction, inference** • conclusion inferred from a limited number of instances: **generalization** • unstated conclusion: **implication** • conclusion wrongly inferred: **non sequitur**

concrete • concrete reinforced with steel: **ferroconcrete, reinforced concrete** • denoting concrete strengthened by rods inserted under tension: **prestressed** • large flat piece of concrete: **slab** • concrete layer under a building: **oversite, raft** • planking supporting setting concrete: **shuttering**

condiments • table condiment-holder: **cruet** • mixture of oil, vinegar, and herbs: **dressing**

condition • *combining forms*: **-acy** (*e.g.* lunacy), **-hood** (*e.g.* falsehood), **-ness** (*e.g.* silliness), **-osis** (*e.g.* neurosis), **-osity** (*e.g.* pomposity), **-tude** (*e.g.* solitude) • in its original condition: **pristine** • agreed conditions:

terms ●essential condition: **prerequisite, sine qua non**

conditioning ●conditioning of cut timber by exposure to the weather: **seasoning** ●raising tolerance levels by regular exposure: **desensitization**

cone ●*adjective*: **conical, conic, conoid** ●cone intersected by a plane: **conic section** ●mathematics of conic sections: **conics**

conference ●academic conference: **colloquium, symposium** ●representative sent to a conference: **delegate**

confinement ●confinement to one's home: **house arrest** ●confinement in a distant part of one's country: **internal exile** ●confinement of enemy aliens during wartime: **internment**

confirm ●confirm formally: **vouch** ●confirm a statement: **corroborate**

conform ●determined refusal to conform: **perversity** ●person not concerned to conform: **dropout, eccentric**

confuse ●confused state of the elderly: **senile dementia** ●confused mass: **welter** ●surprise and confuse: **disconcert, nonplus** ●in headlong confusion: **pell-mell**

connect ●*adjective*: **conjunctive, connective** ●temporary electrical or telephone connection: **patch**

connoisseur ●connoisseur of food and drink: **gourmet, gastronome** ●connoisseur of pictures and antiques: **virtuoso**

conqueror ●Spanish conqueror of South America: **conquistador**

conscience ●*adjective*: **conscientious** ●person refusing to fight as a matter of moral principle: **conscientious objector**

conscious ●temporary loss of consciousness: **blackout** ●below the level of consciousness: **subliminal** ●rigid unconscious state: **catalepsy**

consent ●*adjective*: **consensual** ●permission short of consent: **toleration**

consequence ●inevitable consequence: **corollary** ●have or cause as a consequence: **entail, entrain**

conservation ●open area round a town, with development restrictions: **green belt** ●other area so treated: **Environmentally Sensitive Area** ●listed building's level of importance: **grade**

consonant ●type of consonant produced by a sudden release of air: **plosive** ●type of consonant produced by breath friction: **fricative** ●type of consonant produced by brief contact between palate and tongue tip: **flap** ●type of consonant produced by contact or proximity between palate and tongue blade: **palatal** ●type of consonant produced by contact between tongue tip and the palatal ridge or upper front teeth: **dental** ●type of consonant produced by full or partial lip closure: **labial**

constitution ●partial suspension of the constitution: **state of emergency**

consul ●consul's office or staff: **consulate** ●host government's official recognition of consular staff: **exequatur**

consultation ●opportunity provided by an MP, lawyer, etc. for informal consultation: **surgery**

consume ●consume sparingly: **eke out** ●promotion of consumer interests: **consumerism**

contact ●forcible contact: **impact** ●spread by contact: **contagious**

container ●container for fluids: **reservoir, cistern** ●cylindrical metal container: **canister** ●sealed container holding a measured amount of medicine etc.: **ampoule** ●container for audiotape: **cassette, reel** ●barred container for animal feed: **crib** ●container for film, ink, or a computer program: **cartridge** ● large flexible container for water-transport of liquids: **dracone** ● suspended container with a discharge chute: **hopper** ● container for molten metal: **crucible** ● container for building waste: **skip** ● container for papers: **briefcase, file, portfolio** ● case for unfolded drawings: **portfolio** ● container for petrol or water: **jerrycan** ● container for relics: **reliquary** ● container for tea: **caddy** ● tin-lined wooden container for shipping tea: **tea chest** ● perforated hollow metal sphere to hold infusing tea leaves: **tea ball** ● container for wine or oil: **ampulla, cruse** ● small container for table condiments: **cruet** ● glass container for wine or spirits: **decanter** ● container made from a piece of paper twisted at the ends: **twist** ● earthenware pot or jar: **crock** ● sealed container filled with objects representative of the current time, buried for future discovery: **time capsule** ● batter-proof container: **flight case** ● perforated container for sweet-smelling substances: **pomander** ▶ *see also* **basket, luggage**

containing ● *combining form*: **-fer** (*e.g.* aquifer), **-ferous** (*e.g.* auriferous), **-ous** (*e.g.* dangerous)

contaminate ● contaminate food or drink: **adulterate, doctor** ● contamination of the environment: **pollution**

context ● out of context: **in vacuo**

continent ● large continent of the geological past: **supercontinent** ● supposed original single continent: **Pangaea** ● subsequent land mass in the southern hemisphere: **Gondwana** ● subsequent land mass in the northern hemisphere: **Laurasia** ● continent round the South Pole: **Antarctica** ● continent round the North Pole: **Arctic** ● continent lying east of Europe: **Asia** ● continent running east from the British isles to the Urals: **Europe** ● major section of a continent: **subcontinent** ● creation of continents by the raising of the earth's crust: **epeirogeny** ● gradual movement of the earth's continents: **continental drift**

contraception ● penis sheath: **condom** ● contraceptive cover for the cervix: **cap, diaphragm, Dutch cap** ● intrauterine contraceptive: **coil, loop** ● device for washing out the vagina: **douche** ● substance killing spermatozoa: **spermicide** ● oral contraceptive containing both oestrogen and progestogen: **combined pill** ● oral contraceptive that may be taken after intercourse: **morning-after pill** ● contraceptive method based on body temperature: **sympto-thermal method** ● contraceptive method of avoiding intercourse when conception is most likely: **rhythm method** ● time when a woman is least likely to conceive: **safe period** ▶ *see also* **sterilization**

contract ● *adjective*: **contractual, contractural** ● contract drawn up by deed: **covenant** ● contract for periodic work: **account** ● apprentice's contract: **indenture** ● subordinate contract: **subcontract** ● contract binding in honour only: **gentleman's agreement** ● weakening flaw in a contract: **loophole** ● clause in a contract stipulating exceptions: **saving clause** ● clause freeing a party from obligations under stated conditions: **escape clause** ● clause allowing for price increases: **escalator clause** ● document recording a contract: **deed, memorandum** ● detailed text of a contract: **small print** ● thing given or done in return for another's contracted act: **consideration** ● initial sum paid to validate a contract: **deposit** ● security for the completion of a contract: **pledge** ● changed circumstances making performance impossible: **force majeure** ● payment at early termination of contract: **severance pay** ●performance of a contractual obligation ordered by a court: **specific performance** ●enter into a contract: **engage** ●release from contractual obligation: **discharge** ●person securing and negotiating contracts for a performer or creative artist: **agent**

contradiction ●apparent contradiction used for rhetorical effect: **oxymoron** ●self-contradictory: **inconsistent** ●expression acknowledging that one is contradicting the person specified: **pace**

contrast ●contrast of light and shade: **chiaroscuro** ●volume contrasts in a musical piece: **dynamics**

control ●control from a distance: **remote control** ●controlling influence stifling initiative: **dead hand** ●state economic and social control: **dirigisme** ●control of former dependencies by economic or political pressure: **neocolonialism** ●control panel: **console, fascia** ●loss of control of one's bodily movements: **ataxia** ●loss of control of one's bodily functions: **incontinence** ●absence of any control: **anarchy** ●noisy and hard to control: **obstreperous** ●easy to control: **biddable, pliable, tractable** ●take control of: **commandeer** ●bring under control: **subdue, subjugate** ●enter and take control of: **occupy** ●free from control: **deregulate** ●remove from a position of control: **override** ▶ *see also* **power**

convent ●*adjective*: **conventual** ▶ *see also* **monastery**

convince ●person hard to convince: **sceptic** ●easily convinced: **credulous, gullible**

cook ●senior cook: **chef** ●assistant cook: **commis** ●chef's tall white hat: **toque** ●denoting a first-class cook: **cordon bleu**

cooked ●lightly cooked (of pasta or vegetables): **al dente** ●very lightly cooked (of meat): **saignant** ●lightly cooked (of meat): **rare** ●cooked gently in their own juice (of vegetables): **sweated** ●fried and then stewed: **braised** ●cooked by dipping into a hot oil or sauce: **fondue** ●simmered in or over a little liquid: **poached** ●partly cooked by boiling: **parboiled** ●parboiled and then fried: **sautéed**

cookery ●*adjective*: **culinary** ●type of cookery: **cuisine** ●high quality cooking: **haute cuisine** ●style of cookery emphasizing presentation and fresh ingredients: **nouvelle cuisine** ●cookery as a school subject: **food technology, home economics, domestic science** ●device with a small burner for keeping dishes hot at the table: **chafing dish** ●heated food trolley: **hostess trolley** ●constituent of a dish: **ingredient** ●device extracting juice: **juicer** ●liquidizing and chopping device: **blender, food processor** ●device for whipping liquids: **whisk** ●waxed paper for cookery: **greaseproof paper** ●denoting cookware usable in the oven or on the hob: **flameproof** ●enamel cooking pot with lid and handle: **billy, billycan** ●small metal cooking pot: **skillet** ●large metal cooking pot: **cauldron** ●large metal cooking pot for field use: **dixie** ●large covered cooking pot: **casserole** ●small pot for cooking and serving food: **cocotte, ramekin** ●saucepan cooking food in an upper compartment by means of hot water held in a lower compartment: **bain marie, double boiler, double saucepan** ●airtight saucepan for fast cooking: **pressure cooker** ●broad-bladed serving utensil: **slice** ●blunt wooden blade: **spatula** ●hand-held crushing implement: **pestle** ●strong dish for this: **mortar** ●large cooking stove: **range** ●circular iron cooking plate: **griddle** ●spike for cooking pieces of food: **skewer, spit** ●grill frame of parallel bars: **gridiron** ●cooking appliance with a rotating spit: **rotisserie** ●heating area on the flat top of a cooker: **hob, hotplate** ●partially cook by boiling: **parboil** ●cook at just below boiling point: **simmer, poach, coddle** ●denoting a gentle heat for cooking: **slow** ●denoting a strong heat for cooking: **fast** ●immerse vegetables briefly in boiling water: **blanch** ●fry lightly and then stew: **braise** ●pour juice over cooking meat: **baste** ●liquid remaining after cooking: **liquor**

cooperation ●positive cooperation: **synergy** ●passive cooperation: **connivance** ●covert cooperation: **collusion** ●in close cooperation: **concerted, in concert**

copper ●*combining forms*: **chalc-, cupr-** ●*adjectives*: **cupric, cuprous** ●greenish surface colour of oxidized copper: **verdigris** ●prehistoric era in which copper and stone tools were used: **chalcolithic**

copy ●exact copy: **duplicate, facsimile, diplomatic copy** ●exact genetic copy: **clone** ●copy passed off as the original: **forgery** ●copy taken on paper laid over a raised design: **rubbing** ●copy made by drawing round a shaped piece of card etc.: **stencil** ●copying the work of another and claiming it as one's own: **plagiarism, piracy** ●copying of a rival product after detailed examination: **reverse engineering** ●text spoken for copying down: **dictation** ●original from which copies may be made: **master** ●issue of a stated number of copies: **limited edition** ●in three identical copies: **in triplicate** ●in four identical copies: **in quadruplicate** ●copying machine using stencils and fluid ink: **duplicator** ●copying process using dry powder: **xerography** ●colour copying process using diazonium: **diazo, dyeline**

copyright ●infringement of copyright: **piracy** ●out of copyright: **in the public domain**

coral ●ridge of coral in the sea: **reef** ●circular coral reef or group of islands: **atoll**

cord ●cord holding a whistle etc.: **lanyard** ●cord round a Scout's neckerchief: **woggle**

cork ●spiral device for extracting corks: **corkscrew**

corn ●hand mill for grinding corn: **quern** ●beat corn from the ears: **thresh**

cornea ●*combining form*: **kerato-** ●inflammation of the cornea: **keratitis** ●corneal surgery: **keratoplasty**

corpse ●*combining form*: **necr-** (*e.g.* necropolis, *literally 'city of the dead'*) ●embalmed corpse wrapped in bandages: **mummy** ●corpse used for medical research: **cadaver** ●corpse revived by witchcraft: **zombie** ●reanimated corpse supposed to drink blood from living persons: **vampire** ●corpse-like: **cadaverous** ●dissection of a corpse to establish the cause of death: **post-mortem, autopsy, necropsy** ●preservation of a corpse by injecting chemicals: **embalmment** ●deep-freezing of corpses: **cryonics** ●wrapping for a corpse: **shroud, winding-sheet** ●container for a corpse: **coffin** ●watch kept over a corpse before disposal: **wake** ●place for storing corpses: **mortuary, morgue** ●destruction of a corpse by fire: **cremation** ●fire for burning a corpse: **pyre** ●burial of a corpse: **interment** ●rotting of a corpse: **decomposition** ●fear of corpses: **necrophobia** ●sexual intercourse with corpses: **necrophilia** ●dig up a corpse: **exhume** ●cut up a cadaver for internal study: **dissect** ●denoting a corpse that has not decomposed: **incorrupt**

correct ●*combining form*: ortho- ●conventionally correct: **orthodox** ●correctable: **corrigible**

corset ●light elastic corset: **foundation garment, girdle, roll-on**

cosmetics ●cosmetic improving facial skin: **face mask, face pack** ●cosmetic making the skin firm and smooth: **toner** ●cosmetic removing dead skin cells: **exfoliant** ●cosmetic used for outlines: **liner** ●eyelash cosmetic: **mascara** ●cosmetic giving a warm colour to the cheeks: **blusher** ●red cosmetic: **rouge** ●thin stick of cosmetic: **pencil** ●flesh-toned stick to cover blemishes: **concealer** ●cosmetic applied by a rotating ball: **roll-on** ●fine brush for applying cosmetics: **wand** ●small case containing cosmetics and a mirror: **compact, vanity case** ●cosmetic treatment of the hands: **manicure** ●cosmetic treatment of the feet: **pedicure** ●actors' make-up: **greasepaint** ●testing of cosmetics on rabbits: **Draize testing**

cosmology ●theory that the universe began with an explosion of dense matter: **big bang theory** ●theory that the universe has always maintained an average density: **steady state theory** ▸*see also* **creation**

Cossack ●Cossack commander: **hetman** ●squatting Cossack dance: **kazachoc**

cost ●costs of materials and manufacture, excluding overheads: **prime cost** ●cost of producing one further item: **marginal cost** ●general running costs: **overheads** ●involving acceptable costs: **economic, economical** ●denoting an asset or activity that earns back its original cost: **self-liquidating** ●pay part of the cost: **subsidize** ●progressive write-off of an asset's purchase price: **amortization**

cotton ●cotton seed capsule: **boll** ●cotton-separating machine: **gin** ▸*see also* **fabric**

cough ●*adjective*: **tussive** ●repeated coughing interspersed with rasping gasps: **whooping cough** ●coughed-up mixture of saliva and mucus: **sputum** ●medicine for coughs: **expectorant**

council ●*adjective*: **conciliar** ●council of cardinals: **consistory**

count ●population count: **census** ●counting device with beads on wires: **abacus**

counterpoint ●*adjective*: **contrapuntal** ●counterpoint sung above a melody: **descant**

country ●*adjectives*: **rural, rustic, pastoral, bucolic** ●person coming to live in a foreign country: **immigrant** ●person leaving his or her country: **emigrant** ●person leaving his or her country to escape war, persecution, etc.: **refugee** ●person living outside his native country: **expatriate** ●uncritical loyalty to one's country: **chauvinism**

county ●administrative capital of a county: **county town** ●sovereign's representative in a county: **Lord Lieutenant** ●chief executive of the Crown in a county: **sherriff**

court martial ●barrister advising this: **judge advocate** ●official controlling army and RAF courts martial: **Judge Advocate General**

courtroom ●courtroom section for judges or magistrates: **bench** ●section for the jury or a witness: **box** ●section for the accused: **dock** ●area for the lawyers and court officials: **well** ▸*see also* **lawcourt**

cow ●male cow: **bull** ●castrated bull: **bullock, ox** (*pl.* oxen), **steer** ●young cow: **calf** ●young female cow: **heifer** ●cow's mammary gland: **udder** ●cow's partly digested food:

cud ●fine parchment made from calf-skin: **vellum** ▸*see also* **cattle**

cowardice ●symbol of cowardice: **white feather**

cowboy ●South American cowboy: **gaucho** ●cowboy's leather overtrousers: **chaparajos, chaps** ●cowboys' exhibition of skills: **rodeo** ●cowboy film or story: **western**

crab ●male crab: **cock** ●female crab: **hen** ●astrological term: **cancer**

crack ●full of fine cracks: **crazed** ●small cracks on an old painting's surface: **craquelure**

craftsman ●barrelmaker: **cooper** ●craftsman in brass: **brazier** ●skilled furniture maker: **cabinetmaker** ●craftsman in gold: **goldsmith** ●person shoeing horses: **blacksmith, farrier** ●person working iron by hand: **blacksmith** ●mender of shoes: **cobbler** ●craftsman in silver: **silversmith** ●skilled carver and builder in stone: **mason, stonemason** ●maker of stringed instruments: **luthier, lutist** ●woodworker making stairs, doors, etc.: **joiner**

crane ●crane with a movable pivoted arm: **derrick** ●crane moving on rails: **travelling crane** ●crane's projecting arm: **jib** ●movable beam supporting a crane: **gantry**

cream ●thin cream with little milk fat: **single cream** ●thick cream with much milk fat: **double cream** ●thick cream obtained by heating milk: **clotted cream** ●double cream with added yoghurt: **crème fraiche** ●cream of liquidized fruit or vegetables: **purée**

creation ●*combining form*: **-geny** (*e.g.* orogeny) ●creation of matter throughout time: **continuous creation** ▸*see also* **cosmology**

credit ●estimate of a person's creditworthiness: **credit rating** ●positive information on a person's creditworthiness: **white information** ●company assembling data for credit ratings: **credit agency, credit reference agency**

crescent ●crescent-shaped: **lunate**

cricket[1] ●wooden cross-piece connecting a pair of stumps: **bail** ●stick supporting the bails: **stump** ●set of bails and stumps: **wicket** ●pitch between the two wickets: **wicket** ●line where the batsmen stands: **crease, popping crease** ●lines between which the ball must be delivered: **return creases** ●spell at batting: **innings** ●lengthy innings by a pair of batsmen: **stand** ●batsman's vigorous stroke: **drive** ●batsman's stroke sending the ball to the side: **pull** ●batsman's stroke slightly deflecting the ball: **snick** ●glancing stroke giving the ball spin: **slice** ●hit gaining one run: **single** ●batsman's innings score of zero: **duck** ●batsman sent in at the end of a day's play: **nightwatchman** ●sequence of six balls bowled from one end of the pitch: **over** ●revolving motion imparted to the ball: **spin** ●bowled ball's striking the ground: **pitch** ●distance from the batsman at which the ball pitches: **length** ●denoting a ball pitching too close to the batsman: **overpitched** ●denoting a ball pitching close to the bowler: **short** ●sideways deviation of a bowled ball: **swing** ●batsman's obstruction of the ball: **leg before wicket** ●side of the field behind the batsman: **leg side** ●side of the field facing the batsman: **off side** ●field furthest from the batsman: **outfield** ●denoting a fielding position there: **deep** ●denoting a fielding position opposite the stumps: **square** ●area around the wicket: **infield** ●fielder placed immediately behind the wicket of the batsman receiving the bowling: **wicketkeeper** ●denoting fielding positions near the batsman: **short** ●denoting fielding positions very near the batsman: **silly** ●fielding positions behind the batsman: **slips** ●scoring unit: **run** ●run awarded for a ball not struck: **bye, extra** ●run awarded for a ball striking the batsman: **leg bye** ●run awarded for a ball bowled out of the batsman's reach: **wide** ●over in which no runs are scored: **maiden over** ●ball reaching the batsman without touching the ground: **full toss, full pitch** ●ball pitching immediately under the bat: **yorker** ●ball illegally delivered: **no-ball** ●bowler's style of action: **delivery** ●trophy competed for annually by England and Australia: **the Ashes** ●match that is part of a series between two national teams: **test match, Test** ●large white screen placed behind the bowler: **sight screen** ●netted strip of ground for practice: **net** ●cricketer's genital shield: **box** ●end a team's innings: **dismiss** ●team's second innings played immediately after its first: **follow-on** ●announce an early close to an innings: **declare** ●end of a day's play: **close** ●denoting a game between major county sides: **first class** ●denoting a county not involved in these games: **minor**

cricket² ●shrill sound made by a cricket's rubbing its legs together: **stridulation**

crime ●adjective: **nefarious** ●minor juvenile crime: **delinquency** ●crime triable by a magistrate: **summary offence** ●professional negligence or dishonesty: **malpractice** ●crime motivated by sexual jealousy: **crime passionnel** (*pl.* crimes passionnels) ●denoting a crime punishable by death: **capital** ●facts and circumstances constituting a crime: **corpus delicti** ●involvement in crime: **complicity** ●deliberate hindrance of the police: **obstruction** ●police re-enactment of a crime: **reconstruction** ●establish complicity:

implicate ●bribe someone to commit an unlawful act: **suborn** ●person or organization acting as a cover for illegal activities: **front** ●person who encourages others to commit crimes in order to denounce them: **agent provocateur** (*pl.* agents provocateurs) ●inducement to commit a crime offered by an agent provocateur: **entrapment** ●incriminating item added to someone's belongings: **plant** ●intention to commit a crime: **malice aforethought, mens rea** ●charge someone with a serious crime: **indict** ●person responsible for a crime: **culprit** ●defence showing one was elsewhere when the crime was committed: **alibi** ●facts justifying or excusing a crime: **extenuation** ●police coordination office for investigation of a major crime: **incident room** ●householders' vigilance to discourage crime: **neighbourhood watch** ●study of crime: **criminology** ●civil wrongdoing, other than breach of contract: **tort** ●severe response to undesirable activity: **crackdown**

criminal ●criminal beneath the age of legal responsibility: **juvenile delinquent** ●criminal aged 14–17: **young offender** ●criminal aged 18–20: **young adult offender** ●violent criminal: **thug** ●violent troublemaker: **hoodlum, hooligan** ●criminal who betrays other criminals to the police: **grass, informer** ●convicted criminal who reoffends: **recidivist** ●group of criminals: **family, gang, ring** ●trader in stolen goods: **fence** ●criminal's apparently innocent activities: **cover, front** ●criminal's admission of guilt: **confession** ●criminal's evidence against his accomplices: **Queen's** (*or* **King's**) **evidence** ●criminal's assistant: **accomplice** ●person assisting a criminal in planning or committing a crime: **accessory before the fact** ●person assisting a criminal after the crime has been committed: **accessory**

after the fact ●criminal act: **actus reus** ●criminal intent: **mens rea** ● in the criminal act: **in flagrante delicto** ●criminal cooperation: **collusion, connivance, conspiracy** ●betray a criminal to the authorities: **denounce** ● make someone appear to be a criminal: **incriminate** ● group assembled for identification of a suspect: **identity parade** ●science used in criminal investigations: **forensics** ●centre housing young offenders: **community home** ● electronic monitoring of convicted criminals: **electronic tagging** ●picture of a wanted criminal composed of standard elements: **identikit™** ● unpaid social work required of a convicted offender: **community service** ●scientific study of criminals: **criminology** ▸*see also* **execution, punishment**

criticism ●considered critical assessment: **evaluation** ●published critical assessment: **review** ●literary analysis regarding a text as having no fixed meaning: **deconstruction, poststructuralism** ●humorous criticism of public mores: **satire** ●witheringly critical: **scathing** ●criticize severely: **lambaste, pan, rebuke** ●criticize with the benefit of hindsight: **second-guess** ●person or institution held to be above criticism: **sacred cow**

crop ●crop grown for sale: **cash crop** ●crop grown to protect or enrich the soil: **cover crop** ●crop grown to attract pests from another crop: **trap crop** ●crop grown between main crops: **catch crop** ●crop grown in the spaces between another crop: **intercrop** ●crop grown for sale: **cash crop** ●denoting an unharvested crop: **standing** ●cultivation of a single crop throughout a particular area: **monoculture** ●successive cultivation of different crops: **crop rotation** ●area of growing crops flattened to form a pattern: **crop circle** ●spray or powder a crop: **dress** ●aerial powdering of crops: **crop dusting** ●substance added to the soil to improve cropping: **fertilizer** ●science of crop production: **agronomy**

croquet ●croquet stick: **hammer** ●small metal arch: **hoop** ●winning post: **peg** ●strike another player's ball with one's own: **roquet** ●stroke driving two touching balls in different directions: **split shot** ●send another player's ball through a hoop: **peel** ●ball that has passed all the hoops: **rover** ●win the game by hitting the peg: **peg out**

cross ●*combining form*: **cruci-** ●cross with a loop at the top: **ankh** ●cross bearing a figure of Christ: **crucifix** ●cross with equal arms: **Greek cross** ●cross with the lowest arm longer: **Latin cross** ●Latin cross with the arms in a circle: **Celtic cross** ●Greek cross with each arm continued at a right angle: **fylfot, swastika** ●X-shaped cross: **St Andrew's cross** ●T-shaped cross: **St Anthony's cross, tau cross** ●cross-shaped: **cruciform** ●person carrying a processional cross: **crucifer**

crossbow ●arrow for a crossbow: **bolt**

crossword puzzle ●blank space to be filled with a letter: **light** ●hint of the word required: **clue**

crow ●*adjective*: **corvine**

crowd ●disorderly crowd: **melee, mob, rabble** ●crowd-control device ejecting a powerful jet of water: **water cannon** ●irritant gases used in crowd control: **tear gas, CS gas**

crown ●*adjective*: **coronal** ●nobleman's crown: **coronet** ●pope's crown: **tiara** ●jewelled headband: **diadem, tiara**

cruel ●wantonly cruel: **vicious** ●taking pleasure in cruelty: **sadistic**

cry •high-pitched complaining cry: **whine** •soft complaining cry: **whimper** •cry made on discovery: **eureka**

crystal •crystal that is the mirror image of another: **enantiomorph**

Cuba •slow Cuban dance: **habanera**

cucumber •small pickling cucumber: **gherkin**

culture •person having no cultural interests: **philistine** •highly intelligent and cultured: **sophisticated** •derived from, or knowing about, many cultures: **cosmopolitan** •culture at odds with established norms: **counterculture, subculture** •study of Western culture: **humanities** •study of different cultures: **ethnology** •study of human culture: **anthropology** •study of ancient cultures: **archaeology** •amalgamation of different cultures: **syncretism** •cultural coexistence: **pluralism** •acquisition of a culture: **inculturation** •cultural ambience evoked by the decor etc. of a restaurant, pub, or amusement park: **theme**

cup •small coffee cup: **demitasse** •large two-handled cup passed round at feasts: **loving cup** •eucharistic cup: **chalice** •cup used for reservation of the Sacrament: **ciborium** •cup used by Christ at the Last Supper: **Holy Grail, sangrail**

cupboard •cupboard to hang clothes in: **wardrobe** •heated cupboard for drying clothes: **airing cupboard** •lockable cupboard: **locker** •strong locked cupboard for valuables: **safe**

Cupid •*Greek name*: **Eros**

cure •*adjectives*: **sanative, therapeutic**

curling •mark aimed at: **tee** •session of play in one direction: **end** •captain of a curling team: **skip**

currency •currencies of other countries: **foreign exchange** •value of currency as stated upon it: **face value, nominal value** •value of a currency in terms of the goods it can buy: **purchasing power** •former system defining a currency's value in terms of gold: **gold standard** •nominal parity of one currency with another: **exchange rate** •value of one currency in terms of another: **valuta** •denoting a currency with freely changing value: **floating** •denoting currency with a stable value: **hard** •alter a currency's international value: **revalue, devalue** •pound's value for European Union agriculture purchases: **green pound**

current •air or water current behind a propeller or jet engine: **slipstream** •subsurface current running contrary to the surface current: **undercurrent, undertow**

curry •mild curry marinaded in yoghurt: **korma** •hot spicy curry: **madras** •very hot spicy curry: **vindaloo** •dried fish served with curries: **Bombay duck**

curtain •border concealing curtain fittings: **pelmet** •curtain hung in a drooping curve: **swag**

curve •*adjective*: **sinuous** •curve formed by a rope suspended at both ends: **catenary** •part of a curve: **arc** •curving inwards: **concave** •curving outwards: **convex**

cushion •church kneeling cushion: **hassock, kneeler** •cushion to be placed at random: **scatter cushion** •substance for stuffing cushions: **kapok**

custard •custard of egg, sugar, milk, and flour: **crème pâtissière** •crème pâtissière with ground almonds: **frangipane**

custom •established custom: **institution, usage** •traditional customs of a community: **folklore** ●forbidden by social custom: **taboo**

customer ●regular customer: **patron** ●made to a customer's specifications: **bespoke, custom-built**

customs ●customs permit for import of a motor vehicle: **carnet** ●customs charge on imported goods: **duty** ●customs certificate for duty paid: **docket** ●customs form permitting export of goods or removal from a bonded warehouse: **shipping bill** ●route through customs for those with nothing to declare: **green channel** ●route through customs for those with items to declare: **red channel** ●group of states allowing free trade between themselves: **customs union** ●evasion of customs controls: **smuggling**

cut ●*combining forms for surgical terms*: **-tome** (*e.g.* craniotome), **-tomy** (*e.g.* lobotomy) ●make surface cuts: **scarify** ●cut deeply: **lacerate** ●cut up for study: **dissect** ●cut with a sweeping stroke: **slash** ●part by cutting: **sever** ●cut off ends or edges: **crop, pare, prune, trim** ●cut into zigzag edges: **pink** ●very hot cutting flame: **thermic lance** ▸*see also* **surgical cutting**

cutlery ●box for a set of cutlery: **canteen**

cylinder ●cylinder on which thread etc. is wound: **reel, spool** ●hollow metal cylinder supporting a bridge: **pontoon**

Cyprus ●*adjective*: **Cypriot** ●political union of Cyprus with Greece: **enosis**

D d

dagger ●small slim dagger: **poniard** ●short tapering dagger: **stiletto** ●dagger's handle: **hilt**

dam ●low dam in a river: **weir** ●adjustable dam: **barrage**

damage ●deliberate damage: **sabotage, vandalism** ●damage severely: **mangle** ●damage beyond the possibility of repair: **write off**

damp ●cold and damp: **dank** ●ground moisture absorbed into a wall: **rising damp**

dance ●art dancing that ignores the rules of classical ballet: **modern dance** ●sailor's dance: **hornpipe** ●traditional English dance: **country dance** ●traditional English outdoor dance: **morris dance** ●afternoon dance at which tea is served: **tea dance** ●energetic street dance: **break-dance** ●lively dance in triple time: **jig** ●slow 18th-century dance: **minuet** ●interweaving country dance: **hay** ●country dance for four couples: **square dance** ●solo dance: **pas seul** ●dance for two people: **pas de deux** ●dance with voluntary exchange of partners: **excuse-me** ●dance performed in a long line, one behind the other: **conga** ●erotic dancing to popular music: **go-go dancing** ●erotic oriental dance performed by women: **belly dance** ●synchronized ballroom dancing: **sequence dancing** ●ballroom dance with slow and quick steps: **foxtrot** ●ballroom dance with partners side-by-side: **veleta** ●ballroom dance with pronounced hip movements: **rumba** ●ballroom dance in triple time: **waltz** ●fast foxtrot: **quickstep** ●fast Bohemian dance: **polka** ●lively Brazilian dance:

samba ●squatting Cossack dance: **kazachoc** ●Country and Western dancing performed in a row: **line dancing** ●slow Cuban dance: **habanera** ●French high-kicking dance: **cancan** ●Greek folk dance performed in a line: **syrtaki** ●swaying Hawaiian dance: **hula hula** ●fast Hungarian dance: **csardas** ●dramatic dance of southern India: **Kathakali** ●Italian whirling dance: **tarantella** ●Italian and Spanish leaping dance: **saltarello** ●lively Polish dance: **mazurka** ●vigorous Scottish dance: **Highland fling** ●fast Scottish dance: **reel** ●slow Scottish dance: **strathspey** ●South American dance music with elements of jazz and rock: **salsa** ●fast South American dance: **paso doble** ●lively South American dance: **tango** ●lively Spanish dance: **bolero** ●Spanish solo dance: **cachucha** ●Spanish courtship dance: **fandango** ●Spanish dance with castanets: **flamenco** ●West Indian backward-bending dance: **limbo** ●dance about excitedly: **cavort** ●series of steps for a dance: **choreography, figure** ●informal gathering for country dancing: **barn dance** ●person who announces the steps in a barn dance: **caller** ●group of dancers performing together: **ensemble** ●number of participants needed for a square or country dance: **set** ●public dance hall: **palais, palais de danse** ▶*see also* **ballet**

dancer ●dancer's tights: **maillot** ●tubular garment covering a rehearsing dancer's legs: **leg warmers** ●dancer's leap or sitting posture with one leg forward and one back, both at right angles to the trunk: **splits** ▸*see also* **ballet**

Dane ●part of England under Danish rule: **Danelaw** ●tax levied by the Anglo-Saxons to repel the Danes: **Danegeld**

danger ●serious danger: **peril** ●hidden danger: **pitfall** ●danger inherent in a job: **occupational hazard** ●remove from a dangerous place: **evacuate** ●person so moved: **evacuee**

Dante ●*adjectives*: Dantean, Dantesque

dark ●shining in the dark: **luminous** ●night that is never completely dark: **white night**

darts ●tail of a dart: **flight** ●hit on a part of the board where scores are doubled: **double** ●group of games counting as a unit towards a match: **set** ●line behind which the thrower stands: **hockey, oche**

data ●denoting data gathered over a long time: **longitudinal** ●grid for data display: **matrix** ▸*see also* **electronic data**

date¹ ●give a later date to: **post-date** ●latest possible date: **terminus ante quem** ●earliest possible date: **terminus a quo, terminus post quem** ●out of date: **obsolete, passé** ●going out of date: **obsolescent** ●with no date set: **sine die**

date² ●date with a person one has not met before: **blind date**

dating ●dating of timber structures from the tree rings they contain: **dendrochronology** ●dating of geological eras: **chronostratigraphy, geochronology** ●dating of objects from carbon-14 decay: **carbon dating, radiocarbon dating** ●dating system derived from the birth of Christ: **Christian Era, Common Era** ●mistaken dating: **parachronism**

daughter ●*adjective*: filial

dawn ●*adjective*: auroral

day ●*adjective*: diurnal ●day before: **eve** ●day in which hours of daylight and darkness are equal: **equinox** ●longest or shortest day: **solstice** ●important day: **red-letter day** ●first day of the Roman month: **calends** ●each day: **per diem** ●period of morning twilight: **dawn** ●part of the day given over to work: **working day** ●part of the day when many are commuting: **drive time** ●period of evening twilight: **dusk** ●happening in a daily cycle: **circadian** ●process by which the equinoxes occur slightly earlier each year: **precession**

daylight ●right to enjoy daylight in one's windows, unobstructed by subsequent building: **ancient lights**

deacon ●*adjective*: diaconal ●office of deacon: **diaconate** ●deacon's over-vestment: **dalmatic**

dead end ●deadlock in argument or discussion: **impasse, stalemate** ●road with no exit at its far end: **cul-de-sac**

deaf ●progressive deafness due to bone growth in the ear: **otosclerosis** ●surgical opening made in the inner ear to relieve deafness: **fenestration** ●teaching the deaf to communicate by lip-reading and speech: **oralism**

dealer ●dealer in ship's supplies: **chandler** ●dealer in candles: **chandler** ●dealer in cheap and shoddy goods: **cheapjack**

dean ●*adjective*: decanal ●dean's residence: **deanery**

death ●*combining form*: mori-, necr-, -thanasia ●death viewed as a statistical occurrence: **fatality, mortality** ●number of deaths caused by an event: **toll** ●causing death: **fatal, lethal, mortal, terminal** ●connected with death: **macabre** ●bound to die: **mortal** ●die before another does: **predecease** ●Christian ceremonies over a dying person: **last rites** ●gurgling of dying person: **death rattle** ●struggling of a dying person: **throes** ●at the point of death: **moribund, in extremis** ●denoting a condition that will end in death: **terminal** ●revive someone apparently dead: **resuscitate** ●experience at the brink of death: **near-death experience** ●ghostly image of a person seen near their time of death: **wraith** ●death inflicted to end incurable suffering: **euthanasia** ●death-blow: **coup de grâce** (*pl.* coups de grace) ●unexplained death of a sleeping baby: **cot death, sudden infant death syndrome** ●death of body tissue: **gangrene, mortification, necrosis** ●stiffness of joints after death: **rigor mortis** ●decaying flesh of a dead animal: **carrion** ●cessation of vital functions as proof of death: **clinical death** ●bell rung at death: **knell** ●date of death: **obit** ●plaster cast of a dead person's face: **death mask** ●newspaper announcement of a person's death: **obituary** ●government office where deaths are recorded: **register office** ●insurance sum payable at death: **reversion** ●total money and property owned by a dead person: **estate** ●medical examination to find the cause of a person's death: **post-mortem** ●specialist conducting this examination: **pathologist** ●official statement of cause, date, and place of death: **death certificate** ●official investigating the cause of a person's death: **coroner** ●the inquiry a coroner conducts: **inquest** ●service for the dead: **funeral, requiem** ●lament for the dead: **dirge, threnody** ●poem lamenting the dead: **elegy** ●recently dead: **deceased** ●show sorrow at a death: **mourn** ●reminder of death's inevitability: **memento mori** ●picture of Death leading all to the grave: **dance of death, danse macabre** ●person over-interested in death: **ghoul**

●ratio of deaths to living population: **death rate** ●number of deaths from a particular cause: **mortality rate** ●equivalence of birth and death rates: **zero population growth** ●after-death: **posthumous** ●movement of the soul to a different body after death: **transmigration** ●the use of magic to summon up the dead: **necromancy** ●supposed communication with the dead by mediums: **spiritualism** ●meeting of persons wishing to contact the dead by spiritualism: **seance** ●person returning from the dead: **revenant** ●psychological urge to self-destruction: **death instinct** ●life after death: **afterlife, the other world** ●rebirth of the soul in a new body: **reincarnation** ●never-dying: **immortal** ●all dead: **extinct** ●study of death and dying: **thanatology** ●Christian day for general commemoration of the dead: **All Souls' Day** ▸ *see also* **funeral**

debate ●advantage in debate: **high ground** ●subject to debate: **moot** ●question on procedure: **point of order** ●debater's acknowledgement of an opponent's point: **touché** ●motion to end a debate: **closure**

debt ●debt not legally recoverable: **debt of honour** ●debt overdue for repayment: **arrears** ●debt repayable soon: **floating debt** ●debt with a distant, or no, repayment date: **funded debt** ●money owed by a company: **account payable, liability** ●money owed to a company: **accounts receivable** ●total owed by a state: **national debt** ●debt of gratitude: **obligation** ●denoting a debt not yet repaid: **outstanding** ●denoting a debt repayable on demand: **unfunded** ●denoting a debt impossible to recover: **bad** ●denoting a debt whose recovery is unlikely: **doubtful** ●legal permission for late repayment: **moratorium** ●debtor's asset forfeited if repayment is not achieved: **pledge, security**

• money paid to service a debt: **interest** • (of) a person who cannot pay off his debts: **bankrupt, embarrassed, insolvent** • failure to repay a debt: **default** • demand repayment of a debt: **dun** • payment of a debt: **liquidation, redemption, satisfaction** • payment of a debt by instalments: **amortization** • company's issue of shares to pay off debts: **recapitalization** • money raised for gradual repayment of a debt: **sinking fund** • further time granted to repay a debt: **indulgence, roll-over** • easing a debtor's position by modifying the repayment demands: **restructuring** • cancellation of a debt: **remission** • abandon attempts to recover a debt: **write off** • free of debt: **unencumbered, ungeared** • seizure of a debtor's goods: **attachment, distraint, distress, execution, sequestration** • court order seizing a debtor's assets: **Mareva injunction** • right to hold these until the debt is paid: **lien** • seizure of a debtor's money or wages: **garnishment, attachment of earnings** • person appointed to dispose of the assets of an insolvent person or business: **administrator** • agree to release a debtor for a smaller payment: **compound** • terminate gas etc. supply until bills are paid: **disconnect** • potential indebtedness through business commitments: **exposure** • potential indebtedness through falling values of mortgaged property: **negative equity** • ratio of corporate debt to share value: **gearing, leverage** • assessment of a person or firm's likelihood of paying its debts: **credit rating, creditworthiness** • organization making such assessments: **credit reference agency** ▸ *see also* **loan**

decay • *combining form*: **sapr-** • decay of teeth or bones: **caries** • decay of a part of the body: **mortification, necrosis** • decayed organic matter in the soil: **humus** • plant living on decayed matter: **saprophyte** • decay slowly through neglect: **moulder**

deceive • easily deceived: **credulous, gullible** • intent to deceive: **mala fides** • deliberate deception for financial gain: **fraud** • instance of deliberate deception: **hoax** • deceptive behaviour: **false pretences** • deceptive appearance: **illusion** • deception effected by making a true statement seem like a deception: **double bluff** • ploy designed to conceal one's true intentions: **blind**

decision • ability to make one's own decisions: **free will** • not finally decided: **open** • denoting a decision supported by all present: **unanimous** • right to reject a decision made by others: **veto** • state of indecision: **quandary** • wavering indecision: **vacillation**

decline • moral or cultural decline: **decadence**

decompose • able to be decomposed by sunlight: **photodegradable** • able to be decomposed by bacteria: **biodegradable**

decoration • additional decoration: **trim** • decoration of thin strips of shiny metal foil: **tinsel** • decoration of plaited straw: **corn dolly** • hanging decoration turning in the air: **mobile** • decoration of a manuscript: **illumination** • carved or coloured decoration of shells: **scrimshaw** • decoration of wood or leather with a heated point: **pokerwork, pyrography** • cloth items decorating a room: **soft furnishings** • flags and streamers: **bunting** • crinkly paper for decorations: **crêpe paper** • decorative lights: **illuminations** • decorative strip of cloth hung over a window etc.: **valance** • decorative design of intertwining branches etc.: **arabesque** • denoting metal inlaid with gold or silver: **damascened** ●gelatinous solution used in interior decoration: **size** ●merely decorative: **cosmetic**

decrease ●decrease in value: **depreciation** ●decrease the apparent importance of: **downplay, downrate**

deduction ●deduction from wages ordered by a lawcourt: **garnishment, attachment of earnings** ●denoting a deduction derived from observation or experience: **a posteriori** ●denoting a deduction derived from theoretical concepts: **a priori**

deep ●*combining form*: **bath-** (*e.g.* bathyscaphe) ●region of especially deep sea: **trench** ●not deep: **shallow**

deer ●*adjective*: **cervine** ●female deer: **doe, hind** ●male deer: **buck, hart, stag** ●young deer: **fawn** ●deer's short tail: **scut** ●small tailless deer: **roe** ●male roe: **roebuck** ●small deer with a doglike bark: **muntjac** ●stag's branched horns: **antlers** ●antler's sharp point: **tine** ●soft skin covering a growing antler: **velvet** ●deer's annual period of sexual activity: **rut** ●produce offspring: **fawn** ●deer's track: **slot** ●deer's false hoof: **dewclaw** ●disembowel a deer: **gralloch** ●deer's entrails as food: **numbles** ●deer meat: **venison** ●leg and loin of venison: **haunch**

defeat ●defeat soundly: **trounce, vanquish** ●defeat and drive back: **rout** ●admit defeat: **concede**

defecation ●inability to control defecation: **incontinence** ●bedridden person's receptacle for urine and faeces: **bedpan**

defence ●defence of one's conduct: **apologia** ●defence of a theory: **apologetics** ●uncompromising defence of a position: **stand** ●defensive mound before a trench: **parapet** ●defensive mound behind a trench: **parados**

deformity ●medical treatment of bone and muscle deformities: **ortho-**

paedics ●adjustment of tooth and jaw irregularities: **orthodontics**

degree ●bachelor's degree: **baccalaureate** ●degree next above bachelor in certain universities: **licentiate** ●doctor's degree: **doctorate** ●degree awarded to a candidate who was ill at the time of the examination: **aegrotat** ●denoting a degree conferred when the graduand is elsewhere: **in absentia**

delay ●*adjective*: **dilatory** ●delay by non-cooperation: **stonewall** ●delay by making lengthy speeches: **filibuster**

delusion ●visual delusion: **hallucination** ●delusions of being persecuted: **paranoia** ●delusions caused by alcoholism: **delirium tremens**

demand ●final demand, made with threats of sanctions: **ultimatum** ●when demand is low: **off-peak** ●failure to satisfy demand: **shortfall**

Demeter ●*Latin name*: **Ceres**

demolition ●completely destroy a building: **raze** ●structure of a gutted building: **shell** ●fragments of a demolished building: **rubble** ●heavy beam used to knock down walls: **battering ram**

demon ●*combining form*: **demono-** ●*adjective*: **demoniac, demoniacal, demonic** ●demon attending a witch: **familiar, familiar spirit** ●worship of demons: **demonolatry** ●control by a demon: **possession** ●expulsion of demons: **exorcism** ●study of demons: **demonology**

demonstration ●silent static demonstration: **vigil**

dentist ●dentist who corrects the position of teeth: **orthodontist** ●dentist dealing with the structures around the teeth: **periodontist** ●dentist's assistant who cleans teeth: **hygienist** ●dentist's small drill: **bur**

depart ●depart secretly or illegally: **abscond** ●departure from the normal or expected: **aberration**

depression ●atmospheric depression: **cyclone** ●tiredness and depression occurring after a viral infection: **chronic fatigue syndrome** ●drug alleviating depression: **antidepressant**

depth ●*combining form*: **bathy-** ●instrument measuring the depth of seas or lakes: **bathymeter** ●manned chamber for deep-sea observations: **bathysphere**

deputy ●*combining forms*: **pro-** (*e.g.* proconsul), **vice-** (*e.g.* vice-president) ●person deputizing for another: **surrogate**

descent ●line of descent: **blood line, stock** ●step in a line of descent: **generation** ●denoting direct descent: **lineal** ●denoting descent by a parallel line: **collateral** ●denoting the male line of descent: **patrilineal** ●denoting the female line of descent: **matrilineal** ●person from whom one is descended: **ancestor, progenitor** ●one's descendants: **posterity, progeny** ●theory of universal descent from a single couple: **monogenesis, monogeny**

description ●precise and detailed description: **specification** ●short but thorough description: **profile** ●misrepresentation of complex ideas by oversimplified descriptions: **reductionism**

desert ●group of people travelling across a desert: **caravan** ●inn for these people: **caravanserai** ●desert place with water: **oasis** ●dust-laden desert wind: **simoom**

design ●engraved or incised design: **intaglio** ●design identifying a company's products: **logo**

designer ●designer of buildings: **architect** ●designer of fashion clothes: **couturier** ●designer of roads, bridges, etc.: **civil engineer**

desire ●desire another's property: **covet** ●gratify a base desire: **pander**

desk ●large desk for two facing persons: **partners' desk** ●denoting a desk with a sliding flexible cover: **rolltop**

despair ●despair at imagined lack of progress: **accidie, demotivation**

destruction ●covert destruction: **sabotage** ●destruction of revered objects or ideas: **iconoclasm** ●malicious or purposeless destruction: **vandalism** ●period of massive destruction: **apocalypse** ●destruction of all life: **biocide** ●destruction of a race: **genocide** ●total destruction: **eradication, extirpation, holocaust**

detail ●detail needing attention: **loose end** ●subtle detail: **minutiae, nicety, punctilio, quiddity, technicality** ●(over-)attentive to detail: **meticulous, punctilious, pedantic, pettifogging** ●in detail: **in extenso** ●give more detail: **elaborate**

detection ●device detecting moving objects by reflected radio waves: **radar** ●device detecting underwater objects by reflected sound pulses: **sonar**

detective ●detective employed by members of the public: **private detective, private investigator** ●follow and observe secretly: **shadow** ●systematic shadowing: **surveillance**

detergent ●denoting a biodegradable detergent: **soft** ●denoting a detergent operating by enzymes: **biological**

development ●steady and consistent development: **continuity** ●progressive development of living organisms over the centuries: **evolution** ●developing earlier than usual: **precocious** ●highly developed: **sophisticated**

device ●denoting a device seemingly capable of intelligent action: **smart** ●device performing a specific function within a larger apparatus: **unit**

devil ●*adjectives*: **diabolic, diabolical** ●devil's divided foot: **cloven hoof** ●worship of the devil: **diabolism, satanism** ●control by the devil: **possession**

diagram ●block diagram: **histogram** ●diagram laid out like a tree: **dendrogram** ●diagram showing relationships in a family: **family tree, genealogy, pedigree** ●diagram showing relationships between sets: **Venn diagram** ●diagram of a sequence of events: **flow chart**

dial ●denoting a dial with a moving pointer: **analogue** ●denoting a dial with a changing numerical display: **digital** ●pointer on an instrument dial: **needle**

dialect ●popular dialect: **argot, patois** ●dialect of a particular social class: **sociolect** ●study of dialects: **dialectology**

dialogue ●*adjective*: **dialogic**

diameter ●diameter of wire, knitting needles, and bullets: **gauge** ●inner diameter of a gun barrel: **bore, calibre, gauge**

diamond ●*adjective*: **diamantine** ●inferior diamond, used for cutting: **bort**

Diana ●*Greek name*: **Artemis**

diary ●electronic diary: **personal organizer** ●loose-leaf diary: **Filofax™, personal organizer** ●person keeping a diary: **diarist**

dictator ●*adjective*: **dictatorial** ●title of a German dictator: **führer** ●title of an Italian dictator: **duce** ●title of a Spanish dictator: **caudillo** ●small group exercising dictatorial powers: **junta**

dictionary ●*adjective*: **lexical** ●small dictionary at the back of a book: **glossary, vocabulary** ●dictionary of places: **gazetteer** ●dictionary of synonyms and antonyms: **thesaurus** ●dictionary in which the definition precedes the headword (as here): **reverse dictionary** ●person who compiles dictionaries: **lexicographer**

die ●cut out with a die: **stamp**

diet ●*adjectives*: **dietary, dietetic** ●major diet element: **macronutrient** ●organic compound essential to a balanced diet: **vitamin** ●denoting a vegetable wholefood diet: **macrobiotic** ●disease caused by absence of fresh fruit and vegetables from the diet: **scurvy** ●study of diets and nutrition: **dietetics, nutrition** ●postulated nutritional requirement: **recommended dietary allowance** ●diet expert: **dietitian, nutritionist**

difference ●*adjective*: **differential** ●subtle difference: **nuance** ●amount of difference: **differential** ●difference in brightness in a picture: **contrast** ●tell the difference between: **differentiate**

different ●*combining forms*: **allo-** (*e.g.* allopathy), **hetero-, vari-** ●radically different from anything preceding: **novel** ●having many different colours: **motley, pied, variegated** ●including things of different types: **heterogeneous** ●group or area different from its surroundings: **enclave** ●cause to seem different: **differentiate**

difficult ●*combining form*: **dys-** (*e.g.* dyslexia) ●difficult question: **conundrum, poser** ●temporary difficulty due to mechanical failure: **technical hitch** ●in great difficulties: **in extremis** ●avoid a difficulty: **obviate** ●quick and innovative in overcoming difficulties: **resourceful**

dig ●dig out: **excavate** ●dig beneath: **undermine** ●dig up: **unearth** ●dig up a corpse: **exhume** ●spade-depth of soil: **spit** ●dig two spits deep: **double-dig**

digestion ●*adjective*: **peptic** ●having good digestion: **eupeptic** ●digestive passage through the body: **alimentary canal** ●part of this between stomach and anus: **intestine, gut** ●muscular movement of the alimentary canal: **peristalsis** ●build-up of gas in the alimentary canal: **flatulence** ●bodily organs of digestion: **digestive system**

dilemma ●inescapable dilemma: **catch-22, double bind**

dinner ●*adjective*: **prandial** ●after-dinner: **postprandial**

dinosaur ●dinosaur with a very long neck and tail: **diplodocus** ●dinosaur with large vertical plates on its back: **stegosaurus** ●dinosaur with short armlike front legs: **brachiosaurus** ●upright carnivorous dinosaur: **tyrannosaurus**

diocese ●*adjective*: **diocesan** ●bishop in charge of a diocese: **diocesan** ●diocesan assembly: **synod** ●Anglican parish's contribution to diocesan funds: **quota**

Dionysus ●*Latin name*: **Bacchus** ●female follower of Dionysus: **maenad** ●staff carried by Dionysus' followers: **thyrsus**

diplomacy ●state's senior diplomat resident in a foreign country: **ambassador** ●diplomat with full powers of decision: **plenipotentiary** ●diplomat on a special assignment: **emissary** ●ambassador's deputy: **chargé d'affaires** ●ambassador's assistant: **attaché** ●diplomatic representative: **envoy, minister** ●minister and staff: **legation** ●group of diplomats sent for a special purpose: **mission** ●diplomatic courier: **Queen's (*or* King's) Messenger** ●army officer serving at an embassy: **military attaché** ●Commonwealth embassy: **high commission** ●diplomat acceptable to the host country: **persona grata** (*pl.* personae gratae) ●diplomat not accept-

able to the host country: **persona non grata** (*pl.* personae non gratae) ●diplomat's spell of duty at a particular location: **posting, tour, tour of duty** ●diplomat's report: **dispatch** ●diplomat's residence: **embassy, legation** ●official letter between diplomats: **note** ●draft or amendment to a diplomatic document: **protocol** ●negotiations brokered by a diplomat travelling between two estranged parties: **shuttle diplomacy** ●rule of diplomatic procedure: **protocol** ●easing of diplomatic tension: **détente** ●pressure placed on another state by restrictions on trade or social interaction: **sanctions** ●deliberate risk-taking in international diplomacy: **adventurism, brinkmanship** ●diplomatic policy of seeking to regain lost territory: **revanchism** ●diplomatic policy of preventing another state's expansion: **containment** ●diplomatic policy of seeking control over other nations: **imperialism** ●diplomacy enforced by displays of military strength: **gunboat diplomacy, power politics, sabre-rattling** ●immunity to local law enjoyed by diplomats and their property: **extraterritoriality, extraterritorial rights** ●host government's order to a diplomat to leave: **expulsion** ●order a diplomat to return home: **recall**

direction ●*combining forms*: **-wards** (*e.g.* eastwards), **-ways** (*e.g.* sideways) ●designed to operate in a particular direction: **directional** ●change direction suddenly: **swerve, veer**

director ●director of a group of orchestral musicians: **conductor** ●director of a brass band: **bandmaster**

disability ●physical or mental disability: **handicap**

disagreement ●minor disagreement: **contretemps** (*pl.* same) ●prolonged and bitter disagreement: **feud,**

strife ●causing disagreement: **con-tentious, controversial, divisive** ●without disagreement: **unani-mously, nem. con.**

disappointing ●disappointing out-come: **anticlimax, bathos, damp squib**

disarmament ●total abandonment of a certain weapon: **zero option** ●denoting disarmament undertaken by some states only: **unilateral**

disaster ●large, sudden and violent disaster: **cataclysm** ●natural disas-ter: **act of God**

disc ●disc thrown by an athlete: **dis-cus** ●metal or plastic disc used in-stead of money: **token** ●disc used to store visual images: **videodisc**

discharge ●*combining forms*: -rrhoea (*e.g.* diarrhoea), -rrhagia (*e.g.* menorrhagia) ●vaginal discharge at the onset of labour or menstruation: **show** ●discharge of gas, radiation, or semen: **emission**

discipline ●strict disciplinarian: **martinet, stickler** ●person practis-ing severe self-discipline: **ascetic**

disc jockey ●radio disc jockey who is deliberately offensive or provoca-tive: **shock jock**

discontent ●cause political or emotional discontent: **destabilize**

discontinue ●discontinue tempor-arily: **put into abeyance** ●discon-tinue meetings of a parliament with-out dissolution: **prorogue**

discourage ●discouraging factor: **disincentive** ●numbing discourage-ment: **demotivation**

discovery ●method of discovery by trial and error: **heuristic** ●faculty of making fortunate discoveries: **seren-dipity** ●cry uttered on making a dis-covery: **eureka**

discrimination ●discrimination on grounds of age: **ageism** ●discrim-ination on grounds of social class:

classism ●discrimination on grounds of skin colour: **colour bar** ●discrimination against individuals: **victimization** ●discrimination against the overweight: **fattism** ●dis-crimination against those with physical disabilities: **ableism** ●dis-crimination on grounds of race: **ra-cism** ●discrimination on grounds of sex: **sexism** ●barrier to advance-ment tacitly imposed upon certain groups: **glass ceiling** ●discrimin-ation in favour of those thought to be unfairly treated: **positive discrimin-ation, reverse discrimination, af-firmative action** ●discrimination in favour of those who are thought to be superior: **elitism** ●freedom from dis-crimination: **equal opportunity**

discussion ●academic discussion: **symposium** ●public discussion of a topic: **ventilation** ●discussion involv-ing three or more persons at different sites using telecommunications: **tele-conference** ●strange object provok-ing discussion: **conversation piece** ●discuss without coming to the true point at issue: **beat about the bush**

disease ●*combining forms*: -itis (*e.g.* conjunctivitis), **nos(o)-**, patho-, -pathy (*e.g.* neuropathy), -osis (*e.g.* psychosis) ●*adjective*: **morbid** ●causes of a disease: **aetiology** ●germ causing a disease: **bacillus, pathogen** ●organism transmitting a disease from one host to another: **vec-tor** ●person or animal unaffected by a disease but transmitting it to others: **carrier** ●time between infection and appearance of symptoms: **latent period, incubation period** ●denot-ing a disease with no assignable cause: **non-specific** ●characteristic indicator of a disease: **symptom** ●de-noting a disease too mild to show clear symptoms: **subclinical** ●indica-tion of a disease: **symptom, stigma** ●disease indicated by a particular set of symptoms: **syndrome**   ●group of symptoms indicating a particular disease: **syndrome**   ●symptom accompanying a disease, but not caused by it: **epiphenomenon**   ●denoting a disease having recognizable symptoms: **clinical**   ●denoting a disease without recognizable symptoms: **occult**   ●symptom that only doctors can detect: **sign**   ●denoting the stage of a disease before symptoms appear: **preclinical**   ●disease identification from symptoms: **diagnosis**   ●temporary abatement of a disease: **remission**   ●patient's decline after a period of recovery: **relapse**   ●(sudden) recurrence of a disease: **flare, recrudescence**   ●regional outbreak of a disease: **epidemic**   ●denoting a disease breaking out throughout a country or the world: **pandemic**   ●denoting a highly infectious or harmful disease: **virulent**   ●denoting a disease expected to end in death: **terminal**   ●deadly disease spreading rapidly: **plague**   ●denoting a disease whose outbreaks must be reported: **notifiable**   ●denoting a disease regularly found at a place: **endemic**   ●denoting a disease passed from one generation to the next: **hereditary, vertical**   ●denoting a disease affecting all the body: **generalized**   ●disease's chief bodily location: **focus**   ●expected course of a disease: **prognosis**   ●turning point of a disease: **crisis**   ●secondary disease aggravating an existing one: **complication**   ●pass on a disease: **communicate, transmit**   ●person associating with someone having a contagious disease: **contact**   ●objects likely to carry infection: **fomites**   ●caused by or involving disease: **pathological**   ●study of causes and effects of disease: **pathology**   ●study of the causes of diseases: **aetiology**   ●study and treatment of the diseases of children: **paediatrics**   ●study of the incidence and control of diseases: **epidemiology**

●study of tissue changes caused by disease: **histopathology**   ●study of the treatment of disease: **therapeutics**   ●denoting a disease occurring in the course of another: **intercurrent**   ●denoting a disease characterized by brief but severe attacks: **acute**   ●denoting a long-lasting disease: **chronic**   ●denoting an uncured disease that currently shows no symptoms: **dormant**   ●denoting a disease starting in hospital: **nosocomial**   ●run-down state of a sufferer of a chronic disease: **cachexia**   ●denoting a disease passed on by physical contact: **contagious**   ●denoting a disease passed on through the environment: **infectious**   ●denoting a contagious or infectious disease: **communicable**   ●denoting a disease contracted through sexual activity: **venereal**   ●disease caused by poor diet: **deficiency disease**   ●denoting a disease causing little or no pain: **indolent**   ●denoting a disease causing progressive deterioration of organs or tissues: **degenerative**   ●denoting a disease growing steadily worse: **progressive**   ●denoting a disease caused by antibodies naturally produced by the sufferer to attack other germs: **autoimmune**   ●denoting a psychologically caused disease: **psychosomatic**   ●denoting a disease often or only found in a certain region or people: **endemic**   ●denoting a disease with no known external cause: **essential, idiopathic**   ●systematic description of diseases: **nosography**   ●scientific classification of diseases: **nosology**   ●preventing disease: **prophylactic**   ●study and practice of disease prevention: **preventive medicine**   ●substance developing bodily immunity to a disease: **vaccine**   ●test for the presence of a disease: **screen**   ●sudden attack of a disease: **seizure**   ●place or time of isolation for incomers thought to carry infectious diseases: **quarantine**   ●regain strength after a disease's cure: **conva-lesce** ●person with an obsessive fear of disease: **hypochondriac** ●suicide of a victim of an incurable disease, using lethal drugs supplied by a doctor for this purpose: **assisted suicide**

diseased ●*combining form*: **-otic** (*e.g.* neurotic)

disentangle ●disentangle by careful combing or unknotting: **tease out**

disgrace ●public disgrace: **igno-miny, obloquy, opprobrium** ●mark of disgrace: **stigma**

dish ●shallow stemmed dish: **coupe** ●large covered dish for serving soup: **tureen** ●small heatproof dish or casserole: **cocotte**

dishonest ●craftily dishonest: **slip-pery** ●dishonest person: **rogue, scoundrel** ●dishonest activities: **graft, sleaze, skulduggery**

disinfection ●disinfection by gases: **fumigation**

disintegration ●*combining form*: **-lysis** ●destruction of cells or tissues by their own enzymes: **autolysis**

dislike ●person or thing particularly disliked: **anathema, bête noire, pet hate**

dismiss ●dismiss with dishonour from the armed forces: **cashier** ●dismiss from a job: **terminate employ-ment**

disobey ●openly disobey: **flout** ●defiant disobedience: **insubordin-ation** ●incitement to disobey those in authority: **sedition**

disorder ●violent disorder: **may-hem**

display ●freestanding supermarket display: **gondola** ●display tank for underwater life: **aquarium** ●display tank for undersea life: **oceanarium** ●speaker's large pad of paper: **flip chart** ●display ostentatiously: **flaunt** ●self-dramatizing: **histrionic**

dispute ●protracted and complex dispute: **wrangle** ●confrontation to resolve a dispute: **showdown**

disrespect ●disrespectful to religion: **impious** ●rudely disrespectful: **insolent** ●disrespectful joking: **lev-ity**

dissolution ●*combining form*: **-lysis** (*e.g.* dialysis) ●able to be dissolved: **soluble**

distance ●*combining forms*: **apo-, tel(e)-** (*e.g.* television) ●distance round something: **circumference** ●distance one can see: **eyeshot, visi-bility** ●point where an orbiting object is furthest from the earth: **apogee** ●point where an orbiting object is furthest from the moon: **apolune** ●instrument measuring miles travelled: **milometer**

distant ●distant person or thing: **outlier** ●far distant spot: **ultima Thule** ●alleged ability to move distant objects: **telekinesis**

distinction ●subtle distinction: **ni-cety, nuance** ●over-subtle distinction: **hair-splitting, quibble**

disuse ●temporary disuse: **abey-ance**

ditch ●ditch dug for battlefield shelter: **trench** ●ditch round a castle etc.: **moat** ●hidden ditch separating gardens from parkland: **ha-ha**

diver ●diver's waterproof rubber suit: **drysuit** ●diver's permeable rubber suit: **wetsuit** ●diver not using a rubber suit: **skin diver** ●diver's compressed-air apparatus: **scuba, aqualung** ●diver's drowsy state from breathing air under pressure: **nitro-gen narcosis** ●diver's enclosed vessel for deep-sea observations: **bathy-scaphe, bathysphere** ●diver's air-filled open-bottomed chamber: **div-ing bell** ●diver's signal rope: **lifeline** ●controlled reduction of ambient pressure when a diver returns to the surface: **decompression** ●room for this: **decompression chamber** ●painful condition suffered by a diver after sudden reduction of ambient pressure: **the bends, caisson disease, decompression sickness**

divide ●*combining form*: **-sect** (*e.g.* dissect) ●tending to divide or be divided: **fissiparous** ●divide into two: **bisect** ●divide into mutually hostile units: **Balkanize**

divided ●*combining form*: **schizo-** (*e.g.* schizophrenia)

divination ●*combining form*: **-mancy** (*e.g.* rhabdomancy) ●Roman official interpreting omens: **augur, haruspex** ▸*see also* **fortune-telling**

division ●*combining form*: **schiz(o)-** ●radical division: **dichotomy** ●division into opposing factions: **polarization, schism**

divorce ●denoting a form of divorce requiring no apportionment of blame: **no-fault** ●spouse initiating a divorce action: **applicant** ●spouse against whom a divorce action is brought: **respondent** ●person cited in a divorce action as having committed adultery with the partner being sued: **co-respondent** ●court's provisional divorce ruling: **decree nisi** ●court's final divorce ruling: **decree absolute** ●divorced person: **divorcee** ●parental rights of divorcees: **custody** ●financial support to be given by a former spouse after divorce: **maintenance** ●state agency enforcing child maintenance payments: **Child Support Agency** ●court order enabling spouses to remain married but live apart: **judicial separation, legal separation**

dizziness ●causing dizziness: **vertiginous**

dock ●dock that can be emptied of water: **dry dock** ●submarine's covered dock: **pen** ●dock worker: **stevedore**

doctor ●*combining form*: **iatro-** ●doctor in charge of health services: **medical officer** ●doctor who administers anaesthetics: **anaesthetist** ●doctor specializing in childbirth: **obstetrician** ●doctor concentrating on diagnosis and medication: **physician** ●family doctor: **general practitioner** ●doctor qualified to perform operations: **surgeon** ●doctor treating animals: **vet, veterinary surgeon** ●junior hospital doctor: **house officer, houseman** ●hospital doctor assisting a consultant: **registrar** ●hospital doctor receiving specialist training: **senior registrar** ●doctor in charge of a particular branch of medicine at a hospital: **consultant** ●group of hospital doctors: **firm** ●doctor visiting his patients by plane: **flying doctor** ●doctor temporarily replacing another: **locum** ●person with some medical training, but not fully qualified: **paramedic** ●unqualified doctor: **quack, empiric** ●Indian or Muslim traditional doctor: **hakim** ●person believed by some peoples to have magical healing powers: **medicine man, shaman, witch doctor** ●doctor's room for seeing patients: **consulting room** ●doctor's tour of bedridden patients: **round** ●general practitioner's consulting rooms: **surgery** ●general practitioner's client base: **practice** ●this run by several doctors: **group practice** ●consulting rooms of a group practice: **health centre** ●general practitioner controlling his own budget: **fundholder** ●area list of doctors taking NHS patients: **panel** ●doctor's non-NHS clients: **private practice** ●resources available to a doctor: **armamentarium** ●doctor's device for hearing the chest organs: **stethoscope** ●doctor's device for seeing inside the ear: **auriscope, otoscope** ●doctor's device for inspectng the retina: **ophthalmoscope** ●doctor's small hammer for testing reflexes: **plexor, plessor** • shield against X-rays worn by doctors etc.: **apron** • projects undertaken by a doctor: **caseload** • doctor's ability to put patients at their ease: **bedside manner** • doctor's assessment of symptoms or treatment: **opinion** • doctor's seeking of a specialist's opinion: **referral** • doctor's order for a medicine to be made or issued: **prescription** • doctor's negligence or dishonesty: **malpractice** • oath (formerly) taken by trainee doctors: **Hippocratic oath** • come to a doctor for treatment: **present** • visit to a doctor: **consultation**

document • archived document: **muniment** • handwritten document: **manuscript** • document written entirely by its author: **holograph** • document signed by its author: **autograph** • standard document: **pro forma** • document on the World Wide Web: **web page** • identity documents: **papers** • document containing a sworn statement: **affidavit** • legal document: **instrument** • legal document authorizing entry and search of premises: **search warrant** • formal delivery of a legal document: **service** • mutual disclosure of documents by parties to a lawsuit: **discovery** • legal document recording ownership or a contract: **deed, memorandum** • appendix to a legal document: **schedule** • deed signed by one person only: **deed poll** • legal document disposing of one's assets after death: **will** • document promising a payment: **bond, promissory note** • document ordering payment: **draft** • document acknowledging payment: **receipt** • document entitling the holder to specified goods or services: **warrant** • document proving identity or qualifications: **credentials** • bank document underwriting specified loans on another bank to be taken out by the bearer: **letter of credit**

• document showing ownership of a property: **title deed** • summary of this: **abstract of title** • document recording the transfer of ownership of a property: **conveyance, grant** • document recording the waiving of a right or claim: **waiver** • document recording hours worked: **time sheet** • document showing a vehicle's ownership: **registration document, log book** • document giving the details of an insurance contract: **policy** • document listing transactions on a financial account: **statement** • state document permitting foreign travel: **passport** • document ensuring safe travel over a specified area: **safe conduct** • document authorizing specified police activity: **warrant** • official statement of cause, date, and place of death: **death certificate** • document used to supply evidence: **source** • denoting a document whose ownership can be changed: **negotiable** • subsidiary part of a document kept by its issuer: **counterfoil** • thin-paper copy of a document: **flimsy** • draft a document: **draw up, make out** • draft or amendment to a diplomatic document: **protocol** • produce a legal document in its final form: **engross** • exact wording of a document: **tenor** • presentation of a document for consideration: **submission** • document accompanying a letter: **enclosure** • set of documents on a particular topic: **dossier** • additional statement on a document, modifying its effect: **endorsement** • piece of stamped wax etc. authenticating a document: **seal** • document's abbreviated title: **short title** • abbreviated version of a document: **precis, summary** • place an official document on record: **enter, file** • obscure language of official documents: **officialese** • work involving documents: **paperwork** • counterfeit a document: **forge** • electronic transfer of documents: **fax**

doer ●*combining forms*: **-ee** (e.g. absentee), **-eer** (e.g. auctioneer), **-ent** (e.g. aperient), **-er** (e.g. writer), **-ete** (e.g. athlete), **-ist** (e.g. plagiarist), **-or** (e.g. actor), **-ress** (e.g. actress), **-rix** (e.g. executrix)

dog ●*combining form*: **cyno-** (e.g. cynopodous) ●*adjective*: **canine** ●female dog: **bitch** ●male dog: **dog** ●young dog: **pup, puppy** ●give birth to dogs: **pup, whelp** ●small pet dog: **lapdog** ●dog in poor condition or showing aggression: **cur** ●dog of uncertain breed: **mongrel** ●large police dog: **Alsatian, German shepherd dog** ●hunting dog: **hound** ●heavy hunting dog: **bloodhound, mastiff** ●small hound used to hunt hares: **beagle** ●set of hounds: **pack** ●person in charge of this: **master** ●dog trained to lead the blind: **guide dog** ●dog trained to assist the deaf: **hearing dog** ●dog trained to stand rigid when scenting game: **pointer, setter** ●dog trained to fetch shot game: **retriever, gun dog** ●dog formerly trained to rescue snowbound travellers: **St Bernard** ●competition for retrievers: **field trial** ●racing dog: **greyhound, whippet** ●wolflike North American wild dog: **coyote** ●Arctic sledge dog: **husky** ●Asian stray mongrel: **pyedog** ●Australian wild dog: **dingo** ●Russian wolfhound: **borzoi** ●Scottish sheepdog: **collie** ●competition for sheepdogs: **trials** ●very small large-eyed dog: **chihuahua** ●long dog with short legs: **dachshund** ●large black-and-tan dog: **Dobermann pinscher** ●front part of a dog's face: **muzzle** ●dog's inner eyelid: **haw** ●erectile hairs along a dog's back: **hackles** ●kind of fever suffered by dogs: **distemper** ●inflammation of a dog's ear: **canker** ●dog's disease causing madness and death: **rabies** ●dog's sense of smell: **nose** ●strap restraining a dog: **lead, leash** ●chain controlling a dog by neck pressure: **choke chain**

●guard preventing a dog biting: **muzzle** ●let a dog off the leash: **slip** ●dog's small shelter: **kennel** ●person in charge of trained dogs: **dog handler** ●details of a dog's previous competitive achievements: **form** ●establishment for boarding or breeding dogs: **kennels**

doing ●*combining form*: **-ent** (e.g. aperient)

doll ●soft black-faced doll with clothes and fuzzy hair: **golliwog**

domain ●*combining form*: **-dom** (e.g. fiefdom)

dome ●small dome: **cupola** ●pointed dome, bulging in the middle: **onion dome** ●dome surfaced by many small triangles: **geodesic dome** ●wall supporting a dome: **drum, tambour** ●corner support for a dome: **squinch** ●denoting a dome costructed from struts following the shortest route between two points on a sphere: **geodesic**

dominance ●political dominance: **hegemony**

done ●something done and unalterable: **fait accompli**

donkey ●male donkey: **jackass** ●female donkey: **jenny** ●offspring of a male donkey and female horse: **mule** ●offspring of a male horse and female donkey: **hinny**

door ●glazed outside door : **French window** ●denoting a door linking two rooms: **intercommunicating** ●access panel in a floor or ceiling: **trapdoor** ●peephole in a door: **judas, spyhole** ●angled slats on a door: **louvres** ●folding section of a door: **leaf** ●sloping board at the foot of an outside door: **weatherboard** ●handle etc. on a door: **door furniture** ●ornamental doorplate for the fingers: **fingerplate** ●door catch: **latch, snib** ●slotted metal plate as door-fastening: **hasp** ●strip sealing a door's edges against draughts etc.: **weatherstrip**

● support across the top of a door: **lintel** ● door's sidepost: **jamb** ● slab at the foot of a door: **sill, threshold** ● wall's side surface beside a window: **reveal** ● angled reveal: **embrasure** ● heavy object to keep a door open: **doorstop** ● attendant at the main door of a public building: **porter, concierge** ● go canvassing or selling from door to door: **doorstep**

door jamb ● inside face of a door jamb: **scuncheon** ● plate set into a door jamb to receive the bolt or lock when closed: **striker plate**

doorman ● doorman at an hotel or theatre: **commissionaire** ● doorman at a block of flats: **concierge** ● doorman at a college or large public building: **porter**

double ● *combining forms*: **di-** (*e.g.* dibasic), **diplo-, zygo-** (*e.g.* zygotic) ● double vision: **diplopia**

dough ● dough of durum wheat and water: **pasta** ● work dough: **knead** ● substance added to dough to make it rise: **leaven, yeast** ● become aerated by the leaven: **prove, rise** ● denoting dough that is heavy through having failed to rise: **sad** ● fermenting dough left over from a previous baking: **sourdough**

downwards ● *combining forms*: **cata-** (*e.g.* catadromous), **de-** (*e.g.* descend)

draft ● first draft: **rough, rough copy**

drain ● manhole for drain clearance: **inspection chamber** ● pit filled with hardcore: **soakaway** ● drain through: **leach**

drainage ● drainage ditch: **dyke** ● area drained by a particular river etc.: **catchment area**

drama ● drama abandoning realism to emphasize the irrationality of human life: **theatre of the absurd** ● drama exploring human behaviour

in extreme conditions: **theatre of cruelty** ▶ *see also* **play**

draughts ● remove an opponent's threatening piece: **huff**

drawing ● *combining form*: **-graphy** (*e.g.* photography) ● *adjective*: **graphic** ● drawing of things actually before the artist: **life drawing** ● satirical drawing: **caricature, cartoon** ● drawing showing exact detail and scale: **technical drawing** ● drawing showing enough detail to serve as an instruction: **working drawing** ● drawing of a mechanism showing its parts as if separated by an explosion: **exploded view** ● drawing of a mechanism with parts of its casing removed to show inner workings: **cutaway** ● drawing of an imagined slice taken through a building, mechanism etc.: **section, cross section** ● drawing of a vertical aspect of a building: **elevation** ● drawing of a floor layout of a building: **plan** ● expert in technical drawing: **draughtsman** ● drawing-based arts: **graphic arts** ● system of drawing to show depth: **perspective** ● perspective system using three axes 120° apart: **isometric system** ● system using lines converging at the horizon: **linear perspective** ● drawing of a three-dimensional object: **stereogram** ● preliminary version of a drawing: **draft, rough, sketch** ● drawing made absentmindedly: **doodle** ● drawings done for a publication: **artwork, graphics** ● line indicating an object's general shape: **outline** ● shade an area with close parallel lines: **hatch** ● hatching done in two directions: **crosshatching** ● shade an area by many small dots: **stipple** ● the representation of light and shade in a drawing: **chiaroscuro** ● denoting drawings made in sight of the items depicted: **life** ● denoting a drawing done without instruments: **freehand** ● instrument for drawing arcs: **com-**

pass, compasses, pair of compasses ●instrument for copying a drawing larger or smaller: **pantograph** ●case for unfolded drawings: **portfolio**

dream ●*combining form*: oneir(o)- ●*adjective*: **oneiric** ●unpleasant dream: **nightmare** ●erotic dream causing an involuntary ejaculation of semen: **wet dream** ●interpretation of dreams: **oneiromancy** ●denoting a dream consciously controlled by the dreamer: **lucid** ●dreamlike sequence of images: **phantasmagoria**

drill ●hand-cranked drill: **brace** ●sharp end of a drill: **bit** ●adjustable holder for the bit: **chuck**

drink ●drink taken to stimulate the appetite: **aperitif** ●carbonated water: **soda** ●concentrate of sweetened fruit juice: **squash** ●mixed drink: **cocktail** ●mixed drink with fruit juices etc.: **cup** ●drink made from the juice of pressed fruit: **crush** ●drink from sugar syrup: **julep** ●drink from fermented honey: **mead** ●drink from fermented pear-juice: **perry** ●drink of a seasoned raw egg: **prairie oyster** ●draught cider and lager: **snakebite** ●iced drink: **frappé, granita** ●drink with lemon or lime juice: **sour** ●soft drink sold in concentrated form: **cordial** ●weaken a drink by adding other liquid: **dilute** ●denoting an undiluted drink: **neat, straight** ●denoting a drink that is not effervescent: **still** ●strengthen a drink with alcohol: **fortify** ●add alcohol surreptitiously to a drink: **spike** ●warm and spice a drink: **mull** ●denoting a drink with low alcohol content: **light** ●denoting a drink that has lost its fizz: **flat** ●short drink taken after a long one: **chaser** ●drink taken to aid digestion: **digestif** ●strong sweet alcoholic drink taken after a meal: **liqueur** ●bedtime drink: **nightcap** ●prepared drink with magical or medi-

cinal powers: **potion** ●drink poured out in offering to a god: **libation** ●drink taken in honour of a person or thing: **toast** ●single act of drinking: **draught** ●set of drinks for all members of a group: **round** ●small mat for a drinking glass: **coaster** ●small stick for stirring drinks: **swizzle stick** ●drinking party: **symposium** ●nausea after heavy drinking: **hangover** ●denoting a region where alcoholic drinks cannot be purchased: **dry** ►*see also* **cocktail, spirits, wine**

drive ●drive animals: **herd, drove** ●drive out: **oust** ●person employed to drive a private or hired motor car: **chauffeur, driver**

driving licence ●cumulative value assigned to driving misdemeanours: **penalty points** ●official note of these on the licence: **endorsement**

drop ●cover with drops: **spatter** ●rain in fine drops: **drizzle**

drought ●area suffering severe drought and erosion: **dust bowl**

drug ●combining forms: **pharmaco-, narco-** ●drug inducing abortion: **abortifacient** ●drug taken by asthmatics to widen the bronchi: **bronchodilator** ●drug narrowing blood vessels: **vasoconstrictor** ●drug widening blood vessels: **vasodilator** ●calming drug: **depressant** ●drug relieving depression: **antidepressant** ●enlivening drug: **stimulant** ●drug preventing or moderating epileptic fits: **anticonvulsant** ●drug reducing fever: **antipyretic, febrifuge** ●drug slowing the heart and reducing blood pressure: **beta blocker** ●drug relieving itching: **antipruritic** ●drug improving the memory: **nootropic** ●drug that dulls the nerves: **neuroleptic** ●drug that eases pain: **analgesic** ●drug that prevents pain being felt: **anaesthetic** ●drug given to prevent rejection of a transplanted organ: **immuno-**

suppressor ●drug that sharpens the senses: **stimulant** ●drug stimulating sexual desire: **aphrodisiac** ●drug inducing sleep: **sedative** ●drug reducing tension or anxiety: **sedative, tranquillizer** ●drug increasing urination: **diuretic** ●drug decreasing urination: **antidiuretic** ●drug inducing vomiting: **emetic** ●drug preventing vomiting: **antiemetic** ●study of medical drugs and their action: **pharmacology** ●denoting a cheaper unbranded form of a proprietary drug: **generic** ●place where medicinal drugs are dispensed: **pharmacy** ●official list of medical drugs, with instructions for preparation and dosages: **pharmacopoeia** ●soporific or mood-changing drug: **narcotic** ●denoting a drug producing hallucinations: **psychedelic, hallucinogenic** ●drug affecting the user's mental state: **psychotropic** ●denoting an illegal or addictive drug: **dangerous** ●denoting a strong and addictive drug: **hard** ●denoting a drug not likely to cause addiction: **soft** ●denoting a fashionable artificial drug: **designer** ●denoting a drug that affects a person's mental state: **psychotropic** ●drug producing muscle contractions: **convulsant** ●drug-induced stupor: **narcosis** ●hormonal drug used by athletes to improve performance: **steroid** ●inject a drug directly into a vein: **mainline** ●drug-impregnated material attached to the skin for gradual absorption: **patch** ●solvent whose fumes are inhaled by drug abusers: **inhalant** ●inhalation of adhesive fumes: **glue-sniffing** ●sell illegal drugs: **peddle** ●person doing this: **peddler** ●legal restriction on use or possession of a drug: **control** ●diminution of bodily response to a drug with continued use: **tolerance** ●inability to do without a drug: **addiction, dependency** ●progressive deprivation of addictive

drugs: **withdrawal** ●sudden and complete deprivation of addictive drugs: **cold turkey** ●clear the body of drug residues: **detoxify** ●terrorism associated with the drugs trade: **narcoterrorism**

drum ●bowl-shaped pitched drum: **kettledrum, timpani** (*pl. only*) ●drum with resonating strings across its underside: **snare drum** ●drum in a Latin American band: **bongo** ●jazz drum beaten with the hands: **tom-tom** ●Indian drum: **tabla** ●drum-like instrument with loose discs in the sides: **tambourine** ●thin stick with wire bristles used on drums: **brush**

drunk ●slightly drunk: **tipsy** ●person who is frequently drunk: **alcoholic, drunkard**

dry ●*combining form*: **xero-** ●dry completely by heating: **parch** ●dry food to preserve it: **dessicate** ●denoting plants or animals adapted to a very dry environment: **xerophilous**

duck ●female duck: **duck** ●male duck: **drake** ●young duck: **duckling**

duel ●duellist's attendant: **second**

duke ●*adjective*: **ducal** ●duke who is also a royal prince: **royal duke** ●duke's wife or widow: **duchess** ●duke's territory: **duchy**

dummy ●jointed dummy used by artists: **lay figure** ●jointed dummy used by artists and to teach anatomy: **manikin**

dung ●*combining form*: **copro-** ●dung-eating: **coprophagous** ●dung of seabirds sold as a fertilizer: **guano**

Dutch ●Dutch mayor: **burgomaster** ●piece of land reclaimed from the sea: **polder**

duty ●*adjective*: **deontic** ●moral or legal duty: **obligation** ●fulfilment of duty: **observance** ●failure to perform a duty: **dereliction** ●beyond the call of duty: **supererogatory** ●study of duty: **deontology** ●avoid one's duty: **shirk** ●free from a duty: **exempt, exonerate** ●free from obligations: **footloose**

dwarf ●dwarf plant or tree as cultivated in Japan: **bonsai**

dwelling ●dwelling of monks or nuns: **abbey, monastery, nunnery, priory** ●makeshift dwelling: **bivouac, shack, shanty**

dye ●red food dye: **cochineal** ●orange-yellow food colouring and dye: **saffron** ●dye indicating acidity or alkalinity: **litmus** ●denoting a dye that does not run or fade: **fast** ●denoting a dye not affected by light: **lightfast** ●make a dye permanent: **fix** ●dyeing method using wax to keep the dye from some parts of the material: **batik**

dynamo ●dynamo generating an alternating current: **alternator** ●rotating coil in a dynamo: **armature**

Ee

each other ●*adjectives*: **mutual, reciprocal**

eagle ●*adjective*: **aquiline** ●young eagle: **eaglet** ●eagle's nest: **eyrie**

ear ●*combining forms*: **aur-, ot(o)-** ●*adjectives*: **aural, auricular** ●inflammation of the ear: **otitis** ●external stucture of the ear: **auricle, pinna** ●lower fleshy part of the external ear: **lobe** ●tube leading to the eardrum: **outer ear** ●membrane of the middle ear: **eardrum** ●structure of the inner ear: **labyrinth** ●inflammation of this: **labyrinthitis** ●spiral tube in the inner ear: **cochlea** ●progressive deafness due to bone growth in the ear: **otosclerosis** ●surgical opening made in the inner ear to relieve deafness: **fenestration** ●ringing or buzzing in the ears: **tinnitus** ●study of the ear and its diseases: **otology** ●study of diseases of the ear and throat: **otolaryngology** ●study and treatment of diseases of the ear, nose, and throat: **otorhinolaryngology** ●boxer's deformed ear: **cauliflower ear** ●drooping ears on an animal: **lop ears** ●plastic surgery on the ears: **otoplasty** ●for two ears: **binaural** ●doctor's device for seeing inside the ear: **auriscope, otoscope** ●drainage tube in the eardrum: **grommet** ●ring worn in a pierced ear to prevent its closing: **sleeper**

earnings ●enforced repayment of a debt from wages: **garnishment, attachment of earnings** ●accounting term for earnings gained from service industries: **invisible**

earth ●*combining form*: **geo-** ●*adjectives*: **terrestrial, terrene** ●outer part of the earth: **crust** ●denoting the earth's crust: **tectonic** ●inner part of the earth: **mantle** ●inmost part of the earth: **core** ●regions of the earth's crust and atmosphere inhabited by living organisms: **biosphere** ●this regarded ecologically: **ecosphere** ●study of the earth's atmosphere, climate, and weather: **meteorology** ●thick part of the crust, forming major land masses: **continental crust** ●thin part of the crust, beneath ocean basins: **oceanic crust** ●rigid crust section: **plate** ●equilibrium of the crust: **isostasy** ●hot liquid beneath the earth's crust: **magma** ●major movement of the earth's crust: **convulsion** ●study of the earth's crust: **tectonics** ●theory of crustal structure: **plate tectonics** ●rigid outer casing of the earth: **lithosphere** ●dense interior of the earth: **barysphere, core** ●supposed original single continent: **Pangaea** ●supposed subsequent land mass in the southern hemisphere: **Gondwana** ●supposed subsequent land mass in the northern hemisphere: **Laurasia** ●half of the earth: **hemisphere** ●imagined circle joining the earth's poles: **longitude, meridian** ●imagined circle round the earth equidistant from its poles: **equator** ●imagined line parallel to the equator: **latitude, parallel** ●range of longitudes using a common time: **time zone** ●longitude opposite to that of Greenwich, at which the date changes: **Date Line, International Date Line** ●hot zone centred on the equator: **torrid zone, tropics** ●moderate zone north and south of this: **temperate zone** ●cold zone about either of the poles: **frigid zone** ●general physical study of the earth and its atmosphere: **earth science** ●chemical study of the earth: **geochemistry** ●study of the surface of the earth: **geomorphology** ●study of the structure of the earth: **geology** ●physics of the earth: **geophysics** ●mathematics of the shape of the earth: **geodesy** ●region round the earth governed by its own magnetic field: **magnetosphere** ●study of the earth's magnetism: **geomagnetics** ●denoting the earth's natural heat: **geothermal** ●denoting an astronomical system centred on the earth: **geocentric** ●beyond the earth: **extraterrestrial** ▸see also **world**

earth moving ●powerful tractor pushing a broad blade: **bulldozer** ●wheeled machine levelling the ground: **grader**

earthquake ●*combining form*: **seismo-** ●*adjective*: **seismic** ●minor earthquake: **tremor** ●minor earthquake preceding the main shock: **foreshock** ●minor earthquake following the main shock: **aftershock** ●tremor on the moon's surface: **moonquake** ●starting point of an earthquake: **focus** ●surface point directly above an earthquake's centre: **epicentre** ●scale for earthquake intensities: **Richter scale** ●instrument recording and measuring earthquakes: **seismograph, seismometer** ●record made by this: **seismogram** ●exceptionally large ocean wave caused by an earthquake or volcano: **tidal wave, tsunami** ●study of earthquakes: **seismology**

east ●*adjective*: oriental

east Asia ●*adjective*: oriental

Easter ●*adjective*: **paschal** ●Friday before Easter: **Good Friday** ●Saturday before Easter: **Holy Saturday** ●Sunday after Easter: **Low Sunday**

easy ●easy to do: **plain sailing** ●make easy: **facilitate**

eat ●eat in small amounts: **nibble** ●(of an animal) eat high-growing vegetation: **browse** ●(of an animal) eat grass: **graze** ●fit to eat: **edible** ●unfit to eat: **inedible** ●become unfit to eat: **spoil** ●pathological refusal to eat, due to a desire to lose weight: **anorexia nervosa**

eating ●*combining forms*: -phagous, -phagy, -vorous ●eating all foods: **omnivorous** ●eating a lot: **voracious** ●eating corpses: **necrophagous** ●eating dung: **coprophagous** ●fish-eating: **piscivorous** ●eating grasses and cereals: **graminivorous** ●insect-eating: **insectivorous** ●meat-eating: **carnivorous** ●nut-eating: **nucivorous** ●plant-eating: **herbivorous** ●eating wood: **xylophagous** ●eating no meat or fish: **vegetarian** ●eating no animal flesh or products: **vegan** ●eating only fruit: **fruitarian** ●person or animal feeding on its own species: **cannibal** ●psychologically induced refusal to eat: **anorexia nervosa** ●psychologically induced desire to overeat: **bulimia nervosa** ●substance added to plants or found naturally in them, discouraging animals or microorganisms from eating them: **antifeedant**

eccentric ●eccentric person: **crank** ●eccentric minority: **lunatic fringe**

echo ●*adjective*: **echoic** ●record of water depth made by reflected sound: **echogram** ●location of objects by reflected sound: **echolocation** ●echo-free: **anechoic**

eclipse ●*adjective*: **ecliptic** ●denoting an eclipse obscuring the whole disc: **total** ●denoting an eclipse obscuring no more than part of the disc: **partial** ●denoting a total eclipse in which the edges of the eclipsed body remain visible: **annular** ●area shaded by a total eclipse: **umbra**

• area shaded by a partial eclipse: **penumbra**

ecology • *combining form*: **eco-** • preservation of the natural environment: **conservation** • deliberate destruction of the natural environment: **ecocide** • cropping just short of long-term depletion: **maximum sustainable yield** • denoting practices that do not permanently impair the ecological balance: **sustainable** • biological community regarded as ecologically self-sufficient: **ecosystem** • number of persons and animals a region can support without environmental degradation: **carrying capacity** • product labelling to indicate ecological soundness: **eco-labelling** • tourism intended to increase ecological awareness: **ecotourism** • sabotage committed for ecological reasons: **ecotage** • violence justified by ecological concerns: **ecoterrororism**

economy • economic system in which all major factors are centrally controlled: **command economy, managed economy, planned economy** • economic system led by free operation of market forces: **free-enterprise system, free-market economy, supply-side economy** • free-market economic system with state provision for those unable to sell their labour: **social market economy** • economic system where businesses are privately owned: **capitalism, private enterprise** • economic system in which the state controls production and the use of capital: **state capitalism** • economic system with means of production in state or popular ownership: **collectivism, socialism** • economic system with state control of industries and services: **communism, state socialism** • denoting an economic system containing a balance of the above: **mixed** • capitalist element in a mixed economy: **private sector**

• state-controlled element in a mixed economy: **public sector** • district for which special economic provision is made: **special development area** • dynamic economy in East Asia: **tiger economy** • general economic factors: **macroeconomics** • economic study of single factors: **microeconomics** • open an economy to competitive trading: **demonopolize** • economic system allowing unrestricted competition: **free enterprise, free market** • economic system taxing imports to protect home manufactures: **protectionism** • economic system controlling imports and the export of capital: **siege economy** • government economic policy of non-intervention: **laissez-faire** • economic plan: **budget** • economic plan in which income equals expenditure: **balanced budget** • excess of expenses over income: **deficit** • economic control via the money supply: **monetarism** • financing of government expenditure by borrowing: **deficit financing** • government expenditure thus financed: **deficit spending** • general reduction in prices: **deflation** • perceived need for a commodity: **demand** • denoting an economy governed by consumer demand: **demand-led** • denoting an economy suffering demand-led inflation: **overheated** • increase in economic activity: **expansion, recovery** • period of rapid economic growth: **boom** • denoting an economy unlikely to expand further: **mature** • highest level of economic activity: **peak** • temporary decline in economic activity: **recession** • sharp and prolonged decline in economic activity: **slump** • severe and prolonged decrease of economic activity: **depression** • low level of economic activity: **trough** • regular alternation of boom and slump: **business cycle, trade cycle** • general increase in prices with a decrease in the purchasing power of money: **inflation** ●high inflation and unemployment coupled with low demand: **stagflation** ●total value of goods and services produced: **gross domestic product** ●this plus income from foreign investments: **gross national product** ●difference between a state's income and expenditure: **balance of payments** ●denoting income from service industries: **invisible** ●ratio between export and import prices: **terms of trade** ●difference between the value of a state's imports and exports: **balance of trade** ●excess value of imports over exports: **trade deficit** ●excess value of exports over imports: **trade surplus** ●policy of acquiring political or economic control over dependent states: **colonialism** ●use of mathematics to explain an economic system: **econometrics** ▸ *see also* **inflation**

eczema ●steroid used to treat this: **hydrocortisone**

edge ●*adjective*: **peripheral** ●having a jagged edge: **serrated**

edit ●edit to remove offensive material: **bowdlerize, expurgate**

education ●basic education: **grounding** ●education of both sexes together: **co-education** ●denoting education aimed at personal fulfilment: **liberal** ●denoting education for those with learning difficulties: **remedial** ●denoting school education for the under-elevens: **primary** ●denoting school education for the over-elevens: **secondary** ●denoting education at university level: **tertiary** ●education through questioning and clarification: **maieutics** ●education through independent study: **open learning** ●official assessment of a child's special educational needs: **statement** ●educational requirements of those with learning difficulties etc.: **special needs** ●institution at which one was educated: **alma mater** ●person or institution offering intensive preparation for examinations: **crammer** ●organized series of lessons: **course** ●intensive course of study: **crash course** ●machine giving programmed instruction: **teaching machine** ●independent unit of study: **module** ●programme of study: **curriculum, syllabus** ●curriculum imposed upon state schools: **national curriculum** ●course alternating between instruction and practical experience: **sandwich course** ●course given during the summer holidays: **summer course, summer school** ●denoting a course aimed at theoretical competence: **pure** ●denoting a course aimed at practical utility: **applied** ●denoting a course embracing several subject-areas: **cross-curricular** ●denoting a course consisting of a series of independent study units: **modular** ●denoting an optional course: **elective** ●denoting a course revising or updating previously acquired skills: **refresher** ●series of lectures etc. on a topic of current public interest: **teach-in** ●fixed stage in the national curriculum: **Key Stage** ●school mathematics courses stressing heuristics and set theory: **new maths** ●full-time education for those beyond school age but not at a university: **further education** ●education at university level: **higher education** ●part-time adult education: **continuing education** ●woman employed to educate children at home: **governess** ●day-long release of employees for education: **day release** ●extended release of employees for full-time education: **block release** ●education conducted by post: **correspondence course, distance learning** ●education in household skills: **domestic science** ●work done by a student while learning: **coursework** ●assessment of progress throughout study: **continuous assessment**

•certificate of completed studies: **diploma**

eel •young eel: **elver** •eel split and cooked: **spitchcock**

effect •mutual effect: **interplay** •indirect effect: **knock-on**

efficiency •analysis of workplace efficiency: **operational research** •increased efficiency by subdivision of tasks: **division of labour** •smoothly efficient: **slick** •designed for efficiency rather than appearance: **utilitarian**

effort •requiring much effort: **laborious** •make great effort: **strive, struggle**

egg •*combining forms*: **oo-, ovi-** •frog or fish eggs: **spawn** •egg-shaped: **oviform, ovoid** •producing young by means of eggs: **oviparous** •set of eggs: **clutch** •sit on eggs: **brood** •(of young) emerge from an egg: **hatch** •keep eggs warm for hatching: **incubate** •artificially controlled hatching environment: **hatchery** •study and collecting of birds' eggs: **oology** •recently hatched animal: **hatchling** •denoting an egg boiled so that the yolk is dry: **hard-boiled** •denoting an egg boiled so that the yolk is runny: **soft-boiled** •dish of fried beaten eggs: **omelette** •light dish of stiffly beaten egg whites: **soufflé** •Chinese egg dish: **foo yong** •test eggs for freshness: **candle** •simmer an egg: **coddle** •hardboiled egg fried in sausage meat: **Scotch egg**

egg-shaped •*adjectives*: **oval, ovate, ovoid**

Egyptian •ancient Egyptian ruler: **Pharaoh** •territorial division of ancient Egypt: **nome** •ancient Egyptian temple gateway: **pylon** •ancient Egyptian picture-writing: **hieroglyphs** •oval plaque for hieroglyphs: **cartouche** •ancient Egyptian

priestly script using simplified hieroglyphs: **hieratic** •ancient Egyptian script used by the laity, a simplified form of hieratic: **demotic** •ancient Egyptian god of the dead: **Osiris** •ancient Egyptian embalmed corpse: **mummy** •ancient Egyptian funeral urn: **Canopic jar, Canopic vase** •ancient Egyptian goddess of fertility: **Isis** •ancient Egyptian god of mummification: **Anubis** •ancient Egyptian god of the sky: **Horus** •ancient Egyptian sun-god: **Amun** •ancient Egyptian tomb: **mastaba** •ancient Egyptian beetle-shaped gem: **scarab** •study of ancient Egyptian culture: **Egyptology** •former viceroy of Egypt: **Khedive** •Egyptian peasant: **fellah** (*pl.* fellahin) •Egyptian boat: **fellucca** •hot Egyptian wind: **khamsin** •Egyptian irrigation device of a bucket on a pole: **shadoof**

eight •*combining form*: **oct-** •eight-sided figure: **octagon** •denoting eight parts: **octuple** •one of eight offspring born at a birth: **octuplet** •ensemble of eight musicians, or music for them: **octet**

eighty •person in his or her eighties: **octogenarian**

elaborate •pretentiously elaborate: **grandiose**

elbow •prod with the elbow: **nudge** •inflammation of elbow tendons: **tennis elbow**

election •*adjectives*: **elective, electoral** •election campaign: **hustings** •election for all constituencies: **general election** •election for one constituency: **by-election** •denoting a constituency won by a small majority: **marginal** •denoting a constituency won by a large majority: **safe** •manipulation of constituency boundaries: **gerrymandering** •denoting an election won by a simple majority: **first past the post** •election system distributing seats proportionately to each party's national share of the poll: **proportional representation** ●person seeking election: **candidate** ●propose or enter a candidate: **nominate** ●list of candidates: **slate** ●ideal set of election candidates: **dream ticket** ●part of a county or borough returning a single parliamentary candidate: **division, constituency** ●area for local election purposes: **ward** ●money paid in by an election candidate: **deposit** ●refuse constituency support to one's previous candidate: **deselect** ●solicit votes at an election: **canvass, electioneer** ●politician's mobile headquarters for use in election campaigns: **battlebus** ●election meeting: **hustings** ●official conducting an election: **returning officer** ●person supervising the conduct of an election: **scrutineer** ●official announcement of an election result: **declaration** ●study of voting at elections: **psephology** ▸*see also* **vote**

electric circuit ●electric circuit serving several power points: **ring circuit, ring main** ●denoting an interrupted electric circuit: **open** ●complete an electric circuit: **close** ●wire used to do this: **jumper** ●connect or disconnect an electrical circuit: **trip** ●conductor by which electicity enters or leaves an object: **electrode** ●temporary electrical connection: **patch** ●board with sockets for this: **patchboard** ●unwanted electrical connection, creating a false circuit: **short circuit** ●aerial short circuit between two exposed conductors: **flashover** ●circuit's resistance to alternating current: **impedance** ●denoting circuits etc. which the current enters in turn: **in series** ●denoting circuits etc. which the current enters simultaneously: **in parallel** ●thin wire breaking an overloaded electric circuit: **fuse**

electric current ●complete closed path for electric current: **circuit** ●difference in potential causing an electric current: **electromotive force** ●sudden increase in electric current: **surge** ●denoting an electric current having frequent and regular reverses of direction: **alternating** ●denoting an electric current flowing in one direction: **direct** ●apparatus converting direct into alternating current: **inverter** ●apparatus converting alternating into direct current: **rectifier** ●instrument controlling an electric current by varying the resistance: **rheostat** ●instruments measuring electric currents: **ammeter, galvanometer** ●maximum current taken by a device: **loading** ●change an alternating current to direct: **commutate** ●electrode device used to generate electric current: **cell** ●device cutting off an electric current: **circuit-breaker** ●degree to which a substance opposes the passage of an electric current: **resistance** ●muscle or nerve stimulation by electric current: **electrotherapy** ●chemical decomposition by electric current: **electrolysis**

electricity ●*combining form*: **electro-** (*e.g.* electroplate) ●electricity supply: **power** ●make electricity: **generate** ●device converting mechanical energy into electricity: **dynamo, generator** ●electric generator using permanent magnets: **magneto** ●electrical conductor wound round a magnet: **winding** ●denoting electricity generated by water power: **hydroelectric** ●electric charge generated by friction: **triboelectricity** ●stationary electric charge produced by friction: **static electricity** ●electric potential produced by mechanical stress: **piezoelectricity** ●producing electricity by temperature differences: **thermoelectric** ●device converting solar radiation into electricity: **solar**

battery, solar cell ●device converting quantitative physical changes into an electric signal, or vice versa: **transducer** ●device storing an electric charge: **capacitor, condenser** ●national electricity supply network: **grid, national grid** ●tall support for grid cables: **pylon** ●person repairing electric power lines: **linesman** ●equipment reducing grid voltages to domestic levels: **substation** ●apparatus changing alternating-current voltages: **transformer** ●sudden increase in voltage or current: **surge** ●electric supply failure: **blackout, outage** ●interruption of electricity supply to prevent generator overload: **load-shedding** ●terminate an electric supply: **cut off** ●complete closed path for electric current: **circuit** ●effect of a sudden electrical discharge upon a person or animal: **electric shock, shock** ●electric shocks administered to treat mental illness: **electroconvulsive therapy** ●light-sensitive electric cell: **electric eye, photoelectric cell** ●difference in potential causing an electric current: **electromotive force** ●substance transmitting electricity: **conductor** ●substance that does not transmit electricity: **insulator** ●device suppressing unwanted electrical waves: **filter** ●flow of electricity: **current** ●maximum electric power demand: **peak load** ●electrical contact set against a moving part: **brush** ●device with pins making an electrical connection: **plug** ●single-pronged electric plug: **jack plug** ●device receiving an electric plug: **socket** ●device making or breaking an electric circuit: **switch** ●wall plate around an electric switch: **escutcheon** ●switch controlling a whole system: **master switch** ●set of electrical switches: **gang** ●switch operated by a sprung lever: **tumbler** ●switches and fuse boxes where the electrical supply en-

ters a house: **consumer unit** ●sprung electrical connection clip: **crocodile clip** ●device varying an electric light's brightness: **dimmer** ●electrical appliances such as televisions and hi-fi: **brown goods** ●electrical appliances such as refrigerators and washing machines: **white goods**

electric light ●thin wire giving light in an electric light bulb: **filament** ●glass container for an electric light filament: **envelope** ●electric light bulb with translucent glass: **pearl bulb** ●electric light fitting with two small projecting pins: **bayonet fitting** ●device receiving an electric light fitting: **socket**

electric wire ●electric wire: **cable, lead** ●long-distance electric cable: **transmission line** ●national network of these: **grid** ●electric wire providing heat: **element** ●electric wire providing light: **filament** ●electric wire running to the ground: **earth** ●ducting for electric cable: **shaft** ●towerlike structure carrying cables above the ground: **pylon**

electrode ●positively charged electrode: **anode** ●negatively charged electrode: **cathode** ●electrode device used to generate electric current: **cell**

electronic data ●electronic data gathering: **data capture** ●denoting data in a form a computer can process: **machine-readable** ●basic data unit: **word** ●identifying character appended to a data item: **tag** ●part of a computer record allocated to a particular data item: **field** ●connected set of data items: **record** ●data stored under a particular name: **file** ●group of records processed together: **batch** ●field identifying a record: **key** ●data's consistency and freedom from corruption: **integrity** ●device displaying data on a screen: **visual display unit** ●data shown on a computer screen: **display** ●section of stored data displayable onscreen at one time: **page** ●steady rolling up or down through displayed data: **scrolling** ●printout of computer data: **hardcopy** ●onscreen display of data: **soft copy** ●electronic data sorting: **data processing** ●operate on data by means of a program: **process** ●defined structure for data processing, storage, or display: **format** ●computer part storing data: **memory** ●flat plate for data storage: **disk** ●copy data to a storage location: **save** ●copy or transfer data: **read** ●transfer data to the memory: **load, write** ●send data to an intermediate store: **spool** ●compact data for storage: **compress** ●immediate access to the data sought: **direct access** ●access to data requiring file readthrough: **sequential access** ●time taken to find stored data: **seek time** ●discovery of a sought data item: **hit** ●re-express data for use with a different program or system: **convert** ●hierarchic arrangement of data: **nesting** ●copy data to a second location: **back-up, dump** ●duplicate storage of data: **mirroring** ●copy data from one computer system to another: **download** ●transfer data to a larger computer system: **upload** ●obtain electronic data: **interrogate, retrieve** ●structured data held in a computer: **database** ●corpus of data formed from several databases: **databank** ●company's management database: **data warehouse** ●creating new databases from existing database material: **data mining** ●database structured to recognize relations between stored items: **relational database** ●restore a database to its previous state: **rollback** ●browser program acessing a large database: **navigator** ●storage device allowing data access from any available disk: **jukebox** ●denoting data on free access: **unprotected** ●restrict access to data: **protect** ●gain

unauthorized access to data: **hack** ●destroy data in a computer's memory: **delete, erase** ●cancel a deletion: **undelete** ●destroy data by entering new data in its place: **overwrite** ●prevent this: **write-protect** ●small data loss due to disk flaw: **dropout** ●make data available to several users simultaneously: **multicast** ●data path between computer components: **bus** ●high speed data connection: **local bus** ●rules for electronic transmission of data between devices: **protocol** ●standard signals regulating data transfer: **handshaking** ●denoting the transfer of data as a single sequence of bits: **serial** ●continuous flow of data: **stream** ●denoting systems processing data as it is generated: **real-time** ●single scan through a set of data: **pass** ●block of data transmitted across a network: **packet** ●separate data into such units: **packetize** ●mode of data transmission by packets: **packet switching** ●rules governing electronic transmission of data: **protocol** ●total of the digits in an item of electronic data: **checksum** ●alter data to minimize storage space: **compress** ●restore such data to a machine-readable state: **decompress** ●denoting data compression discarding inessential information: **lossy** ●microchip compressing and decompressing data: **codec** ●data link allowing simultaneous updates: **hot link** ●long-distance transmission of computerized information: **telematics** ●study of electronic data processing for storage and retrieval: **information science, information technology, informatics** ●introduce errors to a program or database: **corrupt** ●error or fault causing loss of data: **hard error** ●piece of computer code that can corrupt or destroy data: **virus** ●legal controls over use of electronic data: **data protection** .

electronic mail ●processing electronic mail: **messaging** ●abusive electronic-mail message: **flame**

electronics ●electronic aviation equipment: **avionics** ●electronic circuit formed on a small piece of semiconducting material: **integrated circuit** ●integrated circuit containing all the functions of a computer's central processing unit: **microprocessor** ●electronic keyboard able to produce many different types of pitched sound: **synthesizer** ●electronic device attached for monitoring purposes: **tag** ●electronic remote control of machines: **teleoperation** ●restore an electronic signal to intelligible form: **descramble** ●semiconductor used in electronics: **transistor** ●denoting technology based on solid semiconductors: **solid-state** ●minor printed circuit board: **daughterboard** ●semiconducting wafer in an integrated circuit: **chip, microchip** ●denoting an electron emitted at high temperatures: **thermionic** ●technology combining electronics and mechanics: **mechatronics**

elegance ●stylish elegance: **chic** ●over-elaborate elegance: **chichi** ●simple and elegant: **clean** ●slim and elegant: **svelte** ●elegant bodily movements: **deportment**

element ●chemical element present or required in minute amounts: **trace element** ●radioactive form of an element: **isotope, radioisotope** ●smallest particle of a chemical element that can participate in chemical reactions: **atom** ●table of the chemical elements arranged by atomic number: **periodic table** ●vertical column in this: **group** ●horizontal row in this: **period**

elephant ●*adjective*: **elephantine** ●young elephant: **calf** ●prehistoric elephant: **mammoth** ●savage elephant living apart from the herd: **rogue elephant** ●frenzied state of rutting male elephants: **must** ●elephant's long projecting tooth: **tusk** ●elephant driver: **mahout** ●seat on elephant's back: **howdah**

eleven ●*combining form*: hendeca- ●eleven-sided figure: **hendecagon, undecagon** ●verse of eleven syllables: **hendecasyllable**

elf ●elf said to do housework: **brownie** ●elf in Irish folklore: **leprechaun** ●elf in German folklore: **kobold**

elm ●fungal disease of elm trees: **Dutch elm disease**

embarrass ●embarrassment at one's appearance or actions: **self-consciousness** ●embarrassing remark or act: **bêtise, faux pas, gaffe** ●avoiding embarrassment: **discreet**

emblem ●Celtic three-legged emblem: **triskelion** ●Nazi emblem: **swastika** ●company emblem: **logo**

embroidery ●piece of embroidery done as a specimen of skill: **sampler** ●ornamental embroidery with drawing out of threads: **drawn-thread-work** ●embroidery with parts cut out: **cutwork** ●embroidery worked over canvas: **needlepoint** ●canvas embroidery of diagonal stitches: **petit point** ●thin twisted embroidery yarn, or the embroidery made with it: **crewel** ●small loop of twisted thread: **picot** ●embroidery stitch forming an X: **cross-stitch** ●circular frame holding embroidery taut: **tambour**

embryo ●membrane surrounding the embryo: **chorion** ●outermost layer of embryonic tissue: **ectoderm** ●innermost layer of embryonic tissue: **endoderm** ●test-tube development of embryos: **ectogenesis**

emigration ●emigration of intellectuals: **brain drain** ●emigrants from a particular nation: **diaspora**

emotion ●violent emotional attack: **hysteria, paroxysm** ●feeling emotion: **passible, sentimental** ●showing no emotion: **impassive, self-controlled** ●emotional shock: **trauma** ●emotional tension: **stress** ●emotional release in response to a moving work of art: **catharsis** ●attribution of human emotions to animals and things: **pathetic fallacy**

emperor ●*adjective*: **imperial** ●former emperor of Germany: **Kaiser** ●former emperor of Japan: **Mikado** ●former emperor of Russia: **Tsar**

empire ●*adjective*: **imperial**

employee ●employee's improper behaviour: **misconduct** ●list of employees and their wages: **payroll** ●temporary or permanent discharge of workers: **lay-off** ●rate at which employees leave and are replaced: **turnover** ●loss of employees due to resignation and retirement: **natural wastage, wastage**

employment ●short experience of employment arranged for school-leavers: **work experience** ●out of employment: **unwaged**

empty ●empty-headed: **vacant, vacuous**

enamel ●decorative enamel inlay: **champlevé** ●decorative enamels separated by wire: **cloisonné**

enclosure ●enclosure for keeping birds: **aviary** ●trackside enclosure where competitors assemble: **paddock**

end ●*combining forms*: **tel(e)-** (*purpose, e.g.* telelology), **acro-** (*tip, e.g.* acronym) ●final outcome: **denouement** ●disappointing end or outcome: **anticlimax** ●put an end to: **scotch** ●bring to a gradual end: **wind up** ●ending point: **terminus ad quem**

endless ●endlessly: **ad infinitum**

end of the world ●theological study of the end of the world: **eschat-**

ology ●time of judgement then: **doomsday**

enemy ●*adjective*: **inimical** ●person voluntarily assisting enemy occupying forces: **collaborator, quisling**

energy ●tiny discrete amount of energy: **quantum** (*pl.* quanta) ●energy derived from renewable non-nuclear sources: **alternative energy** ●energy derived from movement: **kinetic energy** ●emission of energy as electromagnetic waves or moving particles: **radiation**

engagement ●man engaged to be married: **fiancé** ●woman engaged to be married: **fiancée**

engineer ●engineer designing and building roads etc.: **civil engineer**

English ●*combining form*: **Anglo-** ●English-speaking: **anglophone**

engraving ●*adjective*: **glyptic** ●engraving using a waxed plate: **etching, cerography** ●etching technique using resin and varnish to produce shaded areas: **aquatint** ●engraving without acid: **dry point** ●engraving by incised lines: **line engraving** ●engraving effect achieved by many small dots: **stipple** ●engraved or incised design: **intaglio** ●engraving from a plate partly roughened and partly smooth: **mezzotint** ●engrave a design on metal: **chase** ●steel engraving tool: **burin** ●art of gem engraving: **glyptography** ●black compound set in engraved metal: **niello** ▸*see also* **illustration**

enjoy ●enjoy without hurrying: **savour**

enlarge ●enlarge by internal stretching: **distend**

enlightenment ●theological term in Buddhism or Hinduism: **nirvana**

enough ●be enough: **suffice** ●more than enough: **superfluous**

enquiry ●denoting a process of enquiry conducted by negation: **apophatic** ●denoting a process of enquiry conducted by affirmation: **cataphatic**

ensemble ●ensemble of two performers, or the music for them: **duo** ●ensemble of three performers, or the music for them: **trio** ●ensemble of four performers, or the music for them: **quartet** ●ensemble of five performers, or the music for them: **quintet** ●ensemble of six performers, or the music for them: **sextet** ●ensemble of seven performers, or the music for them: **septet** ●ensemble of eight performers, or the music for them: **octet** ●ensemble of instruments of a single type: **choir** ●small ensemble playing early music: **consort** ●small ensemble playing popular music: **combo, group** ●arrangement of a piece of music for ensemble or orchestral use: **orchestration** ●play several instruments in an ensemble: **double**

enter ●impossible to enter: **impenetrable**

entertainer ●very famous entertainer: **megastar** ●entertainer telling jokes: **comedian** (*fem.* comedienne) ●denoting a comedian entertaining a live audience: **stand-up** ●male entertainer impersonating a woman: **drag queen** ●entertainer twisting his or her body: **contortionist** ●entertainer demonstrating skill in escaping: **escapologist** ●entertainer performing elaborate gymnastic feats: **acrobat** ●entertainer walking a tightrope: **funambulist** ●entertainer passing a sword blade down his or her throat: **sword-swallower** ●entertainer seeming to make his or her voice come from a dummy: **ventriloquist** ●musician who entertains in the street: **busker** ●musician making snakes sway to his or her tunes: **snake charmer** ●busker playing several instruments

simultaneously: **one-man band** ●medieval singer: **minstrel, troubadour** ●performer in popular entertainment: **artiste** ●performer in highbrow entertainment: **artist** ●pair of entertainers working together: **double act**

entertainment ●entertainment industry: **show business** ●entertainment consisting of different kinds of act: **variety** ●entertainment of singing to a recorded accompaniment: **karaoke** ●entertainment by taking one's clothes off: **striptease** ●entertainment using sound and lighting effects upon an architectural background: **son et lumière** ●light theatrical entertainment with topical satire: **revue** ●popular variety entertainment: **music hall** ●variety entertainment with topical satire: **revue** ●theatrical Christmas show: **pantomime** ●comic entertainment based on vigorous horseplay: **slapstick** ●military entertainment with demonstrations of skill: **tattoo** ●public entertainment or social activities available at night: **nightlife** ●entertainment with two items: **double bill** ●entertainment with an educational purpose: **edutainment, infotainment**

enthusiast ●extreme enthusiast: **fanatic, monomaniac, zealot** ●enthusiast for some activity: **fancier** ●foolishly enthusiastic: **gung-ho** ●vigorous enthusiasm: **verve, zest** ●stimulate enthusiasm: **motivate** ●showing little enthusiasm: **lukewarm**

entire ●*combining forms*: pan- (*e.g.* pan-Islamic)

entity ●some further unspecified entity: **tertium quid**

entrails ●take out entrails: **disembowel, eviscerate** ●eviscerate a deer: **gralloch** ●eviscerate a fish: **clean, gut** ●eviscerate a fowl: **draw**

environment ●*combining form*: **eco-** ●social environment: **milieu** ●environmentally aware: **green** ●increased environmental awareness: **green revolution** ●watch for threats to the environment: **doomwatch** ●presence of harmful substances in the environment: **pollution** ●animal's or plant's natural environment: **habitat** ●happening in its natural environment: **in vivo** ●study of the interaction of living organisms and their environment: **ecology** ●reversing environmental damage: **remediation**

enzyme ●*combining forms*: **zym-, -ase** ●mixture of enzymes used in alcoholic fermentation: **zymase**

epilepsy ●*adjective*: **epileptic** ●serious form of epilepsy: **grand mal** ●minor form of epilepsy: **petit mal** ●causing epilepsy: **epileptogenic** ●epileptic fit: **seizure** ●violent movements in epileptic fits: **convulsions** ●person suffering from epilepsy: **epileptic** ●drug preventing or moderating epileptic fits: **anticonvulsant**

epoch ●*adjective*: **epochal**

equal ●*combining form*: **equi-, iso-** (*e.g.* isosceles) ●with sides of equal length: **equilateral** ●equal in power or importance: **equipollent** ●equality of pay or status: **parity** ●person of equal status: **peer** ●on an equal basis: **pari passu** ●other things being equal: **ceteris paribus**

equality ●*adjective*: **egalitarian**

equation ●equations sharing unknowns with identical values: **simultaneous equations** ●move to the other side of an equation: **transpose** ●quantity to be found by solving an equation: **unknown**

equator ●*adjective*: **equatorial**

equinox ●*adjective*: **equinoctial** ●progressively earlier occurrence of the equinoxes: **precession**

equipment ●equipment in a specified area of expertise: **armamentarium** ●complete equipment: **panoply** ●miscellaneous equipment: **paraphernalia** ●setting up equipment for use: **installation**

erase ●erase data from an electronic medium: **wipe** ●impossible to erase: **indelible**

Eros ●*Latin name*: **Cupid**

erosion ●landscape levelling through erosion: **planation** ●projecting wall or fence to limit sea's erosion of coast: **groyne** ●minimization of erosion by ploughing along contours: **contour ploughing**

error ●error in logic: **fallacy** ●grammatical error: **solecism** ●error alleged to reveal subconscious feelings: **Freudian slip** ●capable of error: **fallible** ●incapable of error: **foolproof, infallible** ●correct someone's mistaken impression: **undeceive** ●list of errors in a book etc.: **corrigenda, errata** ●opaque fluid to obliterate written errors: **correction fluid**

escape ●person who entertains audiences by demonstrating his or her skill in escaping from confinement: **escapologist** ●place for escaping or hiding: **bolt-hole**

escort ●female escort for young woman: **chaperone, duenna** ●male escort for older woman: **gigolo**

Eskimo ●Eskimo inhabitant of the islands off Alaska: **Aleut** ●Eskimo inhabitant of northern Canada or Greenland: **Inuit** ●Eskimo canoe: **kayak** ●Eskimo ice-house: **igloo** ●Eskimo sledge-dog: **husky, malamute** ●command to this: **mush!**

essay ●academic essay: **dissertation, paper, memoir, thesis**

essence ●denoting things having the same essence: **consubstantial**

essential ●essential oil of rose petals: **attar** ●not essential: **extrinsic**

estate ●estate manager: **land agent**, (*in Scotland*) **factor** ●colonial estate growing sugar, coffee, etc.: **plantation** ●plantation owner or manager: **planter** ●enclosed pasture and woodland round a country mansion: **park**

estimate ●one who provides a detailed estimate of the cost of a proposed building project: **quantity surveyor** ●estimate unknown results by analogy with those already observed: **extrapolate**

ethics ●theory that acts are justified solely by their usefulness, or the pleasure they create: **utilitarianism** ●theory that moral truths exist independently of any knowledge of them: **objectivism** ●theory that moral truths are culturally determined: **relativism** ●theory that several moral systems may coexist: **ethical pluralism** ●theory that pleasure is the highest good: **hedonism** ●ethics of medical and biological research: **bioethics** ●imagined unchanging and universal system of ethical principles: **natural law** ●abandonment of ethical standards: **anomie**

etiquette ●required by etiquette: **de rigueur** ●subtle point of etiquette: **nicety**

Europe ●*combining form*: **Euro-** (*e.g.* Eurocentric) ●European mainland as viewed from Britain: **the Continent**

European Union ●bureaucrat of the European Union: **Eurocrat** ●person unenthusiastic about the European Union: **Eurosceptic** ●official monetary unit of the European Union: **ecu** ●proposed single currency for the European Union: **Eurocurrency**

evaporate ●liable to rapid evaporation: **volatile**

evasion ●evasive talk: **circumlocution, equivocation**

evening ●period of evening twilight: **dusk**

event ●important event: **occasion, landmark, milestone** ●summer outdoor fund-raising event: **fête** ●event inexplicable by scientific laws: **miracle** ●number participating in an event: **turnout** ●person seeing an event take place: **witness** ●place where an event is held: **venue** ●possible sequence of events: **contingency, scenario** ●series of events, each triggered by its predecessor: **chain reaction** ●first of a series of events: **opener** ●related events adding significance to that under consideration: **context** ●wisdom after the event: **hindsight**

ever ●for ever: **ad infinitum**

every ●*combining form*: **pan-** (*e.g.* pansexual)

everywhere ●*combining forms*: **omni-, per** ●found everywhere: **omnipresent, pervasive, ubiquitous**

evidence ●*adjective*: **evidential** ●evidence given under oath: **deposition** ●lying evidence: **perjury** ●evidence given by an accused person against his accomplices: **Queen's** (*or* **King's**) **evidence** ●denoting legally acceptable evidence: **admissible** ●denoting evidence proving guilt: **damning** ●denoting evidence consistent with, but not proving, the accusation: **circumstantial** ●object shown in court as evidence: **exhibit**

evil ●wishing to do evil: **malevolent, malicious, malign, nefarious** ●averting evil: **apotropaic** ●declare to be evil: **denounce** ●portray as evil: **demonize**

evolution ●evolution of one species to resemble another: **mimicry** ●major evolutionary change: **macroevolution** ●Darwinian model of evolution: **natural selection, survival of the fittest**

examination ●*combining forms*: **-opsy** (*e.g.* biopsy), **-scopy** (*e.g.* endoscopy) ●examination of financial accounts: **audit** ●examination of a substance to determine its constituents: **qualitative analysis** ●examination of a substance to determine the proportion of its constituents: **quantitative analysis** ●spoken academic examination: **oral, viva, viva voce** ●practice examination: **mock** ●oral examination of an applicant: **interview** ●school-leaving examination in certain countries: **baccalaureate** ●level of a music examination: **grade** ●person taking an examination: **candidate** ●supervisor of persons taking a written examination: **invigilator** ●denoting an examination question offering several possible answers: **multiple-choice** ●set of examination questions: **paper** ●instruction on an examination paper: **rubric** ●candidate's completed examination paper: **script** ●examiner ensuring consistent marking: **moderator** ●examination grade denoting a fail: **unclassified** ●medical examination of a corpse: **autopsy, post-mortem** ●medical examination of tissue from a living body: **biopsy** ●body examination by touch: **palpation** ●machine examining the body by radiation, ultrasound, etc.: **scanner** ●image produced by such a machine: **scan** ●theological examination of a heretic: **inquisition** ●mental examination of one's thoughts: **introspection**

example ●perfect example: **archetype, epitome, ne plus ultra, paragon, prototype, quintessence** ●prime example: **byword** ●example to be imitated: **object lesson, paradigm, pattern, role model** ●example cited to justify similar action: **precedent** ●cite as an example: **adduce**

excavation ●refilling of excavations with waste material: **landfill** ●refill an excavation with the material dug from it: **backfill**

exceedingly ●*combining forms*: **super-** (*e.g.* supersensitive), **ultra-** (*e.g.* ultra-polite)

excessive ●excessive supply: **glut** ●use of more words than are needed: **pleonasm**

excessively ●*combining forms*: **hyper-, over-** (*e.g.* overfull), **pleo-** ●excessively critical: **hypercritical**

exchange ●mutual exchange: **reciprocity**

excitement ●thrill of excitement: **frisson**

excrement ●*combining forms*: **copro-, scato-** (*e.g.* scatology) ●eating excrement: **coprophagous** ●excrement of seabirds sold as a fertilizer: **guano** ●receptacle for bedridden persons' excreta: **bedpan**

execution ●execution as a punishment: **death penalty** ●official order for this: **death warrant** ●chair for execution by electric shock: **electric chair** ●apparatus for execution by hanging: **gallows, gibbet** ●apparatus for execution by strangling: **garrotte** ●French beheading machine: **guillotine** ●platform for public executions: **scaffold** ●post for display of executed persons: **gibbet**

exercise ●exercises for fitness and strength: **physical training** ●exercises for strength and good appearance: **callisthenics** ●exercises increasing bodily oxygen intake: **aerobics** ●aerobics performed in water: **aquarobics** ●exercises using counterbalanced muscles: **isometrics** ●exercise of gentle running: **jogging** ●exercise of raising the prone body by arm pressure: **press-up** ●exercise of raising oneself to an overhead bar: **pull-up** ●Chinese exercise systems: **t'ai chi ch'uan, qigong** ●system of exercise based on Hindu principles: **yoga** ●series of exercises: **circuit** ●exercise course with physical obstacles to be negotiated: **assault course** ●session of vigorous physical exercise: **workout** ●exercise involving alternate slow and fast work: **fartlek, wind sprint** ●preliminary exercises: **limbering up, warm-up** ●concluding exercises: **cooldown, warm-down**

exhaust ●purifier of vehicle exhaust gases: **catalytic converter**

exhaustion ●inexplicable persistent exhaustion: **chronic fatigue syndrome, myalgic encephalitis**

exhibition ●exhibition showing work from various periods in an artist's life: **retrospective** ●item assembled at the exhibition venue: **installation** ●exhibition preview for invited guests: **private view, vernissage** ●temporary housing for an exhibition: **pavilion**

existence ●*combining form*: onto- (*e.g.* ontology) ●existing situation: **status quo** ●having no physical existence: **incorporeal** ●no longer existing: **defunct**

expect ●disconcert by an unexpected act: **wrong-foot**

expel ●*combining form*: -fuge (*e.g.* febrifuge) ●expel someone from a property: **evict** ●expel a foreigner: **deport**

expense ●minor expenses: **incidentals** ●basic expense of keeping a firm running: **oncost, operating expenses, overheads** ●expensive-looking: **sumptuous**

experience ●experience in handling tricky social or business situations: **savoir faire** ●denoting someone experienced in coping with modern urban life: **streetwise** ●a short but unpleasant experience: **mauvais quart d'heure** ●derived from experience rather than logic:

empirical ●experienced at second hand: **vicarious**

experiment ●experimental ideas in the arts, or the people practising them: **avant-garde** ●experiments performed on living animals: **vivisection** ●procedures of a scientific experiment: **protocol** ●exact repetition of an experiment: **replication** ●sample for experimentation: **specimen** ●bacteria etc. grown for experimentation: **culture** ●item analogous to those experimented upon, and observed for comparison: **control**

expert ●*combining forms*: -ician (*e.g.* statistician), -ist ●expert in a stated field: **boffin, buff** ●person competent in several fields: **generalist** ●aesthetic expert: **connoisseur** ●expert in church law: **canonist** ●panel of experts: **brains trust** ●group of experts advising those in power: **think tank** ●non-expert: **layman**

explanation ●provisional explanation: **hypothesis** ●explanation of a difficult word in a text: **gloss** ●explanation harder to understand than the problem: **ignotum per ignotius**

explode ●make explode: **detonate**

explosive ●nitroglycerine explosive: **dynamite** ●explosive made of nitroglycerine and nitrocellulose: **gelignite** ●powerful odourless plastic explosive: **Semtex™** ●explosive made of saltpetre, sulphur, and charcoal: **gunpowder** ●explosive material in a missile's warhead: **payload** ●explosive charge to propel a rocket: **propellant** ●explosive railway warning device: **detonator** ●denoting ammunition containing explosive: **live** ●device activating an explosive: **detonator, fuse** ●hole bored to take explosive: **blast hole, shot hole** ●sharp-ended bar drilling blast holes: **jumper** ●explosive situation: **powder keg, tinderbox**

extent ●extent of one's operations or power: **ambit**

extermination ●extermination of an entire nation or people: **genocide, holocaust**

external ●*combining forms*: **ecto-** (*e.g.* ectogenesis), **exo-** (*e.g.* exoskeleton), **out-** (*e.g.* outbuildings)

extra ●*combining forms*: **super-** (*e.g.* supersensitive), **ultra-** (*e.g.* ultrapolite)

extreme ●*combining form*: **ultra-** (*e.g.* ultramicroscopic)

eye ●*combining forms*: **ocul-, ophthalmo-** ●*adjectives*: **ocular, ophthalmic, optic** ●eye with a streaked or opaque white iris: **wall eye** ●white outer layer of the eye: **sclera** ●transparent layer at the front of the eye: **cornea** ●coloured area round the pupil: **iris** ●dark opening at the centre of an eye: **pupil** ●transparent tissue filling the eyeball: **vitreous humour** ●light-sensitive area at the back of the eye: **retina** ●inflammation of the retina: **retinitis** ●retinal cell responding to bright light and colour: **cone** ●retinal cell responding to dull light: **rod** ●point on the retina insensitive to light: **blind spot** ●mucous membrane covering the eye: **conjunctiva** ●inflammation of this: **conjunctivitis** ●lack of eye pigmentation: **albinism** ●distortion of the eye, giving partly unfocused images: **astigmatism** ●increased pressure in the eye, causing blindness: **glaucoma**

●opaqueness of the lens, giving blurred vision: **cataract** ●adjustment of the lens to focus: **accommodation** ●dark specks floating before the eyes: **muscae volitantes** ●inflammation of the eye: **ophthalmia, ophthalmitis** ●yellowing of the eye: **jaundice** ●rapid involuntary eye movement: **nystagmus** ●denoting eyes with poor sight: **dim** ●medical specialist for vision problems: **oculist, optician** ●assessment of eyesight and correction of its defects: **optometry** ●study and treatment of eye diseases: **ophthalmology** ●device for inspecting the retina: **ophthalmoscope** ●for or by one eye: **monocular** ●for or by two eyes: **binocular** ●double vision: **diplopia** ●look directly into someone's eyes: **make eye contact** ●visible to the naked eye: **macroscopic** ●small cup for washing the eyes: **eyebath** ●Arab eye make-up: **kohl** ●horse's eye-screen: **blinker** ●eye tooth: **canine** ●an eye for an eye: **lex talionis**

eyebrow ●*adjective*: **superciliary**

eyelash ●*adjective*: **ciliary** ●eyelash cosmetic: **mascara**

eyelid ●*combining form*: **blephar-** ●*adjectives*: **ciliary, palpebral** ●inner eyelid in certain animals: **nictitating membrane, third eyelid** ●this in dogs or cats: **haw** ●drooping of the upper eyelid: **ptosis** ●inflammation of the eyelid: **blepharitis** ●inflamed swelling on the edge of an eyelid: **sty, stye**

F f

fabric ● woven fabric: **textile** ● fabrics in standard lengths: **piece goods** ● strong fabric for belts etc.: **webbing** ● thick fabric for carpets and upholstery: **moquette** ● high quality clothing fabric: **broadcloth** ● fabric made from fine smooth wool: **worsted** ● wide-meshed fabric: **fishnet** ● printed fabric for curtains and upholstery: **chintz** ● fabric with woven pictures or designs: **tapestry** ● fabric made of two or more different yarns: **union** ● thin transparent fabric: **gauze** ● denoting a thin transparent fabric: **diaphanous, sheer, translucent** ● denoting a loosely woven fabric: **open** ● denoting a fabric faced on both sides: **reversible** ● denoting an undyed fabric: **natural** ● denoting a fabric with warp and weft of different colours: **shot** ● denoting a fabric washed with abrasives: **stonewashed** ● denoting a fabric not needing ironing: **drip-dry** ● denoting a fire-resistant fabric: **flameproof, nonflammable** ● denoting fabric with a worn surface: **threadbare** ● long-napped fabric: **plush** ● towelling fabric with long uncut loops: **terry** ● fabric with a surface of diagonal ridges: **twill** ● such a ridge: **wale** ● fabric woven from flax: **linen** ● fine transparent cotton or linen: **lawn** ● coarse fabric woven from flax or hemp: **sackcloth** ● fabric with a glittering metallic thread: **lurex** ● fabric with gold or silver threads: **lamé** ● textile reinforced by embedded glass filaments: **fibreglass, glass fibre** ● thin silk or crêpe fabric: **georgette** ● silk fabric with a rippled effect: **moire, moiré, watered** ● thin stiff transparent silk fabric: **organza** ● light transparent silk or nylon fabric: **chiffon** ● fine crisp lustrous silk: **taffeta** ● fine soft silk fabric: **sarsanet** ● glossy silk fabric: **satin** ● closely woven silk, cotton or nylon with a soft pile on one side: **velvet** ● kind of linen with an inwoven pattern: **damask** ● smooth hard-wearing linen fabric: **holland** ● cotton or linen fabric woven with a diamond pattern: **diaper** ● strong rough cotton or linen: **huckaback** ● heavy cotton waterproofed with oil: **oilskin** ● heavy printed cotton fabric: **cretonne** ● printed puckered cotton fabric: **seersucker** ● hard-wearing blue cotton fabric: **denim, jean** ● coarse twilled cotton or linen: **drill** ● thick ribbed cotton fabric: **corduroy** ● fine twilled cotton: **chino** ● strong untwilled cotton: **duck** ● unbleached cotton: **calico** ● thin loosely woven cotton: **cheesecloth** ● smooth twilled cotton or worsted: **gaberdene** ● cotton fabric woven with stripes or checks: **dimity** ● cotton fabric with bold checks: **gingham** ● napped cotton fabric: **flannellette** ● light flannellette: **winceyette** ● light cotton fabrics: **jaconet, muslin** ● fine translucent cotton muslin: **organdie** ● light cotton with a corded surface: **poplin** ● soft ribbed cotton fabric: **candlewick** ● cotton got up to resemble satin: **sateen** ● coarse thick-napped woollen fabric: **duffel** ● fine woollen suiting: **barathea** ● tartan twilled wool: **plaid** ● rough woollen fabric in a speckled weave: **tweed** ● soft napped woollen fabric: **flannel** ● strong twilled woollen fabric: **serge** ● twilled worsted or cotton: **gaberdine** ● strong fabric of wool and cotton or linen: **wincey** ● coarse hemp or flax fabric: **canvas** ●coarse jute or hemp fabric: **hessian** ●strong rough hessian: **scrim** ●coarsely woven fabric used as a floor-covering: **drugget** ●fabric or yarn from angora goat hair: **mohair** ●tufty velvety fabric: **chenille** ●fabric used for dressing wounds: **lint** ●elasticated polyurethane material: **elastane** ●synthetic resin used to make synthetic textile fibres: **polyester** ●cellulose used to make synthetic textile fibres: **rayon** ●synthetic polymer used to make synthetic textile fibres: **nylon** ●recycled fabric: **mungo** ●piece of fabric covering the head: **kerchief** ●strip of fabric worn inside an open-necked shirt: **cravat** ●strip of fabric inserted to enlarge or strengthen a garment: **gusset** ●soft fabric used to pad a garment: **wadding** ●triangular piece of fabric: **gore** ●strip of gathered fabric: **frill** ●side of fabric intended for display: **right side** ●fabric scraps for stuffing cushions etc.: **flock** ●raised threads on a fabric surface: **nap, pile** ●small hole in fabric for a lace: **eyelet** ●edge on fabric to prevent unravelling: **selvedge** ●shop selling fabrics: **drapery** ●fabric sample: **swatch** ●wrap in several layers of fabric: **swathe**

face ●*adjective*: **facial** ●facial features: **physiognomy** ●appearance of facial skin: **complexion** ●facial wrinkle: **crow's-foot** ●red facial pimples during adolescence: **acne** ●involuntary facial twitch: **tic** ●denoting an expressive face: **mobile** ●with an unexpressive face: **deadpan, inscrutable, poker-faced** ●disease causing facial swelling: **mumps** ●solid representation of a face: **mask** ●cosmetic improving facial skin: **face mask, face pack** ●picture of someone's face composed from photographs of others: **photofit**

faced ●*combining forms*: **-hedral** (*e.g.* decahedral), **-hedron** (*e.g.* decahedron; *pl.* -hedra)

facility ●basic physical facilities: **infrastructure**

facing ●*combining form*: **-ward** (*e.g.* southward) ●lying facing downwards: **prone** ●lying facing upwards: **supine**

fact ●*adjective*: **factual** ●an unalterable fact: **fait accompli, donnée** ●unpleasant fact about oneself: **home truth** ●basic facts about a subject: **rudiments** ●facts known only by report: **hearsay** ●in actual fact: **de facto** ●assume as a fact: **posit**

factor ●key factor: **determinant**

faeces ●*combining form*: **copro-** ●piece of faeces: **stool** ●small round piece of animal faeces: **pellet** ●eating faeces: **coprophagous, scatophagous** ●discharge faeces from the body: **defecate, evacuate** ●such an event: **movement, bowel movement** ●discharge of liquid faeces: **diarrhoea** ●difficulty in discharging faeces: **constipation** ●pipe taking excrement and waste water down the side of a building: **soil stack** ●underground pipe for excrement and waste water: **sewer** ●system of sewers: **sewerage** ●contents of a sewer: **sewage** ●tank in which sewage is left to decompose: **septic tank** ●excrement in a septic tank: **septage** ●empty the contents of a chamber pot: **slop out** ●unhealthy interest in excrement and excretion: **scatology**

failure ●total failure: **fiasco** ●failure to fulfil an obligation: **default** ●proof against failure: **fail-safe** ●safety mechanism activated by machine failure: **fail-safe**

fair[1] ●permanent outdoor fairground: **amusement park** ●revolving fairground ride: **merry-go-round** ●fairground ride with a sharply twisting railway track: **roller coaster** ●fairground wheel: **Ferris wheel** ●fairground sideshow in which motorcyclists ride up the inner side of a large vertical cylinder: **Wall of Death** ●tall spiral slide: **helter-skelter** ●electric bumper car: **dodgem**

fair² ●*adjectives*: **equitable, even-handed, just** ●anger at unfair treatment: **indignation** ●set right an unfair situation: **redress**

fall ●fall controlled by gravity only: **free fall**

false ●*combining form*: **pseud(o)-** ●false fruit: **pseudocarp** ●writings whose authorship is falsely assigned: **pseudepigrapha**

fame ●someone or something enjoying brief fame: **nine days' wonder**

family ●*adjective*: **familial** ●narrowest family unit, consisting of a couple and their own children: **nuclear family** ●wider family unit, also including grandparents, uncles, etc.: **extended family** ●member of one's extended family: **kin, kindred** ●group of interrelated families: **clan** ●within the family: **domestic** ●as a family: **en famille** ●female side of a family: **distaff side** ●male side of a family: **spear side** ●female head of a family: **materfamilias** (*pl.* **matresfamilias**) ●male head of a family: **paterfamilias** (*pl.* **patresfamilias**) ●family descent: **lineage** ●reversion to earlier generations: **throwback** ●person's nearest living relative: **next of kin** ●descendant of a notable family: **scion** ●line of descent: **stock** ●family system having male heads: **patriarchy** ●family system having female heads: **matriarchy** ●denoting a family system counting descent through the female line: **matrilineal** ●denoting a family system counting descent through the male line: **patrilineal** ●diagram showing relationships in a family: **family tree, genealogy, pedigree, stemma** ●this showing the descent of Christ from Jesse: **Jesse tree**

●genealogy of a group of gods: **theogony** ●study of family history: **genealogy** ●state payment to a family on low income: **family credit** ●prolonged and sometimes violent ill-will between families: **feud, vendetta** ●valuable passed on in the family: **heirloom**

fantasy ●fantasy world: **Cockaigne, cloud cuckoo land, Shangri-La, Utopia, Xanadu** ●person living in a fantasy world: **Walter Mitty**

fare ●cheap fare: **saver** ●system of reduced travel fares on offer to those booking well in advance: **Apex**

farm ●large cattle farm in Canada or USA: **ranch** ●agricultural holding smaller than a farm: **smallholding** ●denoting a farm devoted to milk production: **dairy** ●farm store: **barn** ●farm store with a roof but no walls: **Dutch barn** ●farm store for grain or silage: **silo** ●neat cuboid pile of hay or straw bales: **rick, stack** ●animals kept on a farm for profit: **livestock** ●number of livestock on a farm: **headage** ▸*see also* **agriculture**

fashion ●current fashion: **vogue** ●demanded by fashion: **de rigueur** ●indicating or setting the fashion: **directional** ●person or organization able to influence fashion: **tastemaker** ●wealthy and fashionable people: **glitterati, haut monde, high society, smart set, socialites, society** ●acceptability among the urban young: **street credibility** ●out of fashion: **démodé, outmoded, out of date** ●deliberate abandonment of current fashions: **reaction**

fast¹ ●*combining form*: **tachy-** (*e.g.* tachygraphy)

fast² ●Christian fast before Christmas: **Advent** ●Christian fast before Easter: **Lent** ●Muslim month-long fast: **Ramadan** ▸*see also* **Lent**

fastener ●steel band secured by a screw: **Jubilee clip™** ●short wooden

or plastic rod on coats etc.: **toggle**
●ornamental toggle with a braided
loop: **frog**

fat ●*combining forms*: **lipo-, seb(o)-**
●metabolic formation of fat:
lipogenesis ●cosmetic surgery technique for sucking fat out from under
the skin: **liposuction** ●denoting a
gland etc. containing or secreting fat
or grease: **sebaceous** ●containing
little or no fat: **non-fat** ●excessively
fat: **obese** ●bodily fat disappearing
at adolescence: **puppy fat** ●hard
white fat round the kidneys: **suet**
●fat used for making pastry: **shortening** ●pig's fat used in cooking: **lard**
●rendered fat used in candles and
soap: **tallow** ●melt down fat: **render**
●melt down fat to separate impurities: **clarify**

fate ●fate in Hindu and Buddhist
thought: **karma** ●fate in Islamic
thought: **kismet** ●deserved fate:
comeuppance

father ●*combining form*: **patr(i)-**
●*adjective*: **paternal** ●being
someone's father: **paternity** ●denot-
ing the period during which a father's
child is born: **paternity** ●medical
test to establish fatherhood: **paternity
test** ●killing one's father: **patricide**

fault ●minor personal fault: **foible,
peccadillo** ●fault-finding: **captious,
carping, niggling**

faulty ●*combining form*: **dys-** (*e.g.*
dysentery), **mal-** (*e.g.* malfunction)

Faunus ●*Greek name*: **Pan**

favour ●curry favour: **ingratiate
oneself** ●preferential treatment
given to relatives or friends: **nepotism**

fear ●*combining form*: **-phobia** ●ex-
treme or irrational fear: **phobia** ●un-
controllable fear: **panic** ●fear of cats:
ailurophobia ●fear of computers:
cyberphobia ●fear of confined
spaces: **claustrophobia** ●fear of
corpses: **necrophobia** ●fear of the

dark: **nyctophobia** ●fear of death:
necrophobia ●fear of England or the
English: **Anglophobia** ●fear of foreigners: **xenophobia** ●fear of
heights: **acrophobia** ●fear of homosexuals: **homophobia** ●fear of the
new or unfamiliar: **neophobia** ●fear
of pain: **algophobia** ●fear of public
places: **agoraphobia** ●fear of
spiders: **arachnophobia** ●fear of
strangers: **xenophobia** ●fear of technology: **cyberphobia, techno-
phobia** ●fear of the number thir-
teen: **triskaidekaphobia** ●fear of
water: **hydrophobia** ●fear of women: **gynaecophobia, gynophobia**
●thrill of fear: **frisson** ●fearful apprehension: **foreboding**

feast ●*adjective*: **festal** ●seventh
day after a Church feast: **octave**

feather ●fancy feather: **plume**
●bird's flight feather: **pinion** ●pull
the feathers from bird's carcass:
pluck

fee ●initial fee paid to a barrister: **retainer** ●further fee paid to a barrister: **refresher** ●fee paid to a celebrity
attending an event: **appearance
money** ●fee paid to recompense
someone doing 'unpaid' work: **honorarium** ●percentage fee on business
transacted: **commission** ●fee paid to
an author etc. for copies or recordings
sold or performances given: **royalty**
●legal concept of a 'reasonable' fee for
unpriced goods or services: **quantum
meruit**

feeling ●*combining form*: **-pathy**
●feeling that something is about to
happen: **premonition** ●friendly feelings: **goodwill** ●instinctive feeling:
intuition ●widely held feeling:
groundswell ●general but unspoken
feeling: **undercurrent** ●general feeling of contentment: **euphoria** ●feel-
ing of listlessness and apathy: **leth-
argy** ●strong feeling of guilt or
regret: **remorse** ●feeling of sickness

or revulsion: **nausea** • general feeling of unease: **dysphoria, malaise** • general feeling of inadequacy: **inferiority complex** • rousing intense feelings: **emotive** • provoked by feelings rather than logic: **emotive, subjective** • conveyance of feeling in art or music: **expression** • bodily movements or posture taken to indicate thoughts and feelings: **body language** • ability to share another's feelings: **empathy** • establishment of a close relationship based on shared feelings: **bonding** • able to feel: **sentient** • that can be felt: **palpable** • abnormal physical sensation: **paraesthesia** • lack of feeling or concern: **apathy** • unable to feel: **numb**

fellow • fellow-countryman: **compatriot** • fellow sailor: **messmate, shipmate**

female • *combining forms*: **gyn-, -ess** (*e.g.* authoress), **-ette** (*e.g.* suffragette), **-trix** (*e.g.* executrix) • female chromosome: **X chromosome** • medical study of the female body and its illnesses: **gynaecology** • female members of a family: **distaff side** • female principle in Chinese philosophy: **yin** • female demon seducing sleeping men: **succubus** • denoting descent through the female line: **matrilineal**

feminine • feminine part of a man's personality according to Jungian psychology: **anima**

fence • fence of pointed stakes: **paling** • defensive fence of close-set stakes: **palisade** • movable fence section: **hurdle** • openwork fencing: **lattice** • fencing of stakes interwoven with branches: **wattle** • temporary board fence: **hoarding** • pointed wooden fencing stake: **picket** • fenced area: **compound**

fencing • attacking move: **lunge, pass** • quick evasive movement: **volte** • quick return thrust: **riposte**

• pretended sword-thrust: **feint** • sword blade from middle to point: **foible** • sword blade from middle to hilt: **forte** • blunted fencing sword: **épée** • light blunt-edged fencing sword: **foil** • light tapered fencing sword: **sabre** • knob fixed to a foil point: **button** • sword-length fencing stick: **single stick** • fencer's face-cover: **mask** • fencer's chest-protector: **plastron** • fencer's acknowledgement of an opponent's hit: **touché** • Japanese fencing: **kendo**

fermentation • *combining form*: **zym-** • enzyme mix used in fermentation: **zymase** • study of fermentation: **zymurgy**

fern • fern's compound leaf: **frond** • study of ferns: **pteridology**

ferret • male ferret: **buck, hob** • female ferret: **gill** • young ferret: **kit**

fetus • body fluid surrounding a fetus: **amniotic fluid** • membrane surrounding a fetus: **amnion, amniotic membrane, caul** • cord attaching a fetus to the placenta: **umbilical cord** • denoting a fetus able to survive outside the womb: **viable** ▸ *see also* **birth, childbirth**

feudalism • feudal duty: **fealty** • feudal lord: **seigneur** • feudal subject: **liege, vassal** • tied tenant: **villein** • tied labourer: **serf** • grant of freehold land: **feoffment**

fever • *combining form*: **febri-** • *adjective*: **febrile** • mosquito-borne fever: **malaria** • tropical fever with acute joint pains: **dengue** • tropical fever infecting the liver and kidneys: **yellow fever** • infectious fever with red spots on the chest and abdomen: **typhoid** • typhoid-like fever: **paratyphoid** • infectious fever with delirium and a purple rash: **typhus** • fever following childbirth: **puerperal fever** • fever from exposure to excessive heat: **heatstroke, sunstroke** • children's fever with a bright red rash: **scarlet fever, scarlatina** ● children's fever with a raised pink rash: **measles** ● mild form of measles: **German measles** ● children's fever with swelling of the salivary glands: **mumps** ● denoting a fever recurring every second day: **tertian** ● denoting a fever recurring every third day: **quartan** ● denoting a fever with fluctuating body temperatures: **remittent** ● abatement of a fever: **defervescence** ● drug reducing fever: **antipyretic, febrifuge** ● sudden feeling of cold followed by sweating and a sharp temperature increase: **rigor** ● disturbed mental state caused by fever: **delirium** ● kind of fever suffered by dogs: **distemper**

few ● *combining form*: **oligo-** ● rule by a select few: **oligarchy** ● intended only for the socially select: **exclusive** ● intended for a small number of experts: **esoteric** ● market controlled by a few traders: **oligopoly**

fibre ● natural fibres used for mats, ropes, and sacks: **Manila, jute** ● slender glass fibres used to transmit light: **fibre optics**

fiction ● fiction set in a context of real events: **faction** ● fiction set in a computer-dominated society: **cyberpunk** ● fiction parodying the genre's conventions: **metafiction** ● book-length fictional narrative: **novel** ● denoting low-life fiction: **picaresque** ● denoting popular or sensational fiction: **pulp** ● leading character in a work of fiction: **protagonist** ● remove a fictional character in a dramatically convincing way: **write out** ▶ *see also* **novel, story**

field ● field planted with fruit trees: **orchard** ● field used for grazing: **pasture** ● field used to make hay: **meadow** ● meadow that is periodically flooded: **water meadow** ● small field for horses: **paddock** ● rice field: **paddy** ● seasonal alternation of mountain and valley pasture: **transhumance**

fifty ● denoting a fiftieth anniversary: **golden**

fight ● confused general fight: **melee, scrimmage** ● short confused fight: **scuffle, skirmish, tussle** ● fight between two persons: **single combat** ● arranged fight between two persons: **duel** ● fighting in a war: **action** ● ready to fight: **pugnacious**

file ● sharp metal rod as a file for papers: **spike** ● computer file listing other files: **directory** ● computer file having no internal hierarchy: **flat file** ● computer file giving font and layout settings: **style sheet** ● computer file containing data representing sound: **wavetable** ● search directions for a file: **path** ● description of a file's whereabouts: **pathname** ● suffix to a file name: **extension, file extension** ● denoting a file a computer can run: **executable** ● begin access to a computer file: **open** ● text stored in a file: **document** ● record of file contents at a stated time: **snapshot** ● denoting a search conducted throughout a file: **global** ● immediate data retrieval from any part of a computer file: **direct access** ● network device controlling file access: **file server** ● compress a computer file for storage: **zip** ● link from a hypertext file to another file: **hyperlink** ● remove material from a computer file: **cut** ● move material within a file or between files: **cut and paste** ● storage of a file over scattered segments of the hard disk: **fragmentation** ● end access to a computer file: **close**

film ● *combining form*: **cine-** ● *adjective*: **cinematic** ● art of making motion-picture films: **cinematography** ● film portraying real events: **documentary** ● fictional film based or real events: **docudrama, drama-documentary** ● film's story-line: **plot**

• short film of news and current affairs: **newsreel** • short film advertizing another: **trailer** • film depicting police solving a crime: **policier** • bleak and depressing film: **film noir** • film with singing and dancing: **musical** • continuous amount of film shot at one time: **take** • board with identificatory details shot at the start of each take: **clapperboard** • short extract from a film: **clip** • single picture in a film: **frame** • list of contributors to a film: **credits** • film expert or enthusiast: **cineaste, cinephile** • room or building equipped for filming: **studio** • area where a film is being shot: **set** • wheeled platform for a film camera: **dolly** • liftable platform for a film or television camera: **crane** • pole projecting the microphone over a film camera: **boom** • alternation of contrasting shots: **intercutting** • scene reverting to an earlier dramatic time: **flashback** • consistency of detail between filmed scenes: **continuity** • out-of-studio setting for a film scene: **location** • creation of a film from drawings or models: **animation** • animated film: **cartoon** • filming technique simulating animation: **pixilation** • computer application allowing the combination of animated and live-action elements: **rotoscope** • denoting a filming technique of exposing each frame after a fixed period: **time-lapse** • visual or auditory illusions created for a film: **effects, special effects** • miniaturized film set for special effects: **diorama** • technique using special filters to shoot night scenes in daylight: **day-for-night** • soundtrack commentary by an unseen narrator: **voiceover** • list of films: **filmography** • container for a length of film: **cartridge, cassette, magazine, reel, spool** • flat sheet of film containing microphotographs: **microfiche** • film of which each frame is a microphotograph: **microfilm** • strip at the start or end of a film: **leader** • amount of film: **footage** • denoting film insensitive to red: **orthochromatic** • denoting film sensitive to all colours: **panchromatic** • film giving a positive image directly when processed: **reversal film** • admission of light to a film: **exposure** • long exposure of photographic film: **time exposure** • sensitivity of film to light: **speed** • denoting a film needing only short exposure: **fast** • film's ability to respond to light: **sensitivity** • unused or unprocessed film: **stock, film stock** • make exposed film show a visible image: **develop** • spottiness of film image: **grain** • device steadying the film as it passes the lens: **gate** • film sequence photographed continuously by one camera: **shot** • end of a filming session: **wrap** • processed but unedited film: **rushes** • edit or abridge a film: **cut** • edited version of a film: **cut** • film produced by preliminary cutting: **rough-cut** • section of film omitted in cutting: **out-take** • move abruptly from one film image to another: **cut, jump-cut** • cinematic effect in which a new scene seems to unroll across the screen: **wipe** • cinematic effect in which one scene seems to melt into the next: **dissolve** • end of a scene by gradual darkening of the screen: **fade** • inclusion of images commenting upon the main action: **montage** • facility arresting the image: **freeze-frame** • film caption: **title** • caption at the foot of a film frame: **subtitle** • strip at the edge of a film on which the sound is recorded: **soundtrack** • give a film a new soundtrack: **dub** • music composed for a film: **score** • sequence of drawings etc. outlining film shots: **storyboard** • acting text of a film: **screenplay, script** • screenplay including camera directions: **shooting script** • actor's filmed audition:

screen test •single continuous spell of filming: **take** •person in creative charge of shooting a film: **director** •general manager of a film project: **producer** •person in charge of a film's camerawork: **director of photography** •film production company: **studio** •chief electrician on a film set: **gaffer** •gaffer's assistant: **best boy** •auxiliary group responsible for filming action, special effects, and location sequences: **second unit** •person replacing a film star during dangerous action scenes: **stunt man, stunt woman** •studio's costume department: **wardrobe** •strong light for filming: **klieg light** •film actor's stand-in: **double** •availability of a film for public showing: **release** •public showing of a film: **screening** •advance screening of a new film: **preview** •television broadcast of a cinema film: **telecine** •US film award: **Oscar** •film archive: **cinematheque** ▸*see also* **camera**

filter •filter through gradually: **percolate** •face mask filtering ingested air: **respirator** •filtration process for blood of a patient suffering kidney failure: **dialysis**

final •final part of a piece of music: **coda** •final part of a play: **denouement, epilogue** •final part of a speech: **peroration**

find •lucky find: **trouvaille** •ability to make these: **serendipity** •find for the first time: **discover** •technique of locating persons or objects through the heat they emit: **thermal imaging**

finger •*adjective*: **digital** •first finger: **forefinger, index finger** •finger next to the little finger: **ring finger** •excessive number of fingers: **polydactyly** •sheath for an injured finger: **fingerstall**

fingerprint •powder-blower making fingerprints visible: **insufflator**

Finnish •Finnish steam bath: **sauna** •Finnish traditional legends: **Kalevala**

fire •*combining form*: **pyro-** •*adjective*: **fiery** •fire for burning a corpse: **pyre** •fire set in a high place to convey a signal: **beacon** •fierce fire caused by bombs: **firestorm** •treetop forest fire: **crown fire** •lens used to start a fire: **burning glass** •portable container for a fire: **brazier** •material for starting a fire: **kindling** •halfburnt material in a dying fire: **embers** •slow a fire by reducing its draught: **damp** •extinguish a fire: **douse** •extinguish a fire by covering it: **smother** •water-supply for a fire hose: **hydrant** •fireproof sheet: **fire blanket** •starting fires: **incendiary** •person starting fires for malicious purposes: **arsonist** •obsessive desire to set fire to things: **pyromania** •destroy by fire: **burn, incinerate** •mythical creature said to live in fire: **salamander** •easily set on fire: **flammable, inflammable** •slow to catch fire: **flame retardant** •fireresistant: **flameproof, nonflammable**

fireman •fireman's turn of duty: **watch**

fireplace •fireplace in a steam engine: **firebox** •floor of a fireplace: **hearth** •metal plate adjusting the draught: **register** •side-space in a large fireplace: **inglenook** •grid at front of fireplace to keep in burning material: **fender** •cooking shelf along the side of fireplace: **hob** •cooking stand at the front of fireplace: **trivet** •stand to support logs in a fireplace: **andiron, firedog** •metal plate at the back of a fireplace: **fireback, reredos** •smoke duct above a fireplace: **chimney, flue** •shelf above a fireplace: **mantel, mantelshelf, mantelpiece** •ornamental structure above a fireplace: **overmantel** •implements for tending a fire: **fire irons**

● device for picking up pieces of coal: **tongs** ● container for coal at a fireplace: **hod, scuttle**

fireworks ● *adjective*: **pyrotechnic** ● noisy firework: **banger** ● noisy firework used in simulated battles: **thunderflash** ● firework exploding high in the air: **rocket** ● small hand-held firework: **banger** ● small hissing firework: **squib** ● coiled firework spinning when lit: **Catherine wheel**

first ● *combining forms*: **proto-, ur-** (*e.g.* 'reconstruct an ur-Hamlet') ● first example: **prototype** ● first appearance of a performer: **debut** ● first performance: **premiere** ● first among equals: **primus inter pares** ● first-year student at a university: **freshman** ● be the first to use: **pioneer**

first aid ● restart of breathing: **artificial respiration, ventilation** ● position in which unconscious persons are placed: **recovery position, semiprone position**

fish ● *combining forms*: **ichthy(o)-, pisc-** ● *adjective*: **piscine** ● young of fish: **fry** ● large group of fish: **school, shoal** ● fish living at the bottom: **groundling** ● aggressive sharptoothed fish: **piranha** ● hard plate covering a fish's skin: **scale** ● fish's flipper: **fin** ● fish's breathing organ: **gill** ● cover for this: **operculum** (*pl.* opercula) ● fish sperm or sperm gland: **milt** ● fish eggs: **roe, spawn** ● fish gelatin: **isinglass** ● study of fish: **ichthyology** ● denoting fish with light-coloured flesh: **white** ● denoting fish with darker-coloured flesh: **red** ● denoting fish that swim up-river from the sea to spawn: **anadromous** ● journey made by anadromous fish: **run** ● channels built to assist anadromous fish round natural obstacles: **fish ladder, fishway, pass** ● denoting fish that swim down-river to the sea to spawn: **catadromous** ● denoting freshwater fish other than salmon and trout: **coarse** ● fish-

eating: **piscivorous** ● fish that has not been cooked, smoked, or frozen: **wet fish** ● fish stew from southern France: **bouillabaisse** ● dish of fish, rice, and hard-boiled eggs: **kedgeree** ● dried fish eaten with curries: **Bombay duck** ● finely ground paste of seasoned fish: **pâté, terrine** ● small ball of seasoned fish: **quenelle** ● pickled sturgeon roe: **caviar** ● minced fish rolled in bacon: **kromesky** ● dish of finely minced fish: **timbale** ● dish of pressed fish in aspic: **galantine** ● denoting fish cooked in browned butter with lemon: **meunière** ● thick slice of fish: **steak** ● fried strip of fish: **goujon** ● long thin slice of fish rolled and stuffed: **paupiette** ● small flat round cut of fish: **médaillon** ● skewer for grilling fish: **brochette** ● crab-flavoured stick of mixed fish pieces: **crab stick** ● preserve fish by drying or smoking: **cure, kipper** ● remove fish entrails: **clean, gut** ● remove fishbones: **fillet** ● cultivation of sea fish: **mariculture** ● cultivation of fresh-water fish: **pisciculture** ● establishment where fish are bred commercially: **fishery, fish farm** ● display tank for live fish, or building containing these: **aquarium** ● fish seller: **fishmonger**

fishes ● *astrological term*: **pisces**

fishing ● *adjectives*: **piscatorial, piscatory** ● fisherman's assistant: **gillie** ● fisherman's waterproof garment covering from feet to armpits: **waders** ● fisherman's thick blue sweater: **guernsey** ● catch fish with one's hands: **guddle, tickle** ● fish caught for sport: **game fish** ● total fish caught in one session: **net** ● fish with a bobbing fly: **dap** ● floating artificial fly: **dry fly** ● artificial fly that sinks below the water: **wet fly** ● material to make these: **dubbing** ● insect larva for bait: **gentle, maggot** ● bait thrown into the water: **groundbait** ● fishing rod's handle: **stock**

●fish hook weighted to stay underwater: **drail** ●back-turned spike on a fish hook: **barb** ●weight on a fishing line: **sinker** ●cylinder for winding in the line: **reel, spool** ●throw a baited hook or net: **cast** ●secure the hook in a fish's mouth: **strike** ●tire a hooked fish: **play** ●hooked stick for landing fish: **gaff** ●device removing the hook from a fish: **disgorger** ●net for keeping fish alive: **keepnet** ●angler's equipment: **tackle** ●angler's fish basket: **creel** ●stretch of water used for fishing: **ground** ●fish by trailing a line behind a boat: **troll** ●fishing boat dragging a large net along the sea bed: **trawler** ●fishing boat with processing facilities: **factory ship** ●fishing net that drifts with the tide: **drift net** ●fishing net hanging vertically: **seine** ●seine that can be drawn into a bag shape: **purse seine** ●deep-sea fishing line: **long line** ●amount of fish caught over a specified period: **catch** ●fish captured in a single throw of the net: **draught** ●person unloading fishing boats: **lumper**

fit[1] ●periodic loss of consciousness or convulsions: **epilepsy**

fit[2] ●denoting an object that fits inside another: **nesting**

fit for ●*combining form*: -worthy (*e.g.* roadworthy) ●fit to eat: **edible**

five ●*combining forms*: pent-, quin-, quinque- ●five-sided figure: **pentagon** ●solid figure with five faces: **pentahedron** ●five-pointed star: **pentagram, pentangle** ●set of five: **pentad** ●one of five offspring born at a birth: **quintuplet, quin** ●athletic contest with five events for all competitors: **pentathlon** ●ensemble of five musicians, or music for them: **quintet** ●group of five arranged as on a domino or playing-card: **quincunx** ●occurring every, or lasting for, five years: **quinquennial** ●five-

hundredth anniversary: **quincentenary**

fives ●projecting wall in a fives court: **tambour**

flag ●*adjective*: vexillary ●national flag: **banner, ensign** ●national flag flown at a ship's bow: **jack** ●military or ceremonial flag: **standard** ●flag of the United Kingdom: **Union Jack** ●flag of the Royal Navy: **white ensign** ●flag of naval auxiliary vessels: **blue ensign** ●flag of British-registered ships: **red ensign** ●pirate flag: **Jolly Roger** ●blue flag raised by ship about to leave port: **Blue Peter** ●small triangular flag: **burgee** ●long tapering flag: **pennant, pennon** ●short tapering flag: **guidon** ●long narrow flag with a cleft end: **banderole** ●banner hung from a crossbar: **gonfalon** ●flag signalling the end of a motor race: **chequered flag** ●flags as street decorations: **bunting** ●denoting a flag flown below the pole-top: **at half mast** ●rope to raise a flag: **halyard, lanyard** ●lower a flag: **strike** ●study of flags: **vexillology**

flame ●very hot cutting flame: **thermic lance** ●device producing a hot flame: **blowlamp, blowtorch**

flare ●flare fired from a pistol: **Very light**

flat ●top-floor flat: **penthouse** ●flat consisting of one room: **bedsitter** ●flat having one main room: **studio, studio flat** ●flat on two floors: **duplex** ●flat on two or more floors, with its own outside door: **maisonette** ●flat kept for occasional use: **pied-à-terre** ●rented flat cleaned by the owners: **service flat** ●large building divided into flats: **tenement**

flatter ●servile flatterer: **sycophant** ●excessively or insincerely flattering: **unctuous**

flatulence ●infantile flatulence: **colic, wind** ●medication to relieve flatulence: **carminative**

flavour ●strong flavour: **tang** ●having little flavour: **bland, insipid, mild** ●thick flavouring liquid: **sauce** ●pungent vegetable food flavouring: **spice** ●add a pungent flavouring to food or drink: **spike** ●condiment eaten with plain food to give flavour: **relish** ●chemical used to strengthen food flavour: **flavour enhancer** ●flavour enhancer used in Chinese cuisine: **monosodium glutamate** ●yellow powder used to flavour Asian dishes: **turmeric** ●browned sugar or syrup used as flavouring: **caramel** ●herbs or spices as flavour enhancers: **seasoning** ●bag of herbs used to flavour soups: **bouquet garni** ●fine strips of citrus fruit peel used as flavouring: **zest** ▸ *see also* **taste**

flea ●tropical burrowing flea: **chigger, jigger**

fleet ●fleet of small ships: **flotilla** ●small fleet of warships: **squadron** ●Spanish war fleet sent in 1588: **Armada**

Flemish ●Flemish mayor: **burgomaster**

flesh ●*combining form*: **carn-** ●*adjective*: **carnal** ●sensitive flesh: **quick** ●flesh injury: **wound** ●flesh-eating: **carnivorous** ●decaying flesh of a dead animal: **carrion**

flight ●unpowered flight: **glide** ●ceremonial flight over a certain spot: **fly-past** ●frictional limitation on the speed of flight: **heat barrier** ●extreme tiredness felt after a flight across time zones: **jet lag**

flirt ●flirtatious behaviour: **coquetry**

float ●float attached to the side of a canoe etc: **outrigger** ●float supporting a bridge: **pontoon** ●float used to raise sunken ships: **caisson** ●ability to float: **buoyancy**

flood ●*adjectives*: **diluvial, diluvian** ●sudden flood: **flash flood** ●sudden river flood: **spate** ●flood moving down-river: **freshet** ●severe rain causing flooding: **deluge** ●embankment built as a flood defence: **dyke** ●breach caused by flooding: **washout** ●low-lying area subject to flooding: **flood plain** ●field that is periodically flooded: **water meadow** ●rich soil deposited by flood water: **alluvium** ●the biblical Flood: **the Deluge** ●occurring before this: **antediluvian**

floor ●floor for principal reception rooms: **piano nobile** ●floor between the main floors: **entresol, mezzanine** ●floor of wood blocks: **parquet** ●projecting ridge along the edge of a floorboard: **tongue** ●hollow into which this fits: **groove** ●levelled layer of floor cement: **screed** ●flooring material of marble chips set in concrete: **terrazzo** ●floor covering of small pieces of stone etc. arranged to make pictures or patterns: **mosaic** ●access panel in a floor: **trapdoor**

flour ●*adjective*: **farinaceous** ●flour made from whole grains of wheat: **wholemeal** ●flour made from wheat with some of the germ removed: **wheatmeal** ●hard grains left after flour has been milled: **semolina** ●denoting flour with an added raising agent: **self-raising** ●denoting flour lacking a raising agent: **plain** ●work flour into dough: **knead**

flow ●*combining forms*: **rheo-** (*e.g.* rheostat), **-rrhoea** (*e.g.* menorrhoea), **-rrhagia** (*e.g.* menorrhagia) ●flow rapidly: **gush** ●halt a flow: **stem**

flower ●*combining forms*: **antho-** (*e.g.* anthology, *literally a 'collection of flowers'*), **flor-** ●*adjective*: **floral** ●small flower in a composite flower head: **floret** ●flower that keeps its colour when dried: **immortelle** ●flower of willow and hazel trees: **catkin** ●petals of a flower: **corolla** ●flower's female organ: **pistil** ●flower's male organ: **stamen** ●circle of flowers on a stem, or of petals or sepals in a flower: **whorl**

●compact cluster of flowers on one stalk: **truss** ●denoting a flower with a single whorl of petals: **single** ●small bunch of flowers: **nosegay, posy** ●arranged bunch of flowers: **bouquet, spray** ●spray for a button-hole: **boutonnière** ●fastened arrangement of flowers: **garland** ●garland for the head: **chaplet** ●garland for a grave: **wreath** ●Japanese art of flower arranging: **ikebana** ●flower-growing: **floriculture** ●flower-seller: **florist** ●denoting a flower past its prime: **overblown** ●sweet liquid collected by bees from flowers: **nectar** ●fine dust collected by bees from flowers: **pollen** ●leaf at the edge of a flower: **bract** ●plant bearing clusters of flowers: **floribunda**

fluid ●body fluid in early medicine: **humour** ●body fluid surrounding embryo: **amniotic fluid** ●body fluid around joints: **sinovia** ●fluid accumulation in the brain: **hydrocephalus** ●insufficient fluid in the body: **dehydration** ●semifluidity: **viscosity** ●study of fluids at rest: **hydrostatics** ●study of fluid forces: **hydrodynamics** ●study of fluid mechanics: **hydraulics**

fluorescence ●*combining form*: **fluoro-** ●X-ray viewer with a fluorescent screen: **fluoroscope**

fluorine ●*combining form*: **fluoro-** (*e.g.* fluorocarbon)

flute ●flute's mouth-hole: **embouchure** ●flute player: **flautist**

fly ●fly biting livestock: **gadfly** ●fly biting horses and men: **horsefly** ●fly causing malaria: **mosquito** ●African fly causing sleeping sickness: **tsetse** ●fly laying its eggs on food: **blowfly** ●large blowfly: **bluebottle** ●fruit fly used in genetic research: **drosophila** ●fly larva: **maggot, gentle** ●sticky paper strip as flytrap: **flypaper**

flying ●supernatural flying: **levitation** ●fly high in the air: **soar** ●fly

close to the ground: **hedge-hop** ●fly very close to intimidate: **buzz** ●maintain height without using an engine or wings: **soar**

fodder ●fodder of fermented grass: **silage** ●tall fodder plant with yellow flowers: **rape**

fog ●fog mixed with smoke etc.: **smog** ●audible warning to ships in fog: **foghorn**

follow ●follow and observe secretly: **shadow, tail** ●follow an opposing player to obstruct his activities: **mark**

follower ●follower or imitator of lesser ability: **epigone**

fond ●*combining forms*: **phil(o)-** (*e.g.* philoprogenitive), **-phile** (*e.g.* bibliophile)

food ●*combining forms*: **tropho-, -trophic** (*e.g.* oligotrophic) ●*adjective*: **alimentary** ●food for the gods: **ambrosia** ●food for pigs: **swill** ●food for horses: **tack** ●food for sheep and cattle: **fodder, forage** ●food set out for self-service: **buffet** ●food that is quick and easy to prepare: **convenience food, fast food** ●fast food of little nutritional value: **junk food** ●bland and tasteless food: **pap** ●semi-liquid food: **slops** ●food rich in fibre: **roughage** ●denoting food with minimal processing and additives: **organic, natural, whole** ●small tasty piece of food: **titbit** ●lump of food: **gobbet** ●food regurgitated for further chewing: **cud** ●portion of food for one person: **helping, serving** ●supplies of food and drink: **provisions** ●apportioned food: **ration** ●emergency supply of basic food: **iron rations** ●seasoning for food: **condiment** ●denoting undried or unsmoked food: **green** ●food used to embellish a dish: **garnish** ●food used to give taste to a dish: **relish** ●sweet or savoury mixture cooked inside meat, poultry, etc.: **stuffing** ●chemical used to strengthen food flavour: **flavour enhancer** ●flavour enhancer used in Chinese cuisine: **monosodium glutamate** ●bag of herbs used to flavour soups: **bouquet garni** ●pungent vegetable food flavouring: **spice** ●chopped fresh herbs: **fines herbes** ●shop selling foreign foods: **delicatessen** ●denoting food prepared in accordance with Jewish law: **kosher** ●denoting food unacceptable to Jewish law: **tref** ●denoting food cooked and then refrigerated before distribution: **cook-chill** ●denoting food preserved in a sealed jar: **potted** ●denoting food dried for preservation: **dehydrated** ●denoting food treated to stay fresh: **long-life** ●denoting food that is no longer fresh: **stale, off, rancid** ●denoting food that goes bad quickly: **perishable** ●thaw frozen food before cooking: **defrost** ●clean or prepare food: **dress** ●cut food into small cubes: **dice** ●fry food briefly to brown the outside: **sauté, seal** ●fry food briefly, stirring to avoid browning: **stir-fry** ●dip food briefly into boiling water: **scald** ●add spices to food: **season** ●finely ground paste of seasoned meat or fish: **pâté** ●sprinkle liquid over food: **drizzle** ●sprinkle food with flour or sugar: **dredge, dust** ●thin line of cream or icing decorating food: **piping** ●enrich food with vitamins: **fortify** ●denoting foodstuffs that are new and will not keep: **fresh** ●denoting foodstuffs that are currently available fresh: **in season** ●denoting food covered with grated cheese or breadcrumbs and browned: **au gratin, gratiné** ●denoting food cut into short thin strips: **julienne** ●denoting food served on spinach: **florentine** ●denoting food served in browned butter: **meunière** ●denoting food served with white grapes: **Véronique** ●denoting food soused in spirits and set alight: **flambé** ●set food alight thus: **flame**

●denoting food browned quickly at high temperature: **seared** ●denoting food cooked with spicy seasoning: **devilled** ●denoting food cooked in a pastry case: **en croute** ●denoting food cooked and served in a paper wrapper: **en papillote** ●denoting food that is uncooked, or cooked in the simplest way: **au naturel** ●denoting food cooked in the simplest way: **bonne femme** ●denoting food cooked in cider and cream: **à la normande** ●denoting food prepared by a first-class chef: **cordon bleu** ●denoting food that may be prepared quickly: **Instant** ●denoting food preserved in brine: **corned, soused** ●denoting food preserved by drying: **desiccated** ●denoting food soaked in a marinade: **soused** ●denoting food modified to be unfattening: **diet** ●denoting food free from rich ingredients: **light** ●denoting food that is hard to digest: **heavy** ●(of food) be tasted again after being swallowed: **repeat** ●denoting foodstuffs produced without artificial chemicals: **organic** ●denoting food with no nutritional value: **innutritious** ●rolled food: **roulade** ●small amount of food, rolled in breadcrumbs: **croquette** ●food grilled on a skewer: **kebab** ●food coated in batter and fried: **fritter** ●shiny coating on food: **glaze** ●tough piece of fibre in food: **string** ●constituent of a dish: **ingredient** ●person who enjoys fine food and drink: **bon vivant, bon viveur, epicure, gastronome, gourmand, gourmet** ●creature eating all kinds of food: **omnivore** ●fish-eating creature: **piscivore** ●creature eating no meat or fish: **vegetarian** ●creature eating no animal products: **vegan** ●creature eating only fruit: **fruitarian** ●animal eating only plants: **herbivore** ●eating only one kind of food: **monophagous** ●eating raw food: **omophagous** ●person providing food professionally: **caterer, purveyor** ● food heater for use at the table: **chafing dish** ● list of foods eaten or to be eaten: **diet** ● sterilize food by gamma radiation: **irradiate** ● electrical grinder for waste food: **waste-disposal unit** ● food poisoning: **botulism, salmonellosis** ● fly's eggs on food: **fly-blow** ● bring up swallowed food: **regurgitate** ● food allergy with an itching rash: **hives, nettlerash, urticaria** ● abstention from food: **fast** ● food element giving essential nourishment: **nutrient** ● denoting foods rich in these: **nutritious** ● lack of proper or sufficient food: **malnutrition** ● thin or weak through lack of food: **emaciated** ● undernourishment causing low weight: **marasmus** ● study of food and its use: **nutrition** ● search about for food: **forage** ● series of organisms each depending on the next for food: **food chain** ● interlocking system of these: **food web** ● heated food trolley: **hostess trolley** ● credit voucher exchanged for food: **luncheon voucher** ● establishment serving free food to the poor: **soup kitchen** ● extreme scarcity of food: **famine** ▸ *see also* **pudding, sauce**

foot ● *combining forms*: pedi- (*e.g.* pedicure), -pod(e) (*e.g.* arthropod) ● divided foot of cattle, sheep, etc.: **cloven hoof** ● permanently twisted foot: **club foot** ● having an injured foot: **lame** ● having inturned feet: **pigeon-toed** ● foot bones: **metatarsus** ● arch of the foot: **instep** ● denoting a foot with a low arch: **flat** ● denoting the soles of the feet: **plantar** ● animal having two feet: **biped** ● animal having four feet: **quadruped** ● person going on foot: **pedestrian** ● instrument estimating the distance travelled on foot: **pedometer** ● grip for the feet: **foothold, footing** ● wart growing on feet: **verruca** ● small painful area of thickened skin: **wart** ● painful swelling on the big toe joint: **bunion**

● itchy swelling caused by cold: **chilblain** ● specialist treating the feet: **chiropodist, podiatrist** ● cosmetic treatment of the feet: **pedicure** ● caning the soles of the feet as a punishment or form of torture: **bastinado**

football ● primitive form of football played at Eton College: **wall game** ▸ *see also* **soccer**

football pool ● selection of matches in a pools entry: **perm** ● payment shared between pool winners: **dividend**

footwear ● wooden-soled footwear: **clogs** ● ridge on the sole of footwear: **cleat** ● light footwear with a scanty upper: **sandals** ● slipper with sole and sides in one piece: **moccasin** ▸ *see also* **sandal, shoe**

forbid ● forbid by law: **proscribe** ● forbidden by social custom: **taboo**

force ● force attracting a body towards a larger one: **gravity** ● rotatory force: **torque** ● force moving rotating objects outwards: **centrifugal force** ● force moving rotating objects inwards: **centripetal force** ● force holding quarks, neutrons, and protons together within the nucleus: **strong force** ● force involved in the decay of nuclei: **weak force** ● area in which a force is effective: **field** ● using force: **forcible** ● obtain by force: **extort** ● force upon: **impose** ● impetus gained by a moving object: **momentum** (*pl.* momenta) ● tendency of a body to remain static or in motion unless acted upon by an external force: **inertia**

forehead ● *adjective*: frontal

foreign ● *combining form*: xeno- ● strange and foreign: **exotic** ● foreign girl who does domestic work in return for keep and English lessons: **au pair** ● resident foreigner: **alien** ● area settled by foreigners: **colony** ● expel a foreigner: **deport** ● fear or hatred of foreigners: **xenophobia**

●person living in a foreign country: **expatriate** ●foreign embassy's freedom from local laws: **extraterritoriality**

foreman ●foreman's deputy: **chargehand**

foreskin ●congenital narrowness of the foreskin's opening: **phimosis** ●removal of the foreskin: **circumcision**

forest ●*adjective*: **sylvan** ●damp tropical forest: **rainforest** ●open space in a forest: **glade** ●strip of forest cleared to hamper fires: **firebreak** ●mythical wild man of the forest: **green man**

forgiveness ●priest's sacramental forgiveness of confessed sins: **absolution**

fork ●two-pronged agricultural fork: **pitchfork** ●large two-pronged meat fork: **carving fork** ●fork's sharp prong: **tine**

form ●*combining forms*: **morpho-** (*e.g.* morphology), **-morph** (*e.g.* ectomorph), **-morphic** (*e.g.* anthropomorphic)

formula ●*adjective*: **formulaic**

fort ●coastal defence fort: **Martello tower** ●small concrete fort: **blockhouse, pillbox**

fortification ●fortification of wooden stakes: **palisade, stockade** ●projecting fortification where two walls meet at an angle: **bastion** ●outer fortification: **outwork** ●concrete fortification: **blockhouse** ●underground fortified shelter: **bunker** ●fortified shore area established by an invader: **beachhead** ●denoting a fortification that cannot be captured: **impregnable**

fortune ●piece of unexpected good fortune: **windfall** ●unexpected run of good fortune: **bonanza** ●chance development of events in a fortunate way: **serendipity** ●reflect smugly on

one's good fortune: **gloat** ●object thought to bring good fortune: **talisman** ●animal etc. kept to bring good fortune: **mascot** ●source of ill fortune: **jinx** ●change of fortune: **vicissitude** ●extreme point of ill fortune: **nadir**

fortune telling ●fortune telling from dreams: **oneiromancy** ●fortune telling from lines on the hand: **palmistry, chiromancy** ●fortune telling from playing cards: **cartomancy** ●fortune telling from the stars: **astrology** ●fortune telling by drawing lots: **sortilege** ●fortune teller's globe: **crystal ball** ●foretell the future by this: **scry** ●card pack used in fortune telling: **Tarot**

forwards ●*combining form*: **pro-** (*e.g.* protrude)

fossil ●fossil used to date surrounding strata: **index fossil** ●fuel derived from fossilized remains: **fossil fuel** ●study of fossils: **palaeontology**

four ●*combining forms*: **quadr-, tetr-** ●fourfold: **quadruple** ●having four parts: **quadripartite, quadruple** ●four-sided figure: **quadrilateral** ●one of four offspring born at a birth: **quadruplet, quad** ●four-legged animal: **quadruped** ●four-line verse stanza: **quatrain** ●set of four: **quartet** ●group of four artworks with related themes: **tetralogy** ●ensemble of four musicians, or music for them: **quartet, quartette** ●four-track stereophonic sound: **quadraphony** ●in four identical copies: **in quadruplicate** ●four hundredth anniversary: **quatercentenary** ●period of four years: **quadrennium** ●occurring every, or lasting for, four years: **quadrennial**

fowl ●*adjective*: **gallinaceous** ●female fowl: **hen** ●male fowl: **cock, cockerel** ●young fowl: **chick, chicken** ●young hen: **pullet** ●cock bred for fighting: **gamecock** ●castrated cock: **capon** ●small-sized breed of fowls: **bantam** ●fowl's red crest: **comb** ●red lobe hanging below a fowl's beak: **wattle** ●sharp projection on the back of a cock's leg: **spur** ●young fowl killed for eating: **poussin** ●fowl split open and grilled: **spatchcock** ●remove a fowl's innards: **draw** ●denoting a fowl wishing to incubate eggs: **broody** ●denoting fowls that are allowed out: **free range** ●denoting fowls kept in a large shed: **deep litter** ●denoting fowls kept in small cages: **battery, broiler-house** ●open-air cage for fowls: **coop, run** ●fowl's leg served as food: **drumstick** ●fowl's edible offal: **giblets** ●fried strip of chicken: **goujon** ●poultry influenza: **fowl pest, Newcastle disease** ●poultry disease with thick mucus: **pip**

fox ●*adjective*: **vulpine** ●female fox: **vixen** ●male fox: **dog** ●young fox: **cub** ●group of foxes: **skulk** ●fox's lair: **earth** ●fox's tail: **brush** ●fox's head as a hunting trophy: **mask**

fraction ●fraction with numbers above and below a line: **vulgar fraction** ●fraction with numbers either side of a decimal point: **decimal fraction** ●number placed above the line in a fraction: **numerator** ●number placed below the line in a fraction: **denominator** ●common multiple of the denominators of several fractions: **common denominator** ●smallest common multiple of the denominators of several fractions: **lowest common denominator** ●fraction equal to less than one: **proper fraction** ●fraction equal to more than one: **improper fraction**

fracture ●wrist fracture with the hand pushed back: **Colles' fracture** ●denoting a fracture to the bone only: **simple** ●denoting a fracture where the bone pierces the skin: **compound** ●denoting a fracture with many bone splinters: **comminuted** ●denoting a

partial fracture in children: **greenstick**

framework ●framework with sloping legs, used to support a table, bier, etc.: **trestle** ●light framework supporting fruit trees etc.: **trellis** ●framework for drying washing indoors: **clotheshorse** ●firm supporting framework: **skeleton** ●supporting framework for a roof, bridge, etc.: **truss**

frank ●unrestrainedly frank: **blunt, outspoken**

fraud ●interfere with a process to ensure a desired result: **rig, set up**

free ●*combining form*: **un-** (*e.g.* unburden) ●free from obligations: **footloose** ●denoting a service supplied free of charge: **courtesy** ●free from restrictions: **decontrol**

freedom ●freedom of action: **carte blanche, latitude, leeway, licence** ●freedom from punishment: **impunity** ●favouring individual freedom: **liberal** ●restriction of subordinates' freedoms, allegedly for their own good: **paternalism**

Freemasonry ●Freemasons' brotherhood: **Craft** ●Freemasons' branch: **lodge** ●chief Freemason: **Grand Master** ●Freemason's rank: **degree**

freeze ●*combining form*: **cryo-** ●freeze very rapidly: **flash-freeze** ●freeze a liquid without solidification: **supercool** ●deep-freezing of corpses in hope of subsequent medical advances that could reverse their cause of death: **cryonics, cryogenics** ●surgery undertaken on a part of the body that has been subjected to intense cold: **cryosurgery**

French ●*combining forms*: **Franco-, franco-** ●lover of French culture: **Francophile** ●French-speaking: **francophone** ●French using many English terms: **franglais** ●French castle: **chateau** (*pl.* chateaux)

• French holiday house: **gîte** • French motorway: **auto-route** • French public urinal: **pissoir** • French priest: **curé** • title of a French abbot or (as a courtesy) of any French clergyman: **abbé** • French policeman: **gendarme** • French long-distance lorry driver: **routier** • French flaky pastry roll: **croissant** • French soft white cheeses: **Brie, Camembert** • French soft blue sheep-milk cheese: **Roquefort™** • French yoghurt-like cheese: **from-age frais** • French goat's cheese: **chèvre** • French toasted sandwich with cheese and ham: **croque-monsieur** • French pancake: **crêpe** • French beef stew: **grillade** • French soup with beef and vegetables: **pot-au-feu** • French mutton casserole: **navarin** • French stew of meat and beans: **cassoulet** • fish stew from southern France: **bouillabaisse** • small French restaurant: **bistro** • French shop selling cold cooked meats: **charcuterie** • French aniseed-flavoured aperitifs: **pastis, Pernod™** • French brandy: **cognac** • French blackcurrant liqueur: **cassis** • French vineyard: **domaine** • group of French vineyards: **cru** • description awarded to a French wine guaranteeing its orgin and method of production: **appellation contrôlée, appellation d'origine contrôlée** • category of wines or vineyards: **cru** • French bowls: **boules, pétanque** • French wooden shoe: **sabot** • French soldier's peaked cap: **kepi** • French regiment for foreigners: **Foreign Legion** • member of this: **legionnaire** • French resistance fighter: **maquis, maquisard** • French beheading machine: **guillotine** • Frenchwoman knitting by the guillotine: **tricoteuse** • cart conveying victims to the guillotine: **tumbril** • French high-kicking dance: **cancan** • French medieval poet: **troubadour,**

trouvère • French epic poem: **chanson de geste** • French name for southern France: **Midi** • French administrative region: **department** • French suburb: **faubourg** • French law allegedly excluding females from dynastic succession: **Salic law**

friction • *combining form*: **tribo-** • creation of an electric charge by friction: **triboelectricity** • emission of light by something rubbed or scratched: **triboluminescence**

friend • seek someone's friendship: **cultivate**

frog • *adjective*: **batrachian** • frog's young: **fry** • frog eggs: **spawn** • tailed frog larva: **tadpole**

front • *combining form*: **fore-** (*e.g.* forebrain) • front of a building: **façade** • front of an army: **vanguard** • front of a leaf of paper: **recto**

fruit • *combining forms*: **fruct-, -carp** • small stoneless fruit: **soft fruit** • hard dry fruit: **nut** • fruit of the oak: **acorn** • hawthorn fruit: **haw** • tropical fruit used in chutneys: **mango** • green-fleshed fruit with black seeds: **kiwi fruit** • orange-like fruit with sweet rind and sour pulp: **kumquat** • denoting fruit of the orange type: **citrus** • fruit rotten before it is ripe: **medlar** • fruit blown down by the wind: **windfall** • compact cluster of fruit on one stalk: **truss** • fine powdery deposit found on the surface of certain fruits: **bloom** • fruit's outer covering: **hull** • tough outer skin of certain fruits: **rind** • soft fleshy part of fruit: **pulp** • hard seed of certain fruits: **stone** • covering of a fruitseed: **endocarp** • fruit-growing: **pomiculture** • study of fruit-growing: **pomology** • denoting fruit made shiny by preservation in sugar: **glacé** • (of blossom) form into fruit: **set** • ripening of fruit: **matur-ation** • squeeze fruit to extract the juice: **press** • sour juice obtained from fruit: **verjuice** ●cream of liquidized fruit: **purée** ●dish of mixed chopped fruit: **macédoine** ●dish of fruit cooked in syrup: **compote** ●fruit boiled in sugar: **conserve, preserve** ●natural sugar found in fruits and honey: **fructose** ●fruit sugar used as a setting agent: **pectin** ●hard fruitskin used as a water container: **gourd** ●small fruit fly used in genetic research: **drosophila** ●person eating only fruit: **fruitarian** ●shop selling fruit: **fruiterer** ●study of fruit and seeds: **carpology** ●light fruit basket: **punnet** ●disease caused by absence of fresh fruit and vegetables from the diet: **scurvy**

fry ●fry food briefly to brown the outside: **sauté, seal** ●fry food briefly, stirring to avoid browning: **stir-fry**

fuel ●fuel derived from fossilized remains: **fossil fuel** ●jet fuel: **kerosene, paraffin oil** ●failure of fuel to ignite in the cylinder: **misfire**

full ●*combining form*: **-ulent** (*e.g.* purulent)

function ●*combining form*: **-ate** (*e.g.* electorate), **-ure** (*e.g.* judicature) ●performing no useful function: **redundant**

fund ●pooled fund of money: **kitty** ●funds held by the British government: **Exchequer** ●funding for risky projects: **venture capital** ●decentralized funding in the National Health Service: **internal market** ●impounded funds: **frozen assets** ●inadequate funding: **shoestring** ●receiving no outside funding: **independent** ●person providing funding: **patron, sponsor** ●guarantee funding: **underwrite** ●having funds in excess of one's liabilities: **solvent**

funeral ●*adjective*: **funerary** ●funeral procession: **cortège** ●music for this: **dead march** ●bell rung for this: **knell** ●funeral lament: **dirge** ●vehicle for the coffin: **hearse** ●person carrying the coffin: **pall-bearer** ●framework on which a coffin may be set or carried: **bier, catafalque** ●cloth spread over the bier: **pall** ●public exposition of a corpse: **lying-in-state** ●funeral rites: **exequies, obsequies** ●ceremonial attendant at these: **mute** ●military funeral ceremonies: **military honours** ●bugle call at military funerals: **last post** ●final depositing of the corpse after a funeral: **committal** ●burial with appropriate rites: **interment** ●burning of the dead: **cremation** ●place for this: **crematorium** ●container for a dead person's ashes: **casket** ●tomb-inscription: **epitaph** ●relative or friend attending a funeral: **mourner** ●black clothes worn at a funeral: **mourning** ●mourner's black armband: **crepe** ●person engaged to organize a funeral: **undertaker, funeral director**

fungus ●*combining form*: **myco-** ●*adjectives*: **fungoid, fungous** ●edible fungus growing underground: **truffle** ●fungus cultivated on grapes: **botrytis, noble rot** ●fungal growth: **mould** ●whitish fungal coating: **mildew** ●fungal disease of trees or fruit: **canker** ●fungus-derived protein: **mycoprotein** ●study of fungi: **mycology** ●inhibiting fungus: **fungistatic** ●killing fungus: **fungicidal**

fur ●animal's coat of fur: **pelt** ●coypu fur: **nutria** ●stoat's white fur: **ermine** ●shop selling furs: **furrier**

furnace ●furnace for making steel: **blast furnace** ●furnace for large-scale chemical processes: **retort** ●furnace for firing pottery: **kiln** ●furnace for rubbish: **incinerator**

furniture ●set of furniture: **suite** ●fixed piece of furniture: **fitment** ●furniture permanently attached to the building containing it: **fixture** ●item of furniture designed to fit with others: **unit** ●piece of furniture to hold overcoats, umbrellas, etc.: **hall-stand** ●freestanding set of drawers: **chest of drawers** ●waist-high set of drawers and cupboards: **sideboard** ●sideboard with shelves above: **dresser, Welsh dresser** ●shelved stand for ornaments: **whatnot** ●writing desk with a flap and drawers below: **bureau** ●writing desk with drawers and compartments: **escritoire, secretaire** ●tall writing desk with side drawers: **davenport** ●tall chest of drawers: **tallboy** ●cabinet for television or radio equipment: **console** ●sofa with arms and back curving outwards: **chesterfield** ●sofa open at one end: **chaise longue** ●S-shaped sofa: **sociable** ●low upholstered seat without back or arms: **ottoman** ●upholstered footstool: **pouffe, pouf** ●kneeler with bookrest: **prie-dieu** ●furniture item containing a concealed chamber pot: **commode** ●small wheel fixed to furniture: **castor** ●wheeled board used to move heavy furniture: **skate** ●make furniture look worn: **distress** ●ornamental bracket: **console** ●denoting furniture built for the dimensions of the room it occupies: **fitted** ●denoting furniture sold disassembled: **flat-pack** ●denoting furniture designed for infrequent use: **occasional** ●woodworker making furniture: **cabinetmaker** ●wood inlay decorating furniture: **marquetry** ●giant grass whose woody stems are used to make furniture: **bamboo** ●pliant palm stems used to make furniture: **rattan** ●willow twigs plaited to make furniture: **wicker, wickerwork** ●soft padding attached to furniture: **upholstery** ●thin cord decorating upholstery: **piping** ●fitted removable

covers for upholstered furniture: **loose covers** ●large cloth for covering furniture: **dust sheet** ●sheen on polished furniture: **patina** ●furniture beetle or the damage it causes: **woodworm** ●fine wood powder left by woodworm activity: **frass** ●unwanted furniture: **lumber** ●transfer of furniture to another property: **removal** ●disposal of furniture: **clearance**

fuse ●fuse detonating a bomb at a preset distance from its target: **proximity fuse** ●activate a fuse: **arm** ●remove a fuse: **defuse** ●trail of gunpowder acting as a fuse: **train**

future ●possible sequence of future events: **contingency, scenario** ●expected sequence of future events: **outlook, prospect** ●showing potential for the future: **promising** ●arrangements for the future: **provision, contingency plan** ●belief that the future is fixed: **determinism, fatalism** ●expectation of the best: **optimism** ●confidently optimistic: **sanguine** ●expectation of the worst: **pessimism** ●at some indefinite future date: **mañana** ●indication of some future event: **omen, portent, presage** ●astrological forecast of future events: **horoscope** ●knowledge of future events: **prescience** ●gloomy feelings about the future: **foreboding, presentiment, qualm** ●alleged ability to foresee the future: **second sight** ●person claiming to foresee the future: **prophet, seer, soothsayer** ●forecast of future events: **prediction, prognosis, prognostication, projection, prophecy** ●force said to control future events: **destiny**

galaxy ●*adjective*: **galactic**

gall bladder ●*combining form*: **chole-** ●small hard mass forming in the gall bladder: **gallstone** ●X-ray examination of the gall bladder: **cholecystography** ●surgical removal of the gall bladder: **cholecystectomy**

gallery ●musicians' galley: **loft** ●exterior gallery on an upper floor: **loggia**

gallows ●trapdoor beneath a gallows: **drop**

gambling ●room or building for gambling games: **casino** ●person in charge of a gambling table: **croupier** ●collective amount of stakes laid: **pool** ●gambling game with a ball dropped onto a revolving wheel: **roulette** ●gaming machine showing different combinations of fruits: **fruit machine** ●gaming machine token: **jetton**

game¹ ●children's hopping game: **hopscotch** ●children's game of peeping out from hiding: **peep-bo, peek-a-boo** ●children's chasing game: **tag** ●game of throwing sticks or balls at a wooden dummy: **Aunt Sally** ●game of dropping sticks into a stream: **Poohsticks** ●game of throwing rings over upright pegs: **quoits** ●game of throwing rings over prizes: **hoopla** ●game of catching a top on a tautened string: **diabolo** ●game of skimming stones over water: **ducks and drakes** ●game of sliding stones across ice: **curling** ●game of tossing small pebbles: **jacks** ●game of throwing a wooden disc at nine wooden pins: **ninepins, skittles** ●game of throwing a hard ball at ten plastic skittles: **tenpin bowling** ●game of knocking balls through hoops: **croquet** ●game of throwing a ball against walls: **fives** ●game using rackets to hit a ball against walls: **squash** ●this using basketlike rackets: **jai alai, pelota** ●game of throwing a ball against a person's legs: **French cricket** ●game of hitting a ball and making a circuit of outfield bases: **rounders** ●team ballgame played by swimmers: **water polo** ●Irish game resembling hockey: **hurling** ●hockey-like game played with netted sticks: **lacrosse** ●hockey-like game played on horseback: **polo** ●combat game with shot paint capsules: **paintball** ●game of looping string between the fingers: **cat's cradle** ●game of pulling wrapped objects out of a barrel: **lucky dip** ●game of taking tickets out of a revolving drum: **tombola** ●game of flipping plastic disks into a container: **tiddlywinks** ●game of sliding coins across a board: **shove-halfpenny** ●game of removing pegs from a board: **solitaire** ●game of removing one item from a pile without disturbing the others: **spillikins** ●game of guessing a word from acted clues: **charades** ●game of saying which thimble etc. covers an object: **thimblerig** ●game of finding rhymes for a given word: **crambo** ●game of writing a story by turns: **consequences** ●war game played on maps: **kriegspiel** ●electronic game of looking after a pet: **tamagotchi** ●card games won by gaining tricks bid: **contract bridge, solo whist** ●card games won by gaining the most tricks: **auction bridge, piquet, whist** ●control for computerized video games: **console** •even score at the end of a game: **draw, tie** •denoting a player illegally in front of the ball: **offside** •disadvantage imposed for breach of rules: **penalty** •place where a player or piece is safe: **home** •forgo one's turn of play: **pass** •set of games: **rubber** •leave a game: **retire** •further play allowed to avoid a drawn game: **extra time** •game to decide a championship: **play-off** •call for truce in a children's game: **pax** •player who sets up scoring opportunities: **playmaker** •skill at gaining the psychological advantage in play: **gamesmanship**

game² •game killed during a hunting session: **bag** •denoting game sufficiently decomposed to cook: **high**

gannet •gannets' breeding colony: **gannetry**

garden •garden growing food for domestic use: **kitchen garden** •garden growing food for sale: **market garden** •garden where plants are grown for study: **botanic garden** •garden for medicinal herbs: **physic garden** •formal garden with paths between small hedged flowerbeds: **knot garden, parterre** •garden designed to require minimal irrigation: **xeriscape** •uneven garden bed with large decorative stones: **rockery, rock garden** •garden area devoted to bushes: **shrubbery** •garden shelter: **alcove, arbour, bower, pavilion, summer house** •garden pavilion with view: **belvedere, gazebo** •garden trellis arch: **pergola** •ornamental hedge-clipping in a garden: **topiary** •garden's sunken perimeter wall: **ha-ha, sunk fence**

gardening •art of gardening: **horticulture** •soilless horticulture: **hydroponics** •digging to two spades' depth: **double digging** •shallow furrow made for seeds: **drill** •hand tool making holes for seeds: **dibber, dibble**

•small translucent plant-cover: **cloche** •long polythene-covered cloche: **polytunnel** •pruning clippers: **secateurs** •clipping bushes into ornamental shapes: **topiary** •narrow spade for uprooting weeds: **spud, spudder** •gardening machine for breaking up ground: **cultivator, tiller** •gardening string: **fillis** •gardener's shallow basket: **trug** •construction of ornamental gardens: **landscape gardening**

garland •suspended garland: **festoon**

garlic •*adjective*: **alliaceous** •section of a bulb of garlic: **clove** •set of cloves: **bulb, head** •garlic mayonnaise: **aioli**

gas •*adjective*: **gaseous** •imagined gas showing no irregularities: **ideal gas** •largely unreactive gas: **noble gas, rare gas** •gas causing severe irritation to the eyes: **tear gas** •powerful kind of tear gas: **CS gas** •gas in the digestive tract: **flatulence, wind** •foul-smelling gas: **mephitis, effluvium** •suffocating gas found in mines: **choke-damp** •gas formerly thought to fill all space: **ether** •main constituent of natural gas: **methane** •refrigerant and aerosol gas harmful to the ozone layer: **chlorofluorocarbon** •gases used to replace this: **hydrochlorofluorocarbon, hydrofluorocarbon** •gas absorbing infrared radiation: **greenhouse gas** •methane-based gas found in large underground deposits: **natural gas** •gas burner used in laboratories: **Bunsen burner** •gas oven's temperature setting: **mark** •gas jet's luminescent cover: **mantle** •gas jet kept burning to light others: **pilot light** •discharge of gas: **emission** •terminate the gas supply: **cut off** •gas mask: **respirator** •gas storage tank: **gasometer** •gas store at the end of a pipeline: **terminal** •gas-fired water heater: **geyser** •change from gas into a liquid: **condense** ●change from liquid into gas: **evaporate** ●allowing the passage of gas: **permeable, pervious** ●operated by gas pressure: **pneumatic** ●instruments measuring gas pressure: **manometer, piezometer**

gate ●revolving gate: **turnstile** ●fortified gate: **barbican** ●back gate: **postern** ●small gate set into a larger one: **wicket** ●sliding gate controlling a flow of water: **sluice, sluice gate**

gauge ●gauge for narrow gaps: **feeler gauge, micrometer**

gear ●extra high gear: **overdrive** ●gear allowing each driven wheel to revolve at a different speed: **differential** ●vehicle gear preventing movement: **park** ●gear system causing the parts to revolve at the same speed before engagement: **synchromesh** ●bar or wheel with angled teeth permitting movement in one direction only: **ratchet** ●particular cycle gear ratio: **speed** ●system changing cycle gears by moving the chain: **derailleur** ●disengaged position of the gears: **neutral** ●device engaging and disengaging motor gears: **clutch** ●(of a gear) engage with another gear: **mesh**

gelatin ●natural gelatin found in fish: **isinglass** ●vegetarians' substitute for gelatin: **agar**

gem ●precious or semiprecious stone: **gemstone** ●side of a cut gem: **facet** ●gem that is polished but not faceted: **cabochon** ●gem with an incised design: **intaglio** ●bright green gem: **emerald** ●deep red gems: **garnet, ruby** ●reddish orange gem: **jacinth** ●ancient Egyptian gem cut in the form of a beetle: **scarab** ●denoting an uncut gem: **rough** ●place a gem in a mount: **set** ●close setting of gems: **pavé** ●gem set on its own: **solitaire** ●piece of metal into which a gem is set: **setting** ●gem-cutter: **lapi-**

dary ●revolving device cleaning gemstones: **tumbling barrel** ●machine polishing gems: **lapping machine** ●art of gem engraving: **glyptography**

gene ●*adjective*: **genetic** ●threadlike gene structure: **chromosome** ●self-reproduction of genetic material: **replication** ●replacement of defective genes: **gene therapy** ●laboratory genetic manipulation: **genetic engineering** ●natural copying of genetic information: **transcription** ●alternative form of a gene: **allele** ●change in gene structure: **mutation** ●substance causing this: **mutagen** ●gene so changed: **mutant** ●rearrangement of genetic material: **recombination** ●denoting a genetic characteristic manifested even when inherited from only one parent: **dominant** ●denoting a genetic characteristic manifested only when inherited from both parents: **recessive** ●prediction of a future child's genetic disorders: **genetic counselling**

genitals ●external genitals: **pudenda** ●female external genitals: **vulva** ●male external genitals: **penis, testicles** ●inflammation of the vulva: **vulvitis** ●muscular tube leading from the female genitals: **vagina** ●uncover one's genitals: **expose oneself** ●psychologically induced desire to display one's genitals: **exhibitionism** ●display one's genitals briefly: **flash** ●manual stimulation of the genitals: **masturbation** ●support for the male genitals: **athletic support, jockstrap** ●decorative pouch for the male genitals: **codpiece** ●disease causing genital inflammation: **herpes simplex**

genuine ●prove or test that something is genuine: **authenticate**

geology ●dating of geological eras: **chronostratigraphy, geochronology**

geometry ●*adjective*: **geometric** ●drawing illustrating a geometrical problem: **figure** ●denoting identical figures: **congruent** ●flat surface: **plane** ●outer boundary of a curved figure: **circumference** ●portion of a curve: **arc** ●curve made by repeated subdivision: **fractal** ●quarter of a circle: **quadrant** ●part of a figure cut off by an intersecting line or plane: **segment** ●square magnitude of a two-dimensional figure: **area** ●straight line from centre to circumference of a circle: **radius** ●straight line touching but not crossing a curve: **tangent** ●straight line through the centre of a solid: **axis** ●point of intersection of two lines: **vertex** ●denoting a figure having all sides and angles equal: **regular** ●amount by which an angle is less than 90°: **complement** ●denoting either of two angles whose sum is 90°: **complementary** ●amount by which an angle is less than 180°: **supplement** ●denoting either of two angles whose sum is 180°: **supplementary** ●regular oval figure: **ellipse** ●denoting a three-dimensional figure: **solid** ●measurement of solid bodies: **stereometry** ●cubic magnitude of a solid body: **volume** ●longest side of a right-angled triangle: **hypotenuse** ●four-sided figure: **quadrilateral** ●four-sided plane figure: **quadrangle** ●plane figure with four straight sides and four right angles: **rectangle** ●plane figure with two parallel pairs of straight sides: **parallelogram** ●parallelogram with oblique angles and equal sides: **rhombus** ●quadrilateral with opposite sides and angles equal: **rhomboid** ●plane figure with at least three straight sides and angles: **polygon** ●five-sided figure: **pentagon** ●six-sided figure: **hexagon** ●seven-sided figure: **heptagon** ●eight-sided figure: **octagon** ●ten-sided figure: **decagon** ●eleven-sided figure: **hendecagon** ●star-shaped figure formed from two intersecting triangles: **hexagram** ●three-dimensional figure: **solid** ●surface of a solid: **face** ●solid figure having each face a parallelogram: **parallelepiped** ●round solid figure: **sphere** ●half sphere: **hemisphere** ●quarter of a sphere: **quadrant** ●straight line from centre to circumference of a sphere: **radius** ●solid figure with straight parallel sides and a circular or oval base: **cylinder** ●solid figure rising to a point from a circular base: **cone** ●cone truncated by a line parallel with its base: **frustum** ●solid figure contained by six equal sides: **cube** ●solid figure with six faces: **hexahedron** ●solid figure with more than six faces: **polyhedron** ●polyhedron with all faces but one triangular: **pyramid** ●solid figure with seven faces: **heptahedron** ●solid figure with eight faces: **octahedron** ●solid figure with ten faces: **decahedron** ●solid figure with twenty faces: **icosahedron** ●spiralling three-dimensional curve: **helix** ●straight line joining opposite corners of a straight-sided figure: **diagonal** ●straight line joining the ends of an arc: **chord** ●straight line joining the sides of a circle via its centre: **diameter** ●denoting lines maintaining a constant mutual distance: **parallel** ●divide into two equal parts: **bisect** ●draw one figure within another: **inscribe** ●instruments for drawing circles: **compass, compasses, protractor**

germ ●germ causing a disease: **bacillus, pathogen** ●germ provoking the production of antibodies: **antigen** ●germ that has gained immunity to treatments employed to eradicate it: **superbug** ●molecular germ: **virus** ●denoting a virus with a long incubation period: **slow** ●free from germs: **aseptic, sterile** ●infected with germs: **septic** ●resistant to germs: **immune** ●breeding ground for germs: **nidus** ●having an adequate immune system: **immunocompetent** ●lacking this: **immunocompromised** ●bodily inability to resist germs: **immune deficiency, immunodeficiency** ●medical deactivation of the immune system: **immunosuppression** ●study of immunity: **immunology** ●germ-killing: **antiseptic, disinfectant, germicidal** ●body's automatic reaction to germs: **defence mechanism** ●denoting medical treatment that is effective against a variety of germs: **broad spectrum** ●blood protein counteracting germs: **antibody** ●denoting germs present but not causing infection: **latent** ●free of germs: **disinfect** ●substance destroying germs: **germicide** ●person or animal transmitting germs by which they are not affected: **carrier**

German ●German polite form of address to a man: **Herr** ●German polite form of address to a married woman: **Frau** ●German polite form of address to an unmarried woman: **Fräulein** ●German school-leavers' examination: **abitur** ●German rye bread: **pumpernickel** ●German pork sausage: **bratwurst** ●German dish of chopped pickled cabbage: **sauerkraut** ●German dry white wine: **hock** ●German sparkling white wine: **Sekt** ●German wine made with late-picked grapes: **Spätlese** ●German wine made with selected late-picked grapes: **Auslese** ●German wine made from grapes picked with ice on them: **Eiswein** (*pl.* **Eisweine** *or* Eisweins) ●German potato gin: **schnapps** ●German cherry brandy: **kirsch, kirschwasser** ●German caraway-flavoured liqueur: **kümmel** ●German leather shorts: **lederhosen** ●German shepherd dog: **Alsatian** ●motorway in German-speaking countries: **autobahn** ●German central bank: **Bundesbank** ●title of the former German emperors: **Kaiser** ●title of a German dictator under Fascism: **führer** ●head of the German government: **Chancellor** ●lower house of the German parliament: **Bundestag** ●upper house of the German parliament: **Bundesrat** ●German mayor: **burgomaster** ●German air force: **Luftwaffe** ●former German torpedo boat: **E-boat** ●former German submarine: **U-boat** ●former German armoured unit: **panzer** ●former German prisoner-of-war camp for officers: **Oflag** ●former German prisoner-of-war camp for other ranks: **Stalag** ●German castle: **schloss** ●immigrant worker in Germany: **Gastarbeiter** ●German province: **Land** (*pl.* Länder) ●elf in German folklore: **kobold** ●German measles: **rubella** ●German hymn or its music: **chorale** ●German solo song: **lied** (*pl.* lieder) ●German three-handed card game: **skat** ●vernacular language of north Germany: **Low German** ●literary German: **High German** ●German traditional typeface: **Fraktur**

germ warfare ●denoting germ warfare: **bacteriological, biological**

gesture ●use of gestures: **gesticulation**

ghost ●*adjective*: **spectral** ●ghost that throws things about: **poltergeist** ●ghostly double of a living person: **doppelgänger** ●ghostly image of a person seen near their time of death: **wraith** ●ghostlike figure: **apparition** ●appearance of a ghost: **visitation** ●ghostly emanation from a medium during a seance: **ectoplasm** ●observer's shadow projected onto clouds: **Brocken spectre**

gift ●gift given as a memento: **keepsake** ●person giving a gift: **donor** ●person receiving it: **donee, recipient** ●gift of funding: **endowment**

girl ●vigorously boisterous girl: **tomboy**

give ●person who gives: **donor** ●giving or given generously: **liberal** ●in closest possible fulfilment of a donor's intentions: **cy-pres** ●denoting a gift able to be handed on to others: **transferable** ●refuse to give: **withhold**

give away ●that cannot be given away: **inalienable**

glacier ●deep crack in a glacier: **crevasse** ●ice ridge on a glacier: **serac** ●loose snow at the top of a glacier: **firn, névé** ●material deposited by a glacier: **moraine** ●water from a melting glacier: **meltwater** ●material carried away by this: **outwash**

gladiator ●gladiator fighting with a net and trident: **retiarius** (*pl.* retiarii)

gland ●*combining form*: **adeno-** (*e.g.* adenoma) ●*adjective*: **glandular** ●gland producing antibodies: **thymus** ●gland producing digestive juice and insulin: **pancreas** ●gland controlling growth: **thyroid** ●glands controlling growth and development: **pituitary, thyroid** ●gland lubricating the hair and skin: **sebaceous gland** ●gland producing milk: **mammary gland** ●gland producing ova: **ovary** ●gland releasing a fluid component of semen: **prostate** ●gland producing sperm: **testis** ●gland producing tears: **lacrimal gland** ●gland producing urine: **kidney** ●denoting glands secreting directly into the blood: **endocrine** ●denoting glands secreting onto an exterior surface: **exocrine** ●disease causing swelling of the lymph glands: **glandular fever**

glandular fever ●herpesvirus causing glandular fever: **Epstein–Barr virus**

Glasgow ●*adjective*: **Glaswegian**

glass ●*combining forms*: **hyal-, vitr-** ●like or containing glass: **vitreous** ●looking like glass: **hyaloid, vitriform** ●bright clear glass: **crystal** ●thick quality glass: **plate glass** ●glass poured on to molten metal: **float glass** ●glass strengthened against splintering: **safety glass** ●sheet of glass: **pane, light** ●diamond-shaped pane of glass: **quarry** ●thin glass protecting a microscope specimen: **coverslip** ●glass shaped to concentrate or disperse light: **lens** ●lens separating white light into a spectrum of colours: **prism** ●watchmaker's and jeweller's magnifying glass: **loupe** ●narrow-necked glass container: **flask** ●glass container for plants or small reptiles: **terrarium** ●glass container for fish and water plants: **aquarium** ●block containing coloured glass: **millefiori** ●glass scraps for recycling: **cullet** ●denoting translucent glass: **frosted** ●denoting smooth translucent glass: **ground** ●denoting glass that is neither translucent nor transparent: **opaque** ●become glassy: **vitrify** ●darken glass: **smoke** ●rod for handling molten glass: **pontil** ●shape molten glass by air pressure: **blow** ●scum on molten glass: **sandiver** ●supply and fit panes of glass: **glaze** ●person doing this: **glazier** ●frame holding window glass: **sash** ●supporting strip between panes: **glazing bar** ●transmission of light signals along fine glass fibres: **fibre optics** ●slender glass fibres used for insulation: **glass wool** ●textile etc. reinforced by embedded glass filaments: **fibreglass, glass fibre** ●tall narrow wine glass: **flute** ●slender part of a wine glass between bowl and foot: **stem** ●shallow stemmed glass: **coupe** ●ornate drinking glass: **goblet** ●large rounded drinking glass: **balloon** ●drinking glass with straight sides and no handle or stem: **tumbler** ●machine polishing glass: **lapping machine** ●protective mat placed under a drinking glass: **coaster, drip mat**

glider ●launch of a glider by a powered aircraft's pulling it: **aero-towing**

glove ●glove with a large wrist-guard: **gauntlet** ●glove housing the four fingers together: **mitten** ●glove thrown down as a challenge: **gage** ●knight's armoured glove: **gauntlet**

glow ●glowing through heat: **incandescent** ●glowing without heat: **luminescent, fluorescent, phosphorescent**

glucose ●glucose deficiency in the blood: **hypoglaecaemia**

go ●go across: **traverse** ●go back: **regress** ●go beyond: **exceed, overshoot**

goat ●*adjectives*: **caprine, hircine** ●male goat: **buck, billy goat** ●female goat: **doe, nanny goat** ●young goat: **kid** ●agile mountin goat: **chamois** ●group of goats: **flock** ●goat's mammary gland: **udder** ●goat's woolly coat: **fleece** ●fine soft goat wool: **cashmere** ●fabric made from goat hair: **mohair** ●fine goatskin for bindings: **morocco** ●*astrological term*: **capricorn**

god ●*combining form*: **the-** ●*adjective*: **divine** ●god or goddess: **deity** ●becoming a god: **apotheosis, deification, theosis** ●suggesting a god's presence: **numinous** ●woodland god: **satyr, faun** ●creator-god: **demiurge** ●all the gods of a particular religion: **pantheon** ●killing a god: **deicide** ●treat or consider as a god: **deify** ●rule by a god: **theocracy** ●image of a god: **idol** ●offering made to a god: **oblation** ●belief in a single god: **monotheism, monism** ●offering of reverence to one god only, whilst conceding that others exist: **henotheism, monolatry** ●belief in the existence of two gods: **ditheism** ●belief in many gods: **polytheism** ●Hebrew name for

God: **Jehovah, Yahweh** ●four-character representation of this: **Tetragrammaton** ●belief that God created the world but has had no further involvement with it: **deism** ●belief that God created the world and continues to be active in it: **theism** ●belief that God is identical with the created universe: **pantheism** ●belief that God is greater than the created universe, but interpenetrates it: **panentheism** ●God's permanent presence in the universe: **immanence** ●God's permanent existence outside the universe: **transcendence** ●divine intervention in human affairs: **theurgy** ●belief that there can be no sure evidence of a god's existence: **agnosticism** ●belief in God based upon reason not revelation: **deism** ●belief that there is no god: **atheism** ●study of religions having gods: **theology** ●drink of the gods: **nectar** ●drink poured out in offering to a god: **libation** ●food of the gods: **ambrosia** ●blood of the gods: **ichor** ●genealogy of a group of gods: **theogony** ●war between gods: **theomachy** ●god's appearance to humankind: **epiphany, theophany** ●god's appearance in human form: **incarnation** ●denoting a god taking animal form: **zoomorphic** ●denoting a god taking human form: **anthropomorphic** ●pagan female fertility figure: **earth mother** ●chief of the ancient Greek gods: **Zeus** ●his consort: **Hera** ●ancient Greek god of flocks and herds: **Pan** ●chief of the Roman gods: **Jupiter** ●his consort: **Juno** ●Roman household gods: **lares and penates** ●supreme god in Scandinavian mythology: **Odin** ●thunder god in Scandinavian mythology: **Thor** ●goddess of destiny in Scandinavian mythology: **Norn** ●speech or writing showing disrespect for a god: **blasphemy** ●disrespectful treatment of a religious item or place: **sacrilege** ▸*see* *also* **essence, Mass, religion, theology, Trinity**

gold ●*combining form*: **aur-** ●lump of gold: **nugget** ●gold in solid bars: **bullion** ●gold beaten thin for gilding: **gold leaf** ●gold held to support a currency: **gold reserve** ●measure of purity for gold: **carat** ●fabulous place full of gold: **El Dorado, Golconda** ●imagined substance turning base metals to gold: **philosopher's stone** ●utensils made of gold: **plate** ●coat with gold: **gild** ●partly gilded: **parcel-gilt** ●person making gold articles: **goldsmith** ●stamp on gold attesting purity: **hallmark** ●denoting a rock or mineral containing gold: **auriferous** ●trough separating gold from ore: **sluice** ●alloy of gold and silver: **electrum** ●goldlike alloy of copper and zinc: **pinchbeck**

golf ●golf played on a small course: **pitch and putt** ●golfer's assistant: **caddie** ●golfer's baggy knee-length trousers: **plus fours** ●golf club with a thick sloping head: **wood** ●golf club with a thinner sloping head: **iron** ●golf club with a thin straight head: **putter** ●small support for a golfer's ball when the first shot is taken for each hole: **tee** ●area of level ground where this shot is taken: **tee** ●take this shot: **tee off** ●curving shot: **fade** ●strike the ball above its centre: **thin, top** ●stroke taking the ball to the left: **pull** ●stroke taking the ball to the right: **slice** ●high shot: **loft** ●turf dislodged by golfer's stroke: **divot** ●clear area leading from the tee to the hole: **fairway** ●long grass round the fairway: **rough** ●point where the ball stops: **lie** ●golfing obstruction: **hazard** ●sand-filled hollow: **bunker** ●smooth area with very short grass surrounding the hole: **green** ●gentle stroke to roll the ball: **putt** ●circuit of play at a golf course: **round** ●standard number of strokes required for a round or hole: **par**

●scoring by holes won: **match play** ●scoring by strokes taken: **medal play, stroke play** ●golfer's score of one stroke under par: **birdie** ●golfer's score of one stroke over par: **bogey** ●number of strokes above par needed by a player: **handicap** ●denoting a player's score adjusted for this: **net** ●denoting a player with a zero handicap: **scratch** ●hole(s) unplayed when a match has been decided: **bye** ●golf-club bar: **nineteenth hole**

gonad ●female gonad: **ovary** ●male gonad: **testis**

good ●highest good: **summum bonum** ●exceptionally good: **egregious** ●just good enough: **passable** ●thing partly good and partly bad: **curate's egg** ●making a feigned display of virtue: **canting, pious**

goods ●goods used to make others: **capital goods** ●goods for sale: **merchandise** ●goods regularly kept by a business: **stock-in-trade** ●goods intended for the purchaser's use: **consumer goods** ●goods designed for quick use and replacement: **consumables** ●long-lasting goods: **durables** ●promotional goods: **merchandise** ●miscellaneous goods bought as a unit: **job lot** ●slightly faulty goods: **seconds** ●smuggled goods: **contraband** ●denoting goods in saleable condition: **merchantable** ●denoting goods made imperfect by retailer handling: **shop-soiled** ●denoting goods immediately available: **in stock** ●presentation of goods at the point of sale: **merchandising** ●list of goods held: **inventory** ●batch of goods: **consignment** ●transport of goods: **freight, haulage** ●list of goods carried on a vehicle: **waybill** ●ship or aircraft carrying goods: **freighter** ●wooden platform for stacking goods: **pallet** ●large storehouse for goods: **warehouse** ●document accompanying a delivery of goods: **docket**

•place for official inspection of imported goods: **customs** •rate at which goods are sold: **turnover** •society's pursuit of consumer goods: **consumerism** •promise to replace or repair defective goods: **guarantee, warranty**

goose •*adjective*: **anserine** •male goose: **gander** •female goose: **goose** •young goose: **gosling** •goose under four months old: **green goose** •group of geese: **gaggle** •group of geese flying in formation: **skein** •wild goose's cry: **honk**

government •type of government: **regime** •right-wing and authoritarian system of government: **fascism** •cruel and oppressive government: **tyranny** •incompetent or unjust government: **misrule** •government by a party with less than half the seats: **minority government** •government formed from several minority parties: **coalition** •government formed regardless of party interests: **national government** •government formed from members of all political parties: **government of national unity** •temporary government: **caretaker government** •absence of government: **anarchy** •head of the British government: **Prime Minister** •head of the German government: **Chancellor** •head of government of the Irish Republic: **Taoiseach** •head of government in Northern Ireland: **First Minister** •committee of chief government ministers: **cabinet** •head of a major government department: **Minister, Secretary of State** •cabinet minister not heading a government department: **Minister without Portfolio** •member of Parliament assisting a minister: **Parliamentary Private Secretary** •denoting the opposition counterpart to a government minister: **shadow** •duties or office of a government minister: **portfolio** •government department for domestic affairs: **Home Office** •government department for foreign affairs: **Foreign Office** •government department for financial management: **Treasury** •government department assessing and collecting taxes: **Inland Revenue** •government department registering land ownership: **Land Registry** •government department for military supplies: **ordnance** •government administrative department or its staff: **secretariat** •government report with proposals for public discussion: **Green Paper** •government report with proposals for legislation: **White Paper** •national approval of a government's programme as indicated by its election majority: **mandate** •transfer of governmental power to regional authorities: **decentralization, devolution** •principle of central government performing only those functions which cannot be discharged at local level: **subsidiarity** •system of government allowing much local independence: **federalism** •self-government: **autonomy, self-determination** •self-government in domestic affairs: **home rule** •government policy of non-intervention: **laissez-faire** •temporary cessation of government: **interregnum** •government committee of enquiry: **commission** •government organizations assisting those seeking work: **jobcentre, job club** •organization that is independent but government-sponsored: **quango** •funds held by the British government: **exchequer**

gradual •gradual or natural development: **evolution** •gradual absorption: **osmosis**

graft •plant shoot for grafting: **scion** •graft of tissue from one point to another of the same body: **autograft** •graft of tissue taken from a donor who is of the same species but not genetically identical: **allograft** •graft of tissue taken from a donor of the same species: **homograft** ●graft of tissue taken from a donor of a different species: **heterograft, xenograft**

grain ●*combining form*: grani- ●*adjective*: **granular** ●tied bundle of cut grain stalks: **sheaf** ●group of sheaves leant together: **shock, stook** ●grain stalks left standing after harvesting: **stubble** ●gather leftover grain from a harvest field: **glean** ●separate chaff from grain by the wind: **winnow** ●separate chaff from grain by beating: **thresh** ●grain before or after milling: **grist** ●hard grain left after milling flour: **semolina** ●grain-eating: **granivorous** ●producing grain: **graniferous** ●containing whole unprocessed grains: **wholegrain, wholemeal** ●grain fungus: **ergot** ●funnel for dispensing grain: **hopper** ●storage tower or pit for threshed grain: **silo** ●storehouse for threshed grain: **granary** ●cassava grain: **tapioca**

grammar ●*adjective*: **grammatical** ●mistake in grammar: **solecism** ●mistake in grammar made by inappropriate application of a rule: **hypercorrection**

gramophone ●early gramophone and recording machine: **phonograph** ●combined radio and gramophone: **radiogram** ●combined radio, gramophone, and tape deck: **music centre** ▸*see also* **record player**

gramophone record ●denoting a small record revolving at 45 rpm: **extended-play** ●denoting a full-sized record revolving at 33.33 rpm: **long-playing** ●general term for 45 and 33 rpm records: **vinyl** ●general term for 78 rpm records: **shellac** ●laser-read disk of digital information: **compact disk** ●groove in a long-playing record: **microgroove** ●extraneous noise heard when playing a record: **surface noise**

grape ●grape crop: **growth** ●grape harvest: **vintage** ●fermenting grape juice: **must** ●fermentation of grape juice: **vinification** ●juice produced from a second pressing: **taille** ●remains of grapes after pressing: **marc, rape** ●fungus cultivated on grapes: **botrytis, noble rot** ●study of grape cultivation: **viticulture**

graph ●graph designed like a sliced cake: **pie chart** ●graph designed as a series of strips: **bar chart** ●mark points on a graph: **plot**

grasp ●able to grasp: **prehensile** ●device for grasping lumps of coal or sugar: **tongs** ●similar device for grasping very small objects: **tweezers**

grass ●*adjectives*: **graminaceous, gramineous** ●narrow leaf of grass: **blade** ●coarse grass used for paper and ropes: **esparto, esparto grass** ●expanse or slab of earth with the grass in it: **sod, turf** ●circle of darker grass: **fairy ring** ●clump of long coarse grass: **tussock** ●dislodged clump of grass: **divot** ●dried mown grass: **hay** ●grass at the edge of a road: **verge** ●undried grass stored in airtight conditions: **silage** ●silage store: **silo** ●grass-eating: **graminivorous** ●electric grass cutter for edgings etc.: **strimmer** ●grass-like plant growing in wet ground: **sedge** ●synthetic grass surface used on sports fields: **AstroTurf™**

grasshopper ●chirping grasshopper: **cricket** ●large voracious flying grasshopper: **locust**

grassland ●extensive grassland in Siberia: **steppe** ●extensive grassland in North America: **prairie** ●extensive grassland in South America: **pampas** ●extensive grassland in warm regions: **savannah** ●extensive grassland in South Africa: **veldt**

grave ●prehistoric grave mound: **barrow, tumulus** ●stone at a grave's head: **headstone** ●fastened arrangement of flowers for laying on a grave: **wreath**

gravel ●crushed stone and gravel used in building: **aggregate**

gravity ●weak gravity in a spacecraft: **microgravity** ●point towards which gravitational forces tend: **centre of gravity** ●fall controlled by gravity only: **free fall** ●plant growth in relation to gravity: **geotropism** ●instrument measuring gravity: **gravimeter**

grease ●grease used for waterproofing leather: **dubbin**

greed ●greed for money: **avarice** ●greedy eater: **glutton, gourmand**

Greek ●*combining forms*: **Graeco-** (*e.g.* Graeco-Roman), **Hellen-** ●*adjective*: **Hellenic** ●Greek culture: **Hellenism** ●lover of Greek culture: **philhellene** ●small Greek restaurant: **taverna** ●Greek appetiser of stuffed vine leaves: **dolmades** ●Greek mixed hors d'oeuvre: **mezes** ●Greek relish of cucumber sliced in yogurt: **tzatziki** ●Greek fish-roe paste: **taramasalata** ●Greek goat cheese: **feta** ●Greek cheese pie: **tyropitta** ●Greek spinach and feta pie: **spanakopitta** ●Greek egg and lemon soup: **avgolemono** ●Greek meatballs: **keftedes** ●Greek meat stew: **stifado** ●Greek dish of skewered meat: **souvlakia** ●Greek dish of lamb and aubergines: **moussaka** ●Greek sweet of sesame flour and honey: **halva** ●Greek sweet of honey-soaked pastry with nuts: **baklava** ●Greek resin-flavoured wine: **retsina** ●Greek aniseed-flavoured spirit: **ouzo** ●Greek mandolin: **bouzouki** ●harp-like instrument of ancient Greece: **lyre** ●Greek folk dance performed in a line: **syrtaki** ●Greek woollen rug: **flokati** ●popular form of modern Greek: **demotic, Romaic** ●pure form of modern Greek: **katharevousa** ●short skirt as part of traditional Greek male dress:

fustanella ●Greek soldier wearing this: **evzone** ●Greek freedom fighter: **klepht** ●Greek administrative regions: **deme, nomarchy, nome** ●citadel of ancient Greek city: **acropolis** ●woollen tunic worn in ancient Greece: **chiton** ●ancient Greek overgarment: **himation** ●short cloak worn by men in ancient Greece: **chlamys** ●ancient Greek course for horse and chariot races: **hippodrome** ●ancient Greek female statue: **kore** (*pl.* korai) ●ancient Greek male statue: **kouros** (*pl.* kouroi) ●great public sacrifice in ancient Greece: **hecatomb** ●chief god of ancient Greece: **Zeus** ●his consort: **Hera** ●ancient Greek god of flocks and herds: **Pan** ●ancient Greek spirit: **daemon** ●first mortal woman in Greek mythology: **Pandora** ●ancient Greek and Roman storage jar with two handles and a pointed base: **amphora** ●courtesan in ancient Greece: **hetaira** ●resident alien in ancient Greece: **metic**

green ●*combining form*: **chlor(o)-** ●*adjective*: **verdant** ●richly green: **verdant** ●a pale green colour: **eau de Nil** ●green pepper: **capsicum** ●green pigment in plants: **chlorophyll** ●green rust forming on copper and brass: **verdigris**

greenhouse ●heated greenhouse: **hothouse** ●greenhouse attached to a house: **conservatory** ●conservatory stocked with plants flowering in winter: **winter garden**

greeting ●woman's formal greeting by bending the knees: **curtsy** ●opening greeting in a letter: **salutation** ●former Chinese bow of greeting: **kowtow** ●Indian traditional gesture of greeting: **pranam** ●greeting between Jews: **shalom** ●Maori greeting: **kia ora** ●Muslim gesture of greeting: **salaam**

grey ●painting in shades of grey: **grisaille**

greyhound • young greyhound: **sapling** • starting compartment in a greyhound race: **trap**

grid • metal grid over a pit in a road: **cattle grid** • grid for data display: **matrix**

grief • wailing cry expressive of grief: **ululation**

grill • grill quickly over a strong heat: **chargrill**

grin • lecherous grin: **leer**

grind • grinding mechanism: **mill**

groin • *adjective*: **inguinal**

groove • *adjective*: **sulcate** • groove cut by a plough: **furrow**

ground • at or above ground level: **overground** • ground level at which water is always present: **water level, water table**

group • *combining forms*: **-dom** (*e.g.* officialdom), **-hood** (*e.g.* brotherhood), **-ship** (*e.g.* membership), **-some** (*e.g.* foursome) • *adjectives*: **collegial, generic** • compact homogeneous group: **phalanx** • group of people of equal social status: **peer group** • group drawn from a larger body: **detachment** • group selected to represent a larger body: **deputation** • group breaking away from a larger body: **splinter group** • group of people living in one place: **community** • group inhabiting a particular area: **colony** • group of people living together and sharing all property: **commune** • informal group of young people: **gang** • group of people with common interests: **fraternity, network, set, syndicate** • group of people pressing a common interest: **caucus, interest, interest group, lobby, movement, pressure group** • group pressing for vigorous action: **ginger group** • group of political activists: **cadre** • group of persons with a common

problem or illness, meeting regularly for mutual help: **support group** • group resistant to change: **old guard** • separate into sharply opposed groups: **polarize** • dissident group: **faction, sect** • dissident section within a group: **element** • denoting conflict within a group: **internecine** • specialist group: **cadre** • exclusive group: **clique, coterie, elite, in-group, inner circle** • access to an exclusive group: **entrée** • secret goup: **cabal** • undesirable coterie: **galère** • group assigned a particular task: **squad, task force** • legally constituted group administering money or property for the benefit of others: **trust** • group of people sharing public worship: **congregation** • group worshipping on private premises: **house church** • group with particular religious beliefs: **cult, denomination, sect** • group assembled for identification of a suspect: **identity parade** • group with a common statistical characteristic: **cohort** • group thought to have a hidden but pervasive control of society: **the Establishment** • group of influential high-ranking persons: **the hierarchy** • group nominally advising the sovereign: **Privy Council** • small group ruling after a coup: **junta** • group radically different from those surrounding it: **enclave, ethnic minority, minority** • deliberate eradication of such groups: **ethnic cleansing, ethnocide** • group on the fringes of respectability: **demi-monde** • group appointed to consider specific issues: **committee, panel** • group monitoring monopoly organizations: **watchdog** • small secret group: **cell** • group secretly assisting the enemy: **fifth column** • group gambling or drinking together: **school** • group living by hunting and harvesting wild food: **hunter-gatherers** • group controlling Paris during the French Revolution: **Commune** ●group of actors: **troupe, ensmble** ●cooperative group of wild animals: **pack** ●large group of animals: **herd** ●group of animals moving together: **drove, flock, herd, pack** ●group of draught animals working together: **team** ●group of artists or scholars with similar ideas or style: **school** ●group of attendants upon an important person: **entourage, retinue, train** ●large group of bees: **swarm** ●small group of birds: **covey** ●group of birds, goats, or sheep: **flock** ●group of birds or aircraft: **flight** ●group of bombs: **stick** ●group of buildings: **complex** ●group of businesses: **consortium, syndicate, cartel** ●group of criminals: **family, gang, ring** ●group of Cub Scouts or Brownies: **pack** ●group of dancers or musicians: **ensemble** ●group of hospital doctors: **firm** ●set of eggs: **clutch** ●group of employees meeting to seek output improvements: **quality circle** ●group of experts researching specific government problems: **think tank** ●large group of fish: **school, shoal** ●group of foxes: **skulk** ●group of foxhounds: **pack** ●group of geese: **gaggle** ●group of flying geese: **skein** ●large dense group of insects: **swarm** ●group of islands: **archipelago** ●group of interlinked items: **nexus** ●group of lions: **pride** ●group of manual workers: **gang** ●group of persons sent: **mission** ●group of racehorses: **string** ●group of repressed ideas: **complex** ●group of ships or vehicles travelling together: **convoy** ●group of ships or boats: **flotilla** ●group of major sporting fixtures: **grand slam** ●group of states exercising free trade among themselves: **common market** ●group of states with common import tariffs: **customs union** ●group of flying swans: **skein** ●group of prestigious US universities: **Ivy League** ●group

walking one behind another: **file** ●group of witches: **coven** ●group of two: **duo, duumvirate** ●group of three: **triad, trio, troika, triumvirate** ●group of seven: **heptad, septenary** ●group together: **concentrate** ●living in groups: **gregarious** ●group's beliefs and customs: **folklore** ●group's perceptions of the past: **folk memory** ●group loyalty: **esprit de corps** ●group cameraderie: **team spirit** ●study of relationships within a group of people: **sociometry** ●person sympathetic to a group's aims, but not belonging to it: **fellow traveller** ●advocate of the supremacy of a particular group: **supremacist** ●mutual support between group members: **solidarity** ●psychological interactions between members of a group: **group dynamics** ●gain membership of a group to spy on it: **infiltrate, penetrate** ●shared or done by all group members: **collective** ●close a group: **disband** ●forcibly break up a group: **disperse**

grouse ●stand for grouse shooters: **butt**

grow ●grow too big for: **outgrow** ●excessive growth of an organ: **hyperplasia** ●disproportionate growth of the hands and feet in adolescence: **acromegaly** ●growth hormone: **somatotrophin** ●retard growth: **stunt**

growth ●combining form: **-plasia** ●small stalked growth on a mucous membrane: **polyp**

guarantee ●written guarantee: **warranty** ●person or payment guaranteeing the acts of another: **surety**

guard ●*adjective*: **custodial** ●guard at the Tower of London: **Beefeater, Yeoman of the Guard** ●mounted or motorized escort: **outrider**

guardian ●*adjective*: **tutelary** ●under guardianship: **in statu pupillari** ●person receiving advice and protection: **protegé** (*fem.* **prote-gée**)

guerrilla ●Balkan guerrilla: **chet-nik** ●Nicaraguan guerrilla: **contra**

guess ●unsubstantiated guess: **speculation**

guide ●moral guide: **mentor, guru** ●tourist guide: **cicerone** (*pl.* ciceroni)

Guide ●Guide rally: **jamboree**

guillotine ●cart carrying prisoners to the guillotine: **tumbrel, tumbril** ●woman knitting by the guillotine: **tricoteuse**

guilt ●produce arguments or evidence to lessen someone's guilt: **extenuate, mitigate** ●feeling of guilt: **compunction** ●freedom from guilt: **innocence**

guitar ●small steel-stringed guitar: **Hawaiian guitar** ●small four-stringed Hawaiian guitar: **ukulele** ●Russian guitar with a triangular soundbox: **balalaika** ●guitar with in-built microphones: **electric guitar** ●such a microphone: **pickup** ●small disc used to pluck a guitar's strings: **plectrum** ●plectrum attached to the finger: **fingerpick**

gull ●place where gulls live: **gullery**

gum ●*adjective*: **gingival** ●inflammation of the gums: **gingivitis**

gun ●portable gun: **firearm** ●hand-held gun: **handgun** ●portable guns: **small arms** ●spiral-bore gun shot from the shoulder: **rifle** ●smooth-bore gun firing pellets: **shotgun** ●handgun with revolving chambers: **revolver** ●early long-barrelled shoulder gun: **musket** ●gun firing bullets in quick succession: **machine gun** ●light hand-held machine gun: **sub-machine gun** ●gun having a magazine: **repeater** ●short gun with a high trajectory: **mortar** ●heavy gun with a high trajectory: **howitzer** ●gun's backward movement on firing: **recoil** ●large military guns: **artillery**

●artillery and bombs: **ordnance** ●handgun-holder on a belt: **holster** ●small knob forming a gun's fore-sight: **bead** ●crossed fine wires in a gun's sight: **cross hairs** ●inner diameter of a gun barrel: **bore, cali-bre, gauge** ●spiral grooves inside a gun barrel: **rifling** ●denoting an unrifled gun barrel: **smooth-bore** ●open end of a gun barrel: **muzzle** ●back part of a gun barrel: **breech** ●long rod used in muzzle-loading: **ramrod** ●muzzle's wooden stopper: **tampion** ●wedge supporting a gun barrel: **quoin** ●part of a gun where the bullet is placed: **chamber** ●container for bullet and charge: **cartridge** ●gun's container for several bullets: **magazine** ●single unit of ammunition: **round** ●gun's firing lever: **cock, trigger** ●trigger with minimal resistance: **hair trigger** ●part of a gun placed against the shoulder: **butt, stock** ●gun's angle with the horizontal: **elevation** ●gun's wheeled support: **carriage** ●front part of this: **limber** ●firing platform for a large gun: **emplacement** ●fortified gun emplacement: **battery** ●revolving armoured gun emplacement: **turret** ●gun aperture in a wall: **port** ●warship's projecting gun platform: **sponson** ●simultaneous fire from all the guns on one side of a ship: **broadside** ●period of continuous heavy gunfire: **barrage, cannonade** ●rapid burst of gunfire: **fusillade, salvo, volley** ●continuous rapid gunfire at a certain spot: **curtain fire** ●gunfire along a line of targets: **enfilade** ●shield by gunfire: **cover** ●have within range: **sweep** ●ceremonial firing of guns as a token of respect: **salute** ●train a gun on someone: **cover** ●have within firing range: **cover** ●ground depression used as a shelter from gunfire: **foxhole** ●illegal firearms trade: **gun-running** ●science of firearms: **ballistics** ▸*see also* **rifle**

gunman ●hidden gunman: **sniper**

guru ●Hindu guru: **maharishi** ●hermitage for a guru and his pupils: **ashram**

gut ●*adjective*: **visceral** ▸*see also* **intestine**

gymnastics ●gymnastic exercises aiding graceful movement: **callisthenics** ●gymnastic routine not needing apparatus: **floor exercises** ●narrow horizontal bar for gymnastic exercises: **beam** ●wooden frame with a padded top: **horse, vaulting horse** ●sprung fabric sheet: **trampoline** ●floor padding for landing: **mat** ●heavy exercise ball: **medicine ball**

gypsy ●gypsy person, or their language: **Romany** ●gypsy caravan: **vardo** ●Romany word for 'man': **rom** (*pl.* roma) ●Romany word for a male gypsy: **chal** ●Romany word for a non-gypsy: **gorgio** ●secret language of Irish and Welsh gypsies: **Shelta** ●Italian gypsy: **Zingaro** ●Hungarian gypsy: **tzigane** ●itinerant tinker or scrap-metal dealer: **didicoi**

H h

h ●make an 'h' sound: **aspirate**

habit ●strange habit: **eccentricity, idiosyncrasy, mannerism, quirk** ●denoting an ingrained habit: **inveterate** ●denoting a person possessed by compulsive habits: **inveterate, pathological** ●becoming automatic through habit: **second nature**

haddock ●smoke-cured haddock: **finnan**

hair ●*combining form*: **trich-** ●*adjectives*: **capillary, pilose** ●piece of hair: **lock, tress** ●unkempt mass of hair: **shock** ●hair in interlaced strands: **plait** ●length of plaited hair: **pigtail** ●coil of hair at the back of the head: **chignon** ●bunch of false hair: **hairpiece, switch** ●hair brushed upwards and backwards from the forehead: **quiff** ●strip of hair in front of a man's ears: **sideburn** ●short stiff hairs on a man's unshaven face: **stubble** ●hair on a man's cheeks or jaw: **side whiskers** ●long hair on the neck of certain animals: **mane** ●sheath around a hair root: **follicle** ●bristling of the hair in fear or cold: **goose-flesh** ●erectile hairs along a dog's back: **hackles** ●oily secretion keeping the hair soft: **sebum** ●dark hair pigment: **melanin** ●lack of hair pigmentation: **albinism** ●soap preparation for washing the hair: **shampoo** ●substance applied to the hair to make it look healthy: **conditioner** ●hair fixative: **lacquer** ●hair oil: **Macassar** ●scented hair ointment: **pomade, pomatum** ●arrange the hair: **dress** ●ribbon to bind the hair: **fillet** ●hair grip of a sprung metal strip: **kirby grip** ●ornamental hairnet: **snood** ●lacking hair: **bald** ●pro-gressive baldness: **alopecia** ●abnormal hair growth on a woman's face: **hirsutism** ●removal of unwanted hair: **depilation** ●preparation to remove unwanted hair: **depilatory** ●depilation by an electic current: **electrolysis** ●depilation using a sugar and lemon mixture: **sugaring** ●having tightly-curled hair: **ulotrichan** ●study of the hair and scalp: **trichology** ●dead skin in the hair: **dandruff** ●false hair: **wig**

hairdressing ●*adjective*: **tonsorial** ●hairdresser: **coiffeur** (*fem.* coiffeuse) ●hairdresser's shop: **salon** ●wave the hair with a hot iron: **crimp**

hairstyles ●elaborately styled hair: **coiffure** ●knot of hair at the back of a woman's head: **chignon** ●with hair puffed out from the head: **bouffant** ●hairstyle concealing one eye: **peekaboo** ●short hairstyle: **crop** ●short and bristly style: **en brosse** ●very short male style: **crew cut** ●male style with the hair slicked back on both sides: **duck's arse** ●Rastafarian hairstyle with hair in tight braids: **dreadlocks** ●black hairstyle with tight braids giving a geometrical scalp pattern: **cornrows** ●bright dyed streak: **highlight** ●dark dyed streak: **lowlight**

half ●*combining forms*: **demi-, hemi-, semi-** (*e.g.* semicircle) ●half-board: **demi-pension** ●half-line of verse: **hemistich**

hallucination ●hallucinations suffered by alcoholics: **delirium tremens** ●producing or produced by hallucinations: **psychedelic**

ham ●cured or smoked ham: **gammon** ●Italian ham: **prosciutto**

hammer ●hammer used by auctioneers: **gavel** ●diagnostic hammer used by doctors: **plexor, plessor** ●wooden-headed hammer: **mallet** ●heavy mallet: **beetle** ●large heavy hammer: **sledgehammer** ●heavy pivoted hammer: **tilt hammer, trip hammer** ●hammer for beating meat: **tenderizer** ●handle of a hammer: **helve** ●flat part of a hammer head, used for striking: **face** ●rounded or wedge-shaped part of a hammer head, opposite to the face: **peen** ●V-shaped device for removing nails, set opposite to a hammer's face: **claw** ●striking-head of a piledriver: **tup**

hand ●*combining forms*: chiro-, manu- ●*adjectives*: manual, palmate ●hand bones: **metacarpus** ●hand's inner surface between wrist and fingers: **palm** ●itchy hand swelling caused by cold: **chilblain** ●hand pain from much writing: **writer's cramp** ●hand-operated: **manual** ●done with both hands: **bimanual** ●skill with the hands: **dexterity** ●this when deception is involved: **legerdemain, sleight of hand** ●able to use both hands equally well: **ambidextrous** ●specialist treating the hands and feet: **chiropodist** ●cosmetic treatment of the hands: **manicure**

handicap ●physical or mental handicap: **disability** ●denoting a golfer with a zero handicap: **scratch**

handkerchief ●large and brightly coloured handkerchief, often with white spots: **bandanna**

handle ●handle of an axe, knife, or spear: **haft** ●handle of a hammer or other tool: **helve** ●handle of a sword, dagger, or knife: **hilt** ●handle of a whip or fishing rod: **stock**

hand over ●hand over a person to a foreign power for trial or punishment: **extradite**

handworker ●skilled handworker: **artisan, craftsman**

handwriting ●elegant handwriting: **calligraphy** ●calligrapher's decorative flourish: **curlicue**

hang ●hanging loosely: **pendulous** ●structure for hanging criminals: **gallows**

happen ●about to happen: **forthcoming, imminent, pending, upcoming** ●that has never happened before: **unprecedented** ●happening all the time: **perennial** ●happening occasionally: **sporadic** ●make happen: **instigate** ●prevent happening: **preclude** ●happen again: **recur** ●make happen suddenly or unexpectedly: **precipitate** ●reverse what has happened: **undo**

happiness ●feeling of great happiness: **ecstasy, euphoria, exhilaration** ●happiness based on (wilful) ignorance: **fool's paradise** ●make someone very happy: **elate**

harbour ●harbour with customs facilities: **port** ●harbour for yachts: **marina** ●harbour's protection from rough seas: **jetty, mole** ●waterside platform for loading and unloading ships: **quay, quayside** ●sand etc. deposited in a harbour: **silt** ●steersman with local knowledge bringing a ship in or out of harbour: **pilot** ●floating beam restricting access to a harbour: **boom**

hard ●*combining form for medical senses*: scler(o)- ●abnormal hardening of body tissue: **sclerosis** ●hardening of the arteries: **arteriosclerosis**

hare ●*adjective*: leporine ●female hare: **doe** ●male hare: **buck** ●young hare: **leveret** ●hare's short tail: **scut** ●hare's lair: **form** ●hare-hunting: **coursing** ●stew or boil a hare: **jug**

harlequinade ●Italian harlequinade: **commedia dell'arte** ●principal male character: **harlequin** ●principal female character: **columbine** ●comic old man: **pantaloon**

harm ●person suffering harm: **victim** ●look believed to harm the person regarded: **evil eye** ●able to be harmed: **vulnerable** ●subtly harmful: **pernicious**

harpsichord ●small harpsichord with strings set obliquely to the keyboard: **spinet** ●pin tuning a harpsichord string: **wrest pin** ●block in which these are set: **wrest plank** ●device plucking the string: **jack** ●device muting the strings: **buff stop**

Harrow ●member of Harrow School: **Harrovian**

hat ●wide-brimmed straw hat: **panama** ●hat of stiffened straw with a low flat crown: **boater** ●felt hat with indented crown: **homburg, trilby** ●hard domed hat: **bowler** ●hat with a high cylindrical crown: **top hat** ●soft cloth hat with brims at front and back, and earflaps that may be tied up: **deerstalker** ●centre-folded Highland hat: **glengarry** ●hat tied under the chin: **bonnet** ●academic hat: **square, mortarboard, bonnet** ●three-cornered hat: **tricorne** ●firm lightweight sun hat formerly worn in the tropics: **pith helmet, sola topi** ●knitted covering for the head and neck: **balaclava** ●woman's wide-brimmed decorated hat: **picture hat** ●woman's close-fitting bell-shaped hat: **cloche** ●guard's tall fur hat: **bearskin, busby** ●priest's square liturgical hat: **biretta** ●sailor's oilskin hat: **sou'wester** ●worker's protective helmet: **hard hat** ●cowboy's hat: **tengallon hat** ●Texan hat: **stetson** ●Mexican wide-brimmed hat: **sombrero** ●red conical tasselled hat: **fez, tarboosh** ●rosette or ribbons on a hat: **cockade** ●take off one's hat: **doff, uncover** ●shop selling men's hats: **hatter** ●shop selling women's hats: **milliner** ▸*see also* **cap, clothes, vestments**

hatred ●*combining forms*: **mis-, -phobia** ●hatred of foreigners: **xeno-**phobia ●hatred of homosexuals: **homophobia** ●hatred of men: **misandry** ●hatred of people: **misanthropy** ●hatred of women: **misogyny**

hawk ●female hawk: **falcon** ●male hawk: **tercel** ●young hawk: **eyas** ●adult hawk caught for training: **haggard** ●hawk's feeding board: **hack** ●hawk's leg strap: **jess** ●cage for hawks: **mew** ●device to attract a hawk: **lure**

hay ●machine for turning hay: **tedder** ●loose pile of hay: **haycock** ●neat cuboid pile of baled hay: **rick, stack**

hazel ●flower of the hazel tree: **catkin**

head ●*combining form*: **cephal-** ●*adjective*: **cephalic** ●back of the head: **occiput** ●flat part between the forehead and ear: **temple** ●abnormal smallness of the head: **microcephaly** ●study of the proportions of the head and face: **cephalometry** ●unconsciousness from a blow to the head: **concussion** ●injury caused by a severe jerk to the head: **whiplash** ●cut off the head of: **decapitate** ●thrust with the head: **head-butt** ●removable head-covering of real or artificial hair: **wig**

headache ●severe headache with nausea and impaired vision: **migraine** ●office workers' headaches and respiratory problems, thought to be caused by poor ventilation: **sick building syndrome**

headband ●Arab's headband: **agal** ●Jew's liturgical headband: **frontlet**

heading ●heading to a section of text: **lemma** (*pl.* lemmata) ●newspaper title heading: **masthead** ●printed heading on stationery: **letterhead**

healer ●*combining form*: **-path** ●person offering cures through bone and muscle manipulation: **osteopath**

● person offering cures through minute doses of natural substances producing symptoms of the disease: **homeopath**

health ● health-giving: **salubrious, wholesome** ● person obsessed by his or her own health: **hypochondriac, valetudinarian** ● state of health: **condition, constitution** ● in poor health: **sickly** ● conditions relating to public health: **sanitation** ● substance applied to the hair or skin to make it look healthy: **conditioner**

hearing ● *combining form*: audi- ● *adjectives*: **acoustic, auditory, aural** ● alleged ability to hear what others cannot: **clairaudience** ● device measuring the range and sensitivity of a person's hearing: **audiometer** ● graphic record produced by this device: **audiogram** ● study of hearing and its defects: **audiology** ● theatre sound system for hearing-aid users: **induction loop** ● distance over which one can be heard: **earshot, hearing** ● hear something not intended for one: **overhear**

heart ● *combining form for medical and scientific senses*: **cardi-** ● *adjectives*: **cardiac, coronary** ● upper chamber in the heart: **auricle, atrium** ● lower chamber of the heart: **ventricle** ● membrane enclosing the heart: **pericardium** ● inflammation of the pericardium: **pericarditis** ● denoting the arteries surrounding the heart: **coronary** ● blockage of these: **heart attack, coronary thrombosis** ● denoting the heart and blood vessels: **cardiovascular** ● denoting the heart and lungs: **cardiopulmonary, cardiorespiratory** ● relaxed stage of heartbeat: **diastole** ● contracted stage of heartbeat: **systole** ● disturbed heartbeat: **flutter, fibrillation** ● excessively rapid heartbeat: **palpitation, tachycardia** ● excessively slow heartbeat: **bradycardia** ● soft sound made by a diseased heart: **murmur**

● sudden cessation of the heartbeat: **cardiac arrest** ● rapid and chaotic contraction of various heart muscles: **fibrillation** ● apparatus controlling this: **defibrillator** ● device stimulating and controlling heartbeat: **pacemaker** ● plastic-covered electrode used in this: **paddle** ● drug slowing the heart: **beta blocker** ● inflammation of the heart: **carditis** ● doctor's device for hearing the heart: **stethoscope** ● record of heart sounds: **phonocardiogram** ● electrically traced record of a heartbeat: **electrocardiogram** ● ultrasound display of a heartbeat: **echocardiogram** ● study and treatment of heart diseases: **cardiology**

heat ● *combining forms*: **cal(o)-, therm(o)-, -thermy** ● *adjectives*: **thermal, thermic, caloric** ● heat-producing: **calorific** ● glowing through heat: **incandescent** ● slightly warm: **lukewarm, tepid** ● substance that transmits heat: **conductor** ● substance that does not transmit heat: **insulator** ● transfer of heat in fluids: **convection** ● unit of heat energy: **calorie** ● physics of heat and other forms of energy: **thermodynamics** ● denoting the earth's natural heat: **geothermal** ● heat to near boiling point: **scald** ● heat-treat liquids to increase their shelf-life: **pasteurize** ● heat and then cool slowly as a toughening process: **anneal** ● char by exposure to heat: **scorch** ● decompose by exposure to extreme heat: **pyrolyse** ● heat spiced wine or ale: **mull** ● denoting a gentle heat for cooking: **slow** ● denoting a strong heat for cooking: **fast** ● gas-fired water heater: **geyser** ● thermometer for high temperatures: **pyrometer** ● hottest part of the year: **dog days** ● period of unusually hot weather: **heatwave** ● oppressively hot: **sweltering** ● hot and dry: **torrid** ● illness caused by excessive heat: **heatstroke,**

sunstroke ●liquified by extreme heat: **molten** ●electric wire used to provide heat: **element** ●animal dependent upon external sources of heat: **ectotherm** ●animal creating its own bodily heat: **endotherm** ●denoting substances becoming malleable when heated: **thermoplastic** ●denoting substances becoming rigid when heated: **thermosetting** ●heat required for change of state but not of temperature: **latent heat** ●use of electric currents to heat the body's inner organs: **diathermy** ●make impervious to heat: **insulate** ●designed to retain heat: **thermal** ●device producing motive power from heat: **heat engine** ●location of an object through the heat it exudes: **thermal imaging**

heating ●heating device circulating warm air: **convector** ●single heating system supplying many buildings: **district heating** ●underfloor heating system in Roman houses: **hypocaust** ●electric heating element placed in liquid: **immersion heater** ●electric heater taking in power by night and releasing heat by day: **storage heater** ●progressive heating of the earth's atmosphere due to breaches in ozone layer: **global warming, greenhouse effect**

heaven ●*adjective*: **celestial**

Hebrew ●*adjective*: **Hebraic** ●Hebrew scholar: **Hebraist** ●vowel dots around Hebrew script: **points** ●add the points to Hebrew script: **vocalize** ●Hebrew name for God: **Jehovah, Yahweh** ●four-character representation of this: **Tetragrammaton** ▸*see also* **Israeli, Israelite, Judaism**

hedge ●mixed hedge with trees: **hedgerow** ●ornamental hedge-trimming: **topiary** ●strengthen a hedge by interweaving branches: **lay, layer** ●denoting a hedge grown from cuttings: **quickset**

hedgehog ●*adjective*: **erinaceous** ●male hedgehog: **boar** ●hedgehog's sharp hollow bristle: **quill**

height ●*combining forms*: **acro-, alt-, hyps-** ●height above sea or ground level: **altitude** ●height above sea level: **elevation** ●height difference of landscape elements: **relief** ●dizziness caused by heights: **vertigo** ●nausea and exhaustion experienced at high altitudes: **altitude sickness** ●fear of heights: **acrophobia** ●builder specializing in high work: **steeplejack, spiderman** ●instrument measuring an aircraft's height: **altimeter** ●instrument measuring the height above sea level: **hypsometer**

heir ●*adjective*: **hereditary** ●female heir: **heiress** ●heir whose claim is irrefutable: **heir apparent** ●heir whose claim may be overpassed: **heir presumptive** ●heir by blood: **heir-at-law** ●joint heir: **coparcener**

helicopter ●*combining form*: **heli-** ●helicopter's vertical propeller: **rotor** ●helicopter landing-place: **helipad, heliport** ●skiing with ascents made by helicopter: **heli-skiing**

helix ●*adjectives*: **helical, helicoid**

hell ●*adjective*: **infernal** ●place where sins may be expiated after death: **Purgatory** ●hell in Jewish thought: **Gehenna, Sheol** ▸*see also* **underworld**

helmet ●part of a helmet that protects the face: **visor** ●protective helmet for construction workers: **hard hat** ●protective helmet for motorcyclists: **crash helmet**

help ●person keen to help others: **philanthropist** ●domestic helper provided by a local authority: **home help** ●turning to a source of help: **recourse**

hemp ●*adjective*: **hempen** ●comb hemp before spinning: **card**

Hephaestus ●*Roman name*: Vulcan

Hera ●*Roman name*: Juno

Heracles ●*Roman name*: Hercules

herb ●*adjective*: **herbal** ●bag of herbs used to flavour soups: **bouquet garni** ●chopped fresh herbs: **fines herbes** ●garden for medicinal herbs: **physic garden** ●book listing herbs: **herbal**

Hercules ●*Greek name*: Heracles

heredity ●study of heredity: **genetics**

heresy ●founder of a heresy: **heresiarch** ●follower of a heresy: **heretic** ●public burning of a heretic by the Spanish Inquisition: **auto da fé** (*pl.* autos da fé)

Hermes ●*Latin name*: **Mercury** ●Hermes' winged hat: **petasus** ●Hermes' snake-twined staff: **caduceus**

hermit ●*adjective*: **eremitic** ●hermit's habitation: **hermitage, cell** ●hermit living on the top of a pillar: **stylite**

hernia ●padded belt supporting a hernia: **truss**

hero ●unconventional fictional hero: **anti-hero**

Herod ●children killed by Herod: **Holy Innocents**

herring ●small young of herrings, sprats, etc. eaten as food: **whitebait** ●rolled pickled herring fillet: **rollmop**

heterosexuality ●assumption that heterosexuality is the norm: **heterosexism**

hidden ●*combining form*: **crypt(o)-** (*e.g.* cryptocommunist) ●hidden store: **cache, stash** ●hiding-place: **bolt-hole** ●not hidden: **overt**

hide ●hide one's thoughts or feelings: **dissimulate** ●wait in hiding: **lurk** ●person hiding on a ship or aircraft in order to travel without paying: **stowaway**

Highlands ●traditional Highland language: **Gaelic** ●competition of Highland traditional poets and musicians: **Mod** ●woven fabric pattern associated with a particular clan: **tartan** ●distinctive pattern of a tartan: **sett** ●centre-folded Highland hat: **glengarry** ●Highlander's tartan shoulder cloth: **plaid** ●man's tartan skirt in traditional Highland dress: **kilt** ●pouch worn in front of the kilt: **sporran**

hill ●low hill: **hummock, hurst, knoll, mound** ●low hill flanking a mountain: **foothill** ●gently rolling hill: **down** ●flat-topped steepsided hill: **mesa** ●rocky hill: **tor** ●top of a hill: **crest, summit** ●mass of loose stones on a hillside: **scree**

Hindu ●Hindu nationalism: **Hindutva** ●Hindu hereditary class: **caste, varna** ●member of the Hindu priestly caste: **Brahman** ●member of the Hindu military caste: **Kshatriya** ●member of the Hindu caste of merchants and farmers: **Vaisya** ●member of the Hindu worker caste: **Sudra** ●member of the lowest class of Hindu society: **Dalit, Harijan, untouchable** ●denoting a Hindu belonging to one of the highest castes: **twice-born** ●Hindu scriptures: **Veda** ●commentary upon the Vedas: **Upanishad** ●Hindu mystical text: **tantra** ●word repeated in Hindu meditation: **mantra** ●Hindu mystic syllable: **om** ●Hindu liturgical language: **Sanskrit** ●Hindu teacher: **guru, Maharishi, pandit, swami** ●Hindu teacher's pupil: **chela** ●hermitage of a Hindu teacher and his pupils: **ashram** ●Hindu ascetic: **fakir** ●Hindu ascetic wearing few clothes: **gymnosophist** ●Hindu religious beggar: **sannyasi** (*pl.* same) ●chance to see a Hindu holy man: **darshan** ●selfless action as a way to perfection: **karma yoga** ●Hindu state

of supreme happiness: **ananda**
●Hindu state of blessedness: **nirvana**
●Hindu's personal fate: **karma**
●Hindu soul, individual and universal: **atman** ●earthly incarnation of a Hindu divinity: **avatar** ●Hindu goddess: **devi** ●Hindu supreme goddess: **Devi** ●Hindu supreme god: **Shiva** ●phallus-symbol of Shiva: **lingam** ● vulva-symbol of divine creative energy: **yoni** ●disk symbolizing the universe: **mandala** ●power of the Hindu gods: **maya** ●food-offering to a Hindu god: **prasad** ●Hindu term for cosmic law: **dharma** ●Hindu festival of lights: **Diwali** ●Hindu spring festival: **Holi** ●Hindu principle of nonviolence towards all living things: **ahimsa** ●Hindu tower temple: **pagoda** ●Hindu traditional medicine: **Ayurveda** ●male Hindu's loincloth: **dhoti** ●Hindu forehead mark: **tilak** ● red powder used by Hindu women to mark the forehead: **kumkum** ●Hindu epic: **Mahabharata** ●Hindu treatise on love and sexual technique: **Kama Sutra** ●Hindu seclusion of women: **purdah** ●Hindu place of cremation: **ghat** ●Hindu widow's self-cremation: **suttee** ●Hindu meditation technique popular in the West: **Transcendental Meditation** ●Western system of exercises loosely based on Hindu principles: **yoga**

hip ●*adjective*: **sciatic** ●hip joint: **coxa**

hire purchase ●initial hire purchase payment: **down payment** ●company funding hire-purchase: **finance company, finance house**

history ●history-writing, or the study of it: **historiography** ●historical information gained by recorded interviews: **oral history** ●objects of historical interest: **memorabilia** ●objects of interest to military historians: **militaria** ●Muse of history: **Clio**

hit ●hit reapeatedly: **pound, pummel, thrash** ●hit obliquely: **glance**

●blow with the hand's edge to the back of the neck: **rabbit punch** ●quick sharp blow: **rap** ●flatten with a sharp blow: **swat**

hockey ●start of play in hockey: **bully off** ●advance the ball by successive light taps: **dribble** ●side part of the playing area: **wing**

hoe ●pushing hoe to cut off weed roots: **Dutch hoe**

hoist ●hoisting apparatus of three splayed poles: **sheer legs** ●hoisting device winding rope etc. about a drum: **capstan, winch, windlass** ●ropes and pulleys for lifting heavy objects: **tackle**

hole ●bored or pierced hole: **perforation, puncture** ●hole bored to take explosive: **blast hole, shot hole** ●hole allowing leakage: **puncture** ●enlarge the top of a hole to take the screw flush: **countersink**

holiday ●university or lawcourts' holiday: **vacation** ●holiday of half a day: **half holiday** ●school's short mid-term holiday: **half term** ●inclusive holiday: **package, package tour** ●popular holiday destination: **resort** ●rented holiday home: **cottage, gîte, villa** ●agent accompanying a package tour: **courier** ●holiday camp organizer: **redcoat**

holy ●*combining forms*: **hagio-** (*e.g.* hagiology), **hiero-** (*e.g.* hieroglyph) ●holy place: **shrine** ●journey to a shrine: **pilgrimage** ●declare or make holy: **sanctify** ●violate the holiness of a place or thing: **desecrate** ●ritually impure: **unclean**

Holy Communion ●Holy Communion given to a person near to death: **viaticum** ●multidenominational participation in Holy Communion: **intercommunion, open communion** ●thin bread disc used in Holy Communion: **wafer** ▶*see also* **Mass**

holy war ●by Christians to recover the Holy Land: **crusade** ●by Muslims against infidels: **jihad**

home ●longing for one's home: **homesickness** ●force someone to live far from his home: **banish** ●work from home, with electronic access to the workplace: **telecommute**

homoeopathy ●substance used in homoeopathic treatment: **similars**

homosexuality ●*adjectives*: gay, pink, queer ●female homosexual: **lesbian** ●male homosexual transvestite: **drag queen** ●arousing homosexual desire: **homoerotic** ●concealment of one's homosexuality: **closet** ●not concealing one's homosexuality: **out** ●declare one's homosexuality: **come out** ●announcement by others of a prominent person's homosexuality: **outing** ●public lavatory viewed as a homosexual meeting-place: **cottage** ●homosexual purchasing power: **pink pound** ●hatred of homosexuality: **homophobia**

honesty ●consistently honest: **upright, upstanding** ●system relying on participants' honesty: **honour system**

honey ●honey-producing: **melliferous** ●denoting honey drained from the comb without heat or pressure: **virgin** ●alcoholic drink made from honey: **mead** ●sweetmeat made of honey and sesame flour: **halva** ●liquid collected by bees from flowers to make honey: **nectar** ●natural sugar found in honey and fruits: **fructose**

honeycomb ●small compartment in a honeycomb: **cell**

Hong Kong ●general index of Hong Kong share prices: **Hang Seng index**

hook ●hooked pole used to land large fish: **gaff** ●hooked device used to gain purchase: **grappling iron, grapnel** ●decorative openwork made with hooked yarn: **crochet**

hoop ●hoop attached to a skirt to support it: **farthingale**

hope ●unattainable hope: **pipe dream** ●denoting a hope unlikely to be fulfilled: **pious, vain**

hops ●kiln for drying hops: **oast** ●building for this: **oast house**

horizontal ●device establishing horizontality: **level, spirit level**

hormone ●growth hormone: **somatotrophin** ●hormone used to treat allergies and arthritis: **cortisone** ●pituitary hormone tending to increase blood pressure: **vasopressin** ●hormone used to treat diabetes: **insulin** ●hormone used by athletes to improve performance: **steroid, anabolic steroid** ●hormone secreted when under stress: **adrenalin, epinephrine** ●hormone oxidising body sugar: **insulin** ●hormone governing female secondary sexual characteristics: **oestrogen** ●hormones governing male secondary sexual characteristics: **androgen, testosterone** ●hormone stimulating uterine preparation for pregnancy: **progesterone** ●hormone making the cervix dilate: **relaxin** ●hormone stimulating uterine contractions and milk secretion: **oxytocin** ●hormone stimulating milk production after giving birth: **prolactin**

horn ●*adjective*: **corneous** ●horn of plenty: **cornucopia**

horoscope ●prepare a horoscope: **cast** ●astrological map for casting a horoscope: **birth chart, natal chart**

horse ●*combining forms*: **equi-, hippo-** (*e.g.* hippodrome, *originally a track for horse races*) ●*adjective*: **equine** ●small prehistoric horse: **hyracotherium, eohippus** ●female horse: **mare** ●castrated male horse: **gelding** ●uncastrated male horse: **stallion, entire horse** ●young horse: **foal** ●young male horse: **colt** ●young female horse: **filly** ●offspring of a male donkey and female horse: **mule** ●offspring of a male horse and female donkey: **hinny** ●small horse: **pony** ●strong short-legged horse: **cob** ●pure-bred horse: **thorough-bred** ●thoroughbred horses: **blood-stock** ●horse for ordinary riding: **hack** ●horse bred for hunting and steeplechasing: **hunter** ●horse bred for heavy work: **carthorse** ●large horse bred for heavy work: **heavy horse, shire horse** ●horse with black and white patches: **piebald** ●horse with patches of white and some other colour: **skewbald** ●horse having a coat of one colour interspersed with hairs of another: **roan** ●wild American horse: **mustang, bronco** ●Austrian horse bred for dressage: **Lipizzaner** ●knight's war-horse: **destrier** ●racehorse in the calendar year after that in which it was born: **yearling** ●horse that has not yet won a major prize: **novice** ●horse's cry: **neigh** ●horse's soft high-pitched cry: **whinny** ●front part of a horse's face: **muzzle** ●highest part of a horse's back: **withers** ●horny pad in a horse's hoof: **frog** ●horse's neck hair: **mane** ●horse's mammary gland: **udder** ●straps round a horse's body: **harness** ●strap keeping the head down: **martingale** ●horse's metal mouthpiece: **bit** ●horse's eye-screen: **blinker** ●straps round a horse's head: **bridle** ●harness ring for the reins: **terret** ●attachment from the harness to the shafts: **trace** ●rope round a horse's head: **halter** ●horse's vertical jump: **buck** ●horse's style of movement: **gait** ●horse training in obedience and deportment: **dressage** ●advanced training in this: **haute école** ●horse-trainer's long rein: **lunge** ●skill in horsemanship: **manège** ●spike on a rider's heel: **spur** ●spiked disc attached to this: **rowel** ●horse trained to perform without a rider: **liberty horse** ●place where horses are trained: **manège** ●horse's gait between a trot and a gallop: **canter** ●(of a horse) stand upright on its hind legs: **rear** ●(of a horse) run out of control: **bolt** ●(of a horse) give birth: **foal** ●(of a horse) refuse a jump: **baulk, jib** ●military personnel using horses or armoured vehicles: **cavalry** ●small field for horses: **paddock** ●fodder bag attached to a horse's head: **nosebag** ●rope tying a horse's legs together: **hobble** ●establishment where horses are kept or trained: **stable** ●stable worker: **lad** ●horse food of bran and hot water: **mash** ●open trough for horse fodder: **manger** ●horse's coarse grooming brush: **dandy brush** ●metal device for cleaning horse brushes: **currycomb** ●establishment where horses are kept for breeding: **stud** ●book of horse pedigrees: **stud book** ●person who looks after horses: **groom** ●person who shoes horses: **blacksmith, farrier** ●horse disease with swellings below the jaw: **glanders** ●horse-slaughterer: **knacker** ●horse transporter: **horsebox** ●wooden horse for play: **hobby horse** ●mythical creature half man and half horse: **centaur**

horse-riding ●*adjective*: **equestrian** ●art of horse-riding: **equestrianism, equitation, horsemanship** ●equipment for horse-riding: **tack** ●rider's protective helmet: **skullcap** ●public competition in horse-riding skills: **gymkhana** ●equestrian competition involving several tests: **event** ●competitive sport of riding a horse over obstacles in an arena: **show-jumping** ●show-jumping competition over large obstacles: **puissance** ●final round of a jumping competition: **jump-off** ●details of a horse's previous competitive achievements: **form** ●penalty point in showjumping: **fault** ●shaped trousers for horse-riding: **jodhpurs** ●person who rides horses: **equestrian** ●climb onto a horse for riding: **mount** ●horse's response to the reins: **mouth**

hose ●adjustable fitting at a hose end: **nozzle**

hospital ●small rural hospital: **cottage hospital** ●private residential establishment providing health care: **nursing home** ●hospital set up near a battlefield: **field hospital** ●hospital in which medical students are trained: **teaching hospital** ●NHS hospital administering its own budget: **hospital trust** ●boarding school hospital: **sanatorium** ●hospital for the care of childbirth: **maternity hospital** ●hospital for the chronically sick, or those making a slow recovery: **sanatorium** ●hospital for the terminally ill: **hospice** ●medical post giving preliminary treatment: **dressing station** ●specialist hospital department: **clinic** ●hospital room for patients' beds: **ward** ●NHS hospital bed for which a charge is made: **amenity bed, pay bed** ●hospital room for operations: **theatre** ●theatre garment: **gown** ●room for patients reviving from a general anaesthetic: **recovery room** ●(of a state-run hospital) withdraw from local authority control: **opt out** ●region from which a hospital's patients come: **catchment area** ●admit to hospital: **hospitalize** ●keep in hospital: **detain** ●send home from hospital: **discharge** ●patient staying in a hospital: **inpatient** ●patient visiting a hospital for treatment: **outpatient** ●denoting a patient needing much care: **high-dependency** ●adverse effects of lengthy hospitalization: **hospitalism** ●denoting resident medical staff: **house** ●group of hospital doctors: **firm** ●denoting postgraduate medical training given in a hospital: **clinical** ●person receiving

this: **house officer, houseman** ●hospital attendant: **orderly, porter**

hostel ●hostel for the homeless: **reception centre**

hotel ●hotel for motorists: **motel** ●small Italian hotel: **pensione** ●institution offering cheap accommodation for employees, students, etc.: **hostel** ●private house offering food and lodging for payment: **boarding house, guest house** ●European boarding house: **pension** ●hotel entrance hall: **foyer** ●hotel reception counter: **desk** ●hotel employee carrying guests' luggage: **porter** ●service of food and drinks in customers' rooms: **room service** ●refrigerated drinks cupboard in hotel bedroom: **minibar** ●large hotel room for meetings or parties: **function room, reception room** ●hotel bedroom with several beds: **family room** ●person owning or running a hotel: **hotelier** ●hotel doorman: **commissionaire, porter** ●woman who cleans hotel bedrooms: **chambermaid** ●bed, breakfast, and one main meal daily: **demi-pension, half board** ●bed and all meals: **full board** ●formalities on leaving an hotel: **checkout** ▸ *see also* **restaurant**

hot water ●natural hot spring: **geyser** ●pan of hot water above which food may be cooked or kept warm: **bain-marie**

hour ●*adjective*: **horal**

house ●large elaborate house: **mansion** ●large house in the country: **country seat, manor** ●gatehouse for this: **lodge** ●country house with attached farm: **grange** ●Roman country house: **villa** ●single-storey house for a family and its livestock: **longhouse** ●small house used by hunters: **hunting box, shooting box** ●small country house for sportsmen: **lodge** ●Church of England parish priest's house: **vicarage, rectory** ●Roman Catholic parish priest's house: **presbytery** ●Protestant minister's house: **manse** ●detached town house of moderate size: **villa** ●row of houses built as a single block: **terrace** ●official dwelling of a government minister or diplomat: **residence** ●official accommodation of a judge on circuit: **lodgings** ●official accommodation of the head of an Oxford or Cambridge college: **lodge, lodgings** ●house at a secret location: **safe house** ●sample house on a new development, furnished and decorated: **show house** ●self-contained part of a house for an elderly relative: **granny flat** ●denoting a freestanding house: **detached** ●denoting a house attached to another on one side: **semi-detached** ●denoting a house attached to others on both sides: **terraced** ●denoting a house attached to another on the ground floor only: **link detached** ●children's part of a house: **nursery** ●house with its land and outbuildings: **messuage** ●paved area adjoining a house: **patio, terrace** ●children's play house: **Wendy house** ●hut at a holiday camp: **chalet** ●Eskimo's house made of ice blocks: **igloo** ●traditional conical stone house of southern Italy: **trullo** ●Russian summer residence: **dacha** ●traditional wooden house in Switzerland: **chalet** ●house's occupants: **household** ●person owning the house he or she lives in: **owner-occupier** ●person paying to live in another's house: **lodger, paying guest** ●denoting persons unable to leave home due to infirmity: **housebound** ●official confinement to one's home: **house arrest**

household ●*adjectives*: **domestic, domiciliary** ●money for running a household: **housekeeping** ●education in household skills: **domestic science** ●members of a household: **ménage** ●person employed to organize a household: **housekeeper** ●household servant: **domestic**

House of Commons ●chairman of House of Commons debates: **Speaker** ●Speaker's means of expelling a disruptive member: **naming** ●symbol of the Commons' authority: **mace** ●area represented by a member: **constituency** ●place in the House of Commons, or the constituency it represents: **seat** ●front seats occupied by chief members of the government: **Treasury bench** ●box in the House of Commons by which ministers stand to speak: **Dispatch Box** ●secure a quorum in the Commons: **make a House** ●Commons procedure limiting discussion: **ten-minute rule** ●post sought by resigning MP: **Stewardship of the Chiltern Hundreds** ●person who is not a member or official of the House of Commons: **stranger**

House of Lords ●chairman of House of Lords debates: **Lord Chancellor** ●his seat in the chamber: **Woolsack** ●bishops in the House of Lords: **Lords spiritual** ●lay members of the House of Lords: **Lords temporal** ●member of the House of Lords voting for a motion: **content** ●member of the House of Lords voting against a motion: **non-content** ●Crown document summoning a peer to the House of Lords: **writ** ●peer who seldom attends the House of Lords: **backwoodsman** ●peer acting as a senior judge: **law lord**

house purchase ●overbid another's accepted offer: **gazump** ●decrease one's own accepted offer: **gazunder**

hovercraft ●layer of air supporting a hovercraft: **cushion** ●hanging surround for the cushion: **skirt**

huge ●*combining forms*: **mega(lo)-** (*e.g.* megastore), **macro-** (*e.g.* macrocosm)

human ●*combining forms*: **andro-**, **anthrop(o)-** ●attribution of human form or behaviour to gods, animals, or inanimate objects: **anthropomorph-ism** ●belief that humans are the most important element of existence: **anthropocentrism, humanism** ●belief that humans are no more import-ant than other living beings: **biocentrism** ●resembling a human: **anthropoid** ●study of the origins of humankind: **anthropogeny** ●cul-tural study of humankind: **anthro-pology** ●hatred of humankind: **mis-anthropy** ●assumption of human form by a concept or divinity: **em-bodiment, incarnation** ●attribution of human emotions to inanimate ob-jects: **pathetic fallacy** ●seeking to promote human welfare: **humanitar-ian, philanthropic** ●tiny humanoid creature: **homunculus** (*pl.* homunculi) ●robot designed to resemble a human being: **android** ●beyond human powers: **superhuman**

humour ●humorous statement of the opposite to what is really meant: **irony** ●disrespectful joking: **levity**

hundred ●*combining forms*: **cent-** (*e.g.* century), **hecto-** (*e.g.* hectolitre) ●person who is 100 years old: **centen-arian** ●increase a hundredfold: **cen-tuple**

hundredth ●*combining form*: **centi-** (*e.g.* centilitre) ●*adjective*: **centesimal** ●hundredth anniversary: **centenary** ●two-hundredth anniversary: **bicen-tenary, bicentennial** ●three-hundredth anniversary: **tercentenary, tercentennial** ●four-hundredth anni-versary: **quatercentenary** ●five-hundredth anniversary: **quincenten-ary, quincentennial**

Hungarian ●Hungarian person or his language: **Magyar** ●Hung-arian cavalryman: **hussar** ●Hungar-ian gypsy: **tzigane** ●spicy Hungarian stew: **goulash** ●fast Hungarian dance: **csardas**

hunting ●*adjective*: **venatic** ●il-legal hunting: **poaching** ●hunting trip in East Africa: **safari** ●animal that naturally hunts other animals for food: **predator** ●hare-hunting with dogs: **beagling** ●game-hunting with greyhounds: **coursing** ●hunters' pre-liminary assembly: **meet** ●hunter's assistant: **gillie** ●hunters' camou-flaged shelter: **hide** ●hunter's mov-able screen: **stalking horse** ●animal used by hunters to attract others: **decoy** ●official in charge of hounds: **huntsman** ●huntsman's assistant: **whipper-in** ●hunting dog: **hound** ●heavy hunting dog: **mastiff** ●small hound used to hunt hares: **beagle** ●set of hounds: **pack** ●person in charge of this: **master** ●release of hounds at the start of a hunt: **throw-off** ●hunting dog's rigid stance to in-dicate game: **point, set** ●dog trained to recover dead or injured game: **re-triever** ●hunted bird or animal: **game, quarry** ●quarry's hiding place: **cover** ●thicket in which game may hide: **covert** ●drive game from these: **flush** ●cause game birds to rise from cover: **spring** ●follow game stealthily: **stalk** ●denoting cornered game: **at bay** ●person employed to drive game towards the hunters: **beater** ●the driving of game towards the hunters by beaters: **battue** ●shout when the quarry breaks cover: **view halloo** ●animal etc. used to lure others: **decoy** ●person employed to breed or protect game: **gamekeeper, keeper** ●person employed to super-vise game and hunting: **game warden** ●area reserved for private hunting: **preserve** ●area where no hunting is permitted: **reserve** ●person attempt-ing to disrupt a hunt: **hunt saboteur** ●time of year when hunting is permit-ted: **open season** ●time of year when hunting is not permitted: **close**

season ●loss of the scent in hunting: **check** ●group living by hunting and harvesting wild food: **hunter-gatherers** ●strongly scented object used in sham hunts: **drag** ●fox's head as a hunting trophy: **mask** ●small house used by hunters: **hunting box, shooting box**

husband ●monarch's husband: **consort** ●husband remaining at home to look after the house and children: **househusband** ●husband of an unfaithful wife: **cuckold** ●denoting a husband constantly upbraided by his wife: **henpecked** ●servility of a husband towards his wife: **uxoriousness** ●custom or state of having only one husband at a time: **monandry** ●custom or state of having several husbands at a time: **polyandry**

hut ●holiday-camp hut: **chalet** ●wheeled beach hut: **bathing machine** ●tunnel-shaped cast iron hut: **Nissen hut**

hygiene ●*adjective*: **sanitary** ●make hygienic: **sanitize**

hymn ●hymn sung as the clergy enter the church for a service: **introit** ●hymn sung during a procession: **processional** ●hymn sung as the clergy leave the church after a service: **recessional** ●Lutheran hymn or its music: **chorale** ●Latin hymn on the Last Judgement: **Dies Irae** ●Latin hymn on the sufferings of the Blessed Virgin at the Crucifixion: **Stabat Mater** ●Latin hymn venerating the Blessed Sacrament: **Tantum Ergo**

hyphen ●hyphen used always: **hard hyphen** ●hyphen used only when a word is split: **soft hyphen**

hypnosis ●therapy using hypnosis: **hypnotherapy** ●semiconsciousness induced by hypnosis: **trance** ●instilling of ideas in the mind of a hypnotized patient: **suggestion** ●denoting suggestions intended to influence behaviour after the trance has ended: **posthypnotic**

ice ●*adjectives*: **gelid, glacial** ●ice covering a large area: **ice cap** ●slow-moving mass of ice: **glacier** ●mass of snow, ice, and rocks moving down a mountain: **avalanche** ●tapering piece of ice: **icicle** ●thin transparent layer of ice: **black ice, verglas** ●ice coating on fogbound objects: **rime** ●stratified ice sample gained by a hollow drill: **core** ●floating sheet of ice: **floe, pack ice** ●large floating block of ice: **iceberg** ●area of water crowded with floating blocks of ice: **pack ice** ●clear stretch of water surrounded by ice: **polynya** ●shower of compacted ice pellets: **hail** ●slide down an ice slope: **glissade** ●ship designed to break through ice: **ice-breaker** ●building for storing ice: **ice house** ●sailing vehicle on skids for travelling across ice: **ice boat, ice yacht** ●period when much of the earth was covered by ice: **ice age, glacial period** ●drink poured over crushed ice: **frappé**

ice age ●denoting the milder period between two ice ages: **interglacial**

iceberg ●small iceberg: **growler** ●floating ice detached from an iceberg: **calf**

ice cream ●ice cream made with water: **sorbet, water ice** ●conical wafer for ice cream: **cornet** ●Italian ice cream of various flavours with glacé fruits etc.: **cassata** ●Italian water ice: **granita** ●ice cream served with fruit etc. in a tall glass: **Knickerbocker Glory, parfait, sundae** ●dish of ice cream, peaches, and liqueur: **peach Melba, pêche Melba**

ice hockey ●rubber disk used as a ball: **puck** ●attempt to play a ball in an opponent's possession: **tackle**

Icelandic ●Icelandic parliament: **Althing** ●medieval Icelandic prose narrative: **saga**

icing ●hard white icing made from icing sugar and egg whites: **royal icing**

icon ●icon screen in an Eastern church: **iconostasis**

idea ●clever idea: **conceit** ●key idea: **catchword, catchphrase** ●mistaken but traditional idea: **old wives' tale, shibboleth** ●mistaken but widely popular perception of a certain type of person etc.: **stereotype** ●idea held to be above criticism: **sacred cow** ●obsessive idea: **idée fixe** (*pl.* idées fixes) ●obsessive interest in a single idea: **monomania** ●ideas as property: **intellectual property** ●idea's tangible expression: **embodiment** ●creative idea: **inspiration** ●introduction of new ideas: **innovation** ●system of ideas: **ideology** ●uncritical supporter of this: **ideologue** ●rejecter of this offering no alternative: **negativist**

ideal ●denoting an ideal situation: **idyllic, utopian**

identical ●genetically identical organism: **clone**

identity ●identity documents: **papers** ●hiding one's identity: **incognito** ●item habitually seen with a person or thing, and serving to identify them: **attribute**

ideology ●*combining form*: **-ism** (*e.g.* Fascism) ●generally accepted ideology: **orthodoxy**

idleness ●agreeable idleness: **dolce far niente, flânerie, lotus-eating** ●frustrating but enforced inactivity: **doldrums** ●idle and irresponsible person: **ne'er-do-well** ●physically or mentally lethargic: **torpid** ●idle and unambitious: **shiftless** ●idle about: **loaf**

ignorant ●ignorant person: **ignoramus**

ignore ●deliberately ignore an acquaintance: **cut, snub**

illegal ●denoting things made or sold illegally: **bootleg** ●official's illegal use of powers or funds entrusted to him: **malversation** ●alcohol distilled illegally in Ireland: **poteen** ●alcohol distilled illegally in the USA: **moonshine**

illegitimacy ●alleged heraldic indication of illegitimacy: **bar sinister, bend sinister** ●court order obliging an illegitimate child's father to contribute to its support: **affiliation order**

illness ●*combining form*: **-pathy** (*e.g.* neuropathy) ●illness caused by germs in food: **food poisoning** ●identification of an illness: **diagnosis** ●feign illness to avoid work: **malinger** ●employee's statement that his absence was due to illness: **self-certification** ●constant suffering from imagined illnesses: **hypochondria** ●degree awarded to a person absent from the examinations due to illness: **aegrotat** ●study of airborne micro-organisms as sources of infection: **aerobiology** ●cause of an illness: **aetiology** ●tongue-coating indicating illness: **fur** ●denoting a physical illness that has a psychological cause: **psychosomatic** ●denoting an illness caused by medical intervention: **iatrogenic** ●denoting an illness of short duration: **acute** ●denoting a long-lasting or recurrent illness: **chronic** ●denoting illness

bearing a risk of death: **critical** ●prone to illness: **delicate** ●slightly ill: **below par, seedy, under the weather** ●proneness to a specified illness: **diathesis** ●suddenly become seriously ill: **collapse** ●abnormal sweat caused by illness: **diaphoresis** ●restless tossing of a sick person: **jactitation** ●state of a patient showing no brain activity or response to stimuli: **persistent vegetative state** ●school or workplace area set apart for those taken sick: **sick bay** ●recovery from illness: **convalescence, recuperation**

illusion ●*adjective*: **illusory** ●illusion seen in a desert: **mirage** ●illusion seen on mountain peaks: **Brocken spectre** ●illusionist technique of mural painting: **trompe l'oeil**

illustration ●illustration made from a limestone block: **lithograph** ●illustration made from a cut linoleum block: **linocut** ●illustration printed from a scored or etched metal plate: **engraving** ●illustration printed from a cut block of wood: **woodcut** ●finely detailed woodcut: **wood engraving** ●illustration at the front of a book: **frontispiece** ●illustration used to fill the page at the end of a chapter etc.: **tailpiece** ●illustration across the centre pages of a publication: **centre spread** ●small illustration with edges faded away: **vignette** ●position an illustration to leave no margin: **bleed** ●illustration of a mechanism showing the parts separated for clarity: **exploded view** ●illustration of a mechanism showing its casing cut away: **cutaway** ●illustration depicting an imagined slice through the object represented: **cross section** ▸*see also* **engraving**

image ●*combining form*: **icono-** ●images used to represent a person, idea, etc.: **iconography** ●dreamlike sequence of images: **phantasmagoria**

●worship of images: **iconolatry**
●image's degree of focus: **sharpness,
softness** ●study of the use of images
in the visual arts: **iconography**

imitation ●*combining form*: **-ette**
(*e.g.* flanellette) ●mocking imitation:
parody ●distorted imitation: **travesty** ●artwork in imitative style:
pastiche ●not imitation: **genuine,
original**

immature ●artist's immature
works: **juvenilia**

immigrant ●immigrant worker in
Germany: **Gastarbeiter**

immune response ●immune response causing illness: **allergy**
●study of immune responses: **immunology**

immunity ●immunity offered to
previous offenders: **amnesty** ●(place
giving) immunity from arrest: **sanctuary** ●immunity from local laws enjoyed by foreign diplomats: **extraterritoriality** ●germ or insect that has
gained immunity to treatments employed to eradicate it: **superbug**

import ●taxation of imports to protect native manufacturers: **protectionism** ▶*see also* **taxation, trade**

importance ●of first importance:
paramount ●of critical importance:
of the essence ●of lesser importance: **secondary, subordinate** ●of
little importance: **marginal, nugatory,
peripheral, trivial** ●make, or treat as
if, unimportant: **marginalize** ●place
in order of importance: **prioritize**
●important person: **luminary, notable, panjandrum** ●group of attendants upon an important person: **entourage, retinue** ●person of no
importance: **nobody, nonentity, non-
person** ●inflated ideas of one's importance: **delusions of grandeur**

imprisonment ●wartime imprisonment of enemy aliens: **internment**

●imprisonment with forced labour:
penal servitude ●writ to assess the
legality of someone's imprisonment:
habeas corpus

improve ●improve by basic
changes: **reform**

impulsive ●impulsive and impractical: **quixotic**

impurities ●add impurities to: **contaminate** ●add impurities to food or
drink: **adulterate**

incense ●device in which incense
is burnt: **censer, thurible** ●acolyte
carrying the censer: **thurifer**

incidental ●product incidental to
the main purpose of manufacture:
by-product ●incidental remark in a
legal judgement: **obiter dictum**

include ●include as a subsidiary
element: **subsume**

income ●income of a state or large
organization: **revenue** ●income before taxes are deducted: **gross income**
●income after taxes have been deducted: **net income** ●income after
tax has been deducted and essential
expenses paid: **discretionary income,
disposable income** ●income from
wages: **earned income** ●receiving
no earned income: **unwaged** ●in-
come from the sale of goods or services: **takings, turnover** ●income
from personal property, investments,
etc.: **private income, private means,
unearned income** ●source of income: **livelihood, living** ●adequate
income: **competence** ●excess of income over expenditure: **profit, surplus** ●excess of expenses over income: **negative cash flow** ●state
payment to a family on low income:
family credit ●situation where any
increase in income triggers a counterbalancing withdrawal of state benefits: **poverty trap**

inconsistency ●statement containing two apparently inconsistent
elements: **paradox, oxymoron**

increase ●steadily increasing: **progressive** ●increase rapidly: **escalate, proliferate**

incurable ●care of the incurable: **palliative care** ●hospital for this: **hospice**

indecent exposure ●genital exposure: **flashing** ●exposure of the buttocks: **mooning** ●running naked through a public place: **streaking**

independence ●economic independence: **autarchy, autarky, self-sufficiency, self-support** ●governmental independence: **autonomy, self-determination** ●emotionally self-sufficient: **self-reliant**

Indian ●*combining form*: **Indo-** ●title of a highly-respected Indian: **mahatma** ●Indian traditional gesture of greeting: **pranam** ●Indian polite form of adress to a man: **sahib** ●Indian polite form of address to a mature woman: **memsahib** ●Indian non-theistic religion: **Jainism** ●former Indian rulers: **maharaja, raja** (*fem.* rani), **nabob, nizam** ●maharaja's wife or widow: **maharani** ●grand reception held by an Indian ruler: **durbar** ●Indian judge: **hakim, munsif** ●Indian landowner: **zamindar** ●Indian village council: **panchayat** ●Indian traditional doctor: **hakim** ●Indian holy person: **muni, sadhu** ●Indian soldier under the raj: **sepoy** ●Indian sergeant: **havildar** ●Indian minor official: **jamadar** ●Indian police constable: **sepoy** ●Indian secretary: **munshi** ●Indian dancing girl: **nautch girl** ●Indian bandit: **dacoit** ●Indian elephant-driver: **mahout** ●Indian native labourer: **coolie** ●Indian peasant: **ryot** ●Indian police stick: **lathi** ●Indian fan: **punkah** ●garland of flowers given in welcome: **mala** ●Indian enclosed litter: **palanquin, palankeen** ●Indian clay oven: **tandoor** ●denoting a style of Indian cooking using this: **tandoori** ●Indian postal service: **dak** ●steps leading down to a river in India: **ghat** ●Indian tree with fragrant timber: **sandalwood** ●Indian warehouse: **godown** ●Indian brass water pot: **lota** ●closure of businesses as a protest: **hartal** ●Indian political strategy of passive resistance: **satyagraha** ●Indian washing clothes for payment: **dhobi** ●Indian woman's bodice: **choli** ●Indian woman's loose trousers tapering at the ankle: **salwar** ●Indian woman's garment of a single length of cotton or silk: **sari** ●decorative gold thread used on Indian clothes: **zari** ●Indian loincloth: **lungi** ●Indian snack of lentils, peanuts, etc.: **Bombay mix** ●set meal in an Indian restaurant, or the metal plate on which it is served: **thali** ●Indian dish of aniseed and sugar: **saunf** ●Indian term for aubergine: **brinjal** ●thin cake of Indian bread: **chapatti** ●thin crisp spicy Indian bread: **poppadom** ●Indian unleavened bread: **nan, paratha** ●small fried piece of unleavened bread: **puri** ●Indian clarified butter: **ghee** ●Indian ice cream: **kulfi** ●Indian term for red meat: **gosht** ●Indian meatball: **kofta** ●Indian dish of meat cooked in an onion sauce: **dopiaza** ●Indian dish of small pieces of marinaded meat or vegetables: **tikka** ●Indian dish of curried meat in a tomato sauce: **rogan josh** ●triangular savoury pastry: **samosa** ●Indian dish of split pulses: **dhal** ●Indian dish of fried vegetables: **bhaji** ●Indian dish of boiled vegetables with spices: **chaat** ●Indian dish of spiced rice with vegetables etc.: **biriani** ●Indian ground spice mixture: **masala** ●Indian sauce of spices and turmeric, or a dish using it: **curry** ●Indian term for spinach: **saag, sag** ●Indian side-dish of spiced yoghurt with cucumber: **raita** ●Indian sweetmeat made from milk solids and sugar: **burfi** ●Indian sweetmeat of batter in syrup: **jalebi** ●Indian sweetmeat of cheese in syrup: **gulab jamun** ●Indian term for tea: **chai** ●Indian yogurt drink: **lassi** ●screen in an Indian house concealing women from view: **purdah** ● women's quarters in an Indian house: **zenana** ●upland town popular as a holiday resort: **hill station** ●group of villages in India: **pargana, pergunnah** ●travellers' rest house in India: **dak bungalow** ●seasonal wind in India: **monsoon** ●rainy season in India: **monsoon** ●Indian term for a foreigner: **feringhee** ●Indian alphabet: **Devanagari** ●ancient Indian literary language: **Sanskrit** ●ancient and medieval vernacular of north and central India: **Prakrit** ●Indian term for ten million: **crore** ●Indian bowed lute: **sarod** ●long-necked Indian lute: **sitar** ●Indian four-stringed instrument with a resonator at each end: **veena** ●pair of Indian hand drums: **tabla** ●dramatic dance of southern India: **Kathakali** ●note-pattern for improvisation in Indian music: **rag, raga** ●study of Indian culture: **Indology** ▶*see also* **curry, Hindu**

indigestion ●acid indigestion: **heartburn** ●bloated feeling resulting from indigestion: **flatulence**

individual ●*combining form*: **idio-** ●form of speech particular to one person: **idiolect** ●individual habit: **idiosyncrasy**

indulgence ●debauched man: **roué**

industrial relations ●decision-sharing between management and workers: **co-determination** ●negotiation between management and workforce representatives: **collective bargaining** ●unresolved disagreement between management and workers: **dispute** ●third party requested to resolve a dispute: **arbitrator** ●third party requested to assist the disputants' negotiations: **conciliator, mediator** ●resort to strikes rather than

negotiation: **direct action** ●slowing or stopping work as a protest: **industrial action** ●withdrawal of labour as a protest: **stoppage, strike** ●deliberate reduction of output by minute observance of regulations: **go-slow, work to rule** ●statutory interval for negotiation when strikes are threatened: **cooling-off period** ●worker chosen as a workplace representative but having no union appointment: **shop steward** ●group of strikers stationed outside the workplace: **picket** ●picket willing to serve at other workplaces: **flying picket** ●employer's exclusion of all workers: **lockout** ●alteration of an employee's job to encourage him to resign: **constructive dismissal** ●trade union's claim of exclusive rights to a certain job: **demarcation dispute** ●grant a union workplace negotiation rights: **recognize** ●withdraw such rights: **derecognize** ●worker involvement in company government: **industrial democracy** ▶*see also* **negotiation, strike, trade union**

industry ●new and growing industry: **sunrise industry** ●old and declining industry: **sunset industry** ●industry supplying raw materials for further manufacture: **primary industry** ●this further manufacture: **secondary industry** ●economic activity in the supply of services: **tertiary industry** ●industrial efficiency: **productivity**

inflammation ●inflammation of the abdomen lining: **peritonitis** ●inflammation of the anus: **proctitis** ●inflammation of the bladder: **cystitis** ●bone inflammation: **osteitis** ●inflammation of the brain: **encephalitis** ●inflammation of brain membranes: **meningitis** ●inflammation of the brain and spinal cord: **encephalomyelitis** ●inflammation of the breast: **mastitis** ●inflammation of the caecum: **typhlitis** ●inflammation of the colon: **colitis** ● inflammation of the cornea: **keratitis** ● inflammation of the ear: **canker, otitis** ● inflammation of the inner ear: **labyrinthitis** ● inflammation of the elbow tendons: **tennis elbow** ● inflammation of the eye: **ophthalmia, ophthalmitis** ● inflammation of the eyelid: **blepharitis** ● inflammation of the eye's mucus membrane: **conjunctivitis** ● inflammation of fibrous tissue: **fibrositis** ● inflammation of the gums: **gingivitis** ● inflammation of the heart: **carditis** ● inflammation of the intestine: **enteritis** ● inflammation of the joints: **arthritis, rheumatism, rheumatoid arthritis** ● chronic kidney inflammation: **nephritis, Bright's disease** ● inflammation of the knee: **housemaid's knee** ● inflammation of the larynx: **laryngitis** ● inflammation of the liver: **hepatitis** ● bacterial infection causing inflammation of a lung: **pneumonia** ● inflammation of the mucus membrane of the bronchi: **bronchitis** ● inflammation of the muscles: **rheumatism** ● inflammation of the nose: **rhinitis** ● inflammation of an ovary: **oophoritis, ovaritis** ● inflammation of the pericardium: **pericarditis** ● inflammation of the pancreas: **pancreatitis** ● inflammation of the plurae: **pleurisy** ● inflammation of the prostate: **prostatitis** ● inflammation of the rectum: **proctitis** ● inflammation from skin rubbing on skin: **intertrigo** ● skin inflammation near a nail: **whitlow** ● skin inflammation or peeling from overexposure to sunlight: **sunburn** ● inflammation of the retina: **retinitis** ● inflammation of the spinal cord: **myelitis** ● inflammation of the membrane covering the spinal cord: **meningitis** ● inflammation of the spinal joints: **spondylitis** ● inflammation of the spleen: **splenitis** ● inflammation of the stomach: **gastritis** ● syphilitic inflammation of the brain: **paresis**

● inflammation of a tendon: **tendinitis** ● inflammation of the testicles: **orchitis** ● inflammation of the tissue around teeth: **periodontitis** ● inflammation of the tongue: **glossitis** ● inflammation of the tonsils: **tonsillitis** ● inflammation of the trachea: **tracheitis** ● inflammation of the udder: **garget** ● inflammation of the urethra: **urethritis** ● inflammation of the uterus: **metritis** ● inflammation of the vagina: **vaginitis** ● inflammation of vein walls: **phlebitis** ● patchy inflammation of smaller veins: **angiitis, vasculitis** ● inflammation of the vocal cords or voice box: **laryngitis** ● inflammation of the vulva: **vulvitis** ● inflammation of the windpipe: **tracheitis** ● inflammation of the wrist tendons: **tenosynovitis** ● disease causing genital inflammation: **herpes simplex** ● medicine to ease inflammation: **demulcent** ● soft moist mass applied to relieve inflammation: **poultice**

inflation ● inflation caused by increased production costs: **cost-push** ● inflation caused by unsatisfied demand: **demand-pull** ● inflation accompanied by high unemployment and stagnant demand: **stagflation**

inflection ● inflection of a Latin or Greek noun: **declension** ● inflection of a Latin or Greek verb: **conjugation**

inform ● inform officially: **notify**

information ● information of military or political value: **intelligence** ● information designed to mislead: **disinformation, misinformation** ● information designed to further a particular point of view: **propaganda** ● item of information: **datum** (*pl.* data) ● published information: **literature** ● information booklet: **brochure** ● text and graphic information broadcast by television: **teletext** ● alter information to make it more acceptable: **launder** ● informal suppression of information: **conspiracy of silence** ●information sheet distributed to club members etc.: **bulletin, newsletter** ●study of the processes of storing and retrieving information: **informatics, information science** ●denoting officially secret information: **classified** ●release of information: **disclosure, divulgence** ●deliberate disclosure of secret information: **leak** ●person doing this: **mole** ●loath to give information: **reticent, unforthcoming** ●increased availability of information due to computers: **information revolution** ●person supplying information: **informant, source** ●person sent ahead to reconnoitre: **scout**

informer ●criminal supplying information to the police: **stool-pigeon, nark, grass, supergrass**

inhabitant ●*combining form*: **-ite** (*e.g.* Israelite) ●original inhabitant: **aboriginal, autochthon**

inherit ●person who will inherit: **heir** ●things inherited: **heritage** ●things inherited from one's father: **patrimony** ●inheritance of personal characteristics: **heredity** ●gained by inheritance: **hereditary** ●eldest son's right of inheritance: **primogeniture** ●property inheritance settled over several generations: **entail** ●prevent someone from inheriting as he or she expects to do: **disinherit**

initiative ●controlling influence stifling initiative: **dead hand** ●destroy enthusiasm and initiative: **stultify**

injection ●injection protecting against infection: **inoculation, immunization, vaccination** ●second injection to reinforce the first: **booster** ●instrument for making injections: **syringe** ●disposable injection kit: **syrette**

ink ●container for loading ink: **cartridge**

innocence ●demonstrate or pronounce a person's innocence: **exculpate**

inquiry ●official inquiry into the cause of a death: **inquest**

Inquisition ●national director of the Inquisition: **Grand Inquisitor** ●burning of a heretic by the Spanish Inquisition: **auto da fé** (*pl.* autos da fé)

inscription ●scratched inscription: **graffito** ●small flat slab for an inscription: **tablet** ●study of ancient inscriptions: **epigraphy**

insect ●*combining form*: **entomo-** ●insect in immature grub-like form: **larva, maggot** ●insect in inactive stage between larva and adult: **pupa, chrysalis** ●larva of certain insects which develops directly into the adult stage: **nymph** ●transformation of an insect between these stages: **metamorphosis** ●mature insect: **imago** ●insect of greenfly or blackfly type, living on plant juices: **aphid** ●small black flying insect swarming on still summer days: **thrips** (*pl.* same), **thunderfly** ●insect that has gained immunity to treatments employed to eradicate it: **superbug** ●insect's feeding tube: **proboscis** ●insect excrement: **frass** ●killing insects: **insecticidal** ●eating insects: **insectivorous** ●study of insects: **entomology**

insecticide ●insecticide from powdered plant roots: **derris** ●insecticide made from aldrin, now largely banned: **dieldrin**

insert ●insert between other items: **interpolate, interpose, intersperse**

inside ●*combining forms*: **endo-, intra-** (*e.g.* intracranial) ●device inserted via a body cavity to allow internal examination: **endoscope** ●device giving inside views of the ear: **auriscope** ●device inserted via the anus for internal examination of the colon: **colonoscope**

insight ●intuitive insight: **perception**

inspection ●careful inspection: **scrutiny** ●tour of inspection: **round** ●inspect property as a potential lessor or purchaser: **view** ●without inspection: **sight unseen**

inspiration ●source of inspiration: **muse**

institution ●residential institution for orphans: **orphanage** ●institution established by endowment: **foundation**

instruction ●instruction book: **handbook, manual**

instrument ●observing and recording device: **monitor** ●instrument for measuring altitudes: **sextant** ●instrument for measuring angles: **protractor** ●instrument for making or measuring right angles: **set square** ●instrument estimating the distance travelled on foot: **pedometer** ●instrument recording and measuring earthquakes: **seismograph, seismometer** ●instrument measuring humidity: **hygrometer** ●instrument measuring light intensity: **photometer** ●instrument measuring liquid or gas pressure: **manometer, piezometer** ●instrument monitoring changes in pulse and breathing rates: **polygraph** ●instrument measuring a slope's steepness: **gradiometer** ●apparatus transmitting instrument readings by radio: **telemeter**

insulation ●water tank's insulating cover: **jacket** ●insulating cover for water systems: **lagging** ●substance giving limited insulation: **semiconductor**

insult ●insult by lack of attention: **slight** ●insult by total ignoral: **cut, snub**

insurance ●state insurance system for sickness and retirement: **National Insurance** ●insurance payable on the death of the insured person: **life in-**surance ●insurance against bad debts: **credit insurance** ●insurance against employees' dishonesty: **fidelity insurance** ●insurance against loss or damage to property etc.: **indemnity** ●insurance against the consequences of the insured's acts: **liability cover** ●insurer's own insurance against the risk undertaken: **reinsurance** ●travel company's bankruptcy insurance: **bond** ●motorist's international insurance: **green card** ●denoting insurance covering persons other than the insured: **third-party** ●sum paid to effect insurance: **premium** ●organization receiving the premium: **insurer** ●person paying the premium: **insured, policyholder** ●premium increase reflecting extra risk: **loading** ●premium reduction for claim-free years: **no-claims bonus** ●protection provided by insurance: **cover** ●person who calculates insurance risks and premiums: **actuary** ●person assessing payments to be made on claims: **loss adjuster** ●insurer's payment of claims: **settlement** ●person or company accepting liability for the payments promised by an insurance policy: **underwriter** ●insurance underwriter belonging to a Lloyds syndicate: **name** ●insurance contract: **policy** ●temporary insurance certificate: **cover note** ●clause modifying the cover given: **endorsement, exclusion, limitation, rider** ●time during which an insurance policy is effective: **term** ●cancellation of a life insurance, with partial reimbursement of premiums paid: **surrender** ●sale of a life insurance policy by a holder who is terminally ill: **viatical settlement** ●category of insurance provided by an insurer: **line** ●type of insurance policy where payment is guaranteed regardless of events: **assurance** ●type of insurance policy paying a fixed sum on a stated date: **endowment policy**

● achievement of this date: **maturity** ● denoting an insurance policy entitling the holder to a share in the company's profits: **with-profits** ● denoting an insurance policy covering loss regardless of responsibility: **no-fault** ● insurance sum payable at death: **reversion** ● denoting an insurance policy paying only at the death of the insured: **whole-life** ● item or event specifically not covered by an insurance policy: **exclusion** ● part of an insurance claim that the policyholder must pay: **excess** ● denoting an insurance policy financed by the beneficiary: **contributory** ● denoting a motor vehicle insurance covering most risks: **comprehensive** ● insurance companies' agreement to each reimburse their own clients: **knock-for-knock agreement**

intellect ● denoting interest only to an intellectual minority: **highbrow** ● intellectual people collectively: **highbrows, the intelligentsia** ● denoting general popularity: **middlebrow** ● requiring little or no intellect: **lowbrow, mindless**

intelligence ● scale for child intelligence: **Binet-Simon scale** ● figure expressing a person's intelligence: **intelligence quotient**

intention ● ploy designed to conceal one's true intentions: **blind**

interest ● showing interest or concern: **solicitous** ● of current interest: **topical** ● interest paid on capital only: **simple interest** ● interest paid on capital and on accumulated interest of previous periods: **compound interest** ● lowest available rate of interest on a bank loan: **prime rate** ● Bank of England's interest rate for loans to other banks **bank rate, base rate** ● denoting money available at high rates of interest: **tight** ● growth of a sum of money through interest earned: **accumulation**

interference ● policy of non-interference: **laissez-aller, laissez-faire**

internal ● *combining form*: **endo-** ● having an internal cause: **endogenous**

Internet ● Internet section with addresses sharing a common suffix: **domain** ● list of favourite Internet sites: **hot list** ● Internet network of hypermedia sites: **World Wide Web** ● move from site to site on the Internet: **surf** ● skilled Internet user: **internaut, netizen** ● company providing Internet access: **service provider** ● release material on the Internet: **post** ● denoting a computerized game playable over the Internet: **multi-user** ● program retrieving material from the Internet: **search engine** ● proportion of useful material on the Internet: **signal-to-noise ratio** ● proper way to use the Internet: **netiquette**

interruption ● aggressive verbal interruption of a speech: **heckling**

interval ● interval between two successive reigns etc.: **interregnum** ● entertainment given in a theatre interval: **intermezzo, entr'acte**

intestines ● *combining form*: **enter(o)-** ● *adjective*: **enteric** ● part of the intestine leading from the stomach: **small intestine** ● first part of the small intestine: **duodenum** (*pl.* duodenums *or* duodena) ● surgical diversion of the small intestine: **enterostomy** ● second portion of the small intestine: **jejunum** ● third portion: **ileum** ● surgical operation giving an opening to the ileum through the abdominal wall: **ileostomy** ● pouch at the junction of small and large intestines: **caecum** ● inflammation of the caecum: **typhlitis** ● part of the intestine leading to the anus: **large intestine** ● main part of the large intestine: **colon** ● portion of the colon ascending from the caecum: **ascending colon** ●portion of the colon leading to the rectum: **descending colon** ●horizontal portion of colon connecting these: **transverse colon** ●inflammation of the colon: **colitis** ●small blind tube near the end of the large intestine: **appendix** ●S-shaped section preceding the rectum: **sigmoid colon** ●final straight section of the large intestine: **rectum** ●final opening of the rectum: **anus** ●device inserted via the anus to give inside views of the colon: **colonoscope, fibrescope** ●anal insertion of water to flush out the colon: **colonic irrigation** ●surgical operation giving an opening to the colon through the abdominal wall: **colostomy** ●the opening so formed: **stoma** ●intestinal muscle movement: **peristalsis** ●abdominal protrusion of the intestine: **hernia** ●pig's intestines used as food: **chitterlings** ●inflammation of the intestine: **enteritis** ●disease of the intestine: **enteropathy** ●pain in the intestines: **colic** ●painful intestinal obstruction: **ileus** ●folding of one section of intestine inside the next: **intussusception** ●infection of the small intestine with severe diarrhoea: **cholera, enteritis** ●infection of the intestines with severe diarrhoea and bleeding: **dysentery** ●chronic ulceration of the ileum: **Crohn's disease** ●study of the stomach and intestines and their diseases: **gastroenterology** ▸*see also* **bowel**

into ●*combining form*: **intro-** (*e.g.* introduce, *literally 'lead into'*)

introductory ●*combining form*: **fore-** ●introductory speech or writing: **foreword, preamble** ●without introduction: **in medias res**

intuition ●discover by intuition: **divine**

invalid ●sore place on a bedridden person: **bedsore, decubitus ulcer**

●state payment to the long-term sick: **incapacity benefit**

invention ●document granting an inventor sole right to the exploitation of his work: **patent**

investment ●investment in projects having an element of risk: **speculation** ●sum paid to purchase investments: **principal** ●money for speculative investment: **risk capital, venture capital** ●return on investments: **yield** ●list of investments made: **portfolio** ●certificate attesting ownership of investments: **security** ●investor's net holdings at a particular time: **position** ●substantial holding in the shares of a particular company: **stake** ●denoting a portfolio that avoids investment in morally suspect industries: **ethical** ●denoting an investment made with borrowed capital: **leveraged** ●denoting investments with an early redemption date: **short-dated** ●denoting a constantly adjusted investment portfolio: **managed** ●company holding a wide and changing share portfolio and inviting clients to invest in the whole: **unit trust** ●profitability of investments: **performance** ●tax-free investment scheme: **personal equity plan** ●person living off dividends from investments: **rentier** ●minimize risk through counterbalanced investments: **hedge** ●dispose of investments: **divest** ●sudden withdrawal by many investors: **run**

involvement ●effort made to involve others: **outreach** ●involvement with an expectation of financial gain: **vested interest**

inward ●*combining form*: **intro-** (*e.g.* introspection)

ion ●negatively charged ion: **anion** ●positively charged ion: **cation**

Iranian ●Iranian parliament: **Majlis**

Ireland ●*adjective*: **Hibernian** ●Celtic language of Ireland: **Erse** ●citizen of Ireland, especially if an Erse-speaker: **Gael** ●area of Ireland where Erse is spoken: **Gaeltacht** ●person wishing Northern Ireland to retain political links with the UK: **Unionist, Loyalist** ●person seeking the political unification of Ireland: **Nationalist** ●periods of civil unrest in Ireland: **the Troubles**

Irish ●Irish accent: **brogue** ●Irish bagpipes: **uillean pipes** ●Irish term for a beach: **strand** ●Irish round wickerwork boat: **coracle** ●Irish light carriage: **jaunting car** ●Irish clan: **sept** ●Irish cudgel: **shillelagh** ●Irish dagger: **skean** ●elf in Irish folklore: **leprechaun** ●Irish term for an English person: **Sassenach** ●Irish funeral song: **coronach, keen** ●Irish social gathering: **ceilidh** ●Irish traditional harp: **clarsach** ●Irish game resembling hockey: **hurling** ●Irish lake: **lough** ●parliament of the Irish Republic: **Oireachtas** ●upper house of this: **Seanad** ●lower house of this: **Dail** ●police force of the Irish Republic: **Garda** ●member of this: **garda** (*pl.* gardai) ●Irish potato blight: **murrain** ●title of the prime minister of the Irish Republic: **Taoiseach** ●Irish fortified settlement: **dun** ●Irish female spirit whose wailing portends death: **banshee** ●Irish nationalist terrorist organization: **Irish Republican Army** ●Irish valley: **glen** ●Irish wizard: **pishogue** ●Irish term for a young woman: **colleen** ●ancient Irish alphabet: **ogham** ●traditional Irish language: **Gaelic** ●Irish-speaking part of Ireland: **Gaeltacht** ●Irish gypsies' secret language: **Shelta** ●Irish dish of boiled cabbage and potatoes: **colcannon** ●Irish spirit distilled from malted grain: **whiskey** ●alcohol distilled illegally in Ireland:

poteen ●place where alcohol is sold illegally: **shebeen** ●Irish term for a last drink: **deoch an doris** ●head of government in Northern Ireland: **First Minister** ●Northern Ireland Protestant political society: **Orange Order** ●member of this: **Orangeman** ●police force of Northern Ireland: **Royal Ulster Constabulary**

iron ●*combining forms*: **ferr-, sider-** ●*adjectives*: **ferric, ferrous** ●block of crude cast iron: **pig** ●such iron: **pig iron** ●pure malleable form of iron: **wrought iron** ●coat iron with zinc: **galvanize** ●person working iron by hand: **blacksmith** ●metalworkers' disease caused by an accumulation of iron dust in the lungs: **siderosis**

irrigation ●Egyptian irrigation device of a bucket on a pole: **shadoof** ●Spanish irrigation device of buckets on a wheel: **noria**

island ●*adjective*: **insular** ●small island: **islet** ●small island on a lake or river: **ait, eyot, holm** ●remote uninhabited tropical island: **desert island** ●low coral island: **cay, key** ●circular coral reef, group of islands, etc.: **atoll** ●group of islands: **archipelago**

Isle of Man ●*adjective*: **Manx** ●Manx judge: **deemster** ●Manx national symbol: **triskelion** ●Manx parliament: **Tynwald** ●lower house of this: **House of Keys**

isolation ●ring of troops etc. isolating a place: **cordon** ●ring of troops etc. isolating an infected area: **cordon sanitaire**

Israeli ●Israeli collective farm: **kibbutz** ●Israeli smallholders' cooperative: **moshav** ●Israeli intelligence service: **Mossad** ●Israeli nationalist: **Zionist** ●Israeli parliament: **Knesset** ●Palestinian opposition to the Israeli

West Bank occupation: **Intifada** ▸*see also* **Hebrew, Jew**

Israelite ●promise made by God to the ancient Israelites: **covenant** ●ancient Israelite war leader: **judge** ●tent shrine used by the ancient Israelites: **tabernacle** ●bread-like substance eaten by the ancient Israelites in the desert: **manna** ●wooden chest containing the tablets of the Law, carried by the ancient Israelites in the desert: **ark** ▸*see also* **biblical figures**

Italian ●*combining form*: **Italo-** ●Italian polite form of address to a man: **signore** ●Italian polite form of address to a woman: **signora** ●Italian polite form of address to a young woman: **signorina** ●title of an Italian dictator under Fascism: **duce** ●Italian name for southern Italy: **Mezzogiorno** ●Italian harlequinade: **commedia dell'arte** ●small Italian hotel: **pensione** ●traditional conical stone house of southern Italy: **trullo** ●Italian motorway: **autostrada** ●fine Italian coloured pottery: **maiolica** ●small Italian restaurant: **trattoria** ●Italian public square: **piazza** ●Italian aerated bread made with olive oil: **ciabatta** ●flat Italian bread made with olive oil: **foccaccia** ●Italian bread made with eggs, fruit, and butter: **panettone** (*pl.* panettoni) ●thin Italian breadsticks: **grissini** ●toasted Italian bread drenched in olive oil: **bruschetta** ●Italian hors d'oeuvre: **antipasto** ●Italian vegetable soup: **minestrone** ●Italian omelette: **frittata** ●Italian raw cured ham: **prosciutto** ●Italian garlic sausage: **salami** ●spiced Italian pork sausage: **mortadella** ●Italian peppered pork and beef sausage: **pepperoni** ●Italian potato dumplings: **gnocchi** ●Italian dish of flat dough cooked with a savoury topping: **pizza** ●Italian dish of pizza, folded and filled: **calzone** ●Italian durum wheat dough made into various shapes: **pasta** ●Italian dish of pasta rolled round a meat or vegetable filling: **cannelloni** ●Italian dish of stewed marrowbone: **osso buco** ●Italian dish of rice cooked in stock: **risotto** ●Italian dish of fried seafood: **fritto misto** ●Italian dish of spaghetti in a minced meat sauce: **spaghetti Bolognese** ●Italian dish of spaghetti in a tomato sauce: **spaghetti Napolitana** ●Italian dish of veal with sage leaves and ham: **saltimbocca** ●Italian dish of veal in a tuna and anchovy mayonnaise: **vitello tonnato** ●Italian dessert of egg yolks whipped with sugar and Marsala: **zabaglione** ●Italian dessert of sponge soaked in spirits and coffee: **tiramisu** ●Italian dessert resembling trifle: **zuppa inglese** ●Italian-style ice cream: **gelato** ●Italian ice cream of various flavours with glacé fruits etc.: **cassata** ●Italian-style water ice: **granita** ●Italian soft blue-veined cheese: **Dolcelatte™** ●Italian hard blue-veined cheese: **Gorgonzola** ●Italian hard dry cheese: **Parmesan** ●Italian soft white unsalted cheese: **ricotta** ●Italian ewes'-milk cheese: **pecorino** ●Italian cream cheese: **mascarpone** ●firm white Italian cheese: **mozzarella** ●maize-flower paste: **polenta** ●Italian sauce of bacon, egg, and cream: **carbonara** ●Italian pasta sauces: **marinara, pesto** ●Italian sauce of garlic, capers, anchovies, and oil: **salsa verde** ●Italian thick tomato paste: **passata** ●Italian sparkling white wine: **spumante** ●Italian orange-flavoured liqueur: **Strega™** ●Italian aniseed-flavoured liqueur: **sambuca** ●Italian grape brandy: **grappa**

itch ●itchy feeling as if of ants crawling over the skin: **formication** ●itching blisters on the skin: **eczema** ●tropical groin itch: **dhobi itch** ●drug relieving itching: **antipruritic**

item ●key item: **linchpin** ●first item on which others are modelled: **prototype** ●single mass-produced item: **unit** ●small decorative item: **objet d'art** (*pl.* objets d'art) ●written

item: **entry** ●item kept as a reminder: **memento, souvenir** ●item whose true value is unrealized for some time: **sleeper** ●assorted items: **miscellanea** ●unspecified items: **sundries** ●cost of producing one further item: **marginal cost**

itself ●in itself: **per se**

Jj

Jamaican ●member of a Jamaican criminal gang: **Yardie** ●Jamaican religion regarding Haile Selassie as God: **Rastafarianism** ▸ *see also* **West Indian**

Japanese ●Japanese Buddhism, emphasizing meditation: **Zen** ●Japanese Buddhist teacher: **bonze** ●Japanese Buddhist festival of the dead: **Bon** ●Japanese business philosophy of continuous improvement: **kaizen** ●former titles of Japanese emperors: **Mikado, Tenno** ●Japanese traditional espionage: **ninjutsu** ●expert at this: **ninja** ●Japanese fencing: **kendo** ●hereditary commander in feudal Japan: **shogun** ●Japanese feudal warrior: **samurai** (*pl.* same) ●Japanese painting on paper or silk: **kakemono** ●Japanese art of paperfolding: **origami** ●Japanese art of flower arranging: **ikebana** ●Japanese hostess: **geisha** ●Japanese national religion: **Shinto** ●Japanese arts of self-defence: **aikido, ju-jitsu, karate** ●general index of Japanese share prices: **Nikkei index** ●gate to a Shinto shrine: **torii** ●sliding door in a Japanese house: **shoji** ●Japanese suicide bomber or its pilot: **kamikaze** ●Japanese ritual of serving and drinking tea: **tea ceremony** ●Japanese puppet theatre: **bunraku** ●Japanese traditional theatre: **Noh** ●popular version of this: **kabuki** ●Japanese system of therapy by applying finger pressure: **acupressure, shiatsu** ●Japanese dwarf tree: **bonsai** ●Japanese wrestling: **sumo** ●sumo champion: **yokozuna** ●Japanese loose robe: **kimono** ●sash worn with this: **obi** ●ornamental box suspended from this: **inro** ●Japanese carved buttonlike ornament: **netsuke** ●Japanese dish of grilled chicken pieces: **yakitori** ●Japanese dish of cold rice with vegetables: **sushi** ●Japanese edible seaweed: **nori** ●Japanese alcoholic drink made from rice: **sake** ●Japanese syllabic writing: **kana** ●romanized transliteration for Japanese: **romaji** ●Japanese term for Japan: **Nippon** ●Japanese poem of 17 syllables: **haiku, hokku** (*pls.* same) ●Japanese poem of 31 syllables: **tanka** (*pl.* same)

jar ●glass preserving jar: **Kilner jar**™ ●Greek and Roman storage jar with two handles and a pointed base: **amphora**

jargon ●jargon used by a particular group: **argot** ●incomprehensible technical jargon: **technobabble** ●jargon of popular psychology: **psychobabble**

jaundice ●liver disease producing jaundice: **hepatitis**

Java ●Javan percussion orchestra: **gamelan**

jaw ●*adjectives*: gnathic, maxillary ●animal's fearsome jaws: **maw** ●lower jawbone: **mandible** ●upper jawbone: **maxilla** ●having a projecting lower jaw: **prognathous** ●paralysis of the jaws: **lockjaw, trismus**

jazz ●improvised wordless jazz singing: **scat**

jelly ●*adjective*: gelatinous ●jelly made from meat or fish stock: **aspic** ●jelly-like substance: **gel** ●substance from which jelly is made: **gelatin** ●dish served in aspic: **galantine**

jellyfish ●jellyfish's central disc: **umbrella**

jester ●jester's cap: **coxcomb** ●jester's baton: **bauble** ●jester's particoloured suit: **motley**

jet ●jet fuel: **kerosene, paraffin oil** ●jet engine in which a turbine-driven fan provides extra thrust: **turbofan** ●jet engine whose gases operate a turbine-driven compressor: **turbojet** ●jet engine in which a turbine drives a propeller: **turboprop** ●propulsive force of a jet engine: **thrust** ●air current behind a jet engine: **slipstream** ●extinction of a jet engine's flame: **flameout**

Jew ●*combining form*: **Judaeo-** (*e.g.* Judaeo-Christian) ●*adjectives*: **Judaic, Semitic** ●legendary Jew said to have mocked Christ: **Wandering Jew** ●Jew born in Israel: **sabra** ●Jew of central or eastern European descent: **Ashkenazi** (*pl.* Ashkenazim) ●language used by Jews of central and eastern Europe: **Yiddish** ●Jew of Spanish or Portuguese descent: **Sephardi** (*pl.* Sephardim) ●language used by certain Mediterranean Jews: **Ladino** ●Soviet Jew not allowed to go to Israel: **refusenik** ●worldwide dispersion of the Jews: **diaspora, Dispersion** ●greeting between Jews: **shalom** ●(in Jewish legend) animated automaton: **golem** ●Jewish religious culture: **Judaism** ●college for Orthodox Jews: **yeshiva** ●Jewish quarter in a city: **ghetto** ●Jewish malevolent spirit: **dybbuk** ●organized massacre of Jews in 19th-c. Russia: **pogrom** ●Hitler's programme for the extermination of European Jews: **final solution, Holocaust** ●non-Jew: **Gentile** ●Jewish term for non-Jew: **goy** ●Jewish term for a Christian: **Nazarene**

jewellery ●simple jewellery worn in a pierced ear or nose: **stud** ●small cheap item of jewellery: **trinket** ●sham jewellery worn on dressy occasions: **costume jewellery** ●decorated with such jewellery: **diamanté** ●jewelled headband: **diadem, tiara** ●jewellery hanging from a chain: **pendant** ●small ornamental case on a chain: **locket** ●piece of jewellery with a relief portrait: **cameo** ●jeweller's magnifying glass: **loupe**

job ●*adjective*: **vocational** ●job done at home: **cottage industry** ●secondary or minor job: **avocation, sideline** ●have a second job: **moonlight** ●job in which no work is required: **sinecure** ●easy job: **child's play** ●job requiring formal qualifications: **profession** ●appropriate and congenial job: **niche** ●tiresome job: **chore** ●lengthy undertaking: **marathon** ●denoting a job requiring many workers: **labour-intensive** ●denoting a job not requiring specialist skills: **non-professional** ●reduce or eradicate the element of skill required by a job: **deskill** ●division of a job and its pay between several employees: **job-sharing** ●essential to a job's successful completion: **mission-critical** ●risk involved in a job: **occupational hazard** ●hopeless assignment: **fool's errand** ●unoccupied job: **vacancy** ●person applying for a job: **applicant, candidate** ●oral examination of such people: **interview** ●person testifying to an applicant's suitability: **referee** ●trial period before confirmation of appointment: **probation** ●appoint to a job: **nominate** ●ability to do a job: **competence** ●exclusively assigned to a particular job: **dedicated** ●handing down one's own tasks to a subordinate: **delegation** ●give out such a task: **depute, devolve** ●special or temporary task: **assignment** ●detailed description of this: **terms of reference** ●temporary posting away from the usual workplace: **secondment** ●move to another job in the same organization: **posting, transfer** ●giving jobs to one's relatives and friends: **nepotism**

●power to do this: **patronage** ●guaranteed job-holding: **tenure** ●denoting an activity that is not a paid job: **nonprofessional** ●trade union's claim of exclusive rights to a certain job: **demarcation dispute** ●approach an employed person offering him a job elsewhere: **headhunt** ●give up a job voluntarily: **resign** ●leaving jobs by voluntary retirement or resignation: **natural wastage, wastage** ●jobhunting help given to redundant employees: **outplacement** ●chart showing interrelation of a firm's jobs: **organization chart**

jockey ●jockey's coloured outfit: **silks** ●jockey's helmet: **skullcap** ●official weighing of a jockey before and after a race: **weigh-out, weigh-in**

join ●join metals with an alloy: **solder** ●join ropes by interweaving strands: **splice**

joint ●*combining forms*: **co-** (*e.g.* co-author), **arthr-, zygo-** (*e.g.* zygotic) ●ball and socket joint: **enarthrosis** (*pl.* enarthroses) ●hip joint: **coxa** ●knee joint in horses, dogs, etc.: **stifle** ●bone covering the knee joint: **kneecap, patella** ●having unusually flexible joints: **double-jointed** ●painful inflammation of the joints: **arthritis, rheumatism, rheumatoid arthritis** ●painful twisting of a joint: **sprain** ●displacement of the bones in a joint: **dislocation** ●fusion of bones in a joint: **ankylosis** ●degeneration of bone and cartilage in joints: **osteoarthritis** ●thin cartilage in certain joints: **meniscus** (*pl.* menisci) ●joint with bevelled or notched ends: **scarf** ●joint bisecting a right angle: **mitre, mitre-joint** ●joint for piping: **union** ●joint able to transmit rotary power at any angle: **universal joint** ●mortise and tenon joint: **dovetail** ●step-shaped wood joint: **rebate** ●recessed joint part: **mortise** ●protruding joint part: **tenon** ●board jointing with interlocking ridges and hollows:

tongue and groove ●flat ring sealing a joint: **gasket, washer** ●liquid clay or cement sealing a joint: **lute** ●line made by the edges of a join: **seam**

joke ●joke exploiting a word's different meanings: **pun, quibble** ●joke's crucial final sentence: **punchline**

journey ●journey by ship: **passage, voyage** ●long sea or space journey: **voyage** ●journey to a holy place: **pilgrimage** ●repeated journey over a fixed route: **round, run** ●arduous journey: **trek** ●journey made for a specific purpose: **mission** ●return journey not covering the same ground: **round trip** ●part of a journey: **leg** ●in the course of a journey: **en route** ●established en-route stopping place: **staging post** ●right to make a journey: **passage** ●pay for one's journey by work en route: **work one's passage** ●end a scheduled journey: **terminate** ●official record of a ship's or aircraft's journey: **log**

Judaism ●Jewish mystical interpretation of the Old Testament: **Kabbalah** ●Jewish commentary upon the Old Testament: **Masorah, Midrash, Mishnah** ●Jewish law as contained in the first five books of the Old Testament: **Torah** ●ordinance not found in the Torah but held to have been given by God to Moses: **tradition** ●ancient corpus of Jewish ceremonial and civil law: **Talmud** ●expected Jewish national saviour: **Messiah** ●Jewish movement following the traditional law in its entirety: **Orthodox Judaism** ●Jewish movement following the law as modified for modern conditions: **Reform Judaism** ●ancient Jewish professional theologian and jurist: **scribe** ●Jewish religious leader or teacher: **rabbi** ●senior rabbi: **dayan** (*pl.* dayanim) ●rabbi's wife: **rebbetzin** ●training college for rabbis: **seminary, yeshiva** ●Jewish religious school: **cheder** ●school giving instruction in Jewish traditions: **Talmud Torah** ● study of Jewish traditional law: **Talmud Torah** ● supreme council and court of ancient Jerusalem: **Sanhedrin** ● day of religious observance and abstinence from work: **sabbath** ● strict observer of the sabbath: **sabbatarian** ● Jewish dietary regulations: **kashrut** ● denoting food that conforms to Jewish dietary regulations: **kosher** ● denoting food that does not conform to Jewish dietary regulations: **trefa** ● denoting animals that Jews may eat: **clean** ● Jewish term for leavened food: **chametz** ● Jewish unleavened bread: **matzo** ● bread eaten on the sabbath: **challah** ● Jewish sabbath dish of meat and vegetables: **cholent** ● Jewish dish of stuffed fish: **gefilte fish** ● Jewish blessing of wine before the Sabbath: **kiddush** ● Jewish custom of marrying one's brother's widow: **levirate** ● building for Jewish religious observance and instruction: **synagogue** ● Jewish branched candlestick: **menorah** ● outer chamber of the Jewish temple: **holy place** ● inner chamber of the Jewish temple: **holy of holies** ● curtain closing off the holy of holies: **veil** ● Orthodox Jew's skullcap: **kippa, yarmulke** ● small box worn by Orthodox Jew at prayer: **frontlet, phylactery** ● prayer shawl: **tallith** ● corner tassels on this: **tsitsith** ● Jewish girl's coming of age ceremony: **bat mitzvah** ● Jewish boy's coming of age ceremony: **bar mitzvah** ● Jewish new year festival: **Rosh Hashana** ● Jewish day of repentance: **Day of Atonement, Yom Kippur** ● Jewish commemoration of the deliverance from Egypt: **Passover** ● text recited at this: **Haggadah** ● Passover ceremony and meal: **Seder** ● Jewish harvest festival: **Feast of Weeks, Pentecost, Shavuoth** ● Jewish commemoration of the journey through the wilderness: **Feast of Tabernacles,**

Succoth ● Jewish term for the abode of the dead: **Sheol** ● Jewish term for hell: **Gehenna** ▸ *see also* **Hebrew, Israeli, Israelite**

judge ● *adjective*: **judicial** ● judge in a Church court: **official principal** ● Indian judge: **hakim** ● Muslim judge: **cadi, hakim** ● title of an Appeal Court judge: **Lord Justice** ● title of a High Court judge: **Mr Justice** ● title of a judge in Scotland: **sheriff** ● expert adviser who sits with a judge in technical cases: **assessor** ● barrister serving as a part-time judge: **recorder** ● polite form of address to a judge: **Your Lordship** ● judge's summary of arguments at the end of a case: **summing up** ● judge's direction to a jury on points of law: **charge, instruction** ● judge's order for enforcement of a law: **injunction** ● denoting a judge's provisional ruling: **interlocutory** ● judge's incidental remark: **obiter dictum** ● judge's office for private hearings: **chambers** ● judge's itinerary to various courts: **circuit** ● circuit judge's administrative assistant: **marshal** ● circuit judge's official accommodation: **lodgings** ● judge's wig and robes: **court dress** ● judges regarded collectively: **the bench, the judicature, the judiciary** ● attempt to corrupt a judge: **embracery**

judgement ● judgement on payments or possessions: **award** ● judgement awarded on the defendant's failure to plead: **judgement in default** ● divorce court's judgement: **decree** ● judgement that must be followed in subsequent similar cases: **precedent** ● reference to such a judgement: **citation** ● denoting a provisional judgement: **interlocutory** ● writ ordering the enforcement of a judgement: **writ of execution** ● performance of a contractual obligation ordered by a court: **specific performance** ● having good judgement: **sagacious** ● showing careful judgement: **judicious**

judo ● judo expert: **judoka** ● judo suit: **judogi** ● judo jacket: **gi** ● judo mat: **dojo** ● point scored in judo: **ippon** ● send one's opponent to the ground: **throw** ▶ *see also* **martial arts**

jug ● large water jug: **ewer** ● large narrow-necked jug: **flagon** ● low jug for gravy or sauce: **boat** ● jug shaped and painted to resemble a man's head: **toby jug**

juice ● sour juice obtained from fruit: **verjuice**

jump ● jump made with the aid of the hands or a pole: **vault** ● sideways handspring: **cartwheel** ● jump about playfully: **gambol** ● jump on something to capture it: **pounce** ● sprung stick for making large jumps: **pogo stick** ● sheet stretched taut for jumping on: **trampoline**

junk ● ornamental junk: **bric-a-brac**

Juno ● *Greek name*: **Hera**

Jupiter ● *Greek name*: **Zeus**

jury ● denoting an offence requiring jury trial: **indictable** ● enlist a jury: **impanel** ● fill a jury with persons sympathetic to one's aims: **pack**

● jury member: **juror** ● jury's spokesman: **foreman** ● lawyer's objection to a member of the jury: **challenge** ● denoting a challenge made without reason: **peremptory** ● writ summoning substitute jurors: **tales** ● substitute juror: **talesman** ● judge's direction to a jury: **charge, instruction** ● jury's decision: **verdict** ● jury's comment added to its verdict: **rider** ● period a jury spends in private considering its verdict: **retirement**

justice ● system of justice where the judge or magistrate acts as prosecutor: **inquisitorial system** ● system of justice where the judge or magistrate adjudicates between prosecution and defence: **accusatorial system** ● out-of-court negotiations between prosecution and defence lawyers to secure a reduced charge in return for an admission of guilt: **plea bargaining**

justification ● justification of one's conduct: **apologia** ● logical justification: **rationale** ● justification of a theory: **apologetics** ● justification for an action or opinion: **ground** ● earlier event adduced in justification: **precedent** ● that cannot be justified: **unwarrantable**

kangaroo ●male kangaroo: **buck** ●female kangaroo: **doe** ●young kangaroo: **joey**

karate ●karate expert: **karateka** ●karate exercises: **kata** ●kick made with body rotation: **roundhouse kick** ●point scored in karate: **ippon** ▸*see also* **martial arts**

key ●key opening several locks: **master key, pass key, skeleton key** ●lock opened only by a key: **deadlock** ●perform or score in a different key: **transpose**

keyboard ●standard English-language keyboard layout: **querty**

kick ●reflex kick: **knee-jerk** ●kick made with unbent legs: **scissor kick**

kidney ●*combining forms*: **nephr-, ren-** ●*adjectives*: **renal, nephritic** ●movable kidney: **floating kidney** ●chronic kidney inflammation: **nephritis, Bright's disease** ●mechanical purification of the blood by an artificial kidney: **dialysis, haemodialysis** ●stone-like mass forming in a kidney: **kidney stone, renal calculus** (*pl.* calculi), **renal concretion** ●medical treatment of the kidney: **nephrology** ●surgical removal of a kidney: **nephrectomy**

kill ●kill by deprivation of air: **asphyxiate, suffocate** ●kill by beheading: **decapitate** ●kill by electric shock: **electrocute** ●kill by covering the nose and mouth: **smother** ●kill secretly: **make away with** ●be secretly killed by the state: **disappear** ●kill by strangulation: **garrotte, throttle** ●kill an animal humanely: **destroy, put down, put to sleep** ●kill in large numbers: **massacre, slaughter** ●kill most of: **decimate** ●kill a person condemned to death: **execute** ●kill quickly: **dispatch** ●kill selectively: **cull** ●death-blow: **coup de grâce** (*pl.* coups de grâce) ●list of persons to be killed: **hit list** ●place where animals are killed: **abattoir, slaughterhouse** ●occasion when many persons are violently killed: **bloodbath, bloodletting** ●sport that involves the hunting, wounding, or killing of animals: **blood sport**

killer ●*combining form*: **-cide** (*e.g.* regicide) ●killer's plea of unbalanced mental state: **diminished responsibility** ●money paid as a recompense in certain societies by a killer to his victim's relatives: **blood money**

killing ●*combining form*: **-cide** ●deliberate unlawful killing: **murder, homicide** ●unpremeditated killing: **manslaughter** ●accidental killing of one's own forces: **fratricide** ●killing not considered a crime: **justifiable homicide** ●killing to which no blame can attach: **misadventure** ●killing selected animals: **cull** ●killing one's brother or sister: **fratricide** ●killing of a child less than one year old: **infanticide** ●killing one's father: **patricide** ●killing a god: **deicide** ●killing an incurable person in accordance with their wishes: **euthanasia, mercy killing** ●killing an infant by abandonment in a deserted place: **exposure** ●killing one's mother: **matricide** ●killing oneself: **suicide** ●killing a parent or other near relative: **parricide** ●killing a public figure by a surprise attack: **assassination** ●killing as a punishment: **capital punishment** ●killing a son or daughter: **filicide** ●killing a sovereign:

regicide •killing a tyrant: **tyrannicide** •killing one's wife: **uxoricide** •killing large numbers: **massacre** •killing an entire people: **genocide** •killing all life: **biocide**

king •*adjectives*: **royal, regal** •person governing during a monarch's absence or incapacity: **regent** •disease formerly thought to be cured by the sovereign's touch: **king's evil** •killing a king: **regicide**

kiss •perfunctory kiss: **peck** •deep kiss: **French kiss, soul kiss** •kiss and cuddle: **canoodle**

kitchen •*adjective*: **culinary** •small kitchen: **scullery** •kitchen on a ship or aircraft: **galley** •kitchen tools and equipment: **batterie de cuisine, utensils** •service opening in a kitchen wall: **hatch**

knee •knee joint in horses, dogs, etc.: **stifle** •bone covering the knee joint: **kneecap, patella** •tendon behind the knee: **hamstring** •inflammation of the knee: **housemaid's knee**

knife •knife with a folding handle: **clasp knife, jackknife** •knife with a spring-loaded blade: **flick knife** •knife with a sharp replaceable blade: **Stanley knife™** •pocket knife with several blades and other tools: **Swiss army knife** •heavy jungle knife: **machete, panga** •surgical knife: **lancet, scalpel** •knife handle: **haft, hilt** •shank of a knife blade, encased in its handle: **tang** •cover for a knife blade: **sheath** •knife-maker: **cutler**

knight •knights' mounted mock combat: **joust, tilt** •place for this: **lists** •jousting competition: **tournament, tourney** •knights' exercise of charging against a revolving mark: **tilting** •this mark: **quintain** •place for this: **tiltyard** •knight's warhorse: **destrier** •confer a knighthood on: **dub** ▸ *see also* **chivalry**

knitting •set of knitting instructions: **pattern** •create stitches: **cast on** •terminate stitches: **cast off** •move a stitch from one needle to the other: **slip** •rightwards stitch: **plain** •leftwards stitch: **purl** •alternation of plain and purl stitches: **rib** •fine knitting wool: **fingering** •medium-thick knitting wool: **double knitting** •thick knitting wool: **chunky** •diameter of knitting needles: **gauge**

knot •knot undone by a pull: **slip knot** •knot easily loosened: **hitch** •knot joining two ropes: **bend** •loop with a running knot: **noose** •ornamental knotwork made with string: **macramé** •knotted lace: **tatting**

know •not known: **obscure** •knowing everything: **omniscient**

knowledge •*combining forms*: **-gnosis** (*e.g.* prognosis), **-nomy** (*e.g.* aeronomy), **-sophy** (*e.g.* philosophy) •*adjective*: **epistemic** •basic knowledge: **elements, rudiments** •traditional knowledge: **lore** •scholarly knowledge: **erudition** •shallow knowledge: **sciolism** •slight knowledge: **inkling** •deep knowledge: **erudition** •instinctive knowledge: **intuition** •social knowledge: **savoir-faire** •knowledge before the event: **precognition** •knowledge after the event: **hindsight** •knowledge of many subjects: **polymathy** •knowledge of everything: **omniscience** •knowledge of a specified topic: **literacy** •involving several branches of knowledge: **interdisciplinary** •done in full knowledge: **witting** •people with special knowledge: **illuminati, insiders** •person eager to display his or her knowledge: **pedant** •person pretending to be knowledgeable: **sciolist** •philosophical study of the nature of knowledge: **epistemology**

knuckle •metal knuckle-strengthener: **knuckleduster**

Korean •Korean martial art: **tae kwon do**

label ●label attached to a plant or tree: **tally**

laboratory ●laboratory work table: **bench** ●laboratory worker preparing and maintaining equipment: **technician** ●happening in the laboratory rather than its natural environment: **in vitro** ▸*see also* **scientific equipment**

lace-making ●lace made by hand by twisting weighted threads: **bobbin lace, pillow lace** ●coarse bobbin lace with geometrical designs: **torchon, torchon lace** ●lace made by hand in buttonhole stitch: **needle lace, point lace** ●knotted lace made with a shuttle: **tatting** ●heavy outline thread: **gimp** ●firm cushion on which the lace is made: **pillow**

lack ●lack of the basic necessities of life: **deprivation**

lacking ●*combining form*: **-less** (*e.g.* witless)

ladder ●laddder used for roof work: **catladder** ●crosspiece in a ladder: **rung**

lake ●*adjective*: **lacustrine** ●Scottish lake: **loch** ●Irish lake: **lough** ●small mountain lake: **tarn** ●curved lake in a former river bed: **oxbow lake** ●salt lake separated from the sea by a reef or sandbank: **lagoon** ●animals and plants living on the bed of a lake: **epibenthos** ●mapping of lakes: **hydrography** ●study of lakes: **limnology**

lama ●chief Lama of Tibet: **Dalai Lama** ●polite form of address to him: **Your Holiness** ●second Lama of Tibet: **Panchen Lama, Tashi Lama**

lament ●Irish sung lament: **keen** ●Scottish bagpipe lament: **pibroch** ●poem lamenting the dead: **elegy**

land ●*adjective*: **terrestrial** ●mariner's sighting of land: **landfall** ●arrival on land: **landfall** ●by land: **overland** ●surrounded by land: **landlocked** ●narrow strip of land: **isthmus, neck, spit** ●small area of land: **plot** ●land almost completely surrounded by water: **cape, headland, peninsula, promontory** ●area of level high land: **plateau, tableland** ●large land mass: **continent** ●edge of a land mass covered by ocean: **continental shelf** ●bring waste or flooded land under cultivation: **reclaim** ●gradual sinking of an area of land: **subsidence** ●land in Holland reclaimed from the sea: **polder** ●land in East Anglia reclaimed from the sea: **fen** ●large fenland drainage ditch: **dyke** ●extensive area of eroded and uncultivable land: **badlands** ●marshy land: **wetland** ●open land with poor soil: **heath, heathland, moor** ●denoting land that has not been cleared or cultivated: **unimproved** ●land cleared by slash-and-burn methods: **swidden** ●aesthetic improvement of land: **landscaping** ●land temporarily sown to grass: **ley** ●grazing land: **pasture** ●denoting land producing crops: **arable, fertile** ●denoting land unable to produce crops: **sterile** ●denoting land that cannot be cultivated profitably: **submarginal** ●return of fertile land to desert conditions: **desertification** ●denoting agricultural land left unsown: **fallow** ●land taken out of production: **set-aside** ●land under cultivation: **tillage, tilth** •land attached to a house: **curtilage** •farmland owned by parish clergy: **glebe** •agricultural holding smaller than a farm: **smallholding** •property in buildings and land: **real property, realty** •narrow strip of land projecting into water: **headland, peninsula** •narrow strip of land connecting two larger areas: **isthmus** •narrow strip of land projecting into the holdings of others: **panhandle** •intrusion upon another's land by building etc.: **encroachment** •entering another's land without permission: **trespass** •right to cross another's land: **easement, right of way, way leave** •right to cut turf or peat from another's land: **turbary** •another's right to cross one's land: **servitude** •limitations on land's use imposed by its vendor: **restrictive covenant** •piece of land in public use: **common** •right of pasturage on a common: **commonage** •ownership of land or the land owned: **domain** •denoting land ownership: **territorial** •unlawful interference with an owner's enjoyment of his land: **nuisance** •unlawful occupation of land: **squatting** •medieval system of land tenure: **feudalism** •landholder under this system: **feudatory** •absolute ownership of a piece of land: **freehold, fee simple** •holding of land for a period of years: **leasehold** •land held by lease: **holding** •terms under which land is held: **tenure** •tenancy for a fixed period: **term of years** •person who buys up land in order to build on it: **developer** •a government's right to take privately owned land into public use: **eminent domain** •the taking of such land: **expropriation** •open land upon which development is not permitted: **white land** •preserved open land round a city: **green belt**

landlord •money paid to the landlord by an incoming tenant: **key money** •landlord's expulsion of a tenant: **eviction**

landmark •pile of stones as a landmark: **cairn**

landowner •*adjective*: **landed** •chief landowner in a rural area: **squire** •Scottish landowner: **laird** •landowner's agent: **bailiff**

landscape •snow-covered landscape: **snowscape** •moonlike landscape: **moonscape** •height difference of landscape elements: **relief** •wearing away of the landscape by natural forces: **erosion**

language •*combining forms*: lingu-, -ese (*e.g.* Chinese), -glot •*adjectives*: **lingual, linguistic** •express in a different language: **translate** •everyday language: **vernacular** •pretentious language: **bombast, magniloquence** •harshly critical or abusive language: **invective** •deliberately misleading language: **doublespeak, newspeak** •language of a particular group or profession: **cant** •obscure language of official documents: **officialese** •obscure technical language: **jargon** •confusing or meaningless language: **mumbo-jumbo** •language as people actually use it: **parole** •language as described in grammar books: **langue** •form of a language used by ordinary people: **demotic** •regional or social subform of a language: **dialect** •language spoken by a person from early childhood: **mother tongue** •person who has learnt a language thus: **native speaker** •distinctive language of an individual: **idiolect** •language shared by several nations: **koine** •denoting a language currently spoken: **living** •denoting a language no longer spoken: **dead** •denoting a group of languages that includes Arabic and Hebrew: **Semitic** •denoting a group of languages derived from an earlier form of German: **Germanic**

• denoting a group of languages derived from Latin: **Romance** • denoting a group of languages that includes Russian and Serbo-Croat: **Slavic** • language used by speakers having no common native tongue: **lingua franca** • simple trading language drawn from several sources: **pidgin** • form of a native language that has been heavily influenced by a pidgin: **creole** • artificial language proposed for international use: **Esperanto** • a further language developed from Esperanto: **Ido** • artificial language for scientists and technicians: **Interlingua** • language in which words are inflected by changes of pitch: **tone language** • language used to analyse another: **metalanguage** • denoting a language spoken with many mistakes: **broken** • handbook of useful sentences in a foreign language: **phrase book** • temporary ability to speak in a language normally unknown to the speaker: **glossolalia** • in, or able to speak, two languages: **bilingual** • in, or able to speak, three languages: **trilingual** • in, or able to speak, several languages: **polyglot** • in a mixture of languages: **macaronic** • study of language: **linguistics** • study of language as a series of interrelated systems: **structural linguistics** • use of computer techniques to analyse language: **computational linguistics** • collection of machine-readable texts for computer analysis: **corpus** • analysis of related languages to reconstruct their common source: **comparative linguistics** • study of language in relation to social factors: **sociolinguistics** • study of the history of languages: **philology** • study of language sounds: **phonology** • spelling rules for a language: **orthography** • rules for using a language: **grammar** • basic sound unit in a language: **phoneme** • pitched phoneme in a tone language: **toneme**

• basic meaning unit in a language: **semanteme, sememe** • basic word unit in a language: **morpheme** • person skilled in foreign languages: **linguist** • in or knowing one language: **monoglot, monolingual** • foreign language teaching using only the language taught: **direct method** • room with electronic gadgetry for language-learners: **language laboratory**

large • *combining forms*: **macro-** (*e.g.* macroeconomics), **mega-** (*e.g.* megaphone), **megalo-** (*e.g.* megalopolis) • remarkably or unnaturally large: **gigantic, prodigious** • excessively large: **inordinate** • extra-large: **king-sized, outsize** • quite large: **queen-sized** • large and bulky: **unwieldy**

larynx • *adjective*: **laryngeal** • inflammation of the larynx: **laryngitis** • instrument for examining the larynx: **laryngoscope** • surgical incision into the larynx: **laryngotomy** • study of the larynx: **laryngology**

laser • laser using microwaves: **maser** • laser-generated three-dimensional image: **hologram** • American defence programme using satellite-mounted lasers: **star wars, strategic defence initiative**

last • last event: **finale** • last but one: **penultimate** • last but two: **antepenultimate** • long-lasting: **perennial**

lathe • lathe spindle: **mandrel** • lathe's adjustable holder for the workpiece: **chuck** • person working wood on a lathe: **turner**

laugh • half-suppressed laugh: **chuckle, snigger** • causing laughter: **risible**

lava • denoting rock composed of lava: **igneous**

lavatory ●*adjective*: **lavatorial** ●outside lavatory: **privy** ●denoting a lavatory in use: **engaged** ●denoting a lavatory not in use: **vacant** ●compartment for one person in a lavatory: **stall**

law ●*adjective*: **legal** ●law governing the punishment of offenders: **criminal law** ●law governing relations between citizens: **civil law, private law** ●law governing relations between citizens and the state: **public law** ●law governing doctors: **medical jurisprudence** ●law of retaliation: **lex talionis** ●law of the country in which the offence was committed: **lex loci** ●law of the country in which the case is heard: **lex fori** ●written law made by parliament: **statute law** ●law derived from custom and judicial precedent: **common law** ●law as established by the outcome of former cases: **case law** ●set of basic laws or principles by which a state is governed: **constitution** ●collection of laws: **code, digest** ●complete collection of laws: **pandect** ●draft law submitted for parliamentary discussion: **bill** ●text of a law as approved by parliament: **act** ●local law: **by-law** ●international law: **ius gentium** ●Jewish law: **Halacha** ●church law: **canon law** ●expert in canon law: **canonist** ●collection of canon law decisions: **Decretum** ●law setting time limits for commencement of certain actions: **statute of limitations** ●law no longer observed: **dead letter** ●denoting laws intended to govern past offences: **retroactive, retrospective** ●person below the age of full legal responsibility: **infant, minor** ●person no longer protected by the law: **outlaw** ●universal moral principles: **natural law** ●general law or principle: **canon** ●legal concept of natural justice: **equity** ●legal redress: **remedy** ●legal theory: **jurisprudence** ●legal expert: **jurist**

●suspension or postponement of legal proceedings: **stay** ●denoting a harsh law: **draconian** ●strict enforcement of a law: **zero tolerance** ●freedom of action under the law: **civil liberty, civil rights** ●through lack of concern for the law or facts: **per incuriam** ●breach of a law: **infringement** ●deliberate disobedience of certain laws as a protest: **civil disobedience** ●law's provision for conscientious objection: **conscience clause** ●true sense of a law: **intendment** ●foreign diplomats' immunity to local laws: **diplomatic immunity** ●official ratification of a law: **sanction** ●required by law: (*of a person*) liable, (*of a thing or act*) **compulsory** ●meet the law's requirements: **comply** ●extreme strictness in interpreting or implementing the law: **rigorism** ●break a law: **contravene** ●revoke a law: **repeal, rescind** ●seize after legal infringement: **impound** ●branch of the law dealing with ships and the sea: **admiralty** ●denoting legally acceptable evidence: **admissible** ●legal trickery: **chicanery** ●academic study of law: **jurisprudence** ●denoting a person engaged or acting for the duration of a lawsuit: **ad litem** ●advise an arrested person of his legal rights: **caution** ●denoting a legal system in which a prosecutor argues his case before an independent judge: **accusatorial** ●denoting a legal system in which the judge himself conducts the prosecution: **inquisitorial** ●official order having the force of law: **decree** ●permitted by law: **legal, licit** ●in accordance with the law: **lawful** ●in acordance with a cited law: **pursuant to** ●beyond one's legal power: **ultra vires** ●weakening flaw in a law: **loophole** ●having no legal force: **null** ●declare an activity illegal: **criminalize** ●cease to regard an activity as illegal: **decriminalize** ●failure to perform an act required by law:

nonfeasance ●legal categorization of a minor crime: **common** ●legal term for personal possessions: **goods and chattels** ●legal term for serious deliberate injury: **grievous bodily harm** ●legal term for less serious deliberate injury: **actual bodily harm** ●legal controls over use of electronic data: **data protection** ●legal work on transfer of property: **conveyancing** ●legal charges: **costs** ●temporary suspension of a law: **amnesty** ●suspension of a nation's legal system when under military government: **martial law** ●not legally valid: **void** ●outside legal control: **extralegal** ▶ *see also* document, judge, jury, justice, Muslim, sentence, verdict

lawcourt ●*adjective*: judicial, juridical ●court for under-age offenders: **youth court** ●circuit court taking criminal cases: **Crown Court** ●court for civil cases and judicial review: **High Court of Justice** ●division of this for commercial and maritime cases: **Queen's Bench** ●division of this for probate, bankruptcy, and equity: **Chancery** ●division of this for family law: **Family** ●court for appeals against both civil and criminal judgements: **Court of Appeal** ●general title for the Crown, High, and Appeal courts: **Supreme Court of Judicature** ●rule book of the Supreme Court: **White Book** ●military court: **court martial** (*pl.* courts martial *or* court martials) ●court deciding claims for small sums of money: **small claims court** ●court in which a case is first heard: **court of first instance** ●court trying minor offences: **court of summary jurisdiction** ●court whose decisions have weight as precedents: **superior court** ●unofficial court: **kangaroo court** ●denoting a topic within a court's jurisdiction: **cognizable, justiciable** ●a court's power to decide a matter: **competence, jurisdiction** ●court's written

command: **writ** ●order for a person to attend a court: **summons, subpoena, process** ●bond paid into court to guarantee return: **bail, recognizance** ●argument presented in court: **submission** ●trial conducted in court: **proceedings** ●court's decision: **judgement** ●give this: **pass judgement** ●delay giving this: **reserve judgement** ●court's declaration of guilt: **conviction** ●divorce court's judgement: **decree** ●court's cancellation of a claim: **striking out** ●court's failure to reach a correct decision: **miscarriage of justice** ●higher court's direction to a lower court: **mandamus** ●reconsideration of a lower court's decision: **review** ●overturn the decision of a lower court: **quash, reverse** ●court order seizing a debtor's assets: **Mareva injunction** ●court's seizure of assets: **sequestration** ●court's assessment of an act of some public body: **judicial review** ●person sued: **defendant** ●person bringing a suit: **plaintiff** ●defendant's reply to the charge: **plea** ●understanding that if a lesser charge is admitted a graver charge will be dropped: **plea-bargaining** ●judgement awarded on the defendant's failure to plead: **judgement in default** ●awaiting a court's decision: **sub judice** ●period when lawcourts are active: **law term** ●period when lawcourts are closed: **vacation** ●begin a court session: **sit** ●end a court session: **rise** ●pause in court proceedings: **recess, adjournment** ●denoting an indefinite adjournment: **sine die** ●court official's opening call for order: **oyez** ●fair treatment in a court: **due process** ●attempt to frustrate a court's operation: **contempt of court** ●make atonement for this: **purge contempt** ●done out of court: **extrajudicial** ●deliberate delaying of court business: **obstructionism** ●refusal to obey the court: **contumacy** ▸ *see also* **courtroom, evidence, jury, trial**

lawsuit ●a legal action: **case, proceedings** ●start legal action against: **prosecute, sue** ●lawsuit whose decision will influence future decisions: **test case** ●obligation to prove one's case: **burden of proof** ●essential point of a case: **gist, gravamen** ●case waiting to be heard: **lis pendens** ●during litigation: **pendente lite** ●unreasonable delay in bringing a suit: **laches** ●terminate a case through inadequate prosecution evidence: **dismiss, nonsuit** ●argue a case in court: **plead** ●arguments advanced in a legal action: **case** ●denoting an indisputable case: **open-and-shut** ●risk of a person put on trial: **jeopardy** ●prosecution twice for the same offence: **double jeopardy** ●murderer's plea of mental unbalance: **diminished responsibility** ●document or other object produced as evidence: **exhibit** ●disclosure of documents between parties: **discovery** ●person involved in a lawsuit: **litigant, party** ●in the interests of one party only: **ex parte** ●enter a lawsuit as a third party: **intervene** ●right to bring a suit: **locus standi** (*pl.* loci standi) ●judge's summary of arguments at the end of a case: **summing up** ●accept money to drop a legal action: **compound** ●agreement reached by parties to a lawsuit: **settlement** ●denoting a lawsuit intended to inconvenience the defendant: **vexatious** ●assess just fees for a lawsuit: **tax** ●eager to go to law: **litigious** ●go to law: **litigate** ●listen to and judge a lawsuit: **hear** ●send a case to a higher court: **commit** ●send a case back to a lower court: **remit** ●application to a higher court for a decision to be reversed: **appeal** ●person making such an application: **appellant** ●higher court's request to review proceedings of a lower court: **certior-**

ari ●schedule of cases for trial: **calendar** ●exemption from legal proceedings: **immunity**

lawyer ●senior UK law officers: **Lord Chancellor, Lord Chief Justice, Master of the Rolls, Attorney-General, Director of Public Prosecutions** ●principal Scottish law officer: **Lord Advocate** ●company official ensuring the legality of transactions: **compliance officer** ●legal draughtsman: **notary** ●engage a lawyer: **instruct** ●lawyer who may speak for his clients in the higher courts: **barrister** ●barrister engaged to advise a client or appear for him in court: **counsel** (*pl.* same) ●lawyer advising clients, and appearing on their behalf in the lower courts: **solicitor** ●lawyer's objection to a member of the jury: **challenge** ●lawyer's quotation of a previous case: **citation** ●lawyer's questioning of a witness: **examination** ●lawyer's questioning of a witness he or she has called: **examination-in-chief** ●lawyer's questioning of a person already examined by opposing counsel: **cross-examination** ●state funding of a lawyer's fees: **legal aid** ●lawyer's negligence or dishonesty: **malpractice**

layer ●thin surface layer: **film, veneer** ●layer of laminated material: **ply** ●underlying layer: **substrate, substratum**

lead ●*combining form*: **plumb-** (*e.g.* plumber, *water pipes being formerly made of lead*)

leader ●*combining forms*: **-agogue, -arch** ●nominal leader: **figurehead, front man, puppet** ●leader of the rabble: **demagogue** ●eldest member of a group, perceived as its leader: **patriarch, matriarch** ●person most skilled in a particular field: **doyen** (*fem.* doyenne)

leaf ●*combining forms*: **foli-, phyllo-** ●*adjectives*: **foliaceous, foliate**

●leaves in general: **foliage** ●leaf at the edge of a flower: **bract** ●compound leaf of a fern or palm: **frond** ●denoting leaves of several colours: **variegated** ●decorated with leaves: **foliate** ●leaf-stalk: **petiole** ●circle of leaves: **whorl** ●leaves heaped up by the wind: **drift** ●strip the leaves from: **defoliate** ●chemical used to destroy leaves: **defoliant** ●pest killing vine leaves: **phylloxera**

leap year ●*adjective*: **bissextile**

learner ●person learning a trade by assisting a skilled worker for a fixed period: **apprentice**

learning ●learning from a course in a book or computer: **programmed learning** ●learning through tapes played while asleep: **hypnopaedia** ●learning by controlled trial and error: **heuristic** ●mechanical repetition as a learning tool: **rote** ●repeated practice as an aid to learning: **drill** ●age at which a skill is most easily learnt: **critical period** ●condition causing learning difficulties: **learning disability** ●point in a course at which many give up: **pons asinorum** ●card held up for pupils to see: **flashcard**

lease ●person granting a lease: **lessor** ●person taking a lease: **lessee** ●property's return to its owners at the end of a lease: **reversion**

leather ●supple leather used to clean cars and windows: **chamois, wash leather** ●leather formerly used for writing on: **parchment** ●leather from a young goat: **kid** ●brushed kid: **suede** ●outer surface of leather: **grain, grain side** ●narrow strip of leather: **thong** ●leather strip for sharpening razors: **strop** ●leather strap formerly used to punish Scottish schoolchildren: **tawse** ●impressed ornamentation on leather: **tooling** ●denoting highly polished leather: **glacé, patent** ●chemical process

converting an animal skin to leather: **tanning** ●denoting untanned leather: **green** ●grease used for waterproofing leather: **dubbin**

leave ●long leave granted to missionaries or services personnel: **furlough** ●sailor's time off spent ashore: **liberty, shore leave** ●leave to be absent from school: **exeat** ●paid leave granted to a university teacher: **sabbatical** ●leave taken without asking permission: **French leave** ●leave hastily: **decamp** ●leave out: **omit**

left ●*combining form*: **laevo-** (*e.g.* laevorotatory) ●*adjective*: **sinistral** ●left-hand page in a book: **verso** ●left-handed person: **southpaw** ●left side of a ship as seen by one facing its prow: **port**

leg ●*adjective*: **crural** ●legs curving out at the knee: **bandy legs, bow legs** ●legs curving in at the knee: **knock knees** ●upper leg: **thigh** ●principal bone of the upper leg: **thighbone, femur** ●bone covering the knee joint: **kneecap, patella** ●front of the lower leg: **shin** ●fleshy part of the lower leg: **calf** ●swollen vein on the leg: **varicose vein** ●with an injured leg: **lame** ●imagined one-legged creature: **monopod** ●metal leg-splint: **calliper** ●Manx emblem of three legs: **triskelion**

leisure ●leisure activity: **hobby** ●building housing leisure facilities: **leisure complex**

lemon ●*adjectives*: **citric, citrous, citrine** ●spongy tissue inside an lemon skin: **pith**

lender ●person lending money to finance a film or play: **angel**

lens ●lens nearest the object observed: **objective** ●wide-angle lens: **fisheye** ●lens giving wide-screen effects: **anamorphic lens** ●lens with a long focal length: **telephoto lens** ●camera lens allowing smooth transition from close to long shots: **zoom**

lens ●lens used to start a fire: **burn-ing glass** ●denoting a lens flat one side and convex the other: **planocon-vex** ●denoting a lens flat one side and concave the other: **planoconcave** ●point on a lens at which light rays converge: **focal point, focus** ●vari-able opening for a camera lens: **aper-ture** ●distance between the centre of a lens and its focus: **focal length** ●object as seen through a lens: **image** ●uneven focus of an eye due to a fault in the cornea or lens: **astigmatism** ●counterbalanced camera platform that can be raised or turned: **crane**

Lent ●pre-lenten festivities: **carni-val, Mardi Gras** ●day before Lent: **Shrove Tuesday** ●first day of Lent: **Ash Wednesday** ●penultimate week of Lent: **Passion Week** ●last week of Lent: **Holy Week**

leprosy ●*adjective*: **leprous** ●lep-rous person: **leper**

lesbian ●lesbian who takes the dominant role: **butch** ●lesbian who takes the passive role: **femme** ●les-bian simulating male sexual move-ments upon her partner: **tribade**

letter[1] ●*adjective*: **epistolary** ●let-ter explaining other material ac-companying it: **covering letter** ●am-bassador's letter of introduction: **let-ter of credence** ●letter sent to all bishops by the Pope: **encyclical** ●bishop's letter to all his clergy: **pas-toral letter** ●sovereign's letter nom-inating a bishop: **letter missive** ●sovereign's letter appointing a mili-tary officer: **commission** ●letter sent to many persons simultaneously: **circular** ●letter addressed to one per-son but intended for publication: **open letter** ●letter which each re-cipient is asked to copy out and send to several others: **chain letter** ●ma-licious anonymous letter: **poison pen letter** ●letter sent by a woman break-ing off a relationship: **Dear John** ●conventional letter of thanks for hos-

pitality: **Collins** ●letter with stand-ardized wording: **form letter** ●sheet of thin paper foldable to make its own envelope: **air letter, aerogramme** ●transport of letters by air: **airmail** ●town in which letters are sorted: **post town** ●letter that cannot be de-livered: **dead letter** ●post office de-partment holding letters until col-lected: **poste restante** ●opening greeting in a letter: **salutation** ●com-municate by letter: **correspond** ●person with whom one is acquainted only by letters: **penfriend** ●educa-tion conducted by post: **correspond-ence course, distance learning** ●message added to a letter after the writer's signature: **postscript**

letter[2] ●*adjective*: **literal** ●letter written above the line: **superscript** ●letter written below the line: **sub-script** ●part of a letter that rises above the mid-point of a line of text: **ascender** ●part of a letter that sinks below the line of text: **descender** ●denoting a letter not a capital: **lower-case** ●denoting a capital let-ter: **upper-case** ●pair of letters making a single sound: **digraph** ●se-quence of letters reading the same backwards and forwards: **palindrome** ●design of interwoven letters: **mono-gram** ●consisting of both letters and numbers: **alphanumeric** ●write out in the letters of a different alphabet: **transliterate**

lettuce ●tall thin lettuce: **cos** ●let-tuce's tight head: **heart**

leukaemia ●abnormal white blood cell: **lymphoblast** ●blood cell with an overlarge nucleus: **myeloblast**

level ●*combining form*: **plano-** (*e.g.* planoconvex) ●social level: **stratum, echelon** ●device with an air-bubble in liquid, to show if surfaces are level: **spirit level** ●set level to each other, making a single flat surface: **flush**

lever ●foot-operated lever: **treadle** ●point on which a lever turns: **fulcrum** ●power exerted by a lever: **leverage**

liability ●legal transfer of a liability: **assignment** ●secure against liability: **indemnify**

library ●library entitled to a copy of every new UK book: **copyright library** ●library whose books may be consulted but not borrowed: **reference library** ●library store with compact shelving: **stack** ●library employee: **librarian** ●list of books held in a library: **catalogue** ●consolidated catalogue of a group of libraries: **union catalogue** ●library decimal system of topic classification: **Dewey decimal system** ●note in a library book showing where it is shelved: **shelf mark** ●person entitled to use a library: **reader** ●reader's cubicle in a library: **carrel** ●denoting a library book past its return date: **overdue**

lice ●louse egg: **nit** ●infestation with lice: **pediculosis** ●infested with lice: **lousy**

licence ●licence allowing alcoholic drinks to be served with meals: **table licence** ●licence allowing the sale of alcoholic drinks for consumption elsewhere: **off-licence** ●driving licence's note of penalty points incurred: **endorsement** ●accumulation of these: **totting-up**

lie¹ ●lying face downwards: **prone, prostrate** ●lying face upwards: **recumbent, supine** ●lie about in mud or water: **wallow**

lie² ●*adjective*: **mendacious** ●lie told to avoid a greater evil: **white lie** ●published false and damaging statement: **libel** ●false and damaging oral statement: **slander** ●telling lies when under oath to speak the truth: **perjury** ●alleged lie detector: **polygraph**

life ●*combining forms*: **bio-, vit-** ●*adjectives*: **animate, vital** ●long life: **longevity** ●life of pleasure: **la dolce vita** ●life after death: **afterlife, the other world** ●expected lifespan: **natural life** ●bring back to life: **resuscitate, reanimate, revivify** ●weariness of life: **taedium vitae** ●account of a person's life: **biography** ●person's account of his own life: **autobiography** ●prepare a person to resume normal life: **rehabilitate** ●bodily processes that support life: **metabolism** ●clinical measurement of bodily functions as indication of continued life: **vital signs**

lifeboat ●ship's crane for a lifeboat: **davit**

lifestyle ●organized lifestyle: **regime, regimen** ●lifestyle affording only the basic necessities: **poverty line** ●lifestyle seldom seen by the general public: **underlife** ●study of social statistics as an index of changing lifestyles: **demography**

lift ●lift for food in a restaurant: **dumb waiter** ●continuously moving lift with doorless compartments: **paternoster** ●space within which a lift operates: **shaft** ▸ *see also* **hoist**

light ●*combining forms*: **lumin-, photo-** (*e.g.* photosynthesis) ●*adjective*: **photic** ●soft tremulous light: **shimmer** ●soft light when the sun is just below the horizon: **twilight** ●flash or sparkle of light: **scintillation** ●northern lights: **aurora borealis** ●southern lights: **aurora australis** ●moving light seen over marshes: **will-o'-the-wisp, ignis fatuus** ●light set in a high place to convey a signal: **beacon** ●strong turnable outdoor light: **searchlight** ●bright signal light shot into the air: **flare** ●device emitting a bright light at fixed intervals: **stroboscope, strobe** ●strong light for filming: **klieg light** ●device generating an intense light beam: **laser** ●ultraviolet light for suntanning: **sunlamp** ●oil lamp for high winds: **hurricane lamp, storm lantern** ●overnight bedside light: **night light** ●floor-based lamp with a tall stem: **standard lamp** ●small coloured electric lights: **fairy lights** ●decorative lights: **illuminations** ●ship's or aircraft's position lights: **navigation lights, running lights, sidelights** ●incandescent wire in an electric light: **filament** ●device varying an electric light's brightness: **dimmer** ●electric light fitting with two small projecting pins: **bayonet fitting** ●glass container for an electric light filament: **envelope** ●light made from a hollowed-out turnip: **jack-o'-lantern** ●heatless emission of light: **fluorescence, luminescence, phosphorescence** ●light emission caused by intense heat: **incandescence** ●emission of light from a chemical reaction: **chemiluminescence** ●emission of light by living organisms: **bioluminescence** ●transmission of light signals along fine glass fibres: **fibre optics** ●treatment of light and shade in a painting: **chiaroscuro** ●use of light as a medical treatment: **phototherapy** ●bending of light waves passing between media: **refraction** ●illumination of buildings by natural light: **daylighting** ●allowing the passage of light: **diaphanous, translucent** ●not allowing the passage of light: **opaque** ●reacting to light: **photosensitive** ●moving towards or activated by light: **photopositive** ●extreme sensitivity to light: **photophobia** ●plant's use of light for foodmaking: **photosynthesis** ●plant's turning towards light: **phototropism** ●instrument measuring light intensity: **photometer** ●break light into its constituent colours: **diffract** ●restrict light-wave vibrations to a single direction: **polarize** ●extin-guish a light: **douse** ●study of light and its behaviour: **optics**

lighthouse ●lighthouse beam regularly obscured for a few seconds: **occulting light**

lightning ●jagged lightning flash: **bolt, forked lightning** ●diffused lightning: **sheet lightning** ●wire diverting lightning from a building: **lightning conductor**

like ●*combining forms*: -eous (*e.g.* aqueous), -esque (*e.g.* Junoesque), -ine (*e.g.* asinine), -ish (*e.g.* girlish) -oid (*e.g.* deltoid), -ose (*e.g.* ramose)

liker ●*combining forms*: phil(o)- (*e.g.* philhellene), -phile (*e.g.* bibliophile)

liking ●special liking: **predilection**

limb ●gradual stretching of a dislocated limb: **extension, traction** ●sea animal's broad flat limb: **flipper** ●surgical removal of a limb: **amputation** ●person who has had a limb removed: **amputee**

lime ●lime obtained by heating limestone: **quicklime** ●quicklime after treatment with water: **slaked lime**

limit ●upper limit: **ceiling** ●upper financial limit: **cap** ●having limits: **finite** ●having no preset limit: **open-ended** ●keep within limits: **contain**

line ●*adjectives*: **lineal, linear** ●imaginary line about which a body rotates: **axis** ●line of latitude: **parallel** ●line of longitude: **meridian** ●line of persons walking in pairs: **crocodile** ▶*see also* **straight line**

linen ●fine white linen: **cambric** ●square of linen etc. used at table to wipe the mouth: **napkin**

lion ●*adjective*: **leonine** ●young lion: **cub** ●offspring of a male lion and tigress: **ligon** ●offspring of a male tiger and a lioness: **tigon** ●lion's neck hair: **mane** ●injuries inflicted by a lion: **mauling** ●group of lions: **pride** ●astrological term: **leo**

lip ●*combining form*: labi(o)- ●*adjective*: **labial** ●discontented expression made by turning out the lips: **pout, moue**

liqueur ●liqueur flavoured with almonds or fruit kernels: **ratafia** ●cherry liqueur: **maraschino** ●German caraway-flavoured liqueur: **kümmel** ●Italian aniseed-flavoured liqueur: **sambuca** ●rum-based coffee-flavoured liqueur: **Tia Maria™**

liquid ●liquid to swill round the mouth and throat: **gargle, mouthwash** ●thick sweet liquid for food or medicines: **syrup** ●liquid present naturally in the mouth: **saliva** ●liquid remaining after cooking: **liquor** ●rich liquor used in soups and sauces: **stock** ●remnants of liquid: **dregs** ●vast surplus stock of a liquid: **lake** ●liquid waste or sewage: **effluent** ●milky liquid found in plants: **latex** ●hot liquid beneath the earth's crust: **magma** ●(of a liquid) give off bubbles: **effervesce** ●liquid's curved upper surface: **meniscus** ●become liquid: **deliquesce** ●becoming liquid: **liquescent** ●becoming liquid temporarily when shaken or stirred: **thixotropic** ●liquefied by extreme heat: **molten** ●dip into a liquid: **dunk** ●soak thoroughly in a liquid: **impregnate, saturate, souse, steep** ●soften by soaking in a liquid: **macerate** ●place in a liquid to flavour it etc.: **infuse, steep** ●injure by contact with hot liquid: **scald** ●thickness of a liquid: **consistency** ●instrument measuring this: **densimeter, hydrometer** ●instrument measuring liquid pressure: **piezometer** ●slender tube for transferring liquids: **pipette** ●fine dispersion of one liquid within another: **emulsion** ●pressurized liquid in an aerosol: **propellant** ●remove from the surface of a liquid: **skim** ●drift to the bottom of a liquid: **settle** ●matter settling to the bottom of a liquid: **sedi-**

ment ●draw off liquid from a sediment: **rack** ●denoting a liquid cloudy with suspended matter: **turbid** ●medical device for administering tiny amounts of a liquid: **drip feed** ●medical device producing a fine liquid spray: **nebulizer** ●operated by liquid pressure: **hydraulic** ●allowing the passage of liquid: **permeable, pervious, porous** ●slow passage of a liquid: **seepage** ●loss of liquid through leakage or evaporation: **ullage** ●cool a liquid below freezing point without solidification: **supercool** ●turn from liquid into vapour: **evaporate** ●heat a liquid above boiling point without evaporation: **superheat** ●container for liquid: **jerrycan** ●electric heating element placed in liquid: **immersion heater**

list ●official list: **register** ●unweeded list: **longlist** ●weeded list: **shortlist** ●list of the actors in a play, showing what parts they take: **cast list** ●list of addresses for information to be sent to: **mailing list** ●alphabetical topic list with references: **index** ●exhaustive list: **catalogue** ●annotated list: **catalogue raisonné** ●list of best-selling records: **charts** ●list of biblical readings: **lectionary** ●list of books: **bibliography** ●list of books held in a library: **catalogue** ●publisher's list of earlier books still in print: **backlist** ●list of a book's printing errors: **errata** ●list of candidates for final choice: **shortlist** ●list of a political party's candidates for office: **slate** ●consolidated catalogue of a group of libraries: **union catalogue** ●list of characters in a play: **dramatis personae** ●list of competitors in order of achievement: **league table** ●list of computer files: **directory** ●computer's displayed list of commands or facilities: **menu** ●list of the contents of a house or store: **inventory** ●list of contributors to a film, book, etc.: **credits** ●duty list: **roster** ●list of employees and their wages: **payroll** ●list of events and participants at a race meeting: **card** ●list of events with timings: **schedule** ●list of films: **filmography** ●list of foods eaten or to be eaten: **diet** ●list of goods held: **inventory** ●list of goods sent: **invoice** ●list of important items: **hot list** ●list of items covered by a legal document: **schedule** ●list of items for sale or on show: **catalogue** ●list of map symbols and their meanings: **key** ●list of members of a miltary unit or ship's company: **muster roll** ●list of names: **roll** ●list of addresses, telephone numbers, etc.: **directory** ●list of nobles: **peerage** ●list of passengers or parcels carried on a vehicle: **waybill** ●list of aircraft or ship passengers or cargo: **manifest** ●list of a performer's recordings: **discography** ●list of persons to be attacked or killed: **hit list** ●list of persons considered undesirable: **blacklist** ●list of persons entitled to vote: **electoral roll** ●list of persons refused certain rights or services: **stop list** ●list of priority tasks: **hot list** ●list of recordings broadcast on a radio programme: **playlist** ●restaurant's list of available dishes: **menu** ●list of things to be done: **agenda, checklist** ●list of towns, countries, etc.: **gazetteer** ●list of words in a text: **concordance, glossary, vocabulary** ●official list of medicines, with instructions for preparation and dosage: **pharmacopoeia**

listen ●listen in secretly: **eavesdrop**

literature ●factual literature: **nonfiction** ●person knowing about literature: **littérateur** ●traditional literary theme: **topos**

liturgy ●*adjective*: **liturgical** ●liturgical ceremony, or set of these: **rite, ritual** ●liturgical ceremony bestowing divine grace: **sacrament** ●liturgical march: **procession** ●liturgical direction: **rubric** ●liturgical worship viewed as man's duty to God: **opus Dei** ●daily cycle of public prayers for priests and religious: **Divine Office** ●Roman Catholic Communion service: **Mass** ●Anglican morning service: **matins, morning prayer** ●Anglican evening service: **evensong, evening prayer** ●service on the eve of a feast: **vigil** ●daily services of psalms and prayers: **hours, matins, lauds, prime, terce, sext, nones, vespers, compline** ●final office of the day: **compline** ●sequence of services on nine successive days: **novena** ●denoting a service without music: **plain** ●part of the liturgy unchanged on most occasions: **common** ●liturgical text particular to the day: **proper** ●series of petitions and responses: **litany** ●short sentence said or sung by the minister: **versicle** ●reply by the choir or congregation: **response** ●biblical extract sung in the liturgy: **canticle** ●biblical passage read liturgically: **lesson** ●prayer appointed for the day: **collect** ●money collection at a service: **offertory** ●person singing solo parts of the liturgy: **cantor, precentor** ●cleric in charge of a service: **officiant, celebrant** ●assimilation of the liturgy to a foreign milieu: **inculturation** ●study of liturgies: **liturgics, liturgiology**

live ●living alone: **solitary** ●living for ever: **immortal** ●living on land: **terrestrial** ●able to live on land and in water: **amphibious** ●living in trees: **arboreal** ●living in or near water: **aquatic** ●living in the sea: **marine**

liver ●*combining form*: **hepat-** ●*adjective*: **hepatic** ●inflammation of the liver: **hepatitis** ●degeneration of the liver: **cirrhosis** ●enlargement of the liver: **hepatomegaly** ●liver cancer: **hepatoma** ●anticoagulant occurring in the liver: **heparin** ●damaging liver cells: **hepatotoxic** ●surgical removal of the liver: **hepatectomy** ●ball of seasoned chopped liver: **faggot**

Liverpool ●*adjective*: **Liverpudlian**

livestock ●round up and steal livestock: **rustle** ●livestock diarrhoea: **scours** ●acute skin disease of livestock: **anthrax**

living organisms ●progressive development of living organisms over the millennia: **evolution** ●theory deriving all earthly life from micro-organisms in outer space: **panspermia** ●denoting living organisms: **biotic** ●able to be decomposed by the natural activity of living organisms: **biodegradable** ●regions of the earth's crust and atmosphere inhabited by living organisms: **biosphere** ●test of a substance's strength by applying it to living cells or tissues: **bioassay** ●study of living organisms: **biology, physiology** ●study of chemical processes within living organisms: **biochemistry** ●application of the principles of physics to living organisms: **biophysics** ●belief that humans are no more important than other living beings: **biocentrism** ●destruction of all life: **biocide**

lizard ●*combining forms*: **saur-, -saur, -saurus** (*e.g.* brontosaurus) ●*adjective*: **saurian** ●lizard that can change its colour for camouflage: **chameleon** ●huge prehistoric lizard: **dinosaur** ●mythical lizard said to live in fire: **salamander**

load ●intrinsic weight of a vehicle or structure: **dead load** ●weight of people or goods in a vehicle or structure: **live load** ●maximum load a machine or structure is designed to bear: **working load**

loan ●loan at fixed term and fixed interest: **debenture** ●amount of credit extended to a borrower: **line of credit** ●denoting a loan made under conditions as to how it may be spent:

tied ●denoting a loan whose repayment is guaranteed against another asset: **secured** ●denoting a loan available on easy terms: **soft** ●denoting a loan available at high rates of interest: **tight** ●original sum lent: **principal** ●asset pledged as security for a loan: **collateral** ●conveyance of property as security to a creditor or the loan thus obtained: **mortgage** ●loan certificate promising fixed terms of repayment: **bond** ●bank document underwriting specified loans on another bank to be taken out by the bearer: **letter of credit** ●credit that is automatically renewed as debts are paid off: **revolving credit** ●special credits available to members of the International Monetary Fund: **special drawing rights** ●lender's administration charge: **origination fee** ●company providing loans for hire-purchase agreements: **finance company, finance house** ●inter-bank trading of short-term loans: **money market** ●person lending money at high rates of interest: **usurer** ●person making loans on security of articles deposited with him: **pawnbroker** ●failure to repay a loan: **default** ▶ *see also* **debt**

lobster ●male lobster: **cock** ●female lobster: **hen** ●rich lobster soup: **bisque** ●lobster cooked in a cream sauce: **lobster thermidor**

local ●local and petty: **insular, parish-pump, parochial**

local government ●smallest rural unit: **civil parish** ●smallest region having a council and full bureaucracy: **district** ●administrative tier above this: **county** ●official auditing local authority accounts: **district auditor**

lock ●lock opened by selecting a sequence of figures etc.: **combination lock** ●lock opened only by a key: **deadlock** ●lock that cannot be opened until a preset time: **time lock**

• lock with a pivoted hook: **padlock**
• lock set into a door: **mortise lock**
• ridge or bar in a lock preventing its operation by an incorrect key: **ward**
• pivoted part of a lock restraining the bolt: **tumbler**

locomotive • steam locomotive carrying its own fuel and water: **tank engine** • locomotive's grip of the rails: **traction** • part of a locomotive where its crew work: **cab, footplate** • powered wheel of a locomotive: **driving wheel** • unpowered wheel of a locomotive: **trailing wheel** • extending framework connecting a locomotive with overhead power lines: **pantograph** • truck coupled to a steam locomotive, with supplies of fuel and water: **tender** • revolving platform turning a locomotive: **turntable** • person collecting locomotive numbers as a hobby: **trainspotter**

lodgings • person letting out lodgings: **landlord, landlady**

logic • statement used as a basis for argument: **premise, premiss** • asserted proposition: **position** • assumed proposition: **postulate** • proposition following from one already proved: **corollary** • proposition asserted of all members of a class: **universal** • proposition asserted of some members of a class: **particular** • limit a proposition's scope: **quantify** • false step in reasoning: **fallacy, non sequitur, paralogism** • deceptively plausible step in reasoning: **sophism, paralogism** • disproof of a proposition by demonstrating the absurdity of its consequences: **reductio ad absurdum** (*pl.* reductiones ad absurdum) • disproof of a proposition never advanced: **ignoratio elenchi** (*pl.* ignorationes elenchi) • denoting a proposition verifiable by linguistic analysis: **analytic** • denoting a proposition verifiable by recourse to experience: **synthetic** • logical fault of assuming what one sets out to prove:

circularity, **petitio principii** • system of logic: **organon** • system of logical reasoning that moves from a general rule to a particular instance: **deduction** • system of logical reasoning that derives a general rule from particular instances: **induction** • system of reasoning from two premises to a conclusion: **syllogism** • reasoning expressed by a system of symbols: **symbolic logic** • reasonable assumption from evidence available: **inference** • interminable chain of reasoning: **infinite regress** • set of rules to be followed in performing a logical process: **algorithm** • logical proposition that is verified by the meanings of the words that make it: **analytic proposition** • logical justification: **rationale** • logical refutation: **elenchus**

loin • *adjective*: **lumbar**

London • native of east central London: **cockney**

long • *combining form*: **macro-** (*e.g.* macroevolution) • long and thin: **lank, lanky** • make longer: **elongate** • lengthy undertaking: **marathon**

look • threatening or sullen look: **lour** • lecherous look: **leer, ogle** • look believed to harm the person regarded: **evil eye** • look over carefully or quickly : **scan** • look with the eyes partly closed : **squint**

Lord's Prayer • *Latin name*: **paternoster**

lorry • low-sided lorry: **low-loader, pickup** • large covered lorry: **pantechnicon** • light covered lorry: **van** • small low-sided van: **pickup, pickup truck** • lorry equipped to carry liquids in bulk: **tanker** • lorry's unladen weight: **tare** • denoting a lorry having a pivot between the cab and the load-bearing part: **articulated** • articulated lorry's skid into a V shape: **jackknife** • device recording a lorry driver's speeds and spells of driving: **tachograph** ●radiating set of elastic ties securing the load: **spider**

loss ●temporary loss: **misplacement** ●excess of expenditure over income: **deficit**

loud ●loud and harsh: **strident** ●degree of loudness: **volume**

loudspeaker ●loudspeaker for low-pitched sounds: **woofer** ●loudspeaker for high-pitched sounds: **tweeter**

louse ●louse infestation: **pediculosis** ●louse infecting the genital hair: **crab louse** ●egg of the human head louse: **nit**

love ●*combining forms*: **phil-** (*e.g.* philhellenism), **-philia** (*e.g.* necrophilia) ●*adjectives*: **amorous, amatory** ●adolescent love: **calf love, puppy love** ●intense and uncritical love: **infatuation** ●shortlived infatuation: **crush** ●secret love affair: **intrigue** ●affection feigned in order to obtain something: **cupboard love**

lover ●*combining form*: **-phile** (*e.g.* francophile) ●married woman's male lover: **cicisbeo** ●married man's female lover: **mistress** ●male lover younger that his partner: **gigolo, toy boy** ●lovers' secret meeting: **assignation, tryst**

loyalty ●group loyalty: **esprit de corps** ●loyalty owed to one's superiors: **allegiance** ●extreme loyalty to one's own country, people, sex, etc.: **chauvinism**

luggage ●large rigid-framed case: **trunk** ●small case for cosmetics: **vanity bag** ●rotating luggage delivery system: **carousel**

lump ●lump of flesh or food: **gobbet** ●separate out into lumps: **curdle**

lunch ●breakfast and lunch combined: **brunch**

lung ●*combining form*: **pneumo-** ●*adjective*: **pulmonary** ●membrane surrounding the lungs: **pleura** (*pl.* pleurae) ●inflammation of the plurae: **pleurisy** ●artery supplying the lungs: **pulmonary artery** ●tube carrying air to the bronchi: **trachea, windpipe** ●principal air passage of the lungs: **bronchus** (*pl.* bronchi) ●subsidiary air passage in the lungs: **bronchiole** ●drug taken by asthmatics to widen the bronchi: **bronchodilator** ●inflammation of the mucus membrane of the bronchi: **bronchitis** ●damage to the air sacs of the lungs: **emphysema** ●bacterial infection causing inflammation of a lung: **pneumonia** ●pneumonia affecting both lungs: **double pneumonia** ●rattle heard in unhealthy lungs: **rale** ●'black lung' or 'coal miner's lung' caused by inhalation of coal dust: **anthracosis, pneumoconiosis** ●'brown lung' caused by inhalation of textile dust: **byssinosis** ●lung disease from inhalation of asbestos particles: **asbestosis** ●lung disease from silica inhalation: **silicosis** ●lung disease with growth of nodules: **tuberculosis** ●instruments measuring lung capacity: **peak flow meter, spirometer** ●surgical removal of lung scars: **decortication** ●surgical removal of a lung: **pneumonectomy** ●denoting the heart and lungs: **cardiopulmonary, cardiorespiratory**

lute ●long-necked lute: **theorbo** ●Indian bowed lute: **sarod** ●long-necked Indian lute: **sitar** ●long-necked Italian lute: **chitarrone** ●lute player: **lutenist, lutist** ●lute maker: **luthier, lutist**

lymph ●*combining form*: **lymph-** ●*adjective*: **lymphatic** ●lymph filter: **lymph gland, lymph node** ●cancer of these: **lymphoma** ●white blood cell in the lymphatic system: **lymphocyte**

Mm

machine ●*adjective*: **mechanical** ●rotary machine driven by a flow of water etc.: **turbine** ●machine dispensing money: **cashpoint** ●machine dispensing small items when money is inserted: **vending machine** ●gaming machine showing different combinations of fruits: **fruit machine** ●gaming machine token: **jetton** ●coin-operated machine playing recorded music: **juke box** ●kitchen machine for chopping or mixing food: **food processor** ●kitchen machine for extracting juice: **juicer** ●machine pressing wet laundry: **mangle** ●machine shaping wood, metal, etc.: **lathe** ●machine hammering piles into the ground: **piledriver** ●grinding machine: **mill** ●agricultural machine that reaps and threshes: **combine harvester** ●cotton-separating machine: **gin** ●machine for hoisting or hauling: **winch, windlass** ●machine separating out substances of different densities: **centrifuge** ●machine polishing gems, glass, and metal: **lapping machine** ●machinery and other equipment developed in the light of scientific advances: **technology** ●machine performing a complex series of functions automatically: **robot** ●imagined machine resembling a human being: **robot** ●machine's regulating device: **governor** ●machine's oil reservoir: **sump** ●machine's sudden stop due to overload: **stall** ●person repairing or maintaining machines: **mechanic** ●person designing or constructing machines: **mechanician** ●person who behaves like a machine: **automaton** ●person opposed to the introduction of machines: **Luddite** ●make a machine operational: **commission** ●adjust machinery for smooth running: **regulate, set** ●periodic inspection and maintenance of a machine: **service** ●take a machine apart: **strip down** ●take parts from one machine to repair another: **cannibalize** ●link machinery to a drive: **engage** ●abandon an activity to machines: **mechanize** ●electronic remote control of machines: **teleoperation** ●denoting a machine activated by coins: **coin-op** ●denoting a machine part moving straight forward and backward: **reciprocating** ●raised walkway round a large machine: **catwalk**

mad cow disease ●*technical term*: **bovine spongiform encephalitis** ●disease in humans, thought to be related to this: **Creutzfeldt–Jakob disease**

mad dog ●disease caused by the bite of a mad dog: **rabies**

made ●badly made: **shoddy** ●made to order **bespoke**

Madrid ●*adjective*: **Madrilenian**

Mafia ●Neapolitan Mafia: **Camorra** ●US Mafia: **Cosa Nostra** ●Mafia leader: **padrone** ●leader of US Mafia: **capo, godfather** ●member of the Mafia: **Mafioso** ●Mafia code of silence: **omertà** ●Mafioso's sawn-off shotgun: **lupara**

magazine ●magazine published at regular intervals: **periodical** ●magazine sold with a newspaper: **supplement** ●magazine giving summaries of items published elsewhere: **digest** ●profession's magazine: **journal** ●magazine for fans: **fanzine** ●middle pages of a magazine: **centrefold, cen-**

tre spread ●magazine section to be detached and kept: **pull-out** ●magazine section regularly written by a named person: **column** ●large fold-out page: **gatefold** ●loose page in a magazine: **insert, inset** ●magazine's featured contributor: **columnist** ●magazine's treatment of a topic: **coverage** ●coverage consisting of photographs with linking text: **photoessay** ●general article on a topic: **feature** ●background article on a person in the news: **profile** ●female model appearing on magazine covers: **cover girl** ●send articles to a magazine: **contribute** ●text of a magazine item: **copy** ●pictures in a magazine: **illustrations, plates** ●drawn material in a magazine: **graphics** ●shop selling magazines: **newsagent**

magic ●magic to do good: **white magic** ●magic to do evil: **black magic** ●magic to foretell events: **divination** ●magic to summon up the dead: **necromancy** ●West Indian magic: **obeah, voodoo** ●tribal magician credited with healing powers: **witch doctor** ●object thought to have magic powers: **amulet, fetish, juju, talisman** ●five-pointed star: **pentagram, pentangle** ●talisman with the pentagram on it: **pentacle** ●West African fetish: **juju** ●magical beliefs and practices: **the occult** ●magic ritual imitating the effects desired: **sympathetic magic** ●words said as a magic spell: **conjuration, incantation, invocation** ●magical potion: **elixir** ●'magic eye' used in burglar alarms etc.: **photoelectric cell**

magistrate ●professional magistrate with legal training: **stipendiary magistrate** ●London stipendiary magistrate: **metropolitan magistrate** ●unpaid magistrate with no legal training: **lay magistrate** ●county's chief magistrate: **custos rotulorum** (*pl.* custodes rotulorum) ●Channel Islands magistrate: **jurat** ●magistrates

regarded collectively: **the bench** ●charge entered at a magistrate's court: **information**

magnetism ●*combining form*: **magneto-** ●magnet not needing an inducing current: **permanent magnet** ●magnet activated by an electric current: **electromagnet** ●magnet with poles at the sides: **transverse magnet** ●electromagnet of coiled wire: **solenoid** ●magnet's south-seeking pole: **negative pole** ●magnet's north-seeking pole: **positive pole** ●bar across a magnet's poles: **keeper, yoke** ●area over which magnetism is operative: **magnetic field** ●region round the earth governed by its own magnetic field: **magnetosphere** ●magnetic mineral: **lodestone** ●direction of a magnetic field: **polarity** ●destroy an object's magnetism: **degauss** ●electric generator using permanent magnets: **magneto** ●personal magnetism: **charisma**

making ●*combining forms*: **-facient** (*e.g.* abortifacient), **-faction** (*e.g.* stupefaction), **-fic** (*e.g.* pacific), **-fication** (*e.g.* simplification), **-genic** (*e.g.* carcinogenic), **genous** (*e.g.* erogenous), **-geny** (*e.g.* orogeny)

majority ●largest share of the votes cast: **majority, simple majority** ●share containing more than half the votes cast: **absolute majority** ●overwhelming majority of votes: **landslide** ●denoting a group unable to reach a majority decision: **hung**

malaria ●type of mosquito that carries malaria: **anopheles** ●drug that cures malaria: **quinine**

Malayan ●traditional Malayan village: **kampong** ●Malayan communal house: **longhouse** ●Malayan dagger: **kris** ●Malayan garment: **sarong**

male ●*combining forms*: **andro-** (*e.g.* androgen) ●male chromosome: **Y chromosome** ●relating to male sexuality: **priapic** ● aggressive maleness: **machismo, laddism** ● denoting a person displaying this: **butch, macho** ● deprive of maleness: **emasculate** ● supposed male mid-life crisis: **male menopause** ● male members of a family: **spear side** ● denoting descent through the male line: **patrilineal** ● development of male characteristics is women: **virilism**

mammal ● ape-like mammal: **primate** ● study of primates: **primatology** ● sea mammal: **cetacean** ● thick-skinned mammal (*e.g.* rhinoceros): **pachyderm** ● mammal with incisor teeth: **rodent** ● mammal that chews the cud: **ruminant**

man ● *adjectives*: **male, virile** ● primitive man viewed as uncivilized and uncorrupted: **noble savage** ● unmarried man: **bachelor** ● man whose wife has died: **widower** ● boisterously macho man: **lad** ● man whom women find attractive: **ladykiller, lady's man** ● lustful man: **satyr** ● castrated man: **eunuch** ● man rejecting traditional male attitudes: **new man** ● man in charge of a public house: **landlord** ● man letting out lodgings: **landlord** ● man over-eager to dress smartly: **dandy, fop** ● rich man persuing a life of pleasure: **playboy** ● denoting a womanish man: **effeminate** ● rule by men: **patriarchy** ● hatred of men: **misandry** ● party for men: **stag party** ● mythical creature half man and half horse: **centaur**

management ● management style that reacts to problems rather than anticipating them: **firefighting** ● management philosophy demanding enthusiastic commitment from all staff: **Total Quality Management**

manager ● industrial manager or proprietor: **industrialist** ● person managing large sums of money: **financier** ● senior manager: **executive** ● manager with direct production responsibility: **line manager** ▸ *see also* **businessman**

Manchester ● *adjective*: **Mancunian**

mandrake ● mandrake root as a narcotic: **mandragora**

mania ● mania for books: **bibliomania** ● mania for drink: **dipsomania** ● mania for starting fires: **pyromania** ● mania for power or self-aggrandizement: **megalomania** ● manic obsession with a single idea: **monomania** ● mania for stealing: **kleptomania**

manipulation ● therapeutic manipulation of bones: **osteopathy** ● manipulation of electoral boundaries for party advantage: **gerrymandering**

manner ● *combining form*: **-wise** (*e.g.* otherwise)

manners ● code of good manners: **etiquette** ● considerate politeness: **tact** ● refined politeness: **suavity, urbanity** ● affected good manners: **gentility, primness, prissiness** ● lively and cheeky: **pert** ● excessively familiar: **forward** ● offensively cool: **offhand** ● rough and abrupt in manner: **unceremonious, uncouth** ● denoting pleasant appearance and manner: **personable**

manufacture ● manufacturing machinery or premises: **plant** ● finished article in a manufacturing process: **end product** ● series of items produced at one time: **run** ● savings through increased output: **economy of scale** ● savings though diversification of output: **economy of scope** ● cost varying with level of output: **variable cost** ● theory advocating small flexible manufacturing units: **post-Fordism**

manure ● decayed organic material used as manure: **compost** ● seabird excrement used as manure: **guano**

•semi-liquid manure: **slurry** •surface application of manure: **top dressing** •clean out stables etc.: **muck out**

manuscript •manuscript written by the author of the text it contains: **autograph** •manuscript wholly written by the author of the text it contains: **holograph** •manuscript erased and used again: **palimpsest** •manuscript with a text written over an earlier text: **palimpsest** •manuscript in book form: **codex** •decorate a manuscript: **illuminate** •picture or decorated capital letter in a manuscript: **illumination, miniature** •manuscript's opening words: **incipit** •manuscript's closing words: **explicit** •manuscript's closing statement of production details: **colophon** •sheepskin or goatskin prepared for use as a manuscript: **parchment** •calfskin prepared for use as a manuscript: **vellum** •person assessing manuscripts offered to a publisher: **reader**

Manx •Manx emblem of three legs: **triskelion**

many •*combining forms*: multi- (*e.g.* multistorey), poly- (*e.g.* polyhedron)

Maori •Maori greeting: **kia ora**

map •map for sea or air navigation: **chart** •map of the stars mounted on a sphere: **celestial globe** •map showing contours by tinting or shading: **relief map** •lines used for hill-shading: **hachures** •astrological map for casting a horoscope: **birth chart, natal chart** •large-scale map of a small area: **plan** •map-making: **cartography** •map-maker: **cartographer** •detailed mapping of an area's natural features: **topography** •mapping of seas, lakes, and rivers: **hydrography** •mapping of mountains: **orography, orology** •investigate an area for mapping: **survey** •ratio between actual and mapped

distances: **scale** •system representing the earth's surface upon a flat page: **projection** •mark points on a map: **plot** •altitude of selected points shown on a map: **spot height** •mapping of seas, lakes, and rivers: **hydrography** •map line plotting some equal value: **isogram** •map line joining points of equal height: **contour line** •map line joining points of equal atmospheric pressure: **isobar** •map line joining points of equal temperature: **isotherm** •map line joining points of equivalent winter temperature: **isocheim** •map line joining points of equivalent summer temperature: **isothere** •map line joining points of equal rainfall: **isohyet** •network of lines on a map: **grid** •location of a point using these: **grid reference** •system of letters or numbers by which a point on a map may be identified: **coordinates** •first coordinate in a grid reference: **easting** •second coordinate in a grid reference: **northing** •list of map symbols and their meanings: **key** •transparent sheet placed over a map to give extra information: **overlay** •this with grid markings: **romer**

marble •*adjective*: **marmoreal** •imitation marble made of painted plaster: **scagliola**

march •fast march: **forced march** •marching step with unbent legs: **goose-step**

mark •reference mark: **benchmark** •mark burnt onto livestock: **brand** •dirty mark: **smudge, smut** •blurred mark: **smudge**

market •market selling second-hand goods: **flea market** •oriental market: **bazaar** •small specialized market: **niche** •market in which supply exceeds demand: **buyer's market** •market in which demand exceeds supply: **seller's market** •control of the market: **corner** •portion of the market controlled by a company or product: **market share** ●market control by a single supplier: **monopoly** ●market domination by two suppliers: **duopoly** ●market domination by a few suppliers: **oligopoly** ●market control by a single purchaser: **monopsony** ●market domination by a few purchasers: **oligopsony** ●market that no individual can control: **perfect competition** ●denoting a market with steady prices: **hard** ●denoting a market with steadily high or rising prices: **strong** ●denoting a market unlikely to expand further: **mature** ●denoting a market with falling prices: **soft, weak** ●perceived need for a commodity: **demand, market** ●assessment of this: **market research, market profile** ●obtain orders in a new market: **penetrate** ●exposure to free competition: **marketization** ●action preventing free competition: **restraint of trade, restrictive practice** ●situation where certain traders can influence prices: **imperfect competition** ▸ *see also* **sale, sell, seller, trade**

marriage ●*adjectives*: **bridal, conjugal, connubial, marital, matrimonial, nuptial** ●romantic but impractical marriage: **love match** ●marriage contracted for reasons other than love: **marriage of convenience** ●marriage hastened or compelled by pregnancy: **shotgun wedding** ●ready for marriage: **nubile** ●marriage partner: **spouse** ●suitable person to marry: **match** ●denoting a desirable marriage partner: **eligible** ●occurring before marriage: **premarital** ●person arranging marriages: **marriage broker, matchmaker** ●offer of marriage: **proposal** ●formal promise to marry: **engagement** ●marriage formalized by a legal ceremony only: **civil marriage** ●office where this is conducted and documented: **register office** ●marriage performed with full ceremonies and

formal dress: **white wedding** ●permit to hold a wedding at a time or place not normally permitted: **special licence** ●Church official granting special licences: **surrogate** ●run away to get married: **elope** ●formal announcement in church of a forthcoming marriage: **banns** ●hours between which marriage may be celebrated in the Anglican Church: **canonical hours** ●person showing guests to their seats before a marriage service: **usher** ●wedding Mass: **nuptial Mass** ●woman on her wedding day: **bride** ●man on his wedding day: **bridegroom, groom** ●bridegroom's male attendant: **best man, groomsman** ●married woman attending a bride: **matron of honour** ●young woman attending a bride: **bridesmaid** ●boy attending a bride: **page, pageboy** ●hand over a bride to her husband: **give away** ●coloured paper thrown after a marriage ceremony: **confetti** ●formal meal after a marriage ceremony: **wedding breakfast** ●holiday taken by a newly-married couple: **honeymoon** ●poem celebrating a marriage: **epithalamium, prothalamium** ●clothing etc. collected by a bride before her marriage: **trousseau, bottom drawer** ●property etc. brought by a bride to her marriage: **dowry** ●property arrangement at marriage: **settlement** ●completion of marriage by sexual intercourse: **consummation** ●marriage partners' right to mutual sexual relations: **conjugal rights** ●occurring after marriage: **post-nuptial** ●denoting a marriage in which the partners condone each other's adultery: **open marriage** ●denoting marriage customs expecting the couple to live at the wife's home: **matrilocal, uxorilocal** ●denoting marriage customs expecting the couple to live at the husband's home: **patrilocal, virilocal** ●denoting marriage customs expecting the couple to live away from both sets of relatives: **neolocal** ●married woman's former surname: **maiden name** ●marriage between persons of similar backgrounds: **homogamy** ●marriage with a social inferior: **mésalliance** ●this with reservation of titles and succession: **morganatic marriage** ●marriage between persons of different nationality, religion, etc.: **intermarriage, mixed marriage** ●marriage within the local community: **endogamy** ●marriage beyond it: **exogamy** ●crime of being simultaneously married to several spouses: **bigamy** ●practice of being simultaneously married to several spouses: **polygamy** ●custom of the husband taking many wives: **polygyny** ●custom of the wife taking one husband only: **monandry** ●custom of the wife taking many husbands: **polyandry** ●practice of having only one spouse at a time: **monogamy** ●practice of living together without being married: **cohabitation, common-law marriage** ●person who has never married: **celibate** ●man who has never married: **bachelor** ●woman who has never married: **spinster** ●occurring outside marriage: **extramarital** ●relative by marriage: **in-law** ●relationship by marriage: **affinity** ●unsuitable or unsuccessful marriage: **misalliance** ●advice given to those with marital problems: **marriage guidance** ●court order enabling spouses to remain married but live apart: **judicial separation, legal separation** ●official declaration of a marriage's invalidity: **annulment** ●legal dissolution of a marriage: **divorce** ●denoting a person who has never married: **celibate**

Mars ●*Greek name*: **Ares**

marsh ●*adjective*: **paludal** ●marsh gas: **methane** ●marshy region: **wetland** ●low-lying marshy land in East Anglia: **fen** ●moving light seen over marshes: **will-o'-the-wisp, ignis fatuus**

martial arts ●Chinese martial arts: **kung fu, t'ai chi ch'uan** ●simplified form of kung fu: **wing chun** ●Japanese arts of self-defence: **aikido, ju-jitsu, karate, judo** ●Korean martial art: **tae kwon do** ●place where martial arts are practised: **dojo** ●lower grade of proficiency: **kyu** ●belt worn by a beginner in martial arts: **white belt** ●belt worn by an expert in martial arts: **black belt** ●higher grade of proficiency: **dan** ●send one's opponent to the ground: **throw** ●heel-kick aimed at the opponent's head: **axe kick**

Marxism ●Marxist theory of history: **dialectical materialism** ●class struggle leading to the establishment of communism: **revolution** ●Marxist term for the unpoliticized masses: **lumpenproletariat** ●Marxist term for an advocate of evolutionary or pluralistic socialism: **revisionist**

Mary ●*adjective*: **Marian** ●excessive veneration of the Virgin Mary: **Mariolatry** ●theology of the Virgin Mary: **Mariology**

masculine ●masculine part of a woman's personality in Jungian psychology: **animus** ●development of male characteristics is women: **virilism**

mask ●mask to protect the eyes: **visor** ●mask to aid breathing: **respirator** ●mask with attached cloak: **domino** ●dance at which masks are worn: **masquerade**

masonry ●smooth, square-cut masonry: **ashlar** ●masonry carved to appear rough-hewn: **rustication**

mass ●*adjective*: **molar** ●the masses: **canaille, hoi polloi, lumpenproletariat, proletariat**

Mass ●Mass celebrated by three clergy: **high Mass** ●Mass celebrated by one priest: **low Mass** ●wedding

Mass: **nuptial Mass** ●Mass for the dead: **requiem** ●hymn sung at this: **Dies irae** ●Mass celebrated for a special aim: **Mass of special intention, votive Mass** ●priest performing the Mass: **celebrant** ●Mass book: **missal** ●day all must attend Mass: **day of obligation** ●unchanging part of the Mass: **canon, ordinary** ●variable part of the Mass: **proper** ●text sung or said at the beginning of Mass: **introit** ●response between the Epistle and Gospel: **gradual** ●hymn sung after the gradual: **prose, sequence** ●offering of bread and wine for consecration: **offertory** ●central act of the Mass: **consecration** ●first part of the consecration prayer: **preface** ●bread and wine offered in the Mass: **elements** ●each of these: **kind** ●plate for the bread: **paten** ●cup in which the wine is consecrated: **chalice** ●pair of flasks for the water and wine: **cruet** ●jug for the wine: **flagon** ●cloth upon which the chalice and patten are placed: **corporal** ●liturgical raising of the elements: **elevation** ●bell rung at the elevation: **sacring bell** ●consecrated bread: **Host** ●breaking of the bread: **fraction** ●dipping the bread into the wine: **intinction** ●retention of a portion of the sacred elements for later use: **reservation** ●container for the consecrated bread: **ciborium, pyx** ●stand for exposition of the consecrated bread: **monstrance, ostensory** ●Roman Catholic and Orthodox belief that the consecrated elements are substantially changed into the body and blood of Christ, remaining bread and wine in appearance only: **transubstantiation** ●Lutheran belief that the consecrated elements are both the body and blood of Christ and bread and wine: **consubstantiation** ▸*see also* **Holy Communion**

massage ●massage using circular movements: **effleurage** ●massage re-

lieving muscular tensions at skeletal level: **Rolfing** ●massage system based on zone therapy: **reflexology** ●massage treatment using fragrant oils: **aromatherapy**

mast ●mast aft of the mainmast: **mizzen** ●temporary mast: **jury mast** ●strong pole for a mast: **spar** ●mast's crossbar: **yard** ●rope etc. supporting a mast: **shroud, stay** ●keel block to take the mast: **step** ●deck mast socket: **tabernacle** ●lookout post atop the mast: **crow's-nest** ●masthead platform: **top**

master ●*adjective*: **magisterial**

mat ●fibre used for matting: **jute**

match ●match igniting only on a special surface: **safety match** ●collector of matchbox labels: **phillumenist**

material ●material built up of superimposed thin layers: **laminate**

mathematics ●mathematics of the manipulation of numbers: **arithmetic** ●collection and analysis of numerical data: **statistics** ●mathematics of variable quantities: **calculus** ●mathematics using letters and symbols: **algebra** ●mathematics used for strategic planning: **game theory** ●mathematics of the shape and size of the earth: **geodesy** ●mathematics of motion and forces producing it: **mechanics** ●mathematical description of the motion and interaction of subatomic particles: **quantum mechanics** ●mathematical study of the coding of information: **information theory** ●mathematics of points, lines, surfaces, and solids: **geometry** ●mathematical study of triangles: **trigonometry** ●school mathematics courses stressing heuristics and set theory: **new maths** ●able to understand mathematics: **numerate** ●mathematically ignorant: **innumerate** ●mathematical rule: **theorem** ●symbolic expression of a mathematical rule: **formula** (*pl.* formulae) ●mathematical representation of a system or process: **model** ●regulated manipulation of numbers or quantities: **operation** ●rule for calculations: **algorithm** ●repetition of a mathematical procedure: **iteration** ●record of calculations made: **workings** ●expression containing one or more variables: **function** ●expression or function so related to another that their product is unity: **reciprocal** ●statement that the values of two mathematical expressions are equal: **equation** ●number of entities all satisfying certain conditions: **set** ●association of each element in one set with an element in another: **mapping** ●diagram showing relationships between sets: **Venn diagram** ●positiveness or negativeness of a quantity: **sign** ●move a term to the opposite side of an equation, changing its sign: **transpose** ●quantity with unchanging value: **constant** ●quantity with changing value: **variable** ●quantity having direction as well as magnitude: **vector** ●quantity upon which an operation is to be performed: **operand** ●quantity to be added: **summand** ●quantity to be subtracted: **subtrahend** ●quantity to be multiplied: **multiplicand** ●quantity representing the power to which a number is to be raised: **exponent** ●result of adding one quantity to another: **sum** ●result of subtracting one quantity from another: **difference** ●result of multiplying one quantity by another: **product** ●result of dividing one quantity by another: **quotient** ●product of multiplying a number by itself: **square** ●product of multiplying a number by its square: **cube** ●number producing a specified quantity when multiplied by itself: **square root** ●irrational number: **surd** ●curve made by all points

satisfying certain conditions: **locus** ▶*see also* **number**

matter ●tendency of matter to remain motionless or to continue motion in a straight line: **inertia**

mattress ●inflatable mattress: **lilo** ●mattress stuffed with straw: **pallet, palliasse** ●strong cloth used to cover mattresses, pillows, etc.: **ticking**

maxims ●work expands to fill the time available: **Parkinson's Law** ●employees are always promoted one rank beyond their competence: **Peter Principle** ●anything that can go wrong, will: **Sod's Law, Murphy's Law**

mayor ●city mayor: **lord mayor** ●his residence: **mansion house** ●mayor of an Austrian, Dutch, Flemish, German, or Swiss town: **burgomaster**

meal ●self-service meal: **buffet** ●meal at which food is grilled and served out of doors: **barbecue** ●light meal: **tiffin, collation** ●breakfast and lunch combined: **brunch** ●light meal at mid morning: **elevenses** ●substantial late-afternoon meal: **high tea** ●meal offered to wedding guests after the ceremony: **wedding breakfast** ●formal meal for a large party: **banquet, feast** ●banquet or other formal social occasion: **function** ●guest meal with different courses eaten at different houses: **safari supper** ●restaurant meal with a fixed global price and offering few alternatives: **table d'hôte** ●restaurant meal chosen from a range of separately priced dishes: **à la carte** ●meal of bread and cheese: **ploughman's lunch** ●part of a meal: **course** ●first course of a meal: **appetizer, hors d'oeuvre, starter** ●main course of a meal: **entrée** ●light dish served between courses: **entremets** ●time allotted for service and consumption of a complete meal: **sitting** ●small open sandwich served as an appetizer: **canapé**

●alcoholic drink taken before a meal as an appetizer: **aperitif** ●square of cloth for wiping the hands or face while eating: **napkin** ●provision of meals, or the payment for this: **board** ●military establishment where meals are served: **mess** ●person who receives meals and lodging: **boarder**

meaning ●*adjective*: **semantic** ●specific meaning: **denotation** ●implied meaning: **connotation** ●general meaning of a text: **burden, gist, gravamen, tenor** ●give the meaning: **define** ●having only one possible meaning: **unambiguous, univocal** ●having several meanings: **ambiguous, equivocal, polysemous** ●word having the same meaning as another: **synonym** ●word having the opposite meaning to another: **antonym** ●study of meaning: **semantics**

measles ●mild form of measles: German measles, rubella

measurement ●*combining form*: -metry ●*adjectives*: **mensural, metrical** ●measurement of the depth of seas or lakes: **bathymetry** ●measurement across something: **diameter** ●measurement round something: **circumference** ●measuring device: **gauge** ●device measuring internal and external dimensions: **calipers** ●gauges for fine distances: **feeler gauge, micrometer** ●instrument to measure or draw angles: **protractor, set square** ●instrument measuring angles precisely: **goniometer**

meat ●pale meat from pigs, poultry etc.: **white meat** ●darker meat from sheep, deer, etc.: **red meat** ●meat from wild animals or birds: **game** ●cold cooked meats: **charcuterie** ●meat minced for stuffing: **forcemeat** ●seasoned paste of finely minced meat: **pâté** ●boned piece of meat: **fillet** ●thin slice of meat: **escalope** ●thick slice of meat: **steak** ●small round cut of meat: **médaillon, noisette** ●grilled or fried portion of meat:

cutlet ●large piece of meat cooked whole: **joint** ●joint including the front ribs: **rack** ●joint of meat with its backbone: **chine** ●meat cut from the breast: **brisket** ●joint from below the ribs: **loin** ●joint of meat consisting of both loins: **saddle** ●thick end of a loin of meat: **chump** ●meat cut from the side of a carcass: **flank** ●long thin slice of meat rolled and stuffed: **paupiette** ●cattle meat used as food: **beef** ●calf meat used as food: **veal** ●deer meat used as food: **venison** ●pig meat used as food: **pork** ●sheep meat used as food: **lamb, mutton** ●animal's thymus or pancreas as food: **sweetbread** ●animal's internal organs eaten as meat: **offal, pluck** ●hard white fat round the kidneys: **suet** ●fat falling from roasting meat: **dripping** ●tough cartilage in meat: **gristle** ●meat from a cow's tail: **oxtail** ●meat from a pig's leg: **ham** ●lamb's testicles as food: **fry** ●fried thin slice of white meat coated in breadcrumbs: **schnitzel** ●small pieces of meat cooked on a skewer: **kebab** ●kebab of marinaded meat and vegetables: **shish kebab** ●compressed spiced meat coated in breadcrumbs and fried: **rissole** ●dish of minced meat topped with mashed potato: **cottage pie, shepherd's pie** ●minced meat rolled in bacon: **kromesky** ●dish of chopped recooked meat: **hash** ●dish of finely minced meat: **timbale** ●small seasoned meatball: **quenelle** ●cooked mould of layered chopped meats and/or vegetables: **terrine** ●dish of various grilled meats: **mixed grill** ●dish of pressed meat in aspic: **galantine** ●dish of chopped meat, anchovies, eggs, and seasoning: **salmagundi** ●dish of meat braised in wine: **daube** ●dish of stewed meat in a white sauce: **fricassee** ●casserole of meat and vegetables: **hotpot** ●preserve meat by smoking etc.: **cure** ●leave meat in the air until matured: **hang** ●pressed meat from a pig or calf's head: **brawn** ●compressed cooked offal: **haslet** ●paste of dried meat and melted fat: **pemmican** ●finely ground paste of seasoned meat: **pâté, terrine** ●denoting meat cooked only a little: **rare** ●denoting meat cooked very rare: **au bleu** ●denoting meat cooked rare: **saignant** ●denoting medium-cooked meat: **à point** ●denoting well-cooked meat: **bien cuit** ●denoting meat prepared according to Muslim food regulations: **halal** ●hammer for beating meat: **tenderizer** ●skewer for grilling meat: **brochette** ●rod turning roasting meat: **spit** ●denoting decomposing meat: **high**

mechanics ●mechanics of forces producing equilibrium: **statics** ●mechanics of forces producing motion: **dynamics** ●mathematical description of the motion and interaction of subatomic particles: **quantum mechanics**

medal ●face of a medal: **obverse** ●back of a medal: **reverse** ●award a medal to: **decorate** ●metal strip below a medal's clasp: **bar** ●study of medals: **numismatics**

meddle ●meddle with something so as to cause damage: **tamper**

medical ●*combining form*: **medico-** (*e.g.* medico-social)

medical device ●device for inspecting the anus and rectum: **proctoscope** ●device measuring blood pressure: **sphygmanometer** ●device dilating an orifice: **speculum** ●device for listening to the heart or lungs: **stethoscope** ●device for making injections: **syringe** ●device for administering tiny amounts of a liquid: **drip feed** ●device producing a fine liquid spray: **nebulizer** ●device recording a pulse: **sphygmograph** ●device for inspecting the retina: **ophthalmoscope** ●small rubber-headed hammer: **plexor** ●sponge on a flexible stalk: **probang**

medical examination ●*combining form*: **-opsy** ●general medical examination: **check-up** ●general bodily examination: **physical, physical examination** ●medical examination of tissue from a living patient: **biopsy** ●internal medical examination by an optic device: **endoscopy** ●medical examination by a detector or electromagnetic beam: **scan** ●medical examination using a radioactive tracer: **scintigram, scintiscan** ●medical examination of the retina: **ophthalmoscopy** ●medical examination of the vagina and cervix: **colposcopy** ●ultrasonic sound and other vibrations used in medical imaging: **ultrasound**

medical skills ●denoting medical skills learnt in a hospital: **clinical** ●medical skills used in criminal investigations: **forensic medicine, medical jurisprudence**

medical test ●medical test to establish fatherhood: **paternity test**

medical treatment ●*combining forms*: **iatro-, -iatry, -pathy** ●treatment designed to cure a disorder: **therapy** ●medical treatment provided by general practitioners: **primary care** ●medical treatment provided by hospitals: **secondary care** ●medical treatment provided by specialist institutions: **tertiary care** ●medical treatment removing symptoms but not attacking the underlying cause: **palliative** ●medical treatment imagined to cure all diseases: **panacea** ●medical treatment to cure addiction: **detoxification** ●medical treatment of the blood: **haematology** ●medical treatment of bones and muscles: **orthopaedics** ●medical care during childbirth: **obstetrics** ●medical treatment of children: **paediatrics** ●medical treatment of the eyes: **ophthalmology, orthoptics**

•medical treatment of the hearing system: **audiology** •medical treatment of the kidney: **nephrology** •medical treatment of mental diseases: **psychiatry** •medical treatment of the nervous system: **neurology** •medical treatment of old people: **geriatrics** •medical treatment of the skin: **dermatology** •medical treatment of the urinary system: **urology** •medical treatment of women: **gynaecology** •medical treatment to free the body of toxins: **detoxification** •assiduous treatment of the dangerously ill: **intensive care** •medical treatment providing mechanical substitutes for missing or defective bodily organs: **bioengineering** •temporary provision of these: **life support** •medical burning: **cauterization, cautery** •medical treatment by chemicals: **chemotherapy** •medical treatment using intense cold: **cryotherapy** •medical treatment using drugs: **medication** •medical treatment by small doses of substances producing the same symptoms as the disease: **homoeopathy** •medical treatment by drugs giving effects opposite to the symptoms: **allopathy** •medical treatment by two or more drugs: **combination therapy** •medical treatment using hypnosis: **hypnotherapy** •use of light as a medical treatment: **phototherapy** •medical treatment using radiation: **nuclear medicine** •therapeutic use of sunlight: **heliotherapy** •medical treatment by water: **hydropathy, hydrotherapy** •denoting medical treatment involving body-penetration: **invasive** •denoting medical treatment aimed at containment only: **conservative** •denoting medical treatment that is effective against a variety of germs: **broad spectrum** •medical treatment by activation of the immune system: **immunotherapy** •medical treatment given to reassure

or pacify the patient: **placebo** •denoting medical treatment given at the patient's request: **elective** •denoting medical treatment given at the time of an operation: **perioperative** •medical treatment given before a doctor arrives: **first aid** •systems of medical treatment not favoured by the Western medical establishment: **alternative medicine, fringe medicine** •systems of medical treatment beyond the scope of Western medicine: **complementary medicine** •medical treatment considering the whole patient: **holism** •physical treatment of bodily injuries or deformity: **physiotherapy** •assessment of the urgency of a patient's need for treatment: **triage** •slow injection: **infusion** •sustained pulling of a muscle or limb: **traction** •secondary effect of medical treatment: **side effect** •person requiring or receiving medical treatment: **case, patient** •discussion of such a person and his or her treatment: **case conference** •programme of treatment: **regime, regimen** •record of such a person's situation and treatment: **case history** •symptom suggesting a particular treatment: **indication** •symptom warning against a particular treatment: **contraindication** •acceptance of treatment by a patient aware of the risks involved: **informed consent** •written list of medical treatments acceptable to the bearer in case of unconsciousness etc.: **advance directive, living will** •card authorizing use of parts of the holder's body for medical purposes after his or her death: **donor card** •repeated series of medical treatments: **course** •ability to endure a course of medical treatment: **tolerance** •procedures for a course of medical treatment: **protocol** •abnormal sweating caused by medical treatment: **diaphoresis** •thin tube inserted into the body for medical purposes: **cannula** •denoting medical services having no patient contact: **paraclinical** ●person recovering from medical treatment: **convalescent** ●caused by medical treatment: **iatrogenic** ●establishment offering specialist medical care: **clinic** ▸*see also* **alternative medicine, complementary medicine**

medication ●forcible medication: **gavage** ●medication with extracts from animal organs: **organotherapy** ●medication inhibiting germ growth: **antiseptic** ●medication given before an operation: **pre-medication** ●solid medication inserted to dissolve in the vagina: **pessary** ●solid medication inserted to dissolve in the vagina or rectum: **suppository** ●cancer treatment by drugs: **chemotherapy** ●cancer treatment by X-rays: **radiotherapy** ●preparation to remove unwanted hair: **depilatory** ●substance developing bodily immunity to a diease: **vaccine** ●medical device for administering tiny amounts of a liquid: **drip feed** ●denoting the application of medication through the skin: **transcutaneous, transdermal** ●denoting a drug capsule giving steady content release over a long period: **sustained-release** ●undesirable secondary effect of medication: **side effect**

medicine ●*combining form*: **pharm(aco)**- ●*adjective*: **pharmaceutical** ●denoting commercially available medicine: **patent** ●medicine made by dissolving a drug in alcohol: **tincture** ●medicine used to treat allergies: **antihistamine** ●medicine able to target particular cells: **magic bullet** ●medicine for constipation: **aperient** ●medicine for coughs: **expectorant, linctus** ●medicine to encourage defecation: **laxative** ●medicine to cause some bodily discharge: **evacuant** ●medicine for fever: **antipyretic, febrifuge** ●medicine to relieve flatulence: **carminative**

●medicine to ease inflammation: **demulcent** ●medicine to be inhaled: **inhalation** ●device for taking this: **inhaler** ●medicine taken to invigorate: **tonic** ●medicine for itching: **antipruritic** ●medicine attacking microorganisms: **antibiotic** ●medicine to clear the nose: **decongestant** ●medicine to counteract poison: **antidote, antitoxin, antivenin** ●liquid painkiller rubbed into the skin: **embrocation** ●medicine to reduce nervous or physical activity: **depressant** ●medicine to cause sweating: **diaphoretic** ●medicine to increase urination: **diuretic** ●medicine to cause vomiting: **emetic** ●quack medicine: **nostrum** ●denoting a medicine to be applied to the outside of the body: **external** ●denoting a medicine to be taken into the body: **internal** ●denoting a medicine made from natural ingredients: **galenical** ●denoting a medicine available only on prescription: **ethical** ●denoting a non-branded medicine: **generic** ●treatment by medicines: **pharmacotherapy** ●place where medicines are made up: **dispensary** ●doctor's order for a medicine to be made up or issued: **prescription** ●amount of medicine to be given at one time: **dose** ●size or frequency of a prescribed dose of medicine: **dosage** ●container for an injectable dose of medicine: **ampoule** ●dose of medicine reinforcing a previous one: **booster** ●dose of medicine given to an animal: **drench** ●person trained to prepare and dispense medicines: **chemist, pharmacist** ●place where medicines are dispensed: **pharmacy** ●official list of medicines, with instructions for preparation and use: **pharmacopoeia, codex, formulary** ●remedial substances used in medical practice: **materia medica** ●medical use of radioactive substances: **nuclear medicine** ●study of medicines and their uses: **pharmacology**

medieval ●medieval asociation of craftsmen or merchants: **guild** ●meeting-place for this: **guildhall** ●medieval chemistry, seeking to turn base metals into gold: **alchemy** ●medieval system of land tenure: **feudalism** ●unharmonized medieval Latin church music: **Gregorian chant, plainsong**

meditation ●cross-legged meditation posture: **lotus position** ●repeated word or sound used in meditation: **mantra**

Mediterranean ●dense scrub of the Mediterranean coast: **maquis**

meeting ●unexpected meeting: **encounter** ●point of meeting and interaction: **interface** ●meeting for academic discussion: **colloquium, seminar, symposium** ●meeting to be attended by all qualified to do so: **plenary** ●meeting attended by all qualified to do so: **plenum** ●arranged meeting: **rendezvous** ●arranged meeting with reporters: **press conference** ●meeting for church government: **synod, consistory** ●meeting of cardinals to elect a pope: **conclave** ●meeting of delegates: **congress, convention** ●mass meeting: **rally** ●meeting with various sessions: **conference** ●meeting of heads of state: **summit** ●official who calls meetings: **convener** ●representative sent to a meeting: **delegate** ●minimum attendance required for a meeting to be valid: **quorum** ●denoting a meeting attended by a quorum: **quorate** ●denoting a meeting lacking this: **inquorate** ●list of items to be dealt with at a meeting: **agenda** ●speak at a meeting: **contribute** ●present a topic for discussion: **table** ●proposal laid before a meeting: **motion** ●make such a proposal: **move** ●formally support this: **second** ●modification to a motion: **amendment** ●meeting's approval of a motion: **adoption** ●statement of a meeting's decision:

resolution ●question on procedure: **point of order** ●record of a meeting: **minutes** ▸see also **parliament**

melt ●substance mixed with a solid to lower its melting point: **flux** ●water from a melting glacier: **meltwater**

membership ●list of members: **roll** ●withdraw from membership: **secede** ●deprive of membership: **debar, expel** ●remove from membership of a professional body: **strike off**

membrane ●membrane dividing the thorax from the abdomen: **diaphragm** ●membrane lining the abdomen: **peritoneum** ●membrane surrounding a fetus: **amnion, amniotic membrane, caul** ●membrane blocking a virgin's vagina: **hymen** ●membrane between the toes of a swimming bird: **web** ●open sore on an internal membrane: **ulcer**

memory ●ability to remember: **recall, retentiveness** ●denoting a memory capable of detailed recall: **photographic** ●vivid and detailed memory of an event: **total recall** ●supposed subconscious memory of distant events in human history: **race memory** ●supposed brain change on memorizing something: **engram, memory trace** ●ability to recall objects shown once: **memory span** ●aid to memory: **mnemonic** ●item kept as a reminder: **memento, souvenir** ●memory techniques: **mnemotechnics** ●arousing memories: **evocative** ●discard from one's memory: **unlearn** ●inability to recall a familiar item: **mental block** ●distorted memory resulting from confusion of fact and fantasy: **paramnesia** ●loss of memory: **amnesia, oblivion**

mend ●that cannot be mended: **irreparable**

menstruation ●*adjectives*: **menstrual, menstruous** ●first occurrence of menstruation: **menarche**

● regular cycle of ovulation and menstruation: **menstrual cycle** ● menstrual bleeding: **menorrhoea** ● menstrual blood: **menses** ● absorbent pad for this: **sanitary towel** ● excessive menstrual bleeding: **menorrhagia** ● painful or difficult menstruation: **dysmenorrhoea** ● abnormal absence of menstruation: **amenorrhoea** ● cessation of menstruation in middle age: **climacteric, menopause**

mental illness ● *combining form*: **-mania** ● mild mental illness, with grasp of reality retained : **neurosis** ● severe mental illness, with loss of consciousness of reality: **psychosis** ● acutely disordered state of mind: **delirium** ● mental illness caused by anxiety or depression: **nervous breakdown** ● severe inability to communicate or form relationships with others: **autism** ● delusions of self-importance: **folie de grandeur** ● shared delusions: **folie à deux** ● mental illness causing excitement and violence: **mania** ● retreat into a fantasy world: **schizophrenia** ● nervous breakdown resultant from war experiences: **shell-shock, combat fatigue** ● mentally unstable: **disturbed** ● mentally ill: **non compos mentis** ● mental retardation with shortness of stature: **Down's syndrome** ● person suffering alternating depression and euphoria: **manic-depressive** ● person with chronic mental illness leading to violent behaviour: **psychopath** ● person manifesting extreme anti-social attitudes and behaviour: **sociopath** ● caused by or involving mental illness: **pathological** ● institution offering protection and treatment for the mentally ill: **psychiatric hospital, mental hospital, asylum** ● mental hospital room for violent patients: **padded cell** ● electric shocks administered to treat mental illness: **electroconvulsive therapy** ● strong jacket confining a mental patient's arms: **straitjacket** ● brain surgery to treat mental illness: **psychosurgery** ● psychological treatment of mental illness: **psychotherapy** ● commit compulsorily to a psychiatric hospital: **section** ● order authorizing detention in a mental hospital: **reception order** ● person acting for those unable to manage their own affairs: **guardian** ● study and treatment of mental illness: **psychiatry, psychoanalysis, psychopathology** ● denoting a person free from mental illness: **sane, compos mentis**

menu ● limited menu served at a fixed overall price: **table d'hôte** ● menu with items priced separately: **à la carte**

mercury ● mercury alloy used to fill teeth: **amalgam**

Mercury ● *Greek name*: **Hermes** ● Mercury's snake-twined staff: **caduceus**

mercy ● mercy shown to a defeated enemy: **quarter**

merger ● large company created by mergers: **conglomerate, corporation** ● denoting a merger between companies with parallel functions: **horizontal** ● denoting a merger between companies with sequential functions: **vertical** ● reverse previous mergers: **demerge**

message ● message delivered with a kiss: **kissogram** ● message delivered by a striptease artist: **strippergram** ● message sent by telephone but delivered in written form: **telemessage** ● device for the input and printout of telegraph messages: **teleprinter**

messenger ● messenger carrying important documents: **courier** ● delivery by such a messenger: **express**

metal ● oblong block of metal: **ingot** ● long thin strip of metal: **batten** ● thin and narrow strip of metal: **slat** ● thin flexible sheet of metal: **foil**

• very thin sheet of metal: **leaf** • metal grating: **grille** • made of two metals: **bimetallic** • combination of two or more metals: **alloy** • rough edge on cut metal: **bur** • rough piece of metal for grinding or smoothing: **file** • light metal-coated sheet retaining heat: **space blanket** • thin metal sheet for motor vehicle bodies: **panel** • metal rim: **shoe** • metal cap on the end of a stick: **ferrule** • metal plate on a tap-dancer's shoe: **tap** • discarded metal for reprocessing: **scrap** • substance mixed with metal to ease melting: **flux** • vessel for molten metal: **ladle** • extract metal from ore by heating and melting: **smelt** • stony waste separated off during metal smelting: **slag** • block of smelted metal: **sow, pig** • metal technology: **metallurgy** • hardness and elasticity of metal: **temper** • denoting metal brittle when hot: **hot-short** • denoting metal that can be pressed or hammered into shape: **malleable** • denoting metal hammered into relief: **repoussé** • denoting metal inlaid with gold or silver: **damascened** • denoting a metal resistant to chemical action: **noble** • denoting metal resistant to tension: **high-tensile** • denoting metal shaped by hammering: **wrought** • denoting metal not iron or steel: **non-ferrous** • tool for moulding or stamping out metal: **die** • metal-shaping machine: **lathe** • stone for sharpening metal: **hone, grindstone, whetstone** • machine polishing metal: **lapping machine** • scum on the surface of molten metal: **dross** • place where metal is cast: **foundry** • metal weakness from changing stresses: **fatigue** • surface dulling of metal exposed to air: **tarnish** • surface discoloration of certain metals: **patina** • hard protective coating for metal: **lacquer** • shape metal under heat: **forge** • fast-cool metal by plunging into water or oil:

quench • harden metal by heating and then cooling: **temper** • cut or shape metal: **mill** • cover with a thin coating of metal: **plate** • flatten sheet metal: **planish** • unite heated metal under pressure: **weld** • clean metal by steel-particle bombardment: **shot-blast** • damage metal by gradual chemical action: **corrode** • alloy used to join metal: **solder** • metal-worker: **smith, blacksmith** • skill of chasing and carving metal: **toreutics** • test of metal for purity: **assay** • study of metals and their purification: **metallurgy**

metal detector • person using this as a hobby: **detectorist**

meter • meter measuring off-peak electricity consumption: **white meter**

method • methods used: **methodology** • method of doing something: **modus operandi** • usual method: **practice**

Mexican • Mexican wide-brimmed hat: **sombrero** • Mexican flat maize cake: **tortilla** • tortilla with a spicy filling: **burrito, fajita, taco** • tortilla filled with chillied meat or cheese: **enchilada** • cheese-topped tortilla piece: **nacho** • Mexican dish of mashed avocado: **guacamole** • Mexican dish of fried stuffed chillis: **chiles rellenos** • Mexican sauce of onion, garlic, coriander, and peppers: **salsa verde** • Mexican agave spirit: **tequila** • inhabitant of Mexico at the time of the Spanish conquest: **Aztec** • Spanish conqueror of Mexico: **conquistador**

microchip • design of devices using microchips: **electronics**

microphone • underwater microphone: **hydrophone** • microphone used close to the mouth: **lip microphone**

microscope • microscope using electron beams: **electron microscope** • glass plate for microscope specimens to be examined: **slide** ●thin glass protecting a microscope specimen: **coverslip** ●thin layer of tissue etc. on a microscope slide: **smear** ●plate on which the slide is set: **stage**

middle ●*combining forms*: medi-, meso- (*e.g.* mesolithic), mid (*e.g.* midbrain) ●*adjectives*: **medial, median** ●middle ear: **tympanum** ●middle term in a series: **median** ●middle way of compromise: **via media** ●denoting a middle skill level: **intermediate**

middle age ●loss of self-confidence alleged to occur in early middle age: **midlife crisis** ●cessation of menstruation in late middle age: **menopause**

Middle Eastern ●Middle Eastern rice dish with spices and vegetables: **pilaf** ●Middle Eastern term for money given as a bribe or tip: **baksheesh**

military ●enrol for military service: **enlist** ●person joining the armed forces voluntarily: **recruit, volunteer** ●person made to join the armed forces: **conscript** ●newly enlisted person: **recruit** ●young military trainee: **cadet** ●compulsory peacetime military training: **national service** ●complete one's military training: **pass out** ●military officer assisting a senior officer: **adjutant, aide-de-camp** ●military officers who plan a campaign: **general staff** ●senior staff officer: **chief of staff** ●military officer in charge of a camp: **commandant** ●military officer in charge of security: **orderly officer** ●military officer in charge of supplies: **quartermaster** ●commander of a combined military force: **generalissimo** ●officer in charge of a nation's forces: **commander-in-chief** ●regiment's honorary head: **colonel-in-chief** ●military officer of the first grade: **commissioned officer** ●mili-

tary officer of the second grade: **warrant officer** ●military officer of the lowest grade: **non-commissioned officer** ●military officer's assistant: **orderly** ●military officer's personal servant: **batman** ●military personnel who are not commissioned officers: **other ranks** ●military personnel of the lowest grade: **the ranks, other ranks** ●clergyman attached to a military unit: **chaplain, padre** ●document conferring promotion: **commission, warrant** ●document conferring promotion without extra pay: **brevet** ●list of members of a military unit: **muster roll** ●military force: **contingent** ●front section of a military force: **van, vanguard** ●group of several army divisions: **corps** ●group of several army brigades or regiments: **division** ●infantry unit forming part of a brigade: **battalion** ●specialized military section: **corps** ●military corps preparing roads and terrain: **pioneers** ●military group sent on a special mission: **detachment, detail, picket, squad, task force** ●small detachment: **file** ●execution detachment: **firing squad** ●detachment to fire a military salute: **firing party** ●detachment sent to seize specified persons: **snatch squad** ●military force drawn from various units to deal with a particular situation: **battlegroup** ●military unit specializing in raids: **commando** ●a member of this: **commando** ●military personnel belonging to no established unit: **irregulars** ●member of an irregular resistance force: **guerrilla, paramilitary, partisan** ●such a force: **militia** ●spell of military service at a particular location: **posting, tour, tour of duty** ●military accommodation: **camp, barracks, billet** ●town with a large permanent military presence: **garrison town** ●armoured observation post: **blockhouse** ●small distant military establishment: **outpost** •military establishment serving meals: **mess** •British sovereign's ceremonial guard: **Yeomen of the Guard** •officer in this: **exon** •military personnel fighting on foot: **infantry** •military personnel using horses or armoured vehicles: **cavalry** •military personnel regarded as expendable units: **cannon fodder** •military engineer laying and removing mines: **sapper** •long-term military plans: **strategy** •short-term military plans: **tactics** •military preparations: **dispositions** •display of military power as a persuader: **sabre-rattling, show of force** •planned military attack: **offensive, operation** •sudden and intensive military attack: **blitz** •military campaign based upon this: **blitzkrieg** •accidental damage caused to uninvolved civilians by military activities: **collateral damage** •military action to prevent movement of goods or personnel: **blockade** •reduction of a fortified point by surrounding it: **siege** •provision of military manpower and supplies: **logistics** •military department for food and equipment: **commissariat** •military stores and materials: **materiel, ordnance** •store for military supplies: **magazine** •acquisition of military equipment and supplies: **procurement** •large military guns: **artillery** •military formation in parallel rows: **echelon** •end a parade of troops: **dismiss** •military field training: **exercises, field day, manoeuvres** •forces in the battle zone: **front line** •position military forces: **deploy** •remove forces from a conflict area: **disengage** •move away from a superior enemy: **retreat** •retreaters' tactic of destroying anything of use to the enemy: **scorched earth policy** •decrease of military presence: **drawdown** •remove all military presence: **demilitarize** •take troops out of ac-

tive service: **demobilize** •reduce military forces: **disarm** •military rebellion: **mutiny** •military court: **court martial** (*pl.* courts martial *or* court martials) •barrister advising this: **judge advocate** •official controlling army and RAF courts martial: **Judge Advocate General** •reduce to a lower rank as a punishment: **degrade, demote** •military punishment of doing drill carrying full kit: **pack drill** •dismiss with dishonour from the armed forces: **cashier** •such dismissal: **dishonourable discharge** •unauthorized abandonment of military service: **desertion** •person not belonging to the armed forces: **civilian** •person refusing military service on moral grounds: **conscientious objector** •menial work assigned to military personnel: **fatigues** •military signal to wake up: **reveille** •military flag: **standard, colours** •military ceremony with bands and countermarching: **retreat** •military ceremony and formal inspection: **review** •military entertainment with skill demonstrations: **tattoo** •state policy based on maintenance and use of large military forces: **militarism** ▸ *see also* **uniform, war, weapon**

milk •*combining forms*: **lact-, galact-** •*adjectives*: **dairy, lactic, lacteal** •coagulated milk: **curds** •thin milk remaining after curds have formed: **whey** •dish of sweetened curds: **junket** •soured fermented milk: **yogurt** •drink of flavoured whisked milk: **milkshake** •tinned evaporated and sweetened milk: **condensed milk, evaporated milk** •milk secretion: **lactation** •gland producing milk: **mammary gland** •substance that increases a nursing mother's flow of milk: **galactagogue** •denoting a cow kept to give milk: **milch** •place where milk is processed or sold: **dairy** •small cart or van delivering milk: **float** •denoting milk treated to prevent cream separation: **homogenized** •milk from which the cream has been removed: **skimmed milk** •sterilize milk by heat or irradiation: **pasteurize** •made without milk: **non-dairy**

million •*combining form*: **mega-** •a million deaths, as a unit for stating war fatalities: **megadeath**

millionth •*combining form*: **micro-** (*e.g.* micrometre)

mimicry •mimicry in which an edible animal is protected by its resemblance to one avoided by its predators: **Batesian mimicry**

mind •*adjectives*: **mental, noetic, psychological** •part of the mind of which one is not fully aware: **subconscious** •part of the mind from which memories can easily be recalled: **preconscious** •part of the subconscious filled with shared ancestral memories: **collective unconscious** •part of the unconscious filled with memories unique to the individual: **personal unconscious** •in the mind: **interior** •existing only in the mind: **notional** •part of the mind not normally accessible to consciousness: **inner space** •calmness of mind: **equanimity, equilibrium** •mentally lethargic: **torpid** •sharp-minded: **incisive** •mental powers: **intellect** •index of a person's mental ability expressed as the age at which such an ability level is typical: **mental age** •mental picture: **image** •study of the mind and its functions: **psychology** ▸*see also* **psychology**

mine¹ •horizontal passage leading into a mine: **adit** •vertical passage leading into a mine: **shaft** •top of a mineshaft: **pithead** •mineshaft lift cage: **skip** •mine's ventilation shaft: **upcast** •horizontal underground passage: **gallery** •beam supporting a mine roof: **pit prop** •short post supporting a mine roof: **puncheon**

•shaft lining or partition: **brattice** •part of a mine from which minerals are extracted: **workings** •solid material containing a valuable substance: **ore** •testing of ore for purity: **assay** •stratum of ore: **seam, ledge, lode, vein** •main stratum of ore: **mother lode** •material containing a seam: **gangue, matrix** •surface of a seam: **face** •excavation following a seam: **drift** •simultaneous mining of a whole face: **longwall working** •denoting mining on or near the surface: **opencast, strip-mining** •waste material brought up from a mine: **spoil** •miner detonating blasting charges: **shot-firer** •miner's pick: **mandrel** •safety lamp used in mines: **Davy lamp** •suffocating carbon-monoxide gas found in mines **choke-damp** •methane found in mines: **damp, firedamp** •carbon-dioxide gas left by a firedamp explosion: **after-damp** •land taken or allotted for mining: **claim**

mine² •mine activated by sound waves: **sonic mine** •area full of mines: **minefield** •set out mines: **lay, sow** •military engineer laying and removing mines: **sapper** •anti-mine device towed behind a boat: **paravane**

mineral •magnetic mineral: **lodestone** •discover mineral deposits: **strike** •study of minerals: **mineralogy**

Minerva •*Greek name*: **Athena**

mink •young mink: **kit**

mirror •*adjectives*: **catoptric, specular** •tilting mirror: **cheval glass** •large mirror between windows: **pier glass** •mirror reflecting from one side but transparent from the other: **two-way mirror** •having one side that is the mirror image of another: **symmetrical** •molecule that is the mirror image of another:

enantiomer ●crystal that is the mirror image of another: **enantiomorph**

misfortune ●delight in the misfortunes of others: **schadenfreude** ●reflect smugly upon another's misfortunes: **gloat**

missile ●missile guided by an onboard computer: **cruise missile** ●self-propelled underwater missile: **torpedo** ●denoting a missile using gravity for guidance: **ballistic** ●denoting a missile electronically programmed to find its target: **smart** ●denoting a missile designed to evade radar detection: **stealth** ●send a missile on its course: **launch** ●missile's explosive head: **payload, warhead** ●underground launchpad for missiles: **silo** ●establishment monitoring satellite movements: **tracking station** ●piece of brick used as a missile: **brickbat**

missionary ●missionary's long leave: **furlough**

mix ●mix to make uniform throughout: **homogenize** ●mix to create something different: **synthesize** ●mix socially with: **fraternize, hobnob** ●that cannot be mixed: **immiscible**

mixture ●confused mixture: **farrago** ●composed of mixed parts: **heterogeneous, hybrid** ●harmonious mixture: **integration** ●incongruous mixture: **hybrid, motley** ●metal mixed with some other element: **alloy** ●mixture of particles in a fluid: **suspension** ●mercury mixture used in dental fillings: **amalgam**

mob ●mob rule: **mobocracy, ochlocracy** ●execution by a mob: **lynching**

mockery ●public mockery: **jeer, jibe, lampoon, pasquinade, satire, scoffing, skit** ●mockingly ironic: **sarcastic** ●grimly mocking: **sardonic** ●drily (self-)mocking: **wry**

●mocking misrepresentation: **parody, travesty** ●mocking remark: **taunt** ●with hidden mockery: **snide**

model ●string-controlled model of a person or animal: **puppet** ●modelled scene with a painted backdrop: **diorama** ●lightweight wood used in model-making: **balsa** ●female model appearing on magazine covers: **cover girl** ●raised path used by models in a fashion show: **catwalk**

modification ●modification to a proposal at a public meeting: **amendment** ●modification to parliamentary bill or judicial verdict: **rider** ●modification to suit particular requirements: **customization**

moisture ●*combining form*: **hygro-** ●full of moisture: **saturated** ●void of moisture: **dehydrated, desiccated** ●absorbing moisture from the air: **hygroscopic** ●preserving moisture: **humectant** ●denoting an atmosphere with much moisture: **humid** ●device achieving this: **humidifier** ●devices measuring this: **humidistat, hygrometer, hygroscope**

molecule ●molecule that is the mirror image of another: **enantiomer** ●molecule that can be bonded to other identical molecules to form a polymer: **monomer** ●substance composed of bonded similar molecular groups: **polymer**

mollusc ●study of molluscs: **malacology** ●study of mollusc shells: **conchology**

moment ●at the right moment: **pat** ●for the moment: **ad hoc, ad interim, pro tempore**

momentum ●tiny discrete amount of momentum: **quantum**

Monaco ●*adjective*: **Monégasque**

monastery ●*adjective*: **claustral** ●small monastery: **priory** ●monastery room for conversation: **parlour** ●monastery dining hall: **refectory** ●covered walk in a monastery: **clois-**

ter ●covered passageway: **slype** ●head of a monastery: **abbot** ●head of a small monastery: **prior** ●monastery's governing body: **chapter** ●meeting place for this: **chapter house** ●denoting a monastic chapter: **capitular**

money ●*adjectives*: **pecuniary, monetary, numismatic** ●money held: **capital, finances, reserves** ●money available for investment: **capital** ●capital used in day-to-day transactions: **working capital** ●money in circulation: **money supply** ●money in coin: **specie** ●money in coin or notes: **cash** ●British money: **sterling** ●pooled fund of money: **kitty** ●instalment of money: **tranche** ●amount of money: **sum** ●very small sum of money: **pittance** ●small sum of money for minor expenses: **petty cash, pin money** ●small sum of money given in reward for a service: **tip** ●small sum of money given regularly to a child: **pocket money** ●sum of money devoted to a special purpose: **appropriation** ●money accumulated for the eventual replacement of a wasting asset: **sinking fund** ●money held in trust: **escrow** ●money paid for work done: **remuneration** ●money paid back: **rebate, refund, reimbursement** ●money paid to those one has wronged: **compensation, reparation** ●money regained: **clawback** ●money sent: **remittance** ●money placed out in hope of profit: **investment** ●money made available by a bank: **credit** ●money put into a bank account: **deposit** ●money taken out from a bank account: **withdrawal** ●direct payment of money from one bank account to another: **credit transfer** ●money transferred electronically: **digital cash** ●system for this: **giro** ●money that must be accepted as payment: **legal tender** ●money frequently reinvested: **hot money** ●money gained dishonourably: **dirty**

money, lucre ●money for speculative investment: **risk capital, venture capital** ●denoting money generating no interest: **idle** ●money moved abroad as a precaution: **flight capital** ●public availability of money: **circulation** ●money received: **income** ●money received from a transaction: **proceeds** ●money paid out: **disbursement, expenditure, outlay** ●money given away: **largesse** ●sum of money to be paid annually: **annuity** ●money for living expenses: **keep** ●money paid for professional services: **fee** ●money paid to service a debt: **interest** ●money paid on public transport: **fare** ●money supplied at the start of business: **float** ●money paid to the landlord by an incoming tenant: **key money** ●money paid to secure the release of a prisoner awaiting trial: **bail, recognizance** ●pay this money for another: **stand bail** ●money paid as compensation: **damages** ●money paid to ensure secrecy: **hush money** ●money paid as a political bribe: **slush money** ●money paid to criminals to secure their goodwill: **protection money** ●money paid to assuage one's conscience: **conscience money** ●money paid to cover possible damage: **deposit, caution money** ●money paid in by an election candidate: **deposit** ●money saved for the future: **nest egg** ●financial trickery: **chicanery** ●money gained dishonourably: **dirty money** ●obtain money by deception: **defraud** ●misuse of money entrusted to one: **embezzlement, defalcation, peculation** ●Middle Eastern term for money given as a bribe or tip: **baksheesh** ●money voted annually by parliament to the royal family: **Civil List** ●money paid as consolation for an early termination of contract: **golden handshake, golden parachute** ●extra money paid to employees working where living costs are high: **weighting** ●money paid as a recompense: **compensation** ●money paid as a recompense in certain societies by a killer to his victim's relatives: **blood money** ●money paid to release a captive: **ransom** ●accept money to drop a legal action: **compound** ●money lent for a short period: **bridging loan** ●money lent but repayable on demand: **call money** ●money raised for gradual repayment of a debt: **sinking fund** ●limit on spending or borrowing: **cap** ●grant of money from central to local government: **grant aid** ●this without detailed directions as to its use: **block grant** ●money given to help finance some worthwhile activity: **subsidy** ●plan of anticipated income and expenditure: **budget** ●person managing a school's or college's finances: **bursar** ●person handling money in a shop or bank: **cashier** ●machine dispensing money: **cashpoint** ●provide money to meet expenses: **defray** ●supply money: **finance, fund** ●sum of money given to charity: **donation** ●sum of money paid regularly to someone to cover his expenses: **allowance** ●state money paid to parents: **child benefit** ●state agency organizing child maintenance payments: **Child Support Agency** ●money for running a household: **housekeeping** ●deduct money from wages etc.: **dock** ●grant financing university study: **bursary** ●intended to make money: **commercial** ●greed for money: **avarice, cupidity** ●interested only in money: **mercenary** ●careful with money: **frugal, miserly, niggardly, parsimonious, thrifty** ●having sufficient money: **comfortable, solvent** ●short of money: **hard up, embarrassed, impecunious** ●dispose of money so as to conceal its illegal origins: **launder** ●direct exchange of goods or services without the use of money: **barter** ●money entering and

leaving a business: **cash flow** ●state restrictions on moving money abroad: **exchange control** ●undertaking to pay regular sums of money: **deed of covenant** ●seizure of a debtor's money or wages: **garnishment** ●time of financial prosperity: **boom** ●time of financial depression: **bust** ●money-pouch on a belt: **bumbag** ●face value of a coin or note: **denomination** ●money whose face value has no relationship to that of the material of which it is made: **token money** ●deprive of monetary status: **demonetize** ●official monetary unit of the European Union: **ecu** ●metal or plastic disc used instead of money: **token** ●money affairs: **finances** ●person in charge of much money: **financier** ●influential financier: **gnome** ●study of the getting and spending of money: **economics**

Mongolian ●Mongolian nomad's tent: **yurt**

monitor ●establishment monitoring satellite movements: **tracking station** ●group monitoring monopoly organizations: **watchdog**

monk ●*adjective*: **monastic** ●beginner monk: **novice, oblate, postulant** ●take monastic vows: **be professed** ●monk devoting his life to prayer: **contemplative** ●monk of an unenclosed order: **friar** ●monk mostly concerned with manual work: **lay brother** ●monk's hood: **cowl** ●monk's short cloak: **scapular** ●monk's robe: **habit** ●monk's room: **cell** ●denoting a monk wearing no shoes: **discalced** ●shaven part of a monk's head: **tonsure** ●community of monks: **monastery** ●society of monks under a particular rule: **order** ●chief of certain religious orders: **general** ●belonging to a monastic order: **regular**

monkey ●*adjective*: **simian**

monster •*combining form*: terato- •bearlike creature said to live in the Himalayas: **Abominable snowman, yeti** •being from another world: **alien** •study of abnormal forms and growths: **teratology**

monument •monument to person(s) buried elsewhere: **cenotaph**

monumental brass •alloy of which these are made: **latten** •paper tracing of a brass: **brass rubbing, rubbing** •substance used for this: **heelball**

moon •*combining forms*: lun-, selen- •*adjective*: **lunar** •moon's sickle shape: **crescent** •moon first appearing thus: **new moon** •stage in the moon's appearance and disappearance: **phase, quarter** •denoting a moon increasing in apparent size: **waxing** •denoting a moon decreasing in apparent size: **waning** •autumn full moon: **harvest moon** •lunar plain: **mare** •mapping of the moon: **selenography** •study of the moon: **selenology** •within the moon's orbit: **sublunar** •between the moon and the earth: **cislunar** •beyond the moon, or of space travel towards it: **translunar** •circle of light seen round the moon when rain is expected: **aureole, corona** •apparent circle of light round the moon caused by atmospheric ice crystals: **halo** •bright spot appearing beside the moon: **paraselene** •glow on darkened parts of the moon from sunlight reflected from the earth: **earthlight, earthshine** •tremor on the moon's surface: **moonquake** •small spacecraft for moon landings: **lunar module** •vehicle for travel on the moon: **moon buggy, lunar roving vehicle** •moonlike landscape: **moonscape**

moor •high moorland in north England: **fell, wold** •soft place on a moor: **hag**

morale •tactics designed to weaken an opponent's morale: **gamesmanship, psychological warfare**

morals •denoting a person with strict moral standards: **puritanical, strait-laced** •complacent in one's own moral superiority: **sanctimonious, self-righteous** •doubt as to an action's morality: **scruple** •section of society of questionable morality: **demi-monde** •person with no morals: **libertine** •rejection of moral rules: **immoralism, nihilism**

more than •*combining form*: preter- (*e.g.* preternatural)

Mormon •Mormon place of worship: **tabernacle**

morning •period of morning twilight: **dawn**

mortar •thin mortar: **grout** •mortar filling the joints in brickwork: **pointing**

mortgage •person granting a mortgage: **mortgagee** •person taking out a mortgage: **mortgagor** •mortgagee's repossession of mortgaged property: **foreclosure** •mortgage whose principal is repaid by an insurance policy: **endowment mortgage** •mortgage whose principal and interest are repaid in fixed instalments: **repayment mortgage** •value of a mortgaged property after deduction of charges against it: **equity**

Moscow •*adjective*: **Muscovite**

Moses •*adjective*: **Mosaic**

mosque •mosque tower: **minaret** •mosque's pulpit: **minbar** •niche in a mosque's wall facing Mecca: **mihrab** •direction this should take: **kiblah** •mosque official calling the faithful to prayer: **muezzin**

mosquito •type of mosquito that carries malaria: **anopheles**

moss •*combining form*: bryo- •study of mosses: **bryology**

moth ●moth pupa: **chrysalis** ●pungent pellet deterring moths: **mothball** ●moth expert: lepidopterist

mother ●*combining form*: matri- ●*adjective*: **maternal** ●killing one's mother: **matricide**

motion ●*adjective*: **kinetic** ●energy of motion: **impetus** ● impetus gained by a moving object: **momentum** ●tendency to produce rotatory motion: **moment** ●deprive of the power of motion: **paralyse**

motor ●boat's motor housed inside the hull: **inboard** ●boat's motor housed outside the hull: **outboard** ● motor powered by explosive combustion of fuel: **internal combustion engine** ●motor powered by ignition of fuel in hot compressed air: **compression-ignition engine, diesel engine** ●adjust a motor for efficient running: **tune** ●denoting an motor running while out of gear: **idling** ●motor's starting mechanism: **ignition** ●begin to operate a motor: **cut in** ●stop operating a motor suddenly: **cut out** ●rotating coil in an electric motor: **armature** ●device controlling the flow of fuel to a motor: **throttle** ●air valve on a petrol engine carburettor: **choke** ●proportion of fuel to air: **mixture** ●device increasing the mixture pressure: **supercharger** ●supercharger driven by exhaust gases: **turbocharger** ●device atomizing fuel: **injector** ●petrol engine rattle or explosions due to faulty combustion: **knocking, pinking, backfiring** ● correct sequence of events in the cylinder of an internal combustion engine: **timing**

motorcycle ●light motorcycle: **moped, motor scooter, scooter** ●light motorcycle for rough terrain: **trail bike** ●racing motorcycle with four large tyres: **quad bike** ●support for a motorcycle wheel: **fork** ●motorcycle handgrip that is twisted to open the throttle: **twist-grip** ●motorcycle

passenger seat: **pillion** ●small passenger vehicle attached to a motorcycle's side: **sidecar** ●motorcycle without a sidecar: **solo** ●cinder track for motorcycle races: **dirt track** ●motorcycle cross-country race: **motocross**

motorcyclist ●motorcyclist delivering urgent documents: **dispatch rider** ●motorcyclist's protective helmet: **crash helmet** ●motorcyclist's trick of driving with the front wheel off the ground: **wheelie**

motor fuel ●denoting fuel burning with a high proportion of air: **lean**

motorist ●selfish motorist: **road hog** ●motorist who drives excessively fast: **speed merchant** ●slow-driving motorist in search of prostitutes: **kerb-crawler** ●violence between motorists: **road rage** ●motorist's short coat: **car coat**

motor race ●motor race up a steep hill: **hill climb** ●motor racing over rough terrain: **autocross, rallycross** ●long-distance motor race over rough terrain: **enduro** ●long-distance motor race over public roads and/or rough terrain: **rally** ●motor racing round a banked oval track: **Indy** ●short motor race testing acceleration: **drag race** ●car designed for this: **dragster** ●classification for racing cars: **formula** ●approve a car's formula assignment: **homologate** ●basic racing car: **kart** ●starting area: **grid** ●sharp double bend in motor race track: **chicane** ●trackside area for repairs and refuelling: **pits** ●controlled skid: **drift** ●flag signalling the end of a motor race: **chequered flag**

motor vehicle ●small motor vehicle with lifting prongs: **forklift truck** ●large heavy vehicle: **juggernaut** ●large vehicle carrying cars etc.: **transporter** ●large covered lorry: **pantechnicon** ●horse transporter:

horsebox ● wide wheeled vehicle for travelling over sand: **beach buggy, dune buggy** ● small vehicle for golfers and their equipment: **golf cart** ● motor vehicle for travelling over snow: **snowmobile** ● motor vehicle clearing roads of snow: **snowplough** ● motor vehicle with living accommodation: **camper, camper van, caravanette** ● motor vehicle carrying a coffin: **hearse** ● sturdy vehicle for rough terrain: **jeep™, four-track, off-road vehicle** ● small open single-seater vehicle for rough terrain: **all-terrain vehicle, all-roader** ● strong agricutural motor with large rear wheels: **tractor** ● armour-plated military or police vehicle: **armour, armoured car, armoured personnel carrier** ● tracked armoured fighting vehicle: **tank** ● fire service vehicle: **fire engine, tender** ● motor vehicle pulling or carrying vehicles away for repair: **breakdown lorry, recovery vehicle** ● motor vehicle's base frame: **chassis** ● metal framework of a vehicle body: **shell** ● bodywork constructed over the shell: **coachwork** ● motor vehicle's left side: **nearside** ● motor vehicle's right side: **offside** ● motor vehicle modified to give power and speed: **hot rod** ● motor vehicle's acceleration and handling at speed: **performance** ● vehicle travelling on a cushion of air: **hovercraft** ● denoting a motor vehicle with special bodywork: **coach-built** ● motor vehicle's upholstery etc.: **trim** ● motor vehicle body with integral chassis: **monocoque** ● thin metal sheet for motor vehicle bodies: **panel** ● person shaping this: **panel beater** ● group of motor vehicles travelling together: **convoy** ● motor vehicle's front window: **windscreen** ● hinged eye-screen: **sun visor** ● motor vehicle's instrument panel: **dashboard, fascia** ● instrument indicating speed of travel: **speedometer** ● instrument

indicating engine speed: **tachometer** ● dashboard storage recess: **glovebox, glove compartment** ● shaft connecting a steering wheel to its mechanism: **steering column** ● rod turning the front wheels: **track rod** ● steering-column lever with electrical switches: **stalk** ● mechanism conveying engine-power to the axle: **transmission** ● mechanism giving increased power to steering and brakes: **servo, servo-mechanism** ● denoting such a system: **power-assisted** ● semi-automatic system of vehicle control: **steer-by-wire** ● denoting a transmission system changing gears automatically: **automatic** ● denoting a transmission system controlled by the gear-shift: **manual** ● motor vehicle gear system giving smooth changes: **synchromesh** ● move with gears disengaged: **coast** ● engine cover: **bonnet, hood** ● motor vehicle's base frame: **chassis** ● motor vehicle's streamlining structure: **fairing** ● flattened projection improving stability: **fin** ● protective bar across the front or back of a motor vehicle: **bumper** ● strong metal grille fitted to the front of a motor vehicle: **bull bar** ● metal framework protecting an overturning vehicle: **roll bars, roll cage, safety cage** ● raised strip on a vehicle's sides: **rubbing strip** ● subsidiary side window: **quarter-light** ● flashing lights on a motor vehicle's sides: **hazard lights, indicators** ● small lights indicating a vehicle's position: **sidelights** ● part of a vehicle body between windscreen and bonnet: **scuttle** ● hinged rear door or flap: **tailgate** ● part of a motor vehicle designed to absorb impact: **crumple zone, crush zone** ● vehicle's ability to withstand collision: **crashworthiness** ● uncontrolled sideways movement of a vehicle's rear: **fishtail** ● vehicle's tendency to turn too sharply: **oversteer** ● motor vehicle's grip on the road:

traction ●motor locking system operating all locks: **central locking** ●device maintaining a chosen speed: **cruise control** ●graduated rod for measuring engine oil levels: **dipstick** ●device clearing window condensation: **demister** ●device passing current to each plug in turn: **distributor** ●purifier of vehicle exhaust gases: **catalytic converter** ●road for motor vehicles: **carriageway** ●start a vehicle engine bypassing the starter: **hot-wire** ●trip in a stolen vehicle: **joyride** ●avoid high speeds in a new vehicle: **run in** ●lower the headlights: **dim, dip** ●make of motor vehicle: **marque** ●customs permit for the import of a motor vehicle: **carnet** ●denoting a motor vehicle insurance covering most risks: **comprehensive** ●place to which illegally parked motor vehicles are removed: **pound** ●vehicle's unladen weight: **dead load, tare weight** ●weight of a vehicle's burden: **live load** ●periodic inspection and maintenance of a machine: **service** ●taking away a vehicle for repairs: **recovery** ●device raising a vehicle's axle: **jack** ●sunken area for work on a vehicle's underside: **pit** ●equip troops with motor vehicles: **motorize** ●nausea caused by vehicle travel: **car sickness, motion sickness** ●document showing a vehicle's ownership: **registration document, log book**

motor vehicle repairs ●establishment undertaking these: **garage, service station** ●establishment specializing in bodywork: **body shop**

moulding ●*combining form*: -plasty (*e.g.* keratoplasty) ●easily moulded: **plastic** ●cut out with a mould: **stamp**

mountain ●*combining form*: oro- ●*adjective*: **montane** ●side of a mountain: **face** ●top of a mountain: **peak, summit** ●ridge between two peaks: **col, saddle** ●subsidiary

mountain ridge: **spur** ●route over a mountain: **pass, gap** ●series of mountains: **range** ●compact mountain group: **massif** ●system of parallel mountain ranges: **cordillera** ●geological creation of mountain ranges: **orogeny** ●mapping of mountains: **orography, orology** ●mass of snow, ice, and rocks moving down a mountain: **avalanche, glacier** ●slippage of part of a mountain surface: **landslide** ●small mountain lake: **tarn** ●steep mountain gulley: **couloir**

mouse ●*adjective*: murine

mouth ●*combining forms*: or-, stomato- ●*adjectives*: oral, buccal ●top of the mouth: **roof, palate** ●congenital split in this: **cleft palate** ●rear part of the palate: **soft palate** ●fleshy extension at the back of the mouth: **uvula** ●cartilaginous flap at the back of the mouth: **epiglottis** ●mass of tissue at the back of the mouth: **tonsil** ●space between the vocal cords: **glottis** ●inflamed mouth blister: **cold sore** ●ulcer on the inside of the mouth: **enanthema** ●study of the mouth and its diseases: **stomatology** ●liquid present naturally in the mouth: **saliva** ●saliva running from the mouth: **slaver, slobber** ●liquid to swill round the mouth and throat: **gargle, mouthwash** ●bring swallowed food back into the mouth: **regurgitate** ●brass or wind player's correct mouth shape: **embouchure**

movement ●*adjective*: kinetic ●hasty movement: **scurry, scuttle** ●impatient movement: **fidget** ●skilful or crafty movement: **manoeuvre** ●slow piecemeal movement: **straggling** ●smooth silent movement: **glide** ●sudden sharp movement: **lurch** ●sudden convulsive movement: **spasm** ●incapable of movement: **inert** ●move round the edge of: **skirt** ●move about stealthily: **prowl, skulk, slink, sneak** ●move slowly and awkwardly: **shamble** ●move in a lazy, drooping way: **slouch** ●make incapable of movement: **immobilize, paralyse** ●system of rhythmical movements to music: **eurhythmics**

much ●*combining forms*: **multi-** (*e.g.* multistorey), **poly-** (*e.g.* polyhedron)

mucus ●*combining form*: **myxo-** (*e.g.* myxomatosis) ●*adjectives*: **mucoid, mucous** ●mucus in the nose and throat: **catarrh** ●mucus-secreting tissue: **mucous membrane**

mud ●lie about in mud or water: **wallow**

multiple ●*combining form*: **-fold** (*e.g.* fivefold)

municipality ●governing body of a city or borough: **corporation, council** ●titular head of a municipality: **mayor**

muscle ●*combining form*: **my-** ●muscular system: **musculature** ●ring of muscle: **sphincter** ●muscle bending a limb: **flexor** ●muscle straightening a limb: **extensor** ●muscle of the upper arm: **biceps** ●muscle holding the vocal cords: **larynx** ●muscular movement of the alimentary canal: **peristalsis** ●denoting muscles not under conscious control: **involuntary** ●denoting muscles under conscious control: **voluntary** ●cord connecting a muscle to a bone: **sinew, tendon** ●inability to relax muscle after a vigorous effort: **myotonia** ●muscle pain: **myalgia** ●muscular spasm: **clonus** ●muscular spasm and rigidity caused by contaminated wounds: **tetanus** ●painful contraction of a muscle: **cramp** ●painful muscular inflammation: **rheumatism** ●muscular weakness: **paresis** ●hereditary progressive wasting of the muscles: **muscular dystrophy** ●impaired muscular coordination due to brain damage: **cerebral palsy** ●medical treatment of bone and muscle deformities: **orthopaedics** ●therapeutic manipulation

of bones and muscles: **osteopathy** ●exercises in which the muscles work against each other: **isometrics** ●muscle development through strenuous exercise: **bodybuilding** ●muscle-building drug used by sportsmen: **anabolic steroid** ●muscle stimulation by electric current: **electrotherapy** ●record of a muscle's electrical activity: **electromyogram** ●study of muscles: **myology**

Muse ●Muse of acting, music, and dance: **Polyhymnia** ●Myse of astronomy: **Urania** ●Muse of comedy: **Thalia** ●Muse of epic poetry: **Calliope** ●Muse of the flute: **Euterpe** ●Muse of history: **Clio** ●Muse of lyric poetry and hymns: **Erato** ●Muse of lyric poetry and dance: **Terpsichore** ●Muse of tragedy: **Melpomene**

museum ●preservation of museum objects: **conservation** ●museum's custodian: **curator** ●remove an item from a museum collection: **deaccession** ●science of museum management: **museology, museography**

mushroom ●mushroom-shaped: **fungiform** ●mushroom's flat top: **pileus**

music ●undemanding music: **easy listening** ●music derived from traditional popular culture: **folk music** ●music intended to evoke an emotion, tell a story, etc.: **programme music** ●music composed with no representational purpose: **absolute music** ●music constructed from pre-recorded sounds: **musique concrète** ●background music to a film or play: **incidental music, score** ●recorded background music for public places: **muzak™** ●music for a funeral procession: **dead march** ●secular part-song: **madrigal** ●light-hearted part-song: **glee** ●continuous series of musical items: **medley, sequence** ●published musical piece or set of pieces: **opus** (*pl.* opuses *or* opera)

● denoting music that is bland and undemanding: **middle-of-the-road** ● denoting art music composed on traditional lines: **classical** ● denoting art music composed between 1600 and 1750: **baroque** ● denoting art music composed between 1750 and 1800: **classical** ● denoting music only using notes from the scale in which it is written: **diatonic** ● denoting nondiatonic music: **chromatic** ● denoting a five-note scale: **pentatonic** ● denoting music having notes of fixed durations: **mensural** ● denoting music having notes of unfixed durations: **free, rhapsodic** ● denoting music in which all parts share the same rhythm: **homophonic** ● denoting music whose parts have their own rhythms and melodic content: **polyphonic** ● denoting music with a single line performed by all: **monodic, unison** ● denoting music with repeated rhythm but varied pitch: **isorhythmic** ● denoting music using several rhythms simultaneously: **polyrhythmic** ● denoting music using transformations of a fixed series of notes: **serial, twelve-note, twelve-tone** ● such a series of notes: **tone row** ● relating to a twelve-tone musical scale: **chromatic** ● relating to an eight-tone musical scale: **diatonic** ● music for a few musicians: **chamber music** ● music for a single musician: **solo** ● music for two musicians: **duet, duo** ● music for three musicians: **trio** ● music for four musicians: **quartet** ● music for five musicians: **quintet** ● music for six musicians: **sextet** ● music for seven musicians: **septet** ● music for eight musicians: **octet** ● short piece for brass instruments: **fanfare, flourish** ● rescore a musical piece for different instruments or voices: **transcribe** ● denoting music designed to have a random element in its performance: **aleatoric, aleatory** ● medieval Latin church music: **Gregorian chant, plainsong** ● kind of medieval music with parallel parts: **conductus, organum** ● musical piece where all parts sequentially perform the same notes: **canon, round** ● musical piece whose subject appears in all parts: **fugue** ● music with several melodies set together: **counterpoint** ● musical piece in free style: **fantasia** ● musical piece designed to strengthen the player's technique: **study** ● set of musical pieces: **suite, partita** ● pitch range of a musical composition: **tessitura** ● music made up as it is performed: **extemporization** ● section of a musical piece where the subjects first appear: **exposition** ● group of notes given prominence in a musical piece: **theme** ● modified version of a theme: **variation** ● first theme in a musical piece: **first subject** ● second theme in a musical piece: **countersubject** ● section of a musical piece where the subjects are elaborated: **development** ● final section of a piece of music: **coda** ● recurrent musical theme: **figure, leitmotif** ● repeated musical passage: **reprise** ● composer's personal musical style: **idiom** ● brief melodic or rhythmic formula: **figure** ● repetition of this: **imitation, ostinato** ● group of notes sung to one syllable: **melisma** ● counterpoint sung above a melody: **descant** ● soloist's flourish at the end of a musical piece: **cadenza** ● elaborate vocal ornamentation: **coloratura** ● melodic embellishment: **fioritura** (*pl.* fioriture), **grace note** ● slide from one note to another: **portamento** ● fast alternation between adjacent notes: **trill** ● music with strings of fast notes: **passagework** ● continuous low note: **drone, pedal note, pedal point** ● instrumental piece over a repeated bass: **chaconne, ground, passacaglia** ● this repeated bass line: **ground bass** ● interval of silence: **rest** ● declamatory vocal music reflecting the rhythm and intonation of speech: **recitative** ●denoting choral music designed for unaccompanied performance: **a cappella, alla cappella** ●popular close-harmony music for male voices: **barbershop** ●musical lament: **dirge** ●close of a musical phrase: **cadence** ●point in a musical piece where a performer must start: **entry** ●orchestral piece with extended solo work for one or more instruments: **concerto** ●denoting an orchestral piece giving prominence to certain instruments: **concertante** ●the instruments so featured: **concertino** ●section of a musical piece: **movement** ●suite of light music: **divertimento** ●musical piece's range of loudness: **dynamic range, dynamics** ●conveyance of feeling in music: **expression** ●call for a musical piece to be performed again: **encore** ●musical piece so performed: **encore** ●item in a musical performance: **number** ●music performed between the acts of a performance: **entr'acte** ●public musical performance by one or a few musicians: **recital** ●public musical performance by a number of musicians: **concert** ●unstaged performance of theatre music: **concert performance** ●under public performance conditions: **in concert** ●introductory piece of music: **overture, prelude** ●piece of music played between other events: **interlude, intermezzo** ●closing musical piece: **postlude** ●German hymn or its music: **chorale** ●German solo song: **lied** (*pl.* lieder) ●short musical piece for voices and instruments: **cantata** ●substantial unstaged narrative piece for singers and orchestra: **oratorio** ●oratorio narrating Christ's suffering and death: **Passion** ●substantial staged narrative piece for singers and orchestra: **opera** ●tone heard above a note's fundamental: **overtone** ●set of these:

harmonic series ●sign of musical pitch: **clef** ●musical piece's basic key: **home key** ●perform or score in a different key: **transpose** ●key structure of a musical piece: **tonality** ●movement from one key to another: **modulation** ●denoting music written in no key or mode: **atonal** ●denoting music using several keys simultaneously: **polytonal** ●group of notes sounded together: **chord** ●stable and pleasing chord: **concord, consonance** ●unstable and harsh chord: **discord, dissonance** ●movement from one chord to another: **progression** ●movement from discord to concord: **resolution** ●printed music: **sheet music** ●music college: **conservatoire** ●academic study of music: **musicology** ●study of non-Western music: **ethnomusicology** ●system of rhythmical movements to music: **eurhythmics** ▸*see also* **note, tune**

musical instrument ●musical instrument using a vibrating column of air: **aerophone, wind instrument** ●vibrating mouthpiece element in certain aerophones: **reed** ●generic name for metal aerophones: **brass** ●generic name for wooden aerophones: **woodwind** ●musical instrument using a vibrating string: **cordophone, string instrument** ●single-stringed musical instrument: **monochord** ●musical instrument using pitched wooden blocks: **xylophone** ●deep-toned xylophone: **marimba** ●musical instrument using pitched metal bars: **glockenspiel** ●keyboard instrument: **clavier** ●keyboard with hammers striking metal plates: **celesta, celeste** ●small keyboard instrument with a soft tone: **clavichord** ●keyboard with plucked strings: **harpsichord** ●small harpsichord with strings set obliquely to the keyboard: **spinet** ●electronic instrument able to produce many different types of pitched sound: **synthesizer** •synthesizer imposing speech patterns onto musical sounds: **vocoder** •electronic keyboard giving one note at variable pitch: **ondes martenot** •electronic instrument whose pitch is controlled by the approach and withdrawal of the performer's hand: **theremin** •denoting a musical instrument playable in any key: **chromatic** •notes a particular musical instrument can play: **compass, range** •adjust a musical instrument to the desired pitch: **tune** •current standard tuning for musical instruments: **concert pitch** •regulate the tone of a musical instrument: **voice** •musical instrument whose part is written at a different pitch from that at which it sounds: **transposing instrument** •kind of harp played by the wind: **aeolian harp** •Irish and Scottish traditional harp: **clarsach** •musical instrument stretched and squeezed between the hands: **accordion, concertina** •stringed instrument with drones and melody keys: **hurdy-gurdy** •stringed instrument laid flat and plucked: **zither** •small flute used in military bands: **fife** •small orchestral flute: **piccolo** •graduated series of short pipes: **pan pipes, syrinx** •small rectangular multi-reed wind instrument: **harmonica, mouth organ** •small egg-shaped ceramic wind instrument: **ocarina** •denoting a brass instrument having only the notes of the harmonic series: **natural** •device extending a brass instrument's range of pitch: **piston, valve** •instruments required for a piece: **instrumentation** •early form of oboe: **shawm** •early form of trombone: **sackbut** •early form of violin: **viol** •early form of cello: **viola da gamba** •early form of double bass: **violone** •medieval bowed instrument with three strings: **rebec** •early form of piano: **forte-piano** •early form of guitar: **gittern**

•guitar with a round open-backed soundbox: **banjo** •guitar with a pear-shaped soundbox: **lute** •small Hawaiian guitar: **ukulele** •Russian guitar with a triangular soundbox: **balalaika** •lute-like instrument with paired strings: **mandolin** •Greek mandolin: **bouzouki** •location of the stopping hand on a stringed intrument: **position** •maker of stringed instruments: **luthier, lutist** •medieval woodwind instrument with a curved end: **krummhorn** •wooden support for the strings of a violin-family instrument: **bridge** •tuning pin for a violin-family instrument: **peg** •housing for this: **pegbox** •ridge at the neck of a stringed instrument: **nut** •natural material for instrument strings: **catgut** •fingerboard ridge: **fret** •denoting a string vibrating over its whole length: **open** •denoting a string vibrating over part of its length: **stopped** •sheet of wood set behind strings to increase the sound produced: **soundboard** •hollow body of a stringed instrument: **sound box** •musical instruments that are struck: **percussion** •pitched percussion orchestra of Bali and Java: **gamelan** •mouth-held resonating metal strip: **Jew's harp** •complete pitch-range of a musical instrument: **gamut** •finger technique in playing an instrument: **fingering** •device altering tone and volume: **mute** •instrumental part essential to the piece performed: **obbligato** ▸*see also* **drum, guitar, lute, percussion**

musical interval •denoting a repeated musical interval between two parts: **consecutive**

musical notation •written out notation of a musical piece: **score** •set of five parallel lines upon which music is written: **stave, staff** •symbol at the start of each stave indicating the pitch of the notes written on it: **clef** •symbol indicating the pitch and duration of a musical sound: **note** ● sign indicating silence of a fixed duration: **rest** ● score having a separate stave for each part: **full score** ● score having the parts combined onto a few staves: **short score** ● score showing full voice parts and a reduced accompaniment: **vocal score** ● numbers on the stave indicating rhythm: **time signature** ● sign directing the following note to be sounded half a tone higher than usual: **sharp** ● sign directing the following note to be sounded half a tone lower than usual: **flat** ● flats or sharps indicating the key: **key signature** ● sign indicating a musical embellishment: **ornament** ● unmarked accidentals left to the performer: **musica ficta** ● short line above or below the stave: **leger line** ● notation system indicating the fingering only: **tablature**

musician ● distinguished musician: **maestro, virtuoso** ● freelance musician doing casual work: **sessions man** ● street musician: **busker** ● street musician playing a barrel organ: **organ-grinder** ● person singing solo parts of the liturgy: **cantor, precentor** ● church musicians employed by a monarch: **chapel royal** ● director of a group of musicians: **conductor** ● short stick used by a conductor: **baton** ● gallery for musicians: **loft** ● group of musicians performing together: **ensemble** ● small ensemble of musicians: **consort** ● accompanying group in baroque music: **continuo** ● ensemble of three musicians: **trio** ● ensemble of four musicians: **quartet** ● ensemble of five musicians: **quintet** ● ensemble of six musicians: **sextet** ● ensemble of seven musicians: **septet** ● ensemble of eight musicians: **octet** ● brass or wind player's correct mouth shape: **embouchure**

Muslim ● Muslim name for God: **Allah** ● Muslim religion: **Islam** ● emblem of this: **the Crescent** ● believers in Islam: **the faithful** ● the whole Muslim community, united by Islam: **umma** ● principal branches of Islam: **Shia, Sunni** ● Muslim place of worship: **mosque** ● mosque prayer-leader: **imam** ● Muslim who calls the faithful to prayer: **muezzin** ● Muslim daily prayers: **salat** ● Muslim profession of faith: **shahada** ● Muslim religious law expert: **mufti, mullah** ● Islamic college: **madrasa** ● Muslim student of religious law and theology: **softa** ● group of Islamic scholars: **ulema** ● Islamic law code: **sharia** ● traditional portion of Islamic law: **Sunna** ● ruling on Islamic law: **fatwa** ● Muslim religious festival: **Eid** ● Muslim scriptures: **Koran** ● section of the Koran: **sura** ● Muslim knowing the Koran by heart: **hafiz** ● sayings of Muhammad not found in the Koran: **Hadith, tradition** ● Muslim mystic: **dervish, Sufi** ● Sufi's rhythmic repeated prayer: **dhikr** ● Muslim ascetic: **fakir** ● Muslim hermit in North Africa: **marabout** ● tomb of a Muslim holy man: **dargah** ● expected Muslim ruler restoring religion and justice: **Mahdi** ● Muslim religious leader: **ayatollah, imam, mullah, sharif** ● Muslim month-long fast: **Ramadan** ● Muslim feast at the end of Ramadan: **Eid ul-Fitr, Lesser Bairam** ● Muslim feast at the year's end: **Greater Bairam** ● denoting meat prepared according to Muslim food regulations: **halal** ● Muslim term for forbidden foods: **haram** ● Muslim term for a non-Muslim: **kafir** ● Muslim pilgrimage to Mecca: **haj** ● Muslim who has completed this: **haji** ● feast at the culmination of this: **Eid ul-Adha** ● Muslim term for Jews and Christians: **People of the Book** ● Muslim term for a Christian: **Nazarine** ● Muslim gesture of greeting: **salaam** ● Muslim ruler: **hakim, sharif** ● supreme Muslim ruler: **caliph, sultan** ● sultan's wife: **sultana** ●Muslim leader: **amir, emir, khan, sheikh** ●descendant of Muhammad: **sharif** ●Muslim judge: **cadi, hakim** ●Muslim official: **nabob** ●Muslim princess or married woman: **begum** ●Muslim traditional doctor: **hakim** ●Muslim woman's veil: **yashmak** ●Muslim woman's overgarment: **burka, chador** ●Muslim man's headdress: **turban** ●Muslim man's tasselled felt hat: **fez, tarboosh** ●Muslim man's long coat: **jibba** ●Muslim seclusion of women: **purdah** ●women's quarters in a Muslim house: **harem, serai** ●young woman in Muslim paradise: **houri** ●Muslim holy war: **jihad** ●Islamic guerilla: **mujahedin** ●Islamic fundamentalists involved in terrorism: **Muslim Brotherhood** ●Muslim chronological era: **Hegira** ▸*see also* **mosque**

mussels ●mussels served in their shells with a white wine sauce: **moules marinière**

mustard ●mild dark mustard: **French mustard** ●pale strong mustard: **English mustard**

mutton ●leg of mutton: **gigot** ●cheap end of this: **scrag-end** ●mutton kebab: **shashlik** ●large piece of spiced mutton cooked on a spit: **doner kebab**

Mycenaean ●beehive-shaped Mycenaean tomb: **tholos** ●Mycenaean scripts: **Linear A, Linear B**

mysticism ●secret mystical knowledge: **gnosis** ●teacher of mysticism: **mystagogue**

myth ●*combining form*: **mytho-** ●corpus of myths: **mythology, mythos** (*pl.* mythoi), **mythus** (*pl.* mythi) ●first mortal woman in Greek mythology: **Pandora** ●mythical cupbearer of Zeus: **Ganymede** ●mythical one-eyed giant: **Cyclops** (*pl.* Cyclops *or* Cyclopses *or* Cyclopes) ●mythical snake-haired woman: **gorgon** ●mythical patron of an art or science: **muse** ●mythical abode of the dead: **Hades** ●mythical river of forgetfulness: **lethe** ●mythical watchdog of Hades: **Cerberus** ●mythical ferryman of the dead: **Charon** ●denoting the mythical underworld: **chthonian, chthonic** ●mythical bird said to burn itself every 500 years and rise again from the ashes: **phoenix** ●mythical bird with a floating nest: **halcyon** ●mythical horse with a single central horn: **unicorn** ●mythical creature said to live in fire: **salamander** ●mythical creature with an eagle's head and lion's body: **griffin** ●mythical creature with a lion's head, goat's body, and snakelike tail: **chimera** ●mythical many-headed snake: **Hydra** ●mythical female sea monster: **Scylla** ●mythical creature, half man and half horse: **centaur** ●mythical creature, half man and half bull: **Minotaur** ●mythical creature, half man and half goat: **satyr** ●mythical creature, half woman and half fish: **mermaid** ●mythical winged creature with a woman's head and lion's body: **sphinx** ●mythical creature with a bird's body and woman's head: **harpy** ●mythical craftsman: **Daedalus** ●mythical giant: **ogre** ●mythical Norwegian sea monster: **kraken** ●cave dweller in Scandinavian mythology: **troll** ●mythical Scandinavian dwarf: **Nibelung** ●palace for dead heroes in Scandinavian mythology: **Valhalla** ●world ash tree in Scandinavian mythology: **Yggdrasil** ●mythical wild man of the forest: **green man** ●mythical small man with pointed ears and cap: **pixie** ●make a myth of: **mythologize** ●study of myths: **mythology**

nail ● *adjective*: **ungual** ● dead skin at the base of a nail: **cuticle** ● piece of torn skin beside a nail: **agnail, hangnail** ● inflammation near a nail: **whitlow** ● small nail holding glass in position: **sprig** ● light thin nail with a small head: **panel pin** ● small broadheaded nail: **tack** ● short broadheaded pin: **drawing pin** ● heavy nail fastening a rail to its sleeper: **spike** ● short metal pin with a beaten-out end: **rivet** ● U-shaped nail pointed at both ends: **staple** ● insert a nail flush with the surface: **countersink** ● secure a nail by driving the point sideways: **clinch**

naked ● *combining form*: **gymno-** (*e.g.* gymnosophist) ● run naked through a public place: **streak**

name ● *combining forms*: **onom-, nomin-** (*e.g.* nominal), **-nym** (*e.g.* pseudonym) ● *adjective*: **onomastic** ● name derived from a forebear: **patronymic** ● having a name: **onymous** ● having no name: **anonymous** ● person having the same name as another: **namesake** ● having two names: **binomial** ● system of names: **nomenclature** ● list of names: **roll** ● shortened form of a name: **diminutive** ● wrong or inappropriate name: **misnomer** ● false name: **pseudonym** ● so-called: **soi-disant** ● warrior's pseudonym: **nom de guerre** ● writer's pseudonym: **nom de plume** ● criminal's false name: **alias** ● denoting a person after whom something is named: **eponymous** ● existing in name only: **nominal, titular** ● study of personal names: **onomastics** ● study of place names: **toponymy**

Naples ● *adjective*: **Neapolitan**

nasty ● *combining form*: **mal-** (*e.g.* malodorous) ● very nasty: **obnoxious** ● dirty and unpleasant: **squalid** ● unpleasant but beneficial: **salutary**

nation ● *combining form*: **ethno-** (*e.g.* ethnocentric) ● *adjective*: **ethnic** ● wealthy capitalist nations: **First World** ● nations of the former Eastern European communist bloc: **Second World** ● developing nations: **Third World** ● the poorest of these: **Fourth World** ● emigrants from a particular nation: **diaspora** ● transcending national boundaries and interests: **supranational**

nationality ● *combining form*: **-ish** (*e.g.* English) ● give nationality to a foreigner: **naturalize**

native ● native inhabitant: **aborigine, autochthon** ● native country: **fatherland, motherland** ● native of the Alaskan islands: **Aleut** ● native American: **American Indian, Amerindian, Red Indian** ● native of the central Andes: **Inca** ● native Australian: **Aboriginal, Aborigine** ● native of northern Canada or Greenland: **Inuit** ● native to a particular place: **indigenous**

native American ● native American tent: **tepee, wigwam** ● native American's light axe: **tomahawk** ● land set aside for native American settlement: **reservation**

nature ● intrinsic nature of something: **essence** ● that cannot be explained by natural laws: **supernatural**

navel ● *combining form*: **omphalo-** (*e.g.* omphaloscopy) ● *adjective*: **umbilical**

navigation ●*adjective*: **nautical** ●navigation based on computation of position from speed and direction of travel: **dead reckoning** ●air navigation from landmarks: **contact flight** ●navigation by the heavenly bodies: **celestial navigation** ●navigation pointer showing magnetic north: **compass** ●repeated radio or radar signal emitted as a navigational aid: **beam** ●navigation system using these: **Loran** ●electronic air navigation system: **tacan** ●position relative to a fixed point: **bearing** ●map for sea or air navigation: **chart** ●floating navigation mark: **buoy** ●instrument for taking altitudes: **sextant** ●regularly used sea or air route: **lane** ●deviation from set course due to wind, current, etc.: **drift**

navy ●flag of the Royal Navy: **white ensign** ●flag of naval auxiliary vessels: **blue ensign** ●ships involved in trade: **merchant navy** ●flag of the merchant navy: **red ensign** ●naval rebellion: **mutiny**

Nazi ●official title: **National Socialist** ●Nazi emblem: **swastika** ●Nazi regional governor: **Gauleiter** ●Nazi marching step: **goose step** ●Nazi militia forming Hitler's bodyguard: **Brownshirts, Storm Troops, Sturmabteilung** ●Nazi secret police: **Gestapo** ●Nazi prison camp: **concentration camp** ●Nazi justification for territorial expansion: **Lebensraum** ●Nazi policy of eastward expansion: **Drang nach Osten** ●unification of Austria and Germany achieved by Nazis: **Anschluss** ●Nazi term for the German nation: **Herrenvolk** ●Nazi extermination of European Jews: **final solution, Holocaust**

near side ●*combining form*: **cis-** (*e.g.* cisalpine)

neck ●*adjective*: **cervical, jugular** ●back of the neck: **nape, scruff**

●stretch out one's neck: **crane** ●moving projection at the front of the neck: **Adam's apple** ●principal artery of the neck: **carotid artery** ●swelling on the neck from thyroid dysfunction: **goitre** ●fold of skin hanging from a bird's neck: **wattle** ●fold of skin hanging from the necks of cattle: **dewlap** ●wide fabric strip worn round the neck: **cravat** ●square of cloth worn round the neck: **neckerchief**

neckerchief ●large and brightly coloured neckerchief, often with white spots: **bandanna**

necklace ●close-fitting necklace or neck band: **choker**

need ●pressing need: **exigence, exigency** ●thing needed: **desideratum** (*pl.* desiderata) ●as needed: **ad hoc** ●ability to produce all one needs: **self-sufficiency, autarky** ●more than needed: **supernumerary**

needlework ●ornamental needlework: **embroidery** ●ornamental needlework making patterns with pieces of coloured cloth: **appliqué** ●blunt thick needle with a large eye: **bodkin**

negation ●denoting a process of enquiry conducted by negation: **apophatic**

negotiation ●negotiation between management and workforce representatives: **collective bargaining** ●negotiation by a mediator travelling between the parties: **shuttle diplomacy** ●act as mediator in negotiations: **conciliate** ●denoting negotiation between two parties: **bilateral** ●denoting negotiation between three or more parties: **multilateral** ●statutory interval for negotiation when strikes are threatened: **cooling-off period** ●area of possible compromise: **middle ground** ●set of proposals that must be accepted or rejected en bloc: **pack-**

age •agreement reached at the end of negotiations: **conclusion**

Neptune •*Greek name*: **Poseidon** •Neptune's three-pronged spear: **trident**

nerve •*combining form*: **neur(o)-** •*adjective*: **neural** •nerve transmitting signals from the eye to the brain: **optic nerve** •nerve transmitting signals from the ear to the brain: **auditory nerve** •nerve cell: **neurone** •nerve cells and fibres: **nervous system** •junction between nerve cells: **synapse** •network of nerves: **plexus** •nerve complex: **ganglion** •nerve complex at the foot of the stomach: **solar plexus** •bundle of nerve fibres enclosed in the spine: **spinal cord** •brain and spinal cord: **central nervous system** •denoting a nerve stimulating a muscle or organ: **motor** •electrical signal along a nerve fibre: **nerve impulse** •military gas disrupting this: **nerve gas** •intense pain along a nerve: **neuralgia** •pain from pressure on the spinal nerve: **sciatica** •disease causing progressive deterioration of brain and spinal nerve cells: **multiple sclerosis** •progressive nerve disease causing shaking, muscular rigidity, and emaciation: **Parkinson's disease** •nerve disease causing jerky movements: **chorea** •nerve disease causing paralysis: **poliomyelitis** •muscular weakness caused by nerve damage or disease: **paresis** •tropical disease attacking the nervous system: **sleeping sickness** •nerve stimulation by electric current: **electrotherapy** •medicine calming the nerves: **nervine, neuroleptic** •study of the nervous system and its disorders: **neurology** •biological study of the nervous system: **neurobiology** •surgical removal of a nerve: **neurectomy**

nest •gannets' nesting ground: **gannetry** •group of rooks' nests: **rookery**

net •*adjective*: **retiform** •woman's hairnet: **snood** •Roman gladiator armed with net: **retiarius**

network •wire or thread network: **mesh** •complex network: **labyrinth, maze** •network of lines etc. crossing at right angles: **grid** •point in a network at which lines join or cross: **node** •national electricity supply network: **grid** •network of lines on a map: **grid**

new •*combining form*: **neo-** •objectionably new: **newfangled** •incorporating the latest advances: **state-of-the-art** •new thing: **innovation, novelty** •new word: **neologism** •inexperienced newcomer: **novice**

news •exclusive publication of a major news item: **scoop** •news item given prominence to divert attention from another item: **spoiler** •interruption of broadcasting with a brief report of a major event: **newsflash** •broadcast news report: **news bulletin, newscast** •person reading such a report: **newscaster** •news communication by photographs: **photojournalism** •favourable bias on a news report: **spin** •news agency serving a number of publications: **syndicate**

newspaper •official newspaper: **gazette** •newspaper with large pages: **broadsheet** •newspaper with small pages: **tabloid** •newspapers and journalists: **the press** •newspapers specializing in sensational or titillating material: **gutter press, scandal sheets** •newspaper controlled by a political party: **organ** •newspaper's displayed title: **masthead** •newspaper advertisement presented as editorial material: **advertorial** •newspaper's treatment of a topic: **coverage** •item reported by one newspaper only: **exclusive** •factual report of latest developments: **hard news** •news from an overseas reporter: **dispatch** ●newspaper report of discreditable activities: **exposé** ●newspaper's careful research aimed at exposing malpractices: **investigative journalism** ●general article on a topic: **feature, soft news** ●background article on a person in the news: **profile** ●newspaper announcement of a person's death: **obituary** ●complimentary mention in a newspaper: **puff** ●middle pages of a newspaper: **centrefold, centre spread** ●newspaper section regularly written by a named person: **column** ●newspaper gossip column: **diary** ●principal newspaper item: **lead** ●text for a newspaper item: **copy** ●item inserted during printing: **stop press** ●entry at the head of an item showing place and date of writing: **date line** ●decide not to use an item: **kill, spike** ●worth reporting: **newsworthy** ●government directive forbidding publication of certain news: **D notice** ●high summer, when there is a dearth of serious news: **silly season** ●person in charge of a newspaper's daily contents: **editor** ●column of comment written by him: **editorial** ●newspaper staff dealing with a particular topic: **desk** ●newspaper department dealing with financial news: **city desk** ●organization supplying news stories: **news agency** ●freelance photographer or journalist selling sensational material to the gutter press: **paparazzo** (*pl.* paparazzi) ●payment of large sums by representatives of newspapers to gain exclusive rights to sensational material: **chequebook journalism** ●send articles to a newspaper: **contribute, file** ●send newspaper text to the printer: **put to bed** ●number of copies of a newspaper sold: **circulation** ●shop selling newspapers: **newsagent**

night ●*combining forms*: noct-, nyct- ●*adjective*: **nocturnal** ●night that is never completely dark: **white night**

●while night passes: **overnight** ●night blindness: **nyctalopia**

nine ●*combining form*: **non(a)-** ●nine-sided figure: **nonagon** ●ensemble of nine musicians, or music for them: **nonet**

ninety ●person in his or her nineties: **nonagenarian**

nipple ●*adjective*: **mamillary** ●pigmented area around a nipple: **areola** ●enlarged and rigid state of a nipple: **erection**

nitrogen ●*adjective*: **nitrous** ●cyclic environmental interconversion of nitrogen: **nitrogen cycle**

Noah ●*adjective*: **Noachian**

nobility ●female member of the nobility: **peeress** ●male member of the nobility: **peer** ●foreign nobility: **noblesse** ●list of nobles: **peerage** ●title having no legal validity: **courtesy title** ●small crown worn by a noble person: **coronet** ●denoting the junior branch of a noble family: **cadet** ●preposition forming part of a title: **nobiliary particle**

noise ●loud discordant noise: **cacophony** ●chaotic noise: **hubbub, pandemonium, racket, tumult, uproar** ●noise disturbing or harming others: **noise pollution** ●noise containing equal proportions of many frequencies: **white noise** ●rumbling of intestinal gas: **borborygmus** ●noisy and hard to control: **obstreperous, rowdy** ●noise-reducing device: **silencer** ●phenomenon causing pitch-change in passing noises: **Doppler effect**

Nonconformist ●Nonconformist place of worship: **chapel, tabernacle** ●association of nonconformist churches: **union** ●person claiming to believe in God but denying the existence of the Trinity: **Unitarian**

non-interference ●government policy of non-interference: **laissez-faire**

non-violence ●Hindu and Buddhist principle of non-violence towards all living things: **ahimsa** ●non-violent resistance as a form of political protest: **civil disobedience** ●non-violent resistance as advocated by Gandhi in India: **satyagraha**

norm ●behavioural norm: **convention** ●person following established norms: **conformist**

normal ●beyond what is normal: **preternatural**

north ●*adjective*: **boreal** ●north according to the earth's axis: **true north** ●north according to the compass: **magnetic north** ●distance travelled northwards: **northing** ●northern lights: **aurora borealis**

North African ●citadel in a North African town: **kasbah**

North American ●large cattle farm **ranch** ●cowboy's hat: **ten-gallon hat** ●deep river gorge: **canyon** ●open grassy plain: **prairie** ●North American term for the rural hinterland: **backcountry** ●school or university term: **semester** ●second-year high-school or university student: **sophomore** ●wild horse: **bronco** ●wolflike wild dog: **coyote**

Norway ●*adjective*: **Norwegian** ●sea inlet in Norway: **fjord** ●sweet brown Norwegian cheese: **Gjetost** ●medieval Norwegian wooden church: **stave church** ●mythical Norwegian sea monster: **kraken**

nose ●*combining forms*: **nas(o)-, rhino-** (*e.g.* rhinoplasty) ●*adjectives*: **nasal, rhinal** ●hooked nose: **Roman nose** ●straight nose: **Grecian nose** ●upper, bony part of a nose: **bridge** ●opening of the nose: **nostril** ●build-up of mucus in the nose: **catarrh** ●blockage of the nose by mucus: **congestion** ●nasal inflammation: **rhinitis** ●skull cavity connecting with the nasal cavities: **sinus** ●push with the nose: **nuzzle**

nostril ●*adjective*: **narial** ●division between the nostrils: **septum**

not ●*combining forms*: **a-** (*e.g.* asexual), **an-** (*e.g.* anonymous), **dis-** (*e.g.* dishonest), **in-** (*e.g.* infertile), **mal-** (*e.g.* maladroit), **un-** (*e.g.* unloved)

note¹ ●notes of variant textual readings: **apparatus, apparatus criticus, critical apparatus** ●note at the start of a chapter etc.: **headnote** ●marginal notes: **marginalia** ●note at a page-foot: **footnote** ●note at the end of a chapter etc.: **endnote** ●heading to a note: **lemma** (*pl.* lemmata) ●make a quick note: **jot** ●note provisionally: **pencil in**

note² ●sustained note: **pedal, pedal note, pedal point** ●chromatic sequence of notes used in a serial piece: **tone row** ●set of notes to be performed by a particular instrumentalist or singer: **part** ●embellishment of a note: **ornament** ●slide from one note to another: **glissando, portamento** ●stepwise arrangement of successive notes in a musical system: **scale** ●group of notes sounded together: **chord** ●group of adjacent notes sounded together: **note cluster, tone cluster** ●duration and emphasis of a group of successive notes: **rhythm** ●notes a particular voice or instrument can sing or play: **range** ●height of a note: **pitch** ●two-pronged metal fork struck to give a note of specified pitch: **tuning fork** ●denoting notes having different names but the same pitch: **enharmonic** ●lowest sound that can be heard within a note: **fundamental** ●higher sound heard within a note: **harmonic, overtone, partial** ●movement from one note to another: **progression** ●change in a note's pitch as its source passes by: **Doppler effect** ▸ *see also* **musical notation**

notebook ●notebook containing a personal collection of memorable passages: **commonplace book** ●paper or electronic notebook for business and social engagements etc.: **personal organizer** ●loose-leaf notebook: **Filofax™**

notice ●fail or refuse to notice: **overlook** ●accidental failure to notice: **oversight** ●done cautiously to avoid notice: **stealthy**

noun ●*adjective*: **nominal** ●noun that can form a plural: **count noun** ●noun denoting something which cannot be counted: **mass noun** ●denoting a noun used for an individual person, place, etc.: **proper** ●denoting a noun used for a class of objects: **common** ●denoting a noun naming a material object: **concrete** ●denoting a noun naming an idea, quality, etc.: **abstract** ●verbal noun: **gerund**

novel ●novel depicting real persons or events but with changed names: **roman à clef** ●novel depicting its hero's early life: **Bildungsroman** ●family novel, usually dealing with several generations: **roman-fleuve** ●novel presented as a series of letters: **epistolary novel** ●horror novel with a medieval setting: **gothic novel** ●short light novel: **novelette** ●novel flouting literary conventions: **anti-novel** ●extended short story: **novella** ●novel's story-line: **plot** ●principal character in a novel: **protagonist** ●scene reverting to an earlier dramatic time: **flashback** ▸*see also* **fiction, story**

nuclear reactor ●nuclear reactor producing more nuclear fuel than it consumes: **breeder** ●breeder reactor not using a moderator: **fast breeder** ●nuclear reactor converting fertile into fissile material: **converter** ●denoting a reactor in self-sustaining reaction: **critical** ●minimum fissile material needed for a nuclear reaction: **critical mass** ●conversion of matter to energy in a nuclear reaction: **annihilation** ●central part of a nuclear reactor: **core** ●denoting nuclei that can

be split in a reactor: **fissile, fissionable** ●denoting nuclei that can be made fissile: **fertile** ●denoting nuclear reactions occurring only at very high temperatures: **thermonuclear** ●magnesium-based cladding for nuclear fuel: **magnox** ●substance retarding neutrons: **moderator** ●neutron-absorbing rod used to vary a reactor's output: **control rod** ●enrich a reactor with a particular isotope: **spike** ●water used as a moderator: **heavy water** ●lead-lined container for nuclear waste: **flask** ●denoting highly radioactive nuclear waste: **high-level** ●overheating and destruction of the core: **meltdown** ●meltdown that continues through the core and into the earth: **China syndrome** ●close down and decontaminate a worn-out nuclear reactor: **decommission**

nuclear weapon ●nuclear weapon in which the explosion is caused by a chain reaction: **atom bomb, fission bomb** ●nuclear weapon in which the explosion is caused by a single high-temperature reaction: **fusion bomb, hydrogen bomb, thermonuclear bomb** ●nuclear weapon designed to destroy life but not buildings: **neutron bomb** ●denoting a nuclear weapon producing little fallout: **clean** ●denoting a nuclear weapon producing much fallout: **dirty** ●denoting a nuclear weapon of low explosive force: **low-yield** ●denoting non-nuclear weaponry: **conventional** ●ball of hot gas generated by a nuclear explosion: **fireball** ●atmospheric radioactive particles left by a nuclear explosion: **fallout** ●cold and darkness following the explosion of many nuclear warheads: **nuclear winter** ●possession of nuclear weaponry, imagined to frighten aggressors: **deterrent** ●imagined protection gained by alliance with a nuclear power: **nuclear umbrella**

● nuclear capacity beyond that required for universal destruction: **overkill** ● strengthen against nuclear attack: **harden** ● stage in a war when nuclear weapons might be employed: **nuclear threshold** ● nuclear attack intended to destroy the enemy's nuclear arsenal: **first strike, pre-emptive strike** ● retaliatory nuclear attack: **second strike** ● point on the earth's surface directly above or below an exploding nuclear bomb: **ground zero**

nucleus ● positively charged particle in an atom's nucleus: **proton** ● negatively charged particle in an atom's nucleus: **neutron** ● negatively charged particle orbiting an atom's nucleus: **electron** ● reaction causing the splitting of a nucleus: **fission** ● reaction causing the fusion of several nuclei: **fusion** ● force involved in the decay of nuclei: **weak force**

nudity ● full exposure of the front of the body: **full-frontal nudity** ● social nudity: **naturism, nudism**

number ● *adjective*: **numerical** ● number indicating quantity: **cardinal number** ● number indicating position in a sequence: **ordinal number** ● positive whole number: **natural number** ● number greater than any countable number: **infinity** ● number that can be expressed as a whole-number ratio: **rational number** ● number without fractions: **whole number, integer** ● number consisting of an integer and a proper fraction: **mixed number** ● integer divisible only by itself and 1: **prime number** ● number not so limited: **composite number** ● number to be added to another: **summand** ● number showing the result of addition: **sum** ● number from which another is to be subtracted: **minuend** ● number to be subtracted from another: **subtrahend** ● number showing the result of subtraction: **difference** ● number to be multiplied with another: **multiplicand**

● number multiplying an algebraic variable: **coefficient** ● number showing the result of multiplication: **product** ● number whose product with another stated number is unity: **reciprocal** ● product of multiplying a number by itself: **power** ● product of a number multiplied once by itself: **square** ● product of a number multiplied twice by itself: **cube** ● number that when multiplied to a certain power gives a stated product: **root, radical** ● number to be divided: **dividend** ● number by which division is made: **divisor** ● number by which another is exactly divisible: **factor** ● number showing the result of division: **quotient** ● number left over in division: **remainder** ● number or symbol on which a numeration scale is based: **base, radix** ● numeration scale based on 2: **binary system** ● numeration scale based on 3: **ternary system** ● numeration scale based on 8: **octal system** ● numeration scale based on 10: **decimal system** ● numeration scale based on 12: **duodecimal system** ● numeration scale based on 16: **hexadecimal system** ● number to which a logarithm belongs: **antilogarithm** ● numeric notation beginning 1, 2, 3: **Arabic numerals** ● numeric notation beginning i, ii, iii: **Roman numerals** ● number progression in a fixed ratio: **geometric progression** ● number progression by a fixed sum: **arithmetic progression** ● numerical proportion expressing the relative size of two populations: **ratio** ● denoting a number correct to the nearest 10 or 100 (etc.): **round** ● denoting a number repeated indefinitely: **recurring** ● figure, symbol, etc. denoting a number: **numeral** ● consisting of numbers and letters: **alphanumeric** ● fixed or permitted number: **quota** ● number allocated to an individual to validate his electronic transactions: **personal**

identification number ●person collecting locomotive numbers as a hobby: **trainspotter** ●study of numbers' occult significance: **numerology**

number plate ●dealers' temporary number plate for unlicensed motor vehicles: **trade plates**

nun ●beginner nun: **novice, oblate, postulant** ●chief nun: **abbess, mother superior** ●nun mostly concerned with manual work: **lay sister** ●take monastic vows: **be professed** ●nun's cap: **coif** ●nun's covering for the head and neck: **wimple** ●nun's room: **cell** ●denoting a nun wearing no shoes: **discalced** ●community of nuns, or its buildings: **convent, nunnery** ●school run by nuns: **convent, convent school** ●society of nuns under a particular rule: **order**

nunnery ●*adjective*: **claustral** ●small nunnery: **priory** ●nunnery room for conversation: **parlour** ●nunnery dining hall: **refectory**

nurse ●nurse visiting patients' homes: **district nurse** ●nurse visiting homes to give advice: **health visitor** ●nurse assisting women in labour: **midwife** ●nurse in charge of others: **nursing officer, matron, sister, ward manager**

nursery ●day nursery for pre-school children: **crèche** ●nurse caring for a baby without breastfeeding it: **dry-nurse** ●nurse caring for a baby and breastfeeding it: **wet-nurse**

nut¹ ●*combining forms*: **nuci-** ●nut's soft interior: **kernel** ●large seed of the tropical palm: **coconut** ●nut-eating: **nucivorous**

nut² ●nut screwed down on another: **locknut** ●nut with projections for the fingers to turn: **wing nut** ●flat ring under a nut: **washer**

nylon ●unit of fineness for nylon yarn: **denier**

nymph ●mountain nymph: **oread** ●fresh-water nymph: **naiad** ●sea nymph: **nereid** ●tree nymph: **hamadryad** ●wood nymph: **dryad, hamadryad**

Oo

oath ●oath (formerly) taken by trainee doctors: **Hippocratic oath** ●evidence given under oath: **deposition** ●written statement made under oath: **affidavit** ●solicitor entitled to administer oaths: **Commissioner for Oaths**

obedience ●demanding obedience: **peremptory** ●stubbornly disobedient: **refractory** ●person refusing obedience: **recusant**

objection ●open to objection: **exceptionable**

objective ●compromise between two mutually incompatible objectives: **trade-off**

obligation ●failure to fulfil an obligation: **default**

observation ●close and constant observation: **surveillance** ●judge's observation made in passing: **obiter dictum** ●derived from observation rather than logic: **empirical**

obsolescence ●not prone to obsolescence: **future-proof**

octave below ●*combining form*: **contra-** (*e.g.* contrabass)

odds ●denoting odds that reflect a high probability: **short** ●denoting odds that reflect a remote probability: **long**

offal ●deer's offal: **umbles** ●fowl's offal: **giblets** ●animal lungs as offal: **lights**

offer ●offer to perform a specified job at a specified price: **tender** ●be the first to whom something will be offered: **have first refusal**

office¹ ●*combining form*: **-ship** (*e.g.* ambassadorship) ●current office-holder: **incumbent, occupant** ●formal inauguration of office: **induction, installation** ●period of holding office: **tenure** ●ending a term of office: **outgoing**

office² ●barrister's office: **chambers** ●judge's office for private hearings: **chambers** ●rolling reallocation of office accommodation: **hot-desking, hot-seating** ●office workers' headaches and respiratory problems, thought to be caused by poor ventilation: **sick building syndrome**

official ●chief official: **principal** ●senior administrative official: **chief executive** ●powerful official: **mandarin** ●career official in a large bureaucracy: **apparatchik** ●official in the state bureaucracy: **civil servant** ●official who calls meetings: **convenor** ●official implementing the decisions of others: **executive** ●official ensuring that rules are kept: **referee, umpire** ●state official based abroad to assist his compatriots: **consul** ●official representing a state abroad: **diplomat** ●official controlling the College of Arms: **Earl Marshal** ●official overseeing state ceremonial and grants of arms: **herald** ●official auditing local authority accounts: **district auditor** ●court or municipal official making public announcements: **crier** ●official appointed to manage the affairs of bankrupts: **receiver** ●official examining bus tickets: **inspector** ●church official leading processions etc.: **verger** ●church official in charge of vestments etc.: **sacristan** ●former parish official carrying out minor punishments etc.: **beadle** ●coal mine safety official: **deputy**

● official investigating complaints against public authorities: **Ombudsman, Parliamentary Commissioner for Administration** ● official inquiring into the cause of a person's death: **coroner** ● official conducting an election: **returning officer** ● official supervising the running of some public event: **steward** ● person managing a school's or college's finances: **bursar** ● official in charge of hounds: **huntsman** ● government official inspecting imports: **customs officer** ● official controlling a company's investments: **fund manager** ● senior UK law officer: **Director of Public Prosecutions** ● company official ensuring the legality of transactions: **compliance officer** ● university's ceremonial mace-bearer: **beadle** ● mosque official calling the faithful to prayer: **muezzin** ● official supervising those placed on probation: **probation officer** ● official responsible for records: **registrar** ● official in charge of court or council records: **clerk** ● official in charge of a railway station: **stationmaster** ● officials controlling a river or port: **conservancy** ● Roman official interpreting omens: **augur, haruspex** ● official managing a royal household: **chamberlain** ● official in charge of royal ceremonial: **Lord Great Chamberlain** ● hereditary official offering to fight for the monarch's right to the throne: **Champion of England** ● official suppressing published material held to be obscene or harmful to state security: **censor** ● area tax official: **inspector of taxes** ● court official serving writs etc.: **bailiff, tipstaff** ● denoting an official appointed but not yet in his post: **designate, elect** ● denoting an official receiving no pay: **honorary** ● denoting a retired official: **emeritus** ● appointment of officials in rotation rather than according to merit: **Buggins' turn** ● by virtue of one's of-

ficial status: **ex officio** ● start an official job: **take office** ● use of one's official position for personal gain: **jobbery** ● elaborate establishment with many officials: **bureaucracy** ● stifling effects of excessive bureaucracy: **red tape** ● official permission or approval: **clearance** ● official ban: **embargo** ● official order: **edict** ● official order having the force of law: **decree** ● person exercising power without having any office: **éminence grise**

offspring ● offspring of a cat, rabbit, or ferret: **kitten** ● offspring of a dog: **pup, whelp** ● offspring of a fox, bear, or lion: **cub** ● offspring of a swan: **cygnet** ● group of animals produced at a birth: **litter** ● smallest member of a litter: **runt** ● denoting offspring dependent on their parents for some time after birth: **altricial** ● denoting offspring able to feed themselves soon after birth: **precocial** ▸ *for offspring of other animals see the appropriate entry*

oil ● *combining form:* **ole-** ● *adjective:* **oleaginous** ● oil suitable for most engines: **multigrade** ● diesel oil for road vehicles: **derv** ● flower-petal oil used in scent-making: **attar** ● oil distilled from plants etc.: **essential oil** ● sacramental oil: **chrism, unguent** ● rub with sacramental oil: **anoint** ● sweet-scented tropical essential oil: **ylang-ylang** ● layer of oil floating on water: **slick** ● device collecting this: **skimmer** ● oil store at the end of a pipeline: **terminal**

oil well ● first successful well in a new oilfield: **discovery well** ● well needing no pumps: **gusher** ● structure above an oil well: **platform, rig** ● framework holding the drill: **derrick** ● seabed steel frame supporting a rig: **jacket** ● person directing the drilling on an oil rig: **tool pusher** ● oil rig labourer: **roustabout** ● accommodation ship for offshore rig staff: **floatel**

ointment ●lip-ointment: **lipsalve** ●pain-relieving ointment: **liniment** ●skin ointment: **balm, balsam, salve**

okra ●okra in Indian cuisine: **bhindi**

old ●*combining forms*: **archaeo-** (*e.g.* archaeology), **palaeo-** (*e.g.* palaeobotany)

old age ●*combining form*: **geront-** (*e.g.* gerontocracy) ●*adjective*: **gerontic** ●elderly and infirm: **decrepit** ●shrivelled with old age: **wizened** ●dark skin patches in the aged: **lentigo, senile maculation** ●time of life when fertility and sexual drives decline: **climacteric** ●mental and physical decay characteristic of old age: **infirmity, senescence, senility** ●progressive mental decay of the elderly: **senile dementia, Alzheimer's disease** ●period of senile decay: **dotage** ●medical and social care of old people: **geriatrics** ●place providing daytime social supervision for the elderly: **day centre** ●person in his sixties: **sexagenarian** ●person in his seventies: **septagenarian** ●person in his eighties: **octogenarian** ●person in his nineties: **nonagenarian** ●person a hundred or more years old: **centenarian** ●study of old age: **gerontology** ▸*see also* **senior citizen**

old-fashioned ●attractively old-fashioned: **quaint**

old woman ●adjective: **anile**

olive oil ●denoting oil of the finest quality: **extra virgin** ●denoting oil of the next best quality: virgin

omelette ●open omelette containing chopped vegetables: **Spanish omelette**

one ●*combining forms*: **mon(o)-** (*e.g.* monoplane), **uni-** (*e.g.* unilateral) ●the only one of its kind: **unique** ●done by one party only: **unilateral**

one and a half ●*combining form*: **sesqui-** (*e.g.* sesquicentenary)

onion ●small onion planted instead of seed: **set**

opening ●opening of the nose: **nostril** ●opening for liquids or gases to escape: **vent**

open space ●open space along the sea front in a seaside town: **esplanade, promenade** ●open space in front of a building: **forecourt, concourse**

opera ●opera sung throughout: **grand opera** ●opera comprised of separate musical items: **number opera** ●opera with spoken dialogue: **operetta** ●word-book of an opera: **libretto** ●running translation of an opera displayed above the stage: **surtitles** ●famous female opera singer: **diva** ●person teaching opera singers their music: **répétiteur** ●person staging an opera: **producer** ●general manager of an opera house: **intendant** ●contemporary chamber opera: **music theatre**

operation ●operation to improve one's appearance: **cosmetic surgery** ●operation to remove an appendix: **appendectomy, appendicectomy** ●operation to create an alternative blood vessel: **bypass** ●operation to remove a breast: **mastectomy** ●operation to remove a breast tumour: **lumpectomy** ●operation to replace an organ: **transplant** ●operation to remove the ovaries: **oophorectomy** ●operation to transfer tissue: **graft** ●child delivery by cutting the wall of the womb: **Caesarean section** ●medication given before an operation: **pre-medication** ●hospital room for operations: **theatre** ●denoting a condition that cannot be operated upon: **inoperable**

opinion ●generally accepted opinion: **idée reçue** (*pl.* idées reçues) ●considered opinion: **second thoughts, standpoint** ●ask opinions:

canvass ●assessment of public opinion by canvassing a representative sample: **opinion poll** ●person conducting or analysing opinion polls: **pollster** ●mass meeting to express public opinion: **demonstration, rally** ●hold a contrary opinion: **dissent** ●person with opinions diverging from the general consensus: **nonconformist** ●refusal to consider the opinions of others: **laager mentality, tunnel vision** ●person adjusting his opinions to the mood of the time: **trimmer** ●intolerant of others' opinions: **narrowminded, petty, small-minded** ●written statement of one's opinions and intentions: **position paper** ●person airing contentious opinions to provoke debate: **devil's advocate** ●designed to advance a particular point of view: **tendentious**

opium ●*adjective*: **opiate** ●opium-derived drug: **opiate** ●opium-like compound: **opioid** ●opium-derived addictive painkillers: **heroin, morphine**

opponent ●determined opponent of change etc.: **diehard**

opposite ●*combining forms*: **contra-, counter-** (*e.g.* counteract) ●opposite side of the world: **antipodes** ●word having the opposite sense: **antonym** ●having the opposite effect to that desired: **counterproductive** ●assert the opposite of: **contradict**

opposition ●non-violent opposition: **passive resistance**

optician ●optician testing eyes, prescribing, and making up prescriptions: **ophthalmic optician** ●optician making up prescriptions: **dispensing optician**

oral ●oral examination of an applicant: **interview** ●oral examination of academic candidate: **viva**

orange ●kind of orange having reddish flesh: **blood orange** ●small kinds of orange: **mandarin, tangerine** ●loose-skinned tangerine: **satsuma** ●white spongy tissue inside an orange skin: **pith**

orbit ●orbit that keeps a satellite fixed over a terrestrial point: **geostationary orbit** ●point in an orbit furthest from the earth, moon, sun: **apogee, apolune, aphelion** ●point in an orbit closest to the earth, moon, sun, object orbited: **perigee, perilune, perihelion, periapsis** (*pl.* periapses) ●star etc. round which a satellite orbits: **primary**

orchestra ●large orchestra: **symphony orchestra** ●small orchestra: **chamber orchestra, sinfonia, sinfonietta** ●percussion orchestra of Java and Bali: **gamelan** ●substantial piece of orchestral music: **symphony** ●substantial piece for a soloist and orchestra: **concerto** ●orchestra's first violinist: **leader, concertmaster** ●orchestral players' music stand: **desk** ●play several instruments in an orchestra: **double** ▸*see also* **ensemble**

order ●order for supplies: **requisition** ●order for a regularly repeated supply: **standing order** ●order for work to be undertaken: **commission** ●order for a person to attend a court: **summons, subpoena, process** ●order sent from a higher to a lower court: **mandamus** ●court order requiring a certain action to be performed or avoided: **writ, injunction** ●made to order: **bespoke**

ordinary ●ordinary participants: **rank and file** ●reflecting the wishes or tastes of ordinary people: **populist**

organ¹ ●small organ whose pipes are activated by pins attached to a revolving cylinder: **barrel organ** ●foot-blown reed organ: **harmonium** ●cabinet for an organ's keyboards and stops: **console** ●cabinet housing the expressive section: **swell box** ●chief organ keyboard: **great**

●upper organ keyboard, with expressive section: **swell** ●lower organ keyboard, with soft stops: **choir** ●organ piece played at a church service: **voluntary**

organ² ●organ producing gametes: **gonad** ●imaging of internal organs by high-frequency radio waves: **magnetic resonance imaging**

organism ●organism living on another: **parasite** ●organism visible only by microscope: **micro-organism** ●small organisms floating in water: **plankton** ●small organisms swimming in water: **nekton** ●basic unit of a natural organism: **cell** ●development of an organism: **ontogenesis, ontogeny** ●cooperative interaction between two different organisms: **symbiosis** ●able to be decomposed by living organisms: **biodegradable** ●study of living organisms: **biology, physiology, life sciences** ●study of the forms of living organisms: **morphology** ●study of micro-organisms: **microbiology**

organization ●established organization: **institution** ●separate but dependent organization: **satellite** ●organization sponsored but not controlled by government: **quango** ●organization supplying water, gas, etc.: **public utility, utility** ●organization training and regulating barristers: **Inn of Court** ●organization counselling distressed persons: **Samaritans** ●organization's income: **revenue** ●organizational restructuring for greater efficiency: **streamlining** ●simplification of an organization's hierarchy: **delayering** ●reduction of an organization's size: **downsizing, rationalization** ●put a previously failing organization on the path to success: **turn round** ●statement of an organization's aims and principles: **misson statement** ●committee establishing an organization's general principles of operation: **steering com-**

mittee ●person within an organization who betrays its secrets: **mole** ●separate from an organization's control: **hive off** ●split an organization into a number of independent businesses: **unbundle** ●detailed practical organization required to implement a plan: **logistics**

organ transplants ●person giving organs for transplanting: **donor** ●drug preventing rejection of these: **cyclosporin** ●card authorizing use of the holder's organs for medical purposes after his death: **donor card**

orgasm ●ability to achieve an orgasm: **potency**

orgy ●*adjective*: **orgiastic**

origin ●*combining form*: **-genous** (*e.g.* indigenous) ●ethnic origin: **extraction** ●place of origin of a work of art: **provenance** ●study of the origins of words: **etymology** ●study of the origins of names: **onomastics**

original ●*combining form*: proto- (*e.g.* prototype), ur- (*e.g.* urtext)

origination ●person who originates and activates artistic or commercial projects: **animateur**

Orkneys ●*adjective*: **Orcadian**

ornament ●*combining form*: **-let** (*e.g.* necklet) ●small household ornament: **gewgaw, knick-knack, trinket** ●these collectively: **bric-a-brac** ●small decorative item: **objet d'art** (*pl.* objets d'art) ●ornamental festoon of flowers, fruits, etc.: **swag** ●ornamental pattern: **motif** ●ornamental work of knotted cords: **knotting, knotwork** ●ornamental grooves: **fluting** ●fine ornamental wire work: **filigree** ●intertwining decoration: **meander** ●decorated with leaves: **foliate** ●ornamental patterns of holes: **openwork** ●ornamental embedding of different materials:

inlay ●wood inlay decorating furniture: **marquetry** ●thin cord decorating upholstery: **piping** ●ornamental strip of wood or stone: **moulding** ●ornamental centrepiece for a dining table: **epergne** ●flower-shaped ornament: **fleuron** ●thin line of cream or icing decorating food: **piping** ●panelling ornament: **linenfold** ●ornamental plant pot: **jardinière** ●ornamental support for a rail: **baluster** ●ornamentation imitating plaited straps: **strapwork** ●ankle ornament: **anklet** ●ornament worn round the upper arm: **armlet** ●rigid ornamental band worn round the wrist or ankle: **bangle, bracelet** ●ornamental chain worn round the wrist or arm: **bracelet** ●small ornament worn to give magical protection: **amulet** ●three-lobed ornamental design: **trefoil** ●four-lobed ornamental design: **quatrefoil** ▸see also **architecture**

orphan ●person protecting an orphan's interests: **guardian**

ostrich ●*adjective*: **struthious**

other ●*combining form*: **heter(o)-** (*e.g.* heterosexual), **xeno-** (*e.g.* xenograft) ●among other people: **inter alios** ●among other things: **inter alia**

otter ●male otter: **dog** ●otter's lair: **holt, lodge**

out ●*combining forms*: **e-, ec-** (*e.g.* ecstasy, *literally 'standing out of oneself'*), **ex-** ●way out: **egress, exit** ●come out from somewhere or something: **emanate, emerge** ●force out: **extrude**

outing ●outing to an unspecified destination: **mystery tour**

outline ●outline representation: **schema**

outside ●*combining form*: **ecto-** (*e.g.* ectoplasm), **exo-** (*e.g.* exoskeleton), **extra-** (*e.g.* extracellular) ●originating outside: **exogenous**

ovary ●*combining form*: **oophor-** ●*adjective*: **ovarian** ●ovary cell dividing to form an ovum: **oocyte** ●ovary cavity for the ovum: **follicle** ●tube taking an ovum from the ovary: **oviduct** ●inflammation of an ovary: **oophoritis, ovaritis** ●surgical removal of the ovaries: **oophorectomy, ovariectomy, ovariotomy**

over ●*combining forms*: **hyper-** (*e.g.* hypernym), **super-** (*e.g.* superstructure, supererogation), **supra-** (*e.g.* supramundane), **sur-** (*e.g.* surcharge)

overcome ●that cannot be overcome: **insurmountable**

overeating ●compulsive overeating: **bulimia** ●bouts of overeating followed by self-induced vomiting and fasting: **bulimia nervosa**

overlap ●arrange avoiding overlaps: **stagger**

ovum ●*combining form*: **oo-** ●development of an ovum: **oogenesis** ●fertilized ovum: **zygote** ●tube taking an ovum from the ovary: **oviduct** ●discharge ova from the ovary: **ovulate**

own ●all the money and property owned by a person: **estate**

owner ●*adjective*: **proprietary** ●record of previous ownership: **provenance** ●person using or holding goods but not owning them: **bailee**

Oxford University ●*adjective*: **Oxonian** ●Oxford university annual feast: **Encaenia** ●Oxford university formal dress: **subfusc** ●part of the term when undergraduates are expected to be resident: **full term** ●autumn term at Oxford: **Michaelmas term** ●winter term at Oxford: **Hilary term** ●summer term at Oxford: **Trinity term** ●Oxford classics degree: **Greats, Literae Humaniores** ●member of a university sports team: **blue** ●member of the Oxford university police: **bulldog** ●Oxford and Cambridge universities considered together: **Oxbridge** ●Oxford college examination or progress report: **collections** ●final university examinations at Oxford: **schools** ●Oxford college annual feast: **gaudy** ●Oxford college servant: **scout** ●Oxford college bill for food and accommodation: **battels** ●confine within the college: **gate** ●suspend a student: **rusticate**

oxygen ●*combining form*: **oxy-** ●oxygen mixture giving a very hot flame: **oxyacetylene** ●lack of oxygen: **anoxia** ●enrich with oxygen: **oxygenate** ●combine chemically with oxygen: **oxidize** ●exercises designed to increase the body's oxygen intake: **aerobics** ●continuous cyclic interconversion of oxygen: **oxygen cycle**

ozone layer ●thin area in the ozone layer: **ozone hole** ●refrigerant and aerosol gas harmful to the ozone layer: **chlorofluorocarbon**

Pp

package tour ●tour company employee accompanying clients: **courier** ● tour company employee stationed in a resort to assist its clients: **representative**

packaging ●sealed packaging from which the air has been removed: **vacuum pack** ●denoting packaging designed to show if its contents have been meddled with: **tamper-evident** ●packing sheets containing small air bubbles: **bubble wrap** ●soft cotton or wool fabric used in packing: **wadding** ●soft wood shavings used in packing: **woodwool** ●highlighted text on packaging: **flash**

pad ●absorbent pad: **swab**

page ●blank page at the start or end of a book: **flyleaf** ●right-hand page of an open book: **recto** ●left-hand page of an open book: **verso** ●extra-large page folded in to conform with the rest: **gatefold** ●piece of paper with a page printed on each side: **folio, leaf** ●set of leaves folded inside each other: **signature, quire** ●stitching through the back fold of a signature: **saddle stitch** ●arrangement of material on a page: **layout** ●layout made from existing elements: **paste-up** ●denoting a book with worn pages: **dog-eared** ●turn over pages casually: **leaf through** ●count a book's pages: **paginate**

pain ●*combining forms*: **alg-, -algia** ●sudden sharp pain: **twinge** ●pain felt away from its real source: **referred pain** ●painful state evaporating with continued effort: **pain barrier** ●severe abdominal pain caused by wind or intestinal obstruction: **colic** ●pain in the lower back: **lumbago** ●pain of

the back, hip, and outer leg: **sciatica** ●chest pain felt due to lack of blood in the heart: **angina, angina pectoris** ●stress-related bowel pain: **irritable bowel syndrome** ●pains in children's limbs: **growing pains** ●pain in the ear caused by changes in pressure during air travel: **barotitis** ●kidney pain: **nephralgia** ●muscle pain: **myalgia** ●painful contraction of a muscle: **cramp** ●painful stiffness in the neck or back: **crick** ●pain that shoots along a nerve: **neuralgia** ●pain from pressure on the spinal nerve: **sciatica** ●pain in the side felt while running: **stitch** ●painful swelling on the big toe joint: **bunion** ●shrinking movement caused by pain or its expectation: **flinch, wince** ●sexual pleasure derived from inflicting pain: **algolagnia** ●designed to minimize pain: **humane** ●drug that eases pain: **analgesic** ●pain-relieving ointment: **liniment** ●rubbing the body to ease pain: **massage** ●person skilled at this: **masseur** (*fem.* masseuse) ●liquid painkiller rubbed into the skin: **embrocation** ●drug that prevents pain being felt: **anaesthetic** ●inability to feel pain: **anaesthesia** ●instrument measuring pain: **dolorimeter** ●free from pain: **comfortable**

paint ●glue-based paint for walls: **distemper** ●paint diluted with water: **emulsion, watercolour** ●paint diluted with egg-white: **tempera** ●oil-based paint: **oils** ●kind of paint with a slight sheen: **eggshell** ●kind of paint with a high sheen: **gloss** ●paint for bare surfaces: **primer** ●thin coat of water-based paint: **wash** ●denoting paint that is not completely dry: **tacky** ●liquid with which pigments are mixed to make paints: **medium** ●oil used in mixing paints: **turpentine** ●synthetic resin used in paints and adhesives: **polyurethane** ●liquid giving a clear shiny surface when dry: **varnish** ●solution for painting walls white: **whitewash** ●compressed-air device providing a fine spray of paint: **airbrush** ●stone for grinding pigments: **muller** ●paint cleaner or remover made from soap and soda: **sugar soap** ●portable burner giving a hot flame for removing paint: **blowlamp** ●painted surfaces: **paintwork** ●covering for surfaces not to be painted: **masking**

painter ●*adjective*: **painterly** ●painter's board for mixing colours: **palette** ●painter's stick steadying the brush hand: **maulstick**

painting ●painting made onto a wall: **mural** ●painting on wet plaster: **fresco** ●painting on dry plaster: **secco** ●thin layer of diluted paint: **wash** ●gypsum for painting: **gesso** ●painting on two hinged panels: **diptych** ●painting on three hinged panels: **triptych** ●painting on several hinged panels: **polyptych** ●small easel painting: **cabinet picture** ●very small painting: **miniature** ●circular painting: **tondo** (*pl.* tondi) ●painting set behind an altar: **altarpiece** ●Japanese scroll painting: **kakemono** ●Tibetan religious scroll painting: **tanka** ●kind of abstract painting made by random tipping of paint onto the canvas: **action painting** ●execution of a painting: **facture** ●minor figures in a painting: **staffage** ●representation of light and shade in a painting: **chiaroscuro** ●juxtaposition of different colours in a painting: **contrast** ●painting intended to give a deceptive three-dimensional view: **trompe l'oeil** ●painting in shades of a single colour: **monochrome** ●painting in shades of grey: **grisaille** ●painting with thickened watercolours: **gouache** ●very small but detailed painting: **miniature** ●application of thick layers of paint: **impasto** ●painting with tiny dots of colour: **pointillism, stipple** ●painting of domestic scenes: **genre painting** ●painting of inanimate objects: **still life** ●painting's prepared surface: **ground** ●preliminary design for a painting: **cartoon** ●make detailed alterations to a painting: **retouch** ●clear resin applied to protect the surface of a painting: **varnish** ●small cracks on an old painting's surface: **craquelure** ●reappearance of traces of earlier painting: **pentimento** ●prepared surface for painting: **ground** ●wooden frame over which canvas is fixed for painting: **stretcher** ●gelatinous solution applied to a canvas: **size** ●wooden frame supporting a painting: **easel** ●stick steadying a painter's hand: **maulstick**

pair ●pair of pistols or game birds: **brace** ●lasting relationship between two persons or animals: **pair bond**

Pakistani ●type of Pakistani food that is cooked in a deep two-handled pan: **balti** ●deep two-handled pan used to cook balti dishes: **karahi**

palace ●*adjective*: **palatial**

palate ●*adjective*: **palatine** ●bony front part of the palate: **hard palate** ●fleshy rear part: **soft palate**

pale ●unhealthily pale: **pasty**

Palestinian ●Palestinian opposition to Israeli occupation of the West Bank: **Intifada** ●fundamentalist Palestinian liberation movement: **Hamas**

palm ●palm's compound leaf: **frond** ●large seed of the tropical palm: **coconut** ●palm fibre used for making hats etc.: **raffia** ●edible starch obtained from certain palms: **sago**

palmistry ●line indicating length of life: **lifeline**

pancake ●thin pancake: **crêpe** ●pancake of grated potatoes: **galette** ●flamed dessert pancake: **crêpe Susette** (*pl.* crêpes Susette) ●Russian pancake: **blini**

pancreas ●inflammation of the pancreas: **pancreatitis** ●surgical removal of the pancreas: **pancreatectomy**

pantomime ●leading male role, usually played by a young woman: **principal boy** ●leading female role, usually played by a young woman: **principal girl** ●elderly female pantomime character, usually played by a man: **dame**

paper ●thick drawing paper: **cartridge paper** ●strong brown envelope paper: **Manila** ●waxed paper for cookery: **greaseproof paper** ●very thin book paper: **India paper** ●poor paper used for newspapers: **newsprint** ●crinkly paper for decorations: **crêpe paper** ●small twisted-up piece of paper: **screw** ●thin strip of paper: **spill** ●abrasive paper: **sandpaper** ●sheet of thin paper foldable to make its own envelope: **air letter, aerogramme** ●small printed sheet of paper: **leaflet** ●small piece of paper: **slip** ●single thickness of paper in a book: **leaf** ●front side of a sheet of paper: **recto** ●reverse side of a sheet of paper: **verso** ●roll of paper for continuous printing: **web** ●denoting paper with a finely ribbed surface: **laid** ●denoting paper with a smooth surface: **wove** ●denoting paper discoloured by brown spots: **foxed** ●type of grass used to make paper: **esparto, esparto grass** ●soft mass of fibres for papermaking: **pulp** ●maker's emblem in a sheet of paper: **watermark** ●quality of paper used

for top copies: **bond** ●quality of paper used for carbon copies etc.: **bank** ●paper and glue mix hardening when dry: **papier mâché** ●board made from glued layers of paper: **pasteboard** ●Japanese art of paper folding: **origami** ●apparatus cutting a block of paper: **guillotine** ●device inserting sheets of paper into a machine: **paper feed** ●race following a trail of torn-up paper: **paperchase**

parachute ●cord opening a parachute: **ripcord** ●cord fixed to the aircraft to open a parachute: **static line** ●expanding part of a parachute that arrests and directs its movement: **canopy** ●ropes that hold and control a parachute's canopy: **shrouds** ●parachute used to decelerate a landing aircraft: **drogue** ●parachuting in of supplies: **airdrop, paradrop** ●parachute gliding from a height: **paragliding, parapente, parascending** ●parachute sport of being pulled by a fast boat: **parasailing, parascending** ●sport of being dropped by parachute before skiing or water-skiing: **paraskiing** ●troops trained in parachuting: **paratroops**

parallelism ●parallelism drawn between two things: **analogy** ●quadrilateral with two sets of parallel sides: **rhombus** ●quadrilateral with one set of parallel sides: **trapezium**

paralysis ●*combining form*: -plegia ●paralysis from the neck down: **quadriplegia, tetraplegia** ●paralysis from the waist down: **paraplegia** ●paralysis of one side of the body: **hemiplegia** ●symmetrical paralysis on both sides of the body: **diplegia** ●paralysis of a single limb or area: **monoplegia** ●paralysis of all four limbs: **quadriplegia, tetraplegia** ●sudden temporary paralysis: **cataplexy** ●partial paralysis: **paresis** ●infectious disease causing paralysis: **poliomyelitis**

parasite ●parasite living outside its host: **ectoparasite** ●parasite living inside its host: **endoparasite** ●parasite living upon another parasite: **hyperparasite** ●parasitic flatworm: **fluke** ●blood-sucking parasite: **leech** ●presence of parasites in the blood: **parasitaemia** ●creature on or in which a parasite lives: **host** ●organism transmitting a parasite from one host to another: **vector** ●study of parasites: **parasitology**

pardon ●general pardon: **amnesty**

parent ●state payment made to parents: **child benefit** ●person bringing up children without a partner: **single parent** ●having parental responsibility: **in loco parentis** ●parental responsibility of divorcees: **custody** ●child without living parents: **orphan**

Paris ●underground railway in Paris: **metro** ●pleasure boat on the Seine at Paris: **bateau mouche**

parish ●*adjective*: **parochial** ●senior lay person in an ecclesiastical parish: **churchwarden** ●churchwarden's assistant: **sidesman** ●parish merry-making held at or near the patronal feast: **feast, wakes** ▶*see also* **Church of England**

parking ●park alongside a vehicle that stands at the side of the road: **double-park** ●machine selling parking time: **parking meter** ●railway station offering plentiful parking: **parkway**

Parkinson's disease ●natural compound used to treat this: **dopa**

parliament ●sovereign's speech outlining proposed legislation for a parliamentary session: **Queen's** (*or* **King's**) **Speech** ●section of parliament conducting its own meetings: **house** ●room where this meets: **chamber** ●antechamber to this: **lobby** ●either house of parliament as referred to in debate by a member of the other house: **another place** ●name of certain countries' parliament: **diet** ●lower house of the French parliament: **Assemblée Nationale** ●upper house of the French parliament: **Sénat** ●lower house of the German parliament: **Bundestag** ●upper house of the German parliament: **Bundesrat** ●head of the German and Austrian parliaments: **chancellor** ●parliament in Guernsey, Jersey, and Alderney: **States** ●Iranian parliament: **Majlis** ●Irish parliament: **Oireachtas** ●upper house of this: **Seanad** ●lower house of this: **Dail** ●Manx parliament: **Tynwald** ●lower house of this: **House of Keys** ●Norwegian parliament: **Storting** ●lower house of the Russian parliament: **Duma** ●US parliament: **Congress** ●upper house of this: **Senate** ●lower house of this: **House of Representatives** ●denoting a parliament in which no party has an overall majority: **hung** ●denoting a parliament having a single legislative chamber: **unicameral** ●denoting a parliament having two legislative chambers: **bicameral** ●denoting a parliament having three legislative chambers: **tricameral** ●document laid before parliament by the government: **Command Paper** ●barristers drafting parliamentary bills: **Parliamentary Counsel** ●draft law submitted for parliamentary discussion: **bill** ●person introducing a bill: **sponsor** ●proposed change to a bill: **amendment** ●stage in the progress of a bill through parliament: **reading** ●initial parliamentary presentation of a bill: **introduction, first reading** ●second presentation, seeking general approval: **second reading** ●third stage of a bill's progress, when it is considered in detail by a select group of MPs: **committee stage** ●group from either house examining a bill in detail: **committee** ●committee chairman's report to the house: **report stage** ●debate of this report: **third reading** ●amendment to a bill at its third reading: **rider** ●delaying tactics in debate: **filibuster, obstructionism, talking out** ●time-limit imposed to speed debate: **guillotine** ●text of a law as approved by parliament: **act** ●passing of an act by parliament: **enactment** ●daily record of parliamentary proceedings: **Journal** ●parliamentary vote: **division** ●place for this: **division lobby** ●division where members may vote as they wish: **free vote** ●party direction to members on voting: **whip** ●this couched in the most urgent terms: **three-line whip** ●vote for the motion: **aye** ●vote against it: **no** ●person counting division votes: **teller** ●bell rung to warn that a division is imminent: **division bell** ●make laws: **legislate** ●body doing this: **legislature** ●having power to legislate on all topics: **omnicompetent** ●denoting legislation coming into force unless parliament votes against it: **negative** ●piece of legislation affecting all or most citizens: **public act** ●piece of legislation affecting a company or individual: **private act** ●practice of sitting round a speaker appearing on television: **doughnutting** ●members of a house of parliament viewed collectively: **chamber** ●member of parliament having no government office: **private member** ●member of parliament's immunity from prosecution for remarks made in debate: **parliamentary privilege** ●parliamentary party next in size to that in power: **the Opposition** ●party official responsible for parliamentary members' attendance and discipline: **whip** ●money voted annually by parliament to the royal family: **Civil List** ●parliamentary allowance for the sovereign's private expenses: **privy purse** ●seat-

ing in the chamber for party leaders: **front bench** ●secure the adjournment of the house when inquorate: **count out** ●parliamentary holiday: **recess** ●period during which parliament meets regularly: **session** ●discontinue a parliamentary session: **prorogue** ●resume a parliamentary session: **recall** ●dismissal of parliament: **dissolution** ●Crown document instituting a parliamentary election: **writ** ●contrary to the rules or customs of parliament: **unparliamentary** ▶see also **cabinet, debate, House of Commons, House of Lords, meeting**

parrot ●*adjective*: **psittacine** ●large parrot: **macaw** ●small green parrot: **parakeet** ●pneumonia-like disease caught by humans from parrots: **psittacosis**

part ●principal part: **staple** ●set of parts for assembly: **kit** ●set of parts forming a complex whole: **system** ●interrelation of component parts: **topology** ●composed of similar parts: **homogeneous** ●composed of dissimilar parts: **heterogeneous** ●having two parts: **binary, bipartite, double, dual, duple** ●having three parts: **ternary, tripartite, triple** ●having four parts: **quadripartite, quadruple** ●having five parts: **quintuple** ●having six parts: **sexpartite, sextuple** ●separation into constituent parts: **resolution** ●arrangement of constituent parts: **structure** ●take part: **participate**

participate ●choose to participate: **opt in** ●number participating in an event: **turnout**

particle ●positively charged particle in an atom's nucleus: **proton** ●chargeless particle in an atom's nucleus: **neutron** ●small chargeless particle: **neutrino** ●proton or neutron: **nucleon** ●negatively charged particle orbiting an atom's nucleus: **electron** ●particle representing a quantum of light: **photon** ●highly energized particle travelling through space: **cosmic ray** ●assumed particle carrying a fractional electric charge: **quark** ●assumed one-dimensional particle: **string** ●assumed particle having short life but great energy: **virtual particle** ●binding particle: **meson** ●large meson: **pi-meson, pion** ●large unstable electron: **muon** ●protein particle believed to cause mad cow disease: **prion** ●subatomic particle having the same mass but opposite electrical properties to a named particle: **antiparticle** ●total number of protons and neutrons in a nucleus: **mass number** ●device moving particles at high speeds: **accelerator** ●accelerator for straight-line particles: **linear accelerator** ●temperature at which particle movement would be minimal: **absolute zero** ●study of subatomic particles: **microphysics** ●mathematical description of particles' motion and interaction: **quantum mechanics**

partly ●*combining form*: demi- (*e.g.* demigod), semi- (*e.g.* semiconscious), sub- (*e.g.* subtropical)

partner ●inactive business partner: **sleeping partner**

party ●evening party: **soirée** ●party at a new home: **housewarming** ●party at which food is grilled and consumed out of doors: **barbecue** ●party for women only: **hen party** ●party for men only: **stag party** ●wildly licentious party: **orgy** ●attend a party uninvited: **gatecrash** ▶ *see also* **political party**

pass ●catch up with and pass: **overtake**

passion ●passionate appeal: **cri de cœur** (*pl.* cris de cœur)

Passover ●*adjective*: **paschal** ●Passover ceremonies and feast: **Seder** ●Passover bread: **matzo** ●Jews' name for Passover: **Pesach**

passport ●endorsement on a passport: **visa**

past ●dealing with the past: **retrospective** ●wistful longing for the past: **nostalgia** ●interpretation of the past in terms of the present: **presentism** ●in a style typical of some past era: **period**

pasta ●pasta shaped like butterfly wings: **farfalle** ●ear-shaped pasta: **orecchiette** ●pasta envelopes: **ravioli** ●ribbon-shaped pasta: **fettucine** ●pasta in narrow ribbons: **tagliatelle** ●pasta in small rice-like grains: **orzo** ●small pasta rings stuffed with cheese or vegetables: **tortellini** ●sheet pasta: **lasagne** ●spiral-shaped pasta: **fusilli** ●pasta in long strings: **spaghetti** ●pasta in short thin strips: **linguine** ●pasta in long thin strips: **noodles** ●pasta in long slender threads: **vermicelli** ●pasta in narrow tubes: **macaroni** ●pasta in large tubes: **manicotti** ●pasta in short wide tubes: **penne** ●pasta in short fluted tubes: **rigatoni** ●kind of wheat used for pasta: **durum** ●Italian pasta sauces: **bolognese, carbonara, marinara, napolitana, pesto**

paste ●paste of almonds, sugar, and eggs: **marzipan** ●goose liver paste: **pâté de foie gras** ●maize-flour paste: **polenta** ●seasoned paste of finely minced meat or fish: **pâté** ●coarse paste of pork and liver: **pâté de campagne** ●thick paste of sugar and water: **fondant**

pastry ●soft light pastry: **choux pastry** ●light flaky pastry: **puff pastry** ●pastry rolled into thin leaves: **filo pastry** ●pastry with a high proportion of fat: **short pastry** ●pastry envelope: **puff** ●pastry envelope filled with seasoned meat and vegetables: **pasty** ●this with meat and potato: **Cornish pasty** ●sweet pastry enclosing chocolate: **pain au chocolat** ●sweet pastry filled with currants: **Eccles cake** ●puff pastry filled with jam and cream: **millefeuille** ●soft pastry finger filled with cream: **eclair** ●open pastry case with filling: **flan** ●flan with a savoury egg-thickened filling: **quiche** ●crescent-shaped pastry roll: **croissant** ●denoting food cooked in a pastry case: **en croute** ●fat used for making pastry: **shortening** ●place where pastries are sold: **patisserie**

patch ●having black and white patches: **piebald** ●having patches of white and of some other colour (not black): **skewbald**

path ●broad public path along the seaside: **esplanade, promenade** ●path alongside a canal: **towpath** ●country path for walkers and horseriders: **bridlepath, bridleway** ●country path signposted to show natural features: **nature trail** ●raised path over land liable to flooding: **causeway** ●raised path used by models in a fashion show: **catwalk** ●puzzling network of paths etc.: **maze**

pathological condition ●*combining form*: -ism (*e.g.* alcoholism)

patient ●patient staying in hospital overnight: **inpatient** ●hospital patient not staying overnight: **day patient, outpatient** ●patient recovering from illness or treatment: **convalescent** ●denoting a patient whose condition is not deteriorating: **stable** ●involving patients: **clinical** ●bedridden patient's receptacle for urine and faeces: **bedpan** ●record of a patient's previous illnesses, treatments, etc.: **case history**

pattern ●area of growing crops flattened to form a pattern: **crop circle** ●rigid sheet containing a cut-out pattern: **stencil** ●shaped piece used as a pattern for a cutting process: **template** ●pattern of differently coloured squares: **chequers**

pause ●brief pause in a court or parliamentary session: **adjournment** ●pause for holidays in a court session: **vacation** ●pause for holidays in a parliamentary session: **recess** ●pause in the middle of a line of verse: **caesura**

paving ●paving with irregular flat stones: **crazy paving** ●paving with rounded stones: **cobbles**

payment ●single complete payment: **lump sum** ●money sent as payment: **remittance** ●fixed annual payment: **annuity** ●forced payment: **exaction** ●payment demanded from a defeated adversary: **indemnity, reparation** ●additional payment: **supplement** ●increase the value of a payment: **uprate** ●extra payment for good performance: **bonus** ●payment made before due date: **advance** ●advance payment for a series of benefits: **subscription** ●sum paid to the author for each copy sold: **royalty** ●initial payment made to a barrister: **retainer** ●subsequent payment made to a barrister in a long case: **refresher** ●payment calculated on distance travelled: **mileage** ●payment calculated on the number of persons served: **capitation fee** ●payment at early termination of contract: **severance pay** ●payment of someone's living expenses: **maintenance** ●payment for travelling etc. expenses incurred on duty: **subsistence allowance** ●initial hire purchase payment: **down payment** ●payment made in kind: **truck** ●payment made to redundant executive: **golden handshake, golden parachute** ●one of a series of payments: **instalment** ●make a single payment instead of a series: **commute** ●divorced person's payment to former spouse: **maintenance** ●payment made by the state to a certain category of needy persons: **benefit** ●tenant's payment: **rent** ●union payment to striking members: **strike pay**

●payment for work done: **remuneration, wage, salary** ●payment for extra work: **overtime** ●payment made for services not officially charged for: **honorarium** ●denoting a payment made without any admission of obligation: **ex gratia** ●arrangement to pay for goods on delivery to purchaser: **cash on delivery** ●written order for payment: **draft** ●document acknowledging payment: **receipt** ●make persistent demands for payment: **dun** ●day on which quarterly payments become due: **quarter day** ●event at which each participant pays for him- or herself: **Dutch treat** ●denoting deductions etc. taken from a payment before it is made: **at source** ●partial return of payment made: **rebate** ●complete return of payment made: **refund** ●done without payment: **honorary, voluntary**

pea ●large type of pea: **marrowfat pea** ●pea eaten with its pod: **mangetout**

peafowl ●*adjective*: **pavonine** ●female peafowl: **peahen** ●male peafowl: **peacock**

peanut ●paste of ground roasted peanuts: **peanut butter**

pear ●alcoholic drink made from pear-juice: **perry**

pearl ●pearl of the highest quality: **orient** ●pearl formed by deliberate seeding: **cultured pearl**

pedestrian ●safe area for pedestrians between traffic lanes: **island, refuge** ●pedestrian crossings controlled by traffic lights: **pelican crossing, puffin crossing** ●flashing yellow globe at either end of a pedestrian crossing: **Belisha beacon** ●pedestrian tunnel: **underpass, subway**

peer ●peer who seldom attends the House of Lords: **backwoodsman** ●peer with a heritable title: **heredi-** tary peer ●peer with a non-heritable title: **life peer**

peg ●headless cylindrical peg: **dowel**

Peking ●currently preferred transliteration: **Beijing**

pen ●pen made from a feather: **quill** ●pen with an ink reservoir or cartridge: **fountain pen** ●fluorescent marker pen: **highlighter** ●pen's writing end: **nib**

penalty ●surrender as a penalty: **forfeit**

pencil ●pencil that can write on shiny surfaces: **chinagraph** ●coloured pencil: **crayon** ●crayon of powdered pigments: **pastel**

penguin ●penguin breeding ground: **rookery**

penis ●*adjective*: **penile** ●an erect penis or a representation of one: **phallus** (*pl.* phalli) ●phallus as a Hindu symbol of Shiva: **lingam** ●erectile tissue in the penis: **corpus cavernosum** (*pl.* corpora cavernosa), **corpus spongiosum** (*pl.* corpora spongiosa) ●penis bone in certain mammals: **baculum, os penis** ●rounded end of the penis: **glans** ●skin hood covering this: **foreskin, prepuce** ●enlarged and rigid state of the penis: **erection** ●having an erect penis: **ithyphallic** ●ability to achieve an erection: **potency** ●persistent and painful erection: **priapism** ●sebaceous secretion under the foreskin: **smegma** ●oral stimulation of the penis: **fellatio** ●cover for the penis during sexual activity: **condom, sheath** ●surgery to construct, repair, or enlarge a penis: **phalloplasty** ●surgical removal of the penis: **penectomy**

pension ●denoting a pension financed by the beneficiary: **contributory** ●regular contributions funding such a pension: **superannuation** ●denoting a pension solely financed by the beneficiary: **personal** ●denoting a pension transferrable to the beneficiary's subsequent employers: **portable** ●denoting a pension scheme whose payments are made out of current contributions: **unfunded** ●person receiving a pension or lodgings in return for prayers for the donor's soul: **beadsman**

people ●people constantly on the move: **nomads** ●the common people: **canaille, hoi polloi, rabble, riff-raff** ●intended for or done by the common people: **popular** ●make accessible to ordinary people: **popularize** ●representing or concerned with the interests of ordinary people: **populist**

pepper ●red sweet pepper: **pimento, pimiento** ●husked pepper berries: **white pepper** ●whole unripe pepper berries: **black pepper**

perception ●popular but inaccurate or oversimplified perception: **stereotype** ●alleged ability to perceive other than with the normal senses: **extrasensory perception** ●quick to notice things: **observant** ●lacking in perception: **imperceptive, impercipient** ●impossible to perceive: **imperceptible**

percussion ●gourd filled with beans or stones: **maraca** ●small pieces of wood clicked by the fingers: **castanets** ●musical instrument using pitched wooden blocks: **xylophone** ●deep-toned xylophone: **marimba** ●musical instrument using pitched metal bars: **glockenspiel** ●pitched percussion orchestra of Bali and Java: **gamelan**

percussion instruments ●pitched set of bells or metal tubes: **chimes** ●musical instrument using pitched wooden blocks: **xylophone** ●deep-toned xylophone: **marimba** ●concave brass plate: **cymbal** ●metal disk with a turned rim: **gong**

●musical instrument using pitched metal bars: **glockenspiel** ●small pieces of wood clicked together by Spanish dancers: **castanets** ●gourd filled with beans or stones: **maraca** ●percussion orchestra of Java and Bali: **gamelan** ▶ *see also* **drum**

performance ●preparation of material to be performed: **rehearsal** ●performance of material not previously prepared: **improvisation, sight-reading** ●performance showing exceptional skill: **tour de force** (*pl.* tours de force) ●first performance: **first night, opening, premiere** ●performance before the official first night: **preview** ●single performance or the persons attending it: **house** ●single performance at a particular venue: **one-night stand** ●continuous series of performances: **run, season** ●performance repeated at a series of venues: **tour** ●rotating performances of a number of works: **repertory** ●short performance contributed to a larger programme: **turn** ●performance given while the audience eat and drink: **cabaret** ●variety show featuring glamorous young women: **follies** ●short or minor piece performed before the main work: **curtain-raiser** ●wordless theatrical performance: **mime** ●costumed static group representing a scene from a play etc.: **tableau** ●visually striking performance: **spectacle** ●denoting a theatrical performance given surrounded by spectators: **in the round** ●performance of a programme of music by a soloist or chamber group: **recital** ●live performance by pop musicians: **gig** ●number of pop pieces performed as a sequence: **set** ●impromptu performance by pop musicians: **jam, jam session** ●performance whose profits are given to a named person, charity, etc.: **benefit** ●performance given at the sovereign's request: **command per-**

formance ●special performance: **gala** ●sold-out performance: **full house** ●afternoon performance: **matinee** ●farewell performance: **swansong** ●enclosed area for a circus performance: **ring** ●scenery and properties for a dramatic performance: **set** ●series of venues at which a performance takes place: **circuit** ●semi-official or avant-garde performances: **fringe theatre** ●informal performances given in a public place: **street theatre** ●person arranging performances: **agent, impresario** ●person financing performances: **angel, backer, promoter** ●denoting a performance given before an audience: **live** ●nervousness before or during a performance: **stage fright** ●formal assessment of an employee's performance: **appraisal**

performer ●chief performer: **lead** ●brilliant performer: **virtuoso** ●skilful performer: **exponent** ●person performing in the street: **busker** ●group of performers working regularly together: **ensemble, troupe** ●performer's professional name: **stage name** ●items known by a performer: **repertoire, repertory** ●first public appearance of a performer: **debut**

period ●fixed period: **term** ●critical period: **climacteric** ●tedious period: **longueur** ●immediately preceding period: **run-up, countdown** ●immediately following period: **sequel** ●period when a sport is not played: **close season** ●period of a ruling family's dominance: **dynasty** ●thing out of its time: **anachronism** ●imagined intrusion of one age into another: **time warp**

permission ●permission to be absent from school: **exeat** ●absence without permission: **French leave** ●ecclesiastical permission to publish a book: **imprimatur** ●official permis-

sion: **clearance, sanction** ●permission to use copyright etc. material: **release** ●written permission for medical treatment, organ donorship, etc. found on injured person: **advance directive**

permit ●official permit: **licence** ●customs permit for the temporary import of a motor vehicle: **carnet** ●state-granted monopoly over the exploitation of an invention: **patent** ●holder of this: **patentee** ●permit the existence of something disapproved of: **condone, tolerate**

persecution ●vindictive campaign directed against a group by those prejudiced against them: **witch-hunt** ●person forced by persecution to leave his homeland: **refugee**

Persia ●pre-Islamic religion of ancient Persia: **Zoroastrianism**

persist ●grim persistence: **doggedness, perseverance**

person ●*combining form*: **-ot** (*e.g.* Cypriot), **-nik** (*e.g.* beatnik), **-ster** (*e.g.* youngster) ●affecting a specific person only: **in personam** ●for a particular person: **ad hominem** ●per person: **per caput, per capita**

personality ●personality element: **strain, trait** ●inherited personality traits: **nature** ●environmental influences on personality: **nurture** ●dull and dependable: **stolid** ●subject to unpredictable mood changes: **mercurial** ●ingrained pattern of maladaptive behaviour: **personality disorder** ●personality disorder with extreme antisocial behaviour: **sociopathy**

perspective ●perspective system using three axes 120° apart: **isometric system** ●point in a perspective system at which receding parallel lines seem to merge: **vanishing point**

persuade ●easily persuaded: **pliant** ●persuade by flattery: **cajole, inveigle**

- systematic persuasion: **brainwashing** • refusal to be persuaded: **obstinacy, obduracy**

Peru • original inhabitants of Peru: **Incas** • their supreme ruler: **Inca** • Spanish conqueror of Peru: **conquistador**

petrol • *combining form*: **petro-** • jellied petrol used in incendiary bombs: **napalm** • denoting petrol without added lead: **unleaded** • colourless hydrocarbon in petrol: **octane** • natural liquid from which petrol is distilled: **petroleum** • establishment selling petrol to motorists: **filling station, petrol station, service station** • crude bomb made by filling a bottle with petrol: **Molotov cocktail**

petroleum • colourless volatile liquid distilled from petroleum: **white spirit** • money earnt by exports of petroleum: **petrodollars**

phallus • *adjective*: **priapic**

Philistine • god of the ancient Philistines: **Dagon** • gigantic Philistine warrior: **Goliath**

philosophy • philosophical principle: **tenet** • core of universally valid philosophical maxims: **philosophia perennis** • personal philosophy of life: **world view, Weltanschauung** • medieval Western philosophical and theological system: **scholasticism** • philosophical procedure of questioning in pretended ignorance: **Socratic irony** • supposed ultimate cause of all events: **First Cause** • philosophy of law: **jurisprudence** • explanation of phenomena by the purpose they serve: **teleology** • theory that free will does not exist: **determinism** • theory that moral truths exist independently of any knowledge of them: **objectivism** • theory that concepts of knowledge and morality are shaped by the society in which they are found: **relativism** • theory that an action must be right if it benefits most people: **utilitarianism** • theory that all knowledge is derived from sense-experience: **empiricism, phenomenalism** • theory that knowledge cannot be proved objectively: **subjectivism** • theory that knowledge is validated by reason rather than experience: **rationalism** • theory doubting the possibility of reliable knowledge: **scepticism** • theory that the self is all that can be known to exist: **solipsism** • theory denying the duality of mind and body: **monism** • theory that all valid statements can be subjected to rational proof: **positivism, logical positivism** • theory that all phenomena have natural causes: **naturalism** • theory that natural processes have a purpose: **finalism** • theory that practical utility is speculation's only justification: **instrumentalism, pragmatism** • theory that universals have objective existence: **realism** • theory that universals exist only as mental concepts: **conceptualism, idealism** • theory that universals have no real existence: **immaterialism, nominalism** • theory denying the real existence of anything: **nihilism** • philosophical system centred on human freedom and experience: **existentialism, humanism** • philosophical study of basic concepts such as time and identity: **metaphysics** • philosophical study of the nature of knowledge: **epistemology** • Kant's absolute moral obligation: **categorical imperative** • expected superman of Nietzschean philosophy: **Übermensch**

phosphorus • *adjectives*: **phosphoric, phosphorous**

photocopier • powder used in photocopiers: **toner**

photograph • early photograph using a silvered plate: **daguerreotype** • publicity photograph of actors in a film scene: **still** • magazine item of photographs with linking text: **photoessay** ●news communication by photographs: **photojournalism** ●photograph taken through a microscope: **micrograph, photomicrograph** ●photograph with two semi-superimposed images giving a '3-D' effect: **anaglyph** ●photographic image with lights and shades reversed: **negative** ●photographic print made by direct application of the negative: **contact print** ●photograph printed to a larger size: **blow-up, enlargement** ●printed monochrome photograph: **half-tone** ●photograph printed for projection: **slide, transparency, diapositive** ●microphotograph no larger than a fullpoint: **microdot** ●flat sheet of film containing microphotographs: **microfiche** ●denoting a photograph recording actual events: **documentary** ●denoting a photograph taken without the subject's knowledge: **candid** ●denoting a photograph taken against the light: **contre-jour** ●device measuring the light available for photography: **exposure meter, light meter** ●denoting an undeveloped image: **latent** ●make exposed film show a visible image: **develop** ●room for developing photographs: **darkroom** ●coloured light for darkroom use: **safelight** ●clarity of detail shown by a photograph: **resolution** ●looking good when photographed: **photogenic** ●session for publicity photographs: **photocall, photo opportunity**

phrase ●*adjective*: **phrasal** ●key phrase: **motto, watchword** ●stock phrase: **tag** ●phrase whose meaning is not deducible from those of its component words: **idiom** ●expression of a whole phrase as a single word: **holophrasis** ●symbol standing for a phrase: **logogram, logograph**

physical ●*combining form*: **physico-** (e.g. physico-chemical)

physics ●physics of biological phenomena: **biophysics** ●physics of the earth and its structure: **geophysics** ●electron physics: **electronics** ●physics of heat and other forms of energy: **thermodynamics** ●low-temperature physics: **cryogenics** ●exertion of force: **work** ●area in which a force is effective: **field** ●discrete amount of energy etc.: **quantum** (*pl.* quanta) ●heat required for change of state but not of temperature: **latent heat** ●subatomic unit of matter: **particle** ●action of atomic and subatomic particles upon each other: **interaction** ●dependence of various physical phenomena on the motion of the observer and the thing observed: **relativity** ●single theory for subatomic particle interactions: **grand unified theory** ●theory accounting for two or more of the four interactions: **unified field theory** ●theory that random phenomena are in fact rule-bound: **chaos theory** ●hypothesized four-dimensional fusion of space and time: **space–time** ●imagined distortion of space–time enabling astronauts to breach the laws of physics: **space warp**

piano ●piano with horizontal strings: **grand piano** ●piano with vertical strings: **upright** ●mechanical piano: **player-piano, pianola™** ●piano with modified tunings etc. for performing a particular piece: **prepared piano** ●denoting a piano with crossing strings: **overstrung** ●pad silencing a piano string: **damper** ●pin by which a piano string is tuned: **wrest pin** ●mechanism allowing the hammer to return: **escapement** ●piano-player: **pianist** ●art of piano-playing: **pianism**

pickle ●mustard vegetable pickle: **piccalilli** ●spicy mixed pickle: **chutney**

picture ●picture in a book: **illustration, plate** ●picture of a person:

portrait ●artist's picture of himself or herself: **self-portrait** ●wall portrait poster: **pin-up** ●small picture set inside a larger one: **inset** ●picture etc. that can be printed onto another surface by heat pressure: **transfer** ●picture of Death leading all to the grave: **dance of death, danse macabre** ●picture venerated in the Eastern Church: **icon** ●set of 14 pictures depicting Christ's journey to Calvary: **Stations of the Cross** ●picture of an indoors scene: **interior** ●picture of an outdoors scene: **exterior** ●picture portraying everyday life: **genre scene** ●picture of rural life: **pastoral** ●picture of the sea: **seascape** ●picture of arranged objects: **still life** ●satirical picture: **caricature, cartoon** ●mental picture: **image** ●picture obtained by a camera, telescope, mirror, etc.: **image** ●picture made by attaching items to the canvas: **collage** ●outline picture: **silhouette** ●picture made of small pieces of coloured stone or glass: **mosaic** ●such a piece: **tessera** (*pl.* tesserae) ●denoting a detailed and objective picture: **photorealist** ●clarity of a picture: **definition, focus** ●deliberate slight blurring of an image: **soft focus** ●range of tones in a picture: **contrast** ●picture of a face built up from standard elements: **identikit™** ●picture of someone's face composed from photographs of others: **photofit** ●this built up on a computer screen: **videofit** ●manipulation of a digitized image: **image processing** ●gradual change of an image by computerized techniques: **morphing** ●laser-generated three-dimensional image: **hologram** ●picture in the tones of one colour only: **monochrome** ●simplified picture used to represent a word in certain ancient writing systems: **glyph, pictograph** ●part of a picture nearer the observer: **foreground** ●part of a picture further

from the observer: **background** ●bright area of a picture: **highlight** ●position taken by the living subject of a picture: **pose** ●representation of a word by pictures of objects whose names make its syllables: **rebus** ●picture mount: **matt** ●ornamental wooden strip for picture hooks: **picture rail** ●trim a picture's edges: **crop**

pie ●pie thrown in slapstick comedy: **custard pie** ●small pie: **pasty, patty** ●pastry folded round a sweet filling: **turnover** ●small open pastry case with a savoury filling: **vol-au-vent**

piece ●piece left over: **remainder, remnant**

piety ●excessive piety: **pietism**

pig ●*adjective*: **porcine** ●female pig: **sow** ●male pig: **boar** ●castrated male pig: **hog** ●young female pig: **gilt** ●give birth to piglets: **pig, farrow** ●piglets born at a birth: **litter, farrow** ●smallest piglet in a litter: **runt** ●pig raised for food: **porker** ●pig's grunt: **oink** ●fruit of forest trees as pig food: **mast** ●waste food mixed with water as pig food: **swill** ●meat of a pig: **pork** ●skin of a pork joint, roasted until crisp: **crackling** ●crisp pieces of pork fat: **scratchings** ●pig intestines used as food: **chitterlings** ●loaf of chopped pork offal: **haslet** ●pig's feet used as food: **trotters** ●pig fat used in cooking: **lard** ●place where pigs live: **pigsty, piggery**

pigeon ●young unfledged pigeon: **squab** ●pigeon carrying written messages: **carrier pigeon** ●pigeon able to find its way home from great distances: **homer, homing pigeon**

pigment ●dark body pigment: **melanin**

pill ●pill dissolving in the mouth: **lozenge** ●pill's outer cover: **capsule**

pillar ●*combining form*: **styl-** ●rectangular engaged pillar: **pilaster** ●upright stone erected in prehistoric times: **menhir** ●prehistoric circle of stone or wooden pillars: **henge** ●classical pillar carved to resemble a man: **telamon** ●classical pillar carved to resemble a woman: **caryatid** ●Amerindian carved pillar: **totem pole** ●prehistoric ring of pillars: **henge** ●row of pillars round a courtyard or portico: **peristyle** ●early Christian saint living on the top of a pillar: **stylite** ●denoting a pillar projecting from a wall: **engaged** ●denoting a building having four pillars: **tetrastyle**

pillow ●long thick pillow: **bolster**

pilot ●aircraft pilot for test runs: **test pilot** ●Japanese suicide pilot: **kamikaze** ●pilot's unaccompanied flight: **solo** ●interactive training environment for pilots: **flight simulator** ●denoting automatic piloting devices: **fly-by-wire**

pin ●split pin with openable ends: **cotter pin** ●wooden pin fastening timbers: **treenail, trenail** ●supporting pin: **trunnion**

pipe¹ ●branched pipe: **manifold** ●adjustable tuning pipe: **pitch-pipe** ●chief supply pipe: **main** ●pipe connecting a temporary water tap: **standpipe** ●pipe whose contents move upwards: **riser** ●pipe carrying rainwater from the roof: **downpipe, fall-pipe** ●pipe taking excrement and waste water down the side of a building: **soil stack** ●pipe taking used water from sinks etc. to the sewer: **waste pipe** ●underground pipe for excrement and waste water: **sewer** ●suction device clearing blocked pipes: **plunger** ●bent section in a waste pipe: **trap** ●curve near the top of a waste pipe: **trap** ●joint or coupling for pipes: **union** ●long flexible wire for unblocking pipes: **plumber's snake** ●knocking noise in a water supply pipe: **water hammer** ●oil or gas store at the end of a pipeline: **terminal**

pipe² ●long-stemmed clay pipe: **churchwarden** ●Amerindian peace pipe: **calumet** ●Turkish tobacco pipe: **chibouk** ●pipe in which the smoke is passed through water: **hookah, narghile, water pipe** ●pipe for marijuana: **chillum**

pirate ●pirate flag: **Jolly Roger** ●device on this: **skull and crossbones**

pistol ●beat someone with a pistol butt: **pistol-whip**

pit ●farm storage pit: **silo** ●pit for sewage: **cesspit**

pitch ●correct musical pitch: **intonation** ●correctly pitched: **true** ●coincidence in pitch: **unison** ●above true pitch: **sharp** ●below true pitch: **flat** ●musician's constant slight pitch oscillation: **vibrato** ●pitch a string by pressing it: **stop** ●adjust a musical instrument to the desired pitch: **tune** ●lower a pipe's pitch by plugging its end: **stop** ●pitch range of a voice or musical composition: **tessitura** ●phenomenon causing pitch-change in passing noises: **Doppler effect** ●slow pitch-distortion of recorded sound: **wow** ●fast pitch-distortion of recorded sound: **flutter**

pity ●arousing pity: **pathetic, piteous, pitiable, pitiful** ●quality arousing pity: **pathos**

pivot ●pivot on a rudder: **pintle** ●pivot on a large gun: **trunnion**

place ●*combining forms*: **top-, -orium** (*e.g.* auditorium), **-ory** (*e.g.* dormitory) ●place of origin: **provenance** ●place where something happens: **locale, location** ●place where something is: **locality, site** ●place one is going to: **destination** ●places of touristic interest: **sights** ●visit such places: **sightsee** ●safe place: **haven, sanctuary** ●secluded place: **nook, retreat** ●most distant place: **ultima Thule** ●place name: **toponym** ●find the place of: **locate** ●take the place of: **supersede, supplant** ●list of places: **gazetteer** ●'feel' of a place: **genius loci** ●in its place: **in situ** ●make change places: **transpose** ●place beside: **juxtapose** ●place on top of: **superimpose**

plagiarism ●literary work made from quotations of other authors: **cento**

plague ●swelling symptomatic of bubonic plague: **bubo**

plain ●Arctic plain: **tundra** ●plain in Russia: **steppe** ●plain in South Africa: **veldt** ●grassy plain in warm countries: **savannah**

plainsong ●(sign showing) note(s) to be sung to a syllable: **neume** ●scale used in plainsong: **tone**

plan ●design plan: **blueprint** ●secret plan: **intrigue, plot** ●crafty plan: **gambit, ploy, stratagem** ●make crafty plans: **scheme** ●contingency plan: **fail-safe, fallback** ●timed plan for a series of events: **timetable** ●detailed strategy for sporting or business success: **game plan** ●carefully planned sequence of actions or events: **set piece** ●outline plan of a work of fiction: **scenario** ●planned ultimate fallback: **pis aller** ●denoting long-term planning: **strategic** ●denoting short-term planning: **tactical** ●plan in advance: **premeditate** ●frustrate someone's intentions: **thwart**

planet ●tiny planet: **planetesimal** ●large low-density planet: **gas giant** ●planet orbiting the sun: **major planet, primary planet** ●planets etc. orbiting the sun: **solar system** ●denoting a planet orbiting closer to the sun than the earth does: **inferior** ●denoting a planet orbiting further from the sun than the earth does: **superior** ●side of a planet nearest its primary star: **dayside** ●side of a planet away from its primary star: **nightside** ●bright spot on a planet: **facula** ●natural or artificial object orbiting a planet: **satellite** ●cavity on the surface of a planet: **crater** ●study of life-forms on other planets: **exobiology**

planning ●detailed planning of a complex operation: **logistics** ●planning method that evaluates a complex set of alternatives: **critical path analysis**

plant ●*combining forms*: **phyto-, -phyte** (*e.g.* saprophyte) ●plants of a region or period: **flora** ●simple aquatic plant: **alga** ●simple plant growing on stone and trees: **lichen** ●plant-like organism parasitic upon living or decaying matter: **fungus** ●plant living for one year only: **annual** ●plant living for two years only: **biennial** ●plant living for three or more years: **perennial** ●plant flowering or cropping more than once a year: **remontant** ●plant growing in or on water: **hydrophyte** ●plant storing water in its leaves or stem: **succulent** ●plant living on decayed matter: **saprophyte** ●plant growing in damp conditions: **hygrophyte** ●plant growing in dry conditions: **xerophyte** ●plant growing on another plant: **epiphyte** ●plant growing inside another: **endophyte** ●plant growing along the ground or clinging to vertical supports: **vine** ●plant growing on rock: **lithophyte** ●bushlike plant: **shrub** ●young plant raised fom a seed: **seedling** ●piece cut from a plant for propagation: **cutting** ●shoot inserted into another plant: **graft** ●plant shoot for grafting: **scion** ●sideshoot coming up from the roots of a plant: **sucker** ●offspring of plants of different species: **crossbreed, hybrid** ●plant having green leaves all year: **evergreen** ●denoting a plant losing its leaves each autumn: **deciduous** ●denoting a plant dying down to the ground after flowering: **herbaceous** ●denoting a plant native to a region: **endemic** ●denoting a plant able to live outdoors all year: **hardy** ●denoting a plant able to live outdoors except during frost: **half-hardy** ●denoting a plant needing little water: **xerophilous** ●denoting a plant easily harmed by extreme weather: **tender** ●denoting a plant pale through lack of light: **etiolated** ●denoting a plant with multicoloured leaves: **variegated** ●denoting a pot plant whose roots can expand no further: **potbound** ●plant bearing clusters of flowers: **floribunda** ●flowerless plant with delicate leaves: **fern** ●plant producing hemp and a psychotropic drug: **cannabis, Indian hemp, marijuana** ●tapioca plant: **cassava, manioc** ●plant cats like to smell: **catmint, catnip** ●plant with medicinal or culinary uses: **herb** ●growing plants ploughed under: **green manure** ●plant's swollen undergrown food store: **bulb, corm** ●plant's horizontal underground stem: **rhizome** ●part of a plant around ground level: **crown** ●plant stalk: **haulm** ●shoot extending from a plant at ground level: **runner** ●slender twining extension of a plant stem: **tendril, tentacle** ●use by green plants of sunlight energy: **photosynthesis** ●green pigment in plants, enabling photosynthesis: **chlorophyll** ●fluid circulating in a plant: **sap** ●plant's loss of water vapour: **transpiration** ●female reproductive cell in plants: **egg, ovum** ●asexual reproductive unit of the lower plants: **spore** ●plant's beginning to grow: **germination** ●plant growth in relation to gravity: **geotropism** ●plant's turning towards light: **phototropism** ●plant's turning towards a source of heat: **thermotropism** ●plant's turning in response to touch: **thigmotropism** ●variety of plant developed by breeding: **strain** ●(of a plant) grow too fast: **bolt, shoot** ●denoting a plant needing a larger pot: **pot-bound** ●press a plant's roots into soil: **heel in** ●make a plant grow out of season or

unnaturally fast: **force** ●accustom plants to harsh conditions: **harden, harden off** ●establish a plant in a new habitat: **naturalize** ●relocate a plant: **transplant** ●remove plants to allow others room to grow: **thin, thin out** ●remains of prehistoric plants found in rock: **fossil** ●place where plants are grown for study: **botanic garden** ●place where young plants are grown: **nursery** ●glazed building for raising plants: **greenhouse, hothouse** ●glass-lidded area with low walls to shelter young plants: **cold frame** ●glass container for raising plants: **terrarium** ●glass container for water plants: **aquarium** ●growing plants without soil: **hydroponics** ●feeding on plants: **phtyophagous** ●animal feeding on plants: **herbivore** ●small bug parasitic on plants: **aphid** ●poisonous to plants: **phytotoxic** ●plant out seedlings: **prick out** ●label attached to a plant: **tally** ●droop and shrivel as a sickly plant: **wilt, wither** ●repository of dried plants: **herbarium, hortus siccus** ●study of plants: **botany** ●chemistry of plants: **phytochemistry** ●study of plant diseases: **phytopathology**

plaster ●plaster of lime, cement, and gravel: **roughcast** ●fine plaster: **stucco** ●top coat of plaster: **set** ●decorative plasterwork: **pargeting** ●plaster painted to imitate stone: **scagliola** ●hard white plaster for sculpture or bonesetting: **plaster of Paris** ●gypsum for sculpture or painting: **gesso** ●roughen a plaster surface to aid adhesion: **key** ●thin strip of wood as a base for plaster: **lath** ●plasterer's board: **hawk** ●plasterer's smoothing tool: **float**

plastic ●plastic-coated cloth: **American cloth** ●plastic used as glazing: **Perspex™** ●plastic used for gramophone records: **vinyl** ●plastic used for packing: **expanded polystyrene** ●plastic used in paints: **acrylic,**

vinyl ●thin and narrow strip of plastic: **slat** ●overlay with plastic: **laminate**

plastic surgery ●*combining form*: **-plasty** ●plastic surgery on the ears: **otoplasty** ●plastic surgery on the nose: **rhinoplasty** ●plastic surgery on the penis: **phalloplasty** ●sucking away of excess fat: **liposuction**

plate ●plate strengthening a beam or joint: **fish** ●beam or plate distributing weight onto a wall: **template**

platform ●small platform: **podium, rostrum** ●low platform in a room: **dais** ●narrow platform for fashion models: **catwalk, runway** ●platform for an execution: **scaffold** ●platform for election speeches: **hustings** ●display platform on a lorry: **float**

play ●plays in general: **drama** ●play with a happy ending: **comedy** ●play with grim humour: **black comedy** ●play with a sad ending: **tragedy** ●play intended to cause laughter: **comedy** ●broadly comic play: **farce** ●short comic play: **sketch, skit** ●short play presented to open an entertainment: **curtain-raiser** ●play satirizing a particular social group: **comedy of manners** ●Italian traditional comedy with stock characters: **commedia dell'arte** ●sensational or horrific play: **Grand Guignol, melodrama** ●history play: **costume drama** ●play with singing and dancing: **musical, opera** ●play on Christ's birth: **nativity play** ●medieval play portraying scenes from the life of Christ or the saints: **miracle play, mystery play** ●medieval play featuring personifications of theological concepts: **morality play** ●17th-century musical play: **masque** ●play for one actor: **monodrama** ●play for two actors: **two-hander** ●pay intended to be read rather than acted: **closet drama, closet play** ●text of a play: **script** ●principal section of a play: **act** ●subordinate section of a play: **scene** ●address to the audience at the start of a play: **prologue** ●address to the audience at the end of a play: **epilogue** ●play's story-line: **plot** ●turn (a story) into a play: **dramatize** ●crucial moment in a play: **catastrophe** ●contrived resolution of this, as by divine intervention: **deus ex machina** ●startling moment in a play: **coup de théâtre** (*pl.* coups de théâtre) ●principal character in a play: **protagonist** ●secondary role of a pert young woman: **soubrette** ●performance instruction printed in a script: **stage direction** ●person who writes plays: **dramatist, playwright** ●art of play-writing: **dramaturgy** ●person instructing the actors in a play: **director** ●person responsible for a play's staging: **stage manager** ●lighting, sound, or scenery used in a play: **effects** ●offstage sounds as part of the performance: **noises off** ●scenery and properties used in a play: **mise en scène** ●music composed for a play: **score** ▸*see also* **drama**

please ●eager to please: **complaisant** ●excessively eager to please: **servile** ●denoting pleasant appearance and manner: **personable**

pleasure ●pleasure-loving: **hedonistic** ●a life of pleasure: **la dolce vita** ●pleasure gained from the contemplation of others' misfortunes: **Schadenfreude** ●pleasure derived from the suffering of others: **Roman holiday** ●sexual pleasure derived from inflicting pain: **algolagnia** ●sexual pleasure derived from hurting others: **sadism** ●sexual pleasure derived from hurting oneself: **masochism** ●ethical theory that pleasure is the highest good: **hedonism** ●person devoted to sensual pleasures: **debauchee, epicurean, sybarite, voluptuary** ●instinctive psychological drive to seek pleasure: **pleasure principle** ●rich man persuing a life of pleasure: **playboy** ●pleasure trip: **outing** ●pleasure activity: **pastime, recreation** ●person spoiling others' pleasure: **killjoy**

plot ●crafty plot: **machination** ●denoting a crafty plotter: **Machiavellian** ●engage in devious schemes: **wheel and deal** ●plot outline of a work of fiction: **synopsis**

plough ●cutting blade on the front of a plough: **coulter** ●plough's main cutting blade: **ploughshare, share** ●groove cut by a plough: **furrow** ●ploughing technique minimizing erosion on sloping land: **contour ploughing** ●strip of land left unploughed: **headland**

plug ●single-pin plug used in sound equipment: **jack plug** ●21-pin video plug: **Scart** ●plug for the vent of a cask: **spigot, spile** ●plug for the muzzle of a large gun: **tampion** ●plug for a cannon's touch-hole: **spike** ●depression receiving a plug: **socket**

plum ●virus disease of plum trees and their fruit: **plum pox** ●dried plum: **prune**

pneumonia ●pneumonia affecting both lungs: **double pneumonia** ●kind of pneumonia spread by water droplets: **legionnaires' disease**

pocket ●person stealing from others' pockets: **pickpocket**

poem ●traditional poem for young children: **nursery rhyme** ●narrative poem of several stanzas: **ballad** ●long poem of heroic deeds: **epic** ●short poem in epic style: **epyllion** ●poem celebrating a marriage: **epithalamium, prothalamium** ●poem about rural life: **bucolic, eclogue, georgic, idyll** ●poem retracting a former view: **palinode** ●poem lamenting a person's death: **elegy, threnody** ●four-line comic poem: **clerihew** ●five-line comic poem: **limerick** ●poem of 14 lines: **sonnet** ●Japanese three-line poem of 17 syllables: **haiku**

(*pl.* same) ●Japanese five-line poem of 31 syllables: **tanka** (*pl.* same) ●poem constructed so that certain letters from each line form a word: **acrostic** ●poem conveying part of its message through its printed appearance: **concrete poetry** ●section of a long poem: **canto** ●lines repeated at regular intervals through a poem: **refrain**

poet ●successful poet at an Eisteddfodd: **bard** ●French medieval poet: **troubadour, trouvère** ●Scandinavian medieval poet: **skald** ●bad poet: **poetaster** ●poetic technique: **poetics**

point ●highest point: **acme, apex, zenith** ●lowest point: **nadir** ●point at which rays or waves meet: **focal point** ●tapering to a point: **acuminate, apical** ●point of contact or interaction: **interface** ●avoid the point: **prevaricate** ●point implied or inferred: **subaudition**

poison ●*combining forms*: **tox-, toxico-** ●*adjective*: **toxic** ●poison produced by a fungus on peanuts: **aflatoxin** ●poison produced by a fungus on cereals: **ergot** ●poison secreted by snakes, scorpions, etc.: **venom** ●poison drunk by Socrates: **hemlock** ●poisonous to cells: **cytotoxic** ●poisonous to plants: **phytotoxic** ●study of poisons: **toxicology** ●cure for a poison: **antidote, antitoxin, antivenin**

poker ●poker-player's stake made before receiving cards: **ante** ●equal an opponent's bet and demand to see his cards: **see** ●form of poker in which the loser discards an item of clothing: **strip poker**

pole[1] ●punt pole: **quant** ●strong pole for a mast etc.: **spar** ●pole along the foot of a sail: **boom** ●pole projecting the microphone over a film or television camera: **boom**

pole[2] ●around the pole: **circumpolar** ●continent around the North Pole:

Arctic •continent around the South Pole: **Antarctica**

police •area police force: **constabulary** •police group assigned a special task: **squad** •police group with high mobility: **flying squad** •police department dealing with political security: **Special Branch** •police detachment sent to seize specified persons: **snatch squad** •person trained to act as a policeman in an emergency: **special constable** •member of a self-appointed citizen group policing its locality: **vigilante** •policeman's short thick stick: **truncheon** •police patrol car: **squad car** •police van for transporting prisoners: **Black Maria** •police coordination office for investigation of a major crime: **incident room** •police kit for assembling a likeness of a wanted person: **identikit, photofit** •document authorizing specified police activity: **warrant** •surprise hostile police visit: **raid** •policeman's turn of duty: **watch** •policeman's regular patrol: **beat** •regular assignment of a policeman to a particular beat: **community policing** •police job controlling traffic: **point duty** •lowest police rank: **constable** •officer in charge of a constabulary: **chief constable** •officer in charge of the Metropolitan Police: **chief commissioner** •international police organization: **Interpol**

policy •declared policy: **platform, position** •aspect of this: **plank** •published policy statement: **manifesto** •policy of racial segregation: **colour bar** •policy of passive resistance: **satyagraha** •state policy of having no dealings with its neighbours: **isolationism** •reversal of policy: **about-face, volte-face, U-turn**

polish •polishing machine: **buffer** •sheen on polished furniture: **patina**

political party •political party's declared policy: **party line, platform**

•aspect of this: **plank** •party spokesperson putting a favourable gloss upon events: **spin doctor** •splinter group within a political party: **faction, caucus** •infiltration of a political party: **entryism** •party support based on empathy with its leader: **personalism, personality cult** •sympathizer with a party's aims: **fellow-traveller** •publication controlled by a political party: **organ** •(of a constituency political association) choose as candidate for an election: **adopt** •(of a constituency political association) reject a previously adopted candidate: **deselect** •politician belonging to no party: **independent** •move to a rival political group: **defect** •political opposition in a one-party state: **dissidence**

politician •respected political leader: **statesman** •experienced politician: **elder statesman** •politician manipulating his audience's emotions: **demagogue** •politician belonging to no party: **independent** •denoting a politician's statement concordant with his party's position: **on-message** •denoting a crafty and unscrupulous politician: **Machiavellian**

politics •politics as influenced by geographical factors: **geopolitics** •global balance of political power: **world order** •political agenda driven by practical needs rather than moral principles: **realpolitik** •political coalition for a specific purpose: **front** •political action aimed at increasing power or influence: **power politics** •political policy statement: **manifesto** •persistent dissemination of political propaganda via the media: **agitprop** •make politically aware or active: **politicize** •political system allowing much personal freedom: **open society** •political system with much state control of economic and social life: **statism** •system of political power-sharing or coexistence: **pluralism** ●discarded political system: **ancien régime** ●political dominance: **hegemony** ●source of political influence: **power base** ●international acceptance of a state or its government: **recognition** ●political control of dependent countries: **colonialism** ●theory that one political event causes similar ones elsewhere: **domino theory** ●control of a state by large interest groups: **corporatism** ●political opposition in a one-party state: **dissidence** ●political initiative: **démarche** ●resistance to political change: **immobilism** ●advocate of major political change: **radical** ●politician claiming to represent the interests of ordinary people: **populist** ●political enthusiast: **activist, Young Turk** ●group of political activists: **cadre** ●person with moderate political views: **centrist** ●person favouring socialism: **leftist** ●person with extreme or subversive political views: **Bolshevik, maximalist, radical** ●advocate of violence to obtain political objectives: **militant** ●use of violence or intimidation to achieve political aims: **terrorism** ●advocate of military pressure to obtain international political objectives: **militarist** ●person advocating state or popular ownership of means of production: **collectivist** ●person demanding the return of former national territories: **irredentist** ●advocate of political independence: **nationalist** ●advocate of impractical policies: **impossibilist** ●dishonest means of gaining political advantage: **graft** ●dishonest use of political power: **jobbery, sleaze** ●abandonment of one's former political beliefs: **apostasy** ●move to a rival political group: **defect** ●wholesale ousting from power of disliked elements: **purge, repression** ●remove from the political sphere: **depoliticize** ●the masses having no polit-

ical awareness: **lumpenproletariat** ●renunciation of political interests in an area: **disengagement** ●not concerned with politics: **apolitical**

poll ●public poll on some issue of current concern: **plebiscite, referendum** ●officer who counts the votes cast in a poll: **scrutineer** ●officer administering a poll and announcing its result: **returning officer**

pollen ●index of airborne pollen: **pollen count** ●study of ancient pollen grains: **palynology**

pollution ●polluting substance: **pollutant**

polo ●polo stick: **hammer** ●session of play: **chukka**

polymer ●enzyme forming polymers: **polymerase**

Polynesian ●Polynesian garland: **lei**

pond ●shallow upland pond filled by dew: **dew pond**

pool ●pool-player's stick: **cue**

poor ●poor person: **pauper** ●make poor: **impoverish**

pope ●*adjectives*: **papal, pontifical** ●polite form of address to a pope: **Your Holiness** ●pope's triple crown: **tiara** ●pope's short hooded cape: **mozzetta** ●pope's woollen shoulder vestment: **pallium** ●pope's letter to the Church: **encyclical, brief, bull** ●pope's decision on a question of canon law: **decretal** ●pope's decision on a question of doctrine: **rescript** ●pope's personal edict: **motu proprio** (*pl.* motu proprios) ●pope's special permission: **indult** ●pope's freedom from doctrinal error: **papal infallibility** ●pope's ambassador: **nuncio** ●nuncio sent to a non-Catholic country: **pro-nuncio** ●pope's representative: **legate** ●legate with full powers: **legate a latere** ●pope's administrative staff: **Curia** ●pope's guard: **Swiss guard** ●pope's office or tenure of it: **papacy** • papal court: **Holy See** • body electing the pope: **College of Cardinals** • meeting of this: **conclave** • treaty between the pope and a secular state: **concordat** • advocate of supreme papal authority on questions of faith and dicipline: **ultramontanist** • voluntary donation by Roman Catholics to papal funds: **Peter's pence**

population • *combining form*: **dem(o)-** • population count: **census** • quantitative data on changing population levels: **vital statistics** • study of population statistics: **demography** • surplus population: **overspill** • population improvement by controlled breeding: **eugenics**

porcelain • porcelain made with bone ash: **bone china** • denoting very delicate porcelain: **eggshell** • famous type of medieval Chinese porcelain: **Ming**

porcupine • porcupine's sharp hollow bristle: **quill**

pork • tough outer skin on a joint of pork: **rind** • pork rind made crisp by roasting: **crackling**

pornography • denoting explicit pornography: **hard, hard-core** • denoting inexplicit pornography: **soft, soft-core** • mildly pornographic talk or publications: **smut**

porridge • thin porridge: **gruel**

port¹ • port open to all traders: **free port** • officials controlling a port: **conservancy**

port² • denoting a port kept for only a few years in cask and then fined: **ruby** • denoting a port kept longer than usual in the cask: **late-bottled** • denoting port blended from several vintages: **tawny**

portrait • small portrait: **cameo** • half-length portrait: **kit-cat** • group portrait, the subjects appearing to talk together: **conversation piece**

• piece of jewellery with a relief portrait: **cameo**

Portuguese • Portuguese monarch's son: **infante** • Portuguese monarch's daughter: **infanta** • Portuguese noble of the highest rank: **grandee** • Portuguese magistrate or mayor: **alcalde** • Portuguese wine drunk while new: **vinho verde** • Portuguese red wine: **tinto**

Poseidon • *Latin name*: **Neptune** • Poseidon's three-pronged spear: **trident**

position • position relative to a fixed point: **bearing** • apparent change in relative position of objects viewed from different points: **parallax**

possession • personal possession: **chattel** • useless possession: **white elephant** • possession giving social prestige: **status symbol**

post • strong post with a pointed end: **stake** • defensive wall of wooden stakes: **stockade** • firmly fixed upright post: **stanchion**

postage stamp • stamp perforated with a set of initials: **perfin** • stamp printed upside down: **invert** • sheet of stamps: **pane** • denoting a stamp intended for general use: **definitive** • denoting stamps lacking perforations: **imperforate** • envelope with stamps postmarked on their first day of issue: **first day cover** • printed mark cancelling or substituting for a postage stamp: **frank** • date stamp cancelling a postage stamp: **postmark** • small piece of gummed paper for fixing stamps in an album: **hinge** • stamp collecting and study: **philately**

postal service • service guaranteeing next-day delivery to anywhere in the UK: **special delivery** • service offering next-day delivery to most UK areas: **first-class post** • service offering later delivery: **second-class post**

• service offering proof of posting and delivery: **recorded delivery** • service offering recorded delivery and compensation for loss: **registered post** • conveyance of mail by air: **airmail** • conveyance of mail by land and sea: **surface mail** • post office department holding letters until collected: **poste restante** • numbered box assigned to a person using this regularly: **post office box** • fee required to send an item by post: **postage** • address code assisting mail sorting: **postcode** • person delivering letters: **postman** • shop or counter conducting postal service business: **post office** • person managing a post office: **postmaster** (*fem.* postmistress)

postcard • postcard collector: **deltiologist**

post-mortem • doctor conducting a post-mortem examination: **pathologist** • magistrate conducting a post-mortem judicial inquiry: **coroner**

posture • cross-legged meditation posture: **lotus position** • communication by posture: **kinesics**

potato • baked potato served in its skin: **jacket potato** • potato in Indian cuisine: **aloo** • cooked cabbage and potato fried up together: **bubble and squeak** • potatoes mashed and baked with egg yolk: **duchesse potatoes** • dish of sliced potatoes cooked in milk: **dauphinois** • store of potatoes under straw and earth: **clamp** • dark shoot-spot on a potato: **eye** • edible root of the potato plant: **tuber** • Irish potato blight: **murrain**

potential • realization of one's personal potential: **self-actualization**

pottery • *adjective*: **fictile** • type of pottery: **ware** • clay mix for making pottery: **pug** • form pottery on the wheel: **throw** • unfired pottery: **greenware** • pottery fired but not glazed: **biscuit ware, bisque** • porous clay pottery: **earthenware**

• glazed pottery: **faience** • fine Italian coloured pottery: **maiolica** • English pottery imitating this: **majolica** • blue Chinese scene as pottery decoration: **willow pattern** • unglazed brownish-red earthenware: **terracotta** • denoting pottery made from clay: **ceramic, earthenware** • coloured clay for pottery decoration: **slip** • decorative scratches made through slip: **sgraffito** (*pl.* sgraffiti) • pottery decorated with slip: **slipware** • shiny surface on pottery: **glaze** • second layer of glaze: **overglaze** • iridescent pottery glaze: **lustre** • furnace for pottery: **kiln** • bake pottery in a kiln: **fire** • protective box for pottery being fired: **saggar** • pottery fragment: **shard, sherd, potsherd** • this used as a writing surface: **ostracon**

pouch • pouch worn at the front of a kilt: **sporran** • kangaroo's pouch: **marsupium**

powder • reduce to a powder: **pulverize**

power • *combining form*: **dynam(o)-** (*e.g.* dynamism) • power of an engine indicated by the force needed to brake it: **brake horsepower** • unlimited power: **carte blanche, omnipotence** • absolute power: **autocracy, despotism, dictatorship, totalitarianism** • position of power: **ascendancy, dominance** • power gained through status, contacts, etc.: **influence** • seize power to which one has no right: **usurp** • obsession with the exercise of power: **megalomania** • transfer of power from central to regional authorities: **decentralization, devolution** • reservation of all power to the central authority: **direct rule** • deprive of power: **emasculate, overthrow** • undermine an established power: **subvert** • state economic and social control: **dirigisme**

power holder • *combining form*: **-crat** • person enjoying power because of his noble birth: **aristocrat**

● person deriving power from his position in an organization: **bureaucrat** ● person exercising power without having any office: **éminence grise** ● person enjoying power through wealth: **plutocrat** ● group thought to have a hidden but pervasive control of society: **the Establishment** ● group of influential high-ranking persons: **the hierarchy** ● person seeking to increase his personal power: **empire builder**

practical ● dully practical: **prosaic**

practice ● generally accepted practice: **orthodoxy**

praise ● *adjective*: **laudatory** ● deserving praise: **meritorious** ● laudatory speech or text: **encomium, eulogy, panegyric**

prawn ● large edible prawn: **king prawn**

prayer ● prayer said at mealtimes: **grace** ● prayer said for others: **intercession** ● RC devotion of repeated Hail Marys: **rosary** ● set of beads used with this: **rosary** ● Orthodox devotion of repeated invocation of the name of Jesus: **Jesus Prayer** ● knotted cord used with this: **prayer rope** ● special days of prayer observed in the West: **Ember days** ● season of prayer for the harvest: **Rogationtide** ● times of prayer prescribed in the Roman breviary: **canonical hours** ● practice of prayer leading to a direct apprehension of the divine: **mysticism** ● cushion for prayer: **hassock, kneeler** ● period of seclusion for prayer: **retreat**

preaching ● *adjective*: **homiletic** ● art of preaching: **homiletics**

precede ● thing preceding another, esp. when perceived as influencing it: **antecedent** ● precede in time: **antedate** ● fallacy that preceding events must be the cause of those that follow them: **post hoc ergo propter hoc**

predictable ● person whose behaviour is unpredictable: **loose cannon**

prefer ● personal preference: **predilection** ● political or sexual preferences: **orientation**

pregnancy ● *adjectives*: **antenatal, maternity, prenatal** ● make pregnant: **impregnate** ● become pregnant: **conceive** ● capable of conception: **fertile** ● incapable of conception: **barren, infertile, sterile** ● denoting conception achieved in the womb: **in utero** ● denoting conception achieved in an artificial environment: **in vitro** ● be pregnant with: **carry** ● further conception while pregnant: **superfetation** ● development of a fetus within the Fallopian tube: **tubal pregnancy** ● development of a fetus outside the womb: **ectopic pregnancy** ● woman pregnant for the first time: **primigravida** (*pl.* primigravidae) ● woman pregnant for at least the second time: **multigravida** ● hormone stimulating uterine preparation for pregnancy: **progesterone** ● female reproductive cell: **egg, ovum** ● tube conveying the egg to the uterus: **Fallopian tube** ● attachment of the egg to the wall of the womb: **implantation, nidation** ● unborn offspring: **embryo, fetus** ● carrying this in the womb: **gestation** ● body fluid surrounding a fetus: **amniotic fluid** ● membrane surrounding a fetus: **amniotic membrane, caul** ● cord connecting a fetus to the placenta: **umbilical cord** ● nausea during early pregnancy: **morning sickness** ● craving for strange foods during pregnancy: **pica** ● high blood pressure in pregnancy: **pre-eclampsia** ● convulsions resulting from this: **eclampsia** ● custom in certain cultures of the husband's taking to his bed during the latter stages of a pregnancy: **couvade** ● spontaneous expulsion of the foetus early in pregnancy: **miscarriage** ● completion of the normal length of pregnancy: **term, full term** ●end a pregnancy by artificial means: **terminate** ●medically induced expulsion or destruction of an unviable foetus: **abortion** ●before the normal end of pregnancy: **preterm** ●diagnostic sampling of amniotic fluid during pregnancy: **amniocentesis** ●child's mental and physical retardation caused by the mother's consumption of alcohol during pregnancy: **fetal alcohol syndrome** ●false pregnancy: **pseudocyesis** ●deliberate prevention of pregnancy: **birth control, contraception, family planning** ●periodic uterine discharge when pregnancy has not occurred: **menstruation**

prehistoric ●*combining form*: **archaeo-** ●prehistoric life form preserved in rock: **fossil** ●large prehistoric reptile: **dinosaur** ●study of the physical remains of prehistoric civilizations: **archaeology** ●use of scientific techniques to date prehistoric remains: **archaeometry**

prejudice ●unfair treatment due to prejudice: **discrimination**

preparation ●speak or act without previous preparation: **extemporize, improvise, ad-lib**

present ●call-over of names to establish who is present: **roll-call**

preserve ●preserve by smoking, salting, etc.: **cure**

press ●press to smooth paper or cloth: **calender**

pressure ●pressure exerted on a physical object: **stress** ●illegal pressure or constraint: **duress** ●obtaining money or property by duress: **extortion** ●duress exerted by threats to reveal compromising secrets: **blackmail** ●political pressure applied by deliberate environmental damage: **ecoterrorism** ●elongated region of high atmospheric pressure: **ridge** ●elongated region of low atmospheric

pressure: **trough** ●area of atmospheric pressure lower than those around it: **depression** ●unstable atmospheric pressure: **turbulence** ●press down firmly: **tamp** ●instrument measuring liquid or gas pressure: **manometer, piezometer** ●instrument measuring atmospheric pressure: **barometer**

pretend ●pretended ignorance or innocence: **disingenuousness** ●pretend to be another person: **impersonate** ●person doing this: **impostor**

pretty ●quaintly pretty: **picturesque**

price ●lowest price at which an auctioned item may be sold: **reserve price** ●official price: **list price** ●guaranteed minimum price: **support price** ●contractor's estimated price for a job: **quotation** ●contractor's firm price for a specified job: **tender** ●unvarying price: **flat rate** ●assign a price to: **valorize** ●haggle over a price: **chaffer** ●collaboration of traders to fix prices: **cartel, price ring** ●vendor's increase to cost price: **mark-up** ●sum added to a normal price: **premium** ●offer a higher price than that for which the sale has already been agreed with another: **gazump** ●over-pricing to make an article seem superior: **prestige pricing** ●item sold at a loss to attract customers: **loss leader** ●selling at different prices to different customers: **price discrimination** ●price reduction offered to certain categories of purchaser: **concession, discount** ●printed paper entitling the holder to buy at a reduced price: **voucher** ●agreement between manufacturer and retailer not to discount prices: **retail price maintenance, resale price maintenance** ●market-dominant trader whose prices are shadowed by the competition: **price leader** ●low pricing to force competitors out of the market: **predatory pricing** ●reduce a posted price: **mark down** ●sensitive to price changes: **elastic** ●denoting an irreducible price: **net** ●denoting a sharply increased price: **inflated** ●denoting a price so high as to discourage purchase: **prohibitive** ●table of prices: **tariff** ●figure indicating the average position of selected prices: **index** ●government intervention to keep prices down: **price control** ●government intervention to keep prices up: **price support** ●system linking wage etc. rises to price rises: **indexation** ●general rise in prices: **inflation** ●general reduction in prices: **deflation**

pride ●pride leading to one's downfall: **hubris** ●arrogantly self-righteous person: **prig** ●solemnly self-important: **pompous**

priest ●*combining form*: hiero- ●*adjectives*: clerical, hieratic, sacerdotal ●chief priest: **hierarch** ●high-ranking priest: **pontifex** ●priest presiding over a cathedral chapter: **dean** ●his residence: **deanery** ●priest on a cathdral chapter: **canon** ●priest in charge of cathedral music: **precentor** ●priest's pastoral responsibility: **cure** ●sacramental admission of sins to a priest: **confession** ●priest's sacramental forgiveness of confessed sins: **absolution** ●priest performing the Eucharist: **celebrant** ●ancient Celtic priest: **Druid** ●Buddhist priest in China or Japan: **bonze** ●title of a French abbot or (as a courtesy) of any French clergyman: **abbé** ●Orthodox priest in Greece: **pope, papas** ●Orthodox priest in Russia: **pope** ●denoting a ʻnonastic priest: **regular** ●denoting a non-monastic priest: **secular** ●make someone a priest: **ordain** ●stiff white collar fastened at the back, worn by some clergy: **clerical collar, dog collar** ●priest's robes: **vestments** ●priest's liturgical dress: **canonicals** ●priest's square liturgical hat: **biretta** ●assistant

priest: **curate** ●curate's job: **curacy** ●priest's liturgical attendant: **acolyte, server** ●rule by priests: **hierocracy** ●derivation and transmission of a priest's spiritual authority from that given to the apostles: **apostolic succession** ▸*see also* **Church of England, Roman Catholic Church**

principle ●set of principles guiding or summarizing an activity: **theory** ●principle that if anything can go wrong it will: **Murphy's law, sod's law** ●principle that employees are always promoted beyond their abilities: **Peter principle** ●principle that work expands to fill the time available: **Parkinson's law** ●adhering rigidly to principle, regardless of practicalities: **doctrinaire** ●having strong moral principles: **high-minded** ●rejection of all religious and moral principles: **nihilism**

printer ●printer printing a line at a time: **line printer** ●printer using heated pins: **thermal printer** ●printer character disk: **daisy wheel** ●grid of dots forming printer characters: **dot matrix** ●printer mode giving quick but poorly finished printout: **draft** ●number of characters per inch: **pitch**

printing ●printing giving raised lettering: **die-stamping** ●blurred piece of printing: **mackle** ●unwanted transference of ink from one sheet to the next: **set-off** ●printing error: **misprint, literal, typo** ●add printing instructions to a manuscript: **mark up** ●type set up to print a sheet: **forme** ●container for loose metal printing type: **case** ●denoting a letter not a capital: **lower-case** ●denoting a capital letter: **upper-case** ●assemble type for printing: **compose** ●composition using newly cast type: **hot metal** ●layout of lines of type to give straight margins: **justification** ●exact alignment of printed elements: **register** ●white space between lines of type: **lead** ●dots to guide the eye: **leaders** ●arrange pages for printing in correct sequence: **impose** ●fully finished page for photosetting: **camera-ready copy** ●roll of paper for continuous printing: **web** ●single piece of paper for printing: **sheet** ●sheet folded into pages: **gathering, signature** ●vertical division of a printed page: **column** ●arrangement of material on a page: **layout** ●specimen layout: **mock-up** ●estimate the pages a printed text will fill: **cast off** ●short line at the top of a page or column: **widow** ●opening line of a paragraph set at the foot of a page or column: **orphan** ●trial printing for corrections: **proof, pull** ●proof incorporating previous corrections: **revise** ●printed monochrome photograph: **half-tone** ●final adjustments before printing: **makeready** ●illustration without half-tones: **line block** ●computer-generated camera-ready copy: **desktop publishing** ●printing from a flat surface: **planography** ●printing of a single item from a larger publication: **pre-print, offprint** ●number of copies printed at one time: **run, print run** ●aesthetics of printing: **typography** ▸*see also* **typeface**

prison ●*adjective*: **custodial** ●centre housing young persons in need of custodial care: **community home** ●prison for criminals aged 14–20: **young offender institution** ●prison with few restrictions: **open prison** ●secret dungeon: **oubliette** ●former German prison camp: **stalag** ●former German prison camp for officers: **oflag** ●former Soviet labour prison: **gulag** ●decommissioned ship used as a prison: **hulk** ●person in charge of a prison: **governor** ●prison guard: **warder** ●cleric serving a prison: **chaplain** ●place in custody pending trial: **remand** ●place used for this: **remand centre** ●send to prison:

commit, send down ●keep in prison: **detain** ●imprisonment to prevent further offences: **preventive detention** ●imprisonment alone: **solitary confinement** ●imprisoned person: **inmate** ●imprisonment with hard labour: **penal servitude** ●release from prison: **discharge** ●study of prison management: **penology** ●release on promise of good behaviour: **parole** ●conditional early release: **release on licence** ●wartime imprisonment of resident aliens: **internment** ●confinement to one's home: **house arrest** ●confinement to a distant part of one's country: **internal exile** ●detention allegedly to safeguard the detainee: **protective custody**

prisoner ●prisoner who has won privileges by good behaviour: **trusty** ●prisoner's room: **cell** ●money paid to secure the release of a prisoner awaiting trial: **bail**

private ●in private: **in camera** ●denoting one's private life: **personal**

privilege ●exclusive privilege: **prerogative** ●prisoner who has won privileges by good behaviour: **trusty**

prize ●large cash prize: **jackpot** ●prize money in a horse race: **stakes** ●prize given to the worst contestant: **booby prize, wooden spoon** ●prize awarded to the ship making the fastest eastward commercial crossing of the Atlantic: **Blue Riband** ●reward given to a near-winner: **consolation prize, highly commended, honourable mention, proxime accessit** ●cumulative carry-over of unwon prizes to the next event: **rollover**

probe ●probing instrument: **sonde**

problem ●unexpected problem: **snag** ●problem-solving by informal discussion: **brainstorming** ●problem-solving by application of logic: **vertical thinking** ●problem-solving by an indirect and seemingly illogical approach: **lateral thinking** •problem-solving as a managerial role: **trouble-shooting** •problem-solving by random trial and error: **heuristic** •clue to a problem's solution: **lead** •place where problems regularly occur: **trouble spot** •fresh approach to a problem: **initiative**

procedure •established course of procedure: **order** •procedural rule: **standing order**

process •*combining form*: **-osis** (*e.g.* metamorphosis) •not processed: **raw**

procession •costumed procession: **pageant** •outdoor procession: **cavalcade** •solemn procession: **cortège**

producing •*combining forms*: **-facient** (*e.g.* abortifacient), **-fic** (*e.g.* pacific), **-gen** (*e.g.* carcinogen), **-genic** (*e.g.* pathogenic)

product •incidental product: **by-product, spin-off** •product manufactured for a retailer and sold under his name: **own brand, own-label** •product name registered by the manufacturer: **proprietary name, proprietary term** •denoting a product closely imitating a branded one but sold under a different name: **generic** •version of a product: **model** •request the return of a product for modification: **recall**

professional •young urban professional: **yuppie** •young black urban professional: **buppie** •work in a profession: **practise** •person working in a profession: **practitioner** •below professional standards: **unprofessional** •remove from membership of a professional body: **strike off**

professor •professor's position: **chair**

profit •profit made on investments: **return** •profit from the sale of property or investments: **capital gain** •selling off the assets of a purchased company for quick profit: **asset-**

stripping •easy or dishonest profits: **pickings** •profits gained from prostitution: **immoral earnings** •tax on excessive profits: **windfall tax** •person pursuing large profits by legally marginal means: **profiteer** •financier making hostile takeover bids with a view to resale: **corporate raider** •selling off shares while their value is high: **profit-taking** •pursuit of profit: **commercialism** •producing much profit: **lucrative** •situation offering no profit: **dead loss**

program •start a program's operation: **run** •program instructions: **code** •self-operating program with reasoning capacity: **knowbot** •program for accounting: **spreadsheet** •program searching the World Wide Web: **crawler** •program devised to meet a particular user's needs: **application, application program** •program interfacing between user and operating system: **shell, shell program** •program recording restricted information: **sniffer** •program performing a routine function: **utility program** •program controlling a peripheral device: **manager** •program enabling the rearrangement of online text: **editor** •program giving form letters individual names and addresses: **mail merge** •program providing addresses, diary engagements, etc.: **personal information manager** •program arranging tasks in an appropriate sequence: **scheduler** •program written in high-level language: **source program** •program converting a high-level-language program into machine code and executing it: **interpreter** •program converting assembly language into machine code: **assembler, compiler** •program connecting two items of hard- or software: **interface** •program deleting unwanted data: **garbage collector** •set of related programs: **suite** •set of instructions used several times within a program: **procedure, subprogram, subroutine** ●unit of which programs are composed: **module** ●subprogram able to construct other subprograms: **generator** ●denoting a program responding to user input: **interactive** ●denoting a program that a computer can run: **executable** ●denoting a program compatible with many computers: **cross-platform** ●an extension to this providing multimedia facilities: **hypermedia** ●secret program instructions causing damage if activated: **logic bomb** ●simultaneous execution of several programs: **multiprocessing, multitasking** ●simultaneous execution of different parts of the same program: **pipelining** ●small addition to a program: **patch** ●system of symbols for program-writing: **language** ●end a program's operation: **exit** ●convert a program into a machine-code: **compile** ●program's fall-back option: **default** ●repeated sequence of programmed instructions: **loop** ●single instruction expanding into a set: **macro** ●program variable activating a certain function: **switch** ●list of commands to be expressed in machine code: **source code** ●re-express data for use with a different program or system: **convert**

programme ●programme with times assigned to each event: **schedule**

programming language ●programming language consisting of binary or hexadecimal instructions: **machine code, machine language** ●denoting a programming language that is not machine-dependent: **high-level** ●denoting a programming language that is close to machine code: **low-level**

progress ●make progress without effort: **coast** ●make better progress than expected: **overachieve** ●make poorer progress than expected: **under-**

achieve ●enemy to progress: **reactionary** ●enemy to technical progress: **Luddite** ●block to progress: **obstacle** ●situation permitting no progress: **deadlock, stalemate, stasis**

prohibition ●temporary prohibition: **moratorium** ●official prohibition on trade: **embargo**

projectile ●path described by a projectile: **trajectory**

projector ●projector giving images of opaque objects: **epidiascope** ●device steadying the film as it passes the lens: **gate** ●adjust film passing the gate: **rack**

promise ●solemn promise: **oath, pledge, vow** ●promise to do something: **undertaking** ●promise to do something, often at a fixed time: **engagement** ●promise to perform another's obligation: **guaranty** ●promise to replace or repair defective goods: **guarantee, warranty** ●promise money on another's successful completion of a charitable event: **sponsor** ●go back on a promise: **renege, welsh**

prone to ●*combining form*: **-acious** (*e.g.* audacious), **-philiac** (*e.g.* haemophiliac)

pronunciation ●correct pronunciation, or its study: **orthoepy** ●standard British English pronunciation: **received pronunciation** ●pitch change as an aspect of pronunciation: **intonation**

propaganda ●political propaganda disseminated in literature etc.: **agitprop**

propeller ●air or water current behind a propeller: **slipstream** ●ship's secondary propeller used in manoeuvring: **thruster** ●propeller blade: **vane**

proof ●providing proof: **probative** ●prove the truth of: **demonstrate** ●prove to be wrong: **refute**

property •ideas as property: **intellectual property** •property in buildings and land: **real property, realty** •property other than buildings or land: **movables, personal property, personalty** •inherited property: **patrimony** •inspect property as a potential lessor or purchaser: **view** •sale of property: **disposal** •person selling his or her property to another: **vendor** •conclude a property sale: **complete** •legal document transferring ownership of property: **conveyance** •right to ownership of property: **title** •summary of title documentation: **abstract of title** •right of exclusive use of property on completion of sale: **vacant possession** •charge upon property: **encumbrance** •transfer of property: **devolution** •effect such a transfer: **devolve** •legal arrangement whereby property is nominally owned by one person for the benefit of others: **trust** •leasing of a property back to its vendor: **leaseback** •use in turn of a property by several joint owners: **time-sharing** •value of a mortgaged property after deduction of charges against it: **equity** •collapse of property values due to expected area redevelopment: **planning blight** •arrangement for the inheritance of property over several generations: **entail** •government's right to seize private property for state use: **eminent domain** •seize property: **confiscate, expropriate** •seize property for the repayment of a debt: **distrain, sequester** •repossess a mortgaged property upon failure of payments: **foreclose** •enter another's property without permission: **trespass** •take unauthorized possession of another's premises: **squat** •expel someone from a property: **evict** •company selling and renting out properties: **estate agency** •property owner giving lets to tenants: **landlord** (*fem.* land-

lady) •tenant in current occupation: **sitting tenant** •tenancy for a fixed period: **term of years** •denoting a fixed-term tenancy: **shorthold** •person living on income from property: **rentier** •unlawful occupant of a building or land: **squatter** •terms under which real property is held: **tenure** •absolute and permanent tenure: **freehold** •tenure for a term of years: **leasehold** •person taking out a lease: **lessee** •person granting a lease: **lessor** •return of property to the lessor at termination of lease: **reversion**

prophet •*adjective*: **mantic** •prophet of doom: **Jeremiah** •prophet of doom who is ignored: **Cassandra**

proportion •in proportion: **commensurate, pro rata** •proportional relation: **ratio**

prose •prose writing undertaken principally for aesthetic effect: **belles-lettres**

prostate gland •inflammation of the prostate: **prostatitis** •enzyme found in the blood of men with prostate cancer: **prostate-specific antigen**

prostitute •prostitute seeking clients in the street: **streetwalker** •prostitutes' manager: **pimp** •income from prostitution: **immoral earnings** •person obtaining prostitutes for others: **procurer, pandar** •slow driving in search of prostitutes: **kerb-crawling**

protection •*combining form*: **para-** (*e.g.* parasol) •protective measure taken in advance: **precaution** •(place of) protection offered to the weak, destitute, or those in danger: **asylum**

protein •blood protein transporting oxygen: **haemoglobin** •protein found in the blood of a diseased person: **paraprotein** •protein present in cheese: **casein** •fungus-derived protein: **mycoprotein** ●malnutrition caused by protein deficiency: **kwashiorkor**

protest ●protest by refusal to eat: **hunger strike** ●protest by ignoring certain laws: **civil disobedience** ●protest by refusal to leave: **occupation, sit-in** ●person refusing co-operation as a protest: **refusenik** ●reproachful verbal protest: **remonstrance**

Protestant ●member of a dissenting Protestant Church: **Nonconformist** ●Protestant church government by ministers and elders: **Presbyterianism** ●district so governed: **presbytery** ●Protestant minister's house: **manse**

Provence ●*adjective*: **Provençal**

prune ●dish of prunes wrapped in bacon and served on toast: **devils on horesback**

Prussian ●Prussan aristocrat: **Junker**

psalm ●psalm book: **psalter** ●psalm-singing: **psalmody**

psychiatry ●psychiatric therapy that seeks to cure an undesirable habit by associating it with an unpleasant experience: **aversion therapy** ●phobia cure by gradual exposure to its cause: **systematic desensitization**

psychoanalysis ●person undergoing psychoanalysis: **analysand** ●release of repressed emotions by discovery of their cause: **catharsis** ●psychoanalytic test of describing inkblots: **Rorschach test**

psychology ●imagined continuous flow of a person's thoughts: **stream of consciousness** ●below the threshold of consciousness: **subliminal** ●group of repressed ideas: **complex** ●refuse to allow into consciousness: **inhibit, repress, suppress** ●verbal thought: **inner speech** ●innate urge to attain a goal: **drive** ●innate reaction to a given stimulus: **instinct** ●seemingly random suggestion of one idea by another: **free association** ●unconscious transfer of one's own desires or emotions onto another: **projection** ●offsetting of a psychological difficulty by developing in another direction: **compensation** ●person much concerned with his own thoughts and feelings: **introvert** ●unselfconscious, outgoing person: **extravert** ●person's true but concealed self: **inner child** ●excessive interest in one's appearance or abilities: **narcissism** ●psychologically induced refusal or inability to communicate: **autism** ●psychologically induced inability to make decisions: **abulia** ●psychologically induced desire to display one's genitals: **exhibitionism** ●psychologically induced refusal to eat: **anorexia nervosa** ●psychologically induced desire to overeat: **bulimia nervosa** ●either or both of the preceding: **eating disorder** ●psychologically induced interest in faeces and defecation: **coprophilia** ●psychologically induced fear: **phobia** ●obsessive desire to set fire to things: **pyromania** ●paranoid attitude based on the assumption of others' hostility: **siege mentality** ●fixation with a single idea: **obsession** ●loss of a sense of personal identity, thought to be caused by inability to socialize: **alienation** ●aggressive behaviour masking feelings of inadequacy: **inferiority complex** ●arrogant behaviour masking feelings of inadequacy: **superiority complex** ●trust or affection directed towards a captor by his victims: **Stockholm syndrome** ●psychologically induced obsession with personal power: **megalomania** ●psychological state of impaired reason and memory: **dementia** ●meaningless repetition of another's acts: **echopraxia** ●meaningless repetition of another's words: **echolalia** ●delusions of self-importance or of persecution: **paranoia, persecution complex** ●psychological state of sloth and despondency: **depression** ●apathy induced by prolonged dependency on state benefits: **dependency culture** ●psychologically induced refusal to speak: **mutism** ●psychologically induced use of obscene language: **coprolalia** ●psychologically induced meaningless speech: **paraphasia** ●psychologically induced desire to steal: **kleptomania** ●psychological disturbance from exposure to warfare: **battle fatigue, combat fatigue, shell-shock** ●denoting a physical illness caused or enhanced by psychological factors: **psychosomatic** ●life instinct in Freudian psychology: **Eros** ●death instinct in Freudian psychology: **Thanatos** ●conscious personality factor in Freudian psychology: **ego** ●Freudian self-critical personality factor: **superego** ●Freudian instinctive and largely subconscious personality factor: **id** ●desire of the id to avoid pain and seek pleasure: **pleasure principle** ●ego's control of the id to meet social norms: **reality principle** ●young child's alleged desire for its parent of the opposite sex: **Oedipus complex** ●masculine part of a woman's personality in Jungian psychology: **animus** ●feminine part of a man's personality in Jungian psychology: **anima** ●aspect of the personality presented to others: **persona** ●relational aspect of human activity in Jungian psychology: **eros** ●primitive mental image said by Jungian psychology to be inherited from prehistoric man: **archetype** ●shared stock of such images: **collective unconscious** ●innate drive for self-destruction: **death instinct** ●innate drive for self-preservation: **life instinct** ●rerouting of basic drives into more socially acceptable activities: **sublimation** ●uncertainty as to one's

personal role: **identity crisis** ●psychological interactions between members of a group: **group dynamics** ●struggle for psychological dominance: **war of nerves, power play** ●psychological treatment: **therapy** ●giving of psychological advice: **counselling** ●therapy aimed at neurotic behaviour rather than its cause: **behavioural therapy** ●therapy simulating the trauma of being born: **re-birthing** ●therapeutic enactment of various social roles: **role playing** ●therapy associating undesirable behaviour with pain etc.: **aversion therapy** ●psychological system positing a constant interaction between parental, adult, and childish personality traits: **transactional analysis** ●study of phenomena unexpained by orthodox psychology: **parapsychology**

public house ●public house not under brewery control: **free house** ●person in charge of this: **landlord, landlady** ●public house under brewery control: **tied house** ●person in charge of this: **manager, tenant** ●period when drink prices are reduced: **happy hour** ●moment at which bar sales must cease: **time** ●period allowed after closing time for consumption of previously purchased liquor: **drinking-up time** ●period after closing time when 'private' drinking takes place behind locked doors: **lock-in** ●permission for a public house to stay open longer than usual: **extension** ●bar customer's running account: **score** ●pub bar offering basic comforts: **public bar** ●pub bar offering superior accommodation, and charging higher prices: **lounge bar, saloon bar, snug** ●fixture for inverted spirit bottles: **gantry** ●brew temporarily available: **guest beer**

publicity ●publicity booklet: **brochure** ●publicity material: **literature** ●publicity to trigger public debate:

consciousness-raising ●person gaining publicity for clients: **publicist** ●avoidance of publicity: **low profile** ▸*see also* **advertising**

publishing ●initial payment to an author on signing a contract: **advance** ●publishing undertaken at the author's expense: **vanity publishing** ●publication using personal computers and printers: **desktop publishing** ●publisher's preferred form of presentation and layout: **house style** ●publisher's address details or brand name: **imprint** ●author's text as submitted to a publisher: **manuscript** ●employee commissioning and supervising projects: **editor** ●employee examining manuscripts for style and consistency: **copy editor** ●commissioning and production of a book for subsequent sale to a publisher: **packaging** ●copy of a book made available before publication date: **advance copy** ●part of a book published separately: **fascicle, instalment, offprint, preprint** ●exclusive right to publish a book: **copyright** ●breach of copyright: **piracy** ●unique number code assigned to each book published: **International Standard Book Number** ●short description of a book's contents, for publicity use: **blurb** ●sum paid to the author for each copy sold: **royalty** ●reprint with editorial intervention: **edition** ●reprint with little or no editorial intervention: **impression** ●book achieving huge sales: **bestseller, blockbuster** ●sell off remaining copies of an book cheaply: **remainder** ●designating a book still available from its publisher: **in print** ●publisher's list of books still in print: **backlist** ▸*see also* **book**

pudding ●fruit pudding steamed in a cloth: **duff** ●steamed pudding of suet and flour: **suet pudding** ●suet pudding rolled with layers of jam or fruit: **roly-poly** ●suet pudding with currants: **spotted dick** ●stewed fruit in a bread case: **charlotte** ●soft summer fruits in a bread case: **summer pudding** ●sponge base with a sweet topping: **flan** ●Italian dessert of sponge soaked in spirits and coffee: **tiramisu** ●Russian Easter dessert: **pashka** ●sweet batter baked with a fruit filling: **clafoutis** ●chestnut preserved in sugar: **marron glacé** ●sponge-cased custard: **charlotte russe** ●custard topped with caramelized sugar: **crème brûlée** (*pl* crèmes brûlées) ●egg custard topped with caramel: **crème caramel** (*pl.* crèmes caramels) ●cold pudding of milk and flavoured cornflour: **blancmange** ●choux pastry filled with cream: **profiterole** ●thin pastry baked round a fruit filling: **strudel** ●light beaten dessert: **whip** ●pudding of flavoured whipped cream: **syllabub** ●cold pudding with whipped cream and eggs: **parfait** ●cold pudding of sponge cake and fruit topped with layers of jelly, custard and cream: **trifle** ●beaten eggs, sugar, and flavourings: **flummery** ●sweet of whipped cream and egg-white: **mousse** ●Greek sweet of sesame flour and honey: **halva** ●Greek sweet of honey-soaked pastry with nuts: **baklava** ●almond-flavoured cream: **frangipane** ●sweetened milk curds: **junket** ●small curd tart: **maid of honour** ●cold puréed fruit with cream: **fool** ●meringue filled with fruit and whipped cream: **pavlova** ●pudding of bread, jam, and meringue: **queen of puddings** ●frozen dome-shaped dessert: **bombe** ●ice cream served with fruit etc. in a tall glass: **Knickerbocker Glory, parfait, sundae** ●dish of ice cream, peaches, and liqueur: **peach Melba, pêche Melba** ●sweetmeat eaten at the end of a meal: **bonne bouche**

pulley ●ropes and pulleys for lifting heavy objects: **tackle** ●cased set of pulleys: **block** ●grooved wheel in a pulley block: **sheave**

pulp ●pulp of pressed grapes: **marc** ●pulp of pressed apples: **pomace**

pulse ●*combining form*: **sphygmo-** ●instrument recording the pulse: **sphygmograph**

pump ●pour liquid into a pump before use: **prime**

punishment ●*combining form*: pen(o)- ●*adjectives*: **disciplinary, penal, punitive** ●subject to punishment: **penalize** ●punishment assigned: **sentence** ●denoting a punishment intended to discourage further crime: **deterrent, exemplary** ●punishment seen as society's revenge on the criminal: **retributive punishment** ●unavoidable punishment: **nemesis** ●threatened punishment: **sanction** ●denoting punishment appropriate to the crime: **condign** ●deserved punishment: **retribution** ●court order giving no punishment unless the offence is repeated: **conditional discharge** ●school punishment of being kept in: **detention** ●military punishment of doing drill carrying full kit: **pack drill** ●punishment of heavy manual work: **hard labour** ●punishment of doing unpaid work for the community: **community service** ●punishment by inflicting bodily pain: **corporal punishment** ●punishment of caning the soles of the feet: **bastinado** ●punishment of being sent away: **banishment, exile** ●wooden frame with holes for head and hands: **pillory** ●wooden frame with holes for the hands and feet: **stocks** ●punishment of execution: **death penalty** ●denoting such a punishment: **capital** ●execution by a mob: **lynching** ●unconditional remission of punishment: **free pardon** ●cancellation or postponement of punishment: **reprieve** ●freedom from punishment: **impunity** ●escaping punishment: **scot-free** ●person

punished for another's faults: **scapegoat, whipping boy** ●study of punishment: **penology** ●place to which minor offenders must report regularly: **attendance centre** ●custodial centre for young offenders: **community home** ●harsh custodial regime imagined to have a deterrent effect: **short sharp shock** ▸*see also* **sentence**

pupa ●butterfly or moth pupa: **chrysalis** ●pupa's silky case: **cocoon**

pupil ●former pupil of a school or university: **alumnus** (*fem.* alumna: *pl.* alumni) ●debar a pupil from his school: **expel** ●teacher's periodic asessment of and comments on a pupil's progress: **report**

puppet ●puppet on strings: **marionette**

purchase ●purchase motivated solely by point-of-sale publicity: **impulse buying** ●instalment purchase with immediate use: **hire purchase** ●exclusive right to purchase within a stated period: **option** ●state's legally enforced purchase: **compulsory purchase** ●advancement of purchaser's rights: **consumerism** ●purchasers' refusal to buy: **consumer resistance** ●investigation of purchasers' tastes and opinions: **consumer research**

purification ●purification of the emotions through drama etc.: **catharsis** ●purify by boiling off: **distil**

purpose ●purpose for which something exists: **raison d'être**

pus ●*combining form*: **py-** ●*adjective*: **purulent** ●pus-filled pimple or blister: **pustule** ●blood poisoning caused by pus: **pyaemia** ●create pus: **fester, suppurate**

push ●push forward: **propel** ●push roughly: **jostle**

puzzle ●picture cut into interlocking pieces: **jigsaw** ●plastic cube composed of movable multicoloured squares: **Rubic's cube** ●Chinese geometrical puzzle: **tangram** ●grid of letters containing words written in any direction: **wordsearch** ●word puzzle in which certain letters in each line form a name or message: **acrostic**

●puzzle to find from clues provided words fitting into a framework of squares: **crossword** ●puzzle to find a series of words giving the same letter sequence when read across or down: **word square**

Q q

Quaker ●Quaker assembly for worship: **meeting**

quality ●*combining forms*: **-ence** (*e.g.* impertinence), **-ency** (*e.g.* efficiency), **-ship** (*e.g.* friendship) ●*adjective*: **qualitative** ●indefinable quality: **je ne sais quoi** ●distinctive or awe-inspiring quality: **mystique** ●assessed by quality: **qualitative** ●denoting the best quality: **first class, first rate, prime** ●denoting poor quality: **ersatz, second class, second rate**

quarantine ●place in quarantine: **isolate**

quark ●categories of quark: **colour, flavour, strangeness**

quarter ●quarter of a circle or sphere: **quadrant**

queen ●*adjectives*: **royal, regal**

question ●*adjective*: **interrogative** ●difficult question: **conundrum** ●set of written questions: **questionnaire** ●set of questions and answers used as a means of instruction: **catechism** ●denoting a question suggesting the answer required: **leading** ●denoting a question asked for effect, and not expecting a reply: **rhetorical** ●question an agent about his or her completed misson: **debrief** ●long and severe session of questioning: **grilling, interrogation, third degree**

queue ●long traffic queue: **tailback**

quick ●quick and efficient: **expeditious** ●quick and careless: **perfunctory** ●over-hasty: **precipitate**

quiet ●quiet period: **lull**

quinine ●South American tree yielding quinine: **chinchona**

Rr

rabbit ●female rabbit: **doe** ●male rabbit: **buck** ●young rabbit: **kitten** ●rabbit's short tail: **scut** ●rabbit's underground dwelling: **burrow** ●interconnecting series of burrows: **warren** ●rabbit cage: **hutch** ●inflammation of a rabbit's ear: **canker** ●disease fatal to rabbits: **myxomatosis** ●polecat used to chase rabbits: **ferret** ●stew or boil rabbit: **jug**

rabies ●suffering from rabies: **rabid**

race¹ ●short fast race: **sprint** ●preliminary races: **heats** ●race session: **meet, meeting** ●race in which each section is contested by a participant from each team: **relay** ●test of competitors' speed over a set distance: **time trial** ●denoting a race for all: **open** ●programme for a race meeting: **card, racecard** ●competitor's starting place: **mark** ●end of a race with leaders almost level: **photo finish** ●end of a race with level leaders: **dead heat** ●withdraw from a race before its start: **scratch** ●leave a race before its finish: **retire** ●contestant thought to have little chance of success: **outsider** ●contestant leading at the start of a race: **pacemaker, pacesetter** ●denoting a contestant finishing a race in the first three: **placed** ●short stick or tube passed between members of a relay team: **baton** ●watch for timing races: **stopwatch** ●boat race whose participants each use a pair of oars: **sculls** ●boat race on a course round obstacles: **slalom** ●set of boat races: **regatta** ●racing camel: **dromedary** ●track cycle race with a staggered start and attempts to overtake the rider in front: **pursuit** ●cross-country bicycle race: **cyclocross** ●main bunch of cyclists in a race: **peloton** ●cycle racing team assistant: **soigneur** ●jersey given to a stage winner in a cycle race: **yellow jersey** ●racing dog: **greyhound, whippet** ●starting compartment in a greyhound race: **trap** ●horse race with no jumps: **flat race** ●horse race over natural obstacles: **steeplechase, point-to-point** ●starting-compartment in a horse race: **stall** ●barrier raised at the start of a horse race: **starting gate** ●horse race win by less than a horse's head's length: **short head** ●horse-race prize money: **stakes** ●horse-race prize consisting of all the competitors' stakes: **sweepstake** ●denoting a race for horses that have not won before: **maiden** ●steeplechase organizing body: **National Hunt Committee** ●motor race over rough terrain: **rallycross** ●short motor race testing acceleration: **drag race** ●long distance motor race over public roads: **rally** ●best position at the start of a motor race: **pole position** ●flag signalling the end of a motor race: **chequered flag** ●motor cycle racing: **speedway** ●motor cycle cross-country race: **motocross** ●motor cycle race over rough ground: **scramble** ●cinder track for motor cycle races: **dirt track** ●26-mile running race: **marathon** ●race following a trail of torn-up paper: **paperchase** ●running race across rough and unfamiliar terrain: **orienteering** ●running race including hurdles and water jumps: **steeplechase** ●ski race down a winding course: **slalom** ●swimming race requiring several strokes: **medley** ●set of swimming races: **gala**

race² ●person of mixed race: **half-breed, half-caste** ●person with one white and one black parent: **mulatto** ●person with one Spanish and one American Indian parent: **mestizo** (*fem.* mestiza) ●semi-autonomous area for members of a particular race: **homeland** ●policy of common public provision for all races: **integration** ●policy of separate public provision for each race: **segregation** ●racial prejudice: **racism, racialism** ●advocate of the supremacy of a particular race: **supremacist** ●different treatment for persons of different races: **discrimination** ●deliberately favourable treatment of those thought to be discriminated against: **positive discrimination, reverse discrimination**

racetrack ●cycle racing track: **velodrome** ●cinder track for motor cycle races: **dirt track** ●strip of track for one competitor: **lane** ●sharp double bend in motor race track: **chicane** ●final stretch of a racetrack: **home straight** ●condition of a horse-race track: **going** ●frame for jumping over: **hurdle** ●strip of material broken by the winner: **tape** ●winner's ceremonial circuit of the track: **lap of honour** ●ancient Greek or Roman course for horse and chariot races: **hippodrome** ●trackside area not open to the general public: **enclosure** ●trackside enclosure where competitors assemble: **paddock**

radar ●series of radar signals emitted as a navigational guide: **beam** ●reflected radar beam: **echo** ●locate and track a target by radar: **lock on to** ●electromagnetic wave used in radar: **microwave** ●device strengthening this: **maser** ●radar establishment tracking missiles, satellites, etc.: **tracking station** ●metal foil released to evade radar detection: **chaff, win-**

dow ●aircraft designed to evade radar detection: **stealth plane**

radiation ●penetrating electromagnetic radiation of shorter wavelength than X-rays: **gamma radiation** ●region of intense radiation high above the earth: **Van Allen belt** ●discharge of radiation: **emission** ●discharge of radiation through gradual nuclear dissolution: **radioactive decay** ●emitting ionizing radiation: **radioactive** ●caused by ionizing radiation: **radiogenic** ●denoting penetrating radiation: **hard** ●denoting radiation with little penetrating power: **soft** ●denoting electromagnetic radiation with a wavelength just greater than that of red light: **infrared** ●denoting electromagnetic radiation with a wavelength shorter than that of violet light but longer than that of X-rays: **ultraviolet** ●instruments measuring radiation: **dosimeter, radiometer** ●instrument measuring changes in infrared radiation: **thermograph** ●device generating an intense beam of electromagnetic radiation: **laser** ●break up radiation into high and low densities: **diffract** ●expose to radiation: **irradiate** ●level of exposure to ionizing radiation: **dosage** ●amount of ionizing radiation absorbed: **dose** ●device measuring this: **dosimeter, film badge** ●largest radiation dose that can be taken without harm: **tolerance dose** ●illness resulting from exposure to ionizing radiation: **radiation sickness**

radio ●early type of radio: **crystal set** ●tuning wire in this: **cat's whisker** ●apparatus transmitting instrument readings by radio: **telemeter** ●combined radio and gramophone: **radiogram** ●combined radio, gramophone, and tape deck: **music centre** ●radio that can transmit and receive: **transceiver** ●device receiving a radio signal and automatically transmitting another one: **transponder** ●device detecting radio emissions from the sky: **radio telescope** ●terrestrial radio establishment tracking missiles, satellites, etc.: **earth station, tracking station** ●radio device detecting moving objects: **radar** ●series of radio signals emitted as a navigational guide: **beam** ●small radio device alerting its wearer by beeping when it has received a message: **pager** ●system of interconnected transmitters: **network** ●alter a radio signal to make it incomprehensible: **scramble** ●adjust a receiver to the frequency of the desired signal: **tune** ●radio unit detecting and preamplifying the desired signal: **tuner** ●single-rod radio aerial: **monopole** ●set of earphones and microphone: **headset** ●small cathode display as tuning indicator: **magic eye** ●radio wave of constant amplitude: **continuous wave** ●alter a radio wave's amplitude or frequency: **modulate** ●distance between successive crests of a radio or sound wave: **wavelength** ●radio frequencies for local communication: **Citizen's Band** ●radio wave above 1 km long: **long wave** ●radio wave between 0.1 and 1 km long: **medium wave** ●radio wave between 0.01 and 0.1 km long: **short wave** ●radio wave between 0.001 and 0.3 m long: **microwave** ●range of wavelengths between two given limits: **band, waveband** ●deflection of radio waves passing from one medium to another: **refraction** ●reflected radio beam: **echo** ●imaging of internal organs by high-frequency radio waves: **magnetic resonance imaging** ●radio wave transmitted or received: **signal** ●unwanted signals impairing reception: **interference** ●deliberate creation of this: **jamming** ●signal's strength relative to interference around it: **signal-to-noise ratio** ●international radio distress signal:

Mayday ●amateur radio operator: **ham**

radioactivity ●atmospheric radioactivity after a nuclear explosion: **fallout** ●time needed for radioactivity to halve: **half-life** ●not subject to radioactive decay: **stable** ●radioactive form of an element: **isotope** ●medical use of radioactive substances: **nuclear medicine** ●radioactive substance whose passage though the body is monitored for diagnostic purposes: **tracer** ●instrument for measuring radioactivity: **Geiger counter** ●device for handling radioactive material: **glovebox** ●lose radioactivity: **decay** ●remove radioactivity from: **decontaminate** ●free from radioactivity: **clean**

raft ●inflatable raft for use in shipwreck: **life raft**

railway ●railway line leading towards a major city: **up line** ●railway line leading from a major city: **down line** ●railway with a central toothed rail: **rack railway** ●underground railway in London: **tube, Underground** ●underground railway in Paris: **metro** ●underground railway in Rome: **metropolitana** ●underground railway in New York: **subway** ●wheelless railway system: **maglev** ●railway system with a single track from which the train is suspended: **monorail** ●short track beside a railway line: **siding** ●short branch line: **spur** ●transverse beam supporting railway track: **sleeper** ●nail fastening the rail to the sleeper: **spike** ●plate joining two sections of rail: **fishplate** ●stones forming the bed of a railway track: **ballast** ●this with the track upon it: **permanent way** ●distance between track rails: **gauge** ●earth piled up to carry a railway track: **embankment** ●series of arches supporting a railway track: **viaduct** ●water tunnel under a railway track: **culvert** ●onward slope of a railway track: **gradient, incline** ● area of adjustable intersecting track: **points** ● points designed to derail vehicles coming the wrong way: **catch points** ● barrier at the end of a railway track: **buffers** ● signal for the next section of track: **home signal** ● signal giving advance warning: **distant signal** ● explosive warning device set on the track: **detonator** ● railway track and associated equipment: **trackwork** ● person building or maintaining railway tracks: **navvy, platelayer** ● trackside building from which points, signals, etc. are controlled: **signal box** ● minor railway station: **halt** ● station with extensive parking: **parkway** ● station information board or screen: **indicator** ● station that is a major transport interchange: **railhead** ● station serving several routes: **interchange** ● safekeeping for luggage at a station: **left luggage** ● official in charge of a railway station: **stationmaster** ● point where routes merge or cross: **junction** ● rolling-stock maintenance shed with a turntable: **roundhouse** ● point where vehicles etc. cross railway tracks: **level crossing** ● former famous railway guide: **Bradshaw** ▸ *see also* **train**

rain ● *combining form*: **pluvi(o)-** ● *adjective*: **pluvial** ● light fine rain: **drizzle** ● chemically polluted rain: **acid rain** ● rainfall reaching the ground through trees etc.: **throughfall** ● rainwater not absorbed by the earth: **run-off** ● rain cloud: **nimbus** ● sudden violent rainstorm: **cloudburst, deluge** ● rainy season in southern Asia: **monsoon** ● map line joining points of equal rainfall: **isohyet** ● spraying chemicals into a cloud to produce rain: **seeding** ● period with little or no rain: **drought** ● not washed away by rainfall: **rainfast**

rainbow ● band of colours seen in the rainbow: **spectrum**

rally ● rally of Scouts and/or Guides: **jamboree**

random ● denoting music allowing for some random elements in its performance: **aleatoric**

rank ● ranking by status: **hierarchy** ● of higher rank: **superior** ● of lower rank: **subordinate** ● priority accorded to persons of different rank: **precedence** ● raise to a higher rank: **promote** ● degrade to a lower rank: **demote, relegate** ● titled person: **aristocrat** ● person belonging to neither the royalty nor the aristocracy: **commoner**

rapid ● *combining form*: **tachy-** ● rapid heartbeat due to excitement, fever, etc.: **tachycardia**

rash ● rose-coloured rash: **roseola** ● itching red rash caused by food allergies: **hives, nettlerash, urticaria** ● rash round the waist or head, with extreme nerve pain: **shingles, herpes zoster**

Rastafarian ● Rastafarian hairstyle with hair in tight braids: **dreadlocks** ● Rastafarian's vegetarian food: **ital** ● Rastafarian name for God: **Jah** ● contemptuous Rastafarian term for white society and culture: **Babylon**

rat ● *adjective*: **murine** ● male rat: **buck** ● young rat: **pup**

rates ● reduce or remove rates: **derate**

rather ● *combining form*: **-ish** (*e.g.* biggish)

ratio ● ratio of items to a given area: **density** ● ratio in which one term increases as the other decreases: **inverse ratio**

ration ● free from rationing restrictions: **deration**

raven ● *adjective*: **corvine**

ray ● *adjective*: **radial**

razor ● leather strip for sharpening razors: **strop**

read ●that can be read: **legible** ●read carefully: **peruse, pore over** ●read casually: **browse** ●read patchily: **dip** ●inability to read: **illiteracy** ●inability to read due to brain damage: **alexia, word blindness** ●difficulty with reading due to brain dysfunction: **dyslexia** ●scarcely able to read and write: **semi-literate** ●unable to read or write: **illiterate** ●reading words by their general appearance: **look-and-say** ●reading words by the sounds their letters express: **phonics** ●reader's cubicle in a library: **carrel** ●reading stand: **lectern**

ready ●ready if required: **on alert, on standby** ●release from a state of readiness: **stand down**

reality ●make more concrete or real: **reify** ●avoidance of unpleasant realities: **escapism**

real tennis ●court's winning opening: **hazard** ●built projection in the court: **tambour** ●junction between floor and side walls of the court: **nick** ●courtside spectators' gallery: **dedans**

reason ●*adjective*: **rational** ●reasoning system: **dialectic** ●science of reasoning: **logic** ●reasoning from general to particular: **deduction** ●reasoning from particular to general: **induction** ●faulty reasoning, or a belief based on it: **fallacy** ●showing faulty reasoning: **misguided** ●attractive but fallacious reasoning: **sophism** ●pretended reason: **pretext**

recent ●*combining form*: neo- ●child recently born: **neonate** ●recent beginner: **neophyte**

recipient ●*combining form*: -ee (*e.g.* payee)

reciprocal ●*combining form*: inter- (*e.g.* interaction)

recommend ●recommend publicly: **endorse**

record ●*combining form*: -gram ●systematic record: **log** ●record of a person's education and career: **curriculum vitae** (*pl.* curricula vitae) ●electrically traced record of a heartbeat: **electrocardiogram** ●record of hours worked: **time sheet** ●record of a business meeting: **minutes** ●record of a learned society's meetings: **memoirs, proceedings, transactions** ●record of tasks completed or in progress: **worksheet** ●early Exchequer record: **pipe roll** ●paperwork required for official records: **documentation** ●set of records, papers, etc. on a particular topic: **dossier** ●collection of documents or records: **archive, registry** ●period before written records: **prehistory** ▶*see also* archive

recorder[1] ●*combining form*: -graph ●device recording the distance travelled and speeds achieved by a motor vehicle: **tachograph**

recorder[2] ●recorder mouthpiece: **fipple**

recording ●denoting a recording made at a public performance: **live** ●component transferring electrical signals to the recording medium: **head** ●continuous sequence recorded at one time: **take** ●record a television programme for later viewing: **time-shift** ●general sound quality of a recording: **production** ●laser-read disk of digital information: **compact disk** ●section of a recording containing a single item: **track** ●recording's protective cover: **sleeve** ●information sheet inside a recording's case: **inlay** ●framed disc awarded to artists of a high-selling recording: **gold disc, silver disc, platinum disc** ●take a recording off the market: **delete**

record player ●hard point placed in the record groove: **stylus** ●holder for the stylus: **cartridge** ●revolving disc upon which a record is placed: **turntable** ●base for the turntable: **deck** ▸*see also* **gramophone**

recruitment ●former services' recruitment unit, employing force and trickery: **pressgang** ●entice senior employees away from other companies: **headhunt**

rectum ●*combining form*: **proct(o)-** ●inflammation of the rectum: **proctitis** ●instrument for inspecting the rectum: **proctoscope** ●study of the anus and rectum: **proctology** ●solid medication inserted to dissolve in the rectum: **suppository** ●liquid or gas introduced medicinally into the rectum: **enema**

red ●*combining forms*: **erythr(o)-**, **rhod(o)-** (*e.g.* rododendron, *literally 'red tree'*), **rub(i)-** ●brilliant red: **vermilion** ●red blood cell: **erythrocyte** ●red-faced: **rubicund** ●red-blindness: **daltonism, protanopia**

reef ●circular coral reef or group of islands: **atoll** ●low reef or sandbank: **cay** ●reef enclosing a lagoon: **barrier reef**

referee ●referee's assistant indicating when the ball is out of play: **linesman, touch judge**

refinement ●excessive refinement: **preciosity**

refrigerator ●refrigerator compartment for fruit and vegetables: **crisper** ●rid a refrigerator of excess ice: **defrost**

refugee ●state protection offered to a political refugee: **asylum** ●place to detain a refugee while asylum applications are considered: **detention centre**

refuse ●refuse to do business with: **boycott** ●refuse to give: **withhold** ●refuse to socialize with: **ostracize** ●abrupt refusal or rejection: **rebuff**

regalia ●monarch's short staff: **sceptre** ●monarch's globe surmounted by a cross: **orb**

region ●nearby region: **vicinity** ●region offering government incentives to incoming businesses: **development area** ●region observing a common time: **time zone** ●semi-autonomous area for members of a particular people: **homeland** ●region suffering extreme drought and erosion: **dustbowl**

registration plate ●specially purchased vehicle registration plates that contain the owner's initials etc.: **vanity plates**

regret ●regret and wish undone: **rue** ●feeling no regret: **impenitent**

regulate ●low dam in a river to regulate its flow: **weir** ●device regulating fluid flow: **valve**

rehearsal ●rehearsal taken without stops: **run-through** ●rehearsal to check lighting and other effects: **technical rehearsal** ●final rehearsal: **dress rehearsal**

reign ●*adjective*: **regnal** ●period between two reigns: **interregnum**

rejection ●contemptuous rejection: **spurning** ●formal rejection: **renunciation**

related ●related through a common ancestor: **cognate** ●related through a common male ancestor: **agnate** ●related by blood: **consanguineous, kin** ●related at a distance of *x* generations: ***x* times removed** ●related through marriage or adoption: **affined** ●(of words) related by having a common source: **cognate**

relationship ●harmonious relationship between persons: **rapport** ●interactive relationship between things: **correlation** ●establishment of a close relationship based on shared experiences or feelings: **bonding** ●establishment of harmonious international relations: **rapprochement** ●romantic or sexual relationship: **affair** ●casual romantic relationship: **dalliance** ●brief and unpremeditated sexual relationship: **fling** ●romantic relationship preceding marriage: **courtship** ●secret sexual relationship: **liaison** ●person with whom one has an established romantic or sexual relationship: **significant other** ●person having no established romantic or sexual relationship: **single** ●unable to cope with normal social relationships: **dysfunctional**

relative ●closest relative: **next of kin** ●person related to another by birth: **blood relation** ●person related to another by marriage: **inlaw**

relative density ●apparatus measuring a liquid's relative density: **hydrometer**

relic ●container for relics: **reliquary** ●taking of relics to another place: **translation**

religion ●*combining form*: **religio-** ●religion based on reason: **natural religion** ●system of religious belief: **creed, doctrine, dogma, faith** ●religious belief diverging from those generally accepted: **heresy, heterodoxy** ●inflexible adherence to religious dogma: **fundamentalism** ●change of one's religious beliefs: **conversion** ●desertion or abandonment of a system of religious belief: **apostasy** ●subdivision of religious groups: **schism** ●schismatic group: **sect** ●amalgamation of various religions: **syncretism** ●person maintaining his religion in the face of threats: **confessor** ●openly profess one's religious faith: **witness** ●person vowed to religious service: **votary** ●person travelling to holy places: **pilgrim** ●person sent to make religious converts: **missionary, missioner** ●person shifting his religious allegiance: **proselyte** ●religious instruction by question and answer: **catechism** ●person receiving religious instruction: **catechumen** ●secret religious rites: **mysteries** ●secret mystical knowledge: **gnosis** ●person rejecting standard religious beliefs: **freethinker** ●person rejecting all religious and moral principles: **nihilist** ●newcomer to a religion: **neophyte** ●follow the rules of a religion: **practise** ●affirm one's religious belief: **confess, profess** ●religious veneration: **cult** ●animal or natural object believed to have spiritual powers: **totem** ●pole on which these are hung or depicted: **totem pole** ●annual religious celebration: **feast** ●religious reverence: **piety** ●excessive piety: **religiosity** ●disrespectful of religion: **impious, profane** ●disrespectful treatment of a religious item or place: **sacrilege** ●irreligious talk: **blasphemy, profanity** ●distributor of religious literature: **colporteur** ●deception intended to foster religious belief: **pious fraud** ●purge a religious narrative of fanciful elements: **demythologize** ●study of religions having gods: **theology** ●not religious: **secular** ▸*see also* god, theology

remark ●abrupt remark: **interjection** ●remark intended to provoke anger: **taunt** ●contemptuous remark: **sneer** ●mocking remark: **jeer, jibe, lampoon, taunt** ●oblique remark: **innuendo, insinuation** ●trite remark: **bromide, platitude** ●witty remark: **bon mot, mot, epigram** ●witty remark that occurs to one too late: **esprit de l'escalier**

remedy ●remedy for all problems: **panacea**

remote ●remote area: **ultima Thule**

remove ●*combining form*: **dis-** *e.g.* **disbud, un-** (*e.g.* unman) ●remove completely: **eliminate** ●remove from a dangerous place: **evacuate** ●person so moved: **evacuee** ●remove an item from a museum etc. collection: **deaccession** ● remove the bowels of: **disembowel, eviscerate**

renounce ● renounce the throne: **abdicate** ● person who renounces his faith: **renegade**

rent ● rent paid by the householder to the landowner: **ground rent** ● reduced rent paid during nonoccupancy: **retainer** ● excessive rent: **rack-rent** ● nominal rent: **peppercorn rent** ● person living on rental income: **rentier**

repair ● repair made to an item in use: **running repair** ● shoe-repairer: **cobbler** ● keep in good repair: **maintain** ● inspect and repair if necessary: **overhaul**

repetition ● re-run of film of the crucial moments of a sporting event, often in slow motion: **action replay** ● repetition of words or ideas in inverted order: **chiasmus** ● muscle strain caused by frequent repetition of a movement: **repetitive strain injury**

replacement ● temporary replacement for a doctor, clergyman, etc.: **locum** ● replacement by a better item: **upgrade** ● woman bearing children for an infertile woman: **surrogate**

reply ● sharp reply: **retort, riposte** ● witty reply, or conversation consisting of them: **repartee** ● witty retort that comes to mind after the chance to make it has gone: **esprit de l'escalier** ● person replying: **respondent**

report ● report of a praiseworthy act: **citation** ● government report with proposals for public discussion: **green paper** ● government report with proposals for legislation: **white paper** ● official report: **return** ● report giving the writer's considered opinions: **position paper** ● prepare a detailed report: **write up**

reporter ● newspaper reporter: **journalist, correspondent** ● inexperienced newspaper reporter: **cub** ● reporter engaged by a newspaper on a part-time basis: **stringer** ● newspaper's reporter of artistic performances: **critic** ● newspaper's featured contributor: **columnist** ● reporter's official accreditation: **press card** ● arranged meeting with reporters: **press conference** ● person supplying a reporter with inside information: **source**

reproduction ● *combining forms*: **gon-** (*e.g.* gonad) ● *adjective*: **generative** ● age at which reproduction becomes possible: **puberty** ● reproducing by means of eggs: **oviparous** ● reproducing live offspring: **viviparous** ● reproducing by giving birth from eggs hatched within the body: **ovoviviparous** ● breeding between closely related individuals: **inbreeding** ● external reproductive organs: **genitals** ● female external genitals: **vulva** ● male external genitals: **penis, testicles** ● gland producing ova: **ovary** ● tube conveying the ovum to the uterus: **Fallopian tube** ● gland releasing a fluid component of semen: **prostate** ● gland producing sperm: **testis** ● introduction of semen to the vagina other than by sexual intercourse: **artificial insemination** ● reproductive cell: **gamete** ● organ producing gametes: **gonad** ● keeping an egg warm: **incubation** ● self-reproduction of genetic material: **replication** ● denoting asexual reproduction: **vegetative** ● incapable of reproduction: **sterile**

reptile ● *combining forms*: **herpet(o)-, -saur, -saurus** ● large prehistoric reptile: **dinosaur, saurian** ● glass container for keeping small reptiles: **terrarium** ● study of reptiles: **herpetology**

reputation ● reputation gained by ability or achievement: **stature, sta-**

tus ●public destruction of a person's reputation: **humiliation** ●malicious destruction of a person's reputation: **character assassination, whispering campaign**

request ●formal request: **petition**

require ●whenever required: **on demand**

resin ●amber rubbed on stringed-instrument bows: **rosin** ●synthetic resin used to make synthetic textile fibres: **polyester** ●synthetic resin used in paints and adhesives: **polyurethane** ●flexible synthetic resin used in packaging: **polythene**

resist ●resistance to pressure: **compressive strength** ●resistance to tension: **tensile strength** ●resistance generated when one surface brushes past another: **friction** ●designed for minimum air-resistance: **streamlined** ●that cannot be resisted: **inexorable** ●abandonment of resistance: **capitulation**

resort ●resort having a medicinal mineral spring: **spa** ●spa or seaside resort: **watering place**

resource ●shared resource: **pool** ●careful use of resources: **thrift**

respect ●*combining form*: -**wise** (*e.g.* pricewise) ●admiring respect: **prestige** ●given as a mark of respect: **honorific** ●respect due to family or fatherland: **pietas**

respectable ●slightly disreputable: **raffish, rakish** ●shabby and disreputable: **seedy** ●untidy and disreputable persons: **ragtag and bobtail**

response ●automatic response: **instinct, reflex action** ●reported reaction to a new product, proposal, etc.: **feedback** ●unenthusiastic or hostile reaction: **negative feedback**

responsibility ●area of responsibility: **province** ●shared responsibility: **partnership** ●denial of responsibility: **disclaimer** ●person responsible for another: **sponsor** ●take on excessive responsibilities: **overextend oneself**

rest ●short rest: **respite** ●midday rest taken in hot countries: **siesta**

restaurant ●simple restaurant: **cafe, coffee shop, bistro, brasserie** ●self-service restaurant: **cafeteria** ●staff restaurant: **canteen** ●restaurant selling cooked food to be eaten elsewhere: **takeaway** ●restaurant specializing in roasts: **rotisserie** ●restaurant where meat is carved under the customer's direction: **carvery** ●pancake restaurant: **crêperie** ●pizza restaurant: **pizzeria** ●small Greek restaurant: **taverna** ●small Italian restaurant: **trattoria** ●place setting at a restaurant: **cover** ●restaurant charge for bread, laundry, etc.: **cover charge** ●restaurant's list of available dishes: **menu** ●dish available on a particular day: **plat du jour** (*pl.* plats du jour) ●limited menu served at a fixed overall price: **table d'hôte** ●menu with items priced separately: **à la carte** ●style of restaurant service in which a customer's plate is filled by waiters at the table: **silver service** ●restaurant owner: **restaurateur** ●restaurant's senior cook: **chef** ●restaurant's junior cook: **commis** ●bag for restaurant customer to take home uneaten food: **doggy bag**

restraint ●linked metal rings securing the wrists or ankles: **shackles** ●wrist shackles: **manacles** ●ankle shackles: **fetters** ●hold down someone's arms and legs: **pinion**

restrictions ●free from restrictions: **decontrol**

result ●possible result: **eventuality** ●final result: **upshot** ●anticlimactic outcome: **non-event** ●able to produce the desired result: **efficacious** ●aimed at practical results rather than theoretical purity: **pragmatic** ● achieving poor results: **unproductive** ● achieving no results: **nonproductive** ● based on actual results: **ex post facto**

retaliation ● *combining form*: **counter** (*e.g.* counter-attack)

retirement ● denoting a person who has retired from the office cited: **emeritus**

retort ● witty retort that comes to mind after the chance to make it has gone: **esprit de l'escalier**

return ● return to fashion or success: **comeback**

revenge ● act of revenge: **reprisal, retaliation**

reversal ● *combining forms*: **dis-** (*e.g.* disaffirm), **un-** (*e.g.* untie)

revolution ● incitement to rebellion: **sedition** ● revolutionary uprising: **insurrection** ● sudden seizure of power: **coup, coup d'état** (*pl.* coups d'état), **putsch** ● dissatisfied and rebellious person: **malcontent** ● person taking active part in a revolution: **insurgent** ● opposition to revolutionaries: **counter-insurgency**

reward ● reward offered to encourage greater effort: **incentive** ● reward offered for capturing or killing a wanted person or animal: **bounty**

rhetoric ● words addressed to an absent person or thing: **apostrophe** ● application of one word to two others: **zeugma** ● use of apparent contradictions: **oxymoron** ● picturesque comparison: **simile** ● picturesque description in which the object described is said to be the thing it resembles: **metaphor** ● construction lacking its expected grammatical sequence: **anacoluthon** ● introduction of an irrelevant topic: **digression** ● device of mentioning a subject by saying one is not going to mention it: **apophasis** ● ingenious figure of speech: **conceit** ● omission of words

easily understood from the context: **ellipsis** ● personification of an abstract concept: **prosopopoeia** ● opening a new sentence by repeating the last word of the preceding one: **anadiplosis** ● opening a series of sentences with the same word: **anaphora** ● substitution of an attribute for the thing possessing it: **metonymy** ● deliberate understatement: **litotes, meiosis** ● use of more words than is necessary to convey the bare meaning: **pleonasm, redundancy**

rheumatism ● rheumatism of the joints: **rheumatoid arthritis** ● steroid used to treat rheumatism: **hydrocortisone**

rhinoceros ● young rhinoceros: **calf**

rhyme ● rhyme between final stressed syllables: **masculine rhyme** ● rhyme between final unstressed syllables: **feminine rhyme** ● rhyme involving midline words: **internal rhyme** ● partial rhyme between words with different consonants: **pararhyme** ● near rhyme between words having similar consonant or vowel sounds, but not both: **assonance** ● false rhyme between words that look but do not sound the same: **eye-rhyme, imperfect rhyme** ● game of inventing successive lines of rhyming verse: **crambo** ▸ *see also* **verse**

rhythm ● numbers indicating the rhythm of a musical score: **time signature** ● emphasized beat: **downbeat** ● unemphasized beat: **upbeat** ● displacement of the beat: **syncopation**

rib ● *adjective*: **costal** ● between the ribs: **intercostal** ● unattached rib: **false rib, floating rib**

ribbon ● ribbons on a hat: **cockade**

rice ● rice in the husk: **paddy** ● rice field: **paddy** ● Italian rice dish: **risotto** ● Spanish rice dish with chicken and seafood: **paella** ● Middle Eastern rice dish with spices and vegetables: **pilaf**

rid ●get rid of by passing on: **offload**

ridge ●denoting materials shaped into ridges and grooves: **corrugated** ●natural ridge from each side of which water drains into a different river system: **watershed**

rifle ●light automatic rifle: **carbine** ●back part of a rifle barrel: **breech** ●sliding element of a rifle's breech: **bolt** ●rear end of a rifle: **butt** ●lean rifles together with their butts on the ground: **pile arms** ●rifle range: **butts** ●mound for a target in a rifle range: **butt** ▸ *see also* **gun**

right[1] ●rights thought to be possessed by anyone: **human rights** ●rights to political and social freedom and equality: **civil rights, civil liberty** ●principle that all persons have equal rights: **egalitarianism** ●exclusive right: **prerogative** ●denoting a right established by long use: **prescriptive** ●by right: **de jure** ●having a right: **eligible** ●right to enjoy daylight in one's windows, unobstructed by subsequent building: **ancient lights** ●right to cross another person's land: **easement** ●another's right to cross one's land: **servitude** ●exclusive right to publish or use artistic material: **copyright** ●right to reject a decision made by others: **veto** ●right to speak or collaborate with whoever one wishes: **free association** ●right to express one's opinions: **free speech** ●firstborn child's right of succession: **primogeniture** ●right to vote: **franchise** ●legal transfer of a right: **assignment** ●person to whom a right is legally transferred: **assign, assignee** ●refrain from exercising a right: **waive**

right[2] ●*combining forms*: **dextro-** (*e.g.* dextrorotatory) ●*adjective*: **dex-**

tral ●right side of a ship as seen by one facing its prow: **starboard**

rim ●projecting rim: **flange**

ring ●*adjective*: **annular** ●ring for the leash on a dog's collar: **terret** ●leather ring for Scout's neckerchief: **woggle** ●finger ring having a seal instead of a stone: **signet ring** ●ring worn to keep a more valuable one from slipping: **keeper** ●plain ring worn in a pierced ear to prevent its closing up: **keeper, sleeper** ●ring inserted in the lip: **labret** ●ring of muscle: **sphincter** ●ring of light round the sun or moon: **aureole, corona** ●coloured ring seen in the cross-section of a tree trunk, representing a year's growth: **annual ring, tree ring**

ringing ●persistent ringing sound heard in one or both ears: **tinnitus**

ringworm ●*technical term*: **tinea pedis**

riot ●steal goods during a riot: **loot**

risk ●risk inherent in a particular activity: **occupational hazard** ●willing to take risks: **venturesome** ●deliberate risk-taking: **adventurism, brinkmanship** ●funding for risky projects: **venture capital** ●person at risk: **marked man** ●health or environmental risk posed by microbiological experimentation: **biohazard** ●put at risk: **imperil** ●put to excessive risk: **overexpose**

ritual ●admission ritual: **initiation** ●ritual marking a new stage in life: **rite of passage** ●secret ritual: **mysteries** ●ritual pouring of liquid: **libation**

rival ●use of various ploys to gain psychological advantage over one's rivals: **gamesmanship**

river ●*combining form*: **fluvio-** ●*adjectives*: **fluvial, fluviatile, potamic, riverine** ●ice river: **glacier** ●river flowing into a larger one: **tributary** ●place where a river begins: **source** ●tributary joining a river close to its source: **headwater** ●small island in a river: **ait, eyot, holm** ●shallow river crossing: **ford** ●low dam in a river to regulate its flow: **weir** ●deep river gorge: **canyon** ●straight stretch of river: **reach** ●river's winding curve: **meander** ●horseshoe-shaped bend in a river's course: **oxbow** ●new channel made for a river: **cut** ●junction of two rivers: **confluence** ●area of rough water caused by meeting currents: **rip** ●stretch of fast shallow water: **rapids, white water** ●triangular area, with many streams, at a river's mouth: **delta** ●wide area of tidal water at a river's mouth: **estuary** ●sand etc. deposited on a river bed: **silt** ●clean out a river bed: **dredge** ●animals living in a river bed: **infauna** ●floating beam restricting access to a river: **boom** ●dry river bed: **wadi** ●sudden river flood: **spate** ●flood moving down-river: **freshet** ●high wave moving up a river at the spring tide: **bore, eagre** ●steps leading down to a river in India: **ghat** ●instrument measuring rivers' rise and fall: **fluviometer** ●officials controlling a river: **conservancy** ●riverside scavenger: **mudlark** ●mapping of rivers: **hydrography** ●study of rivers: **potamology**

river bank ●*adjective*: **riparian** ●path along a river bank: **towpath**

road ●major cross-country road: **trunk road** ●scenic coast road: **corniche** ●urban seaside road: **esplanade, promenade** ●road along high ground: **ridgeway** ●raised road across wet ground: **causeway** ●private road leading up to a house: **drive** ●drive passing a house in a curve: **sweep** ●access road: **service road** ●road entering or leaving a dual carriageway: **slip road** ●slip road for a vehicle out of control: **escape road** ●road tunnel: **underpass** ●road on which no stopping is permitted: **clearway** ●road with no exit: **cul-de-sac,**

dead end ●narrow section of road causing congestion: **bottleneck** ●road avoiding a congested area: **bypass, relief road** ●bypass encircling a town: **orbital road, ring road** ●road for motor vehicles: **carriageway, motorway** ●motorway's tarmacked edge: **hard shoulder, shoulder** ●French motorway: **autoroute** ●motorway in German-speaking countries: **autobahn** ●Italian motorway: **autostrada** ●motorway in Spanish-speaking countries: **autopista** ●road with a single expanse of tarmac: **single carriageway** ●two-way traffic on a single carriageway: **contraflow** ●strip of land between paired carriageways: **central reservation** ●road so divided: **dual carriageway** ●grass at the edge of a road: **verge** ●point where roads merge or cross: **junction** ●multilevel junction with connecting slip roads: **cloverleaf junction, interchange** ●bridge for one road to cross another: **flyover, overpass** ●road passing under another: **underpass** ●rounded open space where several roads meet: **circus** ●roadside barrier preventing accidents: **crash barrier** ●road hump to limit speed: **sleeping policeman, speed bump, speed hump** ●roadside camera photographing speeding vehicles: **speed camera** ●charge for using a stretch of road: **toll** ●roadside stopping area: **lay-by** ●roadside establishment selling fuel etc.: **filling station, service station, petrol station** ●roadside establishment offering parking, refuelling, and restaurant facilities: **service area, services** ●belt of land alongside a major road: **corridor** ●building along the sides of a road: **ribbon development** ●rise in a road's surface towards the centre, to assist drainage: **camber** ●rise in a road's surface at one side, to assist cornering: **bank** ●create even slopes for roadbuilding: **grade** ●steepness of a road: **gradient, incline** ●small marker projecting slightly from the road surface: **stud** ●raised strip altering tyre noise when crossed: **rumble strip** ●metal grid over a pit in a road: **cattle grid** ●sharp bend on a road: **dogleg, hairpin bend** ●reflecting road marker: **Catseye** ●section of road marked off for a file of traffic: **lane** ●place where a road divides: **fork** ●road junction marked with yellow hatching: **box junction** ●earth piled up to carry a road: **embankment** ●water tunnel under a road: **culvert** ●rubble for road foundations: **ballast, hardcore** ●sand and gravel for road foundations: **hoggin** ●smooth flat stone formerly used to surface roads: **cobble** ●mixture of pitch with sand or gravel, used for surfacing roads: **asphalt** ●stones of graded sizes, laid as a road surface: **macadam** ●mixture of pitch with stones or slag, used for surfacing roads: **tarmac** ●give a road a smooth firm surface: **make up, metal, pave** ●top layer of a road surface: **wearing course** ●hole in a road surface: **pothole** ●designer of roads, bridges, etc.: **civil engineer** ●motor vehicle clearing roads of snow: **snowplough** ●overcrowding of roads: **congestion** ●charging to use roads at busy times: **road pricing** ●official rules for road users: **Highway Code** ●children's rules for crossing a road: **kerb drill**

robbery ●robbery by breaking a shop window: **smash-and-grab** ●robbery by driving into a shop window: **ram-raid** ●robbery at gunpoint: **hold-up** ●open robbery when law and order breaks down: **looting, plunder, pillage** ●plundering and destruction of a captured town: **sack** ●attack and rob: **mug** ▸*see also* **theft**

robot ●technique of making and operating mechanical robots: **robotics** ●technique of making and operating lifelike robots: **animatronics** ●convert a production line to robotic operation: **robotize**

rock ●*combining forms*: **litho-, petro-, -lite** (*e.g.* chrysolite) ●formation of rocks: **petrogenesis** ●large smooth rock: **boulder** ●pointed rock: **needle** ●natural column of rock: **stack** ●rock visible above the surface: **outcrop** ●solid rock under loose deposits: **bedrock** ●rocks deposited by a glacier: **moraine** ●steep rockface: **crag, precipice** ●ridge of rock in the sea: **reef** ●rock layer: **stratum** ●curvature of rock strata: **fold** ●stratified rock sample gained by a hollow drill: **core** ●break in a rock formation: **fault** ●crack in a rockface: **fissure** ●denoting unquarried rock: **living** ●denoting rock changed by heat or pressure: **metamorphic** ●denoting rock formed from lava: **igneous** ●loose pieces of rock on a hillside: **scree** ●mass of snow, ice, and rocks moving down a mountain: **avalanche** ●plant growing on rock: **lithophyte** ●remains of prehistoric plants or animals found in rock: **fossil** ●prehistoric rock carving: **petroglyph** ●study of rocks: **lithology, petrology** ●dating of rocks: **geochronology**

rocket ●rocket putting a spacecraft into orbit: **launcher, launch vehicle** ●small rocket fired for counterpressure: **retrorocket, retroengine** ●diameter of a rocket: **calibre** ●engined rocket section jettisoned after use: **stage** ●first stage of a rocket: **booster** ●projection improving stability: **fin** ●rocket's curving course: **trajectory** ●support for a space rocket before take-off: **gantry** ●surface for rocket launching: **pad, platform** ●supply line between gantry and rocket: **umbilical** ●shoulder-held rocket launcher: **bazooka** ●piece of solid rocket fuel: **grain** ●reagent in a rocket engine: **propellant**

• propulsive force of a rocket engine: **thrust** • firing of a rocket engine: **burn** ▸ *see also* **spacecraft**

rod • rod used for hand spinning: **distaff** • rod turning roasting meat: **spit** • rod strengthening a framework etc.: **strut** • rod said to indicate underground water by twitching: **dowsing rod** • bundle of rods with an axe, carried before Roman magistrates: **fasces**

role • chief role: **lead** • small character role: **cameo** • silent role: **walking-on part, walk-on** • perform two roles: **double**

roll • roll up and secure: **furl**

Roman • *combining form*: **Romano-** • Roman circular auditorium: **amphitheatre** • fighter in the amphitheatre: **gladiator** • mock sea battle staged in a Roman amphitheatre or artificial lake: **naumachia** • awning sheltering an amphitheatre: **velarium** • Roman oblong auditorium: **circus** • Roman course for horse and chariot races: **hippodrome** • Roman square: **forum** (*pl.* fora) • Roman country house: **villa** • Roman underfloor heating system: **hypocaust** • Greek and Roman storage jar with two handles and a pointed base: **amphora** • either of two chief officials of the Roman republic: **consul** • official attending upon these: **lictor** • Roman magistrate with absolute power: **dictator** • bundle of rods carried before a Roman magistrate: **fasces** • Roman emperor's bodyguard: **praetorian guard** • Roman official interpreting omens: **augur, haruspex** • great public sacrifice at Rome: **hecatomb** • Roman household gods: **lares and penates** • clan at ancient Rome: **gens** (*pl.* gentes) • commoner at ancient Rome: **plebeian** • Roman citizen's formal overgarment: **toga** • processional return of a victorious Roman general and his troops: **triumph** • Roman army division: **legion** • member of

this: **legionary** • company commander in the Roman army: **centurion** • Roman military unit of 6 centuries: **cohort** • summary collection of Roman law: **Digest** • first day of a Roman month: **calends** • mid point of a Roman month: **ides** • ninth day before this: **nones**

Roman Catholic • head of the RC church: **pope** • senior RC priest who elects the pope: **cardinal** • priest in charge of an RC church or religious institution: **rector** • RC parish priest's house: **presbytery** • RC priest's cassock: **soutane** • RC priest deputizing for a bishop: **vicar** • skullcap worn by certain RC clergymen: **zucchetto** • training college for RC priests: **seminary** • RC priest's book for daily prayers: **breviary** • RC prayers commemorating the Incarnation: **angelus** • official teaching of the RC Church: **magisterium** • RC doctrine that the Mother of God was conceived without sin: **Immaculate Conception** • RC Church's statement that a book is doctrinally unobjectionable: **nihil obstat** • RC Church's authorization to print a religious book: **imprimatur** • RC religious society: **sodality** • voluntary donation by Roman Catholics to papal funds: **Peter's pence** • denoting a day on which meat may not be eaten: **maigre**

roof • roof formed by arches: **vault** • roof with four sloping sides: **mansard roof** • roof sloping at the ends as well as the sides: **hip roof, hipped roof** • part of a roof overhanging the walls: **eaves** • ornament at the apex of a roof: **finial** • supporting framework for a roof: **truss** • upright post supporting the apex of a roof: **king post** • beam at the apex of a roof: **ridge piece** • upright post supporting the midpoint of a roof's slope: **queen post** • roof timber running towards the apex: **rafter** • horizontal roof timber: **purlin** • horizontal beam connecting trusses or rafters: **tie beam** ●steepness of a roof: **pitch** ●roof covering of straw or reeds: **thatch** ●metal clip supporting roof glass or slates: **tingle** ●felt or boarding between rafters and slates: **sarking** ●make roof-coverings overlap downwards: **weather** ●board used for roof work: **crawlboard** ●roof-building and the materials used: **roofing** ●sharp edge between two sides of a roof: **hip, ridge** ●drainage slope where roofs meet: **valley** ●drainage hole for a flat roof: **scupper** ●ornament at the apex of a roof: **finial** ●small glazed structure at the top of a roof: **lantern** ●wall filling the end of a pitched roof: **gable** ●room in the roof space: **attic, garret, loft** ●roof space used for storage: **loft**

room ●small room leading into a more important one: **antechamber, ante-room, lobby, vestibule** ●open-sided room: **loggia** ●room used for formal or public events: **hall, chamber** ●large reception room in a public building: **stateroom** ●large hotel room for meetings or parties: **function room, reception room** ●relaxation room in school or college: **common room** ●communal room in an institution: **day room** ●room with comfortable furnishings: **drawing room, lounge, parlour** ●dwelling-house room suitable for receiving guests : **reception room** ●well-appointed bedroom for a house's chief occupants: **master bedroom** ●hotel bedroom with several beds: **family room** ●large communal bedroom: **dormitory** ●private or secret room: **closet, den** ●woman's private room: **boudoir** ●room of prisoner, monk, or nun: **cell** ●room in the roof space: **attic, garret, loft** ●storage room for food, crockery, etc.: **larder, pantry** ●large underground storeroom: **vault** ●room housing a washing machine, freezer, etc.: **utility room** ●room for

coats and baggage: **cloakroom** ●room for disused items: **lumber room** ●room for sunbathing: **solarium** ●room where actors or sports players change: **dressing room** ●church robing room: **vestry** ●room equipped for broadcasting, filming or sound recording: **studio** ●room strengthened against fire or theft: **strongroom** ●denoting a room directly connected to another: **en suite** ●denoting a room running the whole length of a building: **through** ●denoting a room with bespoke matching units: **fitted** ●partitioned section of a room: **cubicle** ●set of rooms: **suite**

root ●*combining form*: **rhiz-** ●*adjective*: **radical** ●principal root: **taproot** ●thick part of an underground root: **tuber** ●rootlike stem growing along or under the ground: **rhizome**

rope ●*adjective*: **funicular** (*often used of things* (*e.g.* a mountain railway) *formerly operated by ropes*) ●ship's heavy rope for mooring etc.: **cable, hawser** ●shore rope used to pull a ship along: **warp** ●rope to raise a sail or flag: **halyard, lanyard** ●ropes to support masts or control sails: **rigging** ●rope at a sail's lower corner: **sheet** ●rope supporting a mast: **shroud, stay** ●securing rope fixed to the ground: **guy, guyrope** ●diver's signal rope: **lifeline** ●rope restricting an animal's movement: **tether** ●rope round a horse's head: **halter** ●rope tying a horse's legs together: **hobble** ●rope for a lasso: **lariat** ●rope for hanging someone: **halter** ●rescue or safety rope: **lifeline** ●rope beside a ship's gangway or ladder: **manrope** ●rope used to climb a ship's rigging: **ratline** ●light rope for pulling a heavier rope: **heaving line** ●ropes and pulleys for lifting heavy objects: **tackle, block and tackle** ●strong nylon-cased rubber band: **bungee** ●secure a moving rope round a pin, cleat, etc.: **belay** ●arrange a rope in loose coils: **flake** ●denoting a rope pulled tight: **taut** ●denoting a rope not pulled tight: **slack** ●loop of rope: **bight** ●interweave two ropes: **splice** ●knot joining two ropes: **bend** ●bind a rope-end to prevent fraying: **whip** ●descend a rock face using a double rope coiled round the body: **abseil** ●metal pin slowing an abseiler's rope: **descendeur** ●crosspiece through a rope eye: **toggle** ●curve formed by a rope suspended at both ends: **catenary** ●revolving cylinder for winding in rope: **capstan, winch, windlass** ●T-piece for attaching a rope: **cleat** ●strand of a rope: **ply** ●tool for separating rope strands: **marlinspike** ●fibres used to make ropes: **hemp, jute** ●place where ropes are made: **ropewalk** ●fibre from old rope: **oakum**

rosary ●small rosary with 55 beads: **chaplet** ●bead at which the Lord's Prayer must be said: **paternoster**

rose ●rose grower: **rosarian** ●decoration resembling a rose: **rosette** ●rosette on a hat: **cockade**

rot ●*combining form*: **sapr-** ●that can be rotted: **putrescible** ●rapidly spreading form of timber rot: **dry rot** ●rot affecting damp timber: **wet rot** ●rotting process: **putrefaction** ●plant living on rotting matter: **saprophyte** ●organism feeding on rotting matter: **saprotroph** ●rotten-smelling: **putrid**

rotation ●*combining form*: **gyro-** (*e.g.* gyroscope)

route ●alternative route: **diversion** ●deviation from a direct route: **detour** ●fixed route followed by a milkman etc.: **round** ●route over a mountain: **pass, gap** ●planned route: **itinerary** ●prescribed route for foreign aircraft through a nation's airspace: **air corridor, airway** ●sharp bend on a route: **dogleg** ●person directing the route to be taken: **navigator**

rowing ●light rowing boat for a single oarsman: **scull, skiff** ●pair of oars for this: **sculls** ●racing boat's covered front end: **canvas** ●steersman in a rowing boat: **cox, coxswain** ●oarsman next to the cox: **stroke** ●seat for an oarsman: **thwart** ●oarsman's footrest: **stretcher** ●support for rowing boat's oar: **rowlock** ●pin against which the oar is turned: **thole, thole pin** ●turn a raised oarblade parallel to the water: **feather** ●circle of disturbed water from each stroke: **puddle** ●make a bad rowing stroke: **catch a crab** ●pull oars into the boat: **ship oars**

royalty ●polite form of address to a royal person: **Your Highness** ●polite form of address to female royalty: **ma'am** ●female attendant upon female royalty: **maid of honour** ●money voted annually by parliament to the royal family: **Civil List** ●male assistant to a member of the royal family: **equerry**

rub ●*combining form*: **tribo-** ●wear away by rubbing: **abrade** ●become worn through rubbing: **fray** ●electric charge generated by friction: **tribo-electricity**

rubber ●become brittle and inelastic: **perish**

rudeness ●blatant or insolent rudeness: **effrontery**

rug ●Greek traditional rug: **flokati** ●flat-woven Turkish rug: **kilim**

rugby ●temporary control of the ball: **possession** ●attempt to bring down the player in possession: **tackle** ●touch ground behind the goal line with the ball: **touch down** ●this achieved behind the opposition's goal line: **try** ●kick made after positioning the ball: **place kick, set kick** ●kick given to a dropped ball: **punt** ●set kick awarded after a foul: **free kick** ●indentation made to indicate the place for this: **mark** ●feigned pass or kick: **dummy** ●kick made by dropping the ball onto the boot: **drop kick** ●goal scored from this: **drop goal** ●successful kick at goal after a try: **conversion** ●interlocked arrangement of opposing forwards: **scrum** ●scrum ordered by the referee: **set scrum** ●loose scrum with the ball on the ground: **ruck** ●loose scrum with the ball off the ground: **maul** ●rugby team's forwards: **pack** ●area beyond the pitch side lines: **touch** ●return to play of a ball in touch: **throw-in** ●forwards' queue at a throw-in: **line-out** ●rugby linesman: **touch judge** ●extra playing time after an injury: **injury time** ●order a player to leave the field: **send off** ●side part of the playing area: **wing** ●match that is part of a series between two national teams: **test match, Test**

rule¹ ●*combining forms*: **-archy, -cracy** ●*adjective*: **hegemonic** ●regional self-government: **home rule** ●rule by those showing ability: **meritocracy** ●rule by persons of indifferent ability: **mediocracy** ●rule by a select few: **oligarchy** ●rule by a god or gods: **thearchy** ●rule by the masses: **mobocracy, ochlocracy** ●rule by men: **patriarchy, phallocracy** ●rule by the nobility: **aristocracy** ●rule by the old: **gerontocracy** ●rule exercised by the whole population: **democracy** ●rule by priests: **hierocracy** ●rule by religious officials: **theocracy** ●rule by the rich: **plutocracy** ●rule by a single person: **autarchy, autocracy, despotism, dictatorship, monarchy, monocracy** ●rule by a sovereign: **monarchy** ●rule by a sovereign bound by the laws of the land: **constitutional monarchy** ●rule by a sovereign not bound by law: **absolute monarchy** ●rule by technical experts: **technocracy** ●rule by two separate authorities: **dyarchy** ●rule by

women: **gynaecocracy, matriarchy** ●harsh rule: **despotism, oppression, tyranny**

rule² ●general rule: **guideline, precept** ●basic rule: **principle** ●rules for social behaviour: **etiquette, protocol** ●procedural rules for formal occasions: **protocol** ●denoting a rule that must be obeyed: **strict** ●denoting someone who follows or enforces rules exactly: **strict** ●situation where few rules are observed: **rough and tumble** ●rules of boxing: **Queensberry Rules** ●set of rules to be followed in making a calculation or following a process of logic: **algorithm** ●rules for the grammatical arrangement of words in a language: **syntax** ●official rules for road users: **Highway Code** ●rule book of the Supreme Court: **White Book** ●official ensuring that rules are kept: **referee, umpire** ●exemption from a rule: **dispensation** ●advocate of strict adherence to the rules: **purist** ●stating or enforcing rules: **prescriptive** ●done according to the rules: **clean** ●situation with no clear rules: **grey area** ●refrain from enforcing a rule: **waive** ●against the rules: **irregular** ●absence of rule or control: **anarchy**

ruler ●*combining forms*: **-arch** (*e.g.* heresiarch), **-crat** ●single absolute ruler: **autocrat, despot, dictator, potentate** ●hereditary ruler: **monarch, dynast** ●generations of a ruling family: **dynasty** ●harsh and oppressive ruler: **despot, tyrant** ●ruler of an empire: **emperor** (*fem.* empress) ●denoting a ruler whose title derives from descent: **legitimate** ●former ruler of the central Andes: **Inca** ●former ruler of Austria or Germany: **kaiser** ●ruler of ancient Egypt: **pharaoh** ●former viceroy of Egypt: **khedive** ●former ruler of Ethiopia: **negus** ●former chief magistrate at Genoa and Venice: **doge** ●Nazi ruler of Germany: **führer** ●Nazi district governor: **gauleiter** ●former Indian rulers: **maharaja, raja** (*fem.* rani), **nabob, nizam** ●former ruler of Iran: **shah** ●Islamic rulers: **ayatollah, caliph, emir, hakim, sheik, sultan** ●Fascist ruler of Italy: **duce** ●former Japanese rulers: **mikado, shogun, tenno** ●Ottoman rulers: **aga, bey, khedive, pasha, sultan** ●former ruler of Russia: **tsar, tsarina** ●Spanish military or political leader: **caudillo** ●Spanish or Portuguese monarch's son: **infante** ●Spanish or Portuguese monarch's daughter: **infanta** ●senior magistrate in ancient Sparta: **ephor** ●former ruler of Tibet: **Dalai Lama** ●person holding power during the ruler's absence or incapacity: **regent** ●ceremony of crowning a ruler: **coronation** ●ruler's spouse: **consort** ●ruler's order having the force of law: **decree** ●ruler's arbitrary command: **diktat** ●oriental ruler's command: **firman** ●remove a ruler from power: **depose** ●removal of a ruler by his senior officials: **palace revolution** ●ruling group following a coup d'état: **junta** ●group of advisers to a ruler: **camarilla** ●oppressed by those in power: **downtrodden** ●person out of favour with those in power, whose existence is ignored or denied: **unperson** ●absence of any rules or ruler: **anarchy** ●advocate of this as a political system: **anarchist**

ruler² ●ruler used for calculations: **slide rule**

rum ●rum diluted with water, formerly served to sailors: **grog**

rumour ●false, often malicious, rumour: **canard** ●deliberate spreading of malicious rumours to discredit a person: **whispering campaign** ●source of rumours: **bush telegraph, grapevine**

run ●slow run: **jog** ●short fast run: **sprint** ●uncompetitive run for charity etc.: **fun run** ●at running speed: **at the double** ●run away wildly: **bolt** ●sharp metal point in the sole of a runner's shoe: **spike**

rune ●runic alphabet: **futhorc**

running ●*combining form*: **-drome** (*e.g.* palindrome), **-dromous** (*e.g.* catadromous) ●runner responsible for the last leg in a relay race: **anchorman** ●varied training for distance runners: **fartlek**

rush ●panicked rush of a number of animals: **stampede**

Russian ●*combining form*: **Russo-** ●Russian administrative division: **oblast** ●Russian alphabet: **Cyrillic** ●former Russian aristocrat: **boyar** ●Russian astronaut: **cosmonaut** ●Russian beer: **kvass** ●Russian open carriage: **droshky** ●Russian three-horse carriage: **troika** ●Russian cavalryman: **cossack** ●Russian citadel: **kremlin** ●Russian Easter dessert: **pashka** ●one of a set of Russian babushka dolls: **matryoshka** ●title of the Russian emperors: **tsar** ●title of a Russian empress: **tsarina** ●tsar's eldest son: **tsarevich** ●tsar's daughter: **tsarevna** ●brimless Russian fur hat: **shapka** ●organized massacre of Jews in 19th-c. Russia: **pogrom** ●Russian guitar: **balalaika** ●opponent of the Communists during the Civil War: **White Russian** ●Russian pancake: **blin** (*pl.* blini) ●lower chamber of the Russian parliament: **Duma** ●wealthy Russian peasant: **kulak** ●Russian plain: **steppe** ●Russian rural summer residence: **dacha** ●Russian beetroot soup: **bortsch** ●Russian spirit made from rye, wheat, or potatoes: **vodka** ●Russian tea urn: **samovar** ●(in Imperial Russia) knotted whip: **knout** ●Russian wolfhound: **borzoi** ●old Russian woman: **babushka**

rust ●*adjective*: **ferruginous**

sabotage ● sabotage committed for ecological reasons: **ecotage**

sack ● fibres used to make sacks: **hemp, jute** ● sacking fabric made from these: **hessian**

sacrament ● purification and admission to the Church: **baptism** ● solemn renewal of baptismal vows: **confirmation** ● absolution for confessed sins: **confession, penitence, reconciliation** ● sacramental commemoration of the Last Supper: **Eucharist, Holy Communion, Lord's Supper, Mass** ● setting apart of clergy: **ordination, consecration** ● exchange of marriage vows: **marriage, matrimony** ● liturgical anointing: **unction** ● Christian ceremonies over a dying person: **last rites**

sacred ● *combining form*: hiero- ● sacred literature: **hierology** ● interpreter of sacred mysteries: **hierophant** ● misuse of sacred things: **sacrilege**

sacrifice ● great public sacrifice in ancient Greece or Rome: **hecatomb** ● sacrifice in which the whole offering is burnt: **holocaust**

saddle ● saddle allowing the rider's legs to be both on the same side of the horse: **side-saddle** ● second saddle on a horse or motorcycle: **pillion** ● saddle's projecting front: **pommel** ● loop suspended from the saddle to support the rider's foot: **stirrup** ● this loop when made of metal: **stirrup iron** ● strap suspending the stirrup: **stirrup leather**

safe ● safe place: **haven, sanctuary** ● deposit for safe keeping: **consign**

safety ● safety switch in a locomotive cab that cuts the engine unless constantly depressed by the driver: **dead man's handle** ● safety mechanism activated by machine failure etc.: **fail-safe** ● buoyancy aid for a person in the water: **lifebelt, lifebuoy, life jacket, life ring** ● rescue or safety rope: **lifeline** ● bag inside a motor vehicle that inflates on impact: **air bag** ● deposit items for safe keeping: **lodge**

sailing ● sail-driven wheeled vehicle: **sand yacht** ● high-masted sailing ship: **tall ship** ● large merchant sailing ship: **windjammer** ● sailing ship's stern deck: **poop** ● mast aft of the mainmast: **mizzen** ● mast's crossbar: **yard** ● rope below this: **foot rope** ● diagonal mast spar: **sprit** ● pivoted pole attached to the bottom of a sail: **boom** ● ropes to support masts or control sails: **rigging** ● ropes supporting a mast: **shrouds** ● rope to raise a sail: **halyard, lanyard** ● rope at a sail's lower corner: **sheet** ● rope used to climb a ship's rigging: **ratline** ● wooden block grooved for a sail rope: **deadeye** ● large three-cornered racing sail: **spinnaker** ● equip a boat with sails and ropes: **rig** ● sail round: **circumnavigate** ● sail's lower corner: **clew** ● (of a sail) be filled with wind: **draw** ● spread sails: **make sail** ● adjust a sail to the wind: **trim** ● reduce sail size: **reef, shorten sail, strike sail, take in sail** ● take down a sail: **strike** ● roll up a sail: **furl** ● unfasten a sail: **unbend** ● denoting a wind in the direction travelled: **favourable** ● sail directly before the wind: **run, scud** ● steer closer to the wind: **luff** ● change course by turning across the wind: **tack** ● change course by swinging the boom across a favourable wind: **gybe** ● change course by swinging the boom across an adverse wind: **go about** ● denoting a sailing vessel kept in port by adverse winds: **windbound** ● zigzag course necessitated by adverse wind or current: **traverse** ● lack of sufficient wind to control the boat: **stall** ● device towed astern to lessen leeway: **sea anchor** ● sailing boat's liftable keel: **daggerboard**

sailor ● *adjective*: **nautical** ● ordinary sailor: **rating** ● sailor steering the vessel: **helmsman** ● steersman with local knowledge bringing a ship into harbour etc.: **pilot** ● ship's officer in charge of accounts and cabin service: **purser** ● ship's officer in charge of equipment and crew: **boatswain** ● ship's officer in charge of navigation: **sailing master** ● ship's officer responsible for steering and signals: **quartermaster** ● ship's clergyman: **chaplain** ● officer in charge of a ship: **captain** ● captain of a merchant ship: **master** ● officer second to the captain: **first mate** ● sailor's bag: **ditty bag** ● sailor's ability to keep his balance and resist seasickness: **sea legs** ● sailor's canvas bed: **hammock** ● dried bread formerly eaten by sailors: **hard tack, ship's biscuit** ● sailor's certificate of competence: **ticket** ● sailor's dance: **hornpipe** ● deficiency disease formerly suffered by sailors: **scurvy** ● sailor's imagined heaven: **Fiddler's Green** ● sailor's short overcoat: **pea coat, pea jacket, pilot jacket** ● punish a sailor by dragging him beneath the ship: **keelhaul** ● rum diluted with water, formerly served to sailors: **grog** ● sailor's skills: **seamanship** ● sailor's tool for unravelling rope: **marlinspike** ● sailor's time off spent ashore: **liberty, shore leave** ● sailor's

turn of duty: **watch** ● sailor's short watch: **dog watch** ● sailor's turn at the helm: **trick** ● sailor's work song: **shanty** ● sea robber: **pirate** ● person without seagoing skills: **landlubber**

saint ● *combining form*: **hagi(o)-** ● veneration of saints: **hagiolatry, hierolatry** ● account of a saint's life: **hagiography** ● light round a saint's head: **halo, nimbus** ● pointed halo: **mandorla, vesica** ● declare a dead person to be in a state of bliss (the first stage in canonization): **beatify** ● title bestowed upon a beatified person: **venerable** ● declare a person to be a saint: **canonize** ● person arguing for a saint's canonization: **postulator** ● person arguing against a saint's canonization: **devil's advocate** ● part of a saint's body or personal property preserved for veneration: **relic** ● feast of the saint after whom one is named: **name day** ● general feast commemorating all Christian saints: **All Saints', All Hallows**

salad ● salad of apples, celery, and walnuts in mayonnaise: **Waldorf salad** ● salad of chopped raw cabbage, carrot, etc.: **coleslaw** ● salad of diced cooked vegetables in mayonnaise: **Russian salad** ● sauce for a salad: **dressing** ● salad dressing of oil and vinegar: **French dressing, vinaigrette** ● this with seasoned egg yolks: **mayonnaise** ● salad dressing of mayonnaise with ketchup and gherkins: **Thousand Island dressing**

sale ● bulk sale to retailers: **wholesale** ● sale of items to end-users: **retail** ● sale by mail order or telephone: **direct marketing** ● sale of cheap second-hand items: **jumble sale** ● sale of a cheaper and purchase of a more expensive item: **trade-up** ● promotion and sale of goods and services: **marketing** ● assessment of an item's sales potential: **market research** ● point at which goods are sold: **outlet** ● put an article into the market:

launch, release ● items offered for sale: **wares** ● item outselling its competitors: **market leader** ● item sold at a loss to attract trade: **loss-leader** ● imperfect item sold off cheaply: **reject, second** ● fit for sale: **merchantable** ● period for which an item remains merchantable: **shelf-life** ● conclude a property sale: **complete** ● making sales by unsolicited telephone calls: **cold-calling, telemarketing, telesales** ● statutory interval for the purchaser to change his mind: **cooling-off period** ▸ *see also* **sell**

salmon ● female salmon: **hen** ● male salmon: **cock** ● young salmon: **fingerling, fry, parr, smolt** ● salmon in its second year: **grilse** ● Scandinavian dish of dry-cured salmon: **gravlax**

salt ● *adjective*: **saline** ● salty water: **brine** ● denoting the taste of such water: **brackish** ● denoting food preserved in brine: **corned** ● evaporation pools for sea salt: **saltern** ● remove salt from water: **desalinate**

salute ● deferential salute: **obeisance** ● dropping to one knee: **genuflection** ● lying flat on one's face: **prostration**

salvage ● salvage items from rubbish heaps and dustbins: **tot**

same ● *combining forms*: **homo-, taut(o)-** ● denoting the same age or time: **coetaneous, coeval, contemporary** ● denoting the same extent or meaning: **coterminous** ● denoting the same kind: **homogeneous** ● having the same meaning: **synonymous** ● denoting the same shape: **congruent** ● denoting the same size: **commensurate** ● saying the same thing twice, but in different words: **tautology**

samurai ● samurai's code of honour: **bushido** ● samurai's sword: **katana** ● ritual suicide required of dishonoured samurai: **hara-kiri**

sand ● windblown sand: **spindrift** ● loose wet sand sucking in objects placed upon it: **quicksand** ● mound of sand: **dune** ● area of shifting dunes: **erg** ● ridge of sand in the sea: **reef** ● low reef or sandbank: **cay** ● clean by pressurized sand: **sandblast**

sandal ● light sandal secured by a strap between the toes: **flipflop** ● such a strap: **thong**

sandalwood ● perfume made from sandalwood: **chypre**

sandwich ● sandwich without a top layer of bread: **open sandwich** ● small open sandwich: **canapé** ● buffet of open sandwiches: **smorgasbord**

satellite ● Soviet artificial satellite: **sputnik** ● large satellite used as a base for manned space operations: **space station** ● satellite relaying or reflecting communications signals: **communications satellite** ● satellite orbiting so as to seem in a fixed position: **geostationary satellite** ● satellite in an orbit synchronous with the earth's rotation: **geosynchronous satellite** ● ground observation by satellite: **remote sensing** ● establishment monitoring satellite movements: **tracking station** ● earth station's communications link to a satellite: **uplink** ● satellite's communications link with earth: **downlink**

satire ● satirical picture: **caricature, cartoon**

satisfaction ● self-satisfaction: **complacency, hubris, smugness** ● satisfy to the full: **sate, satiate** ● that cannot be satisfied: **insatiable**

sauce ● sauce in which food is soaked: **marinade** ● sauce for a salad: **dressing** ● thick sauce into which food is dipped: **dip** ● thicken a sauce by boiling: **reduce** ● reduced sauce: **jus** ● sauce thickener: **liaison** ● sautéed chopped vegetables for sauces: **mirepoix** ● fine vegetable or fruit purée: **coulis** (*pl.* same) ● sauce base of butter and flour: **roux** ● sauce of flour, butter, and milk: **white sauce** ● fish sauce of butter, eggs, and vinegar: **hollandaise sauce** ● meat sauce of savoury jelly: **tracklement** ● sauce of butter with parsley and lemon juice: **maître d'hôtel butter** ● cheese-flavoured white sauce: **mornay sauce** ● onion-flavoured white sauce: **sauce soubise** ● sauce of milk and herbs: **béchamel sauce** ● sauce with egg yolks and tarragon: **Béarnaise sauce** ● sauce of tomatoes, garlic, and olive oil: **sauce provençale** ● potato sauce of white wine and onions: **lyonnaise sauce** ● Chinese sauce with sugar and vinegar or lemon: **sweet and sour sauce** ● Chinese and Japanese sauce of fermented soya beans: **soy** ● southern French sauce of red chillies, garlic, and breadcrumbs: **rouille** ● Indian sauce of spices and turmeric: **curry** ● Italian pasta sauces: **carbonara, marinara, pesto** ● Italian sauce of garlic, capers, anchovies, and oil: **salsa verde** ● Mexican sauce of onion, garlic, coriander, and peppers: **salsa verde** ● sauce of puréed rasberries and icing sugar: **Melba sauce**

saucepan ● double saucepan for custards etc.: **bain-marie**

sausage ● continuous coiled sausage: **Cumberland sausage** ● large smoked sausage made of various meats: **bologna, polony** ● seasoned smoked pork sausage: **saveloy** ● seasoned smoked beef and pork sausage: **frankfurter** ● small thin sausage: **cocktail sausage** ● small thin spicy sausage: **chipolata** ● German pork sausage: **bratwurst** ● Italian peppered pork and beef sausage: **pepperoni** ● Italian garlic sausage: **salami** ● spiced Italian pork sausage: **mortadella** ● Spanish spicy pork sausage: **chorizo** ● sausage baked in Yorkshire pudding: **toad in the hole**

savings ● savings through increased output: **economy of scale** ● savings though diversification of output: **economy of scope**

saw ● coarse wood-saw: **ripsaw** ● fine saw for ornamental work: **fretsaw** ● fine-bladed machine saw: **jigsaw** ● frame saw with a fine-toothed blade: **hacksaw** ● power saw with an endless serrated steel belt: **bandsaw** ● power saw with an endless toothed chain: **chainsaw** ● power saw with a rotating toothed disc: **circular saw** ● saw with a thin blade stretched in a frame: **frame saw** ● small saw with a strong back: **tenon saw** ● projecting point on a saw: **tooth** ● adjust a saw's teeth: **set** ● sawn slit: **kerf** ● frame holding wood to be sawn: **horse, sawing horse** ● guide for angled sawing: **mitre box** ● person who saws for a living: **sawyer**

saying ● wise saying: **adage, aphorism, apophthegm, epigram, golden rule, gnome, maxim, proverb, saw** ● trite saying: **bromide, cliché, platitude, truism** ▸ *see also* **remark**

scale ● *adjective*: **squamous** ● scale for child intelligence: **Binet-Simon scale** ● scale for earthquake intensities: **Richter scale** ● scale for general movements of prices etc.: **index** ● movable scale giving subdivisions: **vernier, vernier scale** ● scale for wind velocities: **Beaufort scale** ● mark out the degrees on a scale: **calibrate, graduate** ● relating to a twelve-tone musical scale: **chromatic** ● relating to an eight-tone musical scale: **diatonic**

scales ● *astrological term*: **Libra**

scandal ● seeking and publication of scandal about celebrities: **muckraking** ● deliberate spreading of scandal to damage a person's reputation: **character assassination, scurrility**

Scandinavian ● Scandinavian goddess of destiny: **Norn** ● Scandinavian medieval poet: **skald** •Scandinavian dish of dry-cured salmon: **gravlax**

scar •scar on a healed wound: **cicatrix** (*pl.* cicatrices)

scenery •*combining form*: -**scape** (*e.g.* landscape) •scenery and properties used in a production: **decor** •scenery, furniture, and properties needed for a particular scene: **set** •piece of two-dimensional scenery projecting from the wings: **flat, coulisse** •painted cloth hung at the back of a stage: **backdrop** •arced cloth at the back of the stage: **cyclorama** •gauze cloth opaque until lit from behind: **scrim** •dismantle theatre scenery: **strike** •area where scenery is built and painted: **scene shop** •onstage item other than scenery and furniture: **property, prop**

scent •scented lotion for use after shaving: **aftershave** •dried petals used for scent: **pot-pourri** •oil from flowers etc. used in scent-making: **attar** •perforated container for sweet-smelling substances: **pomander**

schedule •allotted place in a schedule: **slot**

scholarship •*adjective*: **academic** •academic scholarship offered by a school or college: **exhibition** •scholar proficient in several disciplines: **polymath, polyhistor** •great scholar: **savant** •group of scholars with shared viewpoints: **school**

school •*adjective*: **scholastic** •school at which one was educated: **alma mater** •denoting schools receiving state funding: **maintained** •denoting schools receiving no state funding: **independent** •school for very young children: **kindergarten, nursery, nursery school, playschool** •privately-run fee-paying school: **private school** •privately-run fee-paying school for pupils aged 7–13: **preparatory school** •privately-run fee-paying secondary school: **public**

school •school funded and controlled by the state: **state school** •school for children with physical, intellectual, or behavioural difficulties: **special school** •school offering intensive preparation for examinations: **crammer** •school where young women are taught social graces: **finishing school, charm school** •school run by nuns: **convent, convent school** •institution offering evening classes: **night school** •entrance examination for public schools: **Common Entrance** •reduction in fees offered to outstanding Common Entrance candidates: **bursary, exhibition, scholarship** •state school receiving national funding and free of local authority control: **grant maintained school** •state school partially controlled and funded by a religious denomination: **voluntary-aided school** •state school established by a religious denomination but now funded and controlled by the local authority: **voluntary-maintained school** •state school for children aged 5–11: **primary school** •state school for children aged 5–7: **infant school** •state school for children aged 5–9: **first school** •state school for children aged 7–11: **junior school** •state school for children aged 9–13: **middle school** •state school for children aged 11–18: **secondary school, senior school** •state school for children aged 13–18: **upper school** •school in which the pupils live during term-time: **boarding school, residential school** •school from which the pupils return home each night: **day school** •selective state secondary school: **grammar school** •secondary school providing facilities for local adults: **community college** •non-selective secondary school: **comprehensive** •secondary school in certain European countries: **gymnasium** •school day running from early morning to early afternoon: **continental day** ●unit of tuition time: **lesson, period** ●pupil group: **class, form, set, stream** ●class for children in their first year of schooling: **reception class** ●school's short mid-term holiday: **half term, exeat** ●absence from school without permission: **truancy** ●school celebration with speeches, prize-giving, etc.: **speech day** ●school day devoted to athletics: **sports day** ●school punishment of being kept in: **detention** ●school pupil with disciplinary duties: **monitor, prefect** ●short experience of employment arranged for school-leavers: **work experience** ●former pupil of a school: **alumnus** (*fem.* alumna: *pl.* alumni) ●school financial manager: **bursar** ●relaxation room at a school: **common room** ●teachers' common room: **staffroom** ●residential unit at a boarding school: **house** ●woman in charge of domestic arrangements at a boarding school: **matron** ●boarding school hospital: **sanatorium** ●current official name for an approved school: **community home** ●(of a state school) withdraw from local authority control: **opt out** ●state-funded place at an independent school: **assisted place** ●region from which a school's pupils come: **catchment area** ●list of pupils attending a school: **roll** ●debar a pupil from attending school: **expel**

science ●science of the physical world: **natural science** ●science of communications and automatic control systems: `cybernetics` ●science used in criminal investigations: **forensics** ●practical applications of scientific discoveries: **technology** ●excessive faith in the capacities of science: scientism ●denoting events beyond the scope of science: **paranormal**

scientific equipment ●tube of very fine bore: **capillary tube** ●narrow graduated glass tube with a tap at one end: **burette** ●narrow glass tube attached to a bulb: **pipette** ●glass tube closed at one end: **test tube** ●narrow-necked glass container: **flask** ●lipped cylindrical glass container: **beaker** ●shallow dish for culture development: **petri dish** ●bell-shaped glass cover: **bell jar** ●hand-held crushing implement: **pestle** ●strong dish for this: **mortar** ●small gas burner: **Bunsen burner** ●container for items to be heated fiercely: **crucible** ●ventilated enclosure: **fume cupboard** ●weighing apparatus: **balance** ●closed chamber with sealed-in gloves: **glovebox**

scissors ●tailor's serrated scissors: **pinking shears**

score ●even score at the end of a game: **draw**

scorpion ●poison secreted by scorpions: **venom**

Scottish ●Scottish accent: **brogue** ●Scottish bagpipe music for war or lamentation: **pibroch** ●Scottish beret: **bonnet, tam-o'-shanter** ●Scottish broadsword: **claymore** ●Scottish word for church: **kirk** ●Scottish coroner and public prosecutor: **procurator fiscal** ●Scottish dagger: **dirk, skean** ●fast Scottish dance: **reel** ●slow Scottish dance: **strathspey** ●vigorous Scottish dance: **Highland fling** ●Scottish term for an English person: **Sassenach** ●group of interrelated Scottish families: **clan** ●small Scottish farm: **croft** ●Scottish fishing boat: **coble** ●Scottish term for a flat: **tenement** ●Scottish funeral song: **coronach** ●Scottish game of sliding stones across ice: **curling** ●Scottish traditional harp: **clarsach** ●Scottish word for a steep hill: **brae** ●Scottish minister's house: **manse** ●Scottish hut: **bothy** ●title of a judge in Scotland: **sheriff** ●Scottish lake: **loch** ●Scottish land agent: **factor** ●Scottish landowner: **laird** ●Scottish term for long ago: **lang**

syne ●Scottish mayor: **provost**
●river estuary in Scotland: **firth**
●Scottish schoolmaster: **dominie**
● Scottish word for a narrow sea channel: **kyle** ●Scottish fortified settlement: **dun** ●Scottish sheepdog: **collie**
●Scottish social gathering: **ceilidh**
● Scottish female spirit whose wailing
portends death: **banshee** ●Scottish
sport of throwing a large pole: **tossing
the caber** ●Scottish water spirit: **kel-
pie** ●Scottish word for a stream:
burn ●students' elected representative in Scottish universities: **rector**
●Scottish prehistoric stone tower:
broch ●defensive tower on the Scottish Marches: **peel, pele tower**
●tight-fitting tartan trousers: **trews**
●Scottish valley: **glen** ●broad mountain valley: **strath** ●mountainous
part of Scotland: **Highlands** ●Scot-
tish chicken and leek soup: **cock-
a-leekie** ●Scottish soup of meat and
vegetables with pearl barley: **Scotch
broth** ●Scottish dish of boiled cabbage and potatoes: **colcannon** ●Scot-
tish dish of boiled offal and oatmeal:
haggis ●soft Scottish cheese:
crowdie ●Scottish term for a turnip:
neep ●Scottish spirit distilled from
malted grain: **whisky** ●Scottish term
for a last drink: **deoch an doris**
●place where alcohol is sold illegally:
shebeen ●leather strap formerly
used to punish Scottish schoolchildren: **tawse** ▸ see also **Highlands**

Scout ●junior Scout: **Cub** ●Scout
aged 16–20: **Venture Scout** ●Scout
rally: **jamboree** ●loop for a Scout's
neckerchief: **woggle**

screen ●sliding screen in a Japanese house: **shoji** ●screen in an Indian
house concealing women from view:
purdah ●elongated VDU screen
showing a full page of text: **full-page
display** ●tiny illuminated dot on a
VDU screen: **pixel** ●grid of dots on a
VDU screen: **dot matrix** ●pattern of
scanning lines on a VDU screen: **ras-**

ter ●denoting a VDU giving a very
clear image: **high resolution**

screw ●screw with a cross-shaped
slot: **Phillips screw™** ●screw with a
hexagonal slot: **Allen screw™**
●spiral ridge round a screw: **thread,
screw thread** ●dowel set in a hole for
the screw to grip: **wall plug** ●insert a
screw flush with the surface: **countersink**

script ●person with a script remind-
ing actors of their lines: **prompter**
●device displaying a speaker's or
actor's script onto a clear glass screen
invisible to the audience: **autocue**

scriptures ●Buddhist scriptures:
Tripitaka ●Hindu scriptures: **Veda**
●Islamic scriptures: **Koran** ●Sikh
scriptures: **Adi Granth, Granth,
Granth Sahib** ●Zoroastrian scrip-
tures: **Avesta**

sculpture ●prehistoric rock carving: **petroglyph** ●ancient Greek female statue: **kore** (pl. korai) ●ancient
Greek male statue: **kouros** (pl. kouroi)
●sculpture of the subject's head and
shoulders: **bust** ●sculptor's preliminary model: **maquette** ●gypsum for
sculpture: **gesso** ●raised carving:
relief ●shallow carving: **bas-relief**
●moderately deep carving: **mezzo-
relievo** ●deep carving: **high relief**
●denoting free-standing sculpture: **in
the round**

scurvy ●adjective: **scorbutic**

sea ●adjectives: **marine, maritime,
nautical** ●supposed original single
sea: **Panthalassa** ●denoting the sea
adjacent to a nation's coasts: **inshore**
●coastal seas asserted to be under
state control: **territorial waters** ●sea
beyond this: **high seas, international
waters** ●denoting the open sea: **pela-
gic** ●sea under a single country's
jurisdiction: **mare clausum** (pl. maria
clausa) ●sea open to all: **mare
liberum** (pl. maria libera) ●deep sea
inlet: **gulf** ●narrow sea passage:

channel, neck, sound, strait ●area of sea surrounded by ice: **polynya** ●shallow sea round a land mass: **continental shelf** ●sloping seabed beyond this: **continental slope** ●narrow region of especially deep sea: **trench, ocean trench** ●area of shallow water: **shoal** ●ridge of rock, coral, or sand in the sea: **reef, shoal** ●salt water separated from the sea by a reef: **lagoon** ●area of rough water caused by meeting currents: **rip** ●windblown spray: **scud** ●sea mist: **fret** ●animals and plants living on the seabed: **epibenthos** ●animals living in the seabed: **infauna** ●use of sea water for health treatment: **thalassotherapy** ●display tank for undersea life: **oceanarium** ●measurement of sea depths: **bathymetry** ●mapping of seas: **hydrography** ●change in world sea levels: **eustasy** ●equatorial sea with sudden calms: **doldrums** ●diver's enclosed vessel for deep-sea observations: **bathyscaphe, bathysphere** ●unit of speed at sea: **knot** ●person unfamiliar with the sea: **landlubber, landsman** ●denoting a state without direct sea access: **landlocked** ▸ *see also* **navigation**

seal ●young seal: **pup** ●seal fat: **blubber** ●seals' breeding ground: **rookery**

seaplane ●large seaplane: **flying boat**

search ●long or arduous search: **quest** ●hopeless search: **wild goose chase** ●search thoroughly: **scour, sweep** ●search disruptively: **ransack, rifle, riffle, root, rummage** ●remove a person's clothes and search him or her: **strip-search** ●search the seashore for articles of value: **beachcomb** ●search for mineral deposits: **prospect** ●search a river etc. bed with grapnels or nets: **drag** ●search for underground water with a Y-shaped stick: **dowse**

season ●*combining form*: **-tide** (e.g. yuletide)

seat ●long seat for several persons: **bench** ●high-backed wooden bench: **settle** ●church low-backed wooden bench: **pew** ●long upholstered bench: **banquette** ●low backless upholstered seat: **ottoman, pouffe** ●vehicle seat with a rounded back: **bucket seat** ●vehicle seat with a flat back: **bench seat** ●padded back or side of a vehicle seat: **squab** ●person showing others to their seats: **usher**

seat belt ●reel locking under impact pressure: **inertia reel**

seaweed ●*combining form*: **phyco-** ●large brown seaweed: **kelp** ●coarse brown seaweed: **wrack** ●Japanese edible seaweed: **nori** ●study of seaweed: **phycology**

second ●*combining forms*: **deuter(o)-** (e.g. Deuteronomy, *literally the 'second law'*), **meta-** (e.g. metalanguage), **sub-** (e.g. sublet) ●second signature: **countersignature**

secret ●*combining form*: **crypto-** (e.g. cryptogram) ●secret and dishonest: **underhand** ●secret information of national importance: **official secret** ●denoting information which may be divulged only to certain persons: **restricted** ●declare information an official secret: **classify** ●background investigation of those to have access to official secrets: **positive vetting, security check** ●secret told on trust: **confidence** ●secret known to many: **open secret** ●release of secret information: **disclosure** ●person within an organization who betrays its secrets: **mole** ●threat to disclose compromising secrets in order to force a person to do as one wishes: **blackmail** ●secret trade in items not officially available: **black market** ●secret organization working to frustrate or overthrow the regime: **underground** ●secret opposition organization in an occupied country: **resistance** ●person about whom little is known: **dark horse** ●secret plan: **conspiracy** ●belief that an event results from a conspiracy: **conspiracy theory** ●house at a secret location: **safe house** ●secret stock: **hoard** ●gain secret access or control: **infiltrate** ●in secret: **sub rosa**

secretary ●secretary dealing with confidential work: **private secretary**

secret societies ●18th-c. mystical society: **Rosicrucians** ●international secret society for mutual assistance: **Freemasonry** ●Protestant Afrikaner secret society: **Broederbond** ●nationalist Chinese secret society in 19th century: **Boxers** ●Chinese secret criminal gang: **tong, triad** ●Neapolitan branch of the Mafia: **Camorra** ●Sicilian secret criminal and political organization: **Mafia** ●US branch of the Mafia: **Cosa Nostra** ●Cosa Nostra boss: **capo, godfather** ●US secret society promoting White supremacy: **Klu Klux Klan** ●formally admit someone to a secret society: **initiate** ●secret political group: **cabal**

security ●security given for a loan: **collateral** ●person held as a security: **hostage**

sediment ●accumulated layer of sediment: **deposit** ●sediment produced by erosion: **detritus** ●sediment deposited by a glacier: **moraine** ●sediment deposited on a river bed: **silt** ●sediment deposited at a river mouth: **delta**

see ●ability to see: **sight** ●that can be seen through: **transparent** ●(of a corner etc.) difficult to see round: **blind**

seed ●*adjective*: **seminal** ●edible seed of a pea-type plant: **pulse** ●seed's outer covering: **hull** ●prickly seed case: **bur** ●elongated seed case: **pod** ●seed scar: **hilum** ●covering of

a fruitseed: **endocarp** ●seed's beginning to grow: **germination** ●young plant raised from a seed: **seedling**

seeming ●*combining form*: **quasi-**

seizure ●seizure of a debtor's property: **distraint, sequestration** ●seizure after legal infringement: **impoundment**

self ●*combining form*: **aut(o)-** ●self-government: **autonomy, autarchy** ●self-examination: **introspection** ●self-sufficiency: **autarky** ●attaching great importance to oneself: **egocentric, egoistic** ●excessive talking or thinking about oneself: **egotism** ●extreme egotism: **egomania**

self-confident ●cheerily self-confident: **jaunty**

self-control ●lacking self-control: **intemperate**

selfish ●obstinately selfish: **self-willed** ●unselfish concern for the good of others: **altruism**

sell ●selling by unsolicited promotional mailings: **direct mail** ●selling by sending out unsolicited items and then demanding payment if they are not returned: **inertia selling** ●selling through a hierarchy of agents: **pyramid selling** ●manufacturer's direct sale to the public: **direct marketing** ●put a new product on sale: **launch** ●sell small items: **vend** ●sell goods by association (*e.g.* inscribed sweatshirts at a pop concert): **merchandize** ●sell all available stock: **sell out** ●sell more items than are available: **oversell** ●sell one's stock, premises, etc.: **sell up** ●sell illegal drugs: **peddle** ●person doing this: **peddler** ●sell from house to house: **peddle** ●person doing this: **pedlar** ●sell abroad: **export** ●sell items at cheap rates to be rid of them: **sell off** ●sell goods abroad at a giveaway price, to maintain their home price: **dump** ●low pricing to force competitors out of the market: **predatory pricing**

●miscellaneous items sold as a unit: **job lot** ●rate at which stocks are sold and replaced: **turnover** ●depletion of stocks due to demand: **downturn** ●frequent repurchase encouraged by production of new models, use of non-durable materials, etc.: **planned obsolescence** ▸*see also* **market, sale, seller, trade**

seller ●*combining form*: **-monger** ●travelling salesman: **commercial traveller, representative** ●person selling from door to door: **hawker, huckster, pedlar** ●person selling fruit etc. in a street market: **costermonger, huckster** ●person selling supplies for boats and ships: **chandler** ●salesman's unsolicited visit: **cold call** ●salesman's persuasive patter: **pitch** ●subtly persuasive sales technique: **soft sell** ●aggressive sales technique: **hard sell** ●former seller of quack medicines etc. at fairs: **mountebank** ▸*see also* **market, sale, sell, trade**

semen ●*adjective*: **seminal, spermatic** ●male sex cell in semen: **sperm** (*pl.* same), **spermatozoon** (*pl.* spermatozoa) ●count of spermatozoa in a measure of semen: **sperm count** ●deficiency of sperm cells in semen: **oligospermia** ●natural ejection of semen: **ejaculation, emission** ●erotic dream causing an involuntary ejaculation: **wet dream** ●introduction of semen into the vagina other than by sexual intercourse: **artificial insemination** ●person providing semen for this: **donor** ●place where semen is stored until needed for artificial insemination: **sperm bank**

send ●send on: **forward**

senior citizen ●*adjective*: **elderly** ●state allowance paid to the elderly: **old age pension** ●former National Savings certificate available only to pensioners: **granny bond** ▸*see also* **old age**

sense ●common sense: **mother wit, nous** ●supposed intuitive faculty: **sixth sense** ●stimulation of a sense impression away from the point stimulated: **synaesthesia** ●form of sensory perception: **modality** ●deprived of all senses: **insensate, insensible, insentient**

sentence[1] ●sentence containing every letter of the alphabet: **pangram** ●sentence that tails off uncompleted: **aposiopesis** ●sentence consisting of only one clause: **simple sentence** ●sentence composed of several simple sentences: **compound sentence** ●sentence containing one or more subordinate clauses: **complex sentence** ●part of a sentence that contains the verb: **predicate** ●arrangement of words to make a correct sentence: **syntax** ●create a syntactically correct sentence: **construct** ●analyse the syntax of a sentence: **construe, parse**

sentence[2] ●pronounce a judicial sentence: **condemn** ●sentence of supervision in the community: **probation** ●sum of money to be paid as a punishment: **fine** ●demand a sum of money as surety for good behaviour: **bind over** ●prison sentence to be served only upon re-offending: **suspended sentence** ●reduction of a prison sentence for good behaviour: **remission** ●denoting a prison sentence to be served simultaneously with another: **concurrent** ●facts presented to encourage lenient sentencing: **mitigation** ●reduction of a judicial sentence upon appeal: **commutation** ●denoting a sentence that has not been legally authorized: **extrajudicial** ●list of offences with sentences currently deemed appropriate: **tariff** ●free from a sentence: **pardon** ▸*see also* **punishment**

sentimentality ●sentimentality in music or art: **kitsch, schmaltz** ●tearfully sentimental: **maudlin, mawkish**

sentry ●sentry's call for the password: **challenge**

separate ●separate and distinct: **discrete** ●separate on grounds of sex, race, or religion: **segregate**

sequence ●in unbroken sequence: **consecutive** ●in proper sequence: **seriatim** ●sequence with gradual change of items: **continuum**

series ●interconnected series: **concatenation** ●repeated series: **cycle** ●related series of artworks: **cycle** ●series of events, each triggered by its predecessor: **chain reaction** ●series of shops, hotels, etc. owned by one company: **chain**

sermon ●collection of sermons: **homiliary** ●biblical etc. passage upon which a sermon is preached: **text** ▶ *see also* **preaching**

servant ●chief servant in a large household: **major-domo, steward** ●chief female servant: **housekeeper** ●chief male servant: **butler** ●servant's distinctive uniform: **livery** ●liveried servant: **footman, flunkey, lackey** ●military officer's servant: **batman** ●man's personal servant: **valet** ●Cambridge college servant: **gyp** ●Oxford college servant: **scout** ●female cleaner: **char, charwoman** ●domestic helper provided by a local authority: **home help** ●junior public-school boy who acts as servant to a senior boy: **fag** ●Indian servant operating a large ceiling fan: **punkah wallah**

servility ●showing servility: **obsequious** ●make a calculated display of servility: **fawn**

sesame ●paste made from sesame seeds: **tahini** ●sweet made from sesame seeds: **halva**

set ●set of items fitting inside each other: **nest** ●set of items following each other in a fixed order: **sequence** ●set of related items: **compendium**

●set of similar items: **group** ●batch of goods: **consignment**

settlement ●use of a third party to negotiate a settlement: **conciliation** ●recourse to a third party who adjudicates a settlement: **arbitration**

settler ●early settler: **pioneer** ●incoming settler: **immigrant** ●person leaving his own country to settle elsewhere: **emigrant, emigre**

seven ●*combining forms*: **hept(a)-** (*e.g.* heptagon), **sept(i)-** ●*adjective*: **septenary** ●athletic contest with seven events for all competitors: **heptathlon** ●seven-sided figure: **heptagon** ●solid figure with seven faces: **heptahedron** ●group of seven: **heptad, septenary** ●ensemble of seven musicians, or music for them: **septet** ●one of seven offspring born at a birth: **septuplet** ●having seven parts: **septuple** ●verse-line of seven feet: **heptameter** ●occurring every, or lasting for, seven years: **septennial** ●seven-hundredth anniversary: **septcentenary**

seventy ●person in his seventies: **septuagenarian**

severe ●make less severe: **mitigate, palliate**

sewage ●liquid sewage: **effluent** ●pipe for the removal of sewage: **sewer** ●place where sewage is treated: **sewage farm, sewage works** ●pit for sewage: **cesspit, cesspool, septic tank** ●excrement in a septic tank: **septage** ●sewer system and its maintenance: **sewerage**

sewing ●rough sewing with large stitches: **tacking** ●sewing together of assorted cloth fragments: **patchwork** ●sew over a raw edge of cloth: **overcast, overlock, oversew** ●sewing making a decorative grid across the cloth: **quilting** ●sewing gathering material into small tight pleats: **smocking** ●parallel elastic threadwork used in smocking: **shirr**

• woman skilled at sewing: **needle-woman, seamstress, sempstress** • small case for sewing items: **housewife, lady's companion, nécessaire** • container for sewing items: **workbasket, workbox** • finger-protector worn when sewing: **thimble** • shop selling sewing requisites: **haberdasher** • items used in sewing: **notions**

sex • animal or plant having both male and female sexual characteristics: **hermaphrodite** • of, or appearing to belong to, either sex: **androgynous, epicene** • for persons of either sex: **unisex** • for, or consisting of, persons of either sex: **mixed** • person emotionally and physiologically desiring to belong to the opposite sex: **transsexual** • person deriving pleasure from dressing in clothes appropriate to the opposite sex: **transvestite** • external sexual organs: **genitals** • male reproductive fluid: **semen** • remove the testicles of a male animal: **castrate, geld, neuter** • remove the ovaries of a female animal: **spay, neuter**

sexual activity • *adjectives*: **carnal, venereal** • avoiding sexual activity: **celibate, chaste, continent** • person who has never experienced sexual intercourse: **virgin** • indulging in all sexual activity: **pansexual** • evocative of sexual activity: **suggestive** • sexual activity with precautions against Aids: **safe sex** • denoting sexual activity performed without a condom: **unprotected** • sexual activity regarded as a source of power: **sexual politics** • criminal exploitation of sexuality: **vice** • person easily shocked by mention of sexual matters: **prude** • unhealthy interest in sexual matters: **prurience** • liberalization of western society's attitude towards sexual activity: **sexual revolution** • generalized sexual desire excited and gratified in many ways: **polymorphous perversity** • abnormal sexual activity: **paraphilia** • socially unacceptable sexual activity: **perversion** • point in adolescence at which sexual activity become possible: **puberty** • age at which voluntary sexual activity becomes legal: **age of consent** • point in middle age at which sexual activity declines: **climacteric** • female animal's period of sexual receptivity: **heat, oestrus, season** • female animal's period of sexual inactivity: **dioestrus** • deer's annual period of sexual activity: **rut** • sexual desire: **libido** • act hinting sexual interest: **pass** • intended to arouse sexual desire: **provocative, titillating** • deliberately provoke sexual desire with no intention of satisfying it: **tease** • address a person in order to offer or request sexual favours: **accost, proposition** • entice into sexual activity: **seduce** • casual acquaintance made for sexual purposes: **pickup** • adult voluntarily participating in sexual activity: **consenting adult** • person paid for sexual favours: **prostitute** • right of a feudal lord to sexual intercourse with a vassal's bride: **droit du seigneur** • marriage partners' right to mutual sexual relations: **conjugal rights** • sexual intercourse as the completion of marriage: **consummation** • have sexual relations only with one's partner: **be faithful** • be unfaithful to an established sexual partner: **cheat** • engaging in casual sexual relationships: **promiscuous, philandering** • sexual activity between those too closely related to marry: **incest** • sexual intercourse between a married person and someone not their spouse: **adultery** • sexual activity between three persons: **troilism** • older woman's youthful male lover: **gigolo** • feign sexual interest: **flirt** • flirtatious woman: **coquette** • arousing sexual desire:

erotic ● item of clothing etc. as object of desire: **fetish** ● sexual activity preceding intercourse: **foreplay** ● sexual stimulation by touching or caressing: **petting** ● this stopping just short of intercourse: **heavy petting** ● mutual oral genital stimulation: **soixante-neuf** ● stimulation of the female genitals by tongue or lips: **cunnilingus** ● sensitive to sexual stimulation: **erogenous, erotogenic** ● swelling caused by sexual stimulation: **tumescence** ● excessive sexual desire: **erotomania** ● moments of intense genital pleasure: **climax, orgasm** ● sexual pleasure from inflicting or suffering pain: **algolagnia** ● sexual pleasure from hurting others: **sadism** ● sexual pleasure from watching the sexual activities of others: **voyeurism** ● sexual pleasure from watching urination: **urolagnia, urophilia** ● sexual pleasure from one's own pain or humiliation: **masochism** ● sexual pleasure from rubbing one's clothed body against someone in a crowd: **frottage** ● being tied up for sexual pleasure: **bondage** ● whipping for sexual pleasure: **flagellation** ● sexual stimulation of one's own body: **auto-eroticism** ● manual stimulation of the genitals: **masturbation, onanism** ● oral stimulation of the penis: **fellatio** ● sexual pleasure obtained via computer technology: **cybersex** ● printed or visual material aimed at erotic stimulation: **pornography** ● denoting mildly pornographic material: **racy, titillating** ● sexual activity that is disapproved of: **deviance** ● person who is sexually attracted to members of his or her own sex: **homosexual** ● person who is sexually attracted to members of the opposite sex: **heterosexual** ● person who is sexually attracted to members of either sex: **ambisexual, bisexual** ● person having a sexual relationship with someone much younger: **cradle snatcher** ● person who is sexually attracted towards children: **paedophile** ● sexual activity between a boy and a man: **pederasty** ● boy kept for sexual purposes: **catamite** ● person engaging in anal intercourse: **sodomite** ● sexually unfulfilled: **frustrated** ● sexually unresponsive: **frigid, cold** ● denoting a man unable to achieve erection or orgasm: **impotent** ● containing explicit descriptions etc. of sexual activity: **adult, hard-core** ● strong sexual desire: **lust** ● insatiable sexual appetite in women: **nymphomania** ● insatiable sexual appetite in men: **lechery, satyriasis** ● drug, food, or drink thought to stimulate sexual desire: **aphrodisiac** ● drink thought to stimulate sexual desire: **philtre** ● sexual intercourse: **coition, coitus** ● sexual intercourse with premature withdrawal of the penis: **coitus interruptus, onanism** ● sexual intercourse prolonged by avoidance of ejaculation: **coitus reservatus** ● sexual intercourse with corpses: **necrophilia** ● crime of forcing another to have sexual intercourse with oneself: **rape** ● done or happening after sexual intercourse: **post-coital** ● device worn by a woman to make sexual intercourse impossible: **chastity belt** ● injection of semen into the vagina other than by sexual intercourse: **artificial insemination** ● study of human sexual activity: **sexology** ● study of sexual love: **erotology** ● Hindu treatise on sexual technique: **Kama Sutra** ● legal term for sexual intercourse: **carnal knowledge** ● disease contracted through sexual activity: **venereal disease** ● crime motivated by sexual jealousy: **crime passionnel** (*pl.* crimes passionnels) ▸ *see also* **contraception, homosexuality, relationship**

shade ● canvas sunshade over a shopfront etc.: **awning**

shadow ● observer's shadow projected onto clouds: **Brocken spectre**

• shadow's pale edge: **penumbra** • luminous halo round a shadow on fog: **anthelion**

shake • shaking caused by an impact: **shock**

shape • *combining forms*: **morph(o)-** (*e.g.* morphology), **-form** (*e.g.* vermiform), **-morphic, -oid** (*e.g.* rhomboid) • dark shape on a light background: **silhouette** • taking human shape: **anthropomorphic** • ability to regain shape after distortion: **elasticity**

share • share yielding variable dividends: **ordinary share** • ordinary shares of a company: **equity** • share yielding a fixed dividend: **preference share** • British government irredeemable fixed-interest securities: **Consols** • British government redeemable fixed-interest securities: **gilts** • government-issued bonds etc.: **government paper** • shares offering a guaranteed dividend: **gilts** • apply to purchase shares: **subscribe** • denoting shares traded on a stock exchange: **listed, quoted** • denoting shares considered a safe investment: **blue-chip** • denoting a share issue attracting more purchasers than can be satisfied: **oversubscribed** • denoting a share issue where some stock remains unplaced: **undersubscribed** • institution undertaking to buy up such stock: **underwriter** • price of a share when issued: **nominal value, par** • current price of a share to an investor: **offer price** • current resale price of a share from an investor: **bid price** • shares promising increased value rather than high income: **growth stock** • share of little current worth, bought in hope of an improvement: **penny share, recovery stock** • high-profit, high-risk securities: **junk bonds** • shares bought now but delivered and paid for later: **futures, long stock** • option to buy later at a price agreed now: **put option** • provisional certificate of shares purchased: **scrip** • list of an investor's shares: **portfolio** • shares etc. owned: **holding** • company capital derived from shares: **share capital** • part of company profits distributed to shareholders: **dividend** • this paid on less than a full year's trading: **interim dividend** • declare or pay no dividend: **pass** • certificate entitling a shareholder to a dividend: **dividend warrant** • ratio of dividend to current share price: **dividend yield** • ratio of dividend to total company profits: **dividend cover** • denoting shares purchased when a dividend is about to be paid: **cum dividend** • company's offer of cut-price shares to current shareholders: **rights issue, scrip issue** • opportunity to buy shares at a favourable price: **share option** • option that may itself be bought and sold: **traded option** • company created to control others, whose shares it holds: **holding company** • share-buying company selling to the public shares in its whole portfolio: **investment trust, unit trust** • raw material as an object of speculation: **commodity** • company's issue of shares to pay off debts: **recapitalization** • buy-out of one company by another: **takeover** • denoting a takeover resisted by its victim: **hostile** • company's repurchase of its own shares: **buy-in** • purchase of the majority of a company's shares: **buyout** • this effected on borrowed capital: **leveraged buyout** • buyout effected to force a buy-in: **greenmail** • right to have first refusal on shares: **pre-emptive right** • offer shares for sale for the first time: **float, go public, issue** • find a buyer for shares: **place** • buy back all shares in public hands: **go private** • remove shares from trading: **delist** • reduce share values by issuing more without increasing assets: **dilute** • lottery held to assign oversubscribed shares: **ballot** • value of a share at the end of a day's trading: **closing price** ●rise in share values: **rally** ●sudden collapse of the value of shares: **crash** ●denoting a market with falling prices: **soft, weak** ●steep rise in share values followed by a collapse: **bubble** ●denoting shares having a steady price: **firm** ●denoting a market with steady prices: **hard** ●speculator who sells shares in anticipation of a price fall: **bear** ●speculator who buys shares in anticipation of a price rise: **bull** ●denoting shares sold for a later delivery date: **short** ●selling off shares while their price is high: **profit-taking** ●speculator who buys new share issues for a quick resale: **stag** ●group of speculators buying shares individually with a view to later concerted action: **concert party** ●unobtrusive share purchase through nominees: **warehousing** ●speculator who benefits from currency disparities by buying shares in one country and selling them in another: **arbitrageur** ●possession of the majority of a company's shares: **controlling interest** ●holding giving this: **golden share** ●hostile attempt to purchase a controlling interest: **raid** ●attempt at this by early morning buying: **dawn raid** ●share trading on the basis of privileged information: **insider dealing** ●sale of shares: **disposal** ●share market: **stock exchange, stock market** ●person buying and selling shares for himself: **dealer** ●agent for the sale and purchase of shares: **broker, stockbroker** ●fee charged for such work: **brokerage** ●official controlling a company's investments: **fund manager** ●figure indicating the average position of selected shares: **index** ●general index of American share prices: **Dow Jones index** ●general index of Japanese share prices: **Nikkei index** ●general index of Hong Kong share prices:

Hang Seng index ▸*see also* **investment, stock exchange**

sharp ●*combining form*: **oxy-** ●sharpness of a picture: **definition** ●mental sharpness: **acuity** ●sharp projection: **snag** ●sharpen with a whetstone: **hone**

shed ●shed feathers or fur: **moult** ●shed an outer skin or shell: **slough** ●shedding its leaves annually: **deciduous**

sheep ●*adjective*: **ovine** ●female sheep: **ewe** ●male sheep: **ram, tup** ●young sheep: **lamb** ●castrated male sheep: **wether** ●wether leading the flock: **bellwether** ●sheep that has been shorn once: **shearling** ●sheep in its second year: **teg** ●group of sheep: **flock** ●sheep's divided foot: **cloven hoof** ●sheep's mammary gland: **udder** ●sheep's woolly coat: **fleece** ●greasy substance on this: **suint** ●sheep's matted wool: **dag** ●total wool sheared from a flock in one season: **clip** ●sheep disease of the central nervous system: **scrapie** ●sheep disease ulcerating hoofs and mouths: **foot and mouth disease** ●bacterial disease of sheep hoofs: **foot rot** ●sheep disease affecting the skin and lungs: **anthrax** ●inflammation of the udder: **garget** ●cut off a sheep's winter coat: **shear** ●immerse sheep in medicaments: **dip** ●shelter for sheep: **fold** ●sheep meat: **mutton** ●sheep-rearer: **grazier** ●person in charge of sheep: **shepherd** ●land on which sheep are pastured: **sheepwalk** ●(of a dog) chase and attack sheep: **worry**

sheet ●sheet for a corpse: **shroud** ●light metal-coated sheet retaining heat: **space blanket**

shell[1] ●combining forms: **concho-** ●study of mollusc shells: **conchology** ●tortoise's hard shell: **carapace** ●seashell that may be blown like a trumpet: **conch** ●carved or coloured decoration of shells: **scrimshaw**

shell² ●shell emitting smoke etc. so that its course may be traced: **tracer** ●fragments of an exploding artillery shell: **shrapnel**

shellfish ●shellfish that attaches itself to rocks: **limpet**

shelter ●camouflaged shelter for birdwatchers etc.: **hide** ●shelter for a car, having a roof but no walls: **carport** ●shelter for cattle: **byre** ●ground depression used as a shelter from gunfire: **foxhole** ●shelter for sheep: **fold** ●reinforced underground shelter: **bunker**

shepherd ●*adjective*: **bucolic** ●denoting a shepherd constantly moving to fresh pasture: **nomadic**

sherry ●pale dry sherry: **fino** ●very dry sherry: **manzanilla** ●dark medium-sweet sherry: **oloroso** ●large sherry glass: **schooner**

shield ●shield bearing a coat of arms: **escutcheon** ●knob in the centre of a shield: **boss, umbo** ●Roman legionaries' roof of linked shields: **testudo** ●shield against X-rays worn by doctors etc.: **apron**

shine ●soft shine: **lustre** ●shining in the dark: **luminous** ●having no shine: **matt**

ship ●*adjective*: **marine, maritime** ●ship design: **naval architecture** ●ship carrying goods: **freighter** ●freighter working to no fixed route: **tramp** ●ship transporting coal: **collier** ●ship equipped to carry liquids in bulk: **tanker** ●ship providing a regular service between two points: **ferry** ●luxurious passenger ship: **liner** ●ship equipped to remove mines: **minesweeper** ●old ship stripped of fittings: **hulk** ●sailing ship with banks of oars: **galley** ●Spanish sailing ship: **galleon** ●ship built by Noah: **ark** ●ancient warship

with two files of oarsmen on each side: **bireme** ●ancient warship with three banks of oars: **trireme** ●water craft having little displacement at speed: **skimmer** ●group of ships: **fleet, flotilla** ●group of ships travelling together: **convoy** ●narrow but deep formation of ships: **column** ●ship destroyed at sea: **wreck** ●denoting a ship with hull openings allowing vehicles to drive on and off: **roll-on roll-off** ●plank giving access to a ship: **gangplank** ●rope beside a ship's gangway or ladder: **manrope** ●ship's pointed front: **bow, prow** ●spar running out from a ship's bow: **bowsprit** ●ship's rounded rear: **stern** ●rail round this: **taffrail** ●on the side of a ship: **abeam** ●denoting the front of a ship: **fore** ●denoting the rear of a ship: **aft, astern** ●left side of a ship as seen by one facing its prow: **port** ●right side of a ship as seen by one facing its prow: **starboard** ●distant part of the visible sea: **offing** ●side of a ship sheltered from the wind: **lee, leeward** ●side of a ship exposed to the wind: **windward** ●on the outside of an ship: **outboard** ●from a ship into the water: **overboard, overside** ●lookout post atop the mast: **crow's-nest** ●ship's temporary mast: **jury mast** ●lights showing a ship's position: **navigation lights, running lights, sidelights** ●small boat carried on a ship: **jolly boat** ●small crane for lowering a ship's boat: **davit** ●strong crane with a pivoted arm: **derrick** ●line painted on a ship's side to show permitted submersion levels: **load line, Plimsoll line** ●ship's side above water: **freeboard** ●top of this: **gunwale** ●gunwale hole to let off deck water: **scupper, scuttle** ●main part of a ship, without superstructure or fittings: **hull** ●lowest internal portion of the hull: **bilges** ●lengthwise beam at the base of the hull: **keel** ●structure fastening floor timbers to the keel: **keelson** ● chief timber etc. in the bow: **stem** ● curved transverse strut rising from the keel: **rib** ● section-divider in a ship's hull: **bulkhead** ● area between these: **compartment** ● forward part of a ship below decks: **forecastle, fo'c'sle** ● ship's cargo area: **hold** ● packing to steady a ship's cargo: **dunnage** ● part of a ship built above the hull: **superstructure** ● ship's kitchen: **galley** ● private room on a ship: **cabin** ● superior cabin: **stateroom** ● bed on a ship: **berth, hammock** ● ship's stern deck: **afterdeck, poop, quarterdeck** ● opening in a ship's deck: **hatch** ● raised border round a hatch: **coaming** ● soft stone for cleaning the deck: **holystone** ● stairs between a ship's decks: **companionway** ● ship's small window: **porthole** ● porthole's protective cover: **deadlight** ● ship's leaning from the vertical: **heel, list** ● heavy material placed in a ship's bilges to give stability: **ballast** ● (of a ship) rock from front to back: **pitch** ● (of a ship) rock from side to side: **roll** ● (of a ship) twist from side to side: **yaw** ● (of a ship) halt: **come to** ● (of a ship) fill with water and sink: **founder** ● gyroscopic device reducing a ship's rolling: **stabilizer** ● housing for a ship's compass: **binnacle** ● device to keep the compass level: **gimbal** ● deflection of a ship's compass by iron in the ship: **deviation** ● neutralize a ship's magnetic field: **degauss** ● device for taking bearings of a distant object: **pelorus** ● duty-room for those in charge of a ship: **bridge** ● ship's steering wheel: **helm, wheel** ● vertically hinged flap for steering: **rudder** ● ship's secondary propeller used in manoeuvring: **thruster** ● large stern or side wheel propelling a ship: **paddle wheel** ● direct the steering of a ship: **con** ● ship's forward motion: **headway** ● make headway against the current:

stem ● rate of headway required for a ship to answer the helm: **steerage way** ● ship's backward motion: **sternway** ● direction taken by a ship: **course** ● ship's deviation from course due to wind or current: **drift** ● ship's record book: **journal, log** ● list of members of a ship's company: **muster roll** ● list of a ship's cargo: **bill of lading** ● list of a ship's passengers, crew, and cargo: **manifest** ● clergyman serving a ship: **chaplain** ● person attending to passengers' needs: **steward** ● person hiding on a ship in order to travel without paying: **stowaway** ● maximum width of a ship: **beam** ● depth of water needed by a ship: **draught** ● trail of disturbed water left behind a moving ship: **wake, wash** ● passable by ships and boats: **navigable** ● audible warning to ships in fog: **foghorn** ● weight of a ship's cargo: **deadweight** ● place allotted to a ship in a dock etc.: **berth** ● ship's thick mooring rope: **cable, hawser** ● short thick post to which berthed ship is tied: **bollard** ● move a ship by pulling on its anchor: **kedge** ● move a ship by pulling on a rope attached to the shore: **warp** ● go or place on board a ship: **embark** ● leave or remove from a ship: **disembark** ● secure a ship to an anchor or land: **moor** ● unmoor a ship: **cast off** ● sheltered anchorage: **roads** ● place where ships may moor and load or unload: **dock, quay, wharf** (*pl.* wharves) ● unload a ship: **discharge** ● wharf owner or manager: **wharfinger** ● worker loading and unloading ships: **stevedore** ● place where a ship may be boarded: **jetty, landing stage** ● pad hung over the side as a ship approaches the dockside: **fender** ● prepare a ship for its return journey: **turn round** ● dealer in ship's supplies: **chandler, ship chandler** ● place where ships are built or repaired: **dockyard** ● establishment for building and repairing ships: **ship-yard** • make a ship operational: **commission** • take a ship out of service: **decommission, lay up** • hire a ship for a trip: **charter** • journey by ship, or the right to make it: **passage** • ship's scheduled voyage: **sailing** • official record of a ship's journey: **log** • prize awarded to the ship making the fastest eastward commercial crossing of the Atlantic: **Blue Riband** • nausea caused by a ship's motion: **seasickness** • illegally seize control of a ship: **hijack** • destruction of a ship at sea: **shipwreck** • decorate a ship with flags overall: **dress** • ship's registration abroad to avoid stringent regulations: **flag of convenience** ▸ *see also* **boat, sailing**

shipwreck • deliberately sink a ship: **scupper, scuttle** • denoting a ship in danger of sinking or wreck: **in distress** • shipwrecked person: **castaway** • throw from a ship: **jettison** • cargo thrown overboard from a ship to lighten it in a storm: **jetsam** • cargo washed overboard from a ship: **flotsam** • cargo thrown overboard from a ship but marked with buoys etc. for later recovery: **lagan** • recovery of a disabled ship or its cargo: **salvage** • recovery of a wrecked or abandoned ship: **salvage** • float used to raise sunken ships: **caisson**

shipyard • slope on which a ship is built: **shipway, slipway** • ship's extensive overhaul: **refit** • frame supporting a ship out of water: **cradle, stocks** • turn a ship on its side for cleaning: **careen** • make a ship watertight by sealing seams in the hull: **caulk** • shellfish attaching itself to a ship's hull: **barnacle** • framework suspended by ropes, for working on a ship's side: **cradle** • chair suspended by ropes, for working on a ship's side: **boatswain's chair** • float a ship for the first time: **launch**

shock • shock that may cause lasting psychological harm: **trauma** • electric shocks administered to treat mental illness: **electroconvulsive therapy** • shockingly sensational: **lurid** • shock into inactivity: **stun**

shoe • shoe with perforated decoration: **brogue** • shoes with very thick soles: **platforms** • shoe with a thick wooden sole: **clog** • baby's soft shoe: **bootee** • woman's light low-cut shoe: **court shoe** • light canvas shoe with a plaited fibre sole: **espadrille** • light rubber-soled canvas shoe: **plimsoll** • shoe with a turned-up sole: **moccasin** • rubber overshoe: **galosh** • shoe's underside: **sole** • upper front part of a shoe: **vamp** • shoe's reinforced front: **toecap** • back part of a shoe: **counter** • leather rim round a shoe: **welt** • small tube at the end of a shoelace: **aglet, tag** • strip of leather etc. under the laces of a shoe: **tongue** • heavy nail strengthening a sole: **hobnail** • sharp metal point in the sole of a runner's shoe: **spike** • metal plate on a tap-dancer's shoe: **tap** • ballet shoes with strengthened toes: **pointe shoes** • thin high heel on a woman's shoe: **stiletto** • extra inner sole: **insole, sock** • curved instrument easing in the heel: **shoehorn** • block to keep a shoe in shape: **shoe tree** • shoe-repair shop: **heel bar** • shoe-mender: **cobbler** • shoemaker's shaped block: **last**

shoot • shoot growing from a plant's roots etc.: **sucker** • shoot prepared for planting or grafting: **scion, slip** • climbing plant's shoot used to gain support: **tendril**

shooting • person skilled at shooting: **marksman** • member of a shooting party: **gun** • shooting at an artificial target: **target practice** • mound for a target in a shooting range: **butt** • thrown shooting target: **clay pigeon** • dog trained to fetch shot game: **retriever, gun dog** • shoot at from a hiding place: **snipe** ▸ *see also* **hunting**

shop ●shop selling alcoholic drinks for consumption elsewhere: **off-licence** ●shop selling fancy cakes and pastries: **patisserie** ●shop selling chocolates and sweets: **confectionery** ●shop selling men's clothing: **outfitter** ●shop selling fabrics: **drapery** ●shop selling fish: **fishmonger** ●shop selling flowers: **florist** ●shop selling food: **grocer** ●shop selling cooked food for consumption elsewhere: **takeaway** ●shop selling foreign foods: **delicatessen** ●shop selling fruit: **fruiterer** ●shop selling fruit and vegetables: **greengrocer** ●shop selling furs: **furrier** ●shop selling hardware: **ironmonger** ●shop selling men's hats: **hatter** ●shop selling women's hats: **milliner** ●shop selling magazines and newspapers: **newsagent** ●shop selling milk and milk products: **dairy** ●shop selling perfumes: **parfumerie** ●shop selling pizzas: **pizzeria** ●shop or counter conducting postal service business: **post office** ●shop selling dead poultry and game: **poulterer** ●shop selling sewing requisites: **haberdasher** ●shop selling smokers' requisites: **tobacconist** ●shop selling wine: **vintner** ●shop selling writing and office requisites: **stationer** ●small fashionable shop: **boutique** ●small general shop in a residential street: **corner shop** ●shop with many branches: **multiple, multiple store** ●large shop, each part selling different things: **department store** ●large specialized shop: **megastore** ●wholesale shop not offering credit or delivery: **cash and carry** ●general shop established in a remote area: **trading post** ●booth selling newspapers etc.: **kiosk** ●manufacturer's shop for direct sales: **factory shop** ●denoting a small non-residential shop: **lock-up** ●denoting a shop with a comprehensive stock: **one-stop** ●denoting a shop where customers serve themselves: **self-service** ●row of shops: **parade** ●covered walk with shops along each side: **arcade, galleria** ●enclosed pedestrianized shopping area: **mall** ●look at shop-window displays with no intention of buying: **window-shop** ●name board above a shop's window: **fascia** ●sublet space within a large shop: **concession** ●voucher offered by a shop for returned goods: **credit note** ●display bin in a shop: **dump bin** ●shop supervisor: **floor manager, shopwalker** ●person handling money in a shop: **cashier** ●stealing from a shop while pretending to be a customer: **shoplifting** ●day on which shops are shut from lunchtime: **early closing day**

shore ●*adjective*: **littoral** ●shore between high and low water marks: **foreshore** ●wood washed up on a seashore: **driftwood** ●tidal movement of objects along a shoreline: **longshore drift** ●abandon on a shore: **strand**

shorthand ●early form of shorthand: **tachygraphy** ●word represented by a single sign in shorthand: **grammalogue** ●such a sign: **outline**

shout ●shout of derision or disapproval: **catcall**

Shrewsbury ●member of Shrewsbury School: **Salopian**

shrine ●domed Buddhist shrine: **stupa** ●Tibetan Buddhist shrine: **chorten** ●tent shrine used by the ancient Israelites: **tabernacle** ●shrine dedicated to nymphs: **nymphaeum**

shrub ●shrub with branches trained along a wall: **espalier** ●shrubs etc. growing under woodland trees: **undergrowth**

shutter ●shutter with angled slats: **jalousie** ●articulated metal shutter: **roller blind**

Siberian ●Siberian nomad's tent: **yurt**

Sicilian ●secret criminal and political organization, Sicilian in origin: **Mafia**

sickle ●*adjective*: **falcate**

sickly ●sickly person: **valetudinarian**

side ●*adjective*: **lateral**

sided ●*combining forms*: **-gon, -gonal** ●(denoting a) three-sided figure: **triangle, trilateral** ●(denoting a) four-sided figure: **quadrilateral** ●(denoting a) five-sided figure: **pentagon, pentagonal** ●(denoting a) six-sided figure: **hexagon, hexagonal** ●(denoting a) seven-sided figure: **heptagon, heptagonal** ●(denoting an) eight-sided figure: **octagon, octagonal** ●(denoting a) ten-sided figure: **decagon, decagonal** ●(denoting a) twelve-sided figure: **dodecagon, dodecagonal**

siege ●naval siege: **blockade** ●raise a seige: **relieve**

sieve ●coarse sieve: **riddle**

sight ●*combining forms*: **opto-, -opia, -scopy** (*e.g.* microscopy) ●*adjectives*: **optic, optical, visual** ●distance one can see: **eyeshot, visibility** ●ability to see (only) distant objects clearly: **long sight, hypermetropia, hyperopia, presbyopia** ●inability to see distant objects clearly: **short sight, myopia, near-sightedness** ●inability to see peripheral objects clearly: **tunnel vision** ●inability to focus on the whole of an object: **astigmatism** ●perception of depth gained from binocular sight: **stereopsis** ●measurement of a person's field of vision: **perimetry** ●assessment of eyesight and correction of its defects: **optometry** ●ability to see in the dark: **night vision** ●inability to see in the dark: **night blindness, nyctal-**
opia ●area visible: **field of vision** ●seeing everything: **panoptic** ●alleged ability to see what others cannot: **clairvoyance, second sight** ●delusory sight: **hallucination** ●drug causing this: **hallucinogen** ●at first sight: **prima facie** ●sight test using rows of letters: **Snellen test** ▸*see also* **colour blindness**

signal ●bell rung as an alarm: **tocsin** ●noisy firework used as a distress or warning signal: **maroon** ●light or fire set in a high place to convey a signal: **beacon** ●bright signal light shot into the air: **flare, Verey light** ●international radio distress signal: **Mayday** ●railway signal for the next section of track: **home signal** ●railway signal giving advance warning: **distant signal** ●signal transmitting several messages simultaneously: **multiplex** ●signalling system used by bookmakers' assistants: **tick-tack** ●signalling system based on flags hand-held in various positions: **semaphore** ●signalling system based on combinations of long and short flashes, marks, or sounds: **Morse** ●lamp used for sending Morse code messages: **Aldis lamp** ●signalling system based on flashes of reflected sunlight: **heliography** ●denoting signals based on discrete values of a physical quantity: **digital** ●denoting signals based on variations in a physical quantity: **analogue** ●technical quality of incoming electronic signals: **reception**

signature ●signature given as a memento: **autograph** ●second signature: **countersignature** ●person who has written his signature: **signatory, signee** ●flourish after a signature: **paraph** ●counterfeit a signature: **forge**

Sikh ●Sikh scriptures: **Adi Granth, Granth, Granth Sahib** ●Sikh religious leader: **guru** ●male Sikh's headdress: **turban** ●Sikh place of worship: **gurdwara**

silence ●lapse into silence in the middle of a sentence etc.: **aposiopesis** ●Cistercian monk vowed to silence: **Trappist**

silk ●silk production: **sericulture** ●denoting silk treated to give a wavy lustrous finish: **moire, moiré, watered** ▶see also **fabric**

silo ●preserve in a silo: **ensile** ●fodder so preserved: **silage**

silver ●silver in solid bars: **bullion** ●silver covered by gold: **silver gilt** ●alloy of gold and silver: **electrum** ●silver-like alloy of nickel, zinc, and copper: **nickel silver, German silver** ●utensils made of silver: **plate** ●fine silver tray: **salver** ●stamp on silver attesting purity: **hallmark** ●person making silver articles: **silversmith**

similar ●combining form: **homeo-** (e.g. homoeopathy), **para-** (e.g. paramedic) ●partial similarity: **analogy**

simple ●simple and superficial: **jejune, simplistic** ●(excessively) simplified: **schematic** ●admiration or imitation of the simple or unsophisticated: **primitivism**

sin ●denoting sin leading to damnation: **deadly** ●denoting sin depriving the soul of grace: **mortal** ●denoting lesser sin: **venial** ●admission of sins: **confession** ●person doing this: **penitent** ●remorse for sins: **contrition** ●determination to give up sins: **repentance** ●forgiveness of sins: **remission** ●first lapse of humankind into sin: **the Fall** ●denoting the time before this: **prelapsarian** ●universal proneness to sin inherited from this: **original sin** ●punishment inflicted for confessed sins: **penance** ●reparation made for sin: **atonement, expiation** ●sacramental forgiveness of sins: **absolution** ●deliverance from sin and its consequences: **salvation** ●divine cancellation of sin: **justifica-**tion ●place for expiation of sins after death: **purgatory** ●eternal punishment of the unrepentant: **perdition**

sing ●entertainment of singing to a recorded accompaniment: **karaoke** ●wordless singing exercise: **vocalise** ●smooth and rounded singing style: **bel canto** ●style of male singing with frequent use of falsetto: **yodelling** ●sing softly: **croon** ●sing on one note: **intone**

singer ●singer having a higher female voice: **soprano** ●singer having a lower female voice: **contralto** ●singer having the highest male voice: **alto** ●singer having the next highest male voice: **tenor** ●singer having the next highest male voice: **baritone** ●singer having the lowest male voice: **bass** ●castrated male singer: **castrato** ●boy singer or his voice: **treble** ●famous female opera singer: **diva, prima donna** ●tenor undertaking heroic roles: **Heldentenor** ●medieval singer: **minstrel** ●person teaching opera singers their music: **répétiteur** ●range of notes a singer can sing: **compass, register** ●range within which the majority of notes in a song fall: **tessitura** ▶see also **voice**

single ●combining forms: **hapl-** (e.g. haplography), **mon(o)-** (e.g. monaural), **uni-** (e.g. unilateral) ●single person or thing: **singleton**

sister ●combining form: **soror(i)-** ●sister sharing only one parent: **half-sister** ●killing one's sister: **sororicide, fratricide**

sit ●act of sitting with the legs at right angles to the trunk, one before and one behind: **splits** ●involving much sitting: **sedentary**

situation ●combining form: **-ery** (e.g. slavery) ●current situation: **juncture, state of play, status quo** ●current situation of a political or commercial project: **status** ●previous situation: **status quo ante** ●confused situation: **imbroglio, mare's nest** ●difficult situation: **plight, straits** ●perplexing situation: **dilemma, predicament** ●situation offering no profit: **dead loss** ●situation permitting no progress: **deadlock, impasse, limbo, stalemate** ●denoting a situation in which whatever is gained by one side is lost by the other: **zero-sum** ●in an extremely difficult situation: **in extremis** ●uncomplaining acceptance of the current situation: **quietism** ●feeling, when in a new situation, of having experienced it before: **déjà vu**

six ●*combining forms*: hexa-, sex- ●six-sided figure: **hexagon** ●solid figure with six faces: **hexahedron** ●ensemble of six musicians, or music for them: **sextet** ●perception by a 'sixth sense': **extrasensory perception**

sixty ●denoting a sixtieth anniversary: **diamond** ●person in his sixties: **sexagenarian**

size ●relative size: **proportion** ●unusually small size: **dwarfism**

skating ●choreographed ice skating: **ice dancing** ●area of ice made or prepared for skating: **rink** ●skater's jump with a turn in the air: **lutz** ●movement making a pattern on the ice: **figure**

skeleton ●internal skeleton: **endoskeleton** ●external skeleton: **exoskeleton** ●study of the skeleton: **osteology**

ski ●single ski for both feet: **monoski** ●ski bicycle: **ski-bob** ●ski lift pulling skiers up slopes: **drag lift** ●cabin on a suspended ski lift: **gondola** ●ski slope with compacted snow: **piste, run** ●easy ski slope: **nursery slope** ●machine making artificial snow and blowing it onto a ski

slope: **snow cannon, snow gun** ●artificial ski slope: **dry slope** ●direct route down a slope: **fall line** ●cross-country skiing: **langlauf** ●denoting skiing away from official runs: **off-piste** ●skiing with ascents made by helicopter: **heli-skiing** ●sport of being dropped by parachute before skiing: **paraskiing** ●skiing while pulled by a horse or dog: **skijoring** ●ski race down a winding course: **slalom** ●denoting a ski slope or resort likely to have snow: **snowsure** ●distance between the highest and lowest points in a skiing area: **vertical** ●padded skiing trousers: **salopettes** ●denoting the social activities and entertainment following a day's skiing: **après-ski**

skid ●skid in which the wheels are separated from the ground by a film of water: **aquaplane** ●skid turning an articulated vehicle back on itself: **jackknife**

skill ●*combining form*: -ship (*e.g.* seamanship) ●intuitive skill: **aptitude, gift, talent** ●practical skill: **know-how** ●amateur dabbler in some skill: **dilettante** ●beginner in a skill: **neophyte** ●person highly skilled in a particular field: **expert, specialist, virtuoso** ●person pretending to have a skill: **charlatan** ●denoting a middle skill level: **intermediate** ●lacking skill: **inept** ●display of skill, or opportunity for it: **showpiece** ●field in which skill is shown: **speciality, sphere**

skin ●*combining forms*: **derm-, dermat(o)-** ●*adjective*: **cutaneous** ●outer skin: **epidermis** ●inner skin: **dermis** ●skin on the top and back of the head: **scalp** ●animal's skin: **pelt** ●appearance of facial skin: **complexion** ●small depression in the skin: **dimple** ●fold of loose skin at the throat: **dewlap** ●torn skin at a fingernail root: **hangnail** ●dead skin at the base of a nail: **cuticle** ●dead skin in the hair: **dandruff, scurf** ●through the skin: **percutaneous** ●under the skin: **subcutaneous** ●beneath the skin: **hypodermic, subcutaneous** ●oily substance rubbed into the skin: **ointment** ●cosmetic making the skin firm and smooth: **toner** ●substance applied to the skin to make it look healthy: **conditioner** ●substance that softens the skin: **emollient** ●skin pigment assisting suntan: **melanin** ●tumour of melanin-forming cells: **melanoma** ●lack of skin pigmentation: **albinism** ●small surface opening on the skin: **pore** ●open sore on the skin: **ulcer** ●patch of hard skin: **callus, callosity** ●small hard benign skin growth: **wart** ●skin bubble filled with serum: **blister** ●pus-filled blister: **pustule** ●pitted mark on the skin: **pock, pockmark** ●blemish on the skin: **naevus, macula, stigma** ●skin blemish present from birth: **birthmark** ●small dark blemish on the skin: **mole** ●pale streaks on the skin due to previous stretching: **stretch marks** ●dark skin patches in the aged: **lentigo, liver spot, senile maculation** ●removal of skin blemishes by electric heat: **electrolysis** ●stone used to remove hard skin: **pumice stone** ●blue-tinged skin due to poor circulation: **cyanosis** ●red swollen mark left by a blow: **weal, welt** ●reddened skin area: **rash** ●reddening of the skin from irritation: **erythema** ●inflammation from skin rubbing on skin: **intertrigo** ●yellowing of the skin: **jaundice** ●browning of the skin from exposure to sunlight: **suntan** ●skin inflammation or peeling from overexposure to sunlight: **sunburn** ●reddening of the skin from exposure to wind: **windburn** ●deep reddening of the skin from bacterial infection: **erysipelas** ●pimply state of the skin with hairs erect: **gooseflesh, goose pimples**

●thick-skinned mammal: **pachyderm** ●discoloration of the skin after bleeding: **ecchymosis** ●study and treatment of skin diseases: **dermatology** ●skin disease of adolescents, with black pustules: **acne** ●raised red patch on the skin: **naevus** ●tropical skin rash: **prickly heat** ●tropical skin disease leaving deep ulcers: **yaws** ●skin disease with large red patches and fever: **erysipelas, St Anthony's fire** ●skin rash of purple spots: **purpura** ●skin disease with red itchy scaly patches: **psoriasis** ●severe skin disease, causing deformity: **leprosy** ●swollen red and sore skin, due to irritation: **dermatitis** ●severe itching of the skin: **prurigo, pruritus** ●contagious skin disease with circular itchy patches: **ringworm** ●contagious skin disease with small red itchy spots: **scabies** ●itching blisters on the skin: **eczema** ●ulcerous skin disease: **lupus** ●skin disease of hairy and woolly animals: **mange** ●area of hard skin on a toe: **corn** ●horny growth on the skin: **keratosis** ●skin mark left by a healed wound: **scar** ●extreme dryness of the skin: **xeroderma** ●skin ointment: **balm, balsam, salve** ●cream protecting the skin from sunburn: **sunblock** ●cosmetic removing dead skin cells: **exfoliant** ●cosmetic improving facial skin: **face mask, face pack** ●paste of fuller's earth to do this: **mud pack** ●apparatus with lamps for tanning the skin: **sunbed** ●strip off the skin: **flay, flense** ●natural shedding of a skin: **ecdysis** ●make shallow incisions in the skin: **scarify** ●mark the skin with an indelible design: **tattoo** ●surgical removal of outer layers of skin: **dermabrasion** ●shedding of a skin: **slough, ecdysis** ●chemical process converting an animal skin to leather: **tanning** ●tanned animal skin: **hide** ●tough outer skin of pork, cheese, or fruit: **rind**

skittles ●flat wooden disk thrown in skittles: **cheese**

skull ●*combining forms*: **cephal-, cranio-** ●*adjective*: **cephalic, cranial** ●skull as a symbol of mortality: **death's head** ●front part of the skull: **sinciput** ●back part of the skull: **occiput** ●part of the skull containing the brain: **cranium** ●transverse suture of the skull: **coronal suture** ●skull cavity connecting with the nasal cavities: **sinus** ●space between the parts of an infant's skull: **fontanelle** ●skin across the top and back of the skull: **scalp** ●scientific study of skull sizes and shapes: **craniology** ●such study, supposedly indicating character and mental ability: **phrenology** ●bore a hole in the skull for surgical purposes: **trepan, trephine**

skullcap ●skullcap worn by certain Roman Catholic clergymen: **zucchetto** ●skullcap worn by male Orthodox Jews: **yarmulke**

sky ●sky with rows of small clouds: **mackerel sky** ●denoting a sky covered with grey cloud: **overcast** ●brightness of the night sky over built-up areas: **skyglow**

slang ●slang used by a particular group: **argot**

slat ●angled slat: **louvre**

slave ●*adjective*: **servile** ●release from slavery: **emancipate, manumit** ●emancipated slave: **freedman**

sledge ●horse-drawn sledge: **sleigh** ●light racing sledge: **luge** ●mechanically steered racing sledge: **bobsleigh** ●sloping track for tobogganing: **run**

sleep ●*combining forms*: **hypn-, narc-, somn-** ●short light sleep: **doze, nap** ●sleep taken in the hot part of the day: **siesta** ●sleep lasting through the winter: **hibernation** ●sleep lasting through the summer: **aestivation** ●sleep with dreaming and eye movements: **paradoxical sleep, rapid-eye-movement sleep** ●shallow sleep induced by surgical anaesthesia: **twilight sleep** ●denoting sleep that is easily disturbed: **light** ●denoting sleep not easily disturbed: **deep, heavy, sound** ●inability to sleep: **insomnia** ●period of keeping awake during sleeptime: **vigil** ●inclined to sleep: **drowsy, somnolent** ●tendency to fall asleep in relaxing surroundings: **narcolepsy** ●sleep longer than intended: **oversleep** ●causing sleep: **somniferous, somnolent, soporific** ●drug inducing sleep: **narcotic, sedative** ●learning while asleep: **hypnopaedia** ●(seemingly) in a deep sleep: **dormant** ●sleepwalking: **somnambulance, noctambulism** ●sleeplike state in which the subject obeys instructions: **hypnosis**

sleeping sickness ●African fly causing sleeping sickness: **tsetse**

slice ●thin slice: **sliver**

slip of the tongue ●slip of the tongue thought to reveal the speaker's true thoughts: **Freudian slip**

slogan ●repeated slogan: **mantra**

slope ●*combining form*: **clin-** ●downward slope: **declivity** ●upward slope: **acclivity** ●steep slope: **scarp** ●steep slope at the end of a plateau: **escarpment, shoulder** ●onward slope of a road etc.: **gradient** ●side slope of a road: **camber** ●slope of a stage or auditorium: **rake** ●denoting a slope that is almost vertical: **sheer** ●steepness of a slope: **gradient, pitch** ●create an even slope by earthmoving: **grade** ●skier's diagonal route across sloping ground: **traverse** ●instrument measuring a slope's steepness: **gradiometer** ●surveyor's instrument for measuring slopes: **clinometer**

slow ●*combining form*: **brady-** ●Chinese system of slow exercises:

t'ai chi ch'uan ●slowness of movement observed in sufferers from Parkinson's disease: **bradykinesia** ●slow-motion rerun of film showing a key moment of a sporting contest: **action replay**

slum ●slum occupied by minority groups: **ghetto**

small ●*combining forms*: **micro-** (*e.g.* microscope), **mini-** (*e.g.* miniskirt), **nano-** (*e.g.* nanotechnology), **-cle** (*e.g.* icicle), **-ee** (*e.g.* bootee), **-ette** (*e.g.* kitchenette), **-let** (*e.g.* booklet), **-ule** (*e.g.* globule) ●smallest possible: **marginal, minimal, minimum, minuscule** ●extremely small: **infinitesimal** ●ridiculously small: **derisory, paltry** ●small amount: **modicum, scintilla, smidgen, soupçon, vestige** ●small person: **dwarf, manikin, midget, pygmy**

smell ●*adjectives*: **olfactory** (*sense of smell*), **fetid** *or* **mephitic** *or* **rank** (*foul smell*), **osmic** (*either*) ●pleasant smell: **aroma** ●characteristic smell: **savour** ●characteristic smell of wine or perfume: **bouquet** ●sharp but pleasant smell: **tang** ●strong unpleasant smell: **fetor, reek, stench** ●unpleasant and harmful smell: **effluvium** ●unpleasant smell of a person's unwashed body: **body odour** ●emitting a smell: **odoriferous, odorous** ●omitting a sharp smell: **pungent** ●omitting an unpleasant smell: **putrid, rank** ●granules burnt to make a sweet smell: **incense** ●thin stick burnt to do this **joss stick** ●substance removing smells: **deodorant** ●loss of the sense of smell: **anosmia**

smile ●affected smile: **simper** ●contemptuous smile: **sneer** ●smug smile: **smirk** ●fixed grin: **rictus**

smoke ●smoke mixed with fog: **smog** ●cloud of smoke diffused to conceal military activity: **smokescreen** ●projectile supplying this: **smoke bomb** ●district where smokeless fuel must be used: **smokeless zone**

smoking ●person who smokes continuously: **chain-smoker** ●involuntary inhaling of others' smoke: **passive smoking, secondary smoking** ●area in which smoking is forbidden: **no-smoking zone**

smuggling ●smuggled goods or trade in them: **contraband** ●government agency examining travellers' luggage for contraband: **Customs**

snail ●edible snail: **escargot**

snake ●*adjectives*: **anguine, colubrine, serpentine** ●snake that crushes its prey: **constrictor** ●British poisonous snake: **adder, viper** ●venomous hooded snake: **cobra** ●snake's poison: **venom** ●antidote to this: **serum, antivenin** ●snake's venom-injecting tooth: **fang**

snooker ●snooker-player's stick: **cue** ●cue support: **rest** ●long stick to support the cue: **bridge, jigger** ●stroke made with an inclined cue: **massé** ●stroke in which the cue slips: **miscue** ●frame used to position balls: **triangle** ●ball struck by the cue: **cue ball** ●revolving motion imparted to the ball: **spin** ●backspin given to the ball: **screw** ●sidespin given to the ball: **side** ●ball at which the cue ball is aimed: **object ball** ●stroke in which the cue ball hits two others: **cannon** ●brush past another ball: **kiss** ●pouch into which the ball is stuck: **pocket** ●strike a ball into a pocket: **pot** ●single game at snooker: **frame** ●successful turn at play: **break** ●potting all remaining balls in one break: **clearance** ●impossibility of directly hitting any legal ball: **snooker** ●score-keeper: **marker**

snow ●swirling windborne snow: **flurry** ●severe snowstorm: **blizzard** ●dense blizzard impairing vision: **white-out** ●snow heaped up by the wind: **drift** ●snow-covered landscape:

snowscape ●mass of snow, ice, and rocks moving down a mountain: **avalanche** ●snow on the upper part of a glacier: **firn, nivé** ●altitude at which snow is found: **snowline** ●device for walking on snow: **snowshoe** ●motor vehicle for travelling over snow: **snowmobile** ●motor vehicle clearing roads of snow: **snowplough** ●machine making artificial snow and blowing it onto a ski slope: **snow cannon, snow gun**

soak ●soak thoroughly in a liquid: **impregnate, saturate, souse, steep** ●soften by soaking in a liquid: **macerate**

soap ●*adjective*: **saponaceous** ●aerated soap gel: **mousse** ●rendered fat used to make soap: **tallow**

soccer ●area marked out before the goal: **penalty area, penalty box** ●point within this from which penalty kicks are taken: **penalty spot** ●side part of the playing area: **wing** ●temporary control of the ball: **possession** ●attempt to kick the ball when an opponent has it: **tackle** ●propel the ball by successive small kicks: **dribble** ●denoting passing play where each participant kicks the ball once: **one-touch** ●passing play between two participants: **one-two** ●feigned pass or kick: **dummy** ●shot made with the head: **header** ●prevent the ball entering one's own goal: **save** ●goal scored by knocking the ball into one's team's net: **own goal** ●kick made after positioning the ball: **place kick, set kick** ●kick made before the ball has touched the ground: **volley** ●line of defenders forming a barrier to the ball: **wall** ●foul deliberately committed for strategic reasons: **professional foul** ●order a player to leave the field: **send off** ●card shown to a player being sent off: **red card** ●kick made with unbent legs: **scissor kick** ●set kick awarded after a foul: **free kick** ●set

kick awarded after the ball has been kicked over the goal line: **goal kick** ●area beyond the pitch side lines: **touch** ●return to play of a ball in touch: **throw-in** ●extra playing time after an injury: **injury time** ●tied score resolved by penalty kicks: **penalty shoot-out**

social ●socially correct: **comme il faut** ●social rules or custom: **etiquette** ●social blunder: **gaffe, faux pas** ●socially inept: **gauche** ●denoting a socially confident person: **affable, a mixer, outgoing, suave** ●social skills: **savoir-faire** ●social climber: **arriviste, parvenu** ●socially outgoing person: **extrovert** ●social prestige: **cachet** ●person who has recently gained this: **parvenu** ●gaining social status: **upwardly mobile** ●losing social status: **déclassé** ●people of good social standing: **gentry** ●cut off from one's social origins: **deracinated, déraciné**

socialist ●socialist advocating gradual change: **Fabian**

social work ●social worker's projects: **caseload** ●denoting a community-based social worker: **detached** ●person requiring or receiving the attention of a social worker: **case** ●record of such a person's situation and treatment: **case history** ●discussion of such a person and his treatment: **case conference**

society ●*combining form*: **socio-** (e.g. socioeconomic) ●female-dominated society: **matriarchy** ●male-dominated society: **patriarchy** ●denoting a society having few moral restrictions: **permissive** ●group thought to have a hidden but pervasive control of society: **the Establishment** ●concern for the problems and injustices of society: **social conscience** ●social and moral conventions of society: **mores** ●lack of these: **anomie** ●persuade or compel someone to accept the prevailing social conventions: **socialize** ●opposed to the norms of society: **antisocial** ●person failing or refusing to conform to those norms: **dropout, misfit** ●exclude from society: **ostracize** ●person ostracized by society: **outcast, outsider, pariah** ●person avoiding society: **recluse** ●eccentric minority: **lunatic fringe** ●inner insecurity resulting from a change of social role: **identity crisis** ●advice and assistance given to disadvantaged members of society: **social work** ●society based upon getting and spending: **consumer society** ●essential structure of society: **fabric** ●alleged implicit agreement to surrender certain individual freedoms in return for corporate benefits: **social contract** ●uprooted from one's social environment: **déraciné** ●study of human society: **sociology**

sociology ●*combining form*: socio- (*e.g.* sociolinguistics)

sock ●thick sock with a sole: **slipper sock** ●collective term for socks and stockings: **hosiery** ●trade term for socks and stockings: **hose** ●elastic strap holding stockings up: **garter, suspender**

sofa ●sofa with arms and back curving outwards: **chesterfield** ●sofa open at one end: **chaise longue** ●long sofa without back or arms: **divan**

soften ●soften by soaking: **macerate**

soil ●*combining form*: pedo- ●heavy soil used for brick-making: **clay** ●fertile soil of clay and sand: **loam** ●rich black soil: **chernozem** ●rich soil deposit left by flood water: **alluvium** ●soft loose soil: **mould** ●acidic woodland soil: **podzol** ●soil of acid bogs: **peat** ●prepared surface soil: **tilth** ●denoting easily workable soil: **light** ●denoting soil that is eas-

ily crumbled: **friable** ●denoting a soil deficient in lime: **sour** ●artificial bank of soil: **berm** ●large defensive bank of soil: **earthwork** ●spade-depth of soil: **spit** ●permanently frozen layer of soil: **permafrost** ●fertile upper layer of soil: **topsoil** ●organic content of soil: **humus** ●soil enricher of decaying leaves etc.: **mulch** ●fine sand or clay deposited by running water: **silt** ●soil additive improving cropping: **fertilizer** ●soil overlying some underground feature: **overburden** ●drain through soil: **leach** ●science of soil management: **agronomy** ●study of soils: **pedology, soil science** ●growing plants without soil: **hydroponics**

solar system ●mechanical model of the solar system: **orrery**

solder ●fix by soldering: **braze**

soldier ●experienced soldier: **veteran** ●soldier trained to carry out raids: **commando** ●soldier trained to serve at sea: **marine** ●soldier with parachuting skills: **paratrooper** ●soldier enlisting with any force that will pay him: **mercenary, soldier of fortune** ●private in an artillery regiment: **gunner** ●private in a cavalry regiment: **trooper** ●private in an engineer regiment: **sapper** ●member of the reserve forces: **reservist** ●member of an unofficial military unit: **irregular** ●soldier's canvas bag: **kitbag** ●soldier's water bottle: **canteen** ●soldier's cooking and eating utensils: **mess kit** ▸*see also* **troops**

sole of the foot ●*adjectives*: **plantar, volar** ●walking on the soles: **plantigrade**

solicitor ●solicitor authorized to administer oaths: **commissioner for oaths** ●forbid a solicitor to practise: **strike off the roll**

solitude ●person living in solitude: **hermit**

solution ●denoting a solution that cannot be strengthened further: **saturated** ●weaken a solution by adding further liquid: **dilute**

solve ●able to be solved: **soluble**

solvent ●universal solvent sought by alchemists: **alkahest** ●strong solvent attacking most substances: **aqua regia**

somewhat ●*combining form*: **sub-** (*e.g.* subarctic)

son ●*adjective*: **filial**

song ●song in traditional popular style: **folk song** ●song of established popularity: **standard** ●simple song: **air** ●accompanied song in an opera etc.: **aria** ●song to send a child to sleep: **lullaby** ●gondolier's song: **barcarole** ●sailors' work song: **shanty** ●song of praise or triumph: **paean** ●Renaissance secular part-song: **madrigal** ●German art-song: **lied** (*pl.* lieder) ●improvised West Indian song on a topical theme: **calypso** ●words for a song: **lyrics**

soot ●*adjective*: **fuliginous**

sore ●open sore on an internal or external body surface: **ulcer** ●sore on bedridden person: **bedsore, decubitus ulcer**

sorrow ●*adjective*: **dolorous**

sort ●*combining form*: **-er** (*e.g.* newcomer) ●sort by quality: **grade, triage**

soul ●transmigration of the soul: **metempsychosis**

sound ●*combining forms*: **audi-, phon(o)-, sono-, -phony** ●*adjectives*: **acoustic, sonic** ●sound of frequencies that humans cannot hear: **ultrasound, infrasound** ●pleasant sound: **euphony** ●unpleasant sound: **cacophony** ●sweet-sounding: **mellifluent, mellifluous, mellow, melodious** ●brief high sound: **peep** ●continuous low sound: **drone** ●sound containing many frequencies of equal intensity: **white noise** ●artifically generated sound for use in a performance: **sound effect** ●clarity of sound: **definition, focus** ●height of sound: **pitch** ●strength of sound: **volume** ●quality of sound: **timbre** ●denoting sound below the required pitch: **flat** ●denoting sound above the required pitch: **sharp** ●denoting sound mechanically captured, generated, or reproduced: **audio** ●denoting electronically produced sound: **radiophonic** ●sound pattern derived from durations, not pitches: **rhythm** ●sound pattern derived from pitched durations: **tune** ●device converting sound waves into electrical signals: **microphone** ●room equipped for sound recording: **studio** ●denoting sound recorded and reproduced via a single channel: **monophonic, monaural** ●denoting sound recorded and reproduced via several channels: **stereophonic** ●denoting sound recorded and reproduced via two separate channels: **binaural** ●denoting sound recorded and reproduced via four separate channels: **quadraphonic** ●signal distinction in a stereophonic system: **separation** ●combination of several sound channels: **mixing** ●stereophonic reproduction system with speakers all round the listener: **surround sound** ●device converting electrical signals into sound waves: **speaker** ●crackling or hissing noises in a speaker: **static** ●denoting mechanically captured or reproduced sound and vision: **audio-visual** ●strip at the edge of a film on which the sound is recorded: **soundtrack** ●primitive sound recorder and player: **phonograph** ●quality sound reproduction: **high fidelity** ●slow pitch-distortion of recorded sound: **wow** ●fast pitch-distortion of recorded sound: **flutter** ●device analysing sound into its frequency components: **sound spectro-**

graph ●device balancing various sound frequencies: **graphic equalizer** ●device suppressing unwanted sound waves: **filter** ●range of sound intensities a particular system can reproduce: **dynamic range** ●free-standing components of a sound-reproduction system: **separates** ●turntable and pickup mechanism: **deck** ●vertical arrangement of sound-reproduction units: **stack** ●transfer recorded sound from one medium to another: **dub** ●muffle a sound source: **damp** ●make impervious to sound: **insulate** ●device blanking out unwanted sound: **insulator, sound conditioner** ●board placed to reflect sound: **sounding board** ●unit of sound strength: **decibel** ●vocal sound made with obstructed breath: **consonant** ●vocal sound made with unobstructed breath: **vowel** ●sound made by the close conjunction of two vowels: **diphthong** ●name for the indefinite sound often made by English vowels: **schwa** ●make an 'h' sound: **aspirate** ●study of vocal sounds: **phonetics** ●visual record of sound: **sonogram** ●buoy equipped to detect underwater sound: **sonobuoy** ●device detecting underwater objects by reflected sound pulses: **sonar** ●luminescence excited by the passage of sound: **sonoluminescence** ●making a rich or resonant sound: **sonorous** ●study of sound: **acoustics**

soup ●clear soup: **consommé** ●cold consommé: **madrilene** ●thick soup: **potage** ●meat or vegetable soup thickened with cereals: **broth** ●rich shellfish soup: **bisque** ●spicy meat soup: **mulligatawny** ●chilled soup of potatoes, leeks, and cream: **vichysoisse** ●liquid used as a base for soups: **stock** ●concentrated stock: **fumet** ●large covered dish for serving soup: **tureen**

source ●drawing upon many sources: **eclectic**

south ●*adjectives*: **austral, meridional**

South Africa ●South African barbecue: **braai** ●open bush in South Africa: **bundu, bushveld** ●South African native club: **kierie, knobkerrie** ●South African term for a ford: **drift** ●open grassland in South Africa: **veld** ●small hill on the veld: **kopje** ●South African term for the rural hinterland: **backveld** ●South African identity document: **Book of Life** ●strips of dried and salted meat as eaten in South Africa: **biltong** ●South African miners' dance: **gumboot dance** ●South African term for a wooded ravine: **kloof** ●South African native spear: **assegai** ●backwoods town in South Africa: **dorp** ●South African traditional healer: **inyanga, sangoma** ●South African whip: **sjambok** ●veranda in South Africa: **stoep** ●traditional South African village: **kraal** ●South African wagon encampment: **laager** ●South African of Dutch origin: **Afrikaner, Boer** ●Protestant Afrikaner secret society: **Broederbond** ●Afrikaner term for an English-speaker: **rooinek** ●reactionary white South African: **verkrampte** ●progressive white South African: **verligte** ●former South African policy of racial segregation: **apartheid, colour bar** ▶*see also* **apartheid**

South American ●South American cloak having a hole for the head: **poncho** ●South American cowboy: **gaucho** ●South American dance music with elements of jazz and rock: **salsa** ●fast South American dance: **paso doble** ●lively South American dance: **tango** ●South American dissident who disappears: **desaparacido** ●South American magistrate or mayor: **alcalde** ●South American grassy plain: **pampas** ●South American tree yielding quinine:

chinchona ●Spanish conqueror of South America: **conquistador**

sovereign ●*adjective*: **regal** ●polite form of address to a sovereign: **Your Majesty** ●sovereign's state insignia: **regalia** ●sovereign's ornamental staff: **sceptre** ●sovereign's ceremonial chair: **throne** ●sovereign's period of rule: **reign** ●sovereign's representative in a Commonwealth country: **Governor, Governor General** ●sovereign's representative in a colony: **viceroy** (*fem.* vicereine) ●sovereign's representative in a county: **Lord Lieutenant** ●theory that sovereignty is granted by God, not by the monarch's subjects: **divine right of kings** ●person claiming a right to the throne: **pretender** ●person having control during a sovereign's minority, absence, or illness: **regent, protector** ●persons attending a sovereign: **court, suite** ●sword carried before the sovereign on state occasions: **sword of state** ●denoting accommodation in the sovereign's gift: **grace and favour** ●killing a sovereign: **regicide**

Soviet ●Soviet polite form of address: **tovarish** ●Soviet youth organization: **Komsomol, Young Pioneers** ●Soviet collective farm: **kolkhoz** ●Soviet worker achieving exceptional output: **Stakhanovite** ●Soviet party official: **commissar** ●Soviet secret police: **KGB** ●their Moscow headquarters: **Lubyanka** ●Soviet forced labour camp: **gulag** ●Soviet Jew not allowed to go to Israel: **refusenik** ●founder-member of the Soviet communist party: **Bolshevik** ●Social Democrat opposed to the Bolsheviks: **Menshevik** ●Leninist system of central Party control: **democratic centralism** ●influential Party members holding key posts: **nomenklatura** ●head of a pre-1946 government department: **commissar** ●Soviet administrative division: **oblast** ●local or national elected council: **soviet** ●artistic norms promulgated under Stalinism: **socialist realism** ●Soviet economic imperialism: **Finlandization** ●economic and political reform under Gorbachov: **perestroika** ●open government policy of Gorbachov: **glasnost** ●diplomatic and propaganda offensive between the West and the Soviet bloc: **cold war** ●study of Soviet politics: **Kremlinology** ●Soviet artificial satellite: **sputnik** ▸*see also* **communism**

soya ●soya bean curd: **tofu**

spa ●room at a spa where the waters are dispensed: **pump room**

space ●*adjective*: **celestial** ●space occupied by something: **volume** ●space entirely devoid of matter: **vacuum** ●surrounding area a person likes to keep empty: **personal space** ●space having more than three dimensions: **hyperspace**, **space–time** ●space having more than four dimensions: **superspace** ●expedition into space: **mission** ●international competition to explore space: **space race** ●small particles distributed throughout space: **cosmic dust** ●dust cloud in outer space: **nebula** ●supposed non-luminous material in space: **dark matter** ●atomic nucleus travelling through space at high speed: **cosmic ray** ●region in space having an intense gravitational field: **black hole** ●imagined boundary around this: **event horizon** ●hypothetical expanding celestial object: **white hole** ●creature from outer space: **alien, extraterrestrial, little green man** ●study of life forms in space: **exobiology** ●chemistry of space: **astrochemistry**

spacecraft ●small spacecraft: **space capsule** ●small spacecraft for moon landings: **lunar module** ●unmanned exploratory spacecraft: **probe** ●spacecraft capable of several journeys: **shuttle** ●aliens' spacecraft: **fly-**

ing saucer ●spacecraft manufacture and technology: **aerospace** ●official unveiling of a new spacecraft: **roll-out** ●support for an unlaunched spacecraft: **gantry** ●area on which a rocket or spacecraft stands for launching: **launch pad** ●base from which spacecraft are launched: **spaceport** ●send a spacecraft on its course: **launch** ●successful launch: **blast-off, lift-off** ●spacecraft launch for a specified destination: **shot** ●first-stage rocket of a spacecraft: **booster** ●speed at which a spacecraft overcomes gravity: **escape velocity** ●rocket putting a spacecraft into orbit: **launcher, launch vehicle** ●spacecraft's door: **hatch** ●spacecraft's window: **viewport** ●spacecraft's flat array of solar cells: **paddle** ●spacecraft's telecommunications link with earth: **downlink** ●self-contained unit in a spacecraft: **module, pod** ●weak gravity in a spacecraft: **microgravity** ●spacecraft's repeated elliptical course: **orbit** ●put a spacecraft into orbit or trajectory: **inject, insert** ●alteration of a spacecraft's course made by means of the gravitational pull of a celestial body: **swingby** ●spacecraft's secondary engine for orbit adjustments: **thruster** ●join in space with another spacecraft: **dock** ●activities performed in space outside the spacecraft: **extravehicular activities, space walk** ●detachable module carrying fuel and supplies: **service module** ●manned spacecraft's control compartment: **command module** ●person travelling in a spacecraft: **astronaut** ●astronaut's pressurized suit: **G-suit** ●Russian astronaut: **cosmonaut** ●scans of a planet's surface conducted from space: **remote sensing** ●spacecraft's return to the earth's atmosphere: **re-entry** ●spacecraft's self-destructive landing: **hard landing** ●spacecraft's landing causing little

damage: **soft landing** ●spacecraft's landing contact with earth: **touchdown** ●spacecraft's landing on water: **splashdown** ▶*see also* **rocket**

spade ●top of a spade blade where the foot is placed: **tramp**

Spanish ●*combining form*: **Hispano-** ●Spanish polite form of address to a married woman: **señora** ●Spanish polite form of address to a man: **señor** ●Spanish polite form of address to a young woman: **señorita** ●Spanish military or political leader: **caudillo** ●Spanish monarch's son: **infante** ●Spanish monarch's daughter: **infanta** ●Spanish noble of the highest rank: **grandee** ●Spanish gentleman: **hidalgo** ●Spanish magistrate or mayor: **alcalde** ●Spanish-American day labourer: **peon** ●Spanish conqueror of Mexico or Peru: **conquistador** ●Spanish sailing ship: **galleon** ●palace in Moorish Spain: **alcazar** ●Spanish landed estate: **hacienda** ●Spanish irrigation device of buckets on a wheel: **noria** ●lively Spanish dance: **bolero** ●Spanish solo dance: **cachucha** ●Spanish courtship dance: **fandango** ●Spanish dance with castanets: **flamenco** ●Spanish light opera: **zarzuela** ●Spanish game played with basketlike rackets: **pelota** ●Spanish woman's lacy headscarf: **mantilla** ●Spanish savoury snack: **tapas** ●chilled Spanish vegetable soup: **gazpacho** ●Spanish dish of seafood in a rich sauce: **zarzuela** ●Spanish rice dish with chicken and seafood: **paella** ●Spanish spicy pork sausage: **chorizo** ●Spanish spicy stew: **olio, olla podrida** ●Spanish drink of red wine with lemonade, fruit, and spices: **sangria** ●Spanish red wine: **tinto** ●Spanish blending system for sherry and madeira: **solera** ●legendary Spanish seducer: **Don Juan** ●Spanish festival: **fiesta** ●Spanish bullfighter on foot:

torero ●Spanish mounted bull-fighter: **toreador** ●Spanish bull-fighter killing the bull: **matador** ●matador's mounted assistant: **pica-dor** ●public burning of a heretic by the Spanish Inquisition: **auto da fé** (*pl.* autos da fé) ●student of Spanish language and culture: **Hispanist**

spanner ●cylindrical spanner fitting over the nut: **box spanner** ●adjustable spanner: **wrench, monkey wrench**

spare part ●dismantle a machine to supply parts for another: **cannibalize**

Sparta ●senior magistrate in ancient Sparta: **ephor** ●serf in ancient Sparta: **helot**

speak ●speak at a meeting: **contribute** ●speak in a slow, dragging way: **drawl** ●speak fast and unintelligibly: **gibber** ●speak clearly: **enunciate** ●speak at length: **expatiate** ●that cannot be spoken: **ineffable** ●text spoken for copying down: **dictation**

speaker ●skilled public speaker: **orator** ●persuasive and unscrupulous orator: **demagogue, rabble-rouser** ●speaker's makeshift platform: **soapbox** ●person speaking on behalf of others: **deputy, representative, spokesperson** ●person who speaks too much: **chatterbox, flibbertigibbet**

speaking ●*combining form*: **-phone** (*e.g.* francophone) ●art of public speaking: **oratory, rhetoric** ●speaking readily or persuasively: **articulate, fluent** ●speaking little: **taciturn, terse** ●style of enunciation: **diction**

spear ●light spear: **javelin** ●long spear: **lance** ●three-pronged spear: **trident** ●spear shot at whales: **harpoon** ●spear handle: **haft**

specific gravity ●apparatus measuring a liquid's specific gravity: **hydrometer**

spectacles ●spectacles supported by a nose clip: **pince-nez** ●close-fitting spectacles with side shields: **goggles** ●central link between spectacle lenses: **bridge** ●single eyeglass: **monocle** ●pair of eyeglasses on a long handle: **lorgnette** ●spectacles with combined lenses to give near and far vision: **bifocals** ●spectacles whose lenses allow an infinite number of focusing distances: **varifocals** ●denoting spectacles without bifocal lenses: **single-vision** ●lenses placed directly on the eye: **contact lenses**

speech ●*combining forms*: **logo-, phono-, -logue** (*e.g.* dialogue), **-logy, -phasia, -phone** ●*adjectives*: **lingual, oral** ●ability to express oneself in correct speech: **oracy** ●temporary ability to speak in a language normally unknown to the speaker: **glossolalia** ●understand speech from lip movements: **lip-read** ●visual record of speech: **voiceprint** ●speech sound made with full or partial stoppage of the breath: **consonant** ●speech sound made without stoppage of the breath: **vowel** ●smallest unit of speech sound: **phoneme** ●study and classification of speech sounds: **phonetics** ●study of phonemes: **phonemics** ●inability to express speech due to loss of voice: **aphonia** ●inability to express or understand speech due to brain damage: **aphasia** ●endless speech: **logorrhoea** ●psychologically caused meaningless speech: **dyslalia, paraphasia** ●practice of clear speech: **elocution** ●speech with involuntary sound-repetitions: **stammering, stuttering** ●aggressively abusive speech: **vilification, vituperation** ●lengthy and aggressive speech: **harangue, tirade** ●bitter verbal attack: **diatribe, polemic** ●boastful speech: **fanfaronade, rodomontade** ●affectedly elaborate speech: **euphuism** ●carefully evasive speech: **equivocation** ●exaggerated speech: **hyperbole** ●fast slick speech: **patter, spiel** ●speech that sounds impressive but in fact says little: **rhetoric** ●aggressive interruption of a speech: **heckling** ●lengthy speech saying little: **verbalization, verbiage, verbosity** ●speech skilfully crafted to manipulate or mislead: **rhetoric** ●meaningless speech: **hocus-pocus** ●persistent hortatory speech: **nagging** ●persuasive speech: **eloquence** ●pompous speech: **grandiloquence, orotundity** ●speech full of praise: **encomium, eulogy, panegyric** ●rambling or indirect speech: **periphrasis** ●rambling but impassioned speech: **rant** ●sanctimonious speech: **cant** ●tediously wordy speech: **prolixity** ●wordy and evasive speech: **circumlocution** ●denoting fluent but insincere speech: **glib** ●denoting fluent and incessant speech: **voluble** ●denoting awkward and hesitant speech: **stilted** ●denoting speech uttered for social rather than informative purposes: **phatic** ●excessive correctness in speech, leading to error: **hypercorrection** ●loud and forceful tone of speech: **stridency, vociferation** ●form of speech particular to one person: **idiolect** ●form of speech using many informal terms: **slang** ●formal speech: **oration** ●speech made in a church service: **sermon** ●actor's speech when alone on stage: **soliloquy** ●person speaking a certain language: **-phone** (*e.g.* anglophone) ●beginning of a speech: **exordium** ●final part of a speech: **peroration** ●deliberately prolonged speech: **filibuster** ●speech's basic message: **gist** ●style of speaking: **delivery, locution** ●choice of words in speaking: **parlance** ●non-lexical components of speech: **paralanguage** ●art of effective speaking or writing: **rhetoric** ●transmitted by speech: **oral** ●verbal emphasis: **stress** ●not using speech: **non-verbal** ●synthe-sizer imposing speech patterns onto musical sounds: **vocoder**

speed ●*combining form*: **tach-** ●speed at which an object can defy gravity: **escape velocity** ●object's maximum possible air speed: **terminal velocity** ●ratio between a body's speed and the speed of sound in the surrounding medium: **Mach, Mach number** ●denoting a speed less than that of sound: **subsonic** ●denoting a speed equal to that of sound: **sonic** ●denoting a speed greater than that of sound: **supersonic** ●denoting speeds close to that of sound: **transonic** ●denoting a speed five times that of sound: **hypersonic** ●strong air resistance to vehicles approaching the speed of sound: **sonic barrier, sound barrier** ●noise heard when a vehicle exceeds the speed of sound: **sonic boom** ●device indicating a passing vehicle's speed: **radar gun** ●onboard instrument measuring a vehicle's speed: **speedometer** ●onboard instrument measuring an engine's speed: **rev counter, tachometer** ●instrument recording engine speed: **tachograph** ●automatic regulator of an engine's speed: **governor** ●comfortable and economical speed for long distance travel: **cruising speed** ●denoting an area having a speed limit: **restricted** ●denoting an area having no speed limit: **derestricted** ●road hump to limit speed: **sleeping policeman, speed bump, speed hump** ●break the speed limit: **speed** ●roadside camera photographing speeding vehicles: **speed camera** ●clandestine record of speeding vehicles: **speed trap** ●device recording the distance travelled and speeds achieved by a motor vehicle: **tachograph**

spelling ●system of spelling, or its study: **orthography** ●of a letter included in a spelling but not pronounced: **silent**

spend ●spend less: **economize, retrench**

sperm ●organ producing sperm: **testis** (*pl.* testes) ●this organ and its system of ducts: **testicle** ●duct conveying sperm from the testicle to the urethra: **vas deferens** ●varicose veins on the spermatic cord: **varicocele** ●count of sperm in a measure of semen: **sperm count** ●deficiency of sperm cells in semen: **oligospermia** ●substance killing sperm: **spermicide**

sphere ●quarter of a sphere: **quadrant**

spice ●spice made from nutmeg: **mace** ●powdered orange-red spice: **paprika** ●perforated container for aromatic spices: **pomander**

spider ●large hairy spider: **tarantula** ●venomous American spider: **black widow** ●spider's organ producing the thread: **spinneret**

spin ●*adjective*: **rotary** ●spinning sensation: **giddiness, vertigo** ●spinning device separating substances of different densities: **centrifuge** ●pin used in spinning: **spindle**

spinach ●spinach in Greek cuisine: **spanako** ●spinach in Indian cuisine: **saag**

spindle ●spindle for a swinging object: **gudgeon**

spine ●outward curvature of the spine: **kyphosis** ●inward curvature of the spine: **lordosis** ●lateral curvature of the spine: **scoliosis** ●cartilage displaced in the spine: **slipped disc** ●bundle of nerve fibres enclosed in the spine: **spinal cord** ●inflammation of the spinal cord: **myelitis** ●disease of the spinal cord: **myelopathy** ●congenital exposure of part of the spinal cord: **spina bifida** ●inflammation of the spinal joints: **spondylitis** ●degeneration of the spinal disks: **spondylosis** ●therapeutic manipulation of the spinal column: **chiropractic** ●denoting the brain and spine: **cerebrospinal** ●diagnostic removal of fluid from the lower spine: **lumbar puncture**

spiral ●*combining form*: **helic-** (*e.g.* helicopter, *literally 'spiral-winged'*)

spiral staircase ●step in a spiral staircase: **winder** ●centre post of a spiral staircase: **newel**

spirit ●*combining form*: **pneumat-** ●air spirit: **sylph** ●evil spirit: **cacodemon** ●imagined evil spirit invoked to frighten children: **bogeyman** ●female nature spirit: **nymph** ●mischievous spirit: **gremlin, hobgoblin, imp** ●spirit of a place: **genius** (*pl.* genii), **numen** (*pl.* numina) ●spirit said to take female form to seduce a sleeping man: **succubus** ●spirit said to take male form to seduce a sleeping woman: **incubus** ●spirit said to rob graves: **ghoul** ●spirit in Arab folklore: **genie** (*pl.* genii) ●Jewish malevolent spirit: **dybbuk** ●person posssessed by an evil spirit: **demoniac** ●drive out evil spirits: **exorcize** ●theological study of the spirit world: **pneumatology** ●spirit of the age: **zeitgeist** ●spirit of a culture: **ethos** ●denoting spiritual guidance: **pastoral**

spirits ●small measure of spirits: **dram, tot** ●place where spirits are made: **distillery** ●distilling apparatus: **still** ●spirit distilled from grape refuse: **grappa, marc** ●Chinese sorghum spirit: **mao-tai** ●German potato gin: **schnapps** ●Greek aniseed-flavoured spirit: **ouzo** ●Irish spirit distilled from malted grain: **whiskey** ●Mexican agave spirit: **tequila** ●Middle-Eastern grain spirit: **raki** ●Russian spirit made from rye, wheat, or potatoes: **vodka** ●Scottish spirit distilled from malted grain: **whisky** ●Yugoslavian plum brandy: **slivovitz** ●denoting undiluted spirits: **neat** ●standard strength of spirits: **proof** ●small measure of spirits: **nip** ●sweetened drink of spirits: **sling** ●drink of spirits with hot water and sugar: **toddy**

spiritualism ●person claiming contact with the dead: **medium** ●person receptive to psychic phenomena: **percipient** ●meeting of persons wishing to contact the dead: **seance** ●cause a spirit to appear: **raise** ●substance said to exude from a medium during a trance: **ectoplasm** ●movement of a table round which a seance is being conducted: **table-turning** ●writing device for spirit messages: **Ouija board™, planchette** ●form of spiritualism practised by certain north American and north Asian peoples: **shamanism** ●denoting events beyond the scope of science: **paranormal, psychic** ●alleged ability to move objects by mental powers: **psychokinesis** ●alleged ability to move distant objects: **telekinesis** ●denoting the use of psychic powers: **psionic**

spittle ●pot for spitting into: **spittoon**

spleen ●*combining form*: **splen-** ●*adjective*: **splenic** ●abnormal enlargement of the spleen: **splenomegaly** ●inflammation of the spleen: **splenitis** ●surgical removal of the spleen: **splenectomy**

split ●*combining form*: **schiz(o)-** ●easily split: **fissile, fissionable** ●mental illness popularly called 'split personality': **schizophrenia**

spoon ●large spoon with a vertical handle: **ladle** ●large spoon with an openwork bowl: **slotted spoon**

sport ●outdoor sport: **field sport** ●sport watched by many: **spectator sport** ●sport that involves touching: **contact sport** ●unarmed combat sport: **judo, karate** ●sport of floating

down a mountain stream: **canyoning** ●competitive sport of riding a horse over obstacles in an arena: **showjumping** ●sport that involves hunting, wounding, or killing of animals: **blood sport** ●sport of jumping at a Velcro wall in a Velcro suit: **barfly jumping** ●sport of making parachute descents from a fixed point: **base jumping** ●sport of performing acrobatic manoevres while in free fall: **skydiving** ●sport of being dropped by parachute before skiing or water-skiing: **paraskiing** ●parachute sport of being pulled by a fast boat: **parasailing, parascending** ●sport of sailing on a board: **windsurfing** ●sport of being pulled by a fast boat while standing on a wide board: **wakeboarding** ●sport of shooting birds in flight: **wing shooting** ●sport of surfing through the air: **skysurfing** ●sport of sword fighting: **fencing** ●Scottish sport of throwing a large pole: **tossing the caber** ●denoting a sport with few restrictions on technique employed: **free, freestyle** ●sports trainer: **coach** ●person in charge of the business affairs of a sports team: **manager** ●person enforcing the rules in a sports match: **referee, umpire** ●player's refusal to accept his ruling: **dissent** ●illegal act in a sport: **foul** ●illegal hampering of another player: **obstruction** ●participants in a sport: **field** ●player deriving no income from sport: **amateur** ●player paid to participate in sporting events: **professional** ●player falsely claiming amateur status: **shamateur** ●group of clubs competing over a season: **league** ●disadvantage imposed upon a strong competitor: **handicap** ●junior sports team: **colts** ●sports team of second-choice players: **reserves** ●leave a player out of a team: **rest** ●player replacing another in the course of a team game: **substitute** ●professional player's move to another club: **transfer** ●sports team's distinctive uniform: **colours, strip** ●competitive grouping of teams of similar ability: **division** ●person responsible for assembling a sports team: **selector** ●group of players from whom a team will be chosen: **squad** ●person training players: **coach** ●withdraw from a sports fixture before its start: **scratch** ●sporting competition in which the winners proceed to play against other winners: **knock-out, tournament** ●round in this: **tie** ●sporting fixture not part of a larger competition: **friendly** ●sporting fixture for individual players: **singles** ●sporting fixture for pairs of players: **doubles** ●sporting fixture organized in honour of a particular player: **testimonial** ●group of major sporting fixtures: **grand slam** ●annual sequence of major events in a particular sport: **tour** ●sporting tournament in which each competitor plays in turn against every other: **round robin** ●moment at which a match must end: **time, full time** ●result of a sporting fixture giving no clear winner: **tie, draw** ●means of deciding this: **tiebreak** ●overall winner of a sports meeting: **victor ludorum** (*fem.* victrix ludorum) ●paying audience at a sporting event: **gate** ●principal stand at a sporting event: **grandstand** ●tiered standing area for spectators: **terraces** ●midpoint interval at a sporting event: **half-time** ●entry to a sporting contest without participating in preliminary rounds: **wild card** ●stage in a sporting contest: **round** ●round immediately preceding the last: **semifinal** ●sports ground with spectator accommodation: **stadium** ●sports ground building providing changing and social facilities: **pavilion** ●low shelter at the side of a sports pitch: **dugout** ●equipment required for a sport: **tackle** ●person maintaining

sports pitches: **groundsman** ●building with sports facilities: **leisure centre, leisure complex, sports hall** ●person financing a sporting event: **promoter** ●injection of oxygenated blood to enhance athletic performance: **blood doping**

sprain ●slight sprain: **rick**

spray ●windblown sea spray: **spindrift** ●container with a mechanism for emitting its contents as a fine pressurized spray: **aerosol, atomizer**

spread ●spread gradually through: **suffuse**

spring[1] ●*adjective*: **vernal** ●traditional spring festival: **May Day**

spring[2] ●hot spring: **geyser, thermal spring** ●medicinal mineral spring: **spa**

spring[3] ●vehicle spring of curved metal strips: **leaf spring** ●upholstery spring: **box spring**

spy ●spy obtaining an enemy position of trust: **mole, plant** ●spy remaining inactive while establishing himself: **sleeper** ●gain membership of a group to spy on it: **infiltrate, penetrate** ●spy working simultaneously for two intelligence services: **double agent** ●spy's assumed identity: **cover** ●spying activity: **espionage, intelligence** ●government department organizing spying: **secret service** ●British intelligence service: **Secret Intelligence Service, MI5, MI6** ●Israeli intelligence service: **Mossad** ●US intelligence service: **Central Intelligence Agency** ●spying to gain company secrets: **industrial espionage** ●secret surveillance of telephone calls: **tapping** ●ground observation by satellite: **remote sensing** ●information gathered by spies: **intelligence** ●efforts to frustrate spying: **counter-espionage, counter-intelligence** ●check for electronic listening devices: **sweep**

squash ●squash bat: **racket** ●racket face on which the loops project: **rough** ●racket on which the loops do not project: **smooth** ●junction between floor and side walls of the court: **nick** ●strike the ball to commence play: **serve**

squid ●squid served as food: **calamari** ●black liquid ejected by a squid: **ink**

squirrel ●squirrel's nest: **drey**

stabilizer ●gyroscopic stabilizer: **gyrostabilizer**

stable ●boarding stable: **livery stable** ●group of stables, often now converted into flats: **mews** ●area in a stable for untethered animals: **loose box** ●compartment in a stable: **stall** ●stable fodder rack: **manger** ●stable room for storage of harness etc.: **tack room**

staff ●beadle's staff: **mace** ●bishop's staff: **crosier** ●climber's staff: **alpenstock** ●monarch's staff: **sceptre** ●shepherd's staff: **crook** ●verger's staff: **verge** ●Dionysus' staff: **thyrsus** ●Hermes' staff: **caduceus**

stag ●adult stag's branching horns: **antlers** ●season in which stags fight each other: **rut**

stain ●brownish stain on the paper of a book or engraving: **foxing** ●resistant to staining: **stainless**

stained glass ●lead strip holding pieces of stained glass: **came**

staircase ●moving staircase: **escalator** ●set of stairs: **flight** ●part of a staircase for the feet: **tread** ●tread's rounded edge: **nosing** ●vertical section between treads: **riser** ●height of this: **rise** ●timber in which the sides of the treads are set: **string board, stringer** ●uprights and handrail at the side of a staircase: **banister** ●endpost for this: **newel post** ●level area at the top of stairs:

landing ●shaft for a staircase: **stairwell** ▸*see also* **spiral staircase**

stake ●poker-player's stake made before receiving his cards: **ante**

stamp ●stamps given with purchases for eventual exchange for gifts: **trading stamps** ▸*see also* **postage stamp**

standard ●*adjective*: **normative** ●standard of categorization: **criterion** ●standard of comparison: **benchmark, control, yardstick** ●ethical standards: **morality, morals, mores, principles** ●expected standard: **norm** ●below expected standards: **subnormal, unprofessional** ●following generally accepted standards: **orthodox** ●ordinary decent people: **moral majority** ●person with strict moral standards: **Mrs Grundy**

star ●*combining forms*: **astr-, sider(o)-** ●*adjectives*: **astral, sidereal, stellar** ●system of stars: **galaxy** ●cluster of stars: **asterism** ●band of distant stars: **Milky Way** ●named group of fixed stars: **constellation** ●brightest star in a constellation: **alpha** ●star orbited by another: **primary** ●guiding star: **lodestar** ●star whose brightness changes: **variable star** ●star suddenly becoming much brighter: **nova** ●star suddenly becoming very much brighter and exploding: **supernova** ●large bright star: **giant** ●even bigger star: **supergiant** ●large cool star: **red giant** ●small cool star: **red dwarf** ●even smaller cool star: **brown dwarf** ●dwarf with occasional bursts of radiation: **flare star** ●small very dense star: **white dwarf** ●old collapsed star: **collapsar** ●collapsed supernova: **neutron star** ●nebula round an old star: **planetary nebula** ●star emitting rapid radio and electromagnetic pulses: **pulsar** ●moving tailed star periodically visible: **comet** ●comet's tail: **coma** ●potential metor: **meteoroid** ●small incandescent object travelling the earth's atmosphere: **meteor, shooting star** ●this fallen to earth: **meteorite** ●group of radiant meteors reappearing annually: **meteor shower** ●large bright meteor: **fireball** ●starlike object emitting no light: **dark star** ●large low-density planet: **gas giant** ●non-luminous nebula: **dark nebula, absorption nebula** ●very large and distant celestial object emitting large amounts of energy: **quasar** ●alignment of two stars on the same longitude: **conjunction** ●direction of a celestial body from an observer: **azimuth** ●measure of a star's brightness: **magnitude** ●celestial body orbiting a star: **planet** ●sudden explosion on a star: **flare** ●faint glow seen around a star: **aurora, corona** ●cone of shadow projecting from the side of a celestial body away from the sun: **umbra** ●apparent twinkling of the stars: **scintillation** ●obscuring of a celestial body by another passing in front of it: **eclipse, occultation** ●scientific study of the stars and space: **astronomy** ●study of celestial bodies through their radio emissions: **radio astronomy** ●denoting an astronomical system centred on the sun: **heliocentric** ●denoting an astronomical system centred on the earth: **geocentric** ●celestial object's repeated elliptical course: **orbit** ●small rocky body orbiting the sun: **asteroid, minor planet, planetoid** ●star's measured brightness: **magnitude** ●brightness of a celestial body as measured from the earth: **apparent magnitude** ●brightness of a celestial body as measured from a fixed distance: **absolute magnitude** ●description and mapping of the stars: **uranography** ●measurement of the positions etc. of the stars: **astrometry** ●physics of stars and their movements: **astrophysics** ●chemistry of the stars: **astrochemistry** ●study of the movement of the stars as a means of predicting the future: **astrology** ●table giving positions of a star at different times: **ephemeris** (*pl.* ephemerides) ●theory that the galaxies are moving away from each other: **expanding universe theory** ●displacement towards longer wavelengths of radiation from distant galaxies: **red shift** ●displacement towards shorter wavelengths of radiation from distant galaxies: **blue shift** ●instrument detecting radio emissions from the sky: **radio telescope** ●building with a domed ceiling for displaying images of the stars: **planetarium** ▸*see also* planet

start ●official start: **inauguration** ●start a car from another car's battery: **jump-start** ●start a car by pushing it and then engaging the gears: **bump-start, jump-start**

starvation ●lack of proper or sufficient food: **malnutrition** ●thin or weak through lack of food: **emaciated** ●undernourishment causing low weight: **marasmus**

state ●*combining forms*: **-dom** (*e.g* freedom), **-ency** (*e.g.* presidency), **-mony** (*e.g.* matrimony), **-ness** (*e.g.* emptiness), **-osis** (*e.g.* neurosis), **-tude** (*e.g.* solitude) ●internationally influential state: **power, world power** ●state having predominant international influence: **superpower** ●unaligned state set between hostile states: **buffer state** ●state having some control over another: **suzerain** ●state without major ethnic or cultural divisions: **nation state** ●state guaranteeing its citizens' financial and social well-being: **welfare state** ●small state dependent on foreign capital: **banana republic** ●state where everything is good: **Utopia** ●state where everything is bad: **dystopia** ●state where all have the same rights and duties: **pantisocracy** ●state ruled by a prince: **principality**

● democratic state with an elected head: **republic** ● state controlled by political police: **police state** ● power equilibrium between states: **balance of power** ● group of states cooperating to exert influence: **power bloc** ● group of states cooperating in war: **allies** ● group of states allowing free trade between themselves: **customs union** ● state's right to govern its own affairs: **self-determination** ● denoting a state enjoying this right: **sovereign** ● one state's interference in the affairs of another: **intervention** ● control of another state's territory by continued military presence: **occupation** ● denoting a state where the powers of constituent parts are vested in a central authority: **unitary** ● denoting a state where the constituent parts retain some powers of self-government: **federal, federalist** ● denoting a state demanding complete obedience from its subjects: **totalitarian** ● denoting a state seeking to control the economy and social change: **dirigiste, statist** ● denoting an independent state: **sovereign** ● denoting a state not taking sides in a war: **neutral** ● denoting a state without direct sea access: **landlocked** ● international acceptance of a state or its government: **recognition** ● denoting a state giving no support to power blocs: **non-aligned** ● mutual tolerance between ideologically opposed states: **coexistence** ● state acquisition and exploitation of undeveloped territory: **colonialism** ● state's economic domination of another: **neocolonialism** ● state policy based on maintenance and use of large military forces: **militarism** ● fragment a region into mutually hostile states: **Balkanize** ● state's annual income: **revenue** ● area under a state's jurisdiction: **territory** ● set of basic principles and precedents by which a state is governed: **constitution**

● state-provided community services: **social services** ● state system of care for those in need: **welfare state** ● payment made by the state to a certain category of needy persons: **benefit** ● state payment to the unemployed and individuals on low income: **Job Seekers' Allowance** ● state payment to a family on low income: **family credit** ● state payment to the long-term sick: **incapacity benefit** ● denoting a state benefit paid regardless of tax contributions: **non-contributory** ● booklet of vouchers for a state benefit: **order book** ● state bureaucracy: **administration, civil service** ● administrative region of a state: **canton** ● transfer a business to state management: **nationalize** ● return a state-run concern to the private sector: **corporatize, privatize** ● company operating in several states: **multinational** ● state-granted monopoly over the exploitation of an invention: **patent** ● holder of this: **patentee** ● internal to a state: **domestic** ● divide a state into separate units: **partition** ● person's home state: **domicile** ● leave one state and settle in another: **emigrate** ● enter a state and settle there: **immigrate** ● send back to the state of origin: **repatriate** ● compulsory enlistment for state service: **conscription** ● staunch supporter of one's own state: **patriot**

statement ● intentionally ambiguous statement: **weasel words** ● statement made ambiguous by its grammar: **amphibology, amphiboly** ● statement used as a basis for reasoning: **premise, premiss, thesis** ● statement made about all members of the class discussed: **universal** ● statement made about some members of the class discussed: **particular** ● conflicting or evasive statements: **tergiversation** ● published false and damaging statement: **libel** ● false and damaging oral statement: **slander**

●false and damaging statement whether published or oral: **defamation** ●formal statement of a person's character and qualifications: **testimonial** ●seemingly illogical statement: **paradox** ●statements made in a lawcourt: **evidence, testimony** ●legal statement made under oath: **affidavit, deposition** ●statement's general meaning: **drift** ●statement designed to have a second (usually indecent) meaning: **double entendre, double entente** ●statement circulated to the media: **press release** ●modifying statement: **qualification** ●official statement: **communiqué, representation** ●short official statement: **bulletin** ●statement harming a person's reputation: **slur, smear** ●statement denying responsibility etc.: **disclaimer** ●statement assumed, generally believed, or self-evidently true: **axiom** ●true but trite statement: **truism** ●statement saying the same thing twice: **tautology** ●statement presumed true until proved otherwise: **assumption, presumption, presupposition** ●statement's ability to be checked for truth: **verifiability** ●statement expressed in different words: **paraphrase** ●explicitly stated: **express** ●abbreviated version of a statement: **precis, summary** ●key extract from a recorded speech etc.: **sound bite** ●denoting a statement having an underlying implication: **loaded** ●denoting a statement expressed briefly and clearly: **succinct** ●person making a sworn statement: **deponent** ●confirm a statement: **corroborate** ●withdraw a statement: **retract, unsay** ●implied or understood though unstated: **tacit** ●reject a statement as false: **rebut**

stationery ●stationery on a long perforated sheet: **continuous stationery**

statistics ●life-expectancy statistics: **life tables** ●statistically average: **median** ●collection of items under consideration: **population** ●one of four equal groups to which items in a set of data may be assigned: **quartile** ●one of the hundred equal groups to which items in a set of data may be assigned: **percentile** ●person compiling and analysing statistics: **actuary** ●study of social statistics as an index of changing lifestyles: **demography** ●specious use of statistics: **numbers game**

statue ●huge statue: **colossus** ●small statue: **figurine, statuette** ●classical pillar carved to resemble a man: **telamon** ●classical pillar carved to resemble a woman: **caryatid** ●base for a statue: **pedestal, plinth**

status ●*combining form*: **-ate** (*e.g.* doctorate), **-dom** (*e.g.* earldom), **-ship** (*e.g.* citizenship) ●relative status: **rank, ranking** ●give a special status: **designate** ●fallen in social status: **déclassé** ●rising in social status: **upwardly mobile**

status quo ●actions designed to preserve this: **holding operation**

steal ●steal someone's ideas: **plagiarize** ●steal from money entrusted to one: **embezzle, peculate, defalcate** ●open robbery when law and order breaks down: **looting, plunder, pillage** ●steal small items from the workplace: **pilfer** ●person stealing from others' pockets: **pickpocket** ●person who knowingly buys or stores stolen goods: **receiver** ●person who finds a buyer for stolen goods: **fence** ●compulsive urge to steal, regardless of need: **kleptomania**

steam engine ●powerful mobile steam engine pulling loads or powering equipment: **traction engine** ●powerful mobile steam engine pulling a train: **steam locomotive** ●steam-powered roller: **steamroller**

steel ●denoting steel with a low carbon content: **mild** ●coat steel with zinc: **galvanize** • concrete reinforced with steel: **ferroconcrete** • rolling mill for steel slabs: **strip mill**

stepmother • *adjective*: **novercal**

sterilization • female sterilization by severing the Fallopian tubes: **tubal ligation** • male sterilization by severing the vasa deferentia: **vasectomy** • remove the sexual organs of: **castrate, doctor**

steroid • synthetic steroid hormone taken to improve athletic performance: **anabolic steroid**

stethoscope • listening to bodily sounds with a stethoscope: **auscultation**

stew • stew cooked in the oven: **casserole** • beef stew with onions and beer: **carbonnade** • chilli-flavoured stew of minced beef and beans: **chilli con carne** • mutton stew with potatoes and onions: **Irish stew** • meat stew covered with sliced potato: **Lancashire hotpot** • highly seasoned meat stew: **ragout** • French stew of meat and beans: **cassoulet** • French fish stew: **bouillabaisse** • spicy Hungarian stew: **goulash**

stick • thin stick with wire bristles for playing drums or cymbals: **brush** • stick for prodding cattle: **goad** • conductor's stick: **baton** • small stick for stirring drinks: **swizzle stick** • long stout fighting stick: **quarterstaff** • hooked stick for landing fish: **gaff** • long stick forked at the top: **thumb stick** • hillwalker's iron-tipped stick: **alpenstock** • magician's stick: **wand** • military officer's short stick: **swagger stick** • stick steadying a painter's hand: **maulstick** • policeman's short thick stick: **truncheon** • relay runner's stick: **baton** • thin stick burnt to make a sweet smell: **joss stick** • spiked walking stick with an openable seat: **shooting stick** • walking stick containing a

sword blade: **swordstick** • metal cap on the end of a stick: **ferrule**

stimulant • stimulant in coffee: **caffeine** • stimulant in tobacco: **nicotine**

sting • eight-legged spider-like creature with a stinging tail: **scorpion**

stoat • stoat's white fur, used on ceremonial robes: **ermine**

stock • keep in stock: **carry** • accumulated reserve of stock: **stockpile** • depletion of stock due to demand: **drawdown** • enumeration of stock held: **stocktaking**

stock exchange • stock exchange area where shares were formerly traded orally: **floor** • end of a day's stock exchange trading: **close** • Parisian stock exchange: **Bourse** • US stock exchange: **Wall Street** • radical reform of the British Stock Exchange in 1986: **big bang** • denoting companies whose shares are traded on a stock exchange: **listed** • registration of a company so that its shares may be traded: **quotation** • denoting share transactions conducted outside the stock exchange: **kerb-market, over-the-counter** ▸ *see also* **share**

stocking • elastic strap supporting a stocking: **suspender**

stomach • *combining form*: **gastr(o)-** • *adjective*: **gastric** • muscular part of a bird's stomach: **gizzard** • protruding stomach: **paunch** • complex of nerves at the pit of the stomach: **solar plexus** • liquid produced by the stomach to aid digestion: **gastric juice** • stomach pain: **gripe** • inflammation of the stomach: **gastritis** • inflammation of the stomach and intestines: **gastro-enteritis** • denoting the stomach and intestines: **gastrointestinal** • instrument for seeing inside the stomach: **gastroscope** • surgical removal of the stomach: **gastrectomy** • study of the stomach and intestines and their diseases: **gastroenterology**

stone ●*combining forms*: **lapid-, lith(o)-, -lith** ●*adjectives*: **lapidary, lithic** ●magnetic stone: **lodestone** ●stone that cuts easily: **freestone** ●rounded stone formerly used to surface roads: **cobble** ●mass of loose stones on a hillside: **scree** ●loose beach stone: **pebble** ●small pebbles: **shingle** ●precious or semiprecious stone: **gemstone** ●undressed building stone: **rubble** ●fine-grained building stone: **freestone** ●large flat piece of stone: **slab, flagstone** ●small flat stone slab: **tablet** ●granite paving block: **sett** ●cylindrical stone forming part of a column: **tambour** ●tapered stone for an arch: **voussoir** ●stone laid at right angles to a wall: **header** ●stone laid parallel to a wall: **stretcher** ●large stone set in the corner of a wall: **cornerstone, quoin, quoin stone** ●stone set at the top of a wall: **capstone, coping stone** ●horizontal decorative band of masonry: **string course** ●large mushroom-shaped stone formerly used to support ricks: **staddle stone** ●undressed stone used as a wall-filler: **rubble** ●inscribed stone commemorating a building's erection: **foundation stone** ●wall or floor covering of small pieces of stone etc. arranged to make pictures or patterns: **mosaic** ●arrangement of these stones: **tessellation** ●stone for sharpening metal: **hone, grindstone, whetstone, water stone** ●stone used as an anchor: **killick** ●stone used to remove hard skin: **pumice stone** ●large standing stone in a prehistoric monument: **megalith, menhir** ●single upright block of stone: **monolith** ●large upright stone forming part of a structure: **orthostat** ●single stone pillar: **obelisk** ●prehistoric stone circle: **henge** ●prehistoric stone chamber tomb: **dolmen** ●prehistoric stucture

of two upright stones and a third across their top: **trilithon** ●stone coffin: **sarcophagus** ●stone at a grave's head: **headstone** ●pile of stones as a landmark: **cairn** ●break stone into smaller pieces: **spall** ●shape stone by striking it: **knap** ●person who shapes building stone or builds with it: **mason, stonemason** ●place where stone is extracted: **quarry** ●crushed stone and gravel used in building: **aggregate** ●stony waste separated off during smelting: **slag** ●masonry simulating large rough blocks: **rustication** ●plaster painted to imitate stone: **scagliola** ●turn to stone: **petrify** ●simple plant growing on stone: **lichen** ●grotesque stone figure serving as a rainwater spout: **gargoyle** ●stone believed by alchemists to turn base metals into gold: **philosophers' stone** ●strap to hurl stones: **sling** ●stone formed in the kidney or bladder: **calculus** ●this medical condition: **lithiasis** ●surgical removal of a stone: **lithotomy** ●surgical crushing of a stone: **lithotripsy, lithotrity**

stone age ●denoting the earliest stone age: **Palaeolithic** ●denoting the middle stone age: **Mesolithic** ●denoting the latest stone age: **Neolithic**

stop ●stop temporarily: **intermit** ●temporary stoppage: **abeyance** ●stopping and starting: **intermittent**

store ●secret store: **cache, stash** ●funnel-shaped store: **hopper** ●store for solid fuel: **bunker** ●place for storage: **depository, repository** ●store for documents: **archive**

storm ●sudden brief storm: **squall** ●severe snowstorm with high winds: **blizzard** ●dense blizzard with radically reduced visibility: **whiteout** ●tropical sea storm: **typhoon** ●still area at the centre of a storm: **eye**

story ●book-length story: **novel**
●brief evocative account: **vignette**
●complex and rambling narrative:
saga ●story appearing in regular instalments: **serial** ●lesson to be
gained from a story: **moral** ●story illustrating a moral or spiritual truth:
parable ●short moral story, often
with animal characters: **fable** ●story
of the narrator's past life: **autobiography, reminiscence** ●story of
events preceding those already described in another story: **prequel**
●story of events following those already described in another story: **sequel** ●symbolical story: **allegory**
●traditional story: **folk tale, legend,
myth** ●traditional stories of a particular culture: **folklore** ●story's
chief female character: **heroine**
●story's chief male character: **hero**
●story-teller: **narrator** ●skilled
story-teller: **raconteur** (*fem.* racon-
teuse)

straight ●*combining form*: **ortho-**
(*e.g.* orthodontics)

straight line ●*adjective*: **rectilinear**
●supposed straight line connecting
ancient sites: **ley line** ●straight line
joining opposite corners of a straight-
sided figure: **diagonal** ●straight line
joining the ends of an arc: **chord**

strange ●frighteningly strange:
eerie, uncanny, unearthly

stranger ●fear of strangers: **xenophobia**

strangle ●execute a criminal by
strangling: **garrotte**

strap ●strap to hurl stones: **sling**
●elastic strap holding up socks or
stockings: **suspender** ●toe-strap on
light sandals: **thong**

straw ●decoration of plaited straw:
corn dolly ●animal's bedding of
straw etc.: **litter** ●neat cuboid pile of
baled straw: **rick, stack**

stream ●small stream: **rivulet**
●strong fast stream: **torrent** ●stream
flowing into a larger one: **tributary**

street ●wide tree-lined street:
boulevard ●narrow alley in northern England: **ginnel** ●street fixtures
such as lamp posts and road signs:
street furniture ●improvised barrier
blocking a street: **barricade**

strength ●exercises designed to improve strength and appearance: **callisthenics** ●increase a solution's
strength by removing water: **concentrate** ●person whose strength is increased by mechanical implants: **cy-
borg** ●defeat by superior strength:
overpower ●big and strong: **strap-
ping** ●strongly made: **solid**

stress ●hormone secreted in stress-
ful conditions: **adrenalin, epinephrine** ●stress-related bowel pain: **irritable bowel syndrome**

strike ●sudden strike: **walkout,
wildcat strike** ●strike of all workers:
general strike ●consecutive short
strikes by different sections of the
workforce: **rolling strike** ●recourse
to strikes rather than negotiation: **direct action** ●person who continues
working when others are on strike:
blackleg, scab, strike-breaker
●money paid to strikers by their trade
union: **strike pay** ▸*see also* **industrial
relations**

string ●strong string made of
twisted strands: **twine** ●bind round
with twine: **whip** ●gardening string:
fillis ●decorative string-knotting:
macramé ●maker of stringed instruments: **luthier** ●pitch a string by
pressing it: **stop**

strip ●strip mown: **swathe**

stripe ●V-shaped stripe on military
uniforms: **chevron**

stub ●stub of a cigar or cigarette:
butt

student ● student's book giving instruction in a subject: **coursebook, textbook, workbook** ▶ *see also* **pupil**

study ● *combining form*: **-logy** ● topic of study: **discipline** ● study of abnormal forms and growths: **teratology** ● study of air currents and the movement of objects through them: **aerodynamics** ● study of air travel: **aeronautics** ● study of algae: **algology** ● study of amphibians: **herpetology** ● study of anaesthetics and their uses: **anaesthesiology** ● study of animals: **zoology** ● study of animal behaviour: **ethology** ● study of the physical remains of ancient civilizations: **archaeology** ● study of ancient plant life: **palaeobotany** ● study of animals whose existence is doubted: **cryptozoology** ● study of ants: **myrmecology** ● study of the anus and rectum: **proctology** ● study of the atmosphere: **aerology** ● study of the upper atmosphere: **aeronomy** ● study of atomic nuclei: **nuclear physics, nucleonics** ● study of atoms: **atomic physics** ● study of bacteria: **bacteriology** ● scientific study of human or animal behaviour: **behavioural science** ● study of the concept of 'being': **ontology** ● study of birds: **ornithology** ● study of birds' eggs: **oology** ● study of the blood: **haematology** ● study of blood serum: **serology** ● study of the body's ability to combat infection: **immunology** ● study of the body by dissection: **anatomy** ● study of caves: **speleology** ● study of living cells: **cytology** ● study of childbirth: **obstetrics** ● study of Chinese culture and politics: **Sinology** ● study of church building and decoration: **ecclesiology** ● study of the Church Fathers and their writings: **patristics, patrology** ● study of chromosomes: **cytogenetics** ● study of the rights and duties of citizenship: **civics** ● study of the climate: **climatology** ● study of clock-

and watch-making: **horology** ● study of clouds: **nephology** ● study of codes: **cryptography, cryptology** ● study of coins: **numismatics** ● study of communication by body movements: **kinesics** ● scientific study of crime and criminals: **criminology** ● study of the victims of crime: **victimology** ● study of crop circles: **cereology** ● study of crop production: **agronomy** ● study of crystals: **crystallography** ● study of Western culture: **humanities** ● study of different cultures: **ethnology** ● study of electronic data processing for storage and retrieval: **information science, information technology, informatics** ● study of death and dying: **thanatology** ● study of demons: **demonology** ● study of disease prevention: **preventive medicine** ● study of the causes of diseases: **aetiology** ● study of the incidence and control of diseases: **epidemiology** ● study of causes and effects of disease: **pathology** ● study of the treatment of disease: **therapeutics** ● study and treatment of the diseases of children: **paediatrics** ● study of the ear and its diseases: **otology** ● study of diseases of the ear and throat: **otolaryngology** ● study of diseases of the ear, nose, and throat: **otorhinolaryngology** ● study of sexually transmitted diseases: **venereology** ● study of medical drugs and their action: **pharmacology** ● physical study of the earth and its atmosphere: **earth science** ● study of the earth's atmosphere, climate, and weather: **meteorology** ● chemical study of the earth: **geochemistry** ● study of the surface of the earth: **geomorphology** ● study of the earth's crust: **tectonics** ● study of the structure of the earth: **geology** ● study of earthquakes: **seismology** ● study of the interreactions of elements: **chemistry** ● study of embryos: **embryology** ● study of diseases of the heart: **cardiology** ●study of diseases of the joints and muscles: **rheumatology** ●study of duty: **deontology** ●study of the earth's magnetism: **geomagnetics** ●study of the earth's topography: **geomorphology** ●study of earthquakes: **seismology** ●study of ancient Egyptian culture: **Egyptology** ●theological study of the end of the world: **eschatology** ●study of the interaction of living organisms and their environment: **ecology** ●study of eye diseases: **ophthalmology** ●study of eye irregularities: **orthoptics** ●study of family trees: **genealogy** ●medical study of the female body and its illnesses: **gynaecology** ●study of fermentation: **zymurgy** ●study of ferns: **pteridology** ●study of fish: **ichthyology** ●study of flags: **vexillology** ●study of fluids at rest: **hydrostatics** ●study of fluid forces: **hydrodynamics** ●study of fluid mechanics: **hydraulics** ●study of food and its use: **nutrition** ●study of foot ailments: **chiropody, podiatry** ●study of the form of words: **morphology** ●study of fossils: **palaeontology** ●study of fossil animals and plants: **palaeobiology** ●study of fossil plants: **palaeobotany** ●study of friction and lubrication: **tribology** ●study of fruit: **carpology** ●study of fruit-growing: **pomology** ●study of engraved gems: **glyptography** ●study of glaciers: **glaciology** ●study of grape cultivation: **viticulture** ●study of the hair and scalp: **trichology** ●psychological study of handwriting: **graphology** ●study of the proportions of the head and face: **cephalometry** ●study of hearing and its defects: **audiology** ●study and treatment of heart diseases: **cardiology** ●study of heat and energy: **thermodynamics** ●study of heredity: **genetics** ●study of history-writing: **historiography** ●study of the origins of humankind: **anthropogeny** ●study of human culture and society: **anthropology** ●study of the use of images in the visual arts: **iconography** ●study of inanimate natural objects: **physical sciences** ●study of Indian culture: **Indology** ●study of resistance to infection: **immunology** ●study of ancient inscriptions: **epigraphy** ●study of insects: **entomology** ●comparative study of natural and artificial intelligence: **cybernetics** ●study of the interactions of a group of people: **group dynamics** ●study of Jewish traditional law: **Talmud Torah** ●philosophical study of the nature of knowledge: **epistemology** ●study of local variants of language: **dialectology** ●study of lakes: **limnology** ●study of language: **linguistics** ●study of language as a series of interrelated systems: **structural linguistics** ●study of the history of languages: **philology** ●study of the larynx: **laryngology** ●study of law: **jurisprudence** ●study of librarianship: **library science** ●study of lifeforms on other planets or in space: **exobiology** ●study of liturgies: **liturgics, liturgiology** ●study of mankind: **anthropology** ●study of manuscripts: **codicology** ●study of matter and energy: **physics** ●study of the meaning of words: **semantics** ●study of mechanical systems that function like living organisms: **bionics** ●study of medals: **numismatics** ●study of medicines and their uses: **pharmacology** ●study and treatment of mental illness: **psychiatry, psychoanalysis, psychopathology** ●study of metals and their purification: **metallurgy** ●study of the mind and its functions: **psychology** ●study of minerals: **mineralogy** ●study of molluscs: **malacology** ●study of mollusc shells: **conchology** ●study of the getting and spending of money: **economics** ●study of the moon: **selenology** ●study of moral systems: **ethics** ●study of mosses: **bryology** ●study of the mouth and its diseases: **stomatology** ●study of muscles: **myology** ●academic study of music: **musicology** ●study of non-Western music: **ethnomusicology** ●study of myths: **mythology** ●study of personal names: **onomastics** ●study of place names: **toponymy** ●study of the natural world: **natural history** ●study of the nervous system and its disorders: **neurology** ●biological study of the nervous system: **neurobiology** ●scientific and technological study of nuclear power: **nucleonics** ●study of numbers' occult significance: **numerology** ●study of diets and nutrition: **dietetics, nutrition** ●study of old age: **gerontology** ●study of living organisms: **biology, physiology, life sciences** ●study of currently living organisms: **neontology** ●study of fossil organisms: **palaeontology** ●study of micro-organisms: **microbiology** ●study of the forms of living organisms: **morphology** ●study of the normal functions of living organisms: **physiology** ●study of chemical processes within living organisms: **biochemistry** ●study of organism–enivironment relationships: **ecology** ●study of ancient papyri: **papyrology** ●study of parasites: **parasitology** ●study of phonemes: **phonemics** ●study of plants: **botany** ●study of plant diseases: **phytopathology** ●study of poisons: **toxicology** ●study of airborne pollen etc. as sources of infection: **aerobiology** ●study of pollen from archaeological or geological deposits: **palynology** ●study of population statistics: **demography** ●study of postage stamps: **philately** ●study of primates: **primatology** ●study of primitive cultures: **ethnology** ●study of projectiles and firearms: **ballistics** ●study of pronunciation:

orthoepy ●study of phenomena unexplained by orthodox psychology: **parapsychology** ●study of punishment and prison management: **penology** ●study of relationships within a group of people: **sociometry** ●study of religions having gods: **theology** ●study of religious missions: **missiology** ●study of reptiles: **herpetology** ●study of rivers: **potamology** ●study of rocks: **lithology, petrology** ●study of a community's rubbish: **garbology** ●physical and biological study of the sea: **oceanography, oceanology** ●study of seaweed: **phycology** ●study of seeds: **carpology** ●study of human sexual activity: **sexology** ●study of sexual love: **erotology** ●study of sexually transmitted diseases: **venereology** ●study of sight and light: **optics** ●study of the skeleton: **osteology** ●study of the skin and its diseases: **dermatology** ●study of skull sizes and shapes: **craniology** ●study of human society and social relationships: **social science, sociology** ●study of soils: **pedology, soil science** ●study of soil management: **agronomy** ●study of Soviet politics: **Kremlinology** ●study of sound: **acoustics** ●study of language sounds: **phonology** ●study of vocal sounds: **phonetics** ●study of spelling: **orthography** ●theological study of the spirit world: **pneumatology** ●scientific study of the stars and of space: **astronomy** ●study of celestial bodies through their radio emissions: **radio astronomy** ●study of the physics of stars and their movements: **astrophysics** ●study of the movement of the stars as a means of predicting the future: **astrology** ●study of statistics of births, deaths, and disease: **demography** ●study of the stomach and intestines: **gastroenterology** ●study of precious stones: **gemmology** ●study of subatomic particles: **atomic physics, microphysics, particle physics** ●study of symbols and their significance: **semiotics** ●study of taste: **aesthetics** ●study of teeth: **odontology** ●study of time: **horology** ●study of tissue structure: **histology** ●study of tissue changes caused by disease: **histopathology** ●study of trees: **dendrology** ●study of tumours: **oncology** ●study of unidentified flying objects: **ufology** ●study of the general features of the universe: **cosmography** ●study of the origins of the universe: **cosmogony** ●study of the origin and development of the universe: **cosmology** ●medical study of the urinary system: **urology** ●study of viruses: **virology** ●study of visual images: **iconography, iconology** ●study of volcanoes: **volcanology, vulcanology** ●study of voting at elections: **psephology** ●study of the weather: **meteorology** ●study of wines: **oenology** ●study of word origins: **etymology** ●study of the meaning of words: **semantics** ●study of words for closely related concepts: **onomasiology** ●study of the forms of words: **morphology** ●study of the form, meaning, and behaviour of words: **lexicology** ●study of efficient work methods: **ergonomics, time-and-motion study** ●study of ancient writing systems: **palaeography** ●study of X-rays: **radiography** ●study of medical applications of X-rays: **radiology** ●study of an item in its natural environment: **field study, field trip, fieldwork** ●study intensely: **cram** ●denoting a course of study designed for practical applications: **applied, practical** ●denoting a course of study concentrating on theory: **pure** ●course of study completed at home: **distance learning, correspondence course** ●restudy of completed work before an examination: **revision** ●person who has abandoned a course of study: **dropout** ●certificate of completed studies: **diploma, qualification**

stuffing ●stuffing dead animals: **taxidermy** ●stuffing made of chopped meat or vegetables: **force-meat** ●stuffing mixture of finely chopped ingredients: **salpicon** ●cotton-like substance for stuffing cushions: **kapok**

stupid ●stupid person: **dimwit, dunce, dunderhead, ignoramus, nincompoop** ●boorish and stupid: **lumpen**

stupor ●state of immobility and stupor: **catatonia**

style ●flamboyantly confident style: **panache** ●following current styles: **contemporary** ●in a style typical of some past era: **period** ●stylish elegance: **chic** ●stylish originality: **flair** ●stylish vigour: **elan**

subjective ●subjective impression: **perception**

submarine ●submarine seeking and destroying others: **hunter-killer** ●former German submarine: **U-boat** ●submarine's superstructure: **conning tower** ●tube giving surface views: **periscope** ●submarine's door: **hatch** ●submarine's emergency dive: **crash dive** ●submarine's covered dock: **pen**

subsidy ●organization subsidizing an event in return for free publicity: **sponsor**

substance ●primary substance in matter: **element**

substitute ●person replacing another: **stand-in** ●person acting for another: **proxy** ●fraudulently substituted: **supposititious**

subtraction ●number from which subtraction is to be made: **minuend** ●number to be subtracted: **subtrahend**

success ●brilliant success: **éclat** ●success through notoriety: **succès de scandale** ●success with the perceptive few: **succès d'estime** ●possibility of success: **fighting chance, sporting chance, viability** ●three successive successes: **hat-trick** ●product achieving enormous commercial success: **blockbuster** ●person who gains academic or career success: **achiever** ●realization of one's potential: **self-actualization** ●do less well than expected: **underachieve**

sudden ●sudden and dramatic: **galvanic**

suffer ●cause to be suffered: **inflict**

sufferer ●*combining form*: -path (*e.g.* psychopath) ●person enduring suffering without complaint: **stoic**

sugar ●*combining forms*: **glyc(o)-, racchar-** ●*adjective*: **saccharine** ●light brown cane sugar: **demerara** ●sugar got from cane juice: **moscovado** ●sugar found in carbohydrates: **glucose** ●sugar found in honey and fruits: **fructose** ●moulded conical mass of sugar: **sugar loaf** ●finely granulated white sugar: **caster sugar** ●sugar-coated: **crystallized** ●thick paste of sugar and water: **fondant** ●skill of decorating cakes with sugar paste: **sugarcraft** ●sugar browned by heat: **caramel** ●sugar sprinkler: **castor** ●device for picking up sugar lumps: **tongs** ●hormone regulating the blood sugar level: **insulin** ●disease characterized by excess sugar in the blood and urine: **diabetes mellitus** ●excessive sugar in the urine, a symptom of kidney disease and diabetes: **glycosuria**

suicide ●suicide of a victim of an incurable disease, using lethal drugs supplied by a doctor for this purpose: **assisted suicide** ●suicide attempted to gain attention: **parasuicide**

suitable ●mutually unsuited: **incompatible**

suitcase ●small suitcase: **valise**

summary ●summary of points made: **recapitulation** ●summary of past events: **retrospect, review**

summer ●*adjective*: **aestival** ●temporary resumption of summer weather in the autumn: **Indian summer** ●map line joining points of equivalent summer temperature: **isothere**

summer house ●raised summer house with a view: **gazebo, belvedere**

sumo wrestling ●a push in sumo wrestling: **oshi**

sun ●*combining forms*: **helio-, sol-** ●*adjective*: **solar** ●faint glow seen round the eclipsed sun: **corona** ●apparent circle of light round the sun caused by atmospheric ice crystals: **halo** ●dark patch on the sun: **sunspot** ●bright patch on the sun: **facula** ●bright spot beside the sun: **parhelion** ●sudden explosion on the sun: **flare, solar flare** ●sun's highest point in the sky: **zenith** ●structure used to measure this: **gnomon** ●day in the year at which the sun reaches its highest or lowest noontide position: **solstice** ●faint reflection of the sun seen at night: **gegenschein** ●planets etc. orbiting the sun: **solar system** ●planet directly orbiting the sun: **major planet, primary planet** ●passage of a smaller planet across the face of the sun: **transit** ●orbiting planet's furthest point from the sun: **aphelion** ●orbiting planet's nearest point to the sun: **perihelion** ●small rocky body orbiting the sun: **asteroid, minor planet, planetoid** ●denoting an astronomical system centred on the sun: **heliocentric** ●clockwork model of the solar system: **orrery, planetarium** ●revolving projection system displaying on a domed screen the heavenly bodies in their relative positions: **planetarium** ●contrary to the sun's course: **widdershins** ●signalling system based on flashes of reflected sunlight: **heliography** ●panel absorbing sunlight as a source of energy: **solar panel** ●device converting solar radiation into electricity: **solar battery, solar cell** ●therapeutic use of sunlight: **heliotherapy** ●light umbrella giving shade from the sun: **parasol** ●decomposing in sunlight: **photodegradable**

Sunday ●*adjective*: **dominical** ●keeping Sunday as a day of worship and rest: **Sunday observance, Lord's Day observance** ●religious education class held on Sundays: **Sunday school**

sundial ●sundial's vane: **gnomon**

supermarket ●very large supermarket: **hypermarket** ●wheeled basket used by supermarket customers: **shopping trolley** ●desk where purchases are registered and paid for: **checkout**

supervision ●daytime supervision of children or the elderly: **day care**

supplement ●things added as a supplement: **paralipomena**

supply ●supply of persons or equipment for use as needed: **pool** ●obtain from an outside supplier: **outsource**

support ●upright support: **stanchion** ●three-legged support: **tripod** ●support for an arch etc.: **pier, squinch** ●support for a balcony etc.: **cantilever** ●support framework: **horse** ●support for a row of books: **bookend** ●framework with sloping legs, used to support a table, bier, etc.: **trestle** ●person giving financial support: **angel, backer, contributor, patron, sponsor** ●group of persons with a common problem or illness, meeting regularly for mutual help: **support group** ●attempt to win support by affability: **charm offensive**

supporting ●*combining form*: **pro-** (*e.g.* pro-life)

surface ●flat surface: **plane** ●thin surface layer: **film, veneer** ●on the surface: **superficial** ●insert a screw etc. flush with the surface: **countersink**

surfing ●lightweight surfboard: **Malibu** ●set of surfboards: **quiver** ●hollow formed when a large wave breaks: **pipeline**

surgeon ●surgeon's theatre garment: **gown** ●surgeon's nose and mouth covering: **mask** ●surgeon's assistant: **dresser**

surgery ●*adjective*: **operative** ●surgery performed on a patient: **operation, procedure** ●minor surgery not requiring overnight hospitalization: **day surgery** ●surgery to improve the appearance: **cosmetic surgery, plastic surgery** ●surgery using intense cold: **cryosurgery** ●surgery using electric heat: **electrosurgery** ●surgery using microscopes: **microsurgery** ●surgery involving transfer of tissue: **plastic surgery** ●denoting surgery undertaken at the patient's request: **elective** ●denoting surgery seeking the cause of symptoms: **exploratory** ●denoting simple surgery not life-threatening: **minor** ●denoting complex surgery involving risk to life: **major** ●denoting surgery aiming to preserve tissue: **conservative** ●denoting surgery seeking to remove all diseased tissue: **radical** ●denoting surgery in which the heart is exposed and bypassed: **open-heart** ●surgical installation of artificial body parts: **prosthetics** ●brain surgery to treat mental illness: **psychosurgery** ●corneal surgery: **keratoplasty** ●surgery on the nervous system: **neurosurgery** ●surgery to construct, repair, or enlarge a penis: **phalloplasty** ●surgical scraping: **curettage** ●surgical tying: **ligation** ●tissue etc. inserted into the body by surgery: **implant** ●cloth covering a patient undergoing surgery: **drape** ▸*see also* **plastic surgery**

surgical appliance ●hernia support: **truss**

surgical cutting ●*combining form*: **-tomy** ●surgical cut: **incision** ●surgical cutting out: **resection** ●surgically created opening: **stoma** ●surgical cutting of the abdomen: **laparotomy** ●surgical cutting of the abdomen for childbirth: **Caesarian, Caesarian section** ●surgical cutting of the bladder: **cystotomy** ●surgical cutting of bone: **osteotomy** ●surgical cutting of the brain's white nerve fibres: **leucotomy** ●surgical incision into the chest wall: **thoracotomy** ●surgical cutting of the cornea: **keratotomy** ●surgical incision into the eardrum: **myringotomy** ●surgical incision into the larynx: **laryngotomy** ●surgical cutting of a nerve: **neurotomy** ●surgical cutting of a tendon: **tenotomy** ●surgical cutting of the vagina at childbirth: **episiotomy** ●surgical cutting of the vas deferens: **vasectomy** ●surgical incision of a vein: **phlebotomy, venesection** ●surgical incision of the windpipe: **tracheotomy**

surgical instruments ●blunt instrument for exploring a wound: **probe** ●surgical knives: **lancet, scalpel** ●large pincers: **forceps** ●surgical saw for the skull: **trepan** ●instrument for withdrawing liquid: **trocar** ●surgical cord: **ligature, suture** ●steam sterilizer for surgical instruments: **autoclave**

surgical opening ●*combining form*: **-stomy** ●surgically made passage: **fistula** ●surgical opening into the colon: **colostomy** ●surgical opening made in the inner ear to relieve deafness: **fenestration** ●surgical unblocking of the Fallopian tubes: **salpingostomy** ●surgical opening into the ileum: **ileostomy** ●surgical diversion of the small intestine: **enterostomy** ●surgical opening into the stomach: **gastrostomy**

surgical removal ●*combining form*: **-ectomy** (*e.g.* appendectomy) ●surgical removal of the appendix: **appendectomy** ●surgical removal of the bladder or a cyst: **cystectomy** ●surgical removal of a breast: **mastectomy** ●surgical removal of a breast lump: **lumpectomy** ●surgical removal of the Fallopian tubes: **salpingectomy** ●surgical removal of the foreskin: **circumcision** ●surgical removal of the gall bladder: **cholecystectomy** ●surgical removal of a kidney: **nephrectomy** ●surgical removal of the larynx: **laryngectomy** ●surgical removal of a limb: **amputation** ●surgical removal of the liver: **hepatectomy** ●surgical removal of a lobe: **lobectomy** ●surgical removal of lung scars: **decortication** ●surgical removal of a lung: **pneumonectomy** ●surgical removal of a nerve: **neurectomy** ●surgical removal of the ovaries: **oophorectomy, ovariectomy, ovariotomy** ●surgical removal of the pancreas: **pancreatectomy** ●surgical removal of the penis: **penectomy** ●surgical removal of the prostate gland: **prostatectomy** ●surgical removal of upper layers of skin: **dermabrasion** ●surgical removal of part of the skull: **craniotomy** ●surgical removal of the spleen: **splenectomy** ●surgical removal of the stomach: **gastrectomy** ●surgical removal of a stone: **lithotomy** ●surgical crushing of a stone: **lithotripsy, lithotrity** ●surgical removal of a testicle: **orchidectomy** ●surgical removal of the tonsils: **tonsillectomy** ●surgical removal of a tooth: **extraction** ●surgical destruction of tumours or hair roots by an electric current: **electrolysis** ●surgical removal of a vertebral disc: **discectomy** ●surgical removal of the womb: **hysterectomy** ●surgical removal of facial wrinkles: **face-lift**

surname ● woman's surname prior to marriage: **maiden name** ● denoting a hyphenated surname: **double-barrelled**

surprise ● state of helpless amazement: **stupor**

surrender ● symbol of surrender: **white flag**

surroundings ● usual surroundings: **environment**

surveillance ● detect and remove hidden surveillance devices: **debug** ● subject to covert surveillance: **watch**

survey ● survey of enemy resources and positions: **reconnaissance**

surveying ● surveying system based upon triangles: **triangulation** ● rotating telescope for measuring angles: **theodolite** ● instrument for taking altitudes: **sextant** ● incised survey mark in a wall etc.: **benchmark** ● reference point on a small pillar: **trig point** ● striped sight-pole: **ranging pole**

survive ● capable of surviving independently: **viable**

suspense ● event full of suspense: **cliffhanger**

suspicious ● pathologically suspicious: **paranoid**

swallow ● swallow hastily: **gulp**

swamp ● swamp tree with above-ground roots: **mangrove**

swan ● female swan: **pen** ● male swan: **cob** ● young swan: **cygnet** ● flock of swans in flight: **skein** ● place where swans breed: **swannery** ● catching and marking of swans: **swan-upping**

sweat ● abnormal sweat caused by illness or medication: **diaphoresis** ● causing sweat: **sudorific** ● secreting sweat: **sudoriferous** ● strip of material worn to absorb sweat: **sweatband** ● substance applied to prevent or reduce sweat: **antiperspirant**

sweet ● small sweet: **drop, pastille** ● mixture of small coloured sweets: **dolly mixture** ● jellylike translucent sweet: **gumdrop** ● sweet black chewy substance: **liquorice** ● sweet almond paste: **marzipan** ● sweet made of egg whites and sugar: **meringue** ● marzipan-based sweets served after a meal: **petits fours** ● flavoured gelatin cubes: **Turkish delight** ● nuts ground in sugar: **praline** ● soft mixture of sugar, albumin, and gelatin: **marshmallow** ● crumbly sweet made from sugar, butter, and milk: **fudge** ● sweet of sugar, nuts, and egg-white: **nougat** ● flavoured sweet effervescent powder: **sherbet** ● hardened sugar syrup: **spun sugar** ● excessively sweet: **cloying, saccharine** ● sweet-voiced: **mellifluous** ● artificial sweeteners: **aspartame, cyclamate, saccharin, saccharine**

swell ● swelling caused by abnormal tissue growth: **tumour** ● pus-filled swelling: **abscess, boil** ● serum-filled swelling: **blister** ● swelling up: **tumescent** ● swollen: **tumid** ● swollen with fluid: **engorged** ● reduction of swelling: **detumescence**

swimming ● swimming competition: **gala** ● prescribed movement in swimming: **stroke** ● swimming stroke imitating a dog: **doggy-paddle** ● kick made with unbent legs: **scissor kick** ● swimming race requiring several strokes: **medley** ● swimming exercises as a cure for arthritis: **hydrotherapy** ● expert swimmer monitoring others: **lifeguard** ● underwater swimmer using breathing apparatus: **skin diver** ● underwater swimmer using breathing apparatus and a rubber suit: **frogman** ● underwater swimming using an aqualung: **sub-aqua** ● swimmer's foot-extension: **flipper** ●swimmer's breathing tube: **snorkel** ●man's swimming shorts: **trunks** ●inflated arm-floats for someone learning to swim: **water wings**

swimming pool ●public open-air swimming pool: **lido** ●small cold swimming pool at a sauna: **plunge pool** ●water slide at a swimming pool: **flume**

swing ●swing to and fro: **oscillate**

Swiss ●Swiss breakfast food of cereals, dried fruit, and nuts: **muesli** ●hard Swiss cheese: **Emmental** ●pale Swiss cheese with holes: **Gruyère** ●Swiss mayor: **burgomaster** ●Swiss mountaineers' falsetto song: **yodelling** ●Swiss state: **canton** ●traditional Swiss wooden house: **chalet**

switch ●switch controlling a whole system: **master switch** ●switch operated by moving a lever up or down: **toggle switch** ●switch operated by pushing a sprung lever: **tumbler** ●set of electrical switches: **gang** ●switches and fuse boxes where the electrical supply enters a house: **consumer unit** ●mechanism activating a switch at a preset time: **timer**

sword ●curved sword broadening at the end: **scimitar** ●short slightly curved sword: **cutlass** ●curved cavalry sword: **sabre** ●blunted fencing sword: **épée** ●naval sword: **cutlass** ●short sword fixed to the end of a rifle: **bayonet** ●light sharp-pointed sword: **rapier** ●sword carried before the sovereign on state occasions: **sword of state** ●Scottish broadsword: **claymore** ●sword handle: **hilt** ●knob on a sword handle: **pommel** ●cover for a sword blade: **scabbard, sheath** ●sport of sword fighting: **fencing** ●entertainer passing a sword blade down his or her throat: **swordswallower**

syllogism ●term common to both premises: **middle term** ●failure of this to include all members of a class in at least one premise: **undistributed middle**

symbol ●symbol of cowardice: **white feather** ●identifying symbol used for a company, product, etc.: **logo, trade mark** ●symbol of surrender: **white flag** ●symbol replacing a word: **logogram, logograph** ●visual symbols: **imagery** ●system of musical or mathematical symbols: **notation** ●system of symbols, each representing a syllable: **syllabary** ●system of symbols, each of which represents a word in a certain language: **ideograms** ●study of symbols and their significance: **semiotics** ●narrative or design whose content is to be interpreted symbolically: **allegory**

sympathy ●feeling of sympathy: **elective affinity** ●express sympathy with: **commiserate, condole** ●insincere expression of sympathy: **crocodile tears** ●lack of sympathy or concern: **alienation** ●lacking sympathy: **insensate, insensible**

symptom ●symptom accompanying a disease, but not caused by it: **epiphenomenon** ●symptom suggesting a particular treatment: **indication** ●symptom warning against a particular treatment: **contraindication** ●set of symptoms whose joint presence indicates a particular disease: **syndrome** ●denoting a gradually increasing symptom: **ingravescent** ●sudden fierce outbreak of symptoms: **paroxysm, seizure** ●temporary disappearance of symptoms: **remission** ●recurrence of symptoms after apparent recovery: **relapse**

synagogue ●cupboard in a synagogue for scrolls of the Torah: **ark** ●synagogue storeroom: **genizah** ●synagogue singer and prayer-leader: **cantor, hazzan**

syphilis ● syphilitic inflammation of the brain: **paresis**

syringe ● insert by syringe: **inject**

syrup ● dark syrup from raw sugar: **molasses** ● dark syrup from partly refined sugar: **treacle** ● browned syrup: **caramel**

system ● interconnected system: **network** ● switch a system on or off: **power up, power down**

T t

table¹ ●table for the chief guests: **top table** ●work table in a laboratory or workshop: **bench** ●extending table with hinged legs: **gateleg table** ●folding section of a table: **leaf** ●part of a table for the most important persons present: **head** ●part of a table for the least important persons present: **foot** ●card indicating where a person should sit at table: **place card** ●crockery and cutlery for one person at table: **place setting** ●revolving stand on a table: **lazy Susan**

table² ●table of the elements arranged to group those of similar chemical structure: **periodic table** ●table giving the results of various mathematical calculations: **ready reckoner**

table tennis ●table tennis bat: **paddle**

tact ●denoting a situation requiring tact: **delicate**

tactics ●tactical withdrawal enabling a further advance: **reculer pour mieux sauter**

tail ●*combining form*: **caud-** ●*adjective*: **caudal** ●fox's tail: **brush** ●rabbit's or deer's tail: **scut** ●solid part of an animal's tail: **dock** ●cut short an animal's tail: **dock**

tailor ●*adjective*: **sartorial** ●tailor's serrated scissors: **pinking shears** ●try-on of clothes being made: **fitting**

take ●take for one's own use, without permission or illegally: **appropriate, misappropriate**

talk ●conference between opposing sides: **parley** ●conference between colleagues: **powwow** ●polite but unnecessary conversation: **small talk**

●private conversation: **tête-à-tête** ●denoting indecent talk: **ribald, risqué, salacious, smutty** ●talk foolishly or at length: **prate, prattle**

talkative ●excessively talkative: **garrulous, logorrhoeic**

takeover ●denoting an unwelcome takeover bid: **hostile**

tank ●water storage tank: **cistern** ●display tank for live fish etc.: **aquarium**

tap ●support for the washer: **jumper** ●sleeve round the turning shaft: **gland**

tape recorder ●denoting a recorder with individually threaded reels: **open-reel** ●base for the capstans: **deck** ●strip at the end of a tape: **leader** ●cylindrical container for magnetic tape: **reel, spool** ●sealed unit containing tape and spools: **cassette** ●obliterate a tape recording: **erase** ●combined radio, gramophone, and tape deck: **music centre**

tapioca ●plant yielding tapioca: **cassava, manioc**

tar ●tar used to preserve wood: **creosote** ●distilled tar used for waterproofing: **pitch** ●tar used on roofs and roads: **bitumen** ●tar mixed with stones for road-making: **asphalt**

target ●revolving target in a medieval tiltyard: **quintain** ●centre of a target: **bull's-eye** ●target's outermost division: **outer** ●disk thrown up as a shooting target: **clay pigeon** ●device throwing this: **trap** ●mark aimed at in curling and quoits: **tee**

taste ●*adjective*: **aesthetic, gustatory** ●person of refined taste: **aes-**

thete ●having refined taste: **discriminating, discerning** ●reflecting the tastes of ordinary people: **populist** ●characteristic taste: **savour** ●pleasant to taste: **palatable** ●having a pleasantly sharp taste: **piquant** ●having a sharp taste: **pungent** ●having an unpleasant taste due to decay: **rancid** ▸*see also* **bad taste, flavour**

taxation ●*adjective*: **fiscal** ●taxation of expenditure: **indirect taxation** ●tax on goods entering a town: **octroi** ●tax on local households: **council tax** ●taxation of imports: **protectionism** ●tax on a particular class of imports or exports: **tariff** ●taxation of income: **direct taxation** ●tax etc. removed from gross pay: **deduction** ●this system of tax collection by employers: **pay as you earn** ●tax on company profits: **corporation tax** ●tax on excessive profits: **windfall tax** ●tax on goods imported or exported: **duty** ●tax on legal documents: **stamp duty** ●tax on profits from sale of property or investments: **capital gains tax** ●tax on property or money acquired by gift or inheritance: **inheritance tax** ●tax on sales of certain goods: **excise duty** ●supplementary tax: **levy, supertax, surtax** ●tax on the value added to an item at each stage of its production: **value added tax** ●tax paid to keep a vehicle on the public roads: **road fund tax, road tax** ●before deduction of tax: **gross** ●after deduction of tax: **net** ●denoting taxation levied at reduced rates on below-average incomes: **degressive** ●denoting taxation levied at premium rates on below-average incomes: **regressive** ●denoting taxation levied at premium rates on above-average incomes: **progressive** ●denoting taxation levied at a fixed rate per unit: **specific** ●impose a tax: **levy** ●deflationary effect of progressive taxation: **fiscal drag** ●order for a tax to be lev-

ied by another authority, or the tax so levied: **precept** ●allowances credited to taxed income: **negative income tax** ●tax-free investment scheme: **personal equity plan** ●liability to a tax: **incidence** ●disclose items liable to taxation: **declare** ●point at which a tax comes into effect: **threshold** ●class of tax liability, with appropriate documentation: **schedule** ●calculation of one's own tax liability: **self-assessment** ●sum that can be set against tax liability: **tax credit** ●remission of tax due: **relief** ●government department assessing and collecting taxes: **Inland Revenue** ●area officer of this: **inspector of taxes** ●form filled in for assessment of tax: **tax return** ●Inland Revenue code representing the tax-free part of an employee's income: **tax code** ●avoidance of tax liability by legal means: **tax avoidance** ●avoidance of tax liability by dishonest means: **tax evasion** ●financial arrangement minimizing tax liability: **tax shelter** ●person living abroad to avoid tax: **tax exile** ●place where taxes are low: **tax haven** ●economic activity conducted on a cash basis to evade tax: **black economy** ●group payments made to casual workers, enabling the individual to evade tax: **the lump** ●foreign diplomats' immunity to local taxation: **diplomatic immunity** ●former tax of 10% payable to the Church: **tithe** ●former tax levied upon every adult: **poll tax**

taxi ●taxi that must be ordered in advance: **minicab** ●passenger in a taxi: **fare** ●signal a taxi to stop: **hail** ●place where taxis wait for hire: **rank, stand**

tea ●tea made from unfermented leaves: **green tea** ●tea made from fermented leaves: **black tea** ●herb tea: **tisane** ●gain flavour from the tea leaves: **brew, draw, mash** ●become bitter through prolonged brewing:

stew ●perforated hollow metal sphere to hold tea leaves: **tea ball** ●tin holding tea: **tea caddy** ●cover keeping the teapot hot: **cosy** ●European plant used to make tea: **chamomile** ●Indian name for tea boiled with milk, sugar, and cardamoms: **chai** ●Japanese ritual of serving and drinking tea: **tea ceremony** ●ornamental mat for an afternoon tea plate: **doily**

teacher ●teacher engaged to give a few lessons at each of several schools: **peripatetic** ●teacher working with individuals or small groups: **tutor** ●teacher temporarily substituting for another: **supply teacher** ●teacher of laboratory etc. techniques: **demonstrator** ●private teacher: **tutor, coach** ●watch out for the teacher's approach: **keep cave** ●institution training teachers: **college of education**

teaching ●*adjective*: **didactic, pedagogic** ●art of teaching: **pedagogy** ●tuition given, often in public, by a visiting expert to a group of advanced students: **master class** ●disparaging term for conventional teaching methods: **chalk and talk** ●foreign language teaching using only the language taught: **direct method** ●teaching method proceeding by short self-tested steps: **programmed learning** ●person who has taught himself: **autodidact**

teapot ●teapot cover: **cosy**

tear ●*adjective*: **lachrymal** ●prone to, or inducing, tears: **lachrymose** ●gland producing tears: **lacrimal gland**

technology ●*combining form*: **techno-** ●technology for manipulating atoms and molecules: **nanotechnology** ●technology of distance communication by radio or wire: **telecommunications** ●technology

combining electronics and mechanics: **mechatronics** ●technology of transistor and microchip circuits: **electronics** ●technology of robot design and use: **robotics** ●using advanced technology: **high-tech** ●forefront of technological development: **leading edge** ●technological jargon: **technobabble, technospeak** ●person devising and implementing a new technological device: **imagineer** ●fear of technology: **cyberphobia**

telephone ●*combining form*: **tele-** (*e.g.* telemarketing) ●public telephone activated by coins: **payphone, coin box** ●public telephone activated by a plastic card: **cardphone** ●telephone providing visual as well as aural contact: **videophone** ●telephone at the door of a block of flats: **entryphone** ●subsidiary telephone: **extension** ●cordless telephone using cellular radio: **cellphone, mobile, mobile phone** ●put into telephone contact: **connect, put through** ●waiting to be connected: **on hold** ●telephone speaker and microphone arranged to be held to the head: **handset** ●telephone speaker and microphone arranged to fit over the head: **headset** ●support for a telephone handset: **cradle, hook** ●device preventing the caller hearing one's remarks: **mute button** ●main line of a telephone system: **trunk line** ●telephone connection with an external exchange: **outside line** ●telephone line shared by two subscribers: **party line** ●direct telephone line for emergency use: **hotline** ●telephone link for a computer: **modem** ●temporary telephone connection: **patch** ●place where telephone calls are connected: **exchange** ●manual exchange: **switchboard** ●switchboard connecting in-house extensions to each other and to outside lines: **private branch exchange** ●line connecting two private branch exchanges: **tie line** ●telephone system expressing dialled figures by a series of electronic pulses: **pulse dialling** ●telephone system expressing dialled figures by pitched tones: **tone dialling** ●denoting a telephone with number buttons that generate pitched tones: **touch-tone** ●area served by a single cellphone transmitter: **cell** ●copy the security codes of a mobile phone: **clone** ●change the security codes of a stolen mobile phone: **rechip** ●denoting a telephone needing no wired connection: **cordless, mobile** ●numbers dialled to reach a telephone exchange: **code** ●book listing telephone subscribers and their numbers: **telephone directory** ●telephone service giving this information: **directory enquiries** ●denoting a telephone number not made publicly available: **ex-directory** ●tape machine recording incoming telephone messages: **answering machine, answerphone** ●central telephone facility storing callers' messages: **voicemail** ●call linking several telephones: **conference call** ●conference call providing visual links: **videoconference** ●denoting a call paid for by the recipient: **reverse-charge** ●enclosure giving privacy for telephone calls: **booth** ●similar facility provided by an agency: **answering service** ●secret surveillance of telephone calls: **tapping, telephone tapping, wire tapping** ●make a telephone call unintelligible by electronic alteration: **scramble** ●making sales by unsolicited telephone calls: **telemarketing, telesales** ●ordering goods by telephone: **teleshopping** ●message initiated by telephone but delivered in written form: **telemessage** ●telecommunications service using teleprinters: **telex** ●telecommunications service using document scanning: **fax** ●denoting a telephone line in use: **engaged** ●person repairing telephone

lines: **linesman** ●person working at a telephone switchboard: **operator**

telescope ●telescope operating in space by remote control: **space telescope** ●building housing a large telescope: **observatory**

television ●*combining form*: **tele-** (*e.g.* telecine) ●television channel one must pay a special fee to receive: **pay channel, pay television** ●television service transmitted by wire: **cable television** ●television information service displaying computer data received by telephone: **viewdata** ●denoting a television system in which video signals are transmitted by wire to a restricted set of monitors: **closed-circuit** ●television set throwing its image onto a large screen: **projection television** ●tiny illuminated area on a television screen: **pixel** ●juxtaposition of light and shade on a television screen: **contrast** ●clarity of detail on a television screen: **definition, resolution** ●faint secondary image on a television screen: **ghost** ●white spots on a television screen: **snow** ●irregular movement in lines on a television screen: **strobing** ●remote television controls: **handset** ●free a television of unwanted magnetism: **degauss** ●damage to a television screen from long use: **burn-in** ●caption at the foot of a television picture: **subtitle** ●giving a good impression on television: **telegenic** ●stage manager of a television production: **floor manager** ●person introducing and playing music videos on television: **video jockey** ●television broadcaster's prompt card: **cue card** ●pole projecting the microphone over a television camera: **boom** ●studio screen showing input to a particular camera: **monitor** ●televised studio competition: **game show** ●long television programme raising money for charity: **telethon** ●sample episode of a projected television series broadcast to test audience reaction: **pilot** ●record a television programme for later viewing: **time-shift** ●resolve a television image into pixels for digital use: **pixelate** ●computer chip blocking violent or sexually explicit material: **V-chip** ●text and graphic information broadcast by television: **teletext** ●still picture broadcast outside programme hours for tuning purposes: **test card** ●television broadcast of a cinema film: **telecine**

temper ●temper metal or glass by heating and cooling: **anneal**

temperament ●denoting a gloomy temperament: **saturnine** ●denoting a changeable temperament: **mercurial, volatile**

temperature ●lowest theoretically possible temperature: **absolute zero** ●temperature at which dew begins to form: **dew point** ●temperature scale in which water boils at 100°: **Celsius, centigrade** ●temperature scale in which water boils at 212°: **Fahrenheit** ●high bodily temperature with shivering and headache: **fever** ●excessively low body temperature: **hypothermia** ●denoting creatures maintaining a constant body temperature: **warm-blooded** ●denoting creatures whose body temperature varies with that of their surroundings: **cold-blooded** ●cooling effect of the wind upon air temperature: **chill factor, wind-chill factor** ●denoting wine at room temperature: **chambré** ●instrument measuring temperature: **thermometer** ●instrument recording temperature variations: **thermograph** ●device regulating temperature: **thermostat** ●system controlling temperature, humidity, etc. inside a building: **air conditioning** ●device activated by temperature changes: **thermostat** ●hot zone centred on the equator: **torrid zone** ●moderate zone north and south of this: **temperate zone** ●cold zone

about either of the poles: **frigid zone** ●map line joining points of equivalent winter temperature: **isocheim** ●map line joining points of equivalent summer temperature: **isothere** ●gradual increase in worldwide temperatures: **global warming**

temple ●temple of all the gods: **pantheon** ●classical temple with a single row of columns: **monopteros** ●denoting such a temple: **peripteral** ●temple's built-up entrance: **propylaeum** ●front vestibule of a classical temple: **pronaos** ●inner chamber of a classical temple: **cella, naos** ●masonry platform on which a temple is built: **stereobate** ●monumental gateway to an ancient Egyptian temple: **pylon** ●temple precinct: **temenos** (*pl.* temenoi) ●Hindu or Buddhist tower temple: **pagoda** ●outer chamber of the Jewish temple: **holy place** ●inner chamber of the Jewish temple: **holy of holies, sanctum sanctorum**

ten ●*combining form*: **dec-** ●denoting a number system based on ten: **decimal, denary** ●period of ten years: **decade** ●occurring every, or lasting for, ten years: **decennial** ●plane figure with ten sides: **decagon** ●solid figure with ten faces: **decahedron** ●athletic contest with ten events for all competitors: **decathlon** ●Ten Commandments: **Decalogue**

tenant ●money paid to the landlord by an incoming tenant: **key money** ●landlord's expulsion of a tenant: **eviction**

tendency ●tendency to do something: **penchant**

tendon ●tendon attaching the calf muscles to the heel: **Achilles' tendon** ●tendon at the back of the knee: **hamstring** ●inflammation of a tendon: **tendinitis** ●inflammation of the elbow tendons: **tennis elbow** ●inflammation of the wrist tendons: **teno-**

synovitis ● surgical cutting of a tendon: **tenotomy**

tennis ● tennis scaled down for children: **short tennis** ● period of informal play: **knock-up** ● tennis bat: **racket** ● racket face on which the loops project: **rough** ● racket face on which the loops do not project: **smooth** ● strike the ball to commence play: **serve** ● player who must return the served ball: **receiver** ● superior competitor in a tournament: **seed** ● score of zero: **love** ● score of 40 all: **deuce** ● next point after this: **advantage** ● play for game victory: **game point** ● group of games counting as a unit towards a match: **set** ● play for set victory: **set point** ● play for match victory: **match point** ● match for two players: **singles** ● match for four players: **doubles** ● stroke played after the ball has bounced: **groundstroke** ● stroke played before the ball has bounced: **volley** ● stroke played with the palm towards the opponent: **forehand** ● stroke played with the palm towards oneself: **backhand** ● revolving motion imparted to the ball: **spin** ● glancing stroke giving the ball spin: **slice** ● consecutive series of strokes: **rally** ● illegal service: **fault** ● two consecutive instances of this: **double fault** ● overstepping the base line: **foot fault** ● obstruction of ball or player: **let** ● court between service line and net: **forecourt** ▸ see also **real tennis**

tension ● abnormally tense or anxious: **neurotic** ● tension experienced by certain women immediately before menstruation: **premenstrual syndrome** ● drug reducing tension: **sedative** ● reduction of international tension: **détente** ● reduce a situation's tension: **de-escalate, defuse**

tent ● oblong tent: **ridge tent** ● large tent for social or commercial functions: **marquee** ● Native American tent: **lodge, teepee, wigwam** ● tent shrine used by the ancient Israelites: **tabernacle** ● nomad's tent in Mongolia, Siberia, and Turkey: **yurt** ● tent's over-cover: **flysheet** ● waterproof floor-sheet: **groundsheet** ● rope steadying a tent: **guy rope** ● dismantle a tent: **strike**

tenth ● combining form: **deci-** (e.g. decilitre)

territory ● national policy of regaining former territories: **revanchism, irredentism** ● seizure of territory to add to one's own: **annexation**

terrorism ● Basque separatist terrorist organization: **Eta** ● Irish nationalist terrorist organization: **Irish Republican Army** ● Islamic fundamentalist terrorists: **Muslim Brotherhood** ● Islamic fundamentalist Palestinian terrorists: **Hamas** ● terrorism associated with the drugs trade: **narcoterrorism**

test ● conclusive test: **acid test** ● random test: **spot check** ● test of actors or musicians applying for work: **audition** ● testing of cosmetics on rabbits: **Draize testing** ● test of an item in its intended environment: **field test, field trial** ● test of metal or ore for purity: **assay** ● test of a person's potential for various kinds of training or employment: **aptitude test** ● developer's own test of a new product before it is submitted to beta testing: **alpha test** ● test of a new product requested from independent experts before it is put into mass production: **beta test** ● testing of production samples to ensure maintenance of standards: **quality control** ● test of a student's understanding of a text: **comprehension** ● test of state-school pupils in core subjects: **standard assessment task** ● comprehension test of replacing missing words: **cloze test** ● test of a substance's strength by applying it to living cells or tissues: **bioassay**

---

testicle ●*combining form*: orchi- ●having only one testicle: **monorchid** ●failure of a testicle to enter the scrotum: **cryptorchidism** ●inflammation of the testicles: **orchitis** ●surgical removal of a testicle: **orchidectomy** ●skin pouch containing the testicles: **scrotum** ●lamb's testicles as food: **lamb's fry**

text ●text of a play, film, or broadcast: **script** ●original version of a text: **urtext** ●preliminary version of a text: **draft** ●text circulated for reading or signature: **round robin** ●text expressed in different words: **paraphrase** ●author's unpublished text: **manuscript** ●computer manipulation of texts: **text processing** ●attempts to ascertain a text's original wording: **textual criticism** ●denoting a text whose authorship is thought to be wrongly assigned: **apocryphal, pseudepigraphal** ●text in its author's own handwriting: **autograph, holograph** ●text on a single topic: **monograph** ●text composed of quotations from other authors: **cento** ●text in rhyme or metre: **verse** ●text not in rhyme or metre: **prose** ●text systematically omitting one or more letters of the alphabet: **lipogram** ●text full of praise: **encomium, eulogy, panegyric** ●aggressive or argumentative text: **polemic** ●authoritative text: **locus classicus** (*pl.* loci classici) ●unprepared text set for translation: **unseen** ●opening words of a text: **incipit** ●closing words of a text: **explicit** ●extract from a text: **gobbet, passage, pericope** ●text spoken for copying down: **dictation** ●introduction of errors into a text: **corruption** ●insertion of extra matter into a text: **interpolation** ●insertion of further matter between the lines of a text: **interlineation** ●correction of textual errors: **emendation** ●piece of text repeated elsewhere: **doublet** ●point where text is missing: **lacuna** ●textual mark indicating corruption: **obelus** ●collection of texts: **corpus, sourcebook** ●mark indicating a textual insertion: **caret** ●revised edition of a text: **recension** ●ancient textual commentator: **scholiast** ●detailed comparison of texts: **collation** ●denoting a text edited from several sources: **critical** ●denoting an edition using material from several sources: **variorum** ●meld of several texts: **conflation, harmony** ●relationship between texts: **intertextuality** ●diagram showing the supposed relationship between various versions of a text: **stemma** ●parallel presentation of several versions of a text: **synopsis** ●this using six versions: **hexapla** ●list of words in a text: **concordance, glossary** ●explanation of a text: **commentary, exegesis, gloss** ●analysis of a text's meaning: **explication, hermeneutics** ●text's basic message: **gist** ●textual interpretation denying any fixed meaning: **deconstruction** ●insoluble textual problem: **crux** ●prepare a text for publication: **edit** ●shorten a text whilst retaining its content: **condense** ●edit or abridge a text: **cut** ●legal right to control the publication of a text: **copyright** ●test of a student's understanding of a text: **comprehension** ●translation of a text to help understanding: **crib** ●portion of text having a wider margin: **indent, indentation**

that side ●*combining form*: **trans-** (*e.g.* transalpine)

theatre ●variety theatre: **music hall** ●opera theatre: **opera house** ●theatre doorman: **commissionaire** ●theatre's general manager: **intendant** ●theatre's literary manager: **dramaturge** ●part of a theatre used by the audience: **front of house** ●part of a theatre where the audience sits during the performance: **auditorium, house** ●part of a theatre where costumes are made or stored: **wardrobe** ●part of a theatre used as dressing rooms etc.: **backstage** ●theatre entrance hall: **foyer** ●part of a theatre where scenery is prepared: **scene shop** ●part of a theatre where tickets are sold: **box office** ●area for the orchestra: **pit** ●person checking tickets at the auditorium entrance: **usher** (*fem.* usherette) ●seating on the floor of a theatre: **stalls** ●seating beneath the lowest balcony: **pit** ●lowest balcony in a theatre: **dress circle** ●middle balcony in a theatre: **upper circle** ●highest balcony in a theatre: **gallery** ●separate section of the auditorium for a few spectators: **box** ●door between auditorium and backstage: **pass door** ●arch at the front of the stage: **proscenium** ●fireproof proscenium curtain: **safety curtain** ●stage projecting into the auditorium: **apron, thrust stage** ●at or towards the front of the stage: **downstage** ●at or towards the rear of the stage: **upstage** ●side of the stage to the actor's left: **prompt side** ●side of the stage to the actor's right: **off-prompt side** ●area at the side of a stage: **wings** ●angle of slope of the stage or a part of the auditorium: **rake** ●floor-level lights along the stage front: **footlights** ●area above the stage: **flies** ●dismantle a stage set: **strike** ●area where scenery is built and painted: **scene shop** ●substance to make a stage mist: **dry ice** ●actors' backstage rest room: **green room** ●actors' entrance in a theatre, leading directly backstage: **stage door** ●maker of theatrical costumes: **costumier** ●theatre sound system for hearing-aid users: **induction loop** ●denoting a theatre out of use: **dark** ▶*see also* **scenery**

theft ●unauthorized use of another's work: **piracy** ●presenting another's work as one's own: **plagiarism** ●covert theft of entrusted money: **embezzlement, peculation** ●person who knowingly accepts stolen goods: **receiver** ●round up and steal livestock: **rustle** ▶*see also* **robbery**

theme ●recurrent theme: **leitmotif, motif, motive** ●underlying theme: **subtext**

theology ●theology based on observed facts and experiences: **natural theology** ●theology based on a balanced opposition of good and evil: **dualism** ●theology based on the progressive abandonment of inadequate concepts: **apophaticism, via negativa** ●theology of Christ: **Christology** ●theology of the Holy Spirit: **pneumatology** ●theology of the Virgin Mary: **Mariology** ●theological system based on two opposing forces: **dualism** ●theological basis of church organization: **ecclesiology** ●theological doctrine that the future is foreordained: **predestination** ●unscriptural doctrine held to derive from apostolic teaching: **tradition** ●medieval Western philosophical and theological system: **scholasticism** ●argument that God must exist for ideas about him to exist: **ontological argument** ●argument for the existence of God based on perceived order in nature: **teleological argument** ●argument for the existence of God based on the inability of the universe to have created itself: **cosmological argument**

theory ●provisional theory: **hypothesis** ●denoting an ingenious but simple theory: **elegant** ●explanation of a theory: **exposition** ●theory's basic assumptions: **first principles** ●supporter of a theory: **advocate, exponent, proponent, protagonist**

therapy ●psychological therapy that seeks to cure an undesirable habit by associating it with an unpleasant experience: **aversion therapy** ●psychological therapy simulating the trauma of being born:

rebirthing ●Chinese system of therapy by pricking the skin with needles: **acupuncture** ●Japanese system of therapy by applying finger pressure: **acupressure, shiatsu** ●denoting therapy applied after successful treatment of a cancer to suppress secondary tumours: **adjuvant** ●therapeutic enactment of various social roles: **role playing**

thermometer ●thermometer that plots the temperature on a revolving graph: **thermograph** ●thermometer for low temperatures: **cryometer** ●thermometer for high temperatures: **pyrometer** ●pair of thermometers that measure humidity: **psychrometer**

thief ●thief gaining access by climbing: **cat burglar**

thin ●gracefully thin: **slender, svelte** ●thin and bony: **scrawny** ●thin and haggard: **gaunt** ●thin and unkempt: **scraggy** ●become thin and weak: **waste away**

thing ●thing as perceived by the senses: **phenomenon** ●thing as conceived by the mind: **noumenon**

this side ●*combining form*: **cis-** (*e.g.* cisalpine)

thoroughbred ●thoroughbred horses: **bloodstock**

thoroughly ●*combining form*: **ex-** (*e.g.* excruciate)

thought ●*adjective*: **noetic** ●concentrated thought: **meditation** ●a person's ongoing thoughts and reactions to events: **interior monologue, stream of consciousness** ●thinking in which problems are solved by logical deduction: **vertical thinking** ●thinking in which problems are solved by adopting a novel viewpoint: **lateral thinking** ●human thought mechanisms or processes when compared with those of a computer: **wetware** ●consciousness of one's own thought processes: **meta-**

cognition ●ability to think clearly: **lucidity** ●inability to think: **mental block** ●engaged in deep thought: **pensive** ●tendency to think in a particular way: **thought pattern** ●alleged paranormal ability to communicate thoughts: **telepathy, thought transference** ●bodily movements or posture taken to indicate thoughts and feelings: **body language** ●showing creative thought: **inventive, original** ●showing, or capable of, little thought: **shallow** ●think over carefully: **mull over, muse upon**

thousand ●*combining forms*: **kilo-** (*e.g.* kilojoule), **mill-** ●thousandth anniversary: **millennium, millenary**

thousand million ●*combining form*: **giga-** (*e.g.* gigabyte)

thousand millionth ●*combining form*: **nano-** (*e.g.* nanosecond)

thousandth ●*combining form*: **mill(i)-** (*e.g.* millimetre) ●*adjective*: **millesimal**

thread ●spun thread: **yarn** ●single length of thread: **strand** ●loosely coiled length of thread: **skein** ●cylindrical container for thread: **reel, spool**

threat ●threat made by a hostile military build-up: **sabre-rattling** ●constant threat of disaster: **sword of Damocles** ●crime of threatening and touching a person: **assault and battery** ●extortion of money under threat of revealing incriminating secrets: **blackmail** ●person making idle threats: **paper tiger** ●obtain by threats: **extort**

three ●*combining forms*: **ter-, tri-** ●*adjectives*: **ternary, treble, triple** ●Three Wise Men: **Magi** ●set of three: **triad, trinity, trio** ●three in one: **triune** ●one of three offspring born at a birth: **triplet** ●division into three: **trichotomy** ●occurring once in, or lasting for, three years: **triennial** ●three-hundredth anniversary: **ter-**

centenary, tercentennial, tricentenary, tricentennial •ancient ship with three banks of oars: **trireme** •group of three artworks with related themes: **trilogy** •ensemble of three musicians, or music for them: **trio** •solid figure with three faces: **trihedron** •painting etc. covering three panels: **triptych** •three-dimensional picture produced by lasers: **hologram** •three successive successes: **hat-trick** •in three identical copies: **in triplicate** •having three parts: **tripartite, triple** •involving three participants: **trilateral**

three-dimensional •*combining form*: **stereo-** •drawing of a three-dimensional object: **stereogram** •mental perception of three-dimensionality: **stereocognosis**

threshold •*adjective*: **liminal**

thrift •constant thriftiness: **scrimping**

throat •*adjective*: **gular, jugular** •throat armour: **gorget** •throat membrane folds making voice sounds: **vocal cords** •muscular passage containing the vocal cords: **larynx, voice box** •inflammation of the vocal cords and voice box: **laryngitis** •infection of the throat causing white patches and severe itching: **thrush** •build-up of mucus in the throat: **catarrh** •liquid to swill round the mouth and throat: **gargle, mouthwash** •swollen tissue at the back of the throat: **adenoids** •clear the throat noisily: **hawk**

through •*combining form*: **dia-** (*e.g.* diaphanous), **trans-** (*e.g.* transonic)

throw •throw close over a surface: **skim** •throw hard and frequently: **pelt** •throw a baited hook or net: **cast** •throw out: **eject** •denoting a throw made with the arm passing above the shoulder: **overarm, overhand** •denoting a throw made with the arm kept below the shoulder:

underarm, underhand •stick that returns to its thrower: **boomerang**

thyroid •overactivity of the thyroid gland: **hyperthyroidism** •underactivity of the thyroid gland: **hypothyroidism** •neck swelling caused by an enlarged thyroid: **goitre**

Tibet •former ruler of Tibet: **Dalai Lama** •lama next in rank to him: **Panchen Lama** •honoured Tibetan Buddhist teacher: **Rinpoche** •Tibetan Buddhism: **Lamaism** •Tibetan flag or wheel with inscribed prayers: **prayer flag, prayer wheel** •Tibetan Buddhist monk: **lama** •Tibetan Buddhist monastery: **lamasery** •Tibetan Buddhist mystic syllable: **om** •Tibetan religious scroll painting: **tanka** •Tibetan Buddhist shrine: **chorten** •Tibetan ox: **yak** •Tibetan ritual exposure of the dead: **sky burial**

tick •device set to tick at a preset rate: **metronome**

ticket •ticket valid for an outward journey only: **single** •ticket valid for an outward and return journey: **return** •cheap same-day return: **day return** •ticket valid for a single journey across several networks or interchanges: **through ticket** •ticket valid for a series of successive journeys or events: **season ticket** •area ticket giving unlimited travel for a specified period: **rover** •free tickets distributed to create or enlarge an audience: **paper** •book of tickets: **carnet** •denoting a ticket usable on any date: **open** •mark a ticket to show it has been used: **cancel** •person buying up admission tickets to resell at inflated prices: **tout**

tide •tide that rises highest: **spring tide** •tide that rises least: **neap tide** •rising tide: **flood tide** •falling tide: **ebb tide** •denoting a tide that is neither rising or falling: **slack** •denoting a tide that is out: **low** •denoting a tide that is in: **high** •(of a tide or floods) to trap or isolate someone: **maroon** ●times of high and low tide at a particular place: **tide table**

tiger ●female tiger: **tigress** ●young tiger: **cub** ●offspring of a male tiger and lioness: **tigon** ●offspring of a male lion and tigress: **ligon**

tight ●pulled tight: **taut**

tightrope ●tightrope walker: **funambulist**

tights ●tights for dancing or gymnastics: **maillot** ●actor's flesh-coloured tights: **fleshings** ●vertical strip of unravelled fabric in tights: **ladder, run**

tile ●unglazed ceramic floor tile: **quarry, quarry tile** ●curved interlocking roof tile: **pantile** ●wooden exterior tile for roofs and walls: **shingle** ●thin mortar used in tiling: **grout**

timber ●cutting and preparing timber: **logging** ●drying out of timber: **seasoning, treatment** ●denoting timber that has not been dried: **green** ●rapidly spreading form of timber rot: **dry rot**

time ●*combining forms*: **chron(o)-, temp-** ●*adjective*: **chronological, temporal** ●time when a person was active: **floruit** ●time allowed for a fallen boxer to get up: **count** ●time when everyone must stay indoors: **curfew** ●time that cannot be used productively: **dead time** ●time of exceptional prosperity, achievement, etc.: **golden age** ●time for the optimum psychological effect: **psychological moment** ●particular time: **epoch, era** ●point in time: **juncture** ●duration of time: **span** ●amount of time a person is able to concentrate on a particular topic: **attention span** ●denoting the earliest times: **primeval, primordial** ●final moments before an event: **countdown** ●start time: **zero hour** ●time between start and finish: **duration** ●time between start and completion: **lead time**

●time between midnight and dawn: **small hours** ●ticking device that helps musicians keep time: **metronome** ●device measuring time: **timepiece** ●device showing the time by a shadow from the sun: **sundial** ●sand vessel measuring time: **hourglass** ●science of accurate time measurement: **chronometry** ●study of time: **horology** ●mechanism activating a device at a preset time: **timer** ●imagined device allowing passengers to travel to the future or the past: **time machine** ●imagined time–space distortion allowing people and objects of one period to be moved to another: **time warp** ●region observing a common time: **time zone** ●national time set an hour in advance in summer for daylight saving: **summer time** ●national time set an hour in advance throughout the year for daylight saving: **standard time, daylight saving time** ●tiredness felt after a flight across time zones: **jet lag** ●latest time for completion: **deadline** ●further time granted for completion: **extension, grace** ●evade an issue in order to gain time: **temporize** ●law setting a time limit for initiating a prosecution: **statute of limitations** ●item of short-term interest or utility: **ephemeron** (*pl.* ephemera) ●happening at the same time: **concurrent, simultaneous, synchronous** ●existing at the same time: **contemporaneous, contemporary** ●for an unlimited time: **indefinitely** ●not lasting for long: **temporary, transient, transitory** ●for the time being: **pro tem** ●at an inconvenient time: **inopportunely** ●done or happening at an unsuitable time: **untimely** ●before the proper time: **premature** ●on time: **punctually** ●unaffected by time: **timeless**

times over ●*combining form*: **-fold** (*e.g.* hundredfold)

tin ●tin-mining district: **stannary**

tip ●pool for all tips given in a restaurant or hotel: **tronc**

tiredness ●tiredness and depression occurring after a viral infection: **chronic fatigue syndrome**

tissue ●*combining form*: hist-●firm but flexible connective tissue: **cartilage** ●band of connective tissue: **ligament** ●mucus-secreting tissue: **mucous membrane** ●tissue transferred surgically: **graft** ●strong elastic connective tissue: **cartilage** ●small space in tissue: **vacuole** ●swollen pus-filled tissue: **abscess** ●abnormal hardening of body tissue: **sclerosis** ●abnormal tissue growth caused by cancer: **neoplasm** ●nitrogen compound in tissue: **protein** ●tissue compatibility: **histocompatibility** ●thickening and scarring of connective tissue: **fibrosis** ●inflammation of fibrous tissue: **fibrositis** ●tissue damage from extreme cold: **frostbite** ●localized tissue death and decay: **gangrene, necrosis** ●wasting away of tissue: **atrophy, dystrophy** ●colourless tissue fluid: **lymph** ●thick liquid produced in infected tissue: **pus** ●natural substance controlling tissue activity: **hormone** ●diagnostic examination of tissue: **biopsy** ●medical imaging of tissue: **magnetic resonance imaging** ●imaging of a tissue section: **planigraphy** ●study of tissue structure: **histology** ●study of tissue changes caused by disease: **histopathology**

title ●hereditary right to a title etc.: **succession**

toast¹ ●thin crisp toast: **Melba toast** ●small piece of toast to dip into sauce etc.: **sippet** ●small piece of toast served on soup or a salad: **crouton** ●melted cheese on toast: **Welsh rarebit** ●melted cheese on toast with a poached egg: **buck rarebit**

toast² ●toast drunk to the ruler: **loyal toast**

tobacco ●piece of tobacco for chewing: **plug, quid** ●powdered tobacco for sniffing: **snuff** ●tobacco remaining in a pipe: **dottle** ●stimulant in tobacco: **nicotine** ●dark resin produced as tobacco is burnt: **tar** ●involuntary inhalation of tobacco smoke by non-smokers: **passive smoking, secondary smoking**

toe ●toe bent permanently downwards: **hammer toe** ●disease causing toe pain: **gout** ●area of hard skin on a toe: **corn** ●fungal condition affecting the skin between the toes: **athlete's foot** ●having inturned toes: **pigeon-toed** ●excessive number of toes: **polydactyly** ●denoting animals that walk on their toes: **digitigrade**

together ●*combining form*: com-(*e.g.* combination) ●unable to exist or work together: **incompatible, incongruous**

tolerance ●mutual tolerance: **coexistence, pluralism**

tomb ●*adjective*: **sepulchral** ●large and elaborate tomb: **mausoleum** ●rock-cut or built tomb: **sepulchre** ●ancient Egyptian tomb: **mastaba** ●beehive-shaped Mycenaean tomb: **tholos** ●inscription on a tomb: **epitaph** ●ancient tomb of three large stones: **cromlech, dolmen** ●ancient stone burial chamber: **cist** ●ancient burial mound: **barrow** ●tomblike monument: **cenotaph**

tombstone ●tombstone carver: **monumental mason**

tongue ●*combining form*: **gloss(o)-** ●*adjectives*: **glossal, lingual** ●area of the tongue sensitive to tastes: **taste bud** ●inflammation of the tongue: **glossitis** ●speaking with tongues: **glossolalia**

tonic sol-fah ●first note in this system: **doh** ●second note: **re** ●third note: **mi** ●fourth note: **fah**

●fifth note: **soh** ●sixth note: **lah** ●seventh note: **ti**

tonsil ●inflammation of the tonsils: **tonsillitis** ●surgical removal of the tonsils: **tonsillectomy**

tool ●tool for adjusting wheel nuts: **wheel brace** ●corkscrew-like tool for wood-boring: **auger, bradawl, gimlet** ●tool for breaking up hard ground: **pickaxe** ●adze-ended pickaxe: **mattock** ●heavy chisel for cutting bricks: **bolster** ●concave-bladed chisel: **gouge** ●meat chopper: **cleaver** ●rubber blade for cleaning windows: **squeegee** ●tool for crushing or grinding: **pestle** ●curved cutting tool: **hook** ●powered cutting or shaping tool: **machine tool** ●long-bladed agricultural cutting tool: **scythe** ●short-handled agricultural cutting tool with a curved blade: **sickle** ●steel engraving tool: **burin, graver** ●crowbar for forcing windows: **jemmy** ●agricultural two-pronged fork: **pitchfork** ●grinding tool: **file** ●gripping tools: **pincers, pliers, tongs, tweezers** ●tool for gripping a nut or bolt: **spanner** ●hedgecutting tool: **slasher** ●tool for holding an object firmly: **brace, clamp, vice** ●iron bar with a flattened end: **crowbar** ●tool for marking angles: **bevel** ●mixing and spreading tool: **spatula** ●tool for moulding or stamping out metal: **die** ●tool for piercing leather: **awl** ●tool for applying plaster and mortar: **trowel** ●plaster-smoothing tool: **float** ●pruning clippers: **secateurs** ●pruning tool with a sickle-shaped blade: **billhook** ●hooked pruning tool on a long handle: **pruning hook** ●tool making seedholes: **dibber, dibble** ●tool for separating rope strands: **marlinspike** ●tool for shaping metal: **swage** ●tool for shaping wood: **adze** ●heavy powered tool for shaping wood, metal, etc.: **machine tool** ●metal-smoothing tools: **file,**

rasp ●powered smoothing tool: **sander** ●wood-smoothing tool: **plane** ●wide spade: **shovel** ●small narrow spade for cutting roots: **spud** ●small curved spade: **trowel** ●threshing tool: **flail** ●denoting an adjustable tool: **universal** ●tool's handle: **helve** ●narrow part attaching the handle to the operational end: **shank** ●tool's expanding holder: **chuck** ●cutting or gripping part of a tool: **bit** ●device guiding a tool: **jig** ●person making precision machine tools: **toolmaker**

tooth ●*combining forms*: dent-, odont-, -odon (*e.g.* mastodon) ●*adjective*: **dental** ●child's first teeth: **milk teeth** ●second set of teeth, lasting most of adult life: **permanent teeth** ●narrow-edged tooth used to cut: **incisor** ●pointed tooth between the incisors and molars: **canine** ●canine tooth in the upper jaw: **eye tooth** ●broad grinding tooth: **molar** ●irregular or projecting tooth: **snaggletooth** ●long pointed tooth protruding from the mouth: **tusk** ●tooth emerging at the back of the jaw during adulthood: **wisdom tooth** ●snake's venom-injecting tooth: **fang** ●cut teeth: **teethe** ●rub the teeth together noisily: **grind** ●involuntary grinding of the teeth: **bruxism** ●part of a tooth embedded in the gum: **root** ●firm flesh around a tooth's root: **gum** ●tooth's first emergence through the gum: **eruption** ●part of a tooth above the gum: **crown** ●pointed projection on the top of a tooth: **cusp** ●hard glossy substance covering the crown: **enamel** ●bony part of a tooth below the enamel: **dentine** ●soft tissue inside a tooth: **pulp** ●tooth decay: **caries** ●bacterial film on teeth: **plaque** ●hard yellowish deposit forming on teeth: **calculus, scale, tartar** ●decayed area on a tooth: **cavity** ●block this: **fill** ●passage through a tooth for the nerves and blood vessels: **root canal** ●gap between teeth: **diastema**

(*pl.* diastemata) •denoting a tooth wedged between another tooth and the jaw: **impacted** •alloy used to fill teeth: **amalgam** •filling shaped to fit a tooth cavity: **inlay** •wire device to straighten teeth: **brace** •protective covering for a tooth: **cap** •artificial replacement for the upper part of a tooth: **crown** •artificial replacement for a tooth, supported by the teeth on either side: **bridge, bridgework** •shaped plastic holding false teeth: **denture, plate** •dental repair renewing both appearance and function: **restoration** •surgical removal of a tooth: **extraction** •dentistry of children: **paedodontics** •teeth present in a mouth: **dentition** •numerical formula expressing this: **dental formula** •position of teeth with closed jaws: **occlusion** •bad tooth positioning with closed jaws: **malocclusion** •regularization of the teeth or jaws: **orthodontics** •care of the structures surrounding the teeth: **periodontics, periodontology** •inflammation of the tissue around teeth: **periodontitis** •fine thread pulled between the teeth: **dental floss** •pointed piece of wood or plastic for cleaning between the teeth: **toothpick** •compound added to drinking water to arrest tooth decay: **fluoride** •person treating and extracting teeth: **dentist** •design, manufacture, and fitting of false teeth: **prosthodontics** •person who makes and repairs false teeth: **dental technician** •mould made round a person's teeth: **impression** •study of teeth: **odontology** •toothed wheel: **cog, sprocket** •toothed projection on a wheel or cylinder: **sprocket**

top •top of a hill or mountain: **summit**

topic •text on a single topic: **monograph** •general survey of a topic: **overview, synopsis** •related to a particular topic: **thematic** •depart from the topic: **digress** •wandering from topic to topic: **discursive** •irrelevant to the topic: **extraneous**

torture •caning the soles of the feet: **bastinado** •torture by dripping water: **water torture** •frame on which the victim may be stretched: **rack** •device crushing the thumbs: **thumbscrew**

touch •*adjective*: **tactile** •body examination by touch: **palpation** •able to be touched: **tangible** •that cannot be touched or felt: **impalpable**

tourism •tourism intended to increase ecological awareness: **ecotourism** •period of maximum tourist activity: **high season** •period of least tourist activity: **low season** •agent accompanying a tourist group: **courier** •tourist guide: **cicerone** (*pl.* ciceroni), **dragoman** (*pl.* dragomans)

tournament •tournament for medieval knights: **joust**

towards •*combining form*: **ad-** (*e.g.* advection)

tower •airport tower for traffic control officials: **control tower** •bell tower: **belfry, campanile** •castle's central tower: **keep, donjon** •tower above a gate or drawbridge: **barbican** •industrial tower to condense steam: **cooling tower** •mosque tower: **minaret** •small tower: **turret** •tower projecting from a defensive wall: **bastion** •Hindu or Buddhist tower temple: **pagoda** •stepped temple tower in ancient Mesopotamia: **ziggurat** •ancient Scottish tower: **broch** •tower top tapering to a point: **spire, steeple**

town •*adjective*: **civic, municipal, urban** •planned town with large open spaces: **garden city** •town whose inhabitants mostly work elsewhere: **dormitory** •deserted town: **ghost town** •fusion of several towns: **conurbation** •backwoods town in South Africa: **dorp** •visual appearance of a town: **townscape** •squalid urban area: **slum, twilight zone** ●unsightly suburban development: **subtopia** ●public planning and control of urban development: **town planning** ●list of towns: **gazetteer** ●linkage of a town with a similar one abroad for social and cultural exchanges etc.: **twinning** ●person employed to shout announcements in a town's streets: **town crier**

town planning ●official permission for the erection or alteration of buildings: **planning permission** ●area earmarked by planners for a particular type of development: **zone** ●redevelopment of run-down urban areas: **urban renewal** ●collapse of property values due to expected area redevelopment: **planning blight** ●public facility offered by a developer in return for planning permission: **planning gain**

toy ●wheeled board like a single roller skate: **skateboard** ●wheeled board with steering handles: **scooter** ●pair of disks spun on a string: **yo-yo** ●sprung jumping-stick: **pogo stick** ●toy showing coloured patterns in a tube: **kaleidoscope** ●optical toy producing a moving picture: **thaumatrope, zoetrope** ●stick with curved vanes turning in the wind: **windmill** ●cotton-like substance for stuffing soft toys: **kapok**

trade ●*adjectives*: **economic, mercantile** ●unrestricted trade: **free market, open market** ●main item of trade: **staple** ●trade by exchange rather than sale: **barter** ●international trade by barter: **countertrade** ●secret trade in items otherwise available only from state outlets or not at all: **black market, parallel market** ●trading with immediate payment and delivery: **spot market** ●trading for later payment and delivery: **futures** ●trade brought by a particular client: **custom, account** ●illegal trade: **traffic** ●decline in trade: **downturn**

●trading centre: **entrepôt** ●trade agent abroad: **comprador** ●denoting trade unnoticed by official statistics: **grey, informal** ●denoting the cheap end of a trade: **downmarket** ●denoting trade showing no improvement: **flat** ●group of countries exercising free trade among themselves: **common market, customs union, single market** ●discouragement of foreign imports by high tariffs etc.: **protectionism** ●authority to trade with another's goods: **franchise** ●authority to trade at a specified place: **concession** ●trade restrictions imposed upon a foreign country until it changes its policies: **sanctions** ●official ban on trade: **embargo** ●words used in a trade etc.: **jargon**

trader ●*combining form*: **-monger** (*e.g.* fishmonger) ●local trader: **little man** ●trader selling on: **middleman** ●trader in stolen goods: **fence** ●wholesale trader: **merchant** ●combination of traders to fix prices: **cartel, price ring**

trade union ●senior official of certain unions: **convener** ●branch of certain unions: **chapel** ●supporter of trade unions: **unionist** ●grant a union workplace negotiation rights: **recognize** ●withdraw such rights: **derecognize** ●recruit in a workplace: **organize, unionize** ●workplace where union membership is voluntary: **open shop** ●workplace where employees must join a union within an agreed time: **union shop** ●workplace where union membership is compulsory: **closed shop** ●denoting a workplace with no union presence, or of work produced there: **non-union** ▸*see also* **industrial relations**

tradition ●traditional beliefs, customs, and stories of a community: **folklore** ●abandoning tradition: **innovative, radical**

traffic ●excess traffic: **congestion** ●time of peak traffic: **rush hour** ●denoting traffic whose destination lies beyond its present location: **through** ● fixed post used to prevent traffic access: **bollard** ● deliberate slowing of traffic: **traffic calming** ● right to proceed while other traffic must wait: **right of way** ● flashing yellow globe at either end of a pedestrian road-crossing that is not controlled by traffic lights: **Belisha beacon** ● arrangement for traffic to merge with that on a transverse road: **filter** ● traffic jam affecting several streets: **gridlock** ● close to traffic: **pedestrianize**

train ● train with two engines at its front: **double header** ● train driven by motors beneath its carriages: **multiple unit** ● train travelling on a cushion of air: **hovertrain** ● train with sleeping accommodation: **sleeper** ● train run empty: **ghost train** ● denoting a train running towards a major city: **up** ● denoting a train running away from a major city: **down** ● denoting a freight train with a fixed continuous route: **merry-go-round** ● denoting a train carrying both goods and passengers: **mixed** ● train's scheduled route across the network: **path** ● leave a train: **disembark** ● route indicator on a train's front: **headboard** ● railwayman in charge of a train: **guard** ● vehicles of which a train is composed: **stock, rolling stock** ● wagons or carriages coupled together for a particular service: **train set** ● movement of rolling stock from one line to another: **shunting** ● set of pivoted wheels for rolling stock: **bogie** ● projecting rim on wheels of railway vehicles: **flange** ● luxury railway carriage: **Pullman** ● railway carriage's enclosed entrance area: **vestibule** ● partitioned section of a railway carriage: **compartment** ● carriage with beds: **sleeper, sleeping car, sleeping carriage** ● sleeping-car bed: **berth** ● Continental sleeping carriage: **wagon-lit** ● railway carriage whose

seats convert into bunks: **couchette** ● large-windowed carriage: **observation car** ● sideless goods wagon: **flat** ● fitting on the end of a railway vehicle to join it to another: **coupling** ● safety switch in a locomotive cab that cuts the engine unless constantly depressed by the driver: **dead man's handle** ● token given to driver entering a single-track section: **staff** ▶ *see also* **railway**

training ● interactive training environment for pilots: **simulator, flight simulator**

tram ● extending framework connecting with overhead power lines: **pantograph**

transfer ● transfer of goods giving a right to use only: **bailment** ● person conferring this limited right: **bailor** ● person receiving this limited right: **bailee** ● person receiving a right or property by legal transfer: **assign, assignee** ● arrive in time for passengers to transfer to onward transport: **connect**

transistor ● design of devices using transistors: **electronics**

translation ● computer translation: **automatic translation, machine translation** ● free translation: **paraphrase** ● literal translation: **metaphrase** ● unprepared text set for translation: **unseen** ● person making oral translations: **interpreter**

transplant ● body's hostile reaction to a transplanted organ: **rejection** ● drug given to prevent rejection of a transplanted organ: **immunosuppressor**

transport ● transport of goods: **freight, haulage** ● batch of goods transported: **shipment** ● large flexible container for water-transport of liquids: **dracone** ● transport company: **carrier, haulier, shipper** ● company providing scheduled public air transport: **airline** ● right to operate transport services: **cabotage** ● agent arranging sea transport: **shipbroker** ● involving several kinds of transport: **intermodal** ● chart showing times of transport services: **timetable** ● source of transport travelling regularly between two points: **shuttle** ● high-speed urban public passenger transport: **rapid transit** ● denoting a transport service going right to one's final destination: **through** ● money paid to use public transport: **fare** ● point where several transport services meet: **interchange** ● end of a transport route: **terminus** ● extra vehicle put in service when the regular provision is insufficient: **relief**

trap ● animal trap using a noose: **snare** ● trap closing sharply when entered or trodden upon: **spring trap** ● large spring trap formerly set to catch poachers: **mantrap**

trapdoor ● trapdoor giving access to drains etc.: **manhole**

travel ● that can be travelled over: **navigable** ● travel through an area on the way to somewhere else: **transit** ● travel regularly from home to work: **commute** ● travel a route regularly for commercial purposes: **ply** ● travel by soliciting lifts: **hitch-hike** ● travel carrying one's belongings in a rucksack: **backpack** ● travel without a fixed destination: **roam** ● plan and direct the route of travel: **navigate** ● short distance to travel: **short haul** ● persistent desire to travel: **wanderlust** ● travel agency specializing in cheap flights: **bucket shop** ● area ticket giving unlimited travel for a specified period: **rover** ● instrument measuring miles travelled: **milometer**

traveller ● traveller's public account of his experiences: **travelogue**

tray ● fine silver tray: **salver**

treason ● charge with treason: **impeach**

treat ● treat with excessive kindness: **coddle, spoil** ● treat cruelly or unfairly: **mistreat** ● treat roughly: **manhandle** ● repeated cruel and unjust treatment: **persecution**

treatment ● course of treatment: **therapy**

treaty ● treaty between the pope and a secular state: **concordat** ● draft or amendment to a treaty: **protocol** ● formal acceptance of a treaty: **accession** ● formal rejection of a treaty: **denunciation** ● active treaty enforcement by a third party: **peacekeeping**

tree ● *combining forms*: **arbor-, dendr-, silv(i)-** ● *adjectives*: **arboreal, dendroid** ● young tree: **sapling** ● denoting a tree that sheds its leaves annually: **deciduous** ● type of tree that retains its leaves: **evergreen** ● type of tree having cones as fruit: **conifer** ● tree with branches trained along a wall: **espalier** ● tree with top and branches cut off: **pollard** ● tree growing erect to full height: **standard** ● small group of trees: **copse, grove, spinney, stand** ● dense group of trees: **thicket** ● copse on a steep hillside: **hanger** ● wind-stunted trees high on a mountain: **krummholz** ● stunted trees and shrubs: **scrub** ● point beyond which no trees grow: **treeline** ● upper part of a tree: **crown** ● top branches of a group of trees: **canopy** ● tree's hard inner wood: **heartwood** ● tree's soft outer wood: **sapwood** ● coloured ring seen in the cross-section of a tree trunk, representing a year's growth: **annual ring, growth ring, tree ring** ● dating technique derived from these: **dendrochronology** ● tree trunk's outer covering: **bark** ● cut end of a felled tree: **kerf** ● fruit of forest trees as animal food: **mast** ● sticky substance exuded by certain trees: **gum, resin** ● rough protuberance from a tree trunk: **gnarl, knag** ●abnormal growth on a tree trunk: **gall** ●simple plant growing on trees: **lichen** ●cultivation of trees: **arboriculture, forestry, silviculture** ●botanical garden devoted to trees: **arboretum** ●place where young trees are grown: **nursery** ●entwine tree branches: **pleach** ●cut back a tree for poles: **coppice** ●cut down a tree: **fell** ●cut made round a tree-trunk: **girdle** ●person pruning older trees: **tree surgeon** ●person felling trees: **lumberjack** ●label attached to a tree: **tally** ●bushes etc. growing round a tree: **undergrowth** ●study of trees: **dendrology** ●diagram laid out like a tree: **dendrogram**

trellis ●trellis along which the branches of fruit trees are trained: **espalier** ●trellis carrying climbing plants over a garden path or arbour: **pergola**

trial ●trial invalidated by a legal technicality: **mistrial** ●trial held for publicity purposes: **show trial** ●hand over to a foreign state a person accused of commiting a crime there: **extradite** ●mock trial as an academic legal exercise: **moot** ●trial run of an idea, policy, etc. to gauge public reaction: **ballon d'essai, trial balloon** ▸ *see also* **lawcourt**

trial and error ●trial-and-error method of solving problems: **heuristic**

triangle ●triangle with three equal sides: **equilateral triangle** ●denoting a triangle with two equal sides: **isosceles** ●denoting a triangle with unequal sides: **scalene** ●longest side of a right-angled triangle: **hypotenuse** ●surveying system based on measured triangles: **triangulation**

trick ●legal or financial trickery: **chicanery** ●deliberate deception of a trusting person: **confidence trick**

●easily tricked: **naive** ●trick someone into doing something: **beguile**

Trinity ●three-in-one: **triune** ●individual member of the Trinity: **hypostasis** ●denoting the shared essence of members of the Trinity: **consubstantial** ●assertion that the three members of the Trinity are separate gods: **tritheism** ●person claiming to believe in God but denying the existence of the Trinity: **Unitarian**

trip ●pleasure trip: **outing**

trivial ●trivial remark: **bromide** ●conversational exchange of trivialities: **small talk** ●anticlimax resulting from an unexpected mention of trivialities: **bathos**

troops ●troops in permanent military employment: **regulars** ●extra forces kept for emergency use: **reserves** ●member of such a force: **reservist** ●troops not part of an established force: **irregulars, guerrillas** ●troops stationed in a town or fort: **garrison** ●troops trained to serve on land or sea: **marines** ●troops trained in parachuting: **paratroops** ●place where troops are stationed: **post, posting, garrison** ●troops' living accommodation: **barracks, billet, quarters** ●arrangement of troops: **array, formation** ●narrow but deep formation of troops: **column** ●line of troops drawn up abreast: **rank** ●gathering of troops for inspection etc.: **muster** ●draw up troops in parade formation: **dress** ●position troops for battle: **deploy** ●equip troops with motor vehicles: **motorize** ●long leave granted to troops: **furlough** ▸ *see also* **soldier**

trust ●*adjective*: **fiduciary** ●person administering a trust: **trustee** ●innocently trustful: **naive, unsuspecting**

truth ●true but trite statement: **truism** ●appearance of truth: **verisimilitude** ●allegedly or seemingly true: **ostensible** ●guarantee the truth of:

warrant ●prove the truth of: **demonstrate** ●deny the truth of: **controvert**

tube ●tube conveying liquid from a higher to a lower vessel by atmospheric pressure: **siphon** ●very thin tube: **capillary** ●thin tube inserted into a vein or body cavity: **cannula** ●thin tube inserted into the urethra: **catheter** ●insertion of a tube into the body: **intubation** ●glass tube with a closed end used in laboratory experiments: **test tube** ●tube with mirrors to see over or round an obstacle: **periscope** ●tube giving the image in a television or computer: **cathode ray tube** ●made of tubular sections, each fitting inside the last: **telescopic**

tumour ●*combining forms*: **onco-, -oma** ●denoting a tumour that does not seriously threaten health: **benign** ●benign tumour of fatty tissue: **lipoma** ●denoting a tumour that spreads out of control and returns after treatment: **malignant** ●malignant skin tumour: **carcinoma** ●malignant tumour of the bone marrow: **myeloma** ●tumour of melanin-forming cells: **melanoma** ●malignant tumour of connective tissue: **sarcoma** ●slow-growing malignant facial tumour: **rodent ulcer** ●malignant tumour of the testis: **teratocarcinoma** ●causing tumours: **oncogenic** ●surgical destruction of tumours by an electric current: **electrolysis** ●study and treatment of tumours: **oncology** ▸*see also* **cancer**

tune ●simple tune: **air** ●easily memorable tune: **jingle** ●tune of established popularity: **standard** ●musical embellishment to a note in a tune: **ornament** ●reworking of a complete tune: **variation** ●tune fragment constantly repeated: **ostinato** ●section of a tune regularly repeated: **refrain**

tunnel ●road or pedestrian tunnel: **underpass** ●tunnel dug under an enemy's defences: **sap** ●tunnel-building by digging a trench and roofing it over: **cut-and-cover**

turbine ●*combining form*: **turbo-** ●turbine powered by an engine's exhaust gases: **tubocharger** ●turbine blade: **vane**

turkey ●noise made by a turkey: **gobble** ●fleshy lobe hanging from a turkey's neck: **wattle**

Turkish ●*combining form*: **Turco-** (*e.g.* Turco-Soviet) ●Turkish administrative district: **vilayet** ●flat-woven Turkish carpet: **kilim** ●Turkish mixed hors d'oeuvre: **mezes** ●Turkish dish of stuffed aubergines: **Imam Bayildi** ●Turkish dish of spiced lamb: **doner kebab** ●Turkish dish of dried cracked wheat: **bulgar wheat** ●Turkish robe open at the front: **dolman** ●long Turkish tobacco pipe: **chibouk** ●Turkish summer house: **kiosk** ●Turkish shared taxi: **dolmus** ●Turkish nomad's tent: **yurt** ●former title of a Turkish district governor: **bey** ●former title of a Turkish senior officer: **pasha** ●member of the Turkish sultan's former guard: **janissary**

turn ●*combining forms*: **trop-** (*e.g.* tropism), **-tropic** (*e.g.* heliotropic) ●turn assigned in rotation: **Buggins' turn** ●complete turn of a vehicle in a confined space by moving backwards and forwards: **three-point turn** ●complete turn of a vehicle in a single arc: **U-turn** ●race with constant turns: **slalom** ●pass round in turn: **rotate** ●sudden or unexpected turn: **quirk** ●full of twists and turns: **tortuous** ●crucial turning point: **Rubicon, watershed** ●turning force: **torque** ●turn into bone: **ossify** ●turn into stone: **petrify** ●turn from its course: **deflect** ●turn violently: **slew**

turpentine ●*adjective*: **terebinthine**

turtle ●turtles' breeding ground: **rookery**

twelve ●*combining form*: **dodeca-** ●*adjectives*: **duodecimal, duodenary** ●twelve-sided figure: **dodecagon** ●twelve-tone musical system: **serialism, dodecaphony**

twenty ●*adjective*: **vigesimal** ●set of twenty: **score** (*pl.* same)

twice ●*combining forms*: **bi-, di-** (*e.g.* dioxide) ●occurring twice a month: **bimonthly** ●occurring twice a year: **biannual, semi-annual**

twilight ●*adjective*: **crepuscular**

twins ●denoting twins conjoined at birth: **Siamese** ●denoting twins developed from the same ovum: **identical, monozygotic, monozygous** ●denoting non-identical twins: **dizygotic, dizygous** ●astrological term: **Gemini**

twist ●sudden sharp twist: **wrench** ●(of a ship or aircraft) twist from side to side: **yaw** ●twist unnaturally: **contort** ●be twisted by heat or damp: **distort, warp**

twitch ●uncontrolled facial twitch: **tic**

two ●*combining forms*: **bi-, di-, du(o)-** ●*adjectives*: **binary, double, dual** ●division into two categories: **dichotomy** ●(of a legislative body) having two chambers: **bicameral** ●for two ears: **binaural** ●for two eyes: **binocular** ●two-faced: **duplicitous** ●animal having two feet: **biped** ●in, or able to speak, two languages: **bilingual** ●ability to be in two places simultaneously: **bilocation** ●having two names or terms: **binomial** ●involving two participants: **bilateral, bipartisan, bipartite** ●having two parts: **binary, bipartite, dual** ●thing having two parts: **dyad** ●two-sided:

bilateral ●aircraft having two sets of wings: **biplane** ●athletic contest with two events for all competitors: **biathlon** ●ensemble of two musicians, or music for them: **duet** ●painting etc. covering two panels: **diptych** ●ancient warship with two files of oarsmen on each side: **bireme** ●occurring every two months: **bimonthly** ●occurring once in, or (of a plant) lasting for, two years: **biennial** ●two-hundredth anniversary: **bicentenary, bicentennial** ●cut in two: **bisect**

type ●*combining form*: **-ery** (*e.g.* greenery)

typeface ●set of printing type: **font** ●upright typeface: **roman** ●sloping typeface: **italic** ●slight stroke at the end of a printed letter: **serif** ●serifless typeface: **sans serif** ●thick-looking typeface: **bold** ●typeface imitating handwriting: **script** ●German traditional typeface: **Fraktur** ●English equivalent: **black letter**

typewriting ●moving part of typewriter for positioning paper: **carriage** ●typewriter roller: **platen** ●typewriter key giving capital letters: **shift key** ●typewriter key giving a new line: **carriage return** ●typewriter key giving free movement of paper: **carriage release** ●standard English-language keyboard layout: **querty** ●type using all fingers and without looking at the keys: **touch-type**

tyre ●tyre with diagonal cords: **cross-ply** ●tyre with cords at right-angles to the circumference: **radial** ●tyre's reinforced inner edge that grips the rim of the wheel: **bead** ●thick moulded part of a tyre: **tread** ●groove in a tyre tread: **sipe** ●inflatable tube inside a tyre: **inner tube** ●worn tyre given a new tread: **remould, retread**

U u

ulcer ●denoting an ulcer slow to heal: **indolent**

umbrella ●light umbrella giving shade from the sun: **parasol**

unarmed combat ●sports giving skill in unarmed combat: **martial arts**

uncle ●*adjective*: **avuncular** ●child of one's uncle or aunt: **cousin**

unconsciousness ●semi-conscious state: **stupor** ●long period of deep unconsciousness: **coma** ●temporary loss of consciousness: **blackout** ●state of unconsciousness with bodily rigidity: **catalepsy, catatonia** ●unconsciousness from a blow to the head: **concussion** ●knock unconscious: **stun**

unconventional ●unconventional person: **eccentric** ●deliberately unconventional person: **enfant terrible** (*pl.* enfants terribles) ●shock the staid by unconventional behaviour: **épater les bourgeois**

under ●*combining forms*: **hypo-** (*e.g.* hypodermic), **infra-** (*e.g.* infra-red), **sub-** (*e.g.* sub-zero)

underground ●underground cemetery: **catacomb** ●underground command centre: **bunker** ●underground railway in London: **tube** ●underground railway in Paris: **metro** ●underground railway in Rome: **metropolitana** ●underground railway in the USA: **subway**

undermine ●undermine a fortification by tunnelling beneath it: **sap** ●undermine an organization by establishing agents within it: **infiltrate** ●such an agent: **mole**

understand ●easy to understand: **perspicuous, user-friendly** ●immediate understanding not needing rational thought: **intuition** ●hard to understand: **enigmatic, enigmatical, obscure** ●impossible to understand: **impenetrable, inaccessible, indecipherable, indigestible** ●make hard to understand: **obfuscate**

understanding ●perceptive understanding: **insight, penetration** ●sympathetic understanding: **empathy** ●informal diplomatic understanding between two nations: **entente cordiale**

understatement ●deliberate understatement: **litotes**

underwater ●sealed underwater chamber: **caisson** ●underwater wall reaching to the surface to provide a dry area: **coffer, cofferdam** ●divers' underwater vessel open at the bottom and filled with air: **diving bell** ●submarine-like vessel for deep underwater exploration: **bathyscaphe**

underworld ●denoting the underworld: **chthonian, chthonic** ●god of the Classical underworld: **Hades, Pluto** ●his consort: **Persephone** ●river bordering the Classical underworld: **Styx** ●ferryman of the Styx: **Charon**

unemployment ●unemployment due to change of job: **frictional unemployment** ●unemployment due to industrial reorganization: **structural unemployment**

uniform ●uniform for a specified purpose: **order** ●uniform of a particular regiment: **regimentals** ●ordinary uniform: **undress** ●loose drab uniform: **fatigues** ●uniform for formal but not ceremonial occasions: **service dress** ●officer's uniform for formal dinners: **mess kit** ●tight jacket for this: **mess jacket, monkey jacket** ●tight dress trousers: **overalls** ●close-fitting short coat: **tunic** ●soldier's peaked cap: **forage cap** ●military badge: **insignia** (*pl.* same) ●ornamental shoulderpiece on a uniform jacket: **epaulette** ●coloured patch of cloth indicating regiment: **flash** ●V-shaped stripe on the arm of a uniform: **chevron, stripe** ●cord holding a whistle etc.: **lanyard** ●ornamental fastening: **frog** ●belt worn by certain army officers, with a strap over the shoulder: **Sam Browne** ●military officer's short stick: **swagger stick** ●military boot reaching to the knee: **jackboot** ●herald's emblazoned coat: **tabard** ●jester's outfit: **motley** ●non-uniform clothes: **plain clothes, civvies, mufti**

union ●enforced union of Austria with Germany in 1938: **Anschluss**

unit ●independent unit: **module** ●single or indivisible unit: **monad**

United States ●Texan hat: **stetson** ●New York underground railway: **subway** ●New York stock exchange: **Wall Street** ●general index of New York share prices: **Dow Jones index**

unity ●pursuit of unity between all Christian churches: **ecumenism**

universe ●*combining form*: **cosmo-** ●*adjective*: **cosmic** ●the universe beyond the earth's atmosphere: **outer space, deep space** ●the universe viewed as an ordered system: **cosmos** ●belief that God made the universe: **creationism** ●scientific elaboration of this: **creation science** ●explosion of dense matter said to have begun the universe: **big bang** ●theory that the universe is supported by constant creation of matter: **steady state** ●study of the general features of the universe: **cosmography** ●study of the origins of the universe: **cosmogony** ●study of the origin and development of the universe: **cosmology**

university ●*adjective*: **academic** ●university at which one was educated: **alma mater** ●university enrolment: **matriculation** ●first-year university student: **freshman, fresher** ●university student who has not yet taken his or her first degree: **undergraduate** ●denoting a university member below the grade of master: **in statu pupillari** ●grant financing university study: **bursary** ●partial remission of fees awarded to a promising undergraduate: **exhibition, scholarship** ●such undergraduate: **exhibitioner, scholar** ●undergraduate having neither a scholarship nor exhibition: **commoner** ●university student in his or her final year: **finalist, schoolsman** ●denoting a student examined, but not taught by, a university: **external** ●denoting a student taught and examined by a university: **internal** ●former university student: **alumnus** (*fem.* alumna; *pl.* alumni) ●denoting university teaching given to non-members: **extramural** ●introductory university course: **foundation course** ●university class for a small group: **seminar** ●long university essay: **dissertation, thesis** ●level of merit gained in a university examination: **class, honours** ●university academic award: **degree** ●university degree with the highest honours in two subjects or examinations: **double first** ●degree with gradings for ability: **honours degree** ●degree without honours: **pass degree** ●degree ceremony: **graduation** ●person about to receive a degree: **graduand** ●person who has received a degree: **graduate**

● person holding a first degree: **bachelor** ● person holding a more advanced degree: **master** ● person holding the highest degree: **doctor** ● university robes: **academicals** ● dark clothes worn with university robes: **subfusc** ● title of the head of certain universities: **chancellor, rector** ● senior university administrator: **registrar** ● university official carrying official insignia on ceremonial occasions: **beadle, bedel, bedell** ● university disciplinary official: **proctor** ● students' elected representative in Scottish universities: **rector** ● chief university teacher: **professor** ● university teacher: **don** ● permanent employment as a university teacher: **tenure** ● meeting of university senior members: **congregation** ● meeting of university graduates: **convocation** ● university teaching department: **faculty** ● university teachers' relaxation room: **senior common room** ● head of a university faculty: **dean** ● extended leave granted to a university teacher: **sabbatical** ● university extramural tuition: **extension** ● university finance office: **chest** ● university site and buildings: **campus** ● university accommodation block: **hall of residence** ● university dining hall: **refectory** ● university holiday: **vacation** ● group of prestigious US universities: **Ivy League** ● arrive at university: **come up** ● leave university: **go down** ● expel from university: **send down** ● recruiting agents' tour of universities: **milk round** ● period of student antics to raise money for charities: **rag** ▶ *see also* **academic, Cambridge, college, Oxford**

unorthodox ● unorthodox person: **maverick**

unsuitable ● make or declare unsuitable: **disqualify**

unusual ● unusual or unexpected act or event: **aberration**

up ● *combining form*: **ana-** (*e.g.* anadromous) ● straight up: **vertical**

upon ● *combining form*: **epi-** (*e.g.* epigraphy)

upper ● *combining form*: **over-** (*e.g.* overcoat)

upside down ● turn upside down: **invert**

uranium ● modify uranium, increasing its explosive power: **enrich**

urge ● sudden urge to act: **impulse** ● urge to peform an unwise action: **cacoethes**

urine ● *combining form*: **uro-** (*e.g.* urogenital) ● horse and cattle urine: **stale** ● urine-creating gland: **kidney** ● system conducting urine from kidney to urethra: **urinary tract** ● bodily sac holding urine: **bladder** ● duct by which urine passes from the kidney to the bladder: **ureter** ● duct by which urine is discharged from the bladder: **urethra** ● inflammation of the urethra: **urethritis** ● tube inserted into the body for draining off urine: **catheter** ● painful urination: **dysuria** ● involuntary urination: **enuresis** ● inability to control urination: **incontinence** ● production of exceptionally small amounts of urine: **oliguria** ● excessive urine production: **diuresis** ● production of much dilute urine: **polyuria** ● presence of blood in the urine: **haematuria** ● excessive ketones in the urine: **ketonuria** ● drug increasing urination: **diuretic** ● drug decreasing urination: **antidiuretic** ● study and treatment of the urinary system: **urology**

use ● available for use: **at one's disposal, free** ● easy to use: **user-friendly, user-oriented** ● hard to use: **user-hostile** ● items or persons kept for later use: **reserve** ● to be used once and thrown away: **disposable** ● excessive use: **overkill** ● earmark an item for specific use: **reserve**

● make the best possible use of: **opti-mize**

useful ● very useful thing: **godsend**
● useful in real circumstances: **prac-tical**

user ● *combining form*: **-ist** (*e.g.* motorist)

uterus ● *combining forms*: hyster(o)-, uter(o)- ● *adjective*: **uter-ine** ● within the uterus: **intrauterine**
● neck of the uterus: **cervix** ● en-trance to the cervix: **os** ● uterine organ nourishing the fetus: **placenta**
● attachment of the egg to the uterus wall: **implantation** ● mucous mem-brane lining the uterus: **endometrium**

● inflammation of the uterus: **metritis**
● periodic uterine bleeding: **menstru-ation, period** ● abnormal uterine bleeding: **metrorrhagia** ● diagnostic sampling of fluid from a pregnant uterus: **amniocentesis** ● specimen taken from the cervix to detect cancer: **cervical smear** ● vacuuming the uterus as a means of abortion: **va-cuum aspiration** ● surgical scraping of the uterus: **dilatation and curet-tage** ● surgical removal of the uterus: **hysterectomy** ● hormone stimulating uterine preparation for pregnancy: **progesterone** ● hormone stimulating uterine contractions and milk secretion: **oxytocin**

Vv

vaccine ●supplementary dose of vaccine: **booster** ●treat with vaccine: **inoculate, vaccinate**

vacuum ●denoting a barometer using a vacuum box to measure atmospheric pressure: **aneroid**

vagina ●*combining form*: **colp-** ●sensitive area at the top of the vagina: **clitoris** ●sensitive area inside the vagina: **G spot** ●area surrounding the outer end of the vagina: **vulva** ●membrane partially blocking the entrance of a virgin's vagina: **hymen** ●painful spasmodic contraction of the vagina: **vaginismus** ●inflammation of the vagina: **vaginitis** ●infection of the vagina causing white patches and severe itching: **thrush** ●whitish discharge from the vagina: **leucorrhoea, vaginosis** ●vaginal discharge at the onset of labour or menstruation: **show** ●vaginal ulcer: **enanthema** ●medical examination of the vagina: **colposcopy** ●vaginal plug absorbing menstrual blood: **tampon** ●device inserted in the vagina: **pessary** ●solid medication inserted to dissolve in the vagina: **pessary, suppository** ●surgical cutting of the vagina to ease childbirth: **episiotomy** ●excision of the clitoris and stitching together of the vulva: **infibulation**

vagrant ●vagrant who searches beaches for objects of value: **beachcomber**

vague ●vague and unworldly: **fey** ●vague feeling of unease: **malaise**

valid ●make valid: **ratify** ●end of validity: **expiry**

valley ●valley in northern England: **dale** ●valley in Scotland or Ireland:

glen ●valley in Wales: **cwm** ●steep valley in northern England: **ghyll** ●narrow valley with steep sides: **rift valley** ●deep river gorge: **canyon, ravine** ●mountain valley: **gorge** ●short valley in southern England: **combe** ●steep narrow valley in Dorset or the Isle of Wight: **chine** ●steep narrow valley in northern England: **clough** ●steep narrow valley in North America: **gulch** ●narrow gorge or pass: **defile** ●wooded valley: **dene** ●small wooded valley: **dell**

value ●value stated on an item of currency: **face value** ●item's value in an owner's accounts: **book value** ●item's value if sold: **market value, street value** ●cost to replace an item: **replacement value** ●increase in value: **appreciation** ●decrease in value: **depreciation** ●loss of value due to wear and tear: **depreciation** ●estimation of an item's value: **valuation** ●assign a value to: **valorize** ●former system defining a currency's value in terms of gold: **gold standard** ●amount by which the value of an item is increased at each stage in its production: **value added** ●reduce the nominal value of stock held: **write down** ●proportionate to value: **ad valorem**

value added tax ●denoting liable items that are not in fact taxed: **zero-rated**

valve ●air valve on a carburettor: **choke** ●automatic water refill valve: **ballcock** ●externally operated valve regulating flow through a pipe: **stopcock** ●valve preventing reverse flow: **check valve**

variety ●variety of plant or animal developed by breeding: **strain**

varnish ●hard black or coloured varnish: **japan** ●clear natural varnish: **lacquer** ●very hard varnish: **yacht varnish** ●hard resin used to make varnish: **rosin** ●resin flakes used to make varnish: **shellac** ●oil used in mixing varnish: **turpentine**

vase ●tall vase with a stem and base: **urn**

Vatican ●Vatican agreement with another state: **concordat** ▸*see also* **pope**

vault ●rounded roofing vault: **dome** ●vault forming a half cylinder: **barrel vault** ●pair of intersecting barrel-vaults: **groin vault** ●ornament covering converging vaulting: **boss** ●short vaulting rib: **lierne**

veal ●constricted cage in which calves are reared for veal: **crate**

vegetable ●fibrous element in vegetables: **roughage** ●aperitif of mixed raw vegetables: **crudités** ●cream of liquidized vegetables: **purée** ●vegetables minced for stuffing: **forcemeat** ●dish of mixed chopped vegetables: **macédoine** ●dish of mixed cold vegetables: **salad** ●dish of mixed fried vegetables: **ratatouille** ●garnish of mixed vegetables: **jardinière** ●dish of sliced vegetables cooked in milk: **dauphinois** ●sautéed chopped vegetables: **mirepoix** ●disease caused by lack of fresh fruit and vegetables: **scurvy**

vegetarian ●strict vegetarian who avoids all animal products: **vegan** ●vegetarian also consuming milk products: **lacto-vegetarian** ●person consuming eggs, milk, and vegetables: **lacto-ovo-vegetarian**

vehicle ●vehicle that can operate on land or water: **amphibian** ●amphibian travelling on a cushion of air: **hovercraft** ●vehicle with a flat load-carrying area: **flatbed** ●small vehicle or cart: **float** ●unpowered vehicle towed by another: **trailer** ●light Asian vehicle drawn by one or more persons: **rickshaw** ●group of vehicles travelling together: **convoy** ●vehicle's base frame: **chassis** ●vehicle's outer shell: **body, bodywork, coachwork** ●outer structure added to improve aerodynamics: **fairing** ●springs etc. supporting a vehicle: **suspension** ●distance between a vehicle's front and rear axles: **wheelbase** ●axle wheel-mounting: **hub** ●alignment of a vehicle's wheels: **tracking** ●decorative cover for wheel nuts: **hub cap** ●vehicle part projecting over a wheel: **wing** ●partial vacuum in the wake of a moving vehicle: **slipstream** ●distance a vehicle can travel without refuelling: **range** ●list of passengers or parcels carried on a vehicle: **waybill** ●vehicle's intrinsic weight: **dead load** ●weight of people or goods in a vehicle: **live load** ●weighing apparatus for vehicles: **weighbridge** ●complete turn of a vehicle in a confined space by moving backwards and forwards: **three-point turn** ●complete turn of a vehicle in a single arc: **U-turn** ●device immobilizing an illegally parked vehicle: **wheel clamp**

veil ●Muslim woman's veil: **yashmak**

Velcro ●sport of jumping at a Velcro wall in a Velcro suit: **barfly jumping**

venereal disease ●disease with inflammatory discharge from the urethra or vagina: **gonorrhoea** ●disease attacking the bones, muscles, and brain: **syphilis** ●disease with painful genital blisters: **genital herpes** ●painless genital ulcer: **chancre**

Venice ●former ruler of Venice: **Doge** ●small Venetian passenger boat: **gondola** ●operator of this: **gondolier** ●song of Venetian gondoliers: **barcarole** ●Venetian water bus: **vaporetto**

ventriloquist ●ventriloquist's doll: **dummy**

Venus ●*Greek name*: **Aphrodite**

verb ●recite the forms of an inflecting verb: **conjugate** ●denoting a verb taking a direct object: **transitive** ●denoting a verb not taking a direct object: **intransitive**

verdict ●verdict agreed by all jurors: **unanimous verdict** ●verdict agreed by all but one or two jurors: **majority verdict** ●verdict that the accused is not guilty: **acquittal** ●jury's comment added to its verdict: **rider** ●denoting a verdict against the weight of evidence: **perverse** ●denoting a verdict reached on unreliable evidence: **unsafe, unsatisfactory** ●denoting a verdict reached without a jury: **summary** ●coroner's jury verdict on a suspicious death: **open verdict** ●annul a legal decision: **overturn, set aside**

vermin ●rid of vermin: **disinfest**

vermouth ●dry vermouth: **French vermouth** ●sweet vermouth: **Italian vermouth**

verse ●easily memorable verse: **jingle** ●verse that rhymes but does not scan: **doggerel** ●metrical but unrhymed verse: **blank verse** ●verse without rhyme or rhythm: **free verse** ●rhythmic pattern of a piece of verse: **metre, prosody** ●metrical analysis of verse: **scansion** ●metrical scheme imitating normal speech: **sprung rhythm** ●metrical unit in versification: **foot** ●verse-line of five feet: **pentameter** ●verse-line of six feet: **hexameter** ●verse-line of seven feet: **heptameter** ●verse-line of eleven syllables: **hendecasyllable** ●central pause in a line of verse: **caesura** ●half a line of verse: **hemistich** ●four-line stanza: **quatrain** ●matched pair of verse lines: **couplet, distich** ●group of three rhyming lines: **tercet** ●group of four verse lines: **tetrastich** ●group of verse lines forming a metrical unit: **stanza, strophe, verse** ●style of rhyme with several repeated syllables: **echo verse** ●continuation of the sense beyond the line-end: **enjambement** ●denoting verse having a pause at each line-end: **end-stopped** ●stress in a line of verse: **ictus** ●theory and practice of versification: **prosody** ▶*see also* **poem, rhyme**

vertical ●weighted line establishing verticality: **plumb line** ●weight on a plumb line: **bob, plumb, plumb bob, plummet**

vestments ●small square liturgical hat worn by RC clergy: **biretta** ●skullcap worn by RC clergy: **zucchetto** ●strips of white cloth worn at the neck: **Geneva bands** ●woollen shoulder vestment worn by the pope and RC archbishops: **pallium** ●long garment of black or red cloth worn under other vestments: **cassock** ●hip-length vestment of white linen worn over a cassock: **cotta, surplice** ●bishop's long surplice: **rochet** ●thick white ankle-length vestment: **alb** ●linen neck-covering worn with the alb: **amice** ●cape-like Eucharistic over-vestment: **chasuble** ●over-vestment for bishops and deacons: **dalmatic** ●subdeacons' short over-vestment: **tunicle** ●vestment's embroidered ornament: **orphrey** ●bishop's pointed liturgical hat: **mitre** ●ribbon for this: **infula** (*pl.* infulae) ●bishop's hat: **mitre** ●bishop's staff: **crook, crozier, pastoral staff** ●long liturgical scarf: **stole** ●ornate processional cloak: **cope**

vibration ●strong vibration: **judder**

viceroy ●*adjective*: **viceregal** ●viceroy's wife, or female viceroy: **vicereine**

victory ●denoting a victory so costly as to be futile: **pyrrhic**

video ●video compiled from short clips from other videos: **scratch video** ●video colour substitution system: **chromakey** ●video display showing light text on a dark ground: **reverse video** ●showing of a video: **screening** ●person introducing and playing music videos on television: **video jockey** ●portable video camera and recorder: **camcorder** ●facility arresting the image: **freeze-frame** ●numbers on a video image indicating time of exposure etc.: **time code**

view ●place giving a good view: **vantage point** ●giving a wide view: **commanding** ●all-round view: **panorama** ●extensive view: **prospect** ●side view: **profile** ●apparent change of an object's position when viewed from different points: **parallax**

vigour ●stylish vigour: **elan** ●lack of vigour: **inanition**

Viking ●Viking warship: **longship, dragon ship**

village ●village whose inhabitants mostly work elsewhere: **dormitory** ●small village without a church: **hamlet** ●annual village festival: **feast** ●open grassy area in a village: **green**

vine ●cultivation of vines: **viticulture** ●place where vines are grown: **vineyard** ●insect killing vine leaves: **phylloxera**

vinegar ●*adjective*: **acetic**

violence ●situation bringing a high risk of violence: **flashpoint** ●wantonly violent: **vicious**

violin ●part holding the fingerboard: **neck** ●ornamental inlay on the back or belly: **purfle** ●screw on a violin bow: **nut** ▸*see also* **musical instrument**

virgin ●*astrological term*: **virgo** ●membrane partially blocking the entrance of a virgin's vagina: **hymen** ●virgin birth: **parthenogenesis**

virtual reality ●simulated sequence of aerial views: **fly-through** ●simulated sequence of ground-level views : **walk-through** ●simulation of physical attributes: **force feedback** ●apparent participation in distant events: **telepresence** ●person experiencing virtual reality: **cybernaut** ●device for manipulating virtual reality images: **dataglove**

virus ●virus found in the intestines: **enterovirus** ●virus living on bacteria: **bacteriophage** ●group of viruses causing respiratory infections or meningitis: **echoviruses** ●herpesvirus harmful to the newborn: **cytomegalovirus** ●herpesvirus causing glandular fever and certain cancers: **Epstein–Barr virus** ●hypothetical infectious particle postulated as the cause of bovine spongiform encephalitis: **virino** ●the body's hostile reaction to a harmful virus: **immune response** ●protein inhibiting a virus: **interferon** ●study of viruses: **virology**

visit ●day for public visits to an institution etc.: **open day** ●salesman's unsolicited visit: **cold call** ●visited by few: **secluded**

vocabulary ●*adjective*: **lexical** ●total vocabulary of a language: **lexis** ●vocabulary of a language or topic: **lexicon** ●vocabulary of a trade or profession: **terminology**

voice ●*adjective*: **vocal** ●throat membrane folds making voice sounds: **vocal cords** ●muscular passage containing the vocal cords: **larynx, voice box** ●inflammation of the vocal cords or voice box: **laryngitis** ●notes a particular voice can sing: **compass, range** ●section of a voice's range: **register** ●voice's higher register: **head voice** ●voice's lower register: **chest voice** ●unnaturally high voice obtained by constricting the vocal chords: **falsetto** ●pitch range of a voice: **compass, gamut, tessitura**

● denoting a light singing voice: **lyric**
● denoting a strong singing voice: **dramatic, heroic** ● vocalization intermediate between speech and song: **Sprechgesang, Sprechstimme**
● variation of the speaking voice: **inflection, intonation, lilt, modulation** ● in a soft voice: **sotto voce** ● lack of vocal variation: **monotone** ● entertainer seeming to make his or her voice come from a dummy: **ventriloquist** ● funnel-shaped device amplifying the voice: **megaphone** ▸ *see also* **singer**

volcano ● volcano's pointed peak: **cone** ● volcano's hollow mouth: **crater** ● volcanic vent for sulphurous gases: **fumarole** ● volcanic vent for sulphurous gases, steam, and hot mud: **solfatara** ● large volcanic crater: **caldera** ● volcano's ejection of lava etc.: **eruption** ● volcanic phenomena: **volcanism** ● denoting a volcano that is erupting, or has done so within historical times: **active** ● denoting a volcano that is expected to erupt again, though it has not done so within historical times: **dormant** ● denoting a volcano that is not expected to erupt again: **extinct** ● molten material ejected by a volcano: **lava** ● rock fragments ejected by a volcano: **tephra** ● solidified lava in a volcano's top: **plug** ● rock formed by solidifying lava froth: **pumice** ● exceptionally large ocean wave caused by an earthquake or volcanic eruption: **tidal wave, tsunami** ● study of volcanoes: **volcanology, vulcanology**

vomit ● desire to vomit: **nausea** ● drug inducing vomiting: **emetic** ● drug preventing vomiting: **antiemetic**

voodoo ● voodoo god: **loa** (*pl.* same) ● voodoo charm: **gris-gris** (*pl.* same)

vote ● national vote on an important question: **plebiscite, referendum** ● parliamentary vote: **division** ● informal vote taken to gauge opinion:
straw poll ● vote assessed from the volume of shouts for and against: **voice vote** ● overwhelming vocal support: **acclamation** ● (of a proposal) receive a majority vote: **be carried** ● largest share of the votes cast: **majority, simple majority** ● share containing more than half the votes cast: **absolute majority** ● overwhelming majority of votes: **landslide** ● denoting a decision supported by all votes cast: **unanimous** ● occasion or place of voting: **poll** ● right to vote: **suffrage, franchise** ● right of all to vote: **universal suffrage** ● person having the right to vote: **elector** ● person empowered to vote for another: **proxy** ● list of electors: **electoral roll** ● subgroup of electors acting for the larger body: **electoral college** ● elector not giving regular support to any party: **floating voter** ● building used for voting: **polling station** ● number of votes cast: **poll** ● chairman's vote to decide a tied poll: **casting vote** ● positive vote in the House of Commons: **aye** ● positive vote in the House of Lords: **content** ● positive vote in a church or university assembly: **placet** ● negative vote in the House of Commons: **no** ● negative vote in the House of Lords: **noncontent** ● negative vote in a church or university assembly: **non placet** ● vote given to exclude a candidate: **blackball** ● vote proportional in power to the number of persons its caster represents: **block vote** ● system where each voter has as many votes as there are candidates: **cumulative voting** ● voting strategy aimed at defeating an otherwise strong candidate or party: **tactical voting** ● mark a voting paper incorrectly: **spoil** ● give the right to vote: **enfranchise** ● deliberately refrain from voting: **abstain** ● study of voting patterns: **psephology** ▸ *see also* **election, parliament**

vow ● done in fulfilment of a vow: **vo-tive** ● person vowed to religious service: **votary** ● offering made to fulfil a vow: **ex-voto**

vowel ● vowel with a single consistent sound: **monophthong** ● vowel starting with one sound that merges into another: **diphthong** ● vowel with three successive intermerged sounds:

triphthong ● indeterminate vowel sound: **schwa**

voyage ● pleasure voyage: **cruise**

Vulcan ● *Greek name*: **Hephaestus**

vulva ● Hindu vulva symbol representing divine creativity: **yoni** ● outer folds of the vulva: **labia majora** ● its inner folds: **labia minora**

Ww

wage ● wage based on the number of items produced: **piecework** ● wage equality: **parity** ● benefit given in addition to a money wage: **fringe benefit** ● point on a wage scale: **grade, step** ● working hours paid at the normal rate: **plain time** ● improved rate of pay for work done beyond standard hours: **overtime** ● extra pay offsetting high regional living costs: **weighting** ● employer's deduction from wages: **stoppage** ● note detailing pay and deductions: **payslip** ● wage before deduction of tax and stoppages: **gross wage** ● wage after deduction of tax and stoppages: **net wage, take-home pay** ● wage increase awarded on change of job grade: **increment** ● tendency for actual wages to outstrip negotiated levels, due to overtime etc.: **wage drift** ● system linking wage rises to price rises: **indexation** ● denoting such wages: **index-linked** ● person whose wages support others in a household: **breadwinner** ● list of employees and their wages: **payroll**

wagon ● wagon for condemned prisoners in the French Revolution: **tumbril**

waiter ● head waiter: **maître d'hôtel** (*pl.* maîtres d'hôtel) ● wine waiter: **sommelier** ● waiter clearing used dishes: **débarrasseur**

wake ● signal for waking: **reveille**

walk ● leisurely walk: **saunter** ● pleasure walk: **ramble** ● walk aimlessly: **wander** ● walk arrogantly: **strut, swagger** ● walk dragging the feet: **shuffle** ● walk furtively: **sidle** ● walk through water: **paddle, wade** ● force someone to walk forward while pinning their arms from behind: **frogmarch**

walking ● *combining form*: **-grade** ● manner of walking: **gait** ● walking with arms pinned behind: **frogmarch** ● walking as if lame: **hobbling** ● denoting an animal that walks on the soles of its feet: **plantigrade** ● denoting an animal that walks on its toes: **digitigrade**

walking stick ● walking stick with a handle that makes a seat: **shooting stick** ● walking stick's metal tip: **ferrule**

wall ● *adjectives*: **mural** (*of a building*), **parietal** (*in the body*) ● wall of a body cavity: **paries** ● wall linking a castle's towers: **curtain wall** ● outer wall of a castle: **bailey** ● containing wall: **retainer, retaining wall, revetment** ● defensive wall: **bulwark** ● defensive wall of wooden stakes: **stockade** ● flimsy interior wall: **partition** ● building's wall of two layers with a gap between: **cavity wall** ● sunken perimeter wall: **ha-ha** ● low protective wall: **parapet** ● watertight wall dividing the interior of a ship: **bulkhead** ● wall supporting structures above it: **bearing wall, load-bearing wall** ● walling of interwoven sticks covered with mud or clay: **wattle and daub** ● wall's external angle: **quoin** ● continuation of a wall at right angles: **return** ● wall's side surface at a door or window: **reveal** ● angled reveal: **embrasure** ● section of wall between openings: **pier** ● clay etc. used to make a wall: **daub** ● layer of cement etc. on a wall surface: **pargeting, rendering** ● cement rendering with pebbles: **pebble-dash** ● coat a wall with planking: **clad** ● cladding with each plank overlapping that below: **shiplap** ● mortar between bricks in a wall: **pointing** ● denoting a wall built without mortar: **dry, dry-stone** ● undressed stone used as a wall-filler: **rubble** ● brick or stone laid at right angles to a wall: **header** ● brick or stone laid parallel to a wall: **stretcher** ● horizontal decorative band of bricks or masonry: **string course** ● stone set at the top of a wall: **capstone, coping stone** ● course of rounded bricks at the top of a wall: **coping** ● decorative parapet atop a wall: **castellation, crenellation** ● row of spikes or broken glass set on a wall's top: **cheval-de-frise** ● projecting bricks at the end of a wall, allowing for its continuation: **toothing** ● waterproof layer near the foot of a wall: **damp course, damp-proof course** ● lowest part of a wall: **footings, foundations** ● beam or plate distributing weight onto a wall: **template** ● projecting support for a wall: **buttress** ● buttress shaped like half an arch: **flying buttress** ● prop up a wall with heavy timbers etc.: **shore up** ● heavy metal ball swung at a wall to demolish it: **wrecking ball** ● ornamental wall tablet: **plaque** ● shallow recess in a wall: **niche** ● scribblings on a wall: **graffiti** ● recess in a wall: **alcove, niche** ● groove cut into a wall for piping etc.: **chase** ● gun aperture in a wall: **port** ● ornamental wooden strip for picture hooks: **picture rail** ● wall covering of small pieces of stone etc. arranged to make pictures or patterns: **mosaic** ● lower part of an interior wall: **dado** ● wooden panelling covering the lower half of an interior wall: **wainscot, wainscoting** ● board at the base of an interior wall: **skirting board** ● vertical timber to which laths and plasterboard are nailed: **stud** ● thin strip of wood as a base for wall plaster: **lath**

wallpaper ● wallpaper made of uncoloured strong embossed paper: **Anaglypta™** ● wallpaper made of powdered wool or cloth: **flock paper** ● person putting up wallpaper: **paper-hanger**

walrus ● walrus's long projecting tooth: **tusk**

wandering ● wandering aimlessly: **erratic, meandering, roaming, roving** ● wandering in search of adventure: **errant** ● wandering in search of trade: **itinerant** ● homeless wanderer: **tramp, vagabond, vagrant**

war ● *adjective*: **martial** ● war pursued without restraint: **total war** ● war involving fighting: **action, hot war, shooting war** ● state of hostility without fighting: **cold war** ● war between gods: **theomachy** ● war between many important nations: **world war** ● denoting a war between citizens of one state: **civil, internecine** ● denoting a war damaging to both sides: **internecine** ● denoting a war involving the spreading of germs: **chemical** ● denoting a war waged without nuclear weapons: **conventional, limited** ● stage in a war with little belligerent activity: **phoney war, sitzkrieg** ● stage in a war when nuclear weapons might be employed: **nuclear threshold** ● person favouring recourse to war: **hawk, warmonger** ● belligerent patriot: **jingoist** ● person opposing recourse to war: **dove** ● person refusing to participate in war: **pacifist** ● denoting a state not entering a war: **neutral** ● denoting a place undefended in wartime: **open** ● announce the start of hostilities: **declare war** ● person or state engaged in war: **combatant** ● nation or person engaged in warfare: **belligerent** ● group of states cooperating in war: **allies** ● put forces on a war footing: **mobilize** ● training of civilians for home defence: **civil defence** ● arrangements for mutual support against aggressors: **collective security** ● unprovoked attack: **aggression** ● response to aggression: **counterattack, counteroffensive** ● making friends with the enemy: **fraternization** ● traitorous cooperation with the enemy: **collaboration** ● investigation of a hostile area: **reconnaissance** ● position forces for war: **deploy** ● battle area: **front** ● ditch dug for battlefield shelter: **trench** ● foray into enemy territory: **mission, raid, sortie** ● denoting forces on one's own side: **friendly** ● accidental killing of one's own forces: **fratricide, friendly fire** ● incidental destruction of civilians or their property: **collateral damage** ● proportion of fatalities on each side: **kill ratio** ● persons placed by a target to deter attack: **human shield** ● area not liable to attack: **safe area** ● belligerent's unethical act: **war crime** ● belligerent's right to use neutral property for payment: **angary** ● goods taken from a defeated enemy: **loot** ● nervous breakdown resultant from war experiences: **battle fatigue, combat fatigue, shell-shock** ● men killed in the Great War: **lost generation** ● wartime imprisonment of resident aliens: **internment** ● person forced by war to abandon his homeland: **displaced person, refugee** ● agreement to suspend hostilities for a stated period: **armistice, ceasefire, truce** ● payment demanded from a defeated adversary: **indemnity, reparation** ● simulated military conflict: **war game** ● war game played on maps: **kriegspiel** ● money freed for positive uses when military spending is curtailed: **peace dividend** ▸ *see also* **attack, battle, military, weapon**

ward ● ward for patients not staying in hospital overnight: **day ward** ● ward for patients with infectious or contagious diseases: **isolation ward** ● room off a ward, with a few beds: **side ward**

wardrobe ● antique wardrobe in an ornate style: **armoire**

warship ● large warship: **capital ship** ● largest warship: **battleship** ● heavy battleship with large guns: **dreadnought** ● smaller and faster warship: **cruiser** ● smaller and faster warship: **destroyer** ● smaller and faster warship: **frigate** ● admiral's ship: **flagship** ● small naval patrol boat: **vedette** ● warship with an aircraft runway: **aircraft carrier** ● warship's projecting gun platform: **sponson** ● warship's revolving armoured gun emplacement: **turret** ● common room for a warship's senior officers: **wardroom** ● common room for a warship's junior officers: **gunroom** ● German torpedo boat: **E-boat** ● privately owned armed ship licensed to attack enemy craft: **privateer** ● privateer's government licence: **letters of marque** ● merchant ship with hidden weapons: **Q-ship** ● simultaneous fire from all the guns on one side of a warship: **broadside** ● Viking warship: **longship, dragon ship** ● ancient Greek or Roman warship with several banks of oars: **galley** ● galley with three banks of oars: **trireme** ● galley's sharp point for piercing other ships: **ram** ▸ *see also* **submarine**

wart ● contagious wart on the sole of the foot: **verruca**

washing ● establishment where clothes are washed and ironed: **laundry** ● place with coin-operated washing machines: **launderette, washeteria** ● revolving part of a washing machine: **drum** ● washing machine with separate drums for washing and spin-drying: **twin-tub** ● machine pressing wet laundry: **mangle** ● alkaline washing solution: **lye** ● fluorescent substance added to washing powder: **optical brightener** ● clothes that have been, or need to be, washed: **laundry**

wasp •*adjective*: **vespine** •fertile female wasp: **queen** •sterile wasp performing basic tasks: **worker** •large kind of wasp: **hornet**

waste •liquid waste: **effluent** •remove impurities: **refine** •dump waste illegally: **fly-tip** •refilling of excavations with waste material: **landfill** •search through waste material for reusable items: **scavenge** •convert waste into reusable material: **recycle** •wasting away of an organ or tissue: **dystrophy** •wastefully extravagant: **prodigal, profligate** •waste recklessly: **squander** •preventing waste: **economical, efficient, frugal**

watch[1] •very accurate watch: **chronometer** •watch for timing races etc.: **stopwatch** •denoting a watch dial with moving hands: **analogue** •denoting a watch dial with a changing numerical display: **digital** •watch mechanism: **movement** •second hand moving round the main dial: **sweep second hand** •chain for a watch: **fob** •pocket for a watch: **fob** •pocket watch with an opaque cover over the face: **hunter** •pocket watch having a small window in this cover: **half-hunter** •set a watch to the same time as another: **synchronize** •watchmaker's magnifying glass: **loupe**

watch[2] •constant watch: **surveillance** •naval watch between midnight and 4 a.m.: **middle watch** •naval watch between 4 and 8 a.m.: **morning watch** •naval watch between 8 a.m. and 12.30 p.m.: **forenoon watch** •naval watch between 12.30 p.m. and 4 p.m.: **afternoon watch** •naval watch between 4 and 6 p.m.: **first dog watch** •naval watch between 6 and 8 p.m.: **last dog watch** •naval watch between 8 p.m. and midnight: **first watch** •person keeping watch: **lookout, observer** •keeping careful watch: **vigilant** •watch out for the teacher's approach: **keep cave**

water •*combining forms*: **aqu-, hydr-** •*adjectives*: **aquatic, aqueous** •water droplets appearing on surfaces as air cools: **condensation** •water droplets forming on grass overnight: **dew** •temperature at which this begins: **dew point** •water held in rock or soil: **groundwater** •water from a melting glacier: **meltwater** •salty water: **brine** •denoting the taste of such water: **brackish** •water scented by rose petals: **rose water** •waste water from washing: **grey water** •waste water etc. from lavatories: **black water** •flow of water: **current** •rush of water: **flash** •circular movement of water: **eddy** •denoting water containing no natural salt: **fresh** •denoting static water: **stagnant** •denoting water lathering easily: **soft** •denoting water lathering with difficulty: **hard** •skim over water: **plane, aquaplane** •lie about in mud or water: **wallow** •fetch water from a source: **draw** •search for water with a twitching rod: **divine, dowse** •person doing this: **dowser, water diviner** •find the depth of water: **sound** •supply water for agricultural purposes: **irrigate** •terminate a water supply: **cut off** •rid of water: **drain** •operated by water: **hydraulic** •preventing the passage of water: **watertight** •mixing with water: **hydrophilic** •repelling water: **hydrophobic** •person installing and repairing water piping and equipment: **plumber** •water wheel with buckets: **noria** •deposit formed by hard water: **fur** •white deposit from evaporated hard water: **scale** •volume of water normally filling the space occupied by a floating object: **displacement** •ground level at which water is always present: **water level, water table** •level normally reached by water and the mark it leaves: **waterline** ●saturated with water: **waterlogged** ●temporary vertical water pipe with a tap: **standpipe** ●pipe or channel for water: **conduit** ●channel for water to escape: **sluice, sluiceway** ●sliding gate controlling a flow of water: **sluice, sluice gate** ●water tunnel under a road or railway: **culvert** ●perforated device producing a water spray: **rose** ●crowd-control device ejecting a powerful jet of water: **water cannon** ●large container heating water for drinks: **urn** ●desert place with water: **oasis** ●natural ridge from each side of which water drains into a different river system: **watershed** ●region supplying a reservoir etc. with water: **catchment area** ●decrease in a reservoir's water stocks: **drawdown** ●weighted line finding the depth of water: **plumb line** ●weight on a plumb line: **bob, plumb, plumb bob, plummet** ●device determining water depth by sound waves: **echo sounder** ●hard fruitskin used as a water container: **gourd** ●water barrel: **butt** ●small organisms floating in water: **plankton** ●small organisms swimming in water: **nekton** ●bridge carrying water across a valley: **aqueduct** ●large lake for water supply: **reservoir** ●water-supply for a fire hose: **hydrant** ●series of processes by which water circulates between sea, air, and land: **water cycle** ●medical treatment by water: **hydropathy, hydrotherapy** ●irrational fear of water: **hydrophobia** ●compound added to drinking water to arrest tooth decay: **fluoride** ●chemical decomposition by water: **hydrolysis** ●loss or removal of water: **dehydration**

water-carrier ●*astrological term*: **aquarius**

waterfall ●waterfall in northern England: **force**

water mill ●mill driven by tidal flow: **tide mill**

waterproof ●waterproof layer in a wall: **damp course** ●seal with waterproof material: **caulk**

wave ●large wave: **sea** ●exceptionally large ocean wave caused by an earthquake or volcano: **tidal wave, tsunami** ●long curving wave: **comber** ●long wave moving steadily shorewards: **roller** ●wave that curls over and dissolves into foam: **breaker** ●slow waves that do not break: **swell** ●high wave running up a river at high tide: **bore** ●wave's foamy top: **crest** ●spray blown from wave tops: **spindrift** ●low water between two waves: **trough** ●wavelike effect produced by stadium crowd movements: **Mexican wave**

way ●*combining form*: **-wise** (*e.g.* otherwise) ●way a thing operates: **mode**

wax ●*combining form*: **cero-** ●wax mixture for brass-rubbing: **heelball** ●method of engraving using a waxed plate: **cerography**

weak ●weak spot: **Achilles' heel** ●acute state of weakness caused by injury, emotional stress, etc.: **shock** ●minor weakness of character: **foible** ●weak and unsteady: **groggy** ●feeble and effeminate: **namby-pamby** ●become weak: **languish** ●become weak and emaciated: **waste away**

wealth ●general wealth: **affluence, prosperity** ●wealth or its pursuit seen as a corrupting influence: **Mammon, materialism** ●source of wealth: **bonanza, golden goose** ●display of wealth by an expensive lifestyle: **conspicuous consumption** ●fabulous place of great wealth: **El Dorado, Golconda** ●wealthy and influential person: **plutocrat** ●tasteless person who has recently become wealthy: **nouveau riche, parvenu, upstart** ●wealthy wastrel: **rake** ●total money and property owned by a dead person: **estate** ● official examination of financial circumstances: **means test**

weapon ● weapons generally: **armaments** ● weapons worn at a person's side: **side arms** ● weapon's handle: **helve** ● denoting an attack weapon: **offensive** ● denoting weapons used against enemy forces in battle: **tactical** ● denoting weapons used over a wider area of hostilities: **theatre** ● denoting weapons used against enemy home targets: **strategic** ● denoting weapons harming persons rather than buildings: **antipersonnel** ● denoting weapons designed to pierce armour: **antitank** ● blade fixed to a rifle muzzle: **bayonet** ● metal guard over the knuckles: **knuckleduster** ● combined spear and battleaxe: **halberd** ● forked stick with elastic to hurl stones: **catapult, slingshot** ● long stout stick: **quarterstaff** ● short thick stick: **cudgel** ● strap to hurl stones: **sling** ● short truncheon: **life preserver** ● tube down which a dart is blown: **blowpipe** ● competitive development and stockpiling of weapons: **arms race** ● weapons stockpiling to discourage aggressors: **deterrence** ● weapon store: **armoury, arsenal** ● place where weapons are made: **arsenal** ● reduction in a state's weaponry: **disarmament** ● disarmament by international agreement: **arms control**

wear ● gradual wearing down: **attrition, erosion** ● wear down by surface scraping: **scuff**

weather ● state of the weather: **conditions** ● fine weather in late autumn: **Indian summer, St Luke's summer** ● period of unusually hot weather: **heatwave** ● denoting weather appropriate to the time of year: **seasonable** ● denoting weather without extremes: **mild** ● denoting hot and humid weather: **sultry** ● occasional Pacific weather phenomenon:

El Niño ● trapping of the sun's warmth in the lower atmosphere: **greenhouse effect** ● gradual increase in worldwide temperatures: **global warming** ● absence of protection from bad weather: **exposure** ● low-pressure weather system: **cyclone, low** ● high-pressure weather system: **anticyclone, high** ● elongated region of high pressure: **ridge** ● elongated region of low pressure: **trough** ● area of pressure lower than those around it: **depression** ● unstable atmospheric pressure: **turbulence** ● proportion of moisture present in the atmosphere: **humidity** ● forward edge of an advancing mass of warm or cold air: **front** ● science of weather forecasting: **meteorology** ● line on a weather map linking places with the same atmospheric pressure: **isobar** ● line on a weather map linking places with the same temperature: **isotherm** ● balloon-borne radio transmitter sending weather information: **radiosonde**

weaving ● weaving machine: **loom** ● threads running lengthways in weaving: **weft, woof** ● threads running crossways in weaving: **warp** ● cylinder holding a weaver's thread: **bobbin** ● double-ended bobbin used on a mechanical loom: **shuttle** ● weaver's comb separating threads: **reed** ● threads left in the loom after weaving: **thrum**

wedge ● *adjective*: **cuneate** ● denoting ancient wedge-shaped writing: **cuneiform** ● wedge immobilizing a wheel, or supporting a beached boat: **chock**

week ● *adjective*: **hebdomadal**

weight ● falling weight of a piledriving machine: **ram** ● weighing apparatus with a long calibrated arm: **steelyard** ● weighing apparatus for vehicles: **weighbridge** ● overall weight: **gross weight** ● weight without packaging: **net weight** ● insufficient weight: **short weight** ● vehicle's unladen weight: **dead load, tare weight** ● weight of a vehicle's burden: **live load**

weightlifting ● long metal bar on which the weights are placed: **barbell** ● short bar with weights at each end: **dumb-bell** ● lift using the hands and forearms only: **curl** ● quick lift by straightening arms and legs: **jerk** ● quick lift from the floor to over the head: **snatch** ● lift made from a standing position: **dead lift**

weld ● weld made at a number of points: **spot weld**

well[1] ● *combining form*: **eu-** (*e.g.* euphoria)

well[2] ● well in which the water rises by natural pressure through a borehole: **artesian well** ▸ *see also* **oil well**

Welsh ● *adjectives*: Cambrian, Cymric ● Welsh round wickerwork boat: **coracle** ● Welsh valley: **cwm** ● Welsh competition for poets and musicians: **eisteddfod** (*pl.* eisteddfods *or* eisteddfoddau) ● Welsh language: **Cymric** ● Welsh-speakers' term for Wales: **Cymru** ● Welsh gypsies' secret language: **Shelta** ● Welsh spiced mead: **metheglin** ● Welsh megalithic tomb: **cromlech, dolmen** ● Welsh Nationalist Party: **Plaid Cymru** ● Welsh poet: **bard** ● council of Welsh bards: **Gorsedd** ● Welsh poetry improvised to a traditional harp melody: **penillion**

west ● *adjective*: **occidental**

West Indian ● West Indian backward-bending dance: **limbo** ● West Indian magic: **obeah, voodoo** ● West Indian popular music with a strong secondary beat: **reggae** ● West Indian song improvised on a topical theme: **calypso**

wet ● wet and soft: **soggy** ● wet through: **sodden, sopping** ● make thoroughly wet: **soak**

wetland ● denoting wetlands adjacent to watercourses: **riparian**

whale ● whale fat: **blubber** ● waxy substances found in certain whales: **ambergris, spermaceti** ● spear shot at whales: **harpoon**

wheat ● kind of wheat used for pasta: **durum** ● whole grains of wheat including the husk: **wholewheat** ● wheat husk: **chaff** ● wheat embryos used as food: **wheatgerm** ● flour made from wheat with some of the germ removed: **wheatmeal**

wheel ● heavy wheel used as a regulator: **flywheel** ● powered wheel of a locomotive: **driving wheel** ● unpowered wheel of a locomotive: **trailing wheel** ● spinning self-balancing wheel: **gyroscope** ● small wheel fixed to furniture: **castor** ● wheel having a grooved rim: **pulley** ● toothed wheel: **sprocket, spur wheel** ● large vertical wheel carrying passengers at fairground: **Ferris wheel** ● wheel shaft: **axle** ● central part of a wheel: **hub, nave** ● outer edge of a wheel: **rim** ● bar or rod connecting the hub and rim: **spoke** ● outer rim of a spoked wheel: **felloe** ● projecting point on a wheel: **sprocket, tooth** ● projecting rim on wheels of railway vehicles: **flange** ● continuous articulated metal band round the wheels of a heavy vehicle: **track** ● tool for adjusting wheel nuts: **wheel brace** ● alignment of a vehicle's wheels: **tracking** ● wedge preventing a wheel moving: **chock**

whip ● whip with knotted cords: **cat-o'-nine-tails** ● rhinoceros-hide whip: **sjambok** ● whip's flexible part: **lash** ● whip's handle: **stock** ● person whipping himself or others: **flagellant**

whirl ●whirling column of air: **tornado, whirlwind** ●whirling dervish: **sufi** ●whirling mass: **vortex** ●whirling water: **whirlpool**

whirlwind ●small land whirlwind: **dust devil** ●rotating column of water formed by a whirlwind: **waterspout**

whisky ●unblended whisky: **single malt**

whistle ●shrill whistle expressing derision: **catcall** ●whistle expressing sexual admiration: **wolf whistle** ●cord holding a whistle: **lanyard**

white ●*combining forms*: **leuc-, leuk(o)-** (*e.g.* leukaemia) ●greyish or yellowish white: **off-white** ●white blood cell: **leucocyte** ●white-skinned person: **Caucasian** ●person or animal having white skin and hair due to a pigment defect: **albino**

whole ●*combining form*: **holo-** (*e.g.* holograph) ●unite to form a whole: **coalesce** ●forming a consistent whole: **coherent**

wicked ●notably wicked: **infamous**

widow ●widow deriving a title or property from her late husband: **dowager** ●black clothes worn by a widow in mourning: **widow's weeds** ●property left to a widow by her late husband's will: **dower, jointure** ●widow's house so left: **dower house**

wife ●*adjective*: **uxorial** ●wife who stays at home to care for the house and children: **housewife** ●subservient behaviour towards one's wife: **uxoriousness** ●killing a wife: **uxoricide**

wig ●small wig covering a bald spot: **toupee** ●genital wig: **merkin**

will[1] ●*adjectives*: **volitional, voluntary** ●willpower, or its exercise: **volition** ●done of free will: **voluntary** ●whether one wishes it or not: **willy-nilly, volens nolens**

will[2] ●*adjective*: **testamentary** ●person making a will: **testator** ●woman making a will: **testatrix** (*pl.* testatrices) ●not having made a will: **intestate** ●denoting a verbal will: **nuncupative** ●carry out the terms of a will: **execute** ●person appointed to do this: **executor** (*fem.* executrix), **personal representative** ●thing given in a will: **legacy** ●transfer of assets by will: **disposition** ●give personal property in a will: **bequeath** ●give real estate in a will: **devise** ●give funding in a will: **endow** ●estate settled upon the testator's widow: **jointure** ●gift made in a will: **bequest, legacy** ●supplement to a will: **codicil** ●person receiving a gift from a will: **beneficiary** ●legal authentication of a will: **probate** ●estate left when all charges and bequests have been paid: **residue** ●in closest possible fulfilment of testamentary intentions: **cy-pres**

willow ●willow cropped for basket-making: **osier** ●flower of the willow tree: **catkin** ●flexible willow-shoot: **withy** ●willow twigs plaited to make furniture: **wicker, wickerwork**

win ●win by the length of a horse, boat, etc.: **length** ●horserace win by the length of the horse's head: **head** ●horserace win by less than a horse's head's length: **short head** ●denoting a win of several lengths: **easy**

Winchester ●member of Winchester College: **Wykehamist**

wind ●*combining form*: **anemo-** ●wind blowing from in front: **headwind** ●wind blowing from behind: **tailwind** ●wind blowing landwards: **sea breeze** ●denoting a wind blowing away from the land: **offshore** ●small whirlwind: **dust devil** ●storm with violent winds: **hurricane** ●violent rotating wind: **tornado, whirlwind** ●sudden wind with driving rain: **squall** ●brief burst of wind: **gust** ●constant wind in a certain direction: **trade wind** ●warm wind blowing north off the Alps: **föhn** ●equatorial region of the Atlantic Ocean with uncertain winds: **doldrums** ●hot Egyptian wind: **khamsin** ●westerly air current encircling the globe: **jet stream** ●seasonal wind in India: **monsoon** ●hot wind blowing north across the Mediterranean: **sirocco** ●Mediterranean dry northwesterly wind: **meltemi** ●cold wind blowing down the Rhone: **mistral** ●sound of the wind in trees: **sough** ●against the wind: **upwind** ●with the wind: **downwind** ●revolving pointer showing wind direction: **weathercock, weathervane** ●airfield flexible cylinder showing wind direction and force: **drogue, sleeve, windsock** ●instrument for measuring wind speed: **anemometer** ●instrument for measuring and recording wind speed: **anemograph** ●scale for wind velocities: **Beaufort scale** ●test area where wind effects may be simulated and studied: **wind tunnel** ●cooling effect of wind: **chill factor, wind chill** ●shelter from the wind: **lee** ●thing giving shelter from the wind: **windbreak** ●fruit blown down by the wind: **windfall** ●windblown spray, sand, etc.: **spindrift** ●reddening of the skin from exposure to wind: **windburn** ●oil lamp for high winds: **hurricane lamp** ●small pieces of metal etc. suspended to tinkle in the breeze: **wind chimes** ●set of large wind-driven vanes generating electricity: **wind farm** ●build-up of gas in the digestive tract causing the breaking of wind: **flatulence**

windmill ●windmill sail: **sweep**

window ●*adjective*: **fenestral** ●window made of vertically sliding sections: **sash window** ●side-hinged window: **casement** ●circular window: **oculus, oeil-de-beuf** ●circular window with radiating tracery: **rose window** ●corbelled bay window: **oriel, oriel window** ●large single-

pane window: **picture window** ●narrow window with a pointed top: **lancet** ●projecting window: **bay window, bow window** ●window in a roof or ceiling: **skylight** ●window projecting from a sloping roof: **dormer, dormer window** ●window in the side of a ship: **porthole** ●small window over a door etc.: **fanlight** ●spacecraft's window: **viewport** ●beam between door and fanlight: **transom** ●small pane above a main window: **top light** ●support across the top of a window: **lintel** ●window's sidepost: **jamb** ●vertical window bar: **mullion** ●horizontal window bar: **transom** ●slab at the foot of a window: **sill** ●frame holding window glass: **sash** ●glazing with two spaced panes of glass: **double glazing** ●paste fixing window glass: **putty** ●counterbalance to a sash window: **sash weight** ●small diamond-shaped pane of window-glass: **quarry** ●ornamental stonework subdividing a window: **tracery** ●inside face of a window frame: **scuncheon** ●wall's side surface beside a window: **reveal** ●angled reveal: **embrasure** ●window catch: **snib** ●solid inner or outer cover for a window: **shutter** ●installation of windows: **glazing** ●window cleaner's rubber scraper: **squeegee**

windpipe ●*combining form*: **trache-** ●inflammation of the windpipe: **tracheitis** ●surgical cutting of the windpipe: **tracheotomy**

windsurfing ●windsurfing board giving greater speed: **funboard**

wine ●*combining form*: **vin-** ●*adjective*: **vinous** ●spice and warm wine: **mull** ●cold spiced wine: **sangaree** ●wine for everyday use: **vin de table, vin du pays, vin ordinaire** ●wine flavoured with aromatic herbs: **vermouth** ●new wine: **primeur** ●wine from the first grape-pressing: **tête de cuvée** ●light pink wine: **rosé** ●fortified white wine: **sherry** ●fortified red dessert wines: **madeira, port** ●strong sweet wine: **malmsey** ●white wine with crème de cassis: **Kir** ●German dry white wine: **hock** ●German sparkling white wine: **Sekt** ●German wine made with late-picked grapes: **Spätlese** ●German wine made with selected late-picked grapes: **Auslese** ●German wine made from grapes picked with ice on them: **Eiswein** (*pl.* Eisweine *or* Eisweins) ●Greek resin-flavoured wine: **retsina** ●Italian sparkling white wine: **spumante** ●Portuguese wine drunk while new: **vinho verde** ●Spanish or Portuguese red wine: **tinto** ●denoting a wine that is almost dry: **off-dry** ●denoting medium-dry wine: **demisec** ●denoting a wine that is not sweet: **dry, sec** ●denoting sparkling wine: **pétillant, mousseux** ●denoting unsweetened sparkling wine: **brut** ●denoting slightly sparkling wine: **frizzante** ●denoting wine having a rich sweet taste: **luscious** ●denoting a mature and pleasing wine: **mellow** ●denoting a wine of high quality: **vintage** ●denoting wine spoilt by tannin from the cork: **corked** ●denoting wine at room temperature: **chambré** ●grape juice before or during fermentation: **must** ●wine's aroma: **nose** ●wine's becoming ready to drink: **maturation** ●wine's taste: **mouth** ●final taste of wine: **finish** ●sterilize wine by heat or irradiation: **pasteurize** ●cover for a wine bottle's cork: **capsule** ●spiral device for opening a wine bottle: **corkscrew** ●tartrate deposit left by maturing wine: **crust, tartar** ●wine sediment: **lees** ●wine expert: **oenologist, oenophile** ●gathering to evaluate various wines: **tasting** ●wine merchant: **vintner** ●wine waiter: **sommelier** ●restaurant's charge made for serving a customer's own wine: **corkage** ●official title of wine from a particular harvest or area: **designation** ●description

awarded to a French wine guaranteeing its orgin and method of production: **appellation contrôlée, appellation d'origine contrôlée** ●category of vineyards or wines in France: **cru** ●unmarked bottle for serving wine or water: **carafe, decanter** ●double-sized wine bottle: **magnum** ●wine bottle 4 times the normal size: **jeroboam** ●wine bottle 8 times normal size: **methuselah** ●wine bottle 16 times normal size: **balthazar** ●wine bottle 20 times normal size: **nebuchadnezzar** ●box containing a dozen bottles of wine: **case** ●wine barrel: **butt, cask** ●type or batch of wine: **cuvée** ●stock of wine: **cellar** ●shop selling wine: **vintner** ●study of wines: **oenology**

wing ●*combining form*: ptero- (*e.g.* pterodactyl) ●*adjective*: **alar** ●aircraft having a single set of wings: **monoplane** ●aircraft having two sets of wings: **biplane** ●aircraft's single triangular wing: **delta wing** ●main flight feather in a bird's wing: **primary feather** ●maximum distance across a pair of wings: **wingspan**

winner ●winner's ceremonial circuit of the sports ground: **lap of honour** ●one of the first three or four positions at the end of a race: **place**

winter ●*adjectives*: **hibernal, hiemal** ●live through the winter: **overwinter** ●sleep through the winter: **hibernate** ●map line joining points of equivalent winter temperature: **isocheim**

wire ●single length of wire: **strand** ●electric wire: **cable, lead** ●encased group of insulated electrical wires: **cable** ●wires used to start a car from the battery of another: **jump leads** ●tuning wire in an early radio: **cat's whisker** ●sharp-edged barrier wire: **razor wire** ●make wire by pulling metal through fine holes: **draw**

●thickness of a wire: **gauge** ●fine ornamental wire work: **filigree**

wise ●Three Wise Men: **Magi** ●wise or learned man: **sage** ●person claiming to be wise: **wiseacre** ●wisdom after the event: **hindsight**

wish ●sudden wish: **whim** ●comply with someone's wishes: **humour** ●done regardless of wishes: **compulsory, involuntary**

wit ●witty talk: **repartee** ●witty remark: **bon mot, sally** ●witty retort that comes to mind after the chance to make it has gone: **esprit de l'escalier**

witch ●male witch: **warlock, wizard, sorcerer** ●witch's attendant spirit: **familiar** ●witch's cooking pot: **cauldron** ●gathering of witches: **coven, sabbath** ●Irish warlock: **pishogue** ●modern witchcraft cult: **Wicca**

without ●*combining forms*: **a-** (*e.g.* amoral), **an-** (*e.g.* anonymous), **in-** (*e.g.* instability), **un-** (*e.g.* unattached)

witness ●witness who has personally seen what he or she describes: **eyewitness** ●denoting a witness antagonistic to the party questioning him or her: **hostile** ●witness's evidence given in court: **testimony** ●give evidence as a witness: **testify** ●sworn statement made by a witness out of court: **deposition** ●attempt to influence a witness: **interference** ●lying by a witness under oath: **perjury**

wolf ●*adjective*: **lupine** ●young wolf: **pup** ●person who changes into a wolf: **lycanthrope, werewolf**

woman ●*combining form*: **gynaeco-** ●*adjective*: **female, feminine** ●young woman parading with a baton-twirling group: **drum majorette, majorette** ●naive young woman: **ingénue** ●impudent or flirtatious young woman: **minx** ●representations of sexually alluring women: **cheesecake** ●denoting a sexually attractive young woman: **nubile** ●sexually attractive young woman: **nymphette** ●seductive but dangerous woman: **femme fatale** ●fashionable young woman of the 1920s: **flapper** ●dowdy woman: **frump** ●unmarried woman: **spinster** ●ageing unmarried woman: **old maid** ●woman whose husband has died: **widow** ●ugly old woman: **hag** ●intellectual or literary woman: **bluestocking** ●influential woman: **grande dame** ●woman employed to educate children at home: **governess** ●woman employed as resident childminder: **nanny** ●woman employed as a cleaner: **charwoman** ●woman letting out lodgings: **landlady** ●woman in charge of a public house: **landlady** ●arrogant and domineering woman: **prima donna** ●aggressive woman: **virago** ●aggressive old woman: **harridan** ●woman pregnant for the first time: **primigravida** ●woman pregnant for at least the second time: **multigravida** ●woman whose husband is often absent: **grass widow** ●party for women only: **hen party** ●married woman's male lover: **cicisbeo** ●older woman's youthful male escort: **gigolo** ●woman-centred: **gynaecocentric** ●rule by women: **gynaecocracy, gynarchy, matriarchy** ●polite respect shown to women: **chivalry, gallantry** ●school where young women are taught social graces: **finishing school, charm school** ●person supervising a young woman in public: **chaperone, duenna** ●study and treatment of women's diseases: **gynaecology** ●advocate of women's rights: **feminist** ●fear of women: **gynaecophobia, gynophobia** ●hatred of women: **misogyny**

wood ●*combining forms*: **lign-, xylo-** ●*adjective*: **ligneous** ●wood from a conifer: **softwood** ●wood from a broadleaved tree: **hardwood** ●lightweight wood used for model-making: **balsa** • board made of thin layers of wood with alternating grain: **plywood** • board made of compressed wood chips and resin: **chipboard** • board made of compressed and treated wood pulp: **hardboard** • thick piece of wood: **billet** • long thin strip of wood: **batten, lath** • thin and narrow strip of wood: **slat** • piece of thin wood in a chair back: **splat** • bundle of wood: **faggot** • prehistoric wood circle: **henge** • fibre pattern in wood: **grain** • hole in wood where a knot has fallen out: **knothole** • wooden plate: **trencher** • rectangular wooden tile: **shingle** • wood preservative distilled from coal tar: **creosote** • hard protective coating for wood: **lacquer, varnish** • high-gloss wood polish: **French polish** • ripple effect in fine wood grain: **fiddle-back** • thin surface layer of wood: **veneer** • wood inlay decorating furniture: **marquetry** • flooring of wooden blocks: **parquet** • substance painted on wood-knots to prevent resin seepage: **knotting** • fine wood powder left by boring insects: **frass** • feeding on wood: **xylophagous** • (of a plant stem) become woody: **lignify** • giant grass whose woody stems are used in furniture-making etc.: **bamboo** • prepare wood for use by adjusting its moisture content: **season** • wood-shaping machine: **lathe** • person working wood on a lathe: **turner** • musical instrument with pitched wooden blocks: **xylophone**

woodland • woodland nymph: **dryad, hamadryad**

woodworker • woodworker making stairs, doors, etc.: **joiner** • woodworker making furniture: **cabinet-maker**

wool • fine knitting wool: **fingering** • fine soft goat wool: **cashmere** • constituent strand of knitting wool: **ply** • cut wool off a sheep: **shear** • comb wool before spinning: **card** • coil of spun wool: **hank, skein**

word • *combining forms*: lexi-, log-, -nym • *adjectives*: **verbal, lexical** • word of one syllable: **monosyllable** • word of two syllables: **disyllable** • word of two or more syllables: **polysyllable** • word of three syllables: **trisyllable** • word of four syllables: **tetrasyllable** • word formed from the initial letters of other words: **acronym** • word of four letters: **tetragram** • word from which a later word is derived: **etymon** • newly invented word: **coinage, neologism** • word coined for the occasion: **nonce word** • word found only once: **hapax legomenon** • word formed from another word: **derivative** • word formed from the letters of another: **anagram** • word having the combined meanings of two other words, and constructed from some of their sounds: **blend** • word reading the same backwards as forwards: **palindrome** • word taken directly from another language: **loanword** • word or phrase directly translating a term with similar meaning in another language: **calque, loan translation** • denoting a word having the same root as another: **cognate** • word meaning the same as another: **synonym** • word meaning the opposite of another: **antonym** • word spelt and sounding the same as another, but having a different meaning and origin: **homonym** • word spelt the same as another, but having a different meaning: **homograph** • word spelt the same as another, but having a different sound and meaning: **heteronym** • word sounding the same as another, but having a different meaning: **homophone** • more pleasant word: **euphemism** • less pleasant word: **dysphemism** • word used in informal speech: **colloquialism** • important word: **keyword**

• overused word: **cliché** • fashionable and overused word: **buzzword** • denoting such terms: **hackneyed, trite** • misuse of a word: **catachresis** • confusion of similar-sounding words: **malapropism** • accidental transposition of words' opening sounds: **spoonerism** • choice of words: **phraseology, turn of phrase** • choice and use of words: **diction, parlance** • in exactly the same words: **verbatim** • use of more words than are needed: **pleonasm** • words known to a person or used in a sphere of activity: **vocabulary** • terminology particular to an individual or profession: **phraseology** • words used in a trade etc.: **jargon** • conventional expression: **formula** • characteristic use of words: **idiom, parlance** • words often found together: **collocation** • word's implied meaning: **connotation** • syntactic category to which a word belongs: **part of speech, word class** • word used to connect clauses or sentences: **conjunction** • secret word(s) used to gain admission: **password** • words for a song: **lyrics** • expression of a whole phrase as a single word: **holophrasis** • words surrounding a word or utterance, which help determine its meaning: **context** • fanciful use of words: **conceit** • using few words: **laconic** • using too many words: **long-winded, prosy, wordy** • word puzzle in which certain letters in each line form a name or message: **acrostic** • puzzle to find a series of words giving the same letter sequence when read across or down: **word square** • grid of letters containing words written in any direction: **wordsearch** • comprehension test of replacing missing words: **cloze test** • use of words all beginning with the same sound or letter: **alliteration** • repetition of words in reverse order: **chiasmus** • words said as a magic spell: **conjuration, in-**

cantation • basic part of a word: **stem** • change in a word's form reflecting its grammatical function: **inflection** • arrangement of words to make a correct sentence: **syntax** • shortened form of a word: **abbreviation, contraction** • symbol standing for a word: **logogram, logograph** • word represented by a single sign in shorthand: **grammalogue** • skilled user of words: **stylist, wordsmith** • statistical analysis of word use: **stylometry** • words of an opera etc.: **libretto** • study of the meaning of words: **semantics** • study of words for closely related concepts: **onomasiology** • study of the forms of words: **morphology** • study of word origins: **etymology** • popular but mistaken account of a word's origins: **folk etymology, popular etymology** • denoting a word imitating the sound of what it describes: **onomatopoeic** • word blending the sounds and meanings of two others: **portmanteau word** • express in words: **verbalize** • utter a word: **vocalize**

word processor • word processor feature fitting text into available line space: **word wrap**

work • *combining form*: **erg-** • hard menial work: **drudgery** • hard work done for little pay: **sweated labour** • place where this is done: **sweatshop** • work paid for according to the amount produced: **piecework** • work involving much travelling: **legwork** • amount of work to be done: **workload** • ratio of work done to energy etc. consumed: **efficiency** • work taken home: **outwork** • work done by a student while learning: **coursework** • work consequent upon previous work: **follow-up** • work produced incidentally to the main project: **by-product, parergon, spin-off** • selection of work shown to a potential employer: **portfolio** • unauthorized use of another's work: **piracy** • presenting another's work as one's own: **plagiarism** ●denoting professional work: **white-collar** ●denoting manual or industrial work: **blue-collar** ●denoting women's work: **pink-collar** ●way of carrying out a task: **technique** ●skilled approach to a task: **technique, workmanship** ●denoting work done to a decent standard: **workmanlike** ●meticulous completion of a task: **follow-through** ●belief that work has an intrinsic moral value: **work ethic** ●projects undertaken by a doctor or social worker: **caseload** ●substantial piece of artistic or scholarly work: **opus** ●person addicted to work: **workaholic** ●conversation about work between colleagues meeting socially: **shop talk** ●work with difficulty: **labour** ●work in a desultory manner: **potter** ●collapse due to overwork: **burnout** ●(in Japan) death caused by overwork: **karoshi** ●method of working: **modus operandi** (*pl.* modi operandi) ●study of efficient work methods: **ergonomics, time-and-motion study, work study** ●person monitoring the scheduled completion of work: **progress chaser** ●time available for a project: **time frame** ●period of work: **stint** ●daily period of work: **shift, working day** ●denoting a period of work done when most people are at leisure: **unsocial** ●shift composed of separate periods of work: **split shift** ●person taking over at the end of a shift: **relief** ●working hours variable by employees: **flexitime** ●section of a flexitime day when everyone must be at work: **core time** ●working hours shorter than usual: **short time** ●time worked beyond one's contractual hours: **overtime** ●record of the number of hours worked: **time sheet** ●day-long release of employees for education: **day release** ●full-time release of employees for education: **block release** ●day's unpaid work given to an over-

lord: **corvée** ●casual work paid daily: **daywork** ●able to work together: **compatible** ●take on an absent colleague's work: **cover** ●change domicile in search of work: **migrate** ●person living off the work of others: **drone** ●slowing or stopping work as a protest: **industrial action** ●government organizations assisting those seeking work: **jobcentre, job club** ●feign illness to avoid work: **malinger** ●forbid an employee to do his normal work: **suspend** ●send an employee home because of a temporary lull in work: **lay off** ●denoting an employee dismissed because there is no more work: **redundant** ●in working order: **operable, operational, operative, serviceable**

worker ●*combining forms*: -er (*e.g.* milliner), -ier (*e.g.* grazier) ●new worker's introductory training: **induction** ●worker receiving a contracted period of training: **apprentice** ●trained worker employed by another: **journeyman** ●experienced worker: **old hand** ●skilled worker: **artisan, craftsman, operative** ●craftsman's assistant: **mate** ●fully skilled worker: **master** ●unskilled manual worker: **labourer** ●person doing dull work: **hack** ●worker doing any job: **factotum** ●ordinary workers: **factory floor, shop floor** ●home-based worker making extensive use of telecommunications: **telecommuter, teleworker** ●workers considered collectively: **labour, labour force, manpower, workforce** ●employees regarded as a business asset: **human resources** ●group of workers and equipment devoted to a particular task: **section, unit** ●group of workers assembled for a specific project: **task force** ●denoting a worker seeking employment on a job-by-job basis: **casual, freelance** ●denoting a paid worker: **employed, stipendiary** ●denoting an unpaid worker: **honorary,**

voluntary ●construction labourer: **navvy** ●person employed to run errands: **gofer, legman** ●skilled maker of wooden furniture: **cabinetmaker** ●worker loading and unloading ships: **stevedore** ●denoting a quick and skilful worker: **deft** ●denoting a careful and productive worker: **conscientious, diligent** ●incompetent and dishonest worker: **cowboy** ●worker making little effort because retirement etc. is near: **time-server** ●workers employed by the commissioning authority: **direct labour** ●relations between workers and management: **industrial relations** ●workers' share in company government: **industrial democracy** ●worker supervising others: **foreman, forewoman** ●secret arrangement between workers to control output: **restrictive practice** ●workers' festival: **Labour Day** ●temporary or permanent discharge of workers: **lay-off** ●immigrant worker in Germany: **Gastarbeiter** ●Spanish-American day labourer: **peon** ●foreign girl who does domestic work in return for keep and English lessons: **au pair** ●not having enough workers: **short-handed, short-staffed, undermanned** ●replace workers by machines: **mechanize**

works ●complete works of a scholar or creative artist: **oeuvre, corpus** ●related series of artworks: **cycle**

world ●the world as a single community: **global village** ●spherical model of the world: **globe** ●worldwide: **global, mondial** ●operating worldwide: **globalist** ●places at opposite sides of the world: **antipodes** ●worldwide temperature increase: **global warming** ●barrier to infrared radiation causing this: **greenhouse effect** ▶*see also* **earth**

World Wide Web ●Internet location maintaining pages on the World Wide Web: **web site**

worm ●*combining form*: **vermi-** ●*adjectives*: **vermicular, vermiform**

worse ●make worse: **exacerbate** ●become worse: **deteriorate** ●deleterious cycle of cause and effect: **vicious circle**

worship ●*combining form*: **-latry** ●*adjective*: **devotional** ●worship due to God: **latria** ●worship of idols: **idolatry** ●(excessive) veneration of the Mother of God: **Mariolatry** ●reverence due to the saints: **dulia** ●pagan worshipped object: **fetish, idol, juju**

wound ●wound made by a bullet leaving the body: **exit wound** ●wound only skin-deep: **flesh wound** ●denoting a purulent wound: **festering** ●examine a wound carefully: **explore** ●clean and bandage a wound: **dress** ●protective material placed on a wound: **dressing** ●loop of thread joining the edges of a wound: **stitch, suture** ●skin mark left by a healed wound: **scar**

wrestling ●wrestling match: **bout** ●pair of wrestlers taking turns to fight: **tag team** ●roped-off area for a bout: **ring** ●man attending to a wrestler between rounds: **cornerman** ●hold pinning arm(s) behind the back: **nelson** ●move pinning the opponent to the ground: **fall** ●send one's opponent to the ground: **throw** ●surrender to an opponent's hold: **submission**

wrinkle ●facial wrinkle: **crow's-foot**

wrist ●*adjective*: **carpal**

writ ●writ ordering a person to attend court: **subpoena, summons, process** ●writ requiring production of an imprisoned person: **habeas corpus** ●writ summoning substitute jurors: **tales** ●formal delivery of a writ: **service**

write ●write in a different alphabet: **transliterate** ●write hastily and care-

lessly: **scribble** ●write quickly: **jot**
●able to read and write: **literate**

writing ●*combining forms*: **-gram**
(*e.g.* telegram), **-graphy** ●*adjective*:
graphic ●unabbreviated handwriting: **longhand** ●type of handwriting:
script ●elegant handwriting: **calligraphy** ●calligrapher's decorative
flourish: **curlicue** ●sloping style of
handwriting, with loops: **copperplate**
●joined-up handwriting: **cursive**
●reverse writing: **mirror writing**
●stroke joining letters: **ligature**
●curved stroke made in handwriting:
pot-hook ●denoting handwriting in
large letters of even height: **majus-
cule** ●denoting writing in lower-case
letters: **minuscule** ●denoting badly
formed handwriting: **crabbed** ●book
with samples of good handwriting:
copybook ●faint lines on paper to
guide handwriting: **feint** ●marks separating written sentences or phrases:
punctuation,   punctuation   mark
●psychological study of handwriting:
graphology ●text in its author's own
handwriting: **autograph, holograph**
●alternative way of writing a particular letter or sound: **allograph** ●sys-
tem of writing: **script** ●system of
symbols for high-speed writing: **shorthand, stenography** ●system of symbols each representing a syllable: **syllabary** ●Japanese syllabic writing:
kana ●simplified picture used to represent a word in certain ancient
writing systems: **glyph, pictograph**
●symbol standing for a word: **logogram, logograph** ●writing indicating the idea of a thing but not
its name: **ideogram,   ideograph**
●signature-symbol of an illiterate person: **mark** ●picture puzzle in which a
word is represented by pictures of objects whose names make its syllables:

rebus ●systems of signs used to
record music, choreography etc.: **notation** ●ancient Egyptian picture-
writing: **hieroglyphs** ●ancient Egyptian priestly script using simplified
hieroglyphs: **hieratic** ●ancient Egyptian script used by the laity, a simplified form of hieratic: **demotic** ●an-
cient wedge-shaped script: **cuneiform**
●ancient system of writing with lines
running alternately left to right and
right to left: **boustrophedon** ●an-
cient waxed writing tablet of two
hinged leaves: **diptych** ●writing instrument used with waxed tablets:
stylus ●ancient writing surface of
pounded sedge stems: **papyrus** (*pl.* papyri) ●writing surface made from
animal skin: **parchment** ●fine parchment made from calfskin: **vellum**
●study of ancient writing systems:
palaeography ●put into writing:
transcribe ●hand pain from much
writing: **writer's cramp** ●short piece
of writing: **essay** ●collection of writings: **anthology, collectanea, commonplace book, florilegium, garland,
miscellany,   omnibus** ●affectedly
elaborate style of writing: **euphuism**
●tediously wordy style of writing:
prolixity ●elaborately   contrived
piece of writing: **purple passage,
purple patch, purple prose** ●denot-
ing a awkward and hesitant style:
stilted ●newspaper reporters' style
of writing: **journalese**

written ●*combining form*: **-graph**
(*e.g.* autograph)

wrongdoing ●minor wrongdoing:
misdemeanour ●in the act of wrongdoing: **in flagrante delicto**

wrongly ●*combining forms*: **cata-**
(*e.g.* catachresis), **mis-** (*e.g.* misalign)

Xx

X ●X-shaped: **decussate**

X-rays ●X-raying a section through the body: **tomography, computerized axial tomography** ●X-ray examination of the bile ducts: **choliangography** ●X-ray examination of the gall bladder: **cholecystography** ●X-ray examination of the lymphatic system: **lymphangiography** ●X-ray examination of a vein: **venography** ●X-ray location of breast tumours: **mammography** ●X-ray picture: **radiograph** ●X-ray or ultrasound picture of a section through the body: **tomogram** ●opaque region in an X-ray picture: **shadow** ●transparent to X-rays: **radiolucent** ●opaque to X-rays: **radiopaque, radio-opaque** ●substance improving the X-ray visibility of body organs: **contrast medium** ●barium mixture consumed by a patient before the digestive system is X-rayed: **barium meal** ●screen for direct viewing of X-ray images: **fluoroscope** ●shield against X-rays worn by health workers: **apron** ●short-range X-rays: **gamma rays** ●use of X-rays: **radiography** ●medical treatment by X-rays: **radiotherapy, radiation therapy** ●study of medical applications of X-rays: **radiology**

yacht ●twin-hulled yacht: **catamaran** ●yacht of standard design: **one-design** ●yacht's open upper bridge: **flybridge, flying bridge** ●yacht harbour: **marina** ●president of a yacht club: **commodore** ▶*see also* **boat, sailing**

yarn ●strand of a yarn: **ply** ●thread used for stockings: **lisle**

year ●*adjective*: **annual** ●remarkable year: **annus mirabilis** ●year having 366 days: **leap year** ●year of 354 days: **lunar year** ●tax or accounting year: **financial year** ●extra days in a solar year: **epact** ●time of year when day and night are of equal length: **equinox** ●part of the year as particularized by climate or events: **season** ●year just beginning or about to begin: **new year** ●first person to enter a house in the new year: **first-footer** ●year just ended or about to end: **old year** ●for each year: **per annum** ●sum of money paid every year, or an insurance scheme securing this: **annuity** ●period of a thousand years: **millennium** ●period of a hundred years: **century** ●period of ten years: **decade** ●occurring twice a year: **semi-annual, biannual** ●occurring each year, or lasting for a year: **annual** ●occurring every other year, or lasting for two years: **biennial** ●occurring every, or lasting for, three years: **triennial** ●occurring every, or lasting for, four years: **quadrennial** ●occurring every, or lasting for, five years: **quinquennial** ●occurring every, or lasting for, seven years: **septennial** ●occurring every, or lasting for, ten years: **decennial**

years old ●*combining form*: **-genarian** (*e.g.* octogenarian)

yeast ●yeast substitute used in baking: **baking powder** ●(of dough) become aerated by yeast: **prove, rise**

yellow ●dull brownish-yellow: **khaki** ●yellowing of the skin or eyes: **jaundice**

yield ●policy of yielding to the demands of a potential aggressor: **appeasement**

yoga ●system of physical exercises: **hatha yoga**

youth ●time of youth: **nonage** ●different attitudes of young and old: **generation gap** ●creations of a writer's or artist's youth, often later suppressed as immature: **juvenilia**

Zz

Zen ●Zen insoluble riddle: **koan** ●zen meditation: **zazen**

Zeus ●*Roman name*: **Jupiter**

zigzag ●zigzag course taken by a vessel sailing into the wind: **tacking, traverse**

zinc ●coat a metal with zinc: **galvanize**

zoo ●zoo whose visitors drive through large paddocks containing wild animals: **safari park**

zoology ●zoology of living creatures: **neontology** ●zoology of fossil forms: **palaeontology**

Zoroastrian ●Zoroastrian scriptures: **Avesta** ●commentary upon the Avesta: **Zend** ●name of God in Zoroastrianism: **Ahura Mazda, Ormazd** ●follower of Zoroastrianism in western India: **Parsee** ●structure upon which Parsees expose their dead: **tower of silence**

Zulu ●group of Zulu warriors: **impi**